Brothers at Arms

Brothers at Arms

American Independence and the Men of France & Spain Who Saved It

LARRIE D. FERREIRO

ALFRED A. KNOPF NEW YORK 2016

THIS IS A BORZOI BOOK
PUBLISHED BY ALFRED A. KNOPF

Published in the United States by Alfred A. Knopf,
a division of Penguin Random House LLC, New York,
and distributed in Canada by Random House of Canada,
a division of Penguin Random House Canada Limited, Toronto.

www.aaknopf.com

Library of Congress Cataloging-in-Publication Data
Names: Ferreiro, Larrie D., author.
Title: Brothers at arms : American independence and the men of France and Spain who saved it / by Larrie D. Ferreiro.
Description: New York : Knopf, 2016
Identifiers: LCCN 2016007136 (print) | LCCN 20160344751 (ebook) | ISBN 9781101875247 (hardback) | ISBN 9781101875254 (ebook)
Subjects: LCSH: United States—Foreign relations—1775–1783. | United States—History—Revolution, 1775–1783—Participation, French. | United States—History—Revolution, 1775–1783—Participation, Spanish. | Great Britain—Foreign relations—1760–1789. | France—Foreign relations—Great Britain. | Great Britain—Foreign relations—France. | Spain—Foreign relations—Great Britain. | Great Britain—Foreign relations—Spain. | BISAC: HISTORY / United States / Revolutionary Period (1775–1800). | HISTORY / Military / United States. | HISTORY / Europe / General.
Classification: LCC E249 .F47 2016 (print) | LCC E249 (ebook) | DDC 327.73009/033—dc23
LC record available at https://lccn.loc.gov/2016007136

Jacket image: *The Surrender of Lord Cornwallis at Yorktown, October 19, 1781* (detail), by John Trumbull. Yale University Art Gallery
Jacket design by Oliver Munday
Maps by Mapping Specialists

Manufactured in the United States of America
First Edition

To my family, Mirna, Gabriel, and Marcel:
an American family, which, like the American nation,
owes its existence to France and Spain

Contents

Illustrations

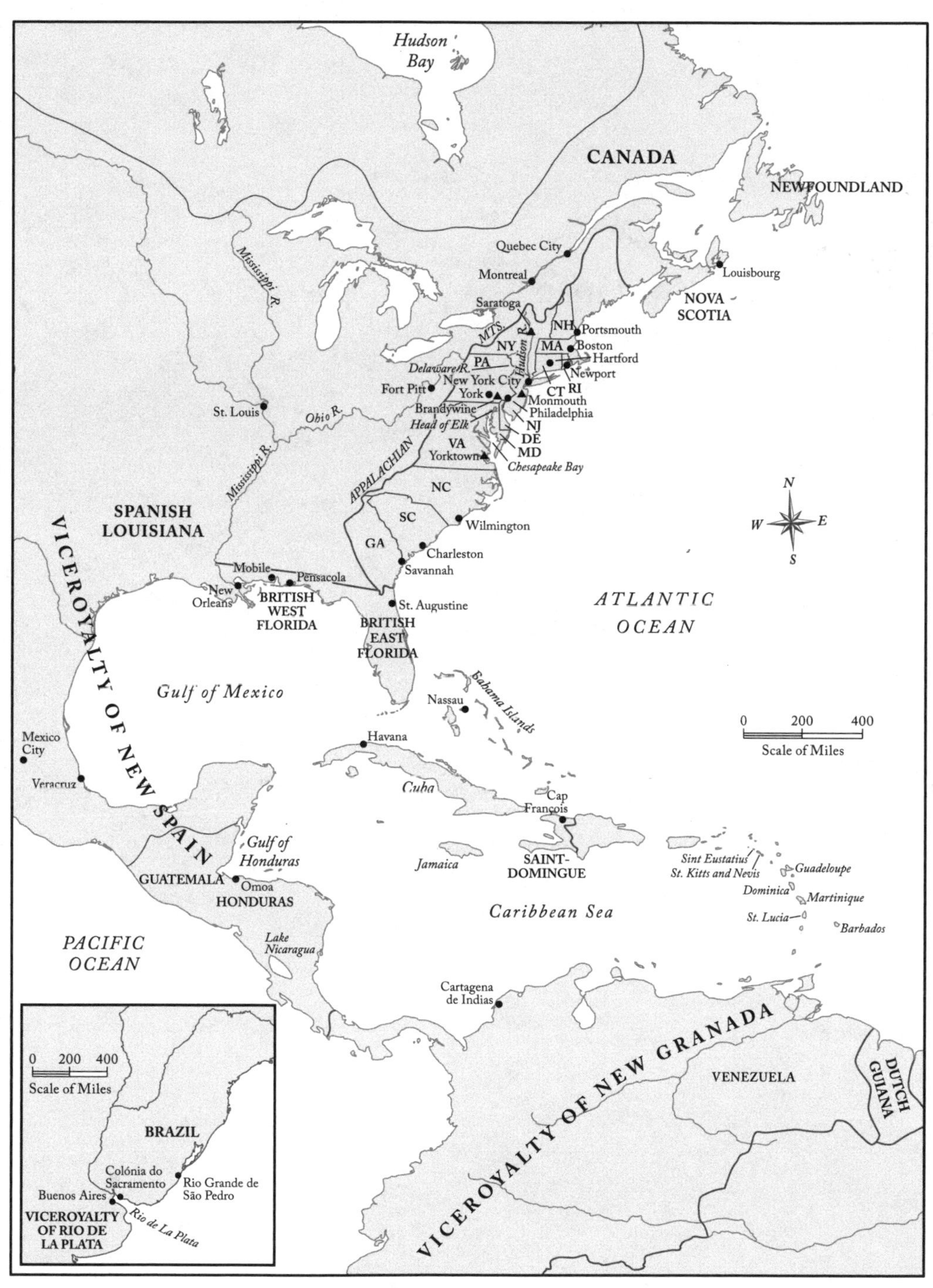

Hudson Bay
CANADA
NEWFOUNDLAND
Quebec City
Montreal
Louisbourg
NOVA SCOTIA
Saratoga
NH
Portsmouth
MA
Boston
Hartford
Newport
RI
CT
NY
PA
MTS.
Hudson R.
Delaware R.
New York City
Fort Pitt
York
Monmouth
Philadelphia
Brandywine
Head of Elk
NJ
DE
MD
VA
Yorktown
Chesapeake Bay
APPALACHIAN
NC
SC
GA
Wilmington
Charleston
Savannah
St. Augustine
Mississippi R.
Ohio R.
St. Louis
SPANISH LOUISIANA
Mobile
Pensacola
New Orleans
BRITISH WEST FLORIDA
BRITISH EAST FLORIDA
ATLANTIC OCEAN
N
W
E
S
VICEROYALTY OF NEW SPAIN
Gulf of Mexico
Nassau
Bahama Islands
0 200 400
Scale of Miles
Mexico City
Veracruz
Havana
Cuba
Cap François
Gulf of Honduras
Jamaica
SAINT-DOMINGUE
Sint Eustatius
St. Kitts and Nevis
Guadeloupe
Dominica
Martinique
St. Lucia
Barbados
GUATEMALA
Omoa
HONDURAS
Caribbean Sea
PACIFIC OCEAN
Lake Nicaragua
Cartagena de Indias
VICEROYALTY OF NEW GRANADA
VENEZUELA
DUTCH GUIANA
0 200 400
Scale of Miles
BRAZIL
Colónia do Sacramento
Rio Grande de São Pedro
Buenos Aires
VICEROYALTY OF RIO DE LA PLATA
Rio de La Plata

0
100
200
Scale of Miles
North Sea
Firth of Forth
GREAT BRITAIN
Flamborough Head
Dogger Bank
Irish Sea
Texel
DUTCH REPUBLIC
Amsterdam
Birmingham
Rotterdam
London
AUSTRIAN NETHERLANDS
Portsmouth
Liège
Boulogne
Douai
Plymouth
English Channel
ATLANTIC OCEAN
Le Havre
Charleville-Mézières
Paris
Strasbourg
Island of Ouessant
Brest
N
W
E
S
Nantes
FRANCE
Rochefort
Lyon
Bordeaux
Sisargas Isles
El Ferrol
Los Pasajes
Bilbao
Placencia
PYRENEES MOUNTAINS
Marseilles
Toulon
SPAIN
Madrid
PORTUGAL
Minorca
Lisbon
Mediterranean Sea
Cape St. Vincent
Cádiz
Málaga
Cape Trafalgar
Gibraltar
Cape Spartel

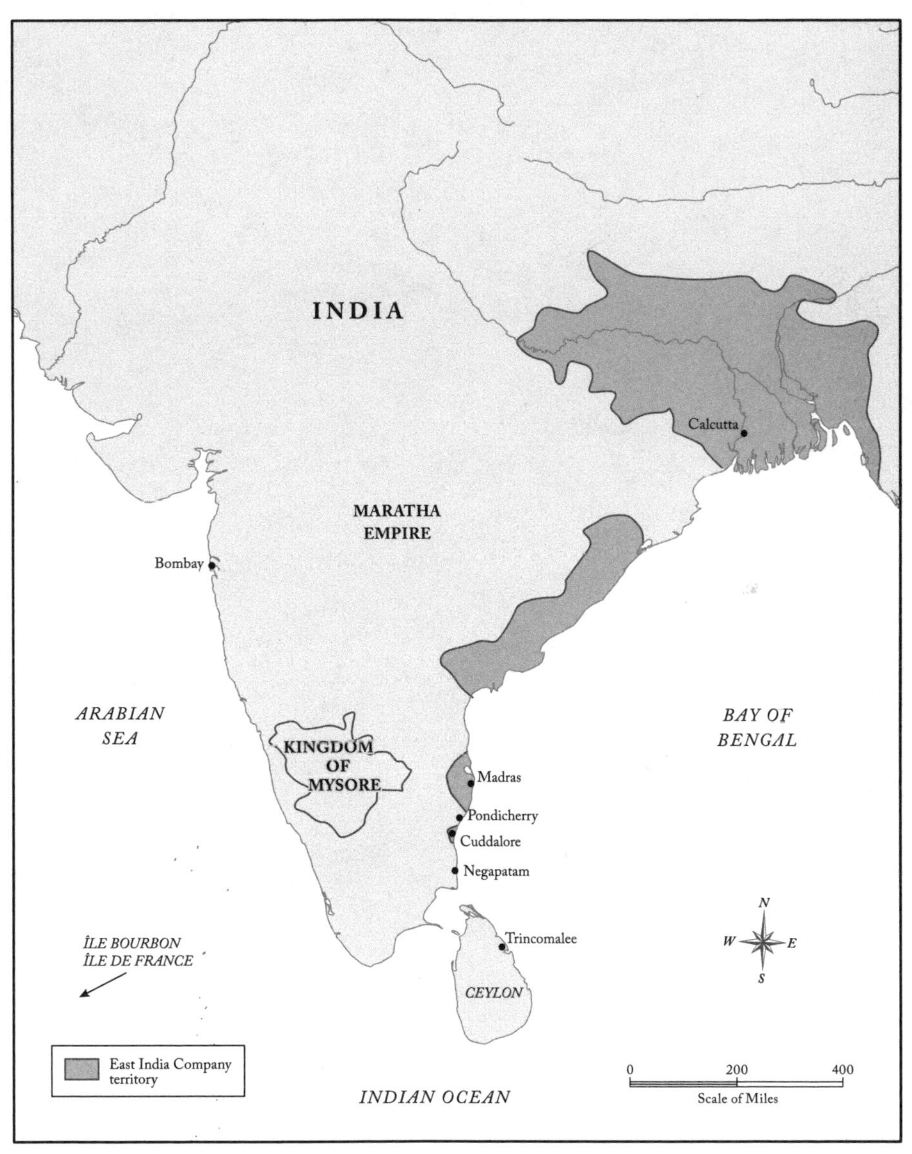
INDIA
MARATHA EMPIRE
Calcutta
Bombay
ARABIAN SEA
BAY OF BENGAL
KINGDOM OF MYSORE
Madras
Pondicherry
Cuddalore
Negapatam
Trincomalee
CEYLON
ÎLE BOURBON
ÎLE DE FRANCE
N
W
E
S
East India Company territory
INDIAN OCEAN
0
200
400
Scale of Miles

Introduction

Not Just the Declaration of Independence, but Also a Declaration That We Depend on France (and Spain, Too)

On a warm summer's day in Philadelphia in 1776, early in the throes of the American Revolution, Thomas Jefferson penned the opening sentences of a document addressed to King Louis XVI of France and King Carlos III of Spain, which the Second Continental Congress hoped would bring much-needed help to the embattled American colonies. Those colonies had been at war with Britain for over a year now, and the military situation was dire. The Continental Army had just suffered disastrous defeats in Canada and on Long Island, and had been driven out of New York City, which General William Howe now occupied. Without the direct intervention of Britain's adversaries, France and Spain, on America's side, the colonies could not hope to prevail against the superior British army and navy to win their independence outright.

The Revolution had been brewing for several years now. The overwhelming British victory over France and Spain in the Seven Years' War in 1763 had been succeeded by increasingly onerous tax duties and export restrictions imposed by London on the American colonies, intended to pay for increased protection, but which the colonists argued were levied without their having any voice in the matter, as would befit British subjects. American protests of these actions grew ever more violent, until war broke out in 1775 with the battles of Lexington, Concord, and Bunker Hill, and the subsequent siege of Boston. Even then, most Americans still hoped for some kind of reconciliation with the Crown. By the beginning of 1776, however, King George III had rejected the colonists' peace overtures, declared them to be in a state of rebellion, and hired regiments from the German states of Hesse-Kassel, Hesse-Hanau, and Brunswick to put down the insurgency. The Continental Congress, particularly appalled by the threat of what they saw as Hessian mercenaries, started clamoring for a complete break from British rule and "to declare the colonies in a state of independent sovereignty." Many of the individual colonial governments began sending their delegates to the Congress instructing them "immediately to cast off the British yoke" and to renounce allegiance to the Crown. The fight that had begun a year earlier to force the mother country to recognize their rights as British subjects had now turned into a war for independence.

The problem was that the new American nation had begun its war against British rule stunningly incapable of fending for itself, like a rebellious adolescent who takes leave of his family without a penny to his name. It had no navy, little in the way of artillery, and a ragtag army and militia that were bereft of even the most basic ingredient of modern warfare: gunpowder. Soon after the Battle of Bunker Hill, Benjamin Franklin noted that "the Army had not five rounds of powder a man. The world wondered that we so seldom fired a cannon; we could not afford it." America, in short, desperately needed to bring France and Spain directly into the war, the only nations powerful enough to carry the fight straight to the British army as well as to bring the British navy into a wider conflict that would draw it away from American shores and sap its strength.

Both France and Spain had allowed clandestine aid to flow to the Americans since before the fighting started, but this was proving insufficient for the scale of the conflict. Neither Louis XVI nor Carlos III would openly take sides in a British civil war; America had to demonstrate that it was an independent nation fighting against a common British enemy. The document that emerged from under Jefferson's hand, clearly stating that "these United Colonies are, and of Right ought to be Free and Independent States," was in fact an engraved invitation to France and Spain asking them to go to war alongside the Americans. The document that was agreed to by the Second Continental Congress on July 4 became known, of course, as the Declaration of Independence, but it was also in a sense a "Declaration That We Depend on France (and Spain, Too)."

COMMON SENSE

Americans today celebrate the July Fourth holiday under somewhat false pretenses. The standard account regarding the Declaration of Independence goes something like this: The colonists could no longer tolerate the British government passing unjust laws and levying taxes without allowing proper representation. The Second Continental Congress voted to write a document explaining to King George III why they needed to be independent, and to justify to the American colonists and the rest of the world the reasons for revolting against the Crown. The truth behind this document was very different. The Declaration was not meant for King George III. The British monarch had already gotten the message, as he told Parliament in October 1775, that the rebellion "is manifestly carried on for the purpose of establishing an independent empire." Nor was it primarily intended to rally the American colonies to the cause of independence, as they had already instructed their congressional delegates to vote for separation. Instead, the Declaration was written as a call for help from France and Spain.

The very idea of a formal document to declare national independence was almost unheard of. In the past, nations that broke from their rulers did not bother to state their intentions in writing, for their actions spoke far louder than any words. The most recent example had been the uprising of the Corsican Republic against the Republic of Genoa in 1755. Its leader, Pasquale Paoli, had simply announced that Corsica was a sovereign nation and established an independent government; no formal declaration was ever printed. The American colonists were well acquainted with these events, and even gave Paoli's name to a town in Pennsylvania that would be the site of a bloody battle with the British. Prior to that, the epic eighty-year battle of the Dutch Republic for independence from Spain had been fought without any written declarations, apart from a single document known as the Act of Abjuration (1581), which was more a casting off of personal allegiances to the Spanish crown than a formal affirmation of a new, independent nation.

Although unprecedented as a formal proclamation of national sovereignty, the American Declaration of Independence was hardly the first declaration that Americans had written in the run-up to the war. Stemming from British legal practice, declarations had a long history of expressing intent or enacting new policy at the national and international levels. Declarations were not simply announcements to the world or documents for the record; each was carefully crafted to influence a particular audience in order to accomplish a specific purpose. In response to the Coercive Acts of 1774, which imposed severe economic and punitive measures on Massachusetts, the First Continental Congress adopted a series of declarations and resolves, as well as addresses to the people of Great Britain and their other colonies, and petitions to the king, which together were intended to change the hated laws either by encouraging the election of a new Parliament more amenable to the colonists' demands or by bringing about a royal intervention to overturn those laws.

When attempts at changing either the laws or the Parliament failed and hostilities erupted in 1775, the Second Continental Congress laid the blame squarely on Parliament and the king's ministers, and assigned a three-man committee, which included Thomas Jefferson, to draft the Declaration of the Causes and Necessity of Taking Up Arms. This declaration was both an explanation of why the colonists felt it necessary to defend their freedoms through force of arms and a final appeal for reconciliation. Although the authors declared that they had written the document out of "respect to the rest of the world," it was quite clearly aimed at George III in an attempt to reverse Britain's course; only by his directing his ministers to negotiate with the colonists "on reasonable terms," the declaration stated, could the "calamities of civil war" be averted. This appeal, and the accompanying Olive Branch Petition asking the king to find a way to "settle peace . . . in our dominions," were roundly rejected by George III. By the end of 1775, the American colonies were in an armed political stalemate; reconciliation was no longer an option, but they could not see a path to winning a separation from Britain.

This impasse was broken at the beginning of 1776, not by the vast intellectual talent then holding forth in congressional debates at the Pennsylvania State House, but by an obscure newspaper editor who, nearly bankrupt, had emigrated from London to Philadelphia just a year earlier. In that brief time Thomas Paine had picked up enough coffeehouse chatter and tavern ramblings to arrive at a conclusion that some politicians were mooting privately: that the various declarations and petitions issued to date by the Congress got the situation backward. It was George III, not his ministers or Parliament, who was to blame for the colonies' current misfortunes; therefore no amount of petitioning the king to change the laws would ever redress the situation; and therefore a complete break with Britain, not a reconciliation, was inevitable to secure a prosperous America. Paine's clear, clean logic led him to a second, even more radical conclusion: Separation could only be achieved militarily, which would only be possible with the support of France and Spain, and their support would be entirely contingent upon the colonies formally and in writing declaring themselves a sovereign nation, independent from Great Britain.

With the assistance of Benjamin Rush, a physician then active in political circles, Paine published a forty-six-page pamphlet titled *Common Sense* that expounded on these views and laid out a course of action for the American colonies to achieve independence. Philadelphia bookstalls began selling it on January 10, 1776, the very same day that news of George III's speech denouncing America's rebellion as an attempt to "[establish] an independent empire" arrived in Philadelphia. Paine's timing was impeccable: His call for independence, which might have been unthinkable just weeks earlier, was unintentionally bolstered by the king's own accusation of the same thing. The pamphlet was widely read, and within months the notion of independence was being openly discussed across the colonies.

Common Sense began by laying out the ideal form of a republic in which citizens have a share in their own governance, and explaining that the British systems of monarchy and aristocracy were the very antithesis of that form of government. By remaining tied to Great Britain three thousand miles away, which evinced little interest or understanding of its problems, America would only suffer further "injuries and disadvantages." Paine then made the plea that would echo in the halls of the Congress and in the local chambers and colonial assemblies from New Hampshire to Georgia: "Every thing that is right or natural pleads for separation. . . . 'TIS TIME TO PART."

The final pages of *Common Sense* made clear the direct link between a declaration of independence and the securing of aid from France and Spain:

> Nothing can settle our affairs so expeditiously as an open and determined declaration for independence.
>
> *First.*—It is the custom of nations, when any two are at war, for some other powers, not engaged in the quarrel, to step in as

> mediators, and bring about the preliminaries of a peace: but while America calls herself the Subject of Great-Britain, no power, however well disposed she may be, can offer her mediation. Wherefore, in our present state we may quarrel on for ever.
>
> *Secondly*—It is unreasonable to suppose, that France or Spain will give us any kind of assistance, if we mean only, to make use of that assistance for the purpose of repairing the breach, and strengthening the connection between Britain and America. . . .
>
> *Thirdly*—While we profess ourselves the subjects of Britain, we must, in the eye of foreign nations, be considered as rebels. . . .
>
> *Fourthly*—Were a manifesto to be published, and despatched to foreign courts . . . [it] would produce more good effects to this Continent, than if a ship were freighted with petitions to Britain.
>
> Under our present denomination of British subjects, we can neither be received nor heard abroad: The custom of all courts is against us, and will be so, until, by an independence, we take rank with other nations.

Paine's scheme to appeal directly to France and Spain for assistance needed no explanation to his American audience, for like him they knew that the two nations had long been spoiling for a rematch with Great Britain. They had come out badly in the Seven Years' War, a global conflict that began in the American colonies in 1754 as a frontier battle between France and Britain, but that quickly engulfed all the major European powers. The war ended in 1763 with France losing Canada to the British Empire, while Spain ceded its dominance over the Gulf of Mexico by giving Florida to Britain. The Americans knew that both nations were now seeking retribution for the territories and prestige they had lost, and that the nascent American conflict could provide them the opportunity for revenge they had long sought.

DECLARING INDEPENDENCE AND JOINING THE WORLD STAGE AS A SOVEREIGN NATION

The effect of *Common Sense* on the American mood was electric, that term already being in popular use due to the widespread accounts of the scientific experiments of Benjamin Franklin, just recently returned to Philadelphia after a decade defending the American cause in London. Where before January 1776 all the talk was of reconciliation, it was now about separation. Calls for independence filled newspapers up and down the continent, and the colonial governments were not deaf to these entreaties. In February and March, South Carolina rewrote its constitution, making it "independent of royal authority." In April, the Virginia county of Charlotte adopted a resolution rejecting any attempts at reconciliation. In May, the Continental Congress sent instructions to all the colonies that effectively urged them to replace any pro-reconciliation governments with new ones more amenable to independence. By the end of the month, John Adams reported that "every post and every day rolls in upon us 'independence' like a torrent."

These same letters to the colonial representatives made it clear that their authors fully embraced Paine's link between a declaration of independence and aid from France and Spain. One of the first to subscribe to that connection was Richard Henry Lee, a Virginia delegate to the Congress and a member of one of the most influential families in colonial America. Long before *Common Sense* was published, he had undoubtedly been inspired in this thinking by his brother Arthur Lee, who while a colonial representative in London along with Benjamin Franklin back in 1774, had told him that in a war with Britain, "America may yet owe her salvation [to European powers] should the contest be serious and lasting." That idea was certainly reinforced by a letter to him in April 1776 from John Washington, one of George Washington's nephews: "I am clearly of opinion that unless we declare openly for Independency there is no chance for foreign aid." That same month Richard Henry Lee explained to his fellow Virginian Patrick Henry back in Williamsburg that the Congress must soon consider independence since the current "danger . . . may be prevented by a timely alliance with proper and willing powers in Europe" and that "no state in Europe will either treat or trade with us so long as we consider ourselves subjects of Great Britain."

In April, colonial delegations began receiving instructions to vote for independence. The Virginia county of Cumberland directed its congressional representatives to "declare for independency [and] procure foreign assistance," while North Carolina instructed its delegates "to concur with the delegates of the other Colonies in declaring independency, and forming foreign alliances." In May, the entire Virginia Convention adopted a resolution that instructed its delegates to "declare the united colonies free and independent states . . . and give assent to whatever measures may be thought proper and necessary for forming foreign alliances." These directions from the colonial governments to their congressional delegates made it clear that, echoing Paine, they saw a declaration of independence as the unique means of obtaining help from France and Spain.

As the movement toward independence gathered momentum, even the Massachusetts delegate John Adams, normally wary of any foreign entanglements, reluctantly admitted:

> We should be driven to the Necessity of Declaring ourselves independent States, and that We ought now to be employed in preparing . . . Treaties to be proposed to foreign Powers, particularly to France and Spain. . . . That foreign Powers could not be expected to acknowledge Us, till We had acknowledged ourselves, and taken our Station among them as a sovereign Power, and Independent Nation; That now we were distressed for Want of Artillery, Arms, Ammunition, Clothing, and even for Flints.

By early June, Richard Henry Lee was ready to follow the Virginia Convention's instructions and call openly for the Congress to declare for independence. Echoing John Adams, he explained to a Virginia landowner, "It is not choice then, but necessity that calls for independence, as the only means by which foreign alliance can be obtained." He wrote those words on Sunday, June 2, then must have spent that week mulling over the wording of a group of resolutions that would set the Congress into motion. On that Friday, June 7, the Congress convened as usual at 10 a.m., addressing pressing concerns from war reports and the more mundane matter of compensating a merchant for goods seized by the Continental Navy. At around 11 a.m., Richard Henry Lee asked for the floor, then introduced the following three interconnected resolutions for consideration:

> That these United Colonies are, and of right ought to be, free and independent States; that they are absolved from all allegiance to the British Crown; and that all political connection between them and the State of Great Britain is, and ought to be, totally dissolved.
>
> That it is expedient forthwith to take the most effectual measures for forming foreign Alliances.

> That a plan of confederation be prepared and transmitted to the respective Colonies for their consideration and approbation.

The resolutions were seconded by John Adams, but the Congress put off consideration until the following day. On Saturday and again on Monday, the Congress debated the three resolutions. While members from southern and New England colonies were for the resolutions, many of the middle Atlantic colonies preferred to postpone the decision. Opponents of independence questioned whether France or Spain would even provide any help to the Americans, given their own colonial interests in the Americas, and argued that France was more likely to form an alliance with Britain and divide up North America between them. Proponents of the resolutions, as Thomas Jefferson's own notes showed, argued that "a declaration of independence alone could render it consistent with European delicacy for European powers to treat with us," and that no time should be wasted in applying for such aid as France and Spain could offer. The arguments went back and forth with no clear consensus.

Instead of taking a vote on the resolution for independence, the Congress postponed further debate until July 1, and instructed a committee to draft a declaration should the Congress decide for it. They addressed the second and third resolutions also by appointing committees, one to draft a model treaty with France, and another to draft a plan of confederation for the thirteen states that would be created from the former colonies once independence was declared. The committee for the plan of confederation was the largest of the three, having a representative from each colony. With such an unwieldy group it was the last to report out, only producing the Articles of Confederation eighteen months later in November 1777 (and those articles would not be ratified by all thirteen states until 1781). The second committee to produce a model treaty for France had just five members, led by John Adams. Adams insisted that the model treaty be commercial in nature only, and not include any political or military alliances that might "entangle us in future wars in Europe." The final Plan of Treaties, which strictly adhered to Adams's principles, was produced on July 18, and adopted by the Congress on September 17. One month later, Benjamin Franklin would embark for France with Adams's model treaty in hand, on his mission to secure the assistance that his nation so desperately needed.

The five-man committee to draft the Declaration of Independence also was headed by John Adams, but the task of drafting it was given to Thomas Jefferson. Jefferson was an accomplished writer and was already working with his fellow Virginia statesmen James Madison and George Mason on a Constitution and Declaration of Rights for their soon-to-be-formed state. Jefferson wrote quickly, borrowing liberally from these and other documents, and produced the first draft in just a few days. He showed it first to Franklin and Adams, who made just a few revisions, then to the whole committee, who wrangled with it for two weeks. By then, the Congress had already settled on the name for the new nation; on June 24, 1776, its president, John Hancock, officially used the term "The United States" for the very first time while commissioning a new French volunteer, Antoine Félix Wuibert, as an officer in the Continental Army.

The revised draft of the Declaration was brought before the Congress on June 28, by which time the mid-Atlantic colonies had authorized their delegates to vote for independence, also with the stipulation that it was the path to obtaining foreign assistance. The motion to adopt Richard Henry Lee's resolution was taken on July 2, after which the Congress debated and revised the draft for two days before approving the final version on July 4, a Thursday. That evening, a broadside sheet was typeset, and about two hundred copies were run off and distributed to the colonies and to the Continental Army headquarters. That the Congress intended the declaration to be read by Louis XVI and Carlos III was underscored by the fact that, on Monday, July 8, the first working day after the weekend, they placed a copy of the Declaration aboard a ship bound for France, with instructions for Silas Deane, a Connecticut merchant and delegate then in Paris negotiating arms deals, to "immediately communicate the piece to the Court of France, and send copies of it to the other Courts of Europe."

Although Richard Henry Lee's resolutions and all of the subsequent congressional debates—as Jefferson himself so clearly noted—tied the Declaration of Independence to the request for foreign aid, nowhere in the text do the words "France" or "Spain" appear. Even in the opening paragraph, Jefferson gave as the sole rationale for the document that "a decent respect to the opinions of mankind" required an explanation for their actions. This statement, like the similar rationale given in the Declaration of the Causes and Necessity of Taking Up Arms, obfuscated the real reason and intended audience for the Declaration of Independence. Even if the Congress had in mind a call for help to Louis XVI and

Carlos III, in all likelihood those monarchs were far from Jefferson's thoughts during the Declaration's actual composition. He was reaching instead for the highest sentiments of Enlightenment thinkers—Locke on natural rights, Voltaire on oppression, Montesquieu on liberty and freedom—to justify the case for independence. Any overt supplication to a foreign power would have debased and demeaned the Declaration that he so carefully crafted. Instead, the very existence of the document would serve as a clarion call for help.

The Declaration became a document for the ages. After the opening apologia that obscured its true purpose, Jefferson launched into his loftiest prose: "We hold these truths to be self-evident, that all men are created equal, that they are endowed by their Creator with certain unalienable Rights, that among these are Life, Liberty and the pursuit of Happiness.—That to secure these rights, Governments are instituted among Men, deriving their just powers from the consent of the governed." He followed this with a litany of charges as to why the British monarch had not lived up to these ideals, from general offenses against the colonies to specific accusations ranging from interference with judicial processes to kidnapping, pillage, and plunder. Jefferson did not hold the British public blameless, calling them "Enemies in War, in Peace Friends." By declaring itself a member of the world's sovereign nations, Jefferson reminded its hoped-for allies that the United States now had "full Power to levy War, conclude Peace, contract Alliances, establish Commerce, and to do all other Acts and Things which Independent States may of right do."

It was only at the very end of the Declaration of Independence that Jefferson included a passage that the kings of France and Spain might have taken particular notice of: "And for the support of this Declaration, with a firm reliance on the protection of divine Providence, we mutually pledge to each other our Lives, our Fortunes and our sacred Honor." In other words: To become an independent, self-governing nation, we have staked everything on winning this war with Britain. Without a military alliance, there is no hope that we can continue. Now please come to our aid.

Across the Atlantic, France and Spain weighed their options. Just thirteen years had passed since they had fought a disastrous war with Britain, losing trade, colonies, and influence. A new war, on the side of the rebellious Americans, could redress their old humiliations—or plunge them into ruination.

Brothers at Arms

CHAPTER 1

The Road to War

On the surprisingly warm evening of February 10, 1763, a carriage bearing two officials, one from France and the other from Spain, clattered down rue Saint-Dominique on Paris's Left Bank, just a few blocks from the Seine. Amid rows of stately buildings, it entered under the round arch and through the double doors of a simple but dignified *hôtel particulier*, stopping in the courtyard. The officials disembarked, turned to the right toward the main entrance, walked through a series of rooms decorated with blue-and-white wallpaper *"à l'anglaise"* and into the red-draped reception hall where hung a portrait, not of the French king Louis XV, but of King George III of Britain. Walking across that short distance, the two men had left the comfortable French world they had known and were now effectively in British territory.

The two men were César Gabriel de Choiseul-Praslin, the French foreign minister, and Pablo Jerónimo Grimaldi y Pallavicini, the Spanish ambassador to France. The dignified Paris town house in which they stood was the residence and de facto embassy of John Russell, Duke of Bedford, who received them sitting down as he was suffering a recurrence of gout. Just five months earlier he had arrived in France as minister plenipotentiary—effectively an ambassador—to negotiate for peace. Together the three were about to sign a treaty that would formally end the ruinous war that had engulfed not just the three countries, but also most of Europe and nations as far away as India and in North America.

The Seven Years' War, as it became known, had begun in 1754 as a series of skirmishes between French and British forces in the Ohio Valley. Within two years it had spread to continental Europe and across the globe. The turning point in the conflict came in 1759, when Britain began a stunning string of victories at sea and on land, eventually decimating the French and Spanish fleets and taking control of their strongholds from Canada to the Caribbean to Asia.

By 1762, France and Spain had no choice but to sue for peace. Choiseul-Praslin led the negotiations on behalf of France. Spain sent Grimaldi at the request of the French ministers, a man with whom they previously had negotiated treaties and whom they saw as "supremely gifted in the art of reconciling political agreement with friendship in opposing parties." The British cabinet selected the enormously wealthy Duke of Bedford, whose social connections and consistent support of peace made it likely he would gain France's trust. The three men were of very different temperaments. Choiseul-Praslin was described as "sensible, laborious . . . [with a] dry manner, an almost impenetrable reserve . . . and total absence of graces." The Italian-born Grimaldi, by contrast, impressed the British historian Edward Gibbon, then on his Grand Tour of Europe, as a well-heeled socialite who "gives balls every week, the magnificence of which is only exceeded by their politeness & elegance" (the diplomats, in fact, had just attended one of Grimaldi's famous soirées the night before the treaty signing, which ended at ten o'clock in the morning). Gibbon was less impressed with Bedford, whose "stateliness and avarice," he claimed, "make him the joke of Paris." The French minister, for his part, found Bedford "a very good man, very polite, well-intentioned, anxious to conclude the peace treaty."

Although Bedford was certainly "anxious to conclude the peace treaty," he was scrupulous about acting only on his government's terms. He could afford to do so, for Britain held the high ground both literally and metaphorically. Over the course of several months, the three men hammered out a treaty that recognized Britain's supremacy and reset the world stage in its favor. Even as they were negotiating the details, Bedford was also furnishing his town house on rue Saint-Dominique with the latest trappings from London, from the exquisite silver service to the first water closets in all of Paris. This sumptuous redecoration was not "stateliness and avarice" on the British ambassador's part, but rather a political statement. When Choiseul-Praslin and Grimaldi crossed the threshold of Bedford's residence on the evening of February 10, the Londonesque surroundings served as a reminder that they were now entering a new, British-dominated world.

THE SEVEN YEARS' WAR—A GLOBAL CONFLICT

The Seven Years' War was unlike any previous conflict those experienced diplomats had ever known. Every decade or so since 1625, Europe had been racked by wars that involved its major powers France, Spain, and England (Britain after the 1707 union with Scotland). Though the proximate causes for the wars varied from controlling seaborne trade to outright land grabs, they could all be traced to the prevailing political system known as "balance of power," which an eighteenth-century encyclopedia described as "a system of equilibrium used in modern politics in which each power contains the other, so that none will become so predominant in Europe that it threatens invasion and total control." In other words, when any one nation became too strong (say, Britain), weaker powers like France and Spain would ally to keep the stronger power in check. Allies and adversaries frequently changed sides from one war to the next as the balance of power shifted.

For most of the previous century and a half, the wars that resulted from these shifting alliances had rarely been decisive and had generally maintained the European balance of power, preventing any one nation from overwhelming the continent. One of the most consequential of these conflicts was the War of the Spanish Succession (1701–14). When the Spanish king Carlos II of the Hapsburg dynasty died without issue in 1700, he willed his crown to his grandnephew the French Bourbon prince Philippe d'Anjou (who became Felipe V), setting off a war that pitted Britain, the Dutch Republic, and Austria against France and Spain for control of the Spanish crown. France and Spain emerged victorious, with the result that the Spanish Empire became aligned with the French Bourbon dynasty instead of the Austrian Hapsburg dynasty supported by Britain. Spain, however, lost to Britain its vital Mediterranean strongholds of Minorca and Gibraltar, though it retained its profitable overseas possessions in the Americas and the Philippines. More recently, the War of the Austrian Succession, in which many of the same belligerents had fought in roughly the same alliances from 1740 to 1748 with losses and victories on both sides, ended largely *status quo ante bellum,* with Louis XV reportedly declaring that he would hand back all the captured territories, "as he wished to conduct the peace, not as a merchant, but as a King."

The Seven Years' War, which actually lasted closer to nine years, began in part precisely because those previous conflicts had left the balance of power largely intact without actually resolving the underlying territorial disputes, particularly in North America. Spain was the first European power to establish a permanent North American colony, in Puerto Rico in 1508, followed in 1535 by the Viceroyalty of New Spain that eventually encompassed modern-day Mexico, Florida, and much of the western United States. France established its Viceroyalty of New France in 1534, though it did not establish permanent settlements in Canada and Louisiana until 1608 and 1686 respectively. Britain's first permanent settlement in 1607 at Jamestown gave rise to the thirteen colonies that by 1733 extended from the eastern seaboard to the Appalachian Mountains. As the three colonial powers expanded their territories across North America over the course of two centuries, fights inevitably broke out between them and with the Native American nations whose lands they were steadily usurping.

The immediate cause of the Seven Years' War was a conflict in the Ohio Valley, part of the undefined border between New France and the British colonies that was left unresolved in the haste to bring the War of the Austrian Succession to a close. Even though the region was inhabited by the Iroquois nations, France saw it as a strategic corridor that linked Canada and Louisiana, while Britain saw it as the natural western extension of its colonies that could be sold to farmers and land speculators.

The Ohio Company of Virginia was established in 1748 by Virginia plantation owners like Lawrence and Augustine Washington in order to profit from this westward expansion. Virginia's lieutenant governor, Robert Dinwiddie, who was also a major shareholder, granted the company a half million acres of the Ohio Valley. In 1752, the company signed a treaty with the Iroquois nations that allowed it access and the right to build a fort at the strategic confluence of the Allegheny and Monongahela Rivers, at present-day Pittsburgh. The only problem was that Dinwiddie's counterpart, Michel-Ange, Marquis de Duquesne, the governor of New France, also had the idea to build fortifications in the same area.

In order to establish control over the region, both Duquesne and Dinwiddie began issuing a series of increasingly belligerent orders to their troops that heightened tensions. Duquesne's instructions from France required him to stop the British by "preventing them from coming there to trade, by seizing their merchandise, and destroying their outposts." As he began building a series of forts to prevent the British from doing the same, Dinwiddie dispatched a letter to the French commander demanding their withdrawal. He charged its delivery to a new member of the Ohio Company, the twenty-one-year-old half brother of Lawrence and Augustine Washington. George Washington, already an experienced surveyor and a major in the Virginia militia, led a small party through the harsh winter landscape to Fort LeBoeuf on the shores of Lake Erie. The French commander sent Washington back with a short reply stating, "I do not think myself obliged to obey it."

In early 1754, Dinwiddie again sent Washington, now promoted to lieutenant colonel in the newly formed Virginia Regiment, to reinforce Ohio Company workers sent to build a fort at the junction of the Allegheny and Monongahela Rivers. Washington soon learned that they had been evicted by a French garrison that was already constructing its own Fort Duquesne on the site. His orders from Dinwiddie regarding the French were quite clear: "in case of resistance to make prisoners of or kill & destroy them." Washington decided to ambush the French scouting party sent to look for him. On May 28, with the help of some Iroquois warriors, his troops descended on the French encampment and in fifteen minutes killed, wounded, or captured all but one of the soldiers.

The Battle of Jumonville Glen (named for the fallen leader of the French troops) was later identified as the spark that ignited the Seven Years' War and precipitated the War of American Independence. At that moment, Washington could not have imagined the global dimensions of that first war, nor have even dreamed that he would lead the second one. All he would have thought about was returning to his nearby Fort Necessity to prepare for the expected French counterattack. When it came on July 4, Washington (now a full colonel) was forced to surrender to the far larger French force and return to Virginia. News of the battles reached Europe later that summer. Britain and France began dispatching ships and soldiers to reinforce their colonies: a thousand British troops under General Edward Braddock to enter the Ohio Valley, and thirty-six hundred French troops to Canada. What had started as a series of frontier skirmishes was quickly escalating into a war between the two European superpowers.

France's determined defense of its New France colony had more to do with European politics than with colonial economics. The income from Canada's fur trade and the Acadian cod fisheries paled in comparison to the far more profitable sugar plantations in the French Caribbean islands of Saint-Domingue (Haiti), Grenada, Saint Vincent, Martinique, and Guadeloupe. Canada's growing season was so limited that it could barely feed its own populace, much less a surge of troops from France. Its seaward approaches were protected by the naval base of Louisbourg in Nova Scotia, one of the most expensive naval fortifications built in North America. The French author and polemicist Voltaire, always with his finger on the social pulse, frequently disparaged Canada as "a few acres of snow," not worth the massive investments France kept pouring into it.

New France, however, acted as a counterweight to the rich British colonies to its south, and marked France as a major power in the eyes of its European allies and adversaries alike; to lose it would, in the view of the French government, undermine France's standing in Europe and threaten its security. The British government equally believed that it needed to confront France's North American incursions in order to shore up its own standing in Europe.

The skirmishes of 1754 had been limited to colonial forces. In 1755, the armies of the two European powers collided head-on. Major General Edward Braddock marched on Fort Duquesne in July with British regulars as well as colonial troops, which included his aide-de-camp Colonel George Washington. Braddock suffered a crushing and bloody defeat at the Battle of the Monongahela by a French contingent heavily reinforced by Native American warriors (British colonials referred to the Seven Years' War as the "French and Indian War" because those were their primary adversaries). The French and Native Americans also turned back British soldiers in northern New York, while British troops drove out the French population in Acadia and Nova Scotia.

By 1756 it was clear in both London and Paris that the so-far-undeclared war in North America could unleash an attack by France on the northern German state of Hanover, which was under the protection of its native son, Britain's King George II, in order to hold that territory hostage in exchange for American lands. The political preparations for this eventuality became known alternatively as the "Diplomatic Revolution," "Reversal of Alliances," or, most poetically, the "Stately Quadrille," referring to the popular dance in which couples frequently changed partners. The previous alliances that had held through the two previous wars of succession were quickly broken in favor of new ones. In January 1756, Britain signed a treaty with its former enemy Prussia to protect Hanover, while Prussia sought Britain's protection from a newly resurgent Russia. Several months later, Bourbon France allied with its old nemesis, Hapsburg Austria, so that French and Austrian forces could threaten Hanover while Austria could count on French help to regain the mineral-rich region of Silesia it had lost to Prussia in the previous war. As these new alliances took shape, France captured Minorca, which Britain had pried from Spain fifty years earlier. Britain declared war on France in May 1756; France reciprocated the following month. At this point, the conflict turned into a global war, roughly divided into two separate struggles—the first one between Britain and France that took place on the high seas and in their colonies, and the second one in continental Europe, primarily between Prussia and Austria.

The European conflict began first, just weeks after war was declared. In the opening stages, French troops defeated German and British troops to occupy Hanover, much to King George II's chagrin, while Austria achieved part of its goal by capturing Breslau in Silesia. As the war progressed, Prussia found itself fighting not just France and Austria but also Russia and Sweden. Time and again, Prussia's King Friedrich II ("the Great") proved himself a brilliant hands-on strategist as well as an innovative leader. Of Friedrich's Prussia it was later remarked that it "was not a country with an army, but an army with a country." Under his rule, Prussia became a highly militarized society—one person in fourteen was a soldier, compared with one in a hundred in France and Britain. Prussian soldiers were highly trained, spending three months of every year in military maneuvers, and their precision and discipline were rarely matched on the battlefield. Time and again during the Seven Years' War, Prussia was able to fight against long odds and superior numbers, ultimately retaining Silesia and eking out a draw with Austria.

By contrast, the conflict between France and Britain became decidedly one-sided in Britain's favor, despite some early victories by France. In 1757, France successfully repelled a major British assault on Louisbourg, built the strategically located Fort Carillon at the southern end of Lake Champlain in New York, and destroyed the British Fort William Henry on Lake George, just a few miles away. That same year, a new British government came to power, led by Prime Minister and First Lord of the Treasury Thomas Pelham-Holles, Duke of Newcastle, and William Pitt "the Elder," Earl of Chatham, who was secretary of state for the Southern Department, which at the time controlled defense and policy toward the American colonies. When it came to the conduct of the war, Pitt held the reins while Newcastle held the purse strings.

Pitt believed in taking the fight directly to the enemy. He first ordered a series of "descents" (amphibious assaults) on French ports and dockyards, but these were largely unsuccessful. In 1758 the fight began to turn in Britain's favor with the capture of Louisbourg in Canada and descents on the profitable French slaving settlements in West Africa. The British navy aggressively captured French warships and merchant ships, severely depleting the ranks of experienced sailors available to man its navy. In North America, Britain began clawing back territory it had lost in the previous two years. A British peace treaty with the Lenape (Delaware), Shawnee, and other Native American nations led to their withdrawing of support for the French in the Ohio Valley. Under Brigadier General John Forbes's command, British soldiers and a large contingent of colonial troops, including Colonel George Washington's First Virginia Regiment, immediately exploited this weakness by attacking Fort Duquesne, which the understrength French garrison blew up before retreating. On the same spot the British colonials built Fort Pitt and the surrounding settlement of Pittsborough (later Pittsburgh), named in honor of the statesman who had initiated the campaign.

The year 1759 was termed by London wags the annus mirabilis, but for France it was the annus horribilis—the beginning of a four-year string of British victories that threatened its possessions around the world and sealed its fate in North America. In the Caribbean, the British navy seized Guadeloupe, which would be followed by the fall of Martinique and Grenada. Farther north, French forts fell across the Ohio Valley, while the British captured Fort Carillon in the east, rebuilding it and renaming it Fort Ticonderoga. With Louisbourg neutralized, Britain began a siege of Quebec City, the capital of New France, which ended with a fierce fifteen-minute battle on the Plains of Abraham outside the city, pitting the British general James Wolfe against the French general Louis-Joseph, Marquis de Montcalm, both of whom would die in the battle. With the fall of Montreal the following year, New France would cease to exist as Canada was placed under British control.

These stunning defeats turned French strategy from fighting battles at the periphery to launching an all-out assault on Britain itself. The strategy was the brainchild of Étienne François, Duc de Choiseul, the younger but politically more powerful cousin of César Gabriel de Choiseul-Praslin. After a career as both soldier and diplomat, in October 1758 Choiseul was named secretary of state for foreign affairs. Louis XV, however, needed more than just a foreign minister to help him run his fractious government in time of war. He needed a chief minister, and the short, florid-faced Choiseul, whose boyish looks belied a keen political acumen and enormous appetite for work, assumed that role in all but name.

Like his counterpart William Pitt, Choiseul believed in taking the fight directly to the enemy. He planned to exploit the lack of troops stationed in Britain itself by carrying out an amphibious landing on its shores, diverting British resources from its Europe campaigns, while the blow to investor confidence would cripple its ability to raise war funds in the financial markets. More than three hundred boats were quickly built along the Atlantic coast to carry over forty thousand troops to Portsmouth, with additional troops to be sent in a diversionary raid in Scotland. But a British descent on Le Havre wrecked many of the boats, while a devastating naval battle in November 1759 at Quiberon Bay off Brittany destroyed the escorting warships. These twin events ended any hope of France invading Britain. The news from French India was also bad, with the capture and razing of the colony at Pondicherry (Puducherry) by forces under the British East India Company.

Choiseul soon assumed the role of minister of war while retaining his foreign affairs portfolio. Initial peace negotiations with Britain had failed, so he opened talks with the Spanish government about an alliance. The Spanish king Carlos III was actually the younger cousin of Louis XV, as both belonged to the Bourbon royal family. France and Spain had twice forged what were called Bourbon Family Compacts, in 1733 and 1743, which pledged mutual support and aid in the event of war as a bulwark against British hegemony. Now the two kings and their ministers believed that Britain was once again threatening the balance of power, and resolved to restore that balance. Madrid sent Jerónimo Grimaldi to negotiate the agreement, and the Third Bourbon Family Compact was signed by Choiseul and Grimaldi on August 15, 1761. It provided for Spain to declare war on Britain the following year provided no peace had been concluded, while France promised to support Spain if the latter were attacked. France, however, was hardly in a position to do so, as its fleet was being mauled by the British navy, which outbuilt and outcaptured France's navy by a ratio of ten to one.

Word of the secret Family Compact leaked to Britain, which, despite Newcastle's misgivings about engaging in yet another campaign, preemptively declared war on Spain in January 1762. But Spain had already set its sights on invading Britain's ally Portugal, which had only half the troop numbers as Spain. However, Portugal's shrewd and powerful prime minister, Sebastião José de Carvalho e Melo, Marquês de Pombal, had already requested British military assistance, and with its help turned back the Spanish army in what was later called the *Guerra Fantástica* (Miraculous War). Choiseul now proposed to Spain a combined amphibious invasion of Britain, but this too never happened as the two navies were unable to coordinate their actions. The final blows came later in the year, with the British capture of Manila and Havana. The loss of Havana was particularly devastating; the jewel in the Spanish crown, it boasted the finest and best-defended harbor in the Caribbean, and built more warships than any shipyard in Spain. Spain's rash decision to enter into the Seven Years' War had resulted in a harrowing string of losses that would cost it dearly in the peace negotiations to follow.

THE TREATY OF PARIS

The men who had conducted the war would not be the ones to sign the peace treaty. By 1762, Choiseul had taken over the Ministry of the Navy while still retaining the position of minister of war. His cousin Choiseul-Praslin, like himself a former soldier and diplomat, became the new foreign minister, though in fact they spoke with one voice. They faced a grim task; the French fleet was in a parlous state, largely blockaded in port and so cash-stricken that it was selling materiel just to make ends meet. Canada was lost, as were most of the colonies in the Caribbean, Africa, and Asia. "Since we do not know how to make war," Choiseul admitted privately, "we must make peace."

On the other side of the English Channel, Pitt and Newcastle, the chief architects of the brilliant British campaign, were on their way out. In 1760, George II died, and his grandson George III succeeded him to the throne. The twenty-two-year-old king, although close with his grandfather, made major changes to the government. He appointed as the new prime minister his longtime tutor, John Stuart, Earl of Bute, who was as anxious to make peace as Pitt was to make war. One of Bute's first actions after taking office was to formalize peace negotiations by exchanging diplomats with France, and the well-connected and influential Duke of Bedford was the obvious choice. Though most of the major decisions would be hammered out in Paris, Choiseul-Praslin selected Louis-Jules Mancini-Mazarini, Duc de Nivernais, to negotiate at the British court. In September, Bedford and Nivernais met at Calais before each went on to assume his post.

All sides understood that both France and Spain would have to pay a heavy territorial price for the war. Although Bute knew that the terms of peace had to be as generous as possible to avoid another conflict breaking out at a later date, Nivernais reported back that the prime minister was under enormous pressure by Pitt's still-powerful supporters to limit British concessions, so as to permanently hobble the French navy. Preliminary negotiations at Fontainebleau Palace stalled when Spain's ambassador, Jerónimo Grimaldi, appalled that British territorial demands would give it almost complete control of the Gulf of Mexico, refused to accept the peace terms offered. Choiseul was furious. "Does the king of Spain want war or peace?" he demanded of the French ambassador in Madrid, Pierre Paul, Marquis d'Ossun. "He must adopt the articles" or keep fighting, said Choiseul, "there is no middle ground." The impasse broke when news of Havana's fall arrived in October, and Louis XV offered French Louisiana to his cousin Carlos III in compensation for any territory Spain might lose in the peace negotiations, which would return to it at least some control over the Gulf of Mexico. Confronted with such a heavy loss and offered such a face-saving measure, the Spanish king relented. Choiseul-Praslin, Grimaldi, and Bedford signed the preliminary treaty at Fontainebleau on November 3. The same day, unbeknownst to Bedford, Choiseul-Praslin and Grimaldi agreed on a separate treaty handing Louisiana to Spain.

The three men negotiated the final terms between November 1762 and February 1763. France felt most keenly its loss of Canada, Acadia, and Nova Scotia to Britain. With Louisiana also gone, France was now almost entirely out of North America. It did, however, maintain access to the fisheries off Newfoundland and in the Gulf of Saint Lawrence, and retained the small, rocky islands of Saint-Pierre and Miquelon for drying and processing the fish. Their strategic importance went far beyond the provision of foodstuffs; the French navy's greatest weakness had historically been manpower, and these fisheries trained roughly one-third of the navy's sailors.

Britain returned to France the main sugar-producing islands of Martinique and Guadeloupe, while retaining Grenada and Saint Vincent. It also cut France off from its former African trading posts, except the slave-trading island of Gorée off modern-day Senegal. French Indian territory was dramatically reduced to just a few trading posts, of which the largest, the beautiful white town of Pondicherry, would be rebuilt in just two years. France, in its turn, relinquished Minorca to British rule.

Britain was also generous in returning Manila to Spain, but demanded either Puerto Rico or Florida in exchange for Havana. Puerto Rico was too valuable to Spain, so instead Britain got Florida, which one politician huffed, was "an uninhabited country." Spain also had to allow Britain logging rights in the Honduras region of Guatemala in Central America. In Europe, the situation returned more or less to *status quo ante bellum*. The residual Spanish troops departed Portugal, while Prussia and Austria withdrew their remaining armies from each other's territories and signed a separate peace accord.

The final Treaty of Paris, according to Bedford, "succeed greatly beyond my expectations," as he made "no one concession contrary to my instructions." The unchanging physical landscape of Europe belied the tectonic shift that had upended its political geography. Although Britain had lost almost all its allies in Europe, they were now thought to be of little consequence, as the global balance of power was now overwhelmingly in its favor. Britain controlled most of North America, its worldwide colonies could trade unmolested, and for the first time Britannia could truthfully be said to "rule the waves," as the popular song claimed. Therefore, when Choiseul-Praslin, Grimaldi, and Bedford signed the treaty on the evening of February 10, it was fitting that the ceremony took place in a thoroughly British drawing room rather than in an anteroom in the royal palace at Versailles.

News of the treaty was celebrated in Britain with a spectacular fireworks display in London's Green Park. Perhaps surprisingly, France and Spain also celebrated the treaty with a series of fireworks in front of the Hôtel de Ville in Paris and in the Parque del Buen Retiro in Madrid. After the War of the Austrian Succession, the French people had coined the phrase "as stupid as the peace" (*bête comme la paix*) in exasperation for having shed so much blood with nothing to show for it. Now, aware that the outcome could have been far worse than losing "a few acres of snow," there was a general sense that life could return to normal, even in the shadow of Europe's new superpower.

THE BOURBON STRATEGY OF *REVANCHE*

Life in France did appear to return to normal, as prices and trade quickly returned to prewar levels. Tourism rebounded in both directions across the English Channel. The celebrated Grand Tour that most young British aristocrats took to see the culture, history, and art of Europe (primarily in France and Italy) was seriously interrupted during the Seven Years' War. When fighting ended in late 1762, well-to-do gentlemen like the aforementioned Edward Gibbon quickly resumed the practice even before the peace treaty was signed. The postwar Grand Tour would, however, be more restrained than the previous lavish-spending ways of Britons on the Continent. The author of the *Gentleman's Guide, in His Tour through France* advised travelers "not to spend more money in the country of our natural enemy, than is requisite to support, with decency, the character of an Englishman."

The end of the war also sparked a reverse Grand Tour from France to Britain, with a sudden French fascination for all things British. The term "anglomania" was popularized to describe the sudden wave of British fashion on Paris streets, French plays about British life, and even the introduction of English-style natural landscaping into staid, formal French *jardins*. French tourists began descending on Britain in droves, causing one British aristocrat to complain that "London abounds in French." Frenchmen saw London in the way future generations of Americans would come to regard Paris, as the place to expand their horizons. Jean-Jacques Rousseau, the writer and philosopher, immersed himself in botanical science, while the scientists Jérôme Lalande and Charles-Marie de La Condamine dined with famous British authors like Samuel Johnson. Johnson, for his part, attributed French anglomania to the recently concluded war: "We had drubbed those fellows into a proper reverence for us. . . . Their national petulance required periodical chastisement."

Not all French visitors acknowledged this idea of "periodical chastisement," nor were they in Britain to absorb the culture. Almost before the ink was even dry on the Treaty of Paris, French military officers were spreading out across the south of England, undoubtedly hoping to pass unnoticed among the throng of foreign tourists while they gathered intelligence on the British navy and potential landing sites on the coast. Those officers were part of an invasion scheme secretly being devised in the halls of Versailles and in Madrid. France and Spain hoped to build on the hard-won experience of the previous failed attempts to make a new invasion a success.

Choiseul in particular had fixed on the strategy of invading England almost from the moment he entered high office. The first invasion attempt in 1759 had foundered because France was unable to match Britain's superior command of the seas. The second attempt in 1762 failed because France and Spain could not coordinate their fleets. The third time, Choiseul would have told himself, the situation would be very different. With his longtime ally Jéronimo Grimaldi now back in Spain as chief minister to King Carlos III, the two began planning a comprehensive Bourbon strategy of *revanche* (revenge) against Britain whose centerpiece would be a combined assault on England. The focus of planning was on their navies, for while Britain's coasts were protected by its "wooden walls" of warships, the island itself had only a smattering of regular troops and militia. If France and Spain could land their troops, Britain could easily be overrun.

Both Choiseul and Grimaldi knew it would take five or more years for both navies to rebuild a credible offensive capability against the British fleet. They therefore undertook two projects simultaneously—first, intelligence-gathering, and second, creating an effective, unified Bourbon armada—all the while pretending to the British that they were only interested in keeping the peace.

For its part, the British government was not fooled. The very first instructions to the Earl of Hertford, Bedford's successor as ambassador to France, demanded

> constant information from you of every step that is taken in France which may tend to strengthen the military force of that Kingdom, and especially in what concerns the augmentation of their navy. . . . You will doubtless be entertained with the strongest declarations of their love of peace and their desire to perpetuate

> it upon the foot of the present settlement, but . . . it is not easy to imagine that the Court of France as well as that of Spain, should not have thoughts of putting themselves in a condition to recover in time their lost possessions and retrieve the reputation of their arms. And though their ability to carry such views into execution may indeed be at a considerable distance, yet it equally behooves us to be upon our guard and to watch every motion that may have such a dangerous tendency.

It was therefore under intense British scrutiny that French spies began arriving in Britain to gather critical intelligence on the British navy and on potential landing sites. In 1764, Choiseul dispatched a young navy cadet, Henri Fulque, Chevalier d'Oraison, to enter the British naval bases of Plymouth and Portsmouth, as well as shipyards on the Thames. "Everything is closed to civilians and foreigners," he boasted, "although I showed that their vigilance is not infallible." He reported back on the number and type of ships under repair and construction, and on technical innovations that could potentially give the British ships an edge in battle.

At the same time as Oraison was visiting shipyards, military spies were reconnoitering the English countryside for landing sites and invasion routes. Jean-Charles-Adolphe Grant de Blairfindy, a Scottish officer in the French service, showed a keen sense of history when he recommended a town in Kent as the ideal landing spot: "It was at Deal where Julius Caesar, having been repulsed at Dover, debarked his army to conquer England." Another army officer, Pierre-François de Béville, recommended attacking Portsmouth in order to cripple the navy, before moving on to London.

Unknown to Choiseul, other French spies were also on the ground in England to scout the best invasion sites. The reason Choiseul, easily one of the best-informed ministers in France, was unaware of these agents was that they were operating under Louis XV's shadow network, the *Secret du Roi* (King's Secret). It had been started by the king twenty years earlier as a surreptitious attempt to obtain the Polish throne for his cousin Louis-François, Prince de Conti. The king bypassed his foreign minister and sent clandestine orders directly to key ambassadors in nations like Sweden, Poland, and Ottoman Turkey, in order to garner political support for his cousin. Although this subterfuge did not succeed in getting Conti the throne, Louis XV kept the *Secret du Roi* and enlarged it so that he was soon passing orders to and getting intelligence from over two dozen ambassadors and embassy officers, all the while keeping his foreign ministers in the dark. In effect, there were now *two* foreign policies operating, the first under the secretary of state for foreign affairs, and the second under the king. With ambassadors and officers getting conflicting orders from Versailles, while at the same time depending upon clandestine agents of sometimes questionable loyalties, the *Secret du Roi* would prove to be a corrosive and ultimately destructive system.

Charles-François de Broglie, who had served as both an ambassador to Britain and a general during the Seven Years' War, was Louis XV's most trusted member of the *Secret*. De Broglie (pronounced *de Broy;* the original Italian family name Broglio means "intrigue") knew that after the Treaty of Paris was signed, the ambassador, the Duc de Nivernais, would return from London and that his place would be taken by the chargé d'affaires Charles de Beaumont, Chevalier d'Éon, another member of the *Secret*. De Broglie, like Choiseul, also hit upon the idea of planning a future invasion of England, but in his case the spies would work from the French embassy in London. Louis XV approved the project in 1765 but kept Choiseul out of the picture.

De Broglie sent to Britain one of his former army engineering officers, Louis-François Carlet de La Rozière, who in turn used a network of his own spies and paid British informants to map out potential invasion sites. La Rozière made detailed drawings and notes of more than one hundred miles of coastline and access routes to London, which he forwarded to de Broglie via d'Éon. Even though the invasion plot had to be kept secret, lest the British get wind of it and use it as an excuse for a preemptive assault, d'Éon kept copies of the correspondence for himself. At the same time, he began ingratiating himself with the British aristocracy, throwing lavish parties at the French embassy's expense. Also, he began dressing as a woman. De Broglie ignored d'Éon's increasingly aberrant behavior, while still badgering Louis XV to put his invasion plans into action. Finally, after years of inaction on the king's part, in 1768 de Broglie was finally allowed to contact Choiseul and send him his hard-won intelligence. Choiseul, in turn, quickly incorporated de Broglie's plans into his own.

Even as the first part of the invasion project—intelligence-gathering—was being finalized, the second part, creating an effective, unified Bourbon fleet, was already well under way. At the beginning of

1763, France had only forty-seven ships of the line (large warships that could fight in a line of battle against other fleets), while Spain had just thirty-seven, far short of the numbers needed. The French treasury after the war was deeply in the red—the portion of revenues that went to debt service and interest had doubled to over 60 percent—and at first Choiseul depended mostly on the program he had instituted during the war, called the *don des vaisseaux* (gift of ships). Individuals, towns, and entire cities were encouraged to donate money to build and outfit ships, accounting for over half of the thirty new ships added to the fleet over seven years. The massive ninety-gun *Ville de Paris,* which would become one of the flagships of the French fleet, was named in honor of the city that funded its construction. Spain was slower off the mark, building only eight ships in the same period.

Both Choiseul and Grimaldi also recognized that simply building more ships was insufficient to defeat the British navy, given the dismal showing of the Bourbon fleets. A wholesale reformation and integration of the navies on both sides of the Pyrenees was in order. In one of his last official acts as navy minister before he switched places again with his cousin Choiseul-Praslin and reassumed the post of foreign minister, Choiseul issued a sweeping Naval Ordinance in 1765 that streamlined the bureaucracy, enforced a strict series of "rates" that standardized the types and dimensions of ships so they would maneuver and fight as one unit, and set up the world's first professional corps of shipbuilders, whose task was to use scientific principles in the design and construction of vessels, with the goal of making each ship better than its British counterpart. These mechanisms of streamlining, standardizing, and fine-tuning the fleet would, Choiseul hoped, create a more effective navy without greatly increasing its cost.

Grimaldi's task, on the other hand, was to rebuild the Spanish fleet along the same lines as the French fleet, so they could operate in unison. That meant importing not just French technology but also French know-how. In 1765, Grimaldi asked Choiseul to send French engineers who could bring both Spanish shipbuilding and gun manufacture up to French standards. For the first request, Choiseul sent Jean-François Gautier, a midlevel shipbuilder, to be placed in charge of all Spanish ship construction. Gautier quickly discarded the older, sturdier Spanish designs and, starting with the seventy-four-gun *San Juan Nepomuceno,* began constructing lighter, faster warships in the French mode, following the instructions from Choiseul's Naval Ordinance. The French shipbuilder fully understood Grimaldi's objectives: "My duty is to regard French and Spanish vessels as forming a single Armada."

For the second request, Choiseul dispatched, also in 1765, the Swiss French artillery engineer Jean Maritz to Spain, where he established foundries that employed the same technique recently introduced in France of solid-casting the cannon and drilling the bore, which gave cannon greater power and precision. Maritz followed the new French guidelines for gun sizes and calibers, so that the older Spanish hodgepodge of naval guns was soon replaced by a standardized set of cannon that could fire more accurately and at longer ranges. These changes to hulls, masts, and guns meant that the new generation of Spanish warships would maneuver and fight identically to French ships of the line. Now, just a few years after the Treaty of Paris, France and Spain were well advanced in planning a war with Britain, and were on their way to having an armada that could accomplish it.

The war plan that was agreed to by both nations in 1767 called for a surprise assault by a combined fleet of 140 ships of the line (80 French, 60 Spanish) against Britain's 120 ships. The main force would escort a fleet of smaller landing boats to descend on Portsmouth and the Sussex coast, laying waste to critical parts of the naval infrastructure so that the British navy could no longer rule the waves. The invasion would stop short of a full-out assault on London, which could frighten other Continental powers and potentially destabilize France's careful web of alliances. Instead, French diversionary forces would attack Scotland, while Spanish forces would descend on Gibraltar with the aim of recovering the strategic territory that Spain had lost years earlier.

Choiseul outlined the grand strategy of such a war in a memorandum to Louis XV. He reminded his king that he "had been attacked in 1755 in America" by a nation intent on driving them out of the continent. The Treaty of Paris was an "embarrassment." There could be no peace in the foreseeable future: "England is the declared enemy of your power and your state, and will always be." Instead, France must now prepare for a new war against Britain. The objective of this war would not be to destroy the British nation, but rather the more limited goal of restoring the European balance of power. France should no longer seek to fight Britain on the Continent, which would be destabilizing, but should instead attempt to undermine its maritime supremacy. All France's foreign policy would be bent to that aim, strengthening its European alliances—that with Spain above all—and exploiting any opportunity to weaken Britain on the world stage.

Toward the end of his memorandum, the French minister held out the hope that Britain could be weakened, not through a direct attack by France and Spain, but simply as a result of its own colonial policies in North America in the aftermath of the Seven Years' War. With phenomenal prescience, Choiseul predicted that "only the future American Revolution will consign England to a state of weakness where it is no longer feared in Europe," though he worried that "we will likely not see it. . . . This event is far away." His cousin Choiseul-Praslin expressed a similar thought regarding the recently concluded Treaty of Paris: "This peace is a remarkable epoch for the English monarchy, but its power is neither stable nor certain; it must either rise or fall. . . . The vast domains it has recently acquired may lead to its loss. . . . One day its colonies will be powerful enough to separate from London and found a state independent from the English crown." Though both men were certain that an American revolution would happen, and that it would topple Britain from its lofty perch, neither believed they could bet on it in the short term. Nevertheless, they decided to hedge that bet by sending a pair of military officers and a Scottish wine merchant to observe at first hand the effect of Britain's policies on its American colonies, and to report back on whether a revolution was in the offing or not.

FRENCH AGENTS IN THE AMERICAN COLONIES

This first of France's agents in the American colonies, navy lieutenant François de Sarrebourse de Pontleroy de Beaulieu, disembarked in Philadelphia in early 1764. He signed on with an American merchant to command a cargo ship that plied the New England and mid-Atlantic coasts. As a ship's master, he could, unnoticed, make accurate maps and soundings of the principal ports, and could speak with other merchants and tradesmen to obtain a broad understanding of the American mind. Pontleroy had arrived just as the glow of victory celebrations was giving way to stirrings of unrest. Historians often quote John Shy's assertion that "Americans were never more British than in 1763" for good reason: The threat of French forces had been removed, the potential for westward expansion seemed limitless, and Britain now controlled the major ocean routes, which meant more trade for the colonies.

The news in July 1763 that a confederation of Native American nations, led by the Ottawa chief Pontiac, was attacking forts on the western frontiers in response to heavy-handed British incursions, gave American colonists their first indication that they would not have unbridled access to the continent. Pontiac's War, as it became known, helped catalyze the British government to issue the Royal Proclamation of 1763 that attempted to bring order and stability to the continent. It created the colonies of Quebec, East Florida, West Florida, and Grenada, and established the western boundary of the original thirteen colonies with a line running down the Appalachian Mountains. According to London, the territory west of the Proclamation Line was given over to the Native American nations, and no British settlements could be made there. That put the investment plans of land speculators like the Ohio Company and George Washington's newly formed Mississippi Land Company in jeopardy.

A second blow to the collective American purse came in the form of taxation. For generations Britain had taken a largely hands-off approach to governing the American colonies, a policy later referred to as "salutary neglect," in keeping with the theory that fewer restrictions would allow the colonies to prosper and thus profit Britain as a whole. Where the average British citizen in 1763 paid twenty-six shillings per year in taxes (equivalent to $200 today), the average American colonist paid just one shilling. Import taxes and trade restrictions with foreign powers went largely unenforced in the American colonies, and merchants from Boston to Charleston did a brisk trade with nations like Spain and the Netherlands and their Caribbean colonies. But the enormous debts incurred during the Seven Years' War—interest payments alone amounted to over 40 percent of revenue—changed that calculus for the British government. Ministers in London now argued that since the war had largely been fought on behalf of the American colonists, they should help shoulder the costs of their defense, which included stationing British troops in the territories.

For over a century, Britain had sought to prevent its colonies from trading directly with other European powers by instating a series of Navigation Acts that levied duties and restricted foreign commerce. The latest incarnation of these acts was the American Duties Act of 1764, which the colonists quickly dubbed the Sugar Act. It clamped down on smuggling but also reduced the tax on sugar and molasses that the colonists paid for imports from British Caribbean plantations. Since they almost never paid those taxes, the Sugar Act's stricter tax collection and antismuggling measures meant a de facto tax hike and simultaneous reduction in trade. At the same time, Parliament passed the Currency Act that tightened the colonists' paper money supply, which was increasingly used due to lack of hard currency (specie) in silver and gold coin. These two acts created a currency shortage that worsened the effects of the postwar depression.

Despite these economic hardships, Pontleroy reported that the American colonies were prosperous, with productive land and spacious harbors, and were in the middle of a postwar baby boom. He also noted their resentment over the Sugar Act, in particular the sudden appearance of revenue ships that put a halt to their previously overlooked Caribbean trade. The Americans were eager to throw off these restrictions on trade and commerce that were cutting into their business. Nor did they see any need for continued British protection now that France no longer had a presence on the continent. Americans were restive, he concluded, and would one day revolt against their mother country. "England," he argued, "should expect a revolution, for it has hastened that occurrence by freeing the colonies from the fear of the French in Canada."

American colonists soon learned that the Sugar Act was a prelude to more severe measures. In early 1765, Parliament passed the Stamp Act and the Quartering Act, both of which were intended to help fund the estimated ten thousand British troops stationed throughout the colonies that London believed necessary for their protection. Where the Sugar Act incited heated grumbling, these acts resulted in outright revolts. Neither act was particularly onerous on its face. The Stamp Act imposed a relatively modest tax on legal documents, magazines, and newspapers, which fell primarily on lawyers and printers, a small, reasonably prosperous subset of the population. The Quartering Act actually exempted private homes from being used as temporary barracks, only authorizing the use of vacant buildings. The point at issue for the colonists was that Parliament should not have the right to levy taxes on them (the Quartering Act was seen as a tax in kind) because they were not represented in the legislature—"no taxation without representation," as the Boston minister John Mayhew had said as far back as 1750. Further, the Americans also argued that as there were no practical means for colonial representation in a three-thousand-mile-distant Parliament, only their own representative assemblies should have the power to tax and to determine how those revenues were spent. The Stamp Act and the Quartering Act were widely seen as direct attempts by Parliament to circumvent the colonial legislatures, opening the door to future tax measures without their representation or consent. Street riots protesting the taxes broke out in Boston (where the homes of acting governor Thomas Hutchinson and stamp distributor Andrew Oliver were gutted), as well as in Newport and Philadelphia.

In May 1765, the House of Burgesses, Virginia's legislative body, met in Williamsburg to denounce the Stamp Act. A young representative named Patrick Henry led the charge with a series of pronouncements, the Virginia Resolves, which declared that only the state legislature, not Parliament, had the right to tax its colonists. His speech before the House of Burgesses compared the movement against the Stamp Act with Brutus standing up to Caesar and Cromwell to Charles I, a sentiment that other members saw as crossing the line of treason.

One of the eyewitnesses to Patrick Henry's inflammatory speech was Charles Murray, a Scottish representative for a London-based wine merchant. Having arrived via the French Caribbean to Charleston in early 1765, he made his way to New York with many stops along the way, selling barrels of "choice prime" Madeira to the likes of George Washington. At the same time, he was furiously taking notes that he sent back to the French government on the state of the American colonies. Those notes, written in English and French, did not reveal how or why he became a spy for France, though like many Scottish Catholics he may have had residual Jacobite leanings that favored France over the "perfidious English." They did, however, record the widespread anger, spilling over to rage, that the Stamp Act had provoked. Murray recounted Patrick Henry saying that his diatribe "must be attributed to the interest of his Country's dying liberty which he had at heart." He met a lawyer in Annapolis who, though loyal to the Crown, "would take up arms himself in defense of his liberty and property." And Choiseul, who undoubtedly read Murray's report, would have been heartened to learn of a group of Virginia taverngoers who proclaimed, "Let the worst come to the worst, we'll call the French to our succor."

The Stamp Act never fully took effect before Parliament, taken aback by the vehemence of the colonists' response, repealed it in early

1766. At the same time it passed the Declaratory Acts, asserting that it superseded colonial legislatures and had complete power to tax the colonies. Parliament stuck another finger in the colonists' eye the following year with the Townshend Acts, named for the chancellor of the exchequer, who proposed duties on colonial imports of glass, lead, paints, paper, and most notably tea, all of which were only available from Britain. Colonists chafed at these continuous infringements upon their rights and livelihoods. Although this time the response was neither as swift nor as violent as with the Stamp Act, resentment against the Crown continued to build.

Once again, an agent from France was in America to witness and report the colonists' response at first hand. Johann de Kalb was a Bavarian-born officer who had acquired his French nobiliary "de" while serving in the French army under Charles-François de Broglie during the Seven Years' War. De Broglie saw that de Kalb, although not part of the *Secret du Roi,* had the intelligence, discretion, and language skills requisite for espionage. In 1767, he proposed to Choiseul that de Kalb be dispatched to America "to identify the views of the American colonists towards Great

Johann, Baron de Kalb (1721–1780).
Charles Willson Peale, from life,
oil on canvas

Britain, and in the case that they envisage a rupture with London, what are their capabilities to wage war or defend themselves."

De Kalb arrived in January 1768, and spent the next four months assessing the revolutionary climate of the colonies from Philadelphia to Boston. This time, the climate was almost as cold as the icy marshes de Kalb braved overnight when soon after his arrival in America, his ship sank just off Staten Island. Compared with Patrick Henry's fiery rhetoric just three years earlier, the sentiment de Kalb heard most often was that of resignation. He reported to Choiseul on his return that yes, the residents were angry about the Townshend Acts, resentful at having to lodge soldiers in their towns and cities, and unhappy with the tight money supply and restrictions on trade that were cutting into profits, all of which could lead to an uprising. "There is no doubt that this country will liberate itself at some point," he speculated, but immediately dashed Choiseul's hopes for an immediate break with the mother country; such a revolution would only happen "when its population exceeds that of Great Britain," many years hence. More damning was his assessment of the chances for the French leading the rebellion. Even though the colonies had no navy and no arsenals with which to support a fight against the motherland, "they will never accept any foreign help, especially that of France, which they view with suspicion and alarm against their liberty; they would rather submit to the English Parliament for a while."

Choiseul, who had hoped for news of a French-led revolutionary war on the horizon, did not take de Kalb's report well, refusing to meet with him upon his return and denying him a long-sought promotion. Not only did it dash Choiseul's carefully thought-out plans for fomenting an American insurrection, it did not square with the previous reports from his spies. Yet de Kalb was reporting a real sentiment that the other observers had either missed or intentionally omitted—as much as the colonials hated the continuous barrage of taxes and trade restrictions, many were still proud to be part of the great British Empire and believed that this "family quarrel" could be resolved equitably. In the American colonies, allegiances did not line up neatly inside borders, as they seemed to do in Europe. Choiseul, who had mastered the European chessboard, was only beginning to understand how much more complex the American game would be.

SPANISH OBSERVERS IN THE AMERICAN COLONIES

The American game was getting more complicated by the month as the effects of the Treaty of Paris became clearer. With the transfer of so much territory from one nation to another, a great reordering of the British, French, and Spanish population took place. From 1763 until the start of the War of American Independence, North America was a continent on the move. Émigrés came in record numbers from across Europe—Britain, Ireland, the German states—lured by the promise of land, resources, and relative peace. Landowners like George Washington put pressure on the British government to open up more western territory for settlement. The government responded by pushing colonial boundaries well past the Proclamation Line and ever closer to the Mississippi River, slowly encroaching on Native American territories.

Farther south, British efforts to populate the two Florida colonies were more disappointing. Spain had relinquished Florida to Britain, which then divided the territory into East Florida (primarily the peninsula, with the capital at Saint Augustine) and West Florida (from the current panhandle to the Mississippi, with the capital at Pensacola). Although Spanish inhabitants were allowed to remain and to practice Catholicism, they overwhelmingly chose to emigrate to Mexico and Cuba. The British government provided land grants to encourage settlement as a means of defense against the Spanish territories, but failed to attract more than a few thousand immigrants to each colony.

Unlike in Florida, the French population of Canada largely chose to stay and live under British rule, though there continued to be some friction between their Catholicism and official Church of England policies. Nevertheless, a substantial minority of Canadians opted to move to Louisiana, a migration that had actually begun during the Seven Years' War when the Acadians were driven from their land. Spanish Louisiana, with its capital at New Orleans, was an enormous territory, twice the size of the thirteen American colonies. The new Spanish governor, Antonio de Ulloa, saw the French settlers as solid bulwarks against potential British encroachment from just across the Mississippi River, and encouraged this migration with transportation and land grants—Saint Louis, for example, was established in 1764 as a French city on Spanish territory.

Britain's occupation of Florida and its continued westward advancement toward the Mississippi River represented a strategic threat to Spanish control of the region. Back in Madrid, the chief minister, Jerónimo Grimaldi, like his counterpart Choiseul, depended upon his intelligence networks to keep tabs on British activities in the Americas. However, he was much more concerned about the potential for surprise attacks on New Orleans and the Louisiana colony than he was about fomenting an American revolution. Part of the reason for concern was that the early years of Spanish Louisiana were fraught with political problems that left the colony potentially vulnerable. The first governor, Ulloa, more of a scientist than an administrator, was forcibly evicted in 1768 during an open rebellion against Spanish authority. He was replaced by the Irish-born Alejandro O'Reilly, who brutally quashed the rebellion. In 1770 a new governor, Luis de Unzaga y Amezaga, finally brought some stability to the colony.

Unzaga served under Antonio María de Bucareli y Ursúa, the captain-general of Cuba, who was military and civilian commander for the northern Caribbean and Gulf of Mexico. Together they developed a network of observers—not trained agents per se, but rather fishermen, merchants, and clergy, all likely to go unnoticed as they entered and departed British territory—who clandestinely reported on ports, fortifications, military garrisons, and fleet movements. The reports that came back to New Orleans and Havana were collected and sent on to Madrid, which helped shape Spain's policy of watchful neutrality toward Britain in the decade after the Treaty of Paris.

Cuba's fishing fleet became a particularly important source for intelligence-gathering and its means of transmission. Not only were fishermen able to observe and track British naval movements across the Caribbean and the Gulf of Mexico, but they also carried messages back and forth to observers in the British colonies, including a group of Spanish priests in East Florida who monitored events in Saint Augustine. Meanwhile, Cuban merchants made regular trips to Pensacola and reported back to Bucareli on the buildup of fortifications around the bay.

Unzaga, meanwhile, was concerned about the British buildup along the Mississippi. Settlers were encouraged to move to the Ohio and Mississippi River valleys both by lack of enforcement of the Proclamation Line, effectively allowing settlement to creep westward, and by prospectuses such as the widely read *Present State of European Settlements on the Mississippi,* published in 1770, that painted a glowing picture of life in the western territories. Wagons and flatboats were soon transporting large numbers of families to towns like Natchez and Baton Rouge.

The year 1770 also brought a political crisis that threatened all-out war and required even closer observation by Unzaga's network. Britain and Spain both maintained small settlements on the Falkland (Malvinas) Islands in the South Atlantic. Acting on orders from Madrid, the governor of Buenos Aires sent a large amphibious force to remove the British garrison. The two nations geared up for war. Madrid advised its overseas colonies to be vigilant against surprise attack, but not to make any hostile moves that might precipitate it. Meanwhile, Grimaldi called on France to honor the Bourbon Family Compact by coming to its aid. Although Choiseul (once again France's foreign minister) gave the Spanish ambivalent responses, Louis XV came down firmly against it. The crisis was defused the following year when Spain disavowed the military action and sidestepped the question of sovereignty.

Even though Unzaga detected no hostile British activities along the Mississippi as a result of the Falklands/Malvinas crisis, he dispatched Jean Surriret, a French merchant and officer in the Spanish militia from near Baton Rouge, to travel to New York to follow up on vague rumors of British troop redeployments farther north, which he feared might be the prelude to an attack. Surriret arrived in 1772 to learn that Thomas Gage, the commander in chief of the British forces in North America, indeed had redeployed his troops from Canada to reinforce New York, Boston, Philadelphia, and other cities. This redeployment was not to threaten Spanish interests, Surriret learned, but was in response to the civil unrest that had developed over the Townshend Acts, which had already resulted in the 1770 Boston Massacre, where British troops fired into a crowd of civilians and killed five. Although both Unzaga and the ministers back in Madrid were reassured by their observers' report, they kept a close eye on the increasing numbers of British troops and ships coming to North America.

FRANKLIN IN THE COCKPIT

In 1768, Johann de Kalb had seen the American colonies generally resigned to British authority. By 1774, they were on the verge of rebellion. Although Parliament had largely repealed the Townshend Acts, it retained the tax on tea and reinforced it with the Tea Act of 1773. Protesters in Boston responded in December 1773 with what contemporary accounts termed "the destruction of the tea," the dumping of a consignment of East India Company tea into Boston harbor, which sparked an uproar on both sides of the Atlantic. Back in London, the standings of the various colonial agents representing American interests to Parliament, which included Ralph Izard for South Carolina and Arthur Lee for Massachusetts, were irretrievably damaged—none more so than Benjamin Franklin, who had been representing Pennsylvania, Massachusetts, and several other states for the past seventeen years, and had been influential in the repeal of the Stamp Act. In late January 1774, he was called before the Privy Council (the king's advisory body) to defend a petition for the removal of Hutchinson and Oliver from the Massachusetts government. Accompanied by his longtime friend Edward Bancroft, he donned an elegant Manchester velvet suit and entered the Cockpit, the Privy Council's chamber at the Palace of Whitehall. Instead of defending the petition, Franklin found himself accused of being the leader of a "secret cabal" intent on turning the American people against their legitimate government. He stoically bore the hourlong harangue, then left with barely a word. Only days before, he had believed that he was slowly accomplishing with Parliament an "accommodation of our differences." He was now convinced that these personal attacks underscored a deep-seated intransigence on Parliament's part that no amount of accommodation could overcome.

For its part, Parliament saw little use for such concessions. It replied to the rising colonial unrest with the Coercive Acts of 1774, which among other provisions closed the Boston port to trade, stripped Massachusetts of any self-governance, and ordered the quartering of troops in towns and cities. The British government directed Gage to enforce the Coercive Acts and suppress any open rebellion, believing that France would not interfere with British colonial affairs, given its lack of support for Spain during the Falklands/Malvinas crisis. The American colonies reacted by sending delegates to the First Continental Congress in Philadelphia in September 1774 to debate what actions could be taken in response to the acts. They also began forming and training militia to prepare for conflict.

In France, the men who had signed the Treaty of Paris would not be the ones to watch with concern as the American war unfolded. Louis XV had lost confidence in Choiseul after the Falklands/Malvinas crisis, and sacked him soon after. Gone too was his cousin Choiseul-Praslin, and with them the rigid control that had dominated French foreign and naval policy for over a decade. The previous *revanche* strategy toward Britain was replaced with a more pacific tone, as French naval rearmament slowed and invasion plans for Britain were shelved. The crisis had also soured the Bourbon Family Compact and made Spain wary of further dependence on France.

In 1774, just as the situation in the American colonies was coming to a boil, Louis XV died, and his grandson Louis XVI succeeded him to the throne. The nineteen-year-old king, although having drawn close to his grandfather after his own father's death, nevertheless instituted major changes to the government. He brought in a former navy minister who had been out of favor for twenty-five years, Jean-Frédéric Phélypeaux, Comte de Maurepas, to be his principal minister. Upon learning from Charles-François de Broglie of the *Secret du Roi,* the king immediately disbanded it, bringing all diplomatic policy under his new foreign minister, Charles Gravier, Comte de Vergennes, himself a former member of the *Secret.* Unfortunately, there was one member of the *Secret* who remained at large, the Chevalier d'Éon, still in London with France's now-abandoned plans for invading Britain. If London learned of these plans, it could precipitate a war that the new king was hardly willing or prepared to undertake. As it happened, the solution to the d'Éon problem, hatched by Louis XVI and Vergennes, would lead France directly into the War of American Independence.

CHAPTER 2

The Merchants

The American insurrection of 1774 was not the first time the British government had faced down a rebellion of its citizens. A generation earlier, the Jacobite rising of 1745 had attempted to overthrow the Crown and install a Scottish claimant, Charles Edward Stuart, to the throne of Great Britain. The rebellion was quickly and violently ended at the Battle of Culloden, where almost a third of the seven thousand Jacobite troops were killed, wounded, or captured. Britain believed that the swift, brutal enforcement of the Coercive Acts would disrupt a full-blown revolution by isolating and punishing the rebellious Massachusetts colony.

It had exactly the opposite effect on the Americans. The other colonies, fearing the same actions could be meted out to them, rallied behind Massachusetts and convened the First Continental Congress, demonstrating that they could act in unison against their common adversary, Parliament. The delegates still believed in their future as part of the British Empire, but now it would have to be on their own terms. They condemned the Coercive Acts as unconstitutional and prepared a list of grievances to send to King George III. They put teeth into their resolutions by approving the arming of local militias to resist further enforcement of the acts, and applied economic pressure by establishing an effective boycott of all trade with Britain and its Caribbean colonies. As the delegates departed Philadelphia in October 1774, they agreed to reconvene the following May if their grievances had not been addressed.

The raising, organizing, and equipping of militias were to fall under

Committees of Safety and Committees of Supplies appointed in each colony. It soon became apparent that signing men to the militia was one thing, but equipping them with guns, ammunition, and powder was entirely another. In colonial America, personal firearms were of widely different types and caliber. Some were smoothbore muskets acquired from the British army during the Seven Years' War (generally the 0.75 caliber "Brown Bess" Land Pattern muskets), others were lighter "fowling pieces" used primarily for small game, and a few—especially along the Appalachian frontier—were the more accurate but slower-firing spiral-bore rifles. This lack of uniformity presented major logistical problems for keeping a militia company supplied with the right kinds of ammunition and spare parts. The Pennsylvania Committee of Safety, for example, found that some militia companies required seven different kinds of ammunition.

In addition, a number of the militia volunteers arrived at muster unarmed. Although at least half of all wealthholders in colonial America owned guns, some militiamen left them at home for hunting and the protection of their families. For example, while returns for New England showed that on average about three-quarters of the militia brought their own weapons, that percentage varied widely; some regiments in New Hampshire reported only one musket and one pound of gunpowder for every four militiamen, enough for about fifteen rounds per man. Although a company could conceivably train with fewer guns than militiamen, it still needed large quantities of powder for practice firing. In wartime, of course, powder use went up dramatically, and guns would be lost, captured, damaged, or under repair, meaning that several firearms were needed for every militiaman. The Committees of Safety and Supplies would have to make up the difference.

The committees knew that their ability to quickly arm the militias was very limited. In late 1774 the Privy Council had issued a ban on the export of all firearms, gunpowder, and accoutrements to the colonies. Meanwhile, the colonists' access to local stockpiles of arms and powder was methodically cut off as the royal colonial governments moved to secure or confiscate them. In September 1774, the Massachusetts military governor, Thomas Gage, ordered gunpowder and arms removed from the Powder House magazine in modern-day Somerset outside of Boston. Several months later, the Virginia governor, John Murray, Lord Dunmore, ordered a similar action against the Williamsburg magazine.

Nor did the militias have a steady supply of home-built weapons.

To service a free population of almost two million there were only fifteen hundred to three thousand gunsmiths in total across the thirteen colonies, and not all of them supported rebellion. The typical gunsmith built and repaired guns in a small shop with his sons and a few other apprentices, using an assortment of hand tools for carving, casting, forging, welding, boring, and assembling every piece of the weapon, a slow process that yielded perhaps five to ten guns per year. Other types of arms manufacture were nonexistent; in all the colonies there were no cannon forges, and not a single mill to produce that most critical of ingredients for the militia, gunpowder.

The ill-equipped American militia would have to face a formidable British army that was kept well provisioned by its century-old logistics arm, the Board of Ordnance, and the enormous firearms manufacturing centers in London and Birmingham. The board developed standard patterns (notably the Land Patterns) for the components of the musket—locks, stocks, and barrels, as well as breeches, triggers, and ramrods. Each of these standard components was fabricated in bulk by individual specialists, which were then brought to armorers who fitted and assembled the parts into complete weapons. Standardization meant that all the muskets in a regiment would fire the same ammunition and have many spare parts in common (though they were still short of being fully interchangeable). Specialization gave rise to an industrial system of mass production. Birmingham alone produced "a prodigious amount for exportation . . . annually above a hundred fifty thousand [muskets]." The Board of Ordnance also ran several artillery foundries and a series of gunpowder mills that churned out hundreds of tons of powder every year. Against the manufacturing might of the mother country, the colonial Committees of Safety and Supplies could hardly hope to contend.

That colonial America had little in the way of manufacturing was only partly due to Britain's mercantilist policies. Mercantilism was not simply a matter of the colonies producing raw materials while the mother country produced finished goods. British law did not prohibit manufacturing in the colonies so much as it prohibited the export of their manufactured products. What mattered to the government was the taxable trade—more exports from British manufacturers to the colonies meant greater tax revenue for the Crown. Instead, colonial manufacturing was inhibited more by a lack of skilled labor and difficulty in raising capital to erect factories and buy materials.

America did not have trouble raising capital for manufacturing because it was poor. Far from it. On the eve of the revolution against what they saw as the economic tyranny of the British system, American colonials were far wealthier than their British counterparts at almost every level of society, with an average household income of £78 per year compared with £50 in Britain (about $12,000 versus $7,500 today). Americans were in fact richer than any other group of people in the world, attested to by the consistently high rates of immigration from the mother country and Europe. British and European visitors frequently remarked on the high standard of living that was widespread across the American colonies, a sharp contrast to the great disparity between rich and poor found back home. Johann de Kalb, upon his return from his mission to gauge the Americans' readiness for revolution in 1768, was openly amazed that "they experience neither famine nor barren harvests," which were relatively common events across the Atlantic.

Instead of putting their capital into manufacture, colonial merchants focused on domestic procurement and trade of raw goods. Although fisheries, especially in New England, were generally prosperous, land was America's primary commodity and the main source of its wealth. Colonial farmers grew cash crops like indigo and tobacco for export, and enough flour and grain to supply a thriving international trade. Land, and therefore wealth, was more equitably distributed across the American population, rather than amassed as in Europe within the landed gentry. Adam Gordon, a caste-conscious member of the British gentry, condescendingly observed that "everybody has property, and everybody knows it." John Hector St. John de Crèvecoeur, a member of the French landed gentry living as a farmer in New York, more empathetically explained the American attitude toward wealth: "By riches I do not mean gold and silver, we have but little of those metals; I mean a better sort of wealth, cleared lands, cattle, good houses, good clothes, and an increase of people to enjoy them."

Crèvecoeur was correct that America had "but little" of gold and silver, not just ore but also coin (specie). The colonies had no mints to strike coins, and precious few British coins—shillings, crowns, and guineas—were ever brought from the motherland. Instead, the American colonies principally used Spanish currency in their shops and counting houses. Silver coins from the Spanish Viceroyalty of Peru were the most important and widely circulated currency in the world during the eighteenth century. The Spanish milled dollar, also called a *peso de ocho,* or piece of eight, made up half of all coins circulating in the colonies, and could be cut, shaved or sliced into smaller sizes and values. Every merchant's counter, from the smallest shop to the largest quayside counting house, had money drawers with various denominations of Spanish specie, along with a smattering of French, Dutch, and Portuguese coins that were also legal tender. Merchants kept printed conversion tables and a set of scales to weigh the coin for silver content, so that a transaction could take place with a mix of, say, Spanish dollars, French écus, and Dutch rijksdaalders. Even with this variety of coinage, paper money was widely used within the colonies, since merchants tended to reserve hard currency for trade in the foreign markets.

EUROPEAN MERCHANTS PROVIDE THE FIRST ARMS AND SUPPLIES OF GUNPOWDER

Merchants, not manufacture, would provide the answer to arming and equipping the American militia, and later the Continental Army, using both raw goods and hard currency to buy guns, powder, and ammunition from abroad. At the start of the war, American farmers not only fed the entire colonial population but also produced enough surplus to annually export overseas six million bushels of grain—almost a quarter of the production—which brought specie and manufactured goods back into the colonial economy. American sailors had over a century of experience defying the Navigation Acts by smuggling those goods past British naval ships, revenue cutters, and the eyes of customs officials. In theory, American ships trading, say, wheat and cod for Spanish wine and silk products would first be required to land their cargoes in Britain to pay customs duties before crossing to America. Certain crops, notably tobacco, could not be sold at all to foreign nations, but had to be delivered to Britain, from where they were later resold at great profit across Europe. Tea, of course, was only to be bought from Britain.

American merchants would sometimes avoid these restrictions by trading directly in European ports such as Amsterdam, Nantes, and Bilbao, where British consuls could do little but complain to local authorities. More often, they would take the shorter and more expedient route of landing and picking up cargoes in the West Indies, such as the French colonies of Saint-Domingue and Martinique, and most notably the tiny Dutch island of Sint Eustatius, a notorious hub for contraband trade from almost every European nation. On the return to America, shipmasters easily avoided royal customs agents, for as the New York lieutenant governor Cadwallader Colden explained, they "do not come into this port [New York City] but anchor at some distance in the numerous bays and creeks that our coast and rivers furnish, from whence the contraband goods are sent up in small boats." This well-honed system of smuggling was perfectly suited to bringing guns and gunpowder to America.

Over the years, Americans had developed a network of trusted merchants in each overseas port with whom they traded in both licit and illicit goods. In Amsterdam and Sint Eustatius, firms like Robert Crommelin, William Hodshon, and Isaac van Dam had business and family ties to New York City, dating from when it was still a Dutch colony. The French port of Nantes was home to the Montaudouin firm of merchants and slavers, which was instrumental in importing flour and rice from Philadelphia during the terrible famine of 1772 in France. In the Basque port of Bilbao in northern Spain, the firm Casa Joseph Gardoqui e hijos (House of Joseph Gardoqui and Sons) had been trading with fish merchants in Massachusetts since 1741, exchanging American salt cod, tobacco, and rice for Spanish products. These foreign merchants (sometimes called factors), publicly neutral but privately sympathetic to the Americans' grievances with Britain, would prove to be the linchpin in the American arms smuggling campaign that began in 1774. Their governments, meanwhile, professed to be against this illicit smuggling even as they tacitly condoned the activity.

In the summer and autumn of 1774, even before the First Continental Congress had finished its business and before the Committees of Safety and Supplies had organized, American merchants began acquiring arms and ammunition in quantity from Europe and the West Indies, using both hard currency and agricultural surplus as payment. British officials began reporting back to London that ships laden with contraband arms and gunpowder were en route from Amsterdam to Sint Eustatius and the American colonies, their chests and barrels of tea actually containing ammunition and gunpowder. Britain demanded that the Dutch Republic prohibit any further contraband trade. Officially the Dutch government promised to stop "such a dangerous traffic." Unofficially, it had little control over the merchants, who stood to make enormous profits on the smuggling trade; one hundred pounds of gunpowder bought in Amsterdam for eighteen rijksdaalders could be resold in Sint Eustatius for almost a hundred rijksdaalders. The stadtholder William V, Prince of Orange, who was George III's first cousin and a British partisan, even told the British ambassador that the Amsterdam merchants "would sell arms and ammunition to besiege the town of Amsterdam itself."

Amsterdam merchants could sell arms and ammunition to the Americans, but they could not fabricate them. The merchants were in fact just one part of a great series of supply chains that began in manufacturing hubs like Zaandam and Liège, passed through the trade centers of Amsterdam, Nantes, Bilbao, and Sint Eustatius, and finally led to America. Although the Dutch Republic manufactured little in the way of firearms for export, its mills in Zaandam and Zeeland produced some of the finest gunpowder in the world, effective and certain to fire, and thus in great demand worldwide. A few months after Americans began their quest for gunpowder, Dutch mills were so backlogged that even though they were churning night and day, deliveries to foreign customers fell six weeks behind.

The firearms that Dutch merchants like Crommelin, Hodshon, and Van Dam bought for resale to the Americans were manufactured just over the border in the principality of Liège, located in the eastern part of modern-day Belgium. Liège was wedged between two halves of the Austrian Netherlands, a loosely controlled part of the Austrian Empire. Both Liège and the Austrian Netherlands professed strict neutrality, which in practice meant that arms could be manufactured and shipped to all sides in a conflict. As in Birmingham, arms manufacture in Liège consisted of individual specialists like Jean-Claude Nicquet and Jean Gosvin, making and fitting parts in an industrial system of mass production that produced somewhere between two hundred thousand and three hundred thousand stands of arms (i.e., fully assembled muskets plus bayonets) per year, primarily the French 0.69 caliber models.

Liège muskets accounted for most of the firearms imported to America during the first year of the war. As American demand for weapons increased monthly, Dutch merchants or their agents came to Liège in ever-larger numbers to order weapons. Within a year of the arrival of the first American ships, the mayor of the city reported that "our traders, great and small, are giving work to our men; we see nothing but crates of muskets in the streets." Many of these muskets freighted for ports in the Dutch Republic were stamped "Pro Libertate," a sure sign that their final destination was in fact the American colonies. Munitions were sent either by barge down the Meuse/Maas River to the North Sea, or by a system of roads through the Austrian Netherlands to Leuven, then by canal boat to Amsterdam, where they were secretly loaded onto ships bound for America or the West Indies.

As the American colonials became more brazen in their desire to buy or trade for arms and powder, the British navy further tightened the noose around Amsterdam. In response, merchants began consigning shipments of arms and powder to other European ports, where they could be secretly reloaded aboard vessels bound for North America. Lisbon and Nantes soon became favored transshipment ports for contraband munitions, since they already furnished arms for the slaving trade to Portuguese and French plantations in Brazil and Saint-Domingue. Slaving was an incredibly violent trade that annually absorbed thousands of the guns manufactured in Liège and other centers, many of which were then traded as currency for the slaves themselves. With so many arms being loaded onto so many ships, it was fairly easy to smuggle guns and powder onto American-bound vessels. In Nantes, the firm headed by Arthur and Jean-Gabriel Montaudouin used its Philadelphia trade connections to conceal covert arms shipments, aboard ships whose names like *Jean-Jacques* (after Rousseau) and *Contrat Social* (a reference to Rousseau's political rights manifesto, *The Social Contract*) revealed the family's Enlightenment leanings toward the American cause.

Of all the transshipment ports for contraband American weapons, Bilbao appeared to be one of the least likely, since it primarily traded in wool, textiles, and, most important, cod, which was a staple dish (*bacalao*) throughout the Iberian Peninsula. Salt cod came from the French Newfoundland fisheries of Saint-Pierre and Miquelon as well as the colonial Massachusetts towns of Marblehead and Salem. Nevertheless, when Gage's enforcement of the Coercive Acts touched off the first American revolts in Massachusetts, this innocuous trade route quickly turned into one of the most important weapons supply lines in the early days of the conflict, with Casa Joseph Gardoqui e hijos at its hub.

Joseph Gardoqui y Mezeta established his trading firm in Bilbao in 1726, and from the start he had strong commercial ties with Britain. His son Diego María de Gardoqui y Arriquibar was born in 1735, the fourth child of eight, and was groomed from an early age to run the family business. In 1749, at age fourteen, he was apprenticed for five years to George Hayley, a well-to-do London merchant who would later bankroll the import-export ventures of Alexander Hamilton and John Hancock. While learning the ropes of international trade, Diego de Gardoqui (the family name is accented on the "o" in the Basque manner) developed a mastery of English that could put rough-hewn East End merchants to shame. During his apprenticeship, he certainly would have gotten to know Hayley's brother-in-law John Wilkes, a radical journalist whose antigovernment screeds propelled him into a seat in Parliament, from where he later supported American independence.

Diego de Gardoqui took over the family business upon his father's death in 1761, and also held increasingly prominent positions in the Bilbao city government. He continued his strong commercial ties with Massachusetts merchants, especially Jeremiah Lee and Elbridge Gerry of Marblehead, and John Cabot of Salem, who were all part of New England's "codfish aristocracy." If the enormously wealthy John Cabot was referred to as a "nabob" by his contemporaries, then Gardoqui was certainly a *"ricacho,"* with a net family worth of around $50 million in today's dollars. Cabot and Gardoqui did not come by all of their fortunes legally. From 1771 to 1773, for example, they entered into an elaborate smuggling scheme that involved shipping flour from Philadelphia to Spain to Havana, and sending thousands of silk handkerchiefs from Spain to Salem.

Britain's Coercive Acts, in particular the Boston Port Act that closed the port to all trade, hit the merchant class especially hard. The Massachusetts Provincial Congress was established in the town of Concord in October 1774 to coordinate the colonials' military resistance. Its leaders included the Boston merchant John Hancock and polemicist Samuel Adams, while Jeremiah Lee and Elbridge Gerry served on the Committee of Supplies. The Provincial Congress ordered the creation of militias, including a select few dubbed "minutemen" as they were to be ready at a minute's notice, while the Committee of Supplies was charged with furnishing it with cannon, muskets, and gunpowder. In Gage's view, of course, this congress was an illegal attempt to create an independent government, and convinced him not only that a rebellion was inevitable, but that it would have to be put down as quickly and fiercely as that of the Scottish Jacobites of 1745. He began fortifying Boston Neck against attack and visibly training his troops. The American partisans, who had

Diego María de Gardoqui y Arriquibar (1735–1798). Miniature

already begun calling themselves Patriots and calling the Crown's supporters Loyalists, took notice and began arming themselves in earnest. The Provincial Congress called on the towns to equip "each of the minutemen not already provided therewith . . . with an effective firearm, bayonet, pouch, knapsack, thirty rounds of cartridges, and ball," but left it to the Committee of Supplies to actually obtain them.

In November 1774, Jeremiah Lee penned a plea for help to his longtime associate Diego de Gardoqui, asking for arms and gunpowder. In February 1775, Gardoqui replied that although the request was of a "very difficult nature," he had found a supply of "300 muskets & bayonets" manufactured for the Spanish army that he was able to send, and promised to be "at their service" if the struggle continued. Smuggling silk handkerchiefs was one thing, but muskets was entirely another; Spain was a neutral nation at this point, and while the Spanish government apparently knew of his munitions smuggling activities with the Americans, Gardoqui was risking his lucrative business with British merchants. However, he had spent his formative years with George Hayley and John Wilkes, and their sympathies for the American cause likely influenced him.

Gardoqui's arms shipment apparently arrived in Massachusetts in June or July 1775, and the Committee of Supplies soon distributed them around the colony; muster rolls for the Massachusetts Continental Regiment reported "new Spanish guns" issued to the infantry by the New Year. They were undoubtedly put to immediate use, for by then the War of American Independence, after months of delay and hesitation, had finally broken out.

AMERICA'S ABILITY TO PAY FOR ARMS AND GUNPOWDER FALTERS

The opening battle of the War of American Independence began as a skirmish over gunpowder, and the war's first American defeat was due to the lack of it. Even as the Patriots were sending entreaties to Europe pleading for munitions, Thomas Gage had sent dispatches to London asking for instructions on how to deal with the rebellion in the offing. The secretary of state for the colonies, William Legge, Earl of Dartmouth, after consulting with Prime Minister Frederick, Lord North, wrote Gage that "force should be repelled by force" and that he should arrest the leaders of the Provincial Congress, in particular John Hancock and Samuel Adams, to try them for treason. When Dartmouth's dispatch reached Gage's headquarters in Boston on April 14, 1775, he took immediate action to quash the rebellion in its infancy.

On the evening of April 18, Gage sent a large force to capture "a quantity of ammunition and provision" that Loyalist sources had informed him was cached in the town of Concord where the Provincial Congress had met. The Americans had already gotten wind of Dartmouth's letter and Gage's plan, and had moved most of the gunpowder and munitions, as well as Hancock and Adams, to safety. The militia mustered in Lexington on the road from Boston to Concord, where at first light on April 19 they had their first skirmish with British infantry, leaving eight Americans dead and the British regulars still on the march. When the British reached Concord they found themselves outnumbered and outmaneuvered by the militia and minutemen, who quickly routed the redcoats and harried them on their retreat to Boston.

Patriots from across New England converged on Boston, laying siege to the city and its environs. By June, there were fifteen thousand provincials camped around Boston, even as British reinforcements arrived from across the Atlantic, along with generals William Howe, Henry Clinton, and John Burgoyne. With only sixty-five hundred troops at their disposal, Gage and the other three generals prepared to break through the siege by capturing the surrounding areas of Dorchester and Charlestown. The Patriots learned of the British plans and began fortifying two high points on the Charlestown peninsula, Breed's Hill and the adjacent Bunker Hill. On June 17, redcoats under Howe crossed Boston harbor to attack the colonial militia dug in on Breed's Hill, though Bunker Hill became the name associated with the battle. After three bloody assaults that resulted in twice as many British as American casualties, the colonial forces ran out of gunpowder and were forced to retreat to Cambridge.

The devastating want of gunpowder at the Battle of Bunker Hill came despite almost a year of preparation, of "powder cruises" to Sint Eustatius, Amsterdam, and other ports, raids on British magazines, and careful stockpiling by the Patriots. British actions like the one against the Somerset Powder House magazine had removed considerable amounts of gunpowder from the hands of colonials. Meanwhile, the British navy was effectively stoppering the flow of arms to the colonials, blockading overseas ports and combing Caribbean waters.

The newly constituted Second Continental Congress immediately took up the question of munitions when it met in Philadelphia, appropriating money for the purchase of arms and gunpowder to supply the new commander in chief, George Washington. Even as it was preparing for war, the Congress was also pressing for peace. Benjamin Franklin had by then joined the Congress after leaving London in March 1775, a little over a year after his humiliation at the Cockpit. Among his last efforts at compromise before his departure was offering to assist Lord North with his Conciliatory Proposal, aimed at allowing the Americans to tax themselves, but which ultimately fell far short of the colonial demand to control how the revenues were spent. Now the Congress tried for peace one more time, dispatching Richard Penn to London with the Olive Branch Petition, asking the king to "form . . . such arrangements" that would achieve a nonviolent resolution to the conflict.

While Penn was preparing his Olive Branch, Washington arrived at the siege of Boston, just a few weeks after the Battle of Bunker Hill. He quickly learned that the gunpowder situation was even worse than had been reported; in all of Massachusetts there were just thirty-eight barrels on hand, less than half a pound per soldier. "The General was so struck that he did not utter a word for half an hour," reported Brigadier General John Sullivan. The Americans were shocked into action. Washington requested the colonies of Rhode Island and Massachusetts to arm and equip ships for more powder cruises, in order to capture British vessels and depots that might contain powder and munitions. Congress attempted to stimulate the domestic production of saltpeter, the staple ingredient of gunpowder, and called on the colonies to refurbish their derelict powder mills. Massachusetts, meanwhile, enacted a resolve "prohibiting the needless expense of gunpowder" and asking the inhabitants "not to fire a gun at beast, bird, or mark, without real necessity."

These desperate measures could not begin to supply Washington's proposed twenty-thousand-man army with the requisite amount of gunpowder—he estimated it at around four hundred barrels—let alone furnish them with the muskets, blankets, uniforms, tents, and other military supplies they lacked. Instead, the colonies now intensified their search for munitions abroad, and Bilbao became an increasingly important port of call. In July 1775, Elbridge Gerry, on the Massachusetts Committee of Supplies, sent another request to Gardoqui for "good pistol and cannon powder." Gerry admitted that the American cause depended upon the "friendship of foreign factors" like Gardoqui to "supply us with military stores of every kind in the future." The Spanish merchant continued to supply the Americans with arms, even as their ability to pay for them was already diminishing.

Americans were facing trouble paying for imported arms because they were quickly becoming destitute. When the war began in April 1775, the colonies had $22 million in paper currency but only about $6 million in specie. The Second Continental Congress, with no power to tax, continued to issue paper currency without any hard currency to back it up. Foreign factors, even with all the friendship they could muster, could not accept paper money as payment for arms and munitions, and the specie reserve used to buy arms began to dry up. At the same time, the agricultural surpluses available for export, which also were used for arms purchases, shrank by almost 80 percent, due to a combination of manpower shortages on the farms as the men went to war, increased domestic demand to feed the Continental Army and militia, and ever-tighter British blockades of American ports and shipping routes. With the military needs of the Patriots growing exponentially as the conflict expanded, it would be only a matter of time before American merchants could no longer afford to buy sufficient arms on the open market to continue the war effort. The Americans, in short, needed direct assistance from the governments of France and Spain, which until this time had merely looked the other way. Fortunately, a French merchant and playwright had already understood this, even before the Americans realized it themselves.

BEAUMARCHAIS AND COVERT FRENCH SUPPORT FOR THE AMERICANS

In the decade since the end of the Seven Years' War, Charles de Beaumont, Chevalier d'Éon, had been living in precarious exile in London. Having slandered the French ambassador, he faced arrest if he returned to France. However, the fact that he still possessed copies of France's now-abandoned plans for invading Britain, which could cause enormous damage if ever revealed, gave him leverage to remain in the British capital as a spy, where he continued to feed information to the head of the *Secret du Roi,* Charles-François de Broglie. D'Éon entertained many British aristocrats, including John Wilkes, though his modest annual pension of 12,000 livres (about $80,000 today) was not nearly enough to maintain his lavish lifestyle. That lifestyle included a considerable budget for women's clothes, for by 1771 d'Éon had convinced so many gossips that he was a woman who had originally disguised himself as a man in order to serve in the army that London bookies were taking bets totaling £60,000 on whether he in fact was male or female.

Louis XVI ascended to the throne in May 1774 and almost immediately disbanded the *Secret du Roi.* Soon after, he asked de Broglie and foreign minister Charles Gravier, Comte de Vergennes, to neutralize the threat that d'Éon might reveal the invasion plans. Their solution was straightforward: The king, who along with Vergennes was convinced that d'Éon was a woman, would continue granting his pension for life and allow him to return to France, on the condition that d'Éon surrender the secret papers. Several times couriers hand-carried this proposal to d'Éon, who rejected each one with the dramatic claim that he had gone into $2 million in debt in service to his nation, and that in addition to the proposed terms, the king must also pay off his creditors. A stalemate ensued, which would finally be broken by a merchant with an equal flair for the theatric.

Pierre-Augustin Caron was born in 1732 in Paris into a watchmaker's family, and after a successful apprenticeship became "watchmaker to the king" at age twenty-two. He shortly thereafter married a wealthy widow, adopting the more aristocratic-sounding name of her country estate to become Pierre-Augustin Caron de Beaumarchais. Endowed with wit, intelligence, and musical talent, Beaumarchais cut a wide swath in both political and financial circles.

In 1764, shortly after the end of the Seven Years' War, a consortium of French financiers led by Joseph Pâris-Duverney and Jacques Donatien Le Ray de Chaumont sent Beaumarchais to Madrid, to negotiate with the Spanish government to obtain the contract for the commercial monopoly (*asiento*) that supplied slaves and agricultural products to the Caribbean islands and Louisiana. Beaumarchais spent a year in the Spanish capital, involved in the negotiations for the *asiento* and absorbing Spanish literature and culture. As in Paris, he charmed his way into both political

Pierre-Augustin Caron de Beaumarchais (1732–1799). After Jean-Marc Nattier, 1773, oil on canvas

and financial circles. In this he was aided by his old family friend María Teresa Patiño, Condesa de Fuenclara, who presided over a regular *tertulia* (literary salon) in her home on the calle de Hortaleza near the Parque del Buen Retiro, where she had undoubtedly watched the fireworks that accompanied the signing of the Treaty of Paris the prior year.

Beaumarchais, encouraged by his discussions with King Carlos III and his chief minister, Grimaldi, began intermingling the negotiations for the *asiento* with the politics of France and Spain. Much to the dismay of the French minister Choiseul and his ambassador to Madrid, Marquis d'Ossun, he portrayed the French presence in the *asiento* not simply as a lucrative business but also as a means of strengthening the Bourbon Family Compact against a common British adversary. The Council of the Indies, responsible for administering Spain's overseas empire, did not see it this way and awarded the monopoly to the Compañía Gaditana de Negros (Cadiz Slaving Company), whose shareholders included the Havana merchant Juan de Miralles, who would soon play an important role in the coming American conflict.

Beaumarchais returned to France having failed to obtain the monopoly, but with a lifetime's worth of political contacts and literary inspirations. He initially acted on the latter, writing and producing plays including *The Barber of Seville,* a love triangle set in Spain and featuring the irrepressible Figaro, which would soon make him famous. At the same time, he was fighting lawsuits from the estate of Pâris-Duverney that threatened to bankrupt him, which by 1773 had led to charges of corruption and a four-month imprisonment. His counterclaims garnered him public support and cemented the unlikely friendship of his jailer, the Paris chief of police, Antoine Raymond Gabriel de Sartine.

Sartine must have seen extraordinary qualities in his erstwhile prisoner, for in early 1774 he asked him to go secretly to London to undo the work of a blackmailer named Charles de Morande who had threatened libel against Louis XV's mistress. Beaumarchais successfully intercepted Morande and completed his mission to save the court from scandal, though just days after his return to Paris, Louis XV was dead and Louis XVI was on the throne. Now a hero in the eyes of the court, Beaumarchais got wind of the stalemated negotiations with d'Éon over the secret invasion plans and immediately saw through his machinations. "D'Éon's secret," he wrote to Sartine, "is to deceive those who want to trap him, pocket the $2 million and remain in London." The subtext was that only a playwright like himself could direct a performer like d'Éon. Sartine, who had just been named minister of the navy, passed the message to Vergennes and Louis XVI, who were now troubling over the d'Éon problem. Within a few months, Beaumarchais was back in London to negotiate the surrender of the incriminating papers.

During the summer and autumn of 1775, Beaumarchais shuttled a half dozen times between Versailles and London, finally concluding the d'Éon affair in November, with d'Éon handing over an iron safe full of secret papers and receiving a royal agreement that allowed him to return to France, but only in women's clothes and never again in his army uniform. Beaumarchais could hardly make these trips in secret anymore; he was now a well-known figure on each side of the Channel, as *The Barber of Seville* had become a huge success in both Paris and London.

During one of these trips in September, Beaumarchais chanced to meet Richard Penn, newly arrived from America with the Olive Branch Petition, which he and Arthur Lee, the agent for Massachusetts in London, unsuccessfully presented to the Earl of Dartmouth. On his return to Versailles, Beaumarchais related to Vergennes that he had heard from Penn "about the situation in America." The events at Bunker Hill proved that "the Americans would suffer anything rather than bend." He went on to claim that nearly forty thousand Americans surrounded Boston, with an equal number of soldiers scattered across the colonies—the real numbers were about half that—and that "not one farmer had to leave his land nor one worker his factory," since those eighty thousand soldiers were fishermen displaced by the British blockades (in fact, almost all of the troops were untrained but capable farmers). This was the height of stagecraft; he was evidently thinking two scenes ahead to a deal where French arms could be traded for American agricultural products, and it would never do to have his ideas undercut by the reality of wartime farmhand shortages.

By this time, Vergennes was also giving thought to the "situation in America" as a means to keep British troops pinned down there, in order to avoid having them enter into a brewing conflict in South America between Spain and Portugal. When Vergennes ordered Beaumarchais back to London in October to finalize the d'Éon affair, it was apparently with the direction to also renew contact with the Americans in order to see how France might assist in their efforts. Beaumarchais approached his friend John Wilkes, now mayor of London as well as a member of

Parliament, to introduce him to Arthur Lee. Wilkes did so on October 25, 1775, when they all attended a dinner at Wilkes's official residence in the Manor House. It was the evening before the opening of Parliament, at which the king was to make a speech denouncing the American revolt as a move toward independence, so Beaumarchais and Lee would undoubtedly have had an animated discussion. The following day, Wilkes dined with George Hayley, also an MP. As both were vocal opponents of Parliament's attempt "to establish arbitrary power over all America," Wilkes may very well have related the meeting to Hayley. Although it is doubtful the two men knew from personal contacts that Hayley's erstwhile apprentice Diego de Gardoqui had already shipped muskets to the American colonies, they may have been aware of his activities via the diplomatic correspondence from the British ambassador in Madrid. Wilkes's introduction of Beaumarchais and Lee now set in motion the direct arming of America, not only by private merchants but also by the governments of France and Spain.

Neither Beaumarchais nor Lee was an official representative of France or the American colonies, but apparently each believed they could persuade their respective governments to cooperate in an arms deal. Together they scripted a complex arrangement in which French gunpowder could be traded for American tobacco, the colonies' most profitable cash crop. Critical to this scheme was the use of a shell corporation to hide the source of the funds. In January 1776, Beaumarchais addressed the proposal directly to Louis XVI. Beaumarchais proposed that the French government place 1 million livres "at the disposal of your agent, who will style himself Roderigue Hortalez et Compagnie, this being the signature and title of the firm under which I have agreed to conduct the entire business." Using this cash to buy gunpowder directly from the French armories at one-fourth livre per pound, the company would exchange it for tobacco at the market rate of one livre per pound of powder, thus tripling the government's investment. "The principal merit of this plan," suggested the man who had twice nearly gone bankrupt, "is to augment both the appearance and substance of your aid so that a single million . . . will produce the same results for the Americans as if your Majesty really had disbursed nine millions in their favor." As he had attempted in Spain a decade before, Beaumarchais once again aimed at intermingling business and politics.

Why he chose the name Roderigue Hortalez is something of a

mystery—"Roderigue" may have referred to Spain's medieval hero Rodrigo Díaz "El Cid" Campeador, while "Hortalez" almost certainly evoked the Madrid home of the Condesa de Fuenclara where he had spent many a pleasant afternoon at her *tertulias*. That his fictitious company had a Spanish name was less mysterious. He was simply following the advice of a popular business "how-to" book found in the Caron family library, *Le parfait négociant* (The Perfect Merchant), which explained how French merchants set up Spanish business fronts in order to penetrate their lucrative West Indies trade. In addition, Beaumarchais had just been named to the board of directors of the *asiento* Compañía Gaditana de Negros, which gave him enormous leverage to direct funds from both the French and Spanish governments to the American cause.

Vergennes, who actually had received Beaumarchais's proposal before forwarding it to the king, counseled caution. All of the information on the American crisis, he noted in his covering letter, was hearsay. Before committing to a course of action, Vergennes needed better intelligence from the agent he had already placed on the scene. That agent had been chosen by the ex-spymaster Charles-François de Broglie, who had also selected Johann de Kalb a decade earlier. De Broglie's choice was a close family friend, Julien-Alexandre Achard de Bonvouloir et Loyauté, who had been a young militia volunteer at Saint-Domingue despite a childhood accident that left him disabled and disfigured. He had made a trip through the American colonies before returning to France via London in July 1775. Although his English was poor, he had made excellent contacts in Philadelphia and even witnessed the siege of Boston. De Broglie likely received news of Bonvouloir's arrival in London and made him known to the French ambassador there, Adrien-Louis, Duc de Guînes, who in turn proposed to Vergennes that he send Bonvouloir back to America to observe the situation there. Vergennes quickly agreed, instructing Bonvouloir not to act as an official envoy or to reveal the French government's views toward the Americans, but only to "make a faithful account of the events and the general attitude" of the population. Posing as a merchant from the Austrian Netherlands, Bonvouloir departed aboard *Charming Betsy* in October 1775, arriving in Philadelphia just ten days before Christmas, after a harrowing three-month voyage.

Bonvouloir had returned to America just as the battles were widening beyond Boston and its environs. Militias under the command of Benedict Arnold and Ethan Allen had bloodlessly captured Fort Ticonderoga in New York, and even now the artillery colonel Henry Knox was hauling captured cannon and munitions across the frozen New England countryside to reinforce the American siege of Boston. At the same time, Arnold and Richard Montgomery led a two-pronged invasion of Canada, hoping to deny the British any safe haven as well as to rally the French-speaking Canadians to enter the war on the American side. Although two Canadian regiments were formed that fought alongside the Americans, the vast majority of Québécois were as suspicious of the Americans as they were of the British and saw no advantage to joining the fight. Montgomery successfully seized Montreal, but in December their combined assault on Quebec City was defeated, with Montgomery killed and Arnold severely wounded, leaving the Americans to conduct an ineffectual siege that was lifted the following spring.

The Second Continental Congress was wrestling not just with the widening battlefield but also with the escalating war of words coming from London. George III had already declared over the summer that the "colonies are in open and avowed rebellion." His rejection of the Olive Branch Petition was followed by a speech to Parliament on October 26, the day after Wilkes introduced Beaumarchais to Arthur Lee, declaring that the ongoing conflict "is manifestly carried on for the purpose of establishing an independent empire." Immediately afterward, Parliament passed the American Prohibitory Act, a naval blockade that amounted to a declaration of war. Against the coming onslaught of British troops, the munitions provided by the individual colonies' Committees of Safety and Supplies were simply inadequate. In response, the Congress established the Secret Committee of Trade, first headed by financier Thomas Willing and later by his business partner Robert Morris, to commission merchants to supply war materiel for all the colonies. One of their first contracts was with a pair of merchants from Nantes, Pierre Penet and Emmanuel de Pliarne, who had sailed from Cap François (present-day Cap-Haïtien) on Saint-Domingue to Providence, Rhode Island, with a cargo of gunpowder. They then came to Philadelphia, where they signed a contract with the Secret Committee to deliver fifteen thousand stands of arms, using the firm of Willing & Morris as their American agent.

On November 29, just two weeks before Bonvouloir's propitious arrival, the Congress also established the (confusingly named) Committee of Secret Correspondence "for the sole purpose of corresponding with our friends in Great Britain, Ireland, and other parts of the world." While the Secret Committee of Trade handled dealings with private merchants, the Committee of Secret Correspondence became the conduit for all direct assistance from the French and Spanish governments. When the five committee members, which included Benjamin Franklin and New York delegate John Jay, arrived at night to meet Bonvouloir in one of the upstairs rooms of the otherwise empty Carpenters' Hall, they found him in the presence of Francis Daymon, the French émigré serving as librarian for Franklin's Library Company, who knew Bonvouloir from his earlier voyage and would translate for them. John Jay described Bonvouloir as an "elderly lame gentleman," even though at twenty-six he was four years younger than Jay. Over the course of this and two subsequent meetings, always at night, Bonvouloir assured his interlocutors that if they wanted arms, ammunition, or money "[they] shall have it," and would pass along those requests to the French government. The requests were actually transmitted to Guînes using invisible milk-based ink within the blank spaces of an innocent-looking business letter; only Guînes knew that "the writing would only appear when heated over a chafing dish." As Guînes had just been recalled to Paris, one of his last acts was to recopy the secret report and give it directly to Vergennes.

Bonvouloir began his report by pointing out that the Americans "have incredible spirit and determination, and have good leaders," giving them an excellent chance of winning the conflict. However, he noted that "they lack three important things: a good navy, provisions, and money." Though their primary request was French permission to exchange goods for military supplies, Franklin and his colleagues admitted that against Britain they were overmatched: "They are convinced they cannot defend themselves without a seafaring nation to protect them, and the only two powers which are able to help are France and Spain." The Americans asked "whether it would be prudent to send an emissary to France" in order to directly request assistance. The Frenchman told them that "this would be precipitous, and even hazardous, as everything that happens in France is known in London, and vice-versa." Finally, knowing that France's decision on assistance might hinge on how its leaders perceived their willingness to carry the fight through, the American delegation made certain that Bonvouloir understood the depth of their commitment: "They expect to see their cities destroyed and their houses burned. . . . They have all said they are fighting to become free and that they will succeed no matter what the price, that they are mutually bound by a pledge and that they would die together rather than surrender." Six months before Thomas Jefferson sat down to write the Declaration of Independence, Americans were already telling a foreign power that they had mutually pledged their lives, fortunes, and sacred honor to the cause of freedom.

The committee had already sent letters abroad asking for assistance, including to Charles Dumas, a Swiss scholar in The Hague, asking him to discover "the disposition of the several courts with respect to such assistance or alliance," and to Arthur Lee, not knowing that he was already working with Beaumarchais to obtain French support. Despite Bonvouloir's warning that sending an emissary to France would be "hazardous," on March 2, 1776, the committee appointed Silas Deane, a Connecticut merchant and congressional delegate, to travel to France and "make immediate application to Monsieur de Vergennes." The short-term goal was to obtain "clothing and arms for 25,000 men" and a hundred cannon, all on credit. Deane was also instructed to inform Vergennes that with the coming "total separation" from Britain, "France would be looked upon as the power, whose friendship it would be fittest for us to obtain and cultivate." Deane departed from Philadelphia six days later, without knowing if or how he might be received at Versailles.

At Versailles, Bonvouloir's report was received with great interest. Its arrival on February 27 coincided with yet another missive by Beaumarchais, titled "Peace or War." It began prophetically enough: "The famous quarrel between America and England, soon to divide the world and alter the European system, forces each power to carefully examine how this separation will influence it, whether in its service or to its detriment." Beaumarchais got right to the point: "We must aid the Americans," for if not, either America, Britain, or both would attack France's sugar islands, so that the king would be forced to "belatedly start a fruitless war." Beaumarchais stated that "you cannot have the peace you desire unless you prevent at all costs peace between England and America . . . and the only way to accomplish this is to supply aid to the Americans to make them equal to England." Finally, he passed along the promise by Arthur Lee that the Americans "offer France, in exchange for its secret aid, a secret treaty of commerce," a promise that Lee had no authority to make.

Vergennes now had two crucial pieces of information from his agents in London and Philadelphia that convinced him, first, that the American rebellion would weaken Britain, and second, that the Americans had the resolve to continue the fight. These reports confirmed that the conflict in America could keep British troops occupied long enough to prevent them from helping their ally Portugal turn a current skirmish with Spanish forces in Brazil into a full-scale European war, which was then a major concern in both the French and Spanish courts. The French minister decided that the best way to ensure that the American war continued to drag on was to fund the insurgents as Beaumarchais proposed, except that he would go Beaumarchais one better; France and Spain together would become the joint backers of Roderigue Hortalez et Compagnie.

On March 1, 1776, the day before Deane sailed for France, Vergennes sent Grimaldi a letter outlining his proposal to jointly fund materiel assistance for the Americans. Grimaldi agreed almost immediately, but stipulated that they both "consider the best means of doing so without implicating ourselves," which he suggested should be accomplished via "commercial means." Vergennes put the proposal before Louis XVI's council of ministers, where it was accepted with almost no dissent, but with the same stipulation that Grimaldi gave: The aid "must always be cloaked and hidden and only appear to be commercial in nature, so that we may at any time deny it." With all sides in agreement on the Roderigue Hortalez scheme, the French king authorized payment, and a request for Spanish payment was sent to Madrid. On June 10, 1776, Beaumarchais signed a receipt stating, "I received from M. Duvergier [the French court's treasurer], conforming to the orders of the Comte de Vergennes, the sum of one million livres." The second million was sent from Spain a few weeks later. With the equivalent of $1 billion in start-up funds, Roderigue Hortalez et Compagnie was now in business.

Beaumarchais became a whirlwind of activity. His initial five or six staff were mostly friends, not from banking and commerce but rather from journalism and theater; this included his secretary, Jean-Baptiste-Lazare Théveneau de Francy, the younger brother of Charles de Morande, the blackmailer whom Beaumarchais had intercepted and who was now one of his allies. He leased his company office in the affluent Marais district of Paris at the Hôtel des Ambassadeurs de Hollande, a three-story town house at 47 rue Vieille du Temple, where he inhabited the top floor and gave the rest over to work space. As the name indicated, the building had previously been the home of ambassadors from the Dutch Republic, and retained the splendid artwork collected over the years; bookkeepers on the ground floor could look up at a ceiling painted by the same artists who had decorated the Versailles palace. Beaumarchais himself spent little time in these sumptuous surroundings. He traveled to the Atlantic ports of Dunkerque, Le Havre, Rochefort, and Nantes to locate shipowners who would freight cargo to America, and also to Bordeaux, where in a run-down fortress named Château Trompette he located five hundred barrels of gunpowder for shipment to America.

But Beaumarchais did not forget about Arthur Lee, his partner in London. By now they were corresponding in cipher and using code words to disguise the actual transactions. In early June he wrote to "Mary Johnston," the prearranged code name for Arthur Lee, informing him that he would shortly be dispatching a ship loaded with gunpowder and supplies to Cap François. "On your part, do not fail to send a ship loaded with good Virginia tobacco," Beaumarchais insisted. He had sold the idea of Hortalez as a moneymaking operation, and now he was worried that the Americans might not keep their end of the bargain. "Mary Johnston" demurred on sending tobacco in payment for the gunpowder, replying that "I advise my friends [code for the Continental Congress] that the communication of sentiments [tobacco] is difficult, and for that reason we ought to do all in our power, without insisting on a certain and immediate return." Lee, who erroneously believed that Hortalez was simply a front for the French government and not a real business, concluded his letter by saying, "This is not a commercial transaction we are engaged in, but a political one of the widest scope." Beaumarchais was right to be wary of Lee; he was already reneging on an agreement that, in fact, he had neither the ability nor the authority to make. Beaumarchais would soon find that exceeding one's authority was a common trait among Americans, for Silas Deane had just arrived in France.

Beaumarchais was in Bordeaux in June 1776 when he met Deane, just arrived from America and passing himself off as a merchant from Bermuda. Neither man knew that they were both there for the same reason, in search of arms for America, and paid little notice to each other as they went about their tasks. While Beaumarchais was scrambling over the ruined Château Trompette looking for gunpowder, Deane was writing letters to two men he thought could help in his quest. Benjamin Franklin had recommended that Deane contact his friend Jacques Barbeu-Dubourg, an elderly doctor who was already a fierce partisan of the American cause. He also suggested that Deane write to his old friend

Edward Bancroft in London. Bancroft had been Deane's student back in Connecticut, which, coupled with Franklin's recommendation, led him to implicitly trust the man. Neither he nor his American colleagues ever learned that Bancroft, who genuinely liked Deane, was not sympathetic to the idea of American independence and would secretly undermine their efforts.

Deane arrived in Paris on July 6, trailed by British agents. David Murray, Viscount Stormont, was Britain's ambassador to France, and his embassy hosted a network of spies, as Bonvouloir had warned, who sent their reports to the Secret Service run by William Eden. Deane quickly met with Bancroft and Barbeu-Dubourg, who warned him of the espionage but agreed to set up a meeting with Vergennes the following week. On July 11, while the other two stayed in the antechamber, Deane met with the foreign minister, accompanied by one of Vergennes's *premier commis* (first secretaries), Conrad Alexandre Gérard, who translated for them. Deane emphasized that America, which was on the verge of declaring independence—and, unknown to him, had done so the week before—wished to be a trading partner with France. His mission was to "purchase a large quantity . . . of military stores, for which remittances would be made," though, given the delays in shipping and his own lack of hard currency, this would have to be done on credit. Vergennes agreed that France would allow such commercial trade without any interference, and directed that Deane call upon Gérard for any future needs. Deane left the meeting convinced that they had made a good start.

Barbeu-Dubourg imagined himself as the link between America and France, but to his consternation Vergennes instead advised Beaumarchais to contact Deane. The playwright wrote to Deane in French, for even after years shuttling back and forth to Britain his English vocabulary was limited to the occasional "Goddam" in his *Figaro* plays. Deane, who claimed that he never spoke English for fear of spies, was described by Beaumarchais as "the quietest man in France, as I defy him to say more than six words to a Frenchman." Nevertheless, after their first meetings, in which Bancroft acted as translator and adviser, they both were mutually impressed and mutually reassured. Beaumarchais, rightly suspicious of both Arthur Lee's absence of authority and his disregard for payment, found in Deane an authorized representative of the Congress who promised to pay for his merchandise. Deane, disappointed in Barbeu-Dubourg's lack of business acumen, found in Beaumarchais a supplier with both an open line of credit and the full backing of the French government. Indeed, when Beaumarchais wrote to the Continental Congress in August promising them cannon, gunpowder, and muskets, Deane appended a note confirming that "everything he says, writes, or does, is in reality the action of the Ministry," a statement that would unintentionally lose Beaumarchais a fortune.

With Arthur Lee now back in London and firmly out of the picture, Deane and Beaumarchais began hammering out a contract that would promise delivery of a substantial consignment of war supplies to America. At first they had agreed that Beaumarchais would supply the cargo while Deane would supply the ships, but by August 19—two days after news of the Declaration of Independence had reached Paris—they concluded that Deane could not guarantee ships from America at any time in the near future. Beaumarchais began negotiating with Jean-Joseph Carrier de Monthieu, whose family had dominated the arms manufacturing business at Saint-Étienne for over three decades, to supply both the arms and the vessels. By great good fortune, the American request for large numbers of muskets and cannon had come at exactly the same time as the French army was reequipping its forces with lighter, more standardized weapons and was now casting about for a means to divest itself of its older arms. These older arms, still functional but ill-suited to France's new strategic needs, would find an ideal home in a nation whose own strategic needs were even now being debated by the Second Continental Congress.

French shoulder arms were manufactured at three sites, Charleville and Maubeuge in the north, and Saint-Étienne near Lyon. The largest of the three, Saint-Étienne, was, like Birmingham and Liège, populated with a vast number of individual gun manufacturers toiling over their forges that "perpetually shrouded [it] in coal smoke which penetrates everywhere." Most of its twenty thousand muskets produced annually were of a standard model (0.69 caliber), though they were updated on a periodic basis. In the years just before Deane's arrival, the most commonly used muskets were the M1763 and M1766 ("M" was for the model year of introduction). Foundries run by the Maritz family in Lyon, Strasbourg, and Douai used their advanced solid-casting and boring techniques to produce standard infantry cannon, the most common of which were the M1732 and M1740 model four-pounders (shot weight) developed by Jean-Florent de Vallière. These models were adapted for the tactics of the Seven Years' War, which emphasized concentrated firepower on massed troops.

After the war, a new generation of French engineering officers, shocked by their losses in battle after battle, argued for faster, more adaptable maneuvers that required lighter weapons. Leading the charge were Jean-Baptiste Vaquette de Gribeauval, who established a new series of manufacturing systems that produced lighter-weight, standardized weapons—the M1774 cannon and M1777 musket—and Philippe Charles Tronson du Coudray, who developed the military theories for the tactical employment of these weapons. With the new models ordered in huge numbers, France had to find a way to get rid of the older ones to make room. Monthieu had already been buying obsolete but still usable muskets from the French arsenals at cut-rate prices and storing them in his warehouses at Nantes, but the problem of artillery remained. In September 1776, the minister of war sent Coudray to visit the various arsenals around France, to select which excess cannon should be sold off to Spain or America.

On September 18, as Coudray was rounding France on his inspection tour, Deane and Monthieu were having dinner with Beaumarchais to hammer out the terms of contract that would ship sixteen hundred tons of surplus muskets, cannon, and other military supplies to America. Monthieu would charter a fleet of eight ships from the Nantes shipping firm of Jean Pelletier-Dudoyer, with whom Monthieu had often contracted to transport his arms to French colonies and slaving ports. At Beaumarchais's behest, Deane also decided that these arms must be accompanied by French officers who knew how to use them. Although the Congress gave him no authority to grant commissions, that did not stop him from doing so. Soon dozens of officers were preparing to embark for America on Beaumarchais's ships.

On October 15, Deane signed the contract with Roderigue Hortalez and Monthieu, who agreed to send out the first shipments by the following month. Purchase orders and bills of exchange began to flow out of 47 rue Vieille du Temple and across France. Beaumarchais purchased the surplus muskets directly from Monthieu. All of the excess cannon from the arsenals, Coudray and the minister of war agreed, would be sent to America; and though they were provided free, their shipping costs would amount to more than the total price of the muskets. Within just a few weeks orders were being filled and merchandise began to be shipped.

The Continental Congress was now committed to a bill of 320,000 livres (about $200 million today), which Deane would have to pay if they defaulted. This was a distinct possibility, given the just-arrived news from the United Colonies of North America (as Deane referred to them in the contract) that William Howe had routed George Washington's army at the Battle of Long Island and that he had established British headquarters in New York City.

Everything finally seemed to be running to Beaumarchais's script, in which Roderigue Hortalez becomes America's savior, but a series of problems soon arose that would turn the one-act play into a three-part farce. First, Beaumarchais advised Deane that since he was a novice in France, he should "not attempt to buy cannons or other arms" except through him. Even with his poor grasp of French, Deane was too savvy a merchant to sign on to a monopoly agreement. But Vergennes, who also distrusted the notion of an arms monopoly, had already mentioned another source of war materiel to Deane: Beaumarchais's former boss Jacques-Donatien Le Ray de Chaumont, now among France's richest shipping magnates. His wealth was due in part to his close connection to the minister of the navy, Sartine, who ensured that he received the lucrative contract to provision the colonies of Martinique and Saint-Domingue and finance the naval fleet in India. Around the same time he was negotiating with Beaumarchais, Deane also met with Chaumont, who offered, on credit for a future payment in tobacco, fifty tons of saltpeter, two hundred tons of gunpowder, and a load of bronze twelve-pound cannon. Deane quickly accepted. Although Beaumarchais complained loudly and frequently to Vergennes about his competitor, Chaumont's deeper pockets and closer ties to the arms industry would soon give him the edge over his erstwhile employee.

The second problem arose when Bancroft returned to London after Deane's initial meetings with Beaumarchais. Bancroft's friend Paul Wentworth confronted him with the news that even Prime Minister North was aware of his stay in Paris, because the spies trailing Deane had reported Bancroft's comings and goings. Wentworth knew this because he was also in the employ of Eden's Secret Service, and he now offered his friend the opportunity to serve Britain in the same way. For Bancroft's part, not only the breakup of the British Empire, but also the idea of a war between France and Britain—for that was the inevitable result of Deane's attempts to pull France into the American conflict—was utterly repugnant; he had, after all, spent much of his time working with Benjamin Franklin trying to avoid that very outcome. He therefore agreed to supply information to the British government. Returning to Paris in early 1777 to assist the Americans, he would discreetly copy their correspondence, dispatches, and notes of their conversations using invisible ink and ciphers. He would then pass them on to Stormont's courier using increasingly sophisticated tactics, including the infamous technique of placing the messages in a bottle within a hole of a particular box tree on the south terrace of the Tuileries garden, to be picked up every Tuesday night after 9:30 p.m. In this manner, British ministers knew about treaty negotiations and the dates of arms shipments many weeks before the Continental Congress did. The British navy, however, rarely put this information to use in capturing supply ships, for fear of sparking a war.

The third problem was that Wentworth and Bancroft were not the only ones to betray Beaumarchais's secrets; he was quite adept at doing that himself. During the months of November and December 1776, while the first three ships, *Amphitrite, Mercure,* and *Seine,* were being readied in Le Havre and Nantes, supplies began pouring in from across France. From Monthieu's warehouses in Nantes came 16,000 muskets of the M1763, M1766, and other older models, packed into 536 cases; from Strasbourg, Douai, and Metz came 21 M1732 and 173 M1740 cannon selected by Coudray, complete with brick-red carriages, more elegant than the British lead-gray ones, which had to be floated up the Rhine River and down the French coast; 20,000 cannonballs floated in small vessels down the Somme River; 24,000 pounds of gunpowder from Sedan; 53 barrels of sulfur from Versailles; tents, linens, spades, and axes. At Le Havre, the cargo was loaded only at night for secrecy.

While Beaumarchais was supervising the loading, a theater in Le Havre decided to stage *The Barber of Seville* with his assistance. News of both Beaumarchais's stage production and the loading of his ships bound for America immediately crossed the Channel and was published in the *London Chronicle*. It was obvious now that the subtitle of *Barber,* "The Useless Precaution," could also be applied to Roderigue Hortalez. The Spanish-sounding name, the attempts to launder its funds, and its furtive nighttime activities at pierside had fooled no one, least of all Stormont. "I am at a loss to comprehend that Beaumarchais . . . who has neither money nor credit could offer to credit the Americans, to the amount of three millions of livres unless this court [the French government] have secretly engaged some merchants or adventurers here to risk that sum," he fumed to the secretary of state for the Southern Department, Thomas Thynne, Viscount Weymouth. He now demanded to Vergennes that the ships be publicly detained and unloaded. Rather than risk opening a war for which France was still unprepared, Vergennes complied.

Just as two of the ships were being unloaded in Le Havre—the third, *Amphitrite,* had managed to slip out to sea—Benjamin Franklin shot into Paris like the proverbial lightning bolt he had come to embody. He had quietly departed Philadelphia with his two grandsons in October aboard a sloop of war, *Reprisal,* commanded by Lambert Wickes. After capturing two British merchantmen along the way, Wickes landed Franklin in Brittany in early December. Franklin stayed in Nantes with a business associate of Pierre Penet, who was even now attempting to fill the order for fifteen thousand muskets given to him by the Secret Committee of Trade. News of Franklin arrived in the capital long before he did, so that when he came to his hotel on December 21 there were already carriages lined up at the door with well-wishers ready to greet him. One of the first was his old friend Jacques Barbeu-Dubourg, whose letters to the Continental Congress, expressing the willingness of France to help the Americans, had led to this voyage. He may well have been clutching the reply he had recently received from the Congress that succinctly described Franklin's mission: "We look only to heaven and France for succor."

COVERT SPANISH SUPPORT FOR THE AMERICANS IN THE WESTERN THEATER

Perhaps "heaven" meant Spain, for in addition to Gardoqui's shipments to New England—one hundred thousand flints, forty-five thousand pounds of lead for shot, and a thousand Spanish blankets were on their way while *Amphitrite* was still loading at the pier—Spanish aid was already en route to help Americans stave off British attacks in the western theater of operations. Fort Pitt was the American stronghold in that theater, but lack of easy access across the Appalachian Mountains, coupled with the British Atlantic blockade, made it difficult to allocate munitions and supplies to its troops. Major General Charles Lee, commander of the American southern district, sent a delegation from Fort Pitt to New Orleans, carrying letters and paper money to Governor Luis de Unzaga requesting that a new supply line be opened up between the two locations, using the Mississippi and Ohio Rivers for transportation.

The delegation was met in August 1776 by Oliver Pollock, a successful American merchant of Irish descent who represented Willing & Morris in New Orleans. With Pollock translating, the delegation leader Captain George Gibson asked the Spanish governor for war materiel in return for American support in recovering Florida. Unzaga demurred on the idea of the reconquest of Florida, but agreed to release ten thousand pounds of gunpowder, using Pollock as the intermediary. Most of it went back to Fort Pitt on flatboats under the direction of Lieutenant William Linn, where it arrived the following year before the spring fighting season began. Gibson himself agreed to be "arrested" for a few weeks to throw the British consul off the scent. In October, Unzaga "released" Gibson, who took one of Pollock's sloops, *Lady Catherine,* back to Philadelphia with a thousand pounds of much-needed gunpowder and a letter from Pollock to his partner Robert Morris and the Continental Congress in which he offered to "make tender of my hearty service . . . [to] that Country I owe everything but birth." Morris of course agreed, and Pollock was now the official American agent in Spanish Louisiana. Intriguingly, Pollock's invoices to Morris would become more famous than him: As he began to abbreviate dollars as "ps" for pesos, by 1778 he had merged the letters to form the dollar mark "$," which Morris and eventually the rest of the new American government would use.

Unzaga relayed to the Spanish ministers the details of Gibson's mission and the proposed American support for reconquering Florida. It arrived in Madrid with other reports describing the resolve with which the Americans had fought at the Battle of Bunker Hill, and those reports taken together helped shape Spanish policy toward the widening conflict. For some time Grimaldi was searching for ways "to encourage the insurgents" that did not rely on French merchants and supplies. Like his counterpart Vergennes, Grimaldi needed an observer in Philadelphia, a sort of Spanish Bonvouloir, to help him decide how to do so. The previous Spanish observer, Jean Surriret, had been dispatched by Unzaga, but even as chief minister, Grimaldi did not control the governors of the Spanish colonies. Fortunately for him, the new minister of the Indies, José de Gálvez y Gallardo, who did control them, also saw the American revolt as his first order of business.

Both men agreed that Cuba and Louisiana would be the front line for both defense and intelligence-gathering. Following Grimaldi's counsel, José de Gálvez ordered Unzaga to send a new observer to Philadelphia under the guise of merchants looking to import flour. It was a plausible cover story: For the past several years Cuba and Louisiana had experienced a devastating series of droughts and hurricanes that laid waste to the harvests, so for the first time the Spanish colonies opened their markets to American entrepreneurs. Unzaga sent Bartolomé Toutant Beauregard, one of a prominent family of merchants in New Orleans, who arrived in Philadelphia in the autumn of 1776 and met with high-level (but unnamed) American officials. He returned with good intelligence that the Americans were determined and prepared to win their independence.

This and other reports convinced King Carlos III and his ministers that the merchant network from Havana and New Orleans could, like the Roderigue Hortalez scheme, be used to deliver supplies to the American rebels, and gave orders to do so. In January 1777, the Spanish naval commander at La Coruña began shipping munitions and supplies to Havana, where they would be stockpiled and transferred to New Orleans. By this time, the nephew of José de Gálvez, Bernardo de Gálvez y Madrid, had replaced Unzaga as governor of Louisiana. The first shipment of goods finally arrived in New Orleans in May 1777, just as another request for more supplies arrived from Fort Pitt. Bernardo de Gálvez, with an eye on the British consul, declared some of the munitions now being stored in the royal warehouses to be surplus and "auctioned" them to the Beauregard family of merchants, who in turn shipped to Fort Pitt ten thousand pounds of gunpowder and three hundred muskets. From now on, Spanish merchants under the direction of Bernardo de Gálvez and financed through Oliver Pollock would provide munitions, clothing, and medicine, in particular quinine from Peru to combat the ever-present danger of malaria. These supplies proved to be the lifeline that kept American troops fighting the British in the western theater of operations.

BEAUMARCHAIS'S ARMS HELP THE AMERICANS WIN THE BATTLE OF SARATOGA

While the New Orleans merchant network scheme was being launched, Roderigue Hortalez was foundering. Even before its first three ships set sail, Beaumarchais was running out of funds, as the costs of his supply and charter contracts rose well past the initial investments. In October 1776, in some desperation, he wrote a long dispatch to both Vergennes and Grimaldi claiming that he had already advanced over 5 million livres for supplies against the 2 million already given to him, and requested an immediate remittance of the balance. Both courts blanched at seeing the bill; Grimaldi replied that Carlos III could not make any further payments, while the French king demanded that Vergennes "cease working with that man who has played us for fools." Though Beaumarchais did not know it yet, he was on his way out as America's chief arms supplier.

While Beaumarchais was negotiating for more funds, the first American diplomats began negotiating for recognition. Back in September in Philadelphia, the arrival of Barbeu-Dubourg's letters expressing French interest in helping the Americans had prompted Congress to name Benjamin Franklin, Silas Deane, and Arthur Lee as official commissioners to France, to negotiate a treaty of amity and commerce that would open trade and provide recognition as an independent nation. Before this, Deane and Lee held somewhat vague responsibilities and authority from the American government, but with the arrival of Franklin carrying their commissions, they now had clear orders and the full powers of Congress behind them. For Lee, summoned by Franklin to return to Paris, his commission helped to take some of the sting out of having been shunted aside in the running of the Hortalez scheme.

On December 28, just a week after Franklin's arrival, the three commissioners had their first audience with Vergennes to discuss their request to establish a treaty. Franklin carried with him John Adams's Plan of Treaties, which the Congress had adopted in September. The model treaty was strictly commercial in nature, without any mention of political or military alliances. It would guarantee equality of tariffs and duties, protection of cargo on neutral ships in time of war, and freedom to trade in each other's ports. Vergennes assured the Americans that their treaty request would be taken seriously, although in fact he would postpone any decision for almost a year. The following day—actually, well after dark for secrecy—they met the Spanish ambassador, Pedro Pablo Abarca de Bolea, Conde de Aranda, at his sumptuous residence in the Hôtel de Coislin on the north side of the Place Louis XV (today's Place de la Concorde), but the language barrier at first prevented them from making much progress. After several more meetings it became apparent that

Aranda could not offer any guarantees from Spain, so the commissioners focused on the French government for the time being.

Over the next few months the American commissioners expanded their wish list: In addition to a commercial treaty, they wanted munitions directly from the king, and warships. Unbeknownst to the Americans, Vergennes was just then bound up in delicate negotiations with Spain to avoid a disastrous war with Portugal; any overt action to help the Americans could scuttle it, and perhaps even start a war with Britain for which neither France nor Spain was as yet prepared. Vergennes had to politely refuse each request from the commissioners, but softened the blow with a secret loan of 2 million livres, paid in quarterly installments. A month later they arranged for another loan of 2 million livres from the Farmer's General (a consortium of "tax farmers," that is, private merchants who collected taxes on behalf of the government) that would be payable in American tobacco. Within just a few weeks, Franklin and his colleagues had obtained the equivalent of $2 billion in credit for their fledgling nation.

Through the early months of 1777, the three commissioners were besieged by visitors. Some were French army officers looking to join the fight, while others were merchants and bankers looking to profit from the munitions and supply trade that accompanies every conflict. As it was by now clear to the commissioners that Beaumarchais was no longer trusted by Vergennes, the Americans needed to find other go-betweens who could be relied upon to help negotiate trade deals with merchants and to intercede with the French government on their behalf. The firm of Pierre Penet and Emmanuel de Pliarne at first appeared to fit the bill. Pliarne had stayed behind in America to drum up more business, while Penet handled the contracts in France. After some early problems, they had filled their order from the Secret Committee with fifteen thousand muskets from Saint-Étienne. Some twenty-five hundred of these arms were shipped to Robert Morris, and were heroically salvaged after the cargo vessel *Morris* that was carrying them was blown up by British warships off Delaware. Other Secret Committee arms were more successfully delivered to Rhode Island merchant John Brown, who became another of their agents. The Massachusetts Board of War (which replaced its Committees of Safety and Supplies) continued to use Penet and Pliarne as their primary suppliers, even though some of their muskets burst during proofing tests. Vergennes, however, saw Penet as "one of those fortune-seekers who wishes to enrich himself at any price," so even though Penet continued to correspond with the American commissioners in Paris, they did not award him any contracts.

The twin problems of too many supplicants and uncertainty as to their reliability were solved when Franklin was invited by the financier Chaumont to move into his estate, the Hôtel de Valentinois, in the village of Passy on the main road to Versailles, in what is today Paris's 16th arrondissement. For business purposes Deane retained his Paris apartment on the second floor of the Hôtel de Coislin, next to Aranda's suites, but he moved in with Franklin a few months after the elder statesman accepted Chaumont's offer. Chaumont had bought the estate "to house for free the plenipotentiary ministers of Congress, and to preserve them from the ambushes laid for them in Paris," and during their stay he would act as the commissioners' gatekeeper, both literally and metaphorically. In addition to protecting them from the "ambushes" of supplicants looking for positions and contracts, the arrangement similarly gave the Americans a degree of physical security from Stormont's spies. The recently widowed Franklin and the soon-to-be widowed Deane, housed in one of the garden pavilions on the eighteen-acre estate and waited upon by Chaumont's four doting daughters, also enjoyed a measure of hominess at Valentinois during their stay in France.

Vergennes implicitly trusted Chaumont, and that same level of trust was soon extended by the commissioners, primarily Deane, who oversaw most of the materiel contracts. During his long career Chaumont had come to know exactly which firms could be relied upon, and he guided the Americans accordingly. For example, he steered the contract for the manufacture of twenty-five thousand Continental Army uniforms to the textile firm of Sabatier fils et Déspres in Montpellier, and to another textile merchant, John Holker, to supervise the quality. These uniforms, thoughtfully manufactured in various colors—blue, brown, green, red, gray, and sky blue—to denote different regiments, were shipped out by Beaumarchais and others in late 1777, and began arriving in New England in the spring of 1778. Chaumont as well solved the problem of financing these purchases by introducing Franklin to his longtime business associate and neighbor in Passy, Rodolphe-Ferdinand Grand. Part of a Swiss family of bankers that extended from Amsterdam to Cadiz, Grand was the Paris agent of the Amsterdam bank Horneca, Fizeaux et Compagnie, which was well established in freight insurance as well as managing French government bonds. Grand was also a longtime confidant of Vergennes, so he quickly gained Franklin's trust; despite later protests by Robert Morris and even his fellow commissioners, Franklin never let any other European bank touch the financial affairs of the Continental Congress.

The American commissioners wanted to obtain additional supplies from Spain, but did not want to depend upon their French intermediaries to do so. Encouraged by Aranda, Arthur Lee set out for Madrid in early February 1777, hoping to procure not just more aid, but also an alliance. The Spanish government, still publicly professing neutrality in the British-American conflict, did not want to be seen accepting Lee's inopportune overture, so when Grimaldi received the news that Lee was on his way, he asked Diego de Gardoqui, who was in Madrid at the time, to write Lee telling him not to come to the capital. Lee fortunately found Gardoqui's letter waiting for him at the city of Burgos, halfway between the Pyrenees and Madrid. The letter instructed him to wait there until Gardoqui and Grimaldi could arrive: "In such a small place as Madrid, it would be absolutely impossible to remain incognito . . . and you would of course be spied upon." The letter did not mention the other reason for the cold shoulder; Grimaldi was on his way out as chief minister, and the incoming minister, José Moñino y Redondo, Conde de Floridablanca, had not yet fully formulated a policy toward the new American nation.

In his last act as minister (although technically he was already out of office), Grimaldi met with Lee at Burgos from March 4 to 6, with Gardoqui translating. Lee pressed for official recognition by Spain, but Grimaldi explained that "this was not the right moment" as neither France nor Spain was prepared to go to war with Britain, the same message Lee had heard from Vergennes. Spain instead opted for the same strategy as France, to provide secret aid directly to the Americans—and the Bilbao merchant at the table would provide the link. Grimaldi now instructed Lee, who did not know about either Gardoqui's smuggling or the supplies to New Orleans, to work directly with him on all future requests. Where Gardoqui's previous smuggling had been carried out with his own money and at his own risk (though likely with the Spanish court's knowledge), he now became Spain's Beaumarchais, sending money and supplies paid for directly by the Spanish treasury, with the expectation of repayment in "strong Virginia tobacco." Even before he had returned home, Gardoqui began placing orders in the Basque industrial town of

Placencia (today Soraluze-Placencia de las Armas) for uniforms and munitions. The mills began fabricating eleven thousand pairs of shoes, eighteen thousand blankets, and thirty thousand suits of clothing for the Continental Army. Meanwhile, the Real Fábrica de Armas (Royal Arms Factory) in the town supplied one thousand Model 1757 muskets (0.69 caliber) and two hundred thousand pounds of saltpeter, to be delivered to nearby Bilbao for loading. Within a month of their agreement, these supplies were being shipped on a half dozen vessels to Elbridge Gerry in New England. But with the War of American Independence now widening at a dizzying pace, it was hardly clear that the multinational supply network could keep up with the demand.

As Arthur Lee began his triumphant return to Paris in April 1777, he received news from Gardoqui that Washington's forces had triumphed over the British at Trenton on December 26, 1776, and at Princeton a week later. These were sorely needed victories for the Americans; 1776 may have been the year of independence, but it had been marked by a long string of military defeats. At the beginning of the year, Henry Knox had successfully dragged the Ticonderoga artillery to points overlooking Boston, forcing Howe to evacuate his troops to Halifax in March, but by July the British had regrouped on Staten Island to begin the invasion of New York City. Starting with the Battle of Long Island in August, Howe gradually cleared out Washington's troops from the city and its environs, pushing them north and west with British victories at Fort Washington, Fort Lee, and White Plains. Pursued by General Charles Cornwallis, Washington was following what he termed a "war of posts" and others dubbed a Fabian strategy, named for Roman general Quintus Fabius Maximus, who avoided pitched battles with a superior enemy in favor of indirect attacks and attrition. Washington steadily retreated across New Jersey and by December 7 was across the Delaware River and into Pennsylvania. With winter's deprivations and desertions rising daily, the situation was bleak: As Thomas Paine wrote in the first of his *American Crisis* pamphlets, "These are the times that try men's souls."

On December 26, three days after the pamphlet appeared, Washington abruptly shifted from his Fabian maneuvers and counterattacked in strength across the Delaware River. The Battle of Trenton was a swift and decisive raid on a garrison of Hessian soldiers, capturing almost a thousand men with fewer than ten American casualties. On January 3, Washington avoided a clash with Cornwallis's main army at Trenton, and instead attacked his rear guard at Princeton, escaping before British reinforcements arrived. Although these were both minor actions in military terms, they provided a great boost to Washington's reputation and to American morale.

These two battles also demonstrated the impact that the munitions provided by French, Spanish, and Dutch merchants were starting to have on America's fighting ability. By the end of 1776, at least ten thousand muskets and close to one million pounds of gunpowder had arrived in America. Where at the beginning of the war some militias were sharing one musket between four men with only fifteen rounds per man, at Trenton each soldier carried his own musket and sixty rounds into battle. Although there are scarce records of exactly which weapons were carried by Continental Army and militias, a modern archeological survey of shot recovered at the Princeton battlefield shows that almost half belonged to 0.69 caliber muskets fabricated in France, Spain, and Liège and used solely by the Americans, with the other half corresponding to the 0.75 caliber British- and American-manufacture muskets and smaller shot for American-made rifles. In these early battles, Dutch gunpowder and Spanish, French, and Liège muskets were not winning the war, but they were certainly preventing it from being lost.

For Britain, the defeats at Trenton and Princeton were trivial sideshows in their larger plan for dividing the American forces and destroying them piecemeal. In early 1777, George Germain, who had replaced Dartmouth as secretary of state for the colonies, developed with his generals William Howe and John Burgoyne a two-pronged assault that would separate New England, the Revolution's center of resistance, from the rest of the colonies (as they still referred to the states). Howe's army would be carried south from New York by a fleet of more than two hundred transport ships to capture Philadelphia, then wheel north past New York City and take the Hudson River valley. Burgoyne, at the same time, would march his troops south from Montreal, capturing forts along Lake Champlain and then driving down the Hudson River to meet with Howe near Albany. With the nation neatly cut in two down the Hudson, the British forces could subdue each half separately while denying any hope for mutual support.

The logistics of getting troops and materiel into place occupied the British until the summer of 1777. To the south, Howe's forces disembarked at Head of Elk in Maryland in late August and pushed north to the American capital. They overran George Washington at the Battle of Brandywine on September 11 and defeated Anthony Wayne at the Battle of Paoli two weeks later. On September 26, the British filed into Philadelphia, forcing the Congress to flee one hundred miles to York, Pennsylvania. Even a determined counterattack by Washington on October 4 at the Battle of Germantown failed to dislodge Howe from his position. To the north, Burgoyne had begun his march in late June down Lake Champlain toward Fort Ticonderoga, which he attacked on July 2. His army of almost eight thousand men easily surrounded the three thousand American troops, who were ordered by General Philip Schuyler to hold the strategic fort as long as possible. British artillery emplaced on higher ground forced the commanding officer, Major General Arthur Saint Claire, to conduct a nighttime retreat to save his army. Burgoyne, having learned that Howe was not coming up the Hudson Valley anytime soon, now took aim at Albany to set up his winter encampment to await a spring offensive. In mid-August he began marching his army south along the Albany road, where it would pass a hamlet called Saratoga.

While Germain, Howe, and Burgoyne were planning their campaigns, Beaumarchais's ships were on their way to America, carrying both provisions and volunteers for the fight that lay ahead. Having been insufficiently victualed at Le Havre, *Amphitrite* returned to Lorient in Brittany and set sail again for New England on January 25. Another Beaumarchais ship, *Mercure,* departed Nantes a few days later, also bound for New England, followed by *Seine* bound for the West Indies. With another pair of ships clearing harbor by March, five vessels under charter to Roderigue Hortalez were at sea in the spring of 1777, their combined cargoes sufficient to arm, clothe, and outfit an army of thirty thousand men. Meanwhile, many more Beaumarchais vessels, eventually totaling forty cargo ships of various types, were being readied in ports around France.

Mercure was the first to arrive, after forty days at sea dropping anchor in Portsmouth, New Hampshire, on Monday, March 17, 1777. On board were twelve thousand stands of muskets and a thousand barrels of gunpowder, along with blankets and textiles. On hand to receive them was John Langdon, a representative of the Continental Congress and its local marine agent. Word of the arrival of these sorely needed supplies spread rapidly, and a tug-of-war ensued: New Hampshire wanted two thousand stands of arms, Connecticut three thousand, Massachusetts five thousand arms plus three hundred barrels of gunpowder. John Langdon quickly complied with these requests, but George Washington was concerned about the problems of having so many arms so near the coast—"the enemy are determined to destroy our magazines wherever they are accessible"—and of shortchanging the middle states such as New York and New Jersey, so he wrote to Langdon and ordered him to send the remaining muskets to the newly established armory at Springfield, Massachusetts.

On April 20, *Amphitrite* arrived in Portsmouth with sixty-six hundred stands of arms, fifty-two cannon, and thirty-three thousand cannonballs, along with spades, axes, and tents. Now Langdon wasted no time sending the cannon and muskets to the Springfield Armory, where they arrived in early June. In part because there had not been time to set up repair facilities in France, many of the muskets had broken locks and springs due to years of storage and damage in transit. Springfield armorers quickly repaired them and made the guns ready for use. Meanwhile, newspapers from the *Boston Gazette* to the *Pennsylvania Packet* carried stories about the "valuable cargo" that had arrived from France. Although arms from overseas had been pouring in for almost two years, this was the first tangible, large-scale demonstration of French support for the American cause, giving a public boost when most of the news from the battlefields was dismal.

Both sides had been depleted by the Battle of Ticonderoga and its aftermath. The Americans left behind all of their cannon, a fact bemoaned by Schuyler's artillery officer, Ebenezer Stevens. Fortunately, Schuyler had already sent orders to the Springfield Armory to dispatch more cannon to the front lines. Even as the Battle of Ticonderoga was raging, oxcarts and horse-drawn wagons were pulling twenty-two cannon, ten of them M1740 four-pounders from *Amphitrite,* to the Hudson River port of Peekskill. From there they were floated up the Hudson to Albany, whence they were taken by ox teams to Schuyler's camp and depot at Stillwater, a few miles south of Saratoga, arriving on July 26.

The British were also low on provisions. In early August, Burgoyne directed a force of twelve hundred Hessian and British troops to raid the supply depot at the town of Bennington in today's Vermont. New Hampshire militia were among the only troops in position to counter the raid. Had this counterattack been needed before the arrival of Beaumarchais's arms, it is doubtful that it could have been accomplished: The lack of firearms in early 1777 contributed to New Hampshire militia companies being understrength by an average of 40 percent. Now, with the availability of thousands of French muskets provided by John Langdon, New Hampshire's militia general John Stark raised and equipped two brigades (fifteen hundred men) in the space of six days. On August 16, the two sides clashed a dozen miles west of Bennington. Stark's militia routed the Hessian and British troops in two separate engagements, wounding or killing almost a thousand men and capturing cannon and muskets. Burgoyne's forces were now weakened but still intimidating as they continued their march toward Albany.

The Battle of Bennington had slowed but not stopped Burgoyne's advance, but the Congress had already decided that Schuyler was not the man to face him. On August 19, Major General Horatio Gates, who had served in the British army during the War of the Austrian Succession and the Seven Years' War, assumed command of the Northern Department of the Continental Army. As the army's adjutant general, he was most concerned about having sufficient men and supplies for the upcoming battle, and Washington threw his full support behind Gates's requests. Orders flowed out of Gates's camp for ammunition, clothing, and supplies. Meanwhile, militia from New Hampshire, Massachusetts, New York, and Connecticut, now fully armed with Beaumarchais's muskets, flocked to the theater of operations through August and September, as did riflemen from Pennsylvania, Maryland, and Virginia. Gates now had nine thousand troops facing seven thousand British and Hessian forces. In early September, at the advice of his engineer Thaddeus Kosciuszko, Gates ordered Ebenezer Stevens to set up his cannon in defensive emplacements at a rise called Bemis Heights that overlooked the Albany road, the distinctive brick-red carriages of the M1740s neatly complementing the barns and outbuildings of the surrounding farm. There the army awaited Burgoyne.

On September 19, the First Battle of Saratoga was engaged. The innocent-sounding nicknames of the opposing generals, "Gentleman Johnny" Burgoyne and "Granny" Gates, belied the ferocity of the engagements. Around noon the Americans left their fortified position on Bemis Heights and met Burgoyne's troops on the forested fields at Freeman's Farm. The two sides clashed musket-to-musket, with the American lines being pushed forward and backward as the afternoon progressed. British artillery and infantry positions would be captured, only to be turned over with the next counterattack. Ultimately the American side withdrew to its fortification, leaving Burgoyne with heavier casualties but having retained the field. With the results of the battle indecisive, both sides returned to watching and waiting.

For Caleb Stark of the First New Hampshire Militia Regiment (and son of General John Stark), there was no question that the timely arrival of Beaumarchais's shipments spelled the difference between stalemate and defeat at the First Battle of Saratoga. "The first opportunity of testing the qualities of the new French muskets occurred September 19, 1777, when the Americans left their lines and advanced, without trepidation, to meet the veterans of Britain in the open field," he vividly remembered many years later. "On that all important day the Beaumarchais arms, followed by their Yankee comrades, after forcing the enemy from the field with great slaughter, leaped boldly into his camp, drove his forces from part of it, capturing a portion of his artillery, and discomfiting his whole army. . . . I firmly believe that unless these arms had been thus timely furnished to the Americans, Burgoyne would have made an easy march to Albany."

During the several-week lull in action, more American troops arrived on the scene, swelling the ranks to nearly twelve thousand, almost double Burgoyne's now-depleted forces. With his troop strength down and supplies running low, on October 7 Burgoyne ordered a late afternoon assault on the American fortification, supported by forward artillery. American troops surged out to meet the attack head-on, their Beaumarchais artillery remaining in its emplacements to await the assault that never came. The battle lines swung back and forth until a series of desperate charges led by Benedict Arnold finally overwhelmed the Hessian center, forcing Burgoyne to retreat as darkness fell.

On October 17, Burgoyne surrendered to Gates. The five thousand troops of the Convention Army of Saratoga, as they were called, were sent to Virginia as prisoners of war, a devastating loss of nearly a quarter of Britain's forces in America. Both sides saw Saratoga as a turning point in the war. It was the first time that American troops had stood toe-to-toe against the British in a major set-piece battle and had rocked them back on their heels. George Washington declared a day of thanksgiving, which the states also observed. British troops were also stunned by the victory and impressed with the "courage and obstinacy with which the Americans fought." The shock reached all the way to London, where

Germain accepted Howe's resignation and cast aside the strategy of dividing the American nation in two. Instead, a new strategy focusing on conquering the southern states—thought to be more Loyalist than New England—began forming.

Back in France, Beaumarchais learned of Saratoga on December 4 from a courier just arrived from Boston. The following day he reported to Vergennes the "very positive news from America"; if he ever made the connection between his *Mercure* and *Amphitrite* shipments and the stunning American victory, he never mentioned it in his correspondence with the minister. Indeed, most of that correspondence dealt with his precarious financial situation. Even after another series of loans totaling 1 million livres, his creditors were baying at the door: Money was still flowing out the door of his elegant office for even more supplies and ship charters, while he had yet to receive any return cargo from America to pay for all the goods.

Beaumarchais was not the only one losing money on America; dozens if not hundreds of private merchants across Europe were heavily invested in the American trade and saw their losses mount due to British depredations at sea and blockades of the American coast. Chaumont and his associates Sabatier fils et Déspres, in addition to their contracts with the American commissioners, were also privately trading with America, and lost five of seven vessels in one season. Another merchant firm actively supplying arms to the rebels, Reculès de Basmarein et Raimbeaux of Bordeaux, lost thirteen of its twenty-two ships. Although such losses were common early in a war, they were untenable in the long term without protection from naval convoys, and no government would instate a convoy system for a nation it did not formally recognize as an ally.

America had already received recognition after a fashion in late 1776, when two ships in search of supplies entered foreign ports—the Continental Navy brig *Andrew Doria* at Sint Eustatius, and an unnamed schooner at the Danish island of Saint Croix—and received naval salutes in honor of their flags. This form of recognition, however, was hardly sufficient for the fledgling nation. The kingdoms of France and Spain had so far been providing enough secret aid to keep American troops in the fight. They would have to provide more than guns, powder, and blankets for the United States to win the war. France and Spain, in short, would now have to put their entire political and military might behind the American cause to ensure victory against their common British enemy.

CHAPTER 3

The Ministers

Jonathan Loring Austin, the Massachusetts courier who brought the news of Saratoga on December 4, 1777, had barely stopped his coach at the Hôtel de Valentinois to see Benjamin Franklin when the American commissioner asked, "Sir, *is* Philadelphia taken?" "Yes, sir," Austin replied. Franklin began to turn away, his hands clasped behind his back in defeat. Austin continued, "But sir, I have greater news than that: *General Burgoyne and his whole army are prisoners of war!*" The American commissioners quickly swung into action to spread the word, now hopeful of rallying an apparently reluctant France to sign a treaty of alliance. Franklin had not yet set up his soon-to-be-famous printing press, so everyone set about making hand copies of the Saratoga report, sending one by express courier to Versailles and engaging Austin to deliver the news around Paris. Beaumarchais, who was at Valentinois when the courier arrived, hurriedly returned to his bureau so he could do the same, but his carriage flipped over on a Paris street. The playwright emerged from the wreckage cut and bruised, unable to write to Vergennes until the next day.

Many years later, Franklin's secretary and then teenaged grandson, William Temple Franklin, remembered that the news of Burgoyne's defeat "was received in France with as great demonstrations of joy as if it had been a victory gained by their own arms." This may have been a memory of youthful exuberance, or a product of the company the Franklins kept, for the accounts published in French newspapers painted a more sober picture, reporting no overt fanfare or accounts of celebrations in the street. Much of the French press, such as the *Gazette de France, Courier de l'Europe, Affaires d'Angleterre et d'Amérique,* and *Gazette de Leyde,* was under either the direct control or the strong influence of the French government. Vergennes made certain that these papers reflected his pro-American views, such as seeing to it that reports from Benjamin Franklin made it into their pages. Similarly in Spain, where newspapers like the *Gaceta de Madrid* and *Mercurío Histórico y Político* were official mouthpieces for the government, there was no interest in allowing the American war for independence to stoke Spanish anticolonial sentiment, so the accounts of Burgoyne's surrender were factual and unembellished. In both nations, the greater concern of the three estates—clergy, nobility, and commoners—was whether this American victory would lead to them becoming enmeshed in yet another war with Britain, just a decade after the previous one.

Although both the French and Spanish crowns sometimes courted public opinion to maintain the peace, they did not need to pay it much heed when formulating their policies, for the reason that they ruled as absolute, if enlightened, monarchs. Both Carlos III (His Most Catholic Majesty) and Louis XVI (His Most Christian Majesty) were descended from the Sun King, Louis XIV, and continued his philosophy that rulers should better the lives of their subjects through the arts, sciences, and literature, as well as the limited toleration of some individual liberties. That enlightenment did not, however, extend to accepting a representative parliamentary-type government as was found in Britain; the unofficial motto of enlightened absolutism was later described as *"tout pour le peuple, rien par le peuple,"* or roughly, "everything for the people, without the people's consent." In France, the États généraux (Estates General) was the closest thing to a representative body, but it had no legislative authority and in any event had not met since 1614. In Spain, the similar Cortes Generales (General Courts) had languished since the mid-1600s. Absent such an elected body, the policymaking in each Bourbon nation resided solely in the hands of the king and a select group of ministers, who were in turn supported by surprisingly small administrative staffs. Yet from the offices of these few dozen men came the thousands of dispatches, memoranda, and edicts that created armies, moved navies, and made history.

THE KINGS AND THEIR MINISTERS

Carlos III and Louis XVI may have shared a bloodline, but they did not share a worldview. Those were shaped by their upbringing, the events of the day, and by the ministers who surrounded them. Carlos III of Spain was by far the older and more experienced of the two, having reigned for twice as long as his cousin had been alive. Born as Carlos de Borbón in Madrid in 1716, he moved to Italy to assume his title of Duke of Parma, and soon after his eighteenth birthday he conquered the Austrian-controlled Kingdom of Naples. As ruler he successfully led his troops during the War of the Austrian Succession, built the grand palace at Caserta that rivaled Versailles in its opulence, and financed the excavations of the buried cities of Herculaneum and Pompeii. After a quarter century as king of Naples, in 1759 he inherited the Spanish throne from his half brother and returned to the city of his birth to assume the title of Carlos III.

His first major decision as king of Spain was to enter the Seven Years' War, with disastrous results. A few years after the fireworks in the Parque del Buen Retiro signaled the end of the conflict, he narrowly avoided another disaster when bread riots forced him to temporarily leave the government in the hands of his close confidant the Conde de Aranda, who at the time was the military commander for Madrid. Carlos III saw better fortunes in reforming Spain's antiquated economy: rationalizing its shipbuilding and arms production to align with those of France; increasing exports by liberalizing trade with its Spanish American colonies; and promoting manufacturing, arts, and the study of sciences (his son Gabriel de Borbón was an occasional correspondent of Benjamin Franklin's). He also reshaped antique Madrid, which was the center of government as well as Spain's social and economic center, to become a modern European city. *El Rey Alcalde* (the Mayor King), as he became known, ordered the narrow, winding streets torn up and replaced with broad radial avenues lit by streetlamps à la Paris, created parks, and opened museums and palaces. Widowed soon after he ascended to the Spanish throne, his personal life was taken up with his seven surviving children (of thirteen) and his passion for hunting.

While lavishing attention on Madrid, Carlos III and his court led a peripatetic existence driven by the season and the hunt. He would begin the New Year at the Royal Palace of Madrid, which served as the administrative home for the government. After Epiphany (January 6), he and his court would move just a few miles north to the excellent hunting grounds of El Pardo palace, where they stayed until Lent. Aranjuez, thirty miles south, was the next stop until July, after which the court decamped to Madrid for a few weeks before moving to Escorial (thirty miles west) for more hunting, then north to Granja, returning to Madrid by the end of November to repeat the cycle. Tapestries designed by Francisco de Goya, one of Carlos III's favorite artists, decorated the great dining halls of several of the palaces.

The royal family was not the only one to dine beneath Goya masterpieces, for the king's ministers also followed his itinerary. Carlos III was an experienced and decisive king, and well skilled in choosing highly competent ministers. In 1777, the ministers concerned with the conduct of the war consisted of: José Moñino y Redondo, Conde de Floridablanca, chief minister and minister of foreign affairs; Pedro González de Castejón, minister of the navy; Ambrosio de Funes Villalpando, Conde de Ricla, minister of war; and José de Gálvez y Gallardo, minister of the Indies. As they traveled from palace to palace, each minister was accompanied by only a handful of administrative secretaries to assist with his relentless day-to-day work of handwriting and triple-copying every document (although Floridablanca, as chief minister, was granted four secretaries). The rest of the ministry staffs, referred to as *covachuelistas* (cave dwellers) for their former subterranean offices, continued their functions at the Royal Palace of Madrid and communicated with their ministers by regular courier.

As Floridablanca served in two roles, he relied on two different networks of officials to help him formulate and carry out the king's policies. As foreign minister he depended on his ambassadors, such as the Conde de Aranda in Paris and Francisco Escarano in London, to keep him informed on European affairs. As the administrative head of a vast empire he leaned on the king's council of ministers, many of whom had a wealth of personal experience with North America that would guide him in the upcoming conflict there. The minister of the navy, González de Castejón, was the first career naval officer to achieve that political position, having fought the British navy during several wars in the Mediterranean and at Havana. The minister of war, the Conde de Ricla, formerly the military leader of Cuba, was concerned over the possibility of the American conflict spilling over into Spanish territory and sought to bolster troop numbers around the region. The minister of the Indies, José de Gálvez, a lawyer by training, had previously been the *visitador,* or inspector general, for New Spain in the years following the Seven Years' War, and he now administered all of the Spanish colonies in the Americas and Asia. Those colonies were divided into a number of viceroyalties, including Peru and New Granada in South America, and New Spain, which covered today's Mexico, Central America, and the American Southwest. Spanish viceroys were more powerful than governors, as they acted with the full authority of the king. Their viceroyalties were divided into administrative districts, or *audiencias,* such as Guatemala,

José Moñino y Redondo,
Conde de Floridablanca (1728–1808).
Francisco de Goya, eighteenth century,
oil on canvas

Buenos Aires, and Quito. Separately, the captain-general of Cuba was the military leader of that island as well as Florida and Louisiana.

Under Floridablanca, these ministers created a new approach to foreign and domestic policy that was no longer subordinate to France. This had not been the case immediately after the Seven Years' War, when Jéronimo Grimaldi worked hand in hand with Choiseul to rebuild their navies and plan a coordinated assault on Britain. Foreign policy failures such as the Falklands/Malvinas crisis of 1770 and a disastrous attempted invasion of Algiers in 1775, as well as a growing suspicion of Italian influence in Spanish politics, led the king to replace Grimaldi in 1777 with Floridablanca as chief minister. Floridablanca, then forty-nine years old, already had wide experience as a diplomat as well as a criminal prosecutor, and had previously worked on colonial trade policy and domestic fiscal reforms. He thus had a solid understanding of both domestic and foreign affairs, compared with Grimaldi, who had spent most of his career outside Spain. Floridablanca and his king consequently reformulated Spanish policy to become more internally focused and less dependent on alliances.

Even if Spain's new foreign policy was less dependent on the French alliance, both the obligations of the Bourbon Family Compact as well as the realities of facing their mutual British adversary required continual coordination between the two nations. Certainly Louis XVI continued to maintain the same close ties to Carlos III as had his grandfather Louis XV, although the new French king was now the junior partner in the monarchies' personal alliance. Born Louis-Auguste in Versailles in 1754, at age eleven he lost his father, Louis XV's son, so the boy now became the dauphin, the heir to the throne. He spent his adolescent years on the grounds of Versailles learning to hunt with his grandfather, who taught him what he could of governing. In 1770, Louis-Auguste married Marie Antoinette, the daughter of France's Austrian ally the empress Maria Theresa, in an effort to cement the bonds between the Bourbon and Habsburg dynasties. In time, Louis grew to love his wife but never to trust her.

When the nineteen-year-old Louis XVI took the throne in 1774 upon his grandfather's death, he asked the aged but experienced Jean-Frédéric Phélypeaux, Comte de Maurepas, to provide sage counsel. Although Maurepas had been out of politics for over twenty-five years, the former navy minister still knew how to read people the way a great navigator reads maps. He was often referred to as the king's principal minister, but he never had that title, nor did he function as a chief minister who coordinated and executed policy, the way Floridablanca did. Rather, his power lay in controlling access by the council of ministers to Louis XVI. This was made easier for Maurepas by the fact that the king spent most of his time at Versailles, the insular seat of French government that was separated by fifteen miles of heavily trafficked road from Paris, France's economic and social hub (the king himself so seldom visited Paris that his brother-in-law was shocked to learn that he had never seen the Invalides, a veterans' hospital and place of worship that was considered one of the grandest buildings in Europe). Maurepas lived at the Versailles palace in a cramped apartment directly above the king's quarters, connected to it by a private staircase, so he could filter all meetings and correspondence. For several months of the year Louis XVI traveled to the various royal châteaux around Paris—Fontainebleau, Compiègne, Marly-le-Roi, Choisy—generally leaving his ministers back at Versailles, who could only visit him upon invitation, which again was controlled by Maurepas.

Louis XVI was not only young and inexperienced, but in greater contrast to his cousin Carlos III, he was indecisive most of his life—his own brother compared his thinking to "two oiled billiardballs that you are vainly trying to hold together." He was determined, however, to rule within a strict moral code, which was one reason for disbanding his grandfather's *Secret du Roi* as soon as he was made aware of it. The king was fortunate rather than prescient in his choice of capable ministers, which he chose from a list of acceptable candidates that his late father had created years before. In 1777, those ministers involved in the conduct of the war were: Jacques Necker, finance minister; Antoine Raymond Gabriel de Sartine, minister of the navy and colonies; Claude Louis, Comte de Saint-Germain, minister of war; and Charles Gravier, Comte de Vergennes, minister for foreign affairs.

The ministers lived and worked just outside the main courtyard of the Versailles palace. Necker's bureau and apartment were in an older edifice, the Hôtel du Grand Contrôle (Superintendents' Bureau). The other ministers resided in the Ailes des Ministres Nord et Sud (Northern and Southern Ministers' Pavilions) and worked in the newly constructed Hôtels de la Guerre, Marine, et des Affaires Étrangères (Bureaus of War, Navy, and Foreign Affairs). Designed by the military surveyor Jean-Baptiste Berthier with floor-to-ceiling shelves for leather-bound archives, it was sumptuously decorated with gilded archways and paintings of French battle victories by the gifted artist Pierre L'Enfant that stood in brilliant contrast to the black-and-white correspondence and reports that occupied the ministers and their staff. Each minister typically had three or four *premier commis* (first secretaries, i.e., administrative heads of bureaus), eight or nine ordinary *commis,* and a smattering of clerks, drawn mostly from the minor aristocracy. The normal work schedule was from 9 a.m. to 1 p.m., then 6 p.m. to 10 p.m., though the ministers themselves usually worked twelve-hour days. Each bureau had its own on-site printing house, almost unheard of in an age of handwritten-and-copied documents, to rapidly disseminate ordinances, regulations, maps, and other documents.

Necker had replaced Anne-Robert-Jacques Turgot as finance min-

Charles Gravier, Comte de Vergennes (1717–1787).
Vangelisti Vincenzio, after Antoine-François Callet,
engraving [s.n., between 1774 and 1789]

ister in May 1776, after the latter had failed to reform France's economy in the wake of a series of devastating famines, and his unwillingness to finance a new war with Britain. Necker was not a French citizen but instead a wealthy Protestant banker from the Republic of Geneva, so although he could not be given the official title of controller-general of finance (which was reserved for Catholics), he served in that capacity in all but name. As an ex-banker, he was in the best position to obtain funding for the upcoming war through loans instead of the politically infeasible route of increased taxation. Much of the increased budget would go to Sartine's navy, in which Louis XVI showed a particular interest, unlike his grandfather. Sartine, a Spanish-born lawyer who had served as Paris's chief of police, had no maritime experience but was a proven administrator who would get the navy's budget and bureaucracy under firm control. In this he was aided by Charles Pierre Claret, Comte de Fleurieu, who though in title was merely the *premier commis* for ports and arsenals, actually served as Sartine's entire strategic planning staff. Minister of War Saint-Germain also attempted to rein in the army's bureaucracy by reforming the officer corps, but his plans would prove unpopular and by the end of 1777 he would be replaced by Alexandre-Marie-Léonor de Montbarey, an experienced soldier as well as a favorite of Maurepas, and who would prove crucial in the planning of joint French-Spanish operations.

Vergennes was, in several ways, the odd man of the group. He had been serving France by living outside of it as a diplomat for over thirty years, with posts in Portugal, various Germanic states, and the Ottoman Empire. His last posting to Sweden was engineered by the head of the *Secret du Roi,* Charles-François de Broglie. It was a delicate assignment, in which Vergennes, with assistance from the Grand family of bankers, helped finance a coup d'état that enabled the French-leaning King Gustav III to overthrow the pro-British factions of the parliament and to "put a brake on [Russia's] ambitious and despotic projects." Louis XVI selected him in part due to this success, but also because his name was on his late father's list of candidates.

Vergennes was a sober, serious man—Aranda claimed that "I chat with M. de Maurepas; I negotiate with M. de Vergennes"—and he became closer to his king than anyone save Maurepas. Louis XVI, in turn, trusted Vergennes to follow his moral credo that "honesty and restraint [meaning honoring treaties and national boundaries] must be our watchwords."

However much Vergennes understood the external political landscape, his extended time outside France made him inexperienced in the internal workings of the court, and at first made him the subject of ridicule; one critic acidly wrote that Vergennes had "arrived at Versailles as a foreigner become minister, rather than a Minister of Foreign Affairs." He quickly learned court politics thanks to his four long-serving *premiers commis*, including the brothers Conrad Alexandre Gérard (who primarily handled northern Europe) and Joseph Matthias Gérard de Rayneval (mostly southern Europe), both of whom had been privy to the various changes in the Bourbon strategy toward Britain and America.

As Vergennes took the reins of diplomacy, he made changes to his ambassadors. In Britain, the Duc de Guînes, who had sent Bonvouloir to America, was replaced by Emmanuel Marie Louis, Marquis de Noailles. Coming from one of the noblest families in France, whose ancestors had served as ambassadors to Britain for two centuries, he was the epitome of "an honest gentleman sent to lie abroad for the good of his country" (as an earlier diplomat said of the profession), for much of his time would be spent bald-facedly denying any French involvement in the arming of American rebels to British secretary of state Weymouth. In Spain, Vergennes replaced the Marquis d'Ossun, who had grown too close to Carlos III, with Armand Marc, Comte de Montmorin, whose personal ties to Louis XVI—as a child he had been the dauphin's playmate—helped bolster his rather thin diplomatic credentials.

Even with this overhaul of diplomats, diplomacy itself still ran at an almost glacial pace. While couriers between Versailles and London could deliver packets in just a few days, two weeks to two months could elapse for a message to travel the eight hundred miles from Versailles to Madrid and be answered in return. Vergennes and Floridablanca had to make decisions based on very little, often outdated information. These decisions were further complicated by the fact that, despite a half century of alliance, France and Spain still had widely different ambitions on the global front.

A WAR BETWEEN SPAIN AND PORTUGAL TRIGGERS COVERT AID FROM FRANCE TO AMERICA

When Louis XVI took the throne in 1774, the expanding struggle between Britain and its North American colonists was far down on the list of priorities of both France and Spain, for there were other, more imminent threats in Europe and abroad. But by the time the news of the Battle of Saratoga reached Europe at the end of 1777, the War of American Independence occupied center stage in their foreign policies. What brought the American conflict to the fore was the realization that it was not a menace to the two Bourbon powers, but rather an opportunity to contain their greatest potential threat, Great Britain, and would ultimately lead to a de facto revival of their long-dormant *revanche* strategy against the island nation.

Then as now, the conduct of foreign policy balanced many competing interests. As Louis XVI came to his throne, Britain was not the most urgent of his concerns. Although the global balance of power had shifted dramatically in Britain's favor, the island kingdom had been left without any strong allies in Europe, so France was still the dominant force on the Continent. For some time France had used its influence to protect its client states, notably Sweden, Poland, and the Ottoman Empire, from territorial claims by a resurgent Russia. However, the Polish partition two years earlier by Prussia, Austria, and Russia threatened that fragile status. Friedrich II of Prussia had engineered the partition to prevent Russia's Catherine II ("the Great") from further enlarging her empire. Russia had been at war with the Ottoman Empire for several years, and after overrunning the Crimea looked poised to take over Turkey. The Polish partition halted Russia's territorial advance and guaranteed at least a temporary peace in eastern Europe. For France, the loss of its Polish ally, coupled with the territorial gains of Prussia and in particular the possibility of an alliance between its two main rivals, Britain and Russia, raised the fear that French power on the European continent would be diminished. The French king equally suspected that Friedrich II would use Prussia's collaboration with Austria to drive a wedge between Vienna and Versailles. Even though Maria Theresa was Louis XVI's mother-in-law, the French court worried that her ambitious son Joseph II (who was co-ruler of Austria) might use this newfound power to make territorial claims against French interests in Italy and French Lorraine. Therefore, France's overarching strategy regarding "restless and greedy" Britain was to ensure that it did not take advantage of any of these other conflicts to overturn the balance of power in Europe.

Spain was less troubled than France by the Russian-Ottoman War and the partition of Poland; its primary European goals were the recovery of Gibraltar and Minorca. Although it was somewhat concerned by

Russia's territorial aspirations in Alaska and present-day California, of much greater danger were the recent British incursions in the Pacific, such as the voyages of James Cook, which could threaten Spain's Asia trade. This was why the Falkland/Malvinas Islands, an important way station on the sea lanes between Europe and the Pacific, became such a contested territory. Another, separate source of trouble was that the 1763 Treaty of Paris gave Britain two footholds in the Gulf of Mexico: the territory of Florida and logging rights in the Honduras region of Guatemala. Apart from its concerns over the proximity of British forces to Havana and its trade routes, Spain also worried that British logging in Guatemala would be used to mask other activities such as occupying Panama, the transshipment point for Peruvian silver, or even digging a canal across the Nicaragua region of Guatemala, which would create a British link between the Atlantic and Pacific Oceans and cut New Spain in two. In the view of Madrid, the Gulf of Mexico was a Spanish lake, and the British presence in Guatemala and Florida could jeopardize its vital colonial interests in the region. Spain's long-term priority, apart from the recovery of Gibraltar and Minorca, was to remove the British from the Gulf of Mexico.

These disparities in worldview and of the threat represented by Britain were highlighted in the different naval policies of Spain and France during the decade after the Seven Years' War. The British capture of Havana in 1763 had a profound impact on the Spanish psyche. Fear of another British incursion into Spain's lifeline—its American and Caribbean colonies that sent sugar and silver to the mainland—led Carlos III and his ministers to shore up colonial defenses and rebuild the navy. They sent inspectors general like José de Gálvez to the colonies in order to oversee the reinforcement of their defenses. They increased taxes to pay for new ships and armament, which were now being built according to French standards in order to achieve a combined Bourbon fleet. They maintained this high level of spending from 1764 to 1774, during which time the Spanish navy added thirty new ships of the line—eleven of which were built in the newly revamped Havana dockyard—to bring its fighting strength up to sixty-four ships, greater than the sixty ships needed in the original plan for the British invasion.

France was supposed to increase its fleet to eighty ships of the line, so that the overall Bourbon invasion fleet would be superior to the British navy. During the first few years after the Treaty of Paris, French shipyards turned out nine new ships of the line, increasing its size from fifty-nine to sixty-eight ships, well on the way to surpassing Britain. But with the loss of Canada and Louisiana, France no longer faced the same British threat to its colonial lifelines as did Spain, and the navy began to take on less importance. This shift in naval policy was made evident after 1770 when Choiseul was dismissed in the wake of the Falklands/Malvinas crisis. With the growing threat from European events weighing more heavily, the new French government adopted a less aggressive stance toward Britain. Choiseul's invasion plans were shelved, and budgetary pressures forced successive navy ministers to drastically cut back on shipbuilding. The French fleet shrank back to fifty-nine ships; further reductions in spares and supplies meant that in reality, only a fraction of those ships were ready for action. With such differing political goals, French and Spanish policies might have continued moving in different directions; but just as Louis XVI came to power in 1774, a new conflict in the Americas led to the realignment of the two nations' priorities and helped create a unified policy toward the British threat.

The American conflict that helped reunite French and Spanish policies against Britain was not the one that began in Boston, but rather the one that began in Buenos Aires. Since the final days of the Seven Years' War, Spain and Portugal had been disputing the borders between their South American colonies, roughly the line between today's Uruguay and Argentina. Portugal maintained an outpost, Colónia do Sacramento, on the Río de la Plata just opposite from Buenos Aires, while Spain held several fortifications, like Rio Grande de São Pedro, in southern Brazil. Each side accused the other of fomenting incursions into the other's territory, raising the stakes for another war. The governor in Buenos Aires prepared to send in more troops, while Lisbon prepared a fleet to meet them. The Spanish invasion of Portugal in 1762 was still fresh in living memory, and an outbreak of hostilities in far-off South America could touch off yet another war between the neighboring countries that could drag the rest of Europe in with it. Even the fact that the Portuguese king, José I, was Carlos III's brother-in-law (Carlos's sister Mariana Victoria was queen of Portugal) did not deter the danger of a new European conflict breaking out.

As Vergennes assumed his ministry in 1774, one of his first tasks was to find a way to defuse that danger. As he did during the Seven Years' War, Portugal's prime minister, Marquês de Pombal, was counting on

Britain to come to its aid in a fight against Spain. Spain, in turn, was waving the Bourbon Family Compact in the face of the French ambassador to Madrid. While tensions rose between Spain and Portugal over the course of 1774 and 1775, the missives from Madrid to Versailles grew increasingly bellicose. In October 1775, Grimaldi, at the time the Spanish chief minister, sent a long letter to Vergennes warning him (without any actual proof) that since Britain and Portugal were planning an attack, a preemptive attack on Portugal was justified. "War is inevitable," said Grimaldi, promising all of Brazil on behalf of the Spanish king if France would provide troops and ships to help conquer Portugal. While this may have been saber-rattling on Grimaldi's part, Vergennes could take no chances that a war would break out on the European continent. After consulting with the king's council, he replied the following month that although Spain had legitimate grievances, a preemptive war with Portugal would be "unjust" and could cause anxiety throughout Europe; in any event France had no designs on Brazil. Even with all the assurances and diplomatic courtesy the French minister could muster, this rejection of Spain's overture, coming on the heels of France's refusal of assistance during the Falklands/Malvinas crisis, sowed mistrust between the two crowns and threatened to sever the carefully forged bonds between the two nations. Vergennes now needed a way to avoid all-out war and yet still maintain the crucial alliance with Spain.

It was the newly erupted War of American Independence that provided Vergennes with a way to prevent a remote border skirmish in South America from becoming a full-scale war in Europe, and at the same time rekindle the Bourbon coalition against Britain. His missives to Grimaldi in the autumn of 1775 trying to dissuade Spain from invading Portugal had thus far met with little apparent success. In late February 1776, across his richly inlaid Brazilian hardwood desk came almost simultaneously two reports that gave him the clues to ending the impasse. Beaumarchais's memorandum "Peace or War" argued that France "must aid the Americans" by supplying them with arms and munitions, in order to continue the rebellion that had so far kept Britain off balance. Bonvouloir's report agreed that the Americans needed war supplies, and assured Vergennes that those arms would find good use, for the colonials would soon declare for independence as they were "fighting to become free and that they will succeed no matter what the price." For Vergennes, it must have been as if the pieces of a jigsaw puzzle (which had just come into popular use) suddenly fit together: Spain would be less likely to launch a preemptive attack on Portugal if Pombal could not rely on British support to expand the war in South America; Britain would not provide troops and ships for Portugal if it was tied up fighting a rebellion in North America; therefore France and Spain must together supply arms to the Americans in order to prolong the conflict, in order to keep British forces occupied in North America and therefore prevent a war in Europe. The American rebellion, which had scarcely drawn Vergennes's attention just two years earlier, suddenly became the focus of his diplomatic strategy.

On March 1, 1776, Vergennes sent Grimaldi a letter outlining his proposal to provide materiel aid to the Americans, and asked for his views on the matter. Grimaldi replied almost immediately. For utmost secrecy, he avoided alerting Aranda by posting his letter in the regular mail and not via diplomatic courier. He agreed with Vergennes's idea and expressed the "hope that the revolt continues . . . and that the English [and Americans] exhaust each other." The Spanish king certainly thought the action justified, as Britain had often provided arms to the foes of Spain (most recently to the Sultanate of Morocco, which in 1774 had unsuccessfully tried to capture the Spanish outpost of Melilla), and agreed to "contribute to all reasonable costs" of their joint venture. Although Grimaldi did not see the proposal as an alternative to war with Portugal, as Vergennes obviously did, it brought into alignment the priorities of Spain and France, paving the way for joint action against Britain.

With his proposal to avoid a major European war now set in motion, Vergennes and his *premier commis* Rayneval quickly drafted the policy that would make the plan official. In two memoranda distributed to the king's council in March and April 1776—titled simply "Considerations" by Vergennes and "Reflections" by Rayneval—they carefully weighed the "political calculations" of France and Spain, taking cues from both Beaumarchais and Bonvouloir. "England is the natural enemy of France," said Rayneval, and is bent on destroying France; Britain's power must therefore be weakened, and the best way to do this would be to support the American insurgency. Vergennes addressed the concern over the Spanish-Portuguese crisis, contending that a year of the British forces "finding employment against the Colonies" would prevent them from "making a strong showing" elsewhere. Both Vergennes and Rayneval argued that the best way to weaken Britain and at the same time prevent it from helping Portugal "would be . . . to give to the insurgents secret assistance in munitions and in money." This in turn would delay British actions while France and Spain strengthened their navies and the defense of their own colonies in the Western Hemisphere. Following in Choiseul's footsteps, Vergennes closed his case for supporting American independence and rebuilding the French navy by stating that it was the only way "to ensure a long-term peace on the [European] Continent."

The actions proposed in "Considerations" and "Reflections" were clearly preparations for a war with Britain, which Spain had been spoiling for. Vergennes, however, wanted to ensure that France waged it on its own terms; the fight would be across the English Channel and overseas, in order to prevent a war from breaking out between Spain and Portugal on the European continent. He admitted that simultaneously aiding the Americans and overhauling the navy would require a "considerable" amount of money, but saw no alternative. The rest of the king's council agreed that both actions were needed, with one exception: the tightfisted finance minister Anne-Robert-Jacques Turgot, who in the aftermath of one of the coldest winters in living memory, which had decimated crops and livestock, had argued that the need for fiscal responsibility outweighed the risk of a foreign adventure. Although he would be proved correct in the long term, his fiscal mishandling of several recent famines (notably the 1775 Flour War) meant that his coin had lost its value at Versailles. In any event, the decision to begin preparations for war was made, and Turgot was the only man standing in the way.

Louis XVI quickly made several critical pronouncements that moved France onto a war footing. His first action, taken in late April 1776, was to order Sartine to prepare the navy for potential combat by sending frigates to the Caribbean and readying ships of the line in the ports of Brest and Toulon. He also authorized him to begin refitting more vessels to be ready for the 1778 campaign season, a lengthy and expensive process that demanded a massive increase in funding. The money began flowing almost immediately. A year earlier, the navy budget was at a peacetime level of 20 million livres (about $10 billion today, which by coincidence is roughly in line with that of the modern French navy). By mid-1776 that number had gone up by one-third; and by the following year, it had doubled to 41 million livres. The king also replaced Turgot with the more accommodating Jacques Necker, who immediately exchanged France's old debt for new loans at more favorable rates, putting more money into the nation's war chest.

In May 1776, the French court had made the momentous decision to join with Spain in providing 2 million livres' worth of arms and munitions to the American insurgents via Beaumarchais's company Roderigue Hortalez. The chief ministers had looked upon this covert aid as the means to stop Britain from helping Portugal to expand its war against Spain. In actual fact, it was the first official step to creating what would soon become an overt alliance with America. Vergennes's "Considerations" had strongly cautioned that while it was "necessary to assist the insurgents indirectly by supplies of munitions or of money," France should not "make any treaty with them until their independence is established and well known." He knew from Bonvouloir's report that the Americans were ready to declare independence, but when Silas Deane met with Vergennes on July 10, both men had to tiptoe around the issue of official French assistance because neither knew that notice of the Declaration of Independence was already on its way to France. The ship that had set sail on July 8 with the broadsheet copy of the Declaration on board apparently never made it to Europe. Vergennes instead learned of the Declaration on August 17 through a letter from the chargé d'affaires in London, Charles-Jean Garnier, who conveyed a British newspaper account of it, and in his covering letter noted that if the Americans win the war, "Britain will be reduced to the point of no longer being a worry for France."

The news of the Declaration of Independence triggered a stunning reaction in Vergennes, though not the one that the Second Continental Congress had been looking for. Rather than seeking a treaty with the Americans, Vergennes moved beyond the current policy of merely girding for war and proposed a preemptive assault on Britain itself. His new memorandum, dated August 31 and titled "Considerations on the position France should take with regard to England," began with a reminder that Britain was "France's hereditary enemy" and accused it of provoking Portugal's bellicosity. Britain was distracted and enfeebled by its American war, where the insurgents were successfully defending themselves through force of arms. Now was the time to strike, Vergennes argued, in order to erase the shame of the "odious" surprise attacks of 1755. He expanded on this in a later memorandum, describing an amphibious invasion upon the southern coast of Britain based upon the plan Choiseul and Grimaldi had drafted back in 1767, and proposing that the two nations step up their naval construction to achieve the required fleet superiority. He also suggested that the two Bourbon powers officially recognize America to strengthen their military alliance. While the French council accepted these proposals without much debate, Vergennes had to wait to see if the Spanish court would agree to his plan in lieu of attacking Portugal.

As Vergennes waited for the Spanish reply, the news arrived that Howe had defeated Washington at the Battle of Long Island, and that British forces now held New York. Deane, at that moment negotiating with Beaumarchais over the first shipments of arms, could offer no good news, not even an official copy of the Declaration of Independence. Even after the official copy finally arrived in Paris in November, and Franklin just a few weeks after, there was no request from the American commissioners to France for an alliance, only a continual press for the commercial treaty that Franklin proposed upon his arrival, but that offered France little except premature hostilities with Britain. With the American war going badly and no immediate prospect of further diplomatic action, Vergennes settled into a policy he termed *attente expectative* (watchful waiting). Although professing that France had a "connectedness" to America through the war that had erupted, for the moment he could only shore up Beaumarchais's operations through continued infusions of cash and allow French officers to sail across the Atlantic to fight alongside the Americans, all while denying any knowledge of these activities to the British ambassador, Stormont. He also began laying the diplomatic groundwork to ensure that Russia, the Dutch Republic, and other northern nations would not support Britain in the event of war.

The Spanish court debated Vergennes's war plans before definitively rejecting them. In the time between the first and second "Considerations," news that war had indeed broken out in South America reached European shores. Back in February 1776 under orders from Pombal, Portuguese forces had launched a surprise attack and captured the Spanish outpost of Rio Grande de São Pedro in Brazil. Once the news reached Spain several months later, Carlos III sent a fleet of nineteen warships and nine thousand soldiers to South America in order to reconquer the territory, and gave the expedition's leader, Pedro Antonio de Cevallos, a free hand by appointing him as head of the newly created Viceroyalty of Rio de la Plata, which replaced the *audiencia* of Buenos Aires (roughly encompassing today's Argentina). The king also dispatched another squadron of four ships of the line under Miguel José Gastón to sail up the Tagus River, without forewarning, and anchor directly in front of Lisbon.

This was a pointed message to Pombal that Spain was ready to use its military might directly against its neighbor. When Vergennes's invasion plan against Britain reached Spain in the late autumn of 1776, Cevallos's fleet was on the point of departure and Grimaldi was more determined than ever to attack Portugal. He saw no benefit either to invading Britain or to allying with the Americans, who were now on the run after losing New York City. His greatest fear was that Britain would come to terms with its former colonists, and the two would then together launch an assault on Spanish and French territories.

Even as Grimaldi's reply was on its way to France early in February 1777, Grimaldi himself was on his way to Burgos to meet Arthur Lee and, in his last official act, to hammer out a deal to supply arms to America. His replacement, Floridablanca, decided that an invasion of Portugal, or any war with Britain, was premature until both France and Spain had sufficiently rebuilt their navies, which would not happen until the following year. A turn of events soon vindicated the new Spanish minister's caution. In February 1777, Portugal's King José I died, and his daughter Queen Maria I, the niece of Carlos III, immediately dismissed the bellicose Pombal. Coupled with the news that the Spanish fleet had arrived in Buenos Aires, had driven out the Portuguese forces, and had retaken the Spanish outposts in Brazil, the tensions between Spain and Portugal receded. For the time being, Spain was content simply to send aid to the Americans via Diego de Gardoqui and Bernardo de Gálvez and, like France, watch attentively for any changes that could overturn the delicate state of affairs.

FRANCE AND AMERICA SIGN TREATIES OF ALLIANCE, TO SPAIN'S CONSTERNATION

In March 1777, just as Vergennes saw the threat of a Spanish-Portuguese war recede, he was once again petitioned by the American commissioners to take up their proposal for a commercial treaty, this time with the offer of military assistance from the Americans in taking the British West Indies, but which fell short of an actual alliance. Even a commercial treaty with the Americans, Vergennes knew, could ignite a war with Britain before the combined Bourbon fleet was ready for battle in 1778, so he once again put off the decision.

Vergennes's policy of *attente expectative* left the American commissioners perplexed and uncertain of what they should be doing. Franklin, for his part, made a great show of indolence, attending meetings of the Academy of Sciences and its literary equivalent the Académie française, sitting for sculptures and portraits, and regularly visiting his favorite Parisian bathhouse to relieve his psoriasis. Behind the closed doors of his apartments in Passy, however, he was inventing American diplomacy on the fly: arranging for private loans and subsidies from Versailles to keep the arms flowing; petitioning for prisoner exchanges with Britain; and churning out stories for popular consumption that trumped up American successes and minimized its failures. Among his most pressing concerns were the American vessels that regularly sailed from French ports—often despite warnings from Versailles—to prey on British shipping. Lambert Wickes, the naval officer who had brought Franklin to France, managed to elude both British and French authorities as he raided shipping around Britain and Ireland. Similar exploits by another naval officer, Gustavus Conyngham, caught the attention of Stormont, and in order to avoid a diplomatic row with Britain, the French authorities ordered Conyngham thrown into prison. Franklin, with a few well-placed letters, managed to get him freed and also to obtain another ship for him.

By contrast to Franklin, the other commissioners never appreciated that inaction was not the same thing as doing nothing. Silas Deane conspicuously busied himself interviewing the legions of French and European officers clamoring to fight in the American conflict, looking over Beaumarchais's shoulder to criticize the accounts, and assisting his newly arrived brother Simeon Deane in setting up his tobacco import business. Meanwhile, his American agents—William Carmichael, Deane's secretary, in Le Havre, and Jonathan Williams, Franklin's grandnephew, in Nantes—reviewed cargo manifests and inspected the outgoing arms for any obvious defects. Arthur Lee's mission to Spain garnered some success in obtaining aid in the form of war materiel, but he had no luck in obtaining official recognition for the new nation. His subsequent mission to Berlin to obtain similar recognition from Prussia was met with equal disappointment. The same thing happened to his brother William Lee at Maria Theresa's court in Vienna. Another would-be commissioner, Ralph Izard, was supposed to represent the United States to the Grand Duchy of Tuscany, but in fact never left France.

Vergennes, though having professed to the commissioners simply to be waiting for the right moment "to reciprocally bind ourselves by a treaty of commerce," was in fact actively pursuing an agreement with Spain to do just that. Since the beginning of 1777, he had been receiving information from his Spanish ambassador on the state of their fleet and integrating that with information from Sartine on the French navy. In March, his *premier commis* Rayneval drew up plans for commencing hostilities in a year's time (March 1778) with an attack on the British fleet in New York harbor. Meanwhile, with little good news coming from America, another concern loomed large in Vergennes's mind. Although the danger of a war on the European continent had now passed, there was a very real possibility that the United States might either lose the war or sue for peace with Britain. The prospect of American colonies returning to British domination presented too great a danger for the adjacent French and Spanish possessions. In the space of just a few months, Vergennes changed his view, from rejecting a treaty with the Americans to believing that the two Bourbon crowns must now make an alliance with the new nation to forestall a potentially dangerous outcome.

Vergennes made this point to Floridablanca in a lengthy memorandum sent on July 23, just as Burgoyne's troops were advancing toward Saratoga and a fleet under British vice-admiral Richard Howe (William Howe's brother) had set sail to capture Philadelphia. "The time has come to decide," argued Vergennes. "We must either abandon America to its own devices or courageously and effectively come to its side." After January or February 1778 it would be too late. Floridablanca was not convinced. In an equally lengthy response, he agreed to continue providing secret aid, but rejected an alliance with the Americans, which "did not seem decent, fair, or useful . . . the envoys of the colonies have not yet made any offers that merit consideration." In any event, the war with Portugal had exhausted Spain's resources, and it first had to "tie up loose ends" before considering another such venture. Most importantly, Spain had two convoys ready to put to sea, one carrying silver from Veracruz in Mexico, and the other carrying its troops home from Buenos Aires. Any premature action could cause Britain to declare war and prey upon these fleets, causing irreparable damage to Spain's economy and military. With Spain's refusal in hand, Vergennes now was forced to develop his own policies toward America.

The arrival of the news of Saratoga on December 4 came at an opportune moment for Vergennes, for by then he was determined to forge an alliance with the United States, with or without Spain. Although Spanish participation was preferred, he knew that Sartine's naval buildup, coupled with the element of surprise, would give him just enough ships to unilaterally carry out the war that surely would follow France's alliance with America. The American victory at Saratoga, combined with somewhat optimistic reports that Washington had been only narrowly defeated at the Battle of Germantown, provided the outwardly reluctant Vergennes the pretext for the decision he had already made. So prepared was he for this alliance that just twenty-four hours after Jonathan Loring Austin had dashed into the courtyard at Valentinois, Vergennes had Gérard dash off a letter to the American commissioners requesting a meeting for the following day. Arriving the morning of December 6, Gérard congratulated the three men on behalf of Maurepas and Vergennes. Now that there was "no doubt of the ability and resolution of the states to maintain their independency," he said, they should "reassume their former proposition of an alliance," the sooner the better.

The commissioners took Vergennes at his word, and two days later William Temple Franklin delivered a treaty proposal to Versailles. The normally opaque Vergennes, who habitually kept foreign dignitaries at arm's length, now revealed some of his true sentiments; he received young Franklin with "uncommon politeness," and in his correspondence with the Americans' banker, Ferdinand Grand, began referring to the commissioners as "*nos amis*" (our friends) instead of "*vos amis*" (your friends) as in the past. Certainly all of Paris now regarded the Americans as *nos amis;* when Franklin attended one of the weekly Academy of Sciences lectures, which were held at the Louvre, he was mobbed with well-wishers, including Voltaire, whom he embraced. On December 12, Vergennes formally opened treaty talks. He was most struck, he admitted, by the ability of the Americans to raise in just one year an army that could stand against General Howe, which "promised everything." A treaty was forthcoming, he assured them, but first he had to consult with the Spanish court.

Vergennes knew that the negotiations with Spain would likely prove fruitless. Although the Spanish ambassador Aranda was every bit as enthusiastic as the French for an American alliance, Floridablanca had already demonstrated that he did not believe it to be in Spain's best interest, regardless of the terms of the Bourbon Family Compact. Nevertheless, in a series of dispatches to Montmorin, his ambassador in Madrid,

Vergennes tried one last time to offer up arguments in favor of Spain's acceptance: War was coming, and it would be better fought with the Americans on their side; moreover, the Americans could help Spain regain Florida. Time was of the essence: Parliament would reconvene on January 20 and possibly sue for reconciliation with the insurgents; and if America fell back into British hands, they would be an overwhelming menace for the Bourbon powers. The prospect of an alliance was therefore "the most interesting conjunction that the heavens can offer," he said, arguing that "nothing can justify . . . letting slip through our fingers the only opportunity in many centuries to put England in its place."

Even while pretending to ask for Spain's agreement, Vergennes moved quickly to cement an alliance. Under orders from Louis XVI, Gérard met with the American commissioners at Passy on December 17 to inform them that "it was determined to acknowledge [the Americans'] Independence and make a treaty . . . of amity and commerce." Franklin and his colleagues agreed that such a treaty would contain terms for peace that included full independence, so as to preclude any return to the British Empire. Three days later, the frigate *Belle Poule* was ordered to carry the news of the pending treaty to the United States.

Floridablanca's reply, dated December 23, arrived just eight days later on New Year's Eve. As Vergennes anticipated, he once again rejected the idea of a treaty. For France, the timetable was set by the British Parliament; for the Spanish minister, the safe arrival of its convoys from Veracruz and Buenos Aires, not due until mid-1778 at the earliest, "have been, and continue to be, the two concerns that we absolutely cannot set aside." Floridablanca wondered openly why France, which was so insistent on not going to war just eight months earlier, was now barreling ahead with plans to do just that. If it did decide to go to war, France could not count on having Spain at its side; Floridablanca for now would instead take time to gather information and make a decision when it suited him.

Vergennes absorbed this news for about a week, until a new message from Montmorin confirmed that Floridablanca would not budge from his rejection of an alliance with the Americans. The foreign minister conferred with Maurepas and the king, and then ordered Gérard to hammer out the final terms of the treaty with the American commissioners. On January 8, they opened negotiations in Deane's apartment at the Hôtel de Coislin. The Americans promised to ignore any proposal from Britain that "did not have at its basis entire liberty and independence." Gérard, in turn, offered not only the commercial treaty the Americans sought, but also a military treaty of alliance, promising that France would stand with the Americans in the event of war, which was now almost certain.

Deane's next-door neighbor Aranda, who undoubtedly could see their comings and goings, did not have to guess at the proceedings; the same day that negotiations began, Vergennes sent dispatches via Aranda to Floridablanca explaining that France had decided to go ahead with the American alliance. That same day, Louis XVI took the unusual step of writing directly to "my brother [monarch] and uncle" Carlos III to explain that he had taken the decision to act alone because "the destruction of Burgoyne's army . . . has totally changed the face of things; America is triumphant and England beaten." Two weeks later, the dispatches arrived at El Pardo, where the king and his ministers were at their annual hunting retreat. When Montmorin handed Vergennes's letter to Floridablanca, the chief minister flew into a rage. "His whole body trembled," the French ambassador reported, before he regained his composure and asked for a copy of the letter to distribute to his council. The following day he consulted with his other ministers on what to do next. His minister of the Indies, José de Gálvez, who saw Vergennes as "unpredictable," needed time to reinforce Havana, Puerto Rico, and New Spain against a possible British attack. The minister of the navy, González de Castejón, reiterated the absolute necessity to wait until the Veracruz and Buenos Aires convoys returned. Only the minister of war, Ricla, saw any advantage to joining the alliance.

Floridablanca's irate response to Vergennes made it clear that the ties between the two nations had once again been severely strained. Not for the Spanish minister was the nebulous goal of restoring the balance of power in Europe; Spain was instead only concerned with the more concrete aim of "recovering the shameful usurpations of Gibraltar and Minorca," and evicting British forces from the Gulf of Mexico. While Spain's reply was being carried across the Pyrenees, in Versailles the terms of the two treaties were being scrutinized. On February 4, Vergennes read the rejection along with Montmorin's assurance that Spain would eventually follow France into the war. Certain now that France would enter the upcoming war alone, Vergennes had Gérard put the final touches into place. The original outlines of the treaties were preserved, but language was added to clarify fishing rights and commercial trade, and a separate, secret act was drafted inviting Spain to "accede to the said treaties." On February 5, the final embossed documents—a treaty of amity and commerce, a treaty of alliance, and a secret act—were ready for signature.

The signing was delayed by one day due to Gérard's brief bout with a cold. The evening of Friday, February 6, 1778, Franklin left his cottage in Passy wearing the same Manchester velvet suit he had worn in the Cockpit at his humiliation before the Privy Council four years earlier, to "give it a little revenge." His coach stopped before the Hôtel de Coislin, where he ascended the wide stone steps of the grand stairway to find Deane in his second-floor apartment. Also waiting in the salon were Gérard and Arthur Lee, and as a fire blazed in the marble fireplace, the four men compared the English text on the left side of each page with the French text on the right side. Satisfied, Gérard first signed and sealed the documents, followed by Franklin, Deane, and Lee, going from left to right. By nine o'clock the ceremony was complete, after which Gérard departed for Versailles, while Franklin tucked the documents into his well-worn velvet coat and brought them back to Passy to be copied.

A few weeks later, Gérard invited the American commissioners to be presented before the king, in a short ceremony that nevertheless had enormous significance—when the Swiss Guards opened the doors at noon of March 20, they announced them as "the ambassadors of the Thirteen United Provinces," the first official reference by a foreign power to America as a sovereign nation. Louis XVI assured them of his friendship with their government, while Vergennes praised their "wisest, most reserved conduct." Franklin and his delegation were justifiably proud of what they had achieved to date—first, an agreement to provide their new nation with arms and munitions, and second, a treaty allying their nation with France—but in actual fact they had had little influence over the course of those events. Vergennes's initial decision to secretly arm the American insurgents was not due to Deane's entreaties or Beaumarchais's silver tongue, but instead was to prevent Portugal from expanding its war with Spain onto the European continent. The French-American alliance was agreed to not so much because Saratoga was a great American victory, but rather because Vergennes had already decided that their more numerous defeats, such as those at Long Island and Brandywine, demonstrated that despite their growing abilities, the insurgents were still likely to lose the war without direct intervention, and a reunited Britain was simply too dangerous to contemplate.

Vergennes knew that he had very little time to prepare the nation for war before Stormont's spies got wind of the treaties, not realizing that Edward Bancroft had already given it to them the very night of its signature. While the Paris aristocracy may have adulated Franklin and his countrymen after the news of Saratoga, they nevertheless needed reassurance that official French support for this republican insurgency would not directly threaten their carefully constructed social order. Vergennes quickly deployed the French and European press, notably the *Affaires d'Angleterre et d'Amérique* and the *Courier de l'Europe,* to generate a drumbeat of popular imagery among the aristocracy, vilifying the British and exalting the Americans. The Americans themselves would also have to be notified soon, not only to bolster their fighting spirit, but also to prevent them from acceding to any British petitions. Silas Deane's brother Simeon, having had little success in his Paris tobacco ventures—among other handicaps, he spoke no French—had been tasked in December to carry news of the treaty (not the treaty itself) back to America, but the frigate *Belle Poule* turned back after just six weeks at sea. On March 8, Simeon Deane departed Brest aboard another frigate, *Sensible,* this time with a signed copy of the treaty in hand and news of another 6 million livres in loans, to bring back to the United States. The following day, Louis XVI wrote to Carlos III to explain, again, the reasons for so hastily agreeing to a commercial treaty with America, though discreetly leaving out any mention of the military alliance.

Finally, Vergennes needed a clean break with Britain to occur at just the right time to bolster the anti-British message. On March 13 the French ambassador in London, the Marquis de Noailles, after informing his Spanish counterpart Francisco Escarano of the alliance, presented the treaty of amity and commerce (though not the military treaty) to Secretary of State Weymouth. Weymouth's stunned reaction, despite the fact that he had already been tipped off by Bancroft, was only slightly less furious than that of Floridablanca. Weymouth ordered Stormont immediately to leave Paris, and Gérard issued his passports so promptly that one suspects they had been made out in advance. A few days later, Noailles reciprocated and departed London. With both ambassadors now recalled home, hostilities might break out between France and Britain at any time. At just this moment, another group of ambassadors from France, Spain, and the United States was being readied to take up what would soon become wartime duties for the three nations.

AMERICA RATIFIES THE TREATIES OF ALLIANCE AND RECEIVES THE FRENCH AMBASSADOR

Simeon Deane landed in Falmouth, Maine, carrying the French-American treaties on April 16, 1778, after an uneventful six-week voyage from Brest. Deane was not the only courier to carry signed copies of the crucial treaties—two other frigates carrying copies were also en route—but he was the first to arrive, and lost little time delivering them to the Continental Congress now in York, Pennsylvania. Traveling on horseback, he stopped briefly at major cities along the route—Portsmouth, Boston, Providence—and at the Continental Army encampment at Fishkill, New York, to spread the news. On Saturday, May 2, Deane arrived in York, treaties in hand. Congress had by then adjourned for the weekend, so after a hasty reading Saturday night, the ratification was put off until Monday.

There was little real deliberation over the merits of the alliance; despite the victory at Saratoga, the previous winter had been very hard, with George Washington's soldiers suffering the most at their encampment at Valley Forge. Having France now openly on America's side breathed new hope into the cause of independence; instead of depending upon a British misstep or leniency to gain victory, America was now assured of a military campaign on more equal terms. When a messenger brought word of the treaties to Washington at his headquarters, he could barely contain his happiness even though the Congress had not yet ratified them, and impromptu celebrations were held throughout the camp. "I believe no event was ever received with a more heartfelt joy," he reported to Henry Laurens. Several days later, when the formal announcement was made, Washington ordered musket and artillery salutes, followed by celebratory toasts of "Long Live the King of France." One soldier, Henry Brockholst Livingston, gave voice to the widespread feeling of relief when he wrote his cousin that "America is at last saved by almost a miracle."

The civilian reaction to the alliance was no less effusive than the military one. As Simeon Deane made his way across New England, cities and towns fired off gun salutes, while newspapers trumpeted the alliance as if it were a victory in battle. Thomas McKean, a Delaware delegate to the Congress, declared Louis XVI to be "the most wise, most just and most magnanimous prince, not only in the world [but also] in history."

Even in the South, considered more Loyalist than the North, newspapers reported "universal joy," no doubt lubricated by "plenty of liquor" that accompanied the announcement. One Charleston merchant called the alliance "a special act of a kind providence in our favor," while another opined that the news "gave great satisfaction to all except Tories."

That last statement was not quite true. John Adams was by no stretch of the imagination a Tory, but he certainly would have derived no "satisfaction" from the military alliance America had just concluded. Indeed, Adams had drafted the original Plan of Treaties to avoid precisely these sorts of "articles of entangling alliance" with France, a nation he deeply mistrusted. He was not present in York to register his astonishment, for he had departed for Paris back in February after having been appointed to replace Silas Deane in the American commission. Deane's recall had been engineered by Virginia delegate Richard Henry Lee, the brother of Arthur Lee, and soon became the focus of sectarian clashes within the Congress.

Since its inception, the Second Continental Congress had been divided into several factions, generally termed "radical," "moderate," and "conservative," which were split along geographical as well as ideological lines. For some time the most influential had been the radical faction, centering on Richard Henry Lee of Virginia and Samuel Adams of Massachusetts, which had led the charge for the Declaration of Independence and was generally wary of (though not opposed to) foreign alliances. Southern representatives dominated the pro-French conservative bloc, while the smaller moderate bloc from the mid-Atlantic states often held the balance of power, as they might ally with one faction or the other depending upon the matter at hand.

The initial selection of Deane, Arthur Lee, and Franklin as the commissioners in Paris was made in part to satisfy these different factions, but they often found themselves as much at odds with each other as did their congressional brethren back in Philadelphia. Arthur Lee resented Deane in particular, after having been snubbed in their dealings with Beaumarchais, and wrote to his brother and to Samuel Adams that he believed Deane was skimming off money from the munitions trade. In November 1777, Richard Henry Lee moved to have Deane recalled on unspecified charges of corruption and profiteering. The motion was easily passed by the Congress, which also resented Deane for having foisted upon them dozens of French and European officers who arrived demanding a commission with pay, a field command, and the purple or pink sash worn by general officers of the Continental Army, at a time when the congressional larders were empty and Washington already had his hands full with a fractious officer corps. The recall vote was carried and a few days later Samuel Adams's cousin John Adams was nominated to take his place.

On March 31, 1778, Deane slipped out of Paris under an assumed name. This was not from shame but for secrecy, though Deane did not know that Edward Bancroft had already alerted his handlers in London to his departure. Far from being ashamed at the congressional recall, Deane held his head high; he carried with him the memories of the crucial shipments of Beaumarchais's arms, the treaty signing, and of having been among the first American ambassadors to be presented to Louis XVI. He also carried a physical reminder, a present from the king in the form of a diamond-studded gold snuffbox. Vergennes further gilded these tributes by seeing to it that Deane sailed home aboard the massive eighty-gun warship *Languedoc,* the flagship of the first French squadron to directly support the Americans in their War of Independence.

The seventeen ships under Vice Admiral Charles-Henri, Comte d'Estaing, had been organized months earlier to threaten Richard Howe's fleet in North America, and at the same time to draw off British warships from the Gulf of Mexico to help protect the Spanish treasure fleet now sailing from Veracruz. They were scheduled to depart Toulon in mid-April, which left Deane little time for tying up loose ends. He arrived in the port to meet his fellow passenger Conrad Alexandre Gérard, who had also left Paris in haste and under a false name. With the signing of the treaties of alliance, Vergennes needed to establish a French embassy in the United States, and he selected Gérard to be its first ambassador (his formal title would be minister plenipotentiary). His instructions, written by his brother Rayneval and signed by Vergennes, afforded Gérard great leeway in his diplomacy. While the only nonnegotiable stipulation was that "neither party shall make a peace or truce without the consent of the other," Gérard had full authority, on the king's behalf, to negotiate with the Spanish envoys in the United States, pledge military cooperation to Congress, and broker further subsidies.

D'Estaing's fleet left Toulon on April 13, making a slow, circuitous voyage through the Mediterranean and the Strait of Gibraltar in order to avoid any contact with British ships, taking a total of three months to finally reach American shores. During that time, Philadelphia was rocked by the arrival of the Carlisle Commission and the departure of the occupying British forces. With the news of Saratoga and the intelligence about the French-American treaty, British prime minister North ordered a delegation led by Frederick Howard, Earl of Carlisle, to travel to Philadelphia to propose peace terms to the Continental Congress that rescinded taxation and offered wide autonomy within the empire but stopped short of granting independence. Arriving on June 8, they found that Henry Clinton, who had replaced William Howe as Britain's commander in chief, was preparing to evacuate the city and move his troops back to New York City, in anticipation of d'Estaing's arrival. Despite this setback, Carlisle and his delegation promptly sent their peace proposals to York, where they were just as promptly rejected—only an "explicit acknowledgement of the independence of these States," explained the congressional president, Henry Laurens, would be accepted. By June 18, Clinton was on the move with his soldiers to New York City, having ordered the remaining warships to leave quickly to avoid being bottled up by d'Estaing. On July 2, Laurens once again took the gavel at the Pennsylvania State House in Philadelphia, where the Congress sat.

The following week, d'Estaing's fleet arrived off the mouth of the Delaware River, too late to have intercepted the British fleet. He dispatched the frigate *Chimère,* with Deane and Gérard aboard, to travel upriver while the rest of his fleet sailed north to face Richard Howe in New York. Even before *Chimère* anchored, well-wishers alerted to the arrival of Gérard, and recognizing the French frigate by its bright paintwork and white Bourbon ensign, massed along the shore of the Delaware River to greet the new envoy. "You have come to our rescue," they called, "we will come, when you need us, to yours." On July 12 they debarked at Chester, where they were received by John Hancock and his congressional delegation. Gérard, riding to Philadelphia in Hancock's coach-and-four under cavalry escort, was greeted with an artillery salute and columns of soldiers. Benedict Arnold, the newly appointed military commander of the city, lodged Gérard in his mansion on High Street (now Market Street), quite fittingly in the bedroom that had until recently held William Howe. Silas Deane, in the commotion, was all but forgotten.

In the following weeks Gérard met with various congressional delegations, as well as the Board of War and the Marine Committee. In his clumsy English tinged with the long vowels and guttural consonants that betrayed his Alsatian roots, he carefully reiterated that the conditions of the alliance meant that the United States could not negotiate a separate peace with Britain. His negotiations with the Congress became complicated by the fact that Samuel Adams had met with one of the agents of the Carlisle Commission (now in New York and still actively pursuing a truce), though the discussions led nowhere. Gérard soon learned that Adams was also opposed to a congressional resolution approving the terms of the alliance. It was not until January 14, 1779, that ratification came, when Congress publicly resolved that it "will not conclude peace or truce without the formal consent of their ally."

Gérard's experience with Samuel Adams highlighted for him the fact that the United States, despite the effusive celebrations at the news of the treaties, was not unanimous in its support for the French alliance. In his many letters to Vergennes, which were sent in triplicate or quadruplicate via different ships in case they were waylaid or lost in transit across the ocean, he detailed the complex, evolving politics of the new nation. Gérard believed that the competing interests of the thirteen states, absent a strong, centralizing government to marshal their troops and finances, rendered the United States too fractured and feeble to defeat Britain without France's help.

At the same time as Gérard was complaining about an enfeebled American government, he also weakened his own position by becoming enmeshed in the factional fighting over the Silas Deane affair. From the summer of 1778 through the spring of 1779, the Congress held multiple hearings on Deane's alleged mishandling of funds, on whether Arthur Lee should be recalled, and even on replacing Benjamin Franklin, though ultimately neither Franklin nor Lee was recalled, and no official charges of profiteering were ever made against Deane. Despite Vergennes's warnings not to become involved in American domestic politics, Gérard vocally supported Deane and advocated for the removal of Arthur Lee. This of course infuriated the Lee-Adams faction, which began to tie any affiliation with Gérard with support for the French alliance, and openly expressed distrust of French motives. "Why should we bind our interests so closely with those of France?" Samuel Adams asked the Congress in March 1779. "Here," he said, tapping the floor with his foot, "is where our independence must be consolidated."

Gérard's domestic meddling had been largely responsible for the diplomatic rift with the Lee-Adams faction, which he termed "party of the opposition," and this caused him additional troubles during negotiations with the Congress in the spring and summer of 1779 over the war aims of the two nations, and the acceptable terms for peace with Great Britain. The Lee-Adams faction insisted that no peace should be concluded without guarantees of free navigation on the Mississippi, fishing rights on the Grand Banks off Newfoundland, and cession of Nova Scotia to the United States. Gérard argued that those terms should be desirables but not ultimatums, following Louis XVI's insistence that the fighting not be prolonged any longer than needed to ensure American independence. Gérard, a skilled politician as well as a diplomat, managed to secure a majority support for his terms with private entreaties to the conservative and moderate factions, and several audiences before the Congress. He also put public pressure on the representatives by paying the polemicist Thomas Paine to print articles that "inspired the people towards favorable views of France and the alliance." The Congress largely acceded to the French demands, and by August 1779 both sides of the alliance agreed to the final terms for peace with Britain, if and when the war was won.

That Gérard was successful in his negotiations was in no small part due to the fact that he had instant access to the Congress, which considered the French alliance so important that they installed him and his embassy just a block away, in a home on Chestnut Street that was visible through the front windows of the Pennsylvania State House. Through those front doors came not only American politicians but also dozens of French military officers looking for official help in their dealings with the American government. Gérard had been a stalwart supporter of Silas Deane, but he would do nothing to solicit rank for the legions of would-be generals whom Deane had dispatched. Although the vast majority of those officers, such as Johann de Kalb, the Marquis de Lafayette, and Louis Lebègue Duportail, were serving bravely and effectively in the Continental Army, both Congress and George Washington himself were becoming overwhelmed with a seemingly endless stream of supplicants. Washington, writing to Henry Laurens, spoke for both of them when he expressed gratitude that the French ambassador was preventing "many frivolous & unwarrantable applications" from reaching his desk.

Gérard's arrival in Philadelphia meant that French commercial agents now had a sympathetic ear for their complaints. Beaumarchais was still sending a stream of merchant ships to the United States, despite the fact that the American commissioners in Paris had just seized *Amphitrite*'s return cargo of rice and indigo, intended as repayment for the Saratoga arms, as their own (they eventually relinquished it). In September 1777, the Beaumarchais contract ship *Flamand*, commanded by a brash French naval officer named Pierre Landais whom Deane had earlier commissioned into the Continental Navy, departed Marseilles carrying artillery, munitions, volunteer officers including Friedrich Wilhelm von Steuben with his aide-de-camp, Pierre-Étienne du Ponceau, and also Beaumarchais's secretary, Jean-Baptiste-Lazare Théveneau de Francy, who would serve as the American agent for Roderigue Hortalez.

Flamand docked at Portsmouth in December, and by February 1778, Francy was in York to present his credentials to the Congress and to request payment for the seven shipments of arms that had arrived to date. It was a plea made from desperation, for Roderigue Hortalez was near bankruptcy. By the time Francy left Marseilles the previous September, the company had already burned through the original 2 million livres advanced from France and Spain, an additional million from private investors, and another million that Vergennes had granted, all just to pay for the initial five ships that carried the arms that helped the Americans win at Saratoga. Meanwhile, Beaumarchais had spent even more money to outfit and send two more ships across the Atlantic, but not a single return cargo of tobacco had yet been delivered. By Francy's reckoning, the Congress now owed Roderigue Hortalez 5 million livres, nearly $3 billion in today's terms.

Even if many in the Congress were grateful for Beaumarchais's arms and were sympathetic to Francy's claim, the Lee-Adams faction insisted that the munitions were a gift from Louis XVI. Part of this perception was due to Deane's statement to the Congress two years earlier that "everything [Beaumarchais] says, writes, or does, is in reality the action of the Ministry." The other part was Arthur Lee's assertion that "M. de Beaumarchais's demands of payment for the supplies . . . are unjust," because the arms, munitions, and equipment were "a subsidy from the Court [of France]." Richard Henry Lee, in his role as a member of the Committee of Foreign Affairs in charge of settling overseas accounts, insisted that Beaumarchais's claims would be "scrutinize[d] most carefully" before any payments were made, which in practice meant endless delay.

While Francy waited for the Congress to take action during the summer of 1778, he was at Williamsburg overseeing the unloading of another Beaumarchais vessel, *Fier Roderigue,* a converted fifty-gun warship carrying hundreds of tons of gunpowder, cloth, and uniforms for the state of Virginia. After a year of no return cargoes, Francy finally managed to obtain a small payment for the Roderigue Hortalez munitions in the form of 231 hogsheads of tobacco from the Congress and another 479 from Virginia. This was loaded aboard *Fier Roderigue,* which set sail in August for Rochefort. This return cargo, however, did not go nearly far enough to cover the balance owed. In October 1778, out of patience with congressional inaction, Francy approached Gérard to help resolve the issue. The ambassador proposed that the Americans should instead furnish d'Estaing's fleet in equal value to the goods they had received, so that France could repay Beaumarchais directly—an elegant solution that was never enacted, once again leaving the merchant-playwright virtually empty-handed.

Back in France, Chaumont had had better luck and foresight than Beaumarchais in his business ventures, and this continued in America as well. His chosen agent, John Holker, was the scion of the firm that oversaw Chaumont's textile exports to the United States, and was already well known to Vergennes. Holker had arrived in Philadelphia just days before Gérard, who lost no time in appointing him consul-general of France and gave him the job of resupplying d'Estaing's fleet. As Gérard's consul as well as Chaumont's agent, it was easy for Holker to steer government contracts to his own firm and to pocket a tidy commission. He and Gérard worked well together, supplying Washington's army with flour in the autumn of 1778, during a time of shortage. Holker's business acumen caught the attention of Robert Morris, who entered into partnership with him for both international and domestic trade. The profits from his various business ventures enabled Holker to buy Benedict Arnold's mansion shortly after Arnold left, which soon became a de rigueur stop for all French visitors to America.

Another frequent visitor to Gérard's embassy was Juan de Miralles y Trayllón, the Havana merchant representing the Compañía Gaditana de Negros, who had been secretly tasked by Minister of the Indies José de Gálvez to observe and report on the Congress and military activities. The aging Miralles and his secretary, Francisco de Rendón, had arrived in December 1777 in Charleston, South Carolina, to begin the overland journey to the capital. While they were there, a devastating fire had destroyed much of the city, so Miralles arranged a loan from Havana for 21,000 pesos ($40 million today) for repairs, the news of which put him in good stead with the southern congressional delegates. He reached Philadelphia just a few days before Gérard, claiming to be there simply to establish flour trade with Cuba. This was not just a cover story: He already knew Robert Morris through the latter's Havana connections, and the two quickly set up a profitable trading venture—beef, pork, flour, and fish for sugar, rum, and honey—between the two cities. Those same cargo ships also carried sealed reports from Miralles for the new captain-general of Cuba, Diego José Navarro, to relay to Gálvez, covering everything from news from the battlefronts to American and French motives in the war to the personal habits of the congressional leaders.

Spain had not recognized the United States, so Miralles carried no formal accreditation as a diplomat. Nevertheless, the Congress treated him with the same deference given to the French minister plenipotentiary. Gérard, for his part, struck up a cautious friendship with Miralles, suspecting but never certain that he had direct connections to the Spanish court. Vergennes had instructed Gérard to support Spain's diplomatic policies, so when Miralles found himself with actual diplomatic tasks, such as requesting American help in attacking British outposts in Florida, negotiating for the release of Spanish sailors captured by American privateers, or vying for an extension of Spanish fishing rights on the Grand Banks, they worked closely to represent Spain's position to the American government. The two men were even invited, on equal terms, by George Washington to visit the Morristown encampment and witness a formal review and mock battle. Meanwhile, they waited for news from Europe of the real battles with Britain that had already begun.

THE AMERICAN AMBASSADORS IN EUROPE AND THE SPANISH ENTRY INTO THE WAR

On March 31, 1778, the same day Silas Deane departed Paris, the Continental frigate *Boston* anchored in Bordeaux carrying John Adams, his replacement for the American commission. Soon after the Continental Congress had voted to recall Deane, the newly established Committee for Foreign Affairs, which had just taken over from the Committee of Secret Correspondence, emphatically endorsed Adams, and the Congress unanimously approved him. For the American legislators, the fiercely anti-Gallic John Adams was seen as the "one man of inflexible integrity" who could negotiate with the French.

The recall of ambassadors Stormont and Noailles a few weeks before Adams's arrival meant that tensions were high, but hostilities did not immediately commence. Indeed, Adams noted that the countryside was calm and "extremely beautiful" as he made his way from Bordeaux to Paris by post chaise, arriving the evening of April 9. His first few days in the "glittering" capital were filled with a whirlwind of dinner engagements, social calls, and visits to the theater, all orchestrated by Franklin, that could hardly have been expected in a nation girding for war. As Adams settled into the residence at Valentinois, he found that living in France confirmed his worst fears of the nation that at the same time left him breathless. He was impressed with utilitarian things, noting on his journey from the coast that "for thirty miles from Paris or more the road was paved." He loved the garden at Valentinois, where "nature and art have conspired to render everything here delightful." He was at first awed by the sheer opulence that had no equivalent in America—every morning seven thousand barbers rushed through the streets to fix their clients' hair, every afternoon ornate carriages carried handsomely dressed men to and fro, every evening women wore diamonds that amplified the steady glow of windowfront candles and street lanterns that burned all through the night, giving Paris its title "the City of Light." As time wore on, though, he came to distrust this lavishness as a mere assault on the senses that for him offered little for the intellect. The elaborate social rituals and subtle turns of phrase frustrated him; while his French improved to the point where he could comprehend the words being spoken, he often did not understand what was actually being said. Even the opera and concerts left him cold: "There was too much sound for me," he complained to his diary, perhaps his only sympathetic outlet.

Instead, Adams plunged into the busywork of the embassy, rising at five o'clock to fix the American commission's financial accounts that were a haphazard mess. Franklin rarely rose before ten, and had little time for diplomacy before taking afternoon dinner and a nap. In actual fact, there was scant diplomacy to be done. If the American commissioners had little influence over international affairs before the signing of the French-American treaties, they had almost none afterward. The next steps in the war were purely in the hands of Vergennes and Floridablanca, and

Adams and Franklin could only watch powerlessly as events unfolded before them.

For Vergennes, it was critical that Britain, not France, be seen as the instigator of hostilities, in order to call upon its allies for aid in a defensive war. His wishes were answered on June 17, 1778, when the frigate *Belle Poule* (which had earlier been turned back from carrying Simeon Deane and news of the alliance), while patrolling off Cornwall, encountered a squadron of British warships under the command of Admiral Augustus Keppel and refused an order to follow them. When HMS *Arethusa* fired a warning shot across its bow, *Belle Poule* returned fire with a broadside and managed to escape, though not without heavy casualties. The fact that the British had fired the first shot gave Vergennes the cover story he needed, and on July 10, Louis XVI authorized his fleet to carry out reprisals against British shipping, which was tantamount to an official declaration of war. Britain responded with a similar order on July 19. On July 27 off the island of Ouessant (Ushant) near Brittany, Keppel's fleet encountered that of Louis Guillouet, Comte d'Orvilliers, who had been ordered to "show the French flag in all its glory." The resulting Battle of Ouessant was bloody but inconclusive; neither side could claim a clear victory, although d'Orvilliers was hailed as a hero upon his return, while Keppel was court-martialed. For Vergennes, the indecisiveness of the battle gave pause to the notion that France could take on the British navy alone. It was becoming increasingly apparent that he would need to enlist Spain's help very soon.

France was now fully engaged in the War of American Independence, which had suddenly grown from a North American struggle to a transatlantic conflict. Vergennes and his council were forced to plan campaigns on a grand scale, weighing where and how to deploy their ships in Europe, the Caribbean, and North America in order to both protect French interests and bring the fight to the enemy. But while Franklin understood the importance of this shift in French strategy and the need to balance American interests with those of its protector, Adams had eyes only for his home country. When he insisted on trying to persuade Vergennes to detach some of his ships to "secure naval superiority" in American waters, the French minister ignored the request; for, unknown to the Americans, Vergennes had bigger plans afoot to strike at the very heart of the enemy that would require half of the ships of the line in France's fleet.

With the role of the American commissioners now diminished amid the swirl of international affairs, Adams saw that he was superfluous, and wrote to his cousin Samuel Adams that Franklin should be named as the single plenipotentiary minister. Given that Conrad Alexandre Gérard had just been appointed to that same position in Philadelphia, this would provide a certain diplomatic symmetry. Congress agreed, and in September 1778 they named Franklin as sole ambassador, though the letter would not be read in Paris until the following February. Adams had been at his post just over ten months with almost nothing to show for it, and was anxious to return to his wife, Abigail. In mid-June, after several delays, Adams gratefully left the docks at Lorient and boarded the frigate *Sensible,* the same one that had transported Simeon Deane and the treaties to America a year earlier, for the long voyage home.

Vergennes was undoubtedly glad to be well clear of Adams and his importuning, for he needed as few distractions as possible while he was in the final stages of negotiations to get Spain into the war. It had been a delicate process to date. Floridablanca, soon after the signing of the French-American treaty, instructed his London ambassador Escarano that Spain would remain neutral, for Carlos III wanted to "avoid war for as long as possible" without jeopardizing his empire. A few weeks later on April 4, 1778, Escarano was approached by Weymouth to mediate between France and Britain. Floridablanca immediately ordered Escarano to proceed with the discussions, seeing the opportunity to regain lost territory, specifically Gibraltar, in payment for its neutrality, and at the same time to place Spain in a more influential position relative to its French ally. Vergennes, when notified of these talks, believed the Spanish were stalling for time—both the treasure fleet from Veracruz and the troop fleet from Buenos Aires were still at sea and therefore vulnerable to British attack—but had little choice but to agree and to trust in the good faith of the Spanish court.

When in early May Britain rejected the offer to give up Gibraltar, discussion ground to a halt. Spain decided to recall Escarano and send a more experienced negotiator to offer terms for peace. Pedro Francisco, Marqués de Almodóvar del Río, left Spain in June, and, after consulting with Aranda in Paris, met with Weymouth in London in mid-July. Their conversations, like their correspondence, were conducted in French, the language of diplomacy. Almodóvar laid before the British secretary of state three alternatives under which Spain could mediate a peaceful solution: a thirty-year truce between Britain and America, during which time Britain would consider America as an independent nation; a truce between France and Britain, but with the condition that Britain withdraw its troops from America; or an unlimited truce between Britain and America, while Spain mediated a permanent peace. By September, Weymouth had accepted the offer for Spanish mediation along the lines of a truce between France and Britain, and the negotiations began.

Spain began by asking both sides for their conditions for peace. France was willing to negotiate on issues like fishing rights on the Grand Banks, but stuck to the terms of the French-American treaty by making it clear that Britain must acknowledge American independence and withdraw its troops. The British cabinet, by contrast, was instructed in October by George III not to compromise, but rather to play for time by pretending to go along with the mediation. "I have no doubt next spring, Spain will join France," he presciently told Prime Minister North, "but if we can keep her quiet till then I trust the British navy will be in a state to cope with both nations." Britain's initial response in November was therefore ambiguous, but required France to withdraw its forces from America and stop all other aid, which France firmly rejected. In December, Almodóvar put the issue of recovering Gibraltar as a price for Spain's neutrality directly to Weymouth, who replied equally directly that they could discuss the issue only when a truce had been firmly established. Spain's primary—perhaps only—condition for neutrality was now clearly off the table; Floridablanca, in one of his habitual tantrums, railed to Almodóvar that the British were only concerned about "this pile of rocks called Gibraltar, which gives them nothing except worries and expenses, troubles us, and prevents our permanent friendship."

Until this time, as Vergennes had correctly divined, Spain had been reluctant to do anything that might start a war with Britain, so as to protect its two important fleets at sea. The first of these, the treasure fleet from Veracruz, arrived at Cadiz in July 1778. Its commander, Antonio de Ulloa (who had been the first governor of Spanish Louisiana), referred to it as "a most fortunate fleet," an understatement given that its cargo of 22 million pesos (the equivalent of $50 billion today) was one of the largest, and would be the last, of the great silver convoys that kept Spain's economy afloat. The second fleet, carrying troops who had fought in Brazil, finally returned from Buenos Aires in the autumn of that year. With both fleets now safely home and patience with British negotiations wearing thin, by the beginning of 1779 the Spanish court was ready to join France in its fight against Britain. The nature of that alliance, however, would be very much on Spain's own terms. Although Spain could not afford a long, drawn-out war, a sudden invasion of Britain might yield territorial gains that could be used as bargaining chips for the return of Gibraltar and Minorca.

With the defeat of the Seven Years' War and the Falklands/Malvinas debacle clearly in mind, Floridablanca now proceeded with careful deliberation. He knew exactly where Spain's vital interests lay, and he would not prematurely commit his nation to a war if he was not assured of protecting those interests. He knew exactly what his ally's strengths were, and what his enemy's weaknesses were—his special agent Francisco Gil y Lemos, a career naval officer, had secretly visited French and British shipyards to ascertain the state of their fleets. Floridablanca also had the diplomatic upper hand. A year earlier, Vergennes had barreled ahead with the American treaty before Spain was ready. Now France was fully committed to the fight and needed Spain's navy to win a war with Britain; the indecisiveness of the Battle of Ouessant was proof of that to Vergennes, who was also convinced that the Spanish alliance was vital to warding off British attacks on French territories in the West Indies. For its part, Spain would not ally itself directly with the United States, but it would respect the French alliance with the United States by not making peace until Britain recognized American independence. Floridablanca knew that to achieve this result, Vergennes would be willing to accede to almost any demand he would make. However, in return for Spain's participation in the war against Britain, Floridablanca proposed that France agree to a combined invasion of England, to help recover Gibraltar and Minorca, and to help expel British forces from Florida and Central America.

Vergennes was appalled upon learning of these conditions that went well beyond his original proposals—he called the Spanish demands "gigantic"—but reminded his king that without Spanish assistance, the current war would be prolonged and potentially ruinous. With no other European wars on the horizon, Louis XVI consented to the terms. He also allowed Sartine to double the navy's funding, now over 100 million livres, with Necker taking out further loans to cover the costs. Spain, meanwhile, presented an ultimatum to Britain on April 3, 1779, demanding an immediate truce with France, knowing that it would be rejected.

Floridablanca, however, did not wait for the news of Britain's refusal. On April 12 in the palace of Aranjuez, he and the French ambassador Montmorin signed the "Treaty of Defense and Offensive Alliance against England" that activated the mutual assurance clauses of the Bourbon Family Compact. The Treaty of Aranjuez was in fact a long list of Spanish demands punctuated by the occasional concession to French desires. The treaty, which was not made public until many years later, stipulated that Spain and France would make war against Britain with the "intent to acquire" Gibraltar and Minorca, cooperate in an invasion of Great Britain, and expel British forces from the Floridas and its logging colonies in Honduras, which would result in the return of the Gulf of Mexico to full Spanish control and effectively put a stop to any further American expansion west of the Mississippi. France would see a recovery of its African slaving colonies and the fisheries of Newfoundland. The treaty further stipulated that neither country would "lay down its arms until the independence [of the United States] is recognized by the King of Great Britain," a tacit indication of Spain's acknowledgment of America as a sovereign nation. Upon learning the news of the treaty, Louis XVI thanked his "brother and uncle" Carlos III for "joining our forces to combat the common enemy."

From May 18 to 20, José de Gálvez wrote letters to his viceroys and governors in North America, instructing them to begin hostilities against British forces two months after receiving those orders. On June 3, the expected rejection of the Spanish ultimatum arrived. On June 16, after a French/Spanish invasion fleet against Britain had already gotten under way, Almodóvar presented Weymouth with a list of Spanish grievances, including the unsubstantiated claim that Britain "had threatened the American dominions of the Crown," a document that in the British view amounted to a declaration of war. Two days later the Spanish ambassador departed London. On June 21, Carlos III issued a decree authorizing all means necessary to stop British trade, in effect declaring that a state of war now existed. Barely a generation after their humiliating capitulation with the Treaty of Paris, both France and Spain were now once again at war with Britain. In the space of just one year, Britain had gone from fighting what it thought was a minor civil war in a distant colony, to waging a full-scale world war against its two mightiest adversaries. By rejecting Spanish mediation, Britain had in effect sacrificed the United States for that pile of rocks called Gibraltar.

FRANCE PROPOSES TO SEND TROOPS TO AMERICA

When the French frigate *Sensible* arrived in Boston on August 2, 1779, John Adams was not the only diplomat to debark. He had spent the six-week voyage in long conversation with Anne-César de La Luzerne, Vergennes's choice to succeed Gérard as minister plenipotentiary to the United States. Almost from the moment Gérard arrived in Philadelphia, he had been continually laid low by a series of fevers whose symptoms point to bouts of malaria. Despite the important work he knew lay ahead, he pleaded with Vergennes to be recalled. Luzerne, who had been an army officer and recently served as ambassador to Bavaria, had only just returned to Paris when Gérard's request for a replacement came to Vergennes. Luzerne was both experienced and available, so the foreign minister appointed him to fill the post. Apparently alerted to the enormous amount of paperwork that accompanied an American ambassadorship, Luzerne arrived with his first secretary, François Barbé-Marbois, and four other staff in tow. While Adams went quietly back to his home in Braintree, Luzerne spent almost a month in Boston, meeting with a steady stream of both public and private individuals to get a sense of the situation facing the nation he had been sent to assist.

On his way from Boston to Philadelphia, where he would take the reins from a grateful Gérard and be formally presented to Congress, Luzerne stopped at George Washington's headquarters in West Point, New York, on September 16, 1779, to confer on military matters. They discussed the news of Spain's entry into the war, the possibility of American help in recovering Florida for Spain, and plans for the next season's military campaign. During the course of their conversation, Luzerne asked Washington "whether it would be agreeable to the United States . . . to send directly from France a squadron and a few regiments attached to it, to act in conjunction" with American troops. Washington replied that it would be "very advantageous of the common cause." With this almost offhand exchange, the future of American independence was now, for the first time, placed on a firm footing; after almost five years' fighting Britain from Canada to Georgia with very few American successes, it had become clear that Washington's troops could not hope to dislodge the British army without the direct assistance of a large French fighting force.

It would be almost another year before a major French expedition landed on American shores to provide Washington the overwhelming military force he needed to finally defeat Great Britain and secure America's independence. In the meantime, soldiers from France and Spain would carry the fight to the British from Europe to the Gulf of Mexico, giving American troops some breathing room to carry on the struggle.

CHAPTER 4

The Soldiers

The Americans needed far more than breathing room, or even guns, tents, and gunpowder, to defeat the British. If war were merely a matter of numbers, American forces could have overwhelmed their enemies in the first full year of fighting. In 1776, William Howe had 20,700 British and Hessian troops in North America, mostly in New York City, and another 7,000 troops available in Canada. At the same time, George Washington's Continental Army had 46,900 soldiers spread from Massachusetts to Georgia, plus another 26,000 militia on enlistments from four to six months. Despite their apparent numerical disadvantage, the British held the upper hand after the Battle of Long Island, for a number of reasons. British troops were concentrated in a few well-defended strategic positions, while the Continental Army and militia were widely dispersed. The British army had at its disposal an unchallenged naval force that could move its soldiers where they were needed, while the American forces were generally limited to fighting in their local regions. Most important, Howe commanded highly trained soldiers who already knew how to use these attributes to their advantage. Washington, by contrast, had to build up, equip, and train his army and militia even as the war raged, a task rather akin to constructing and outfitting a fleet of warships while engaged in battle at sea.

Washington recognized from the beginning that he had to create a European-style army to wage war both offensively and defensively against the British. Never having received any formal military education or instruction, he had learned at first hand from his experiences in the French and Indian War how European armies fought. American colonists were familiar with wars with and between Native American nations, which typically emphasized hit-and-run tactics to kill or capture the enemy and to take trophies and spoils of war. European-style conflicts, by contrast, involved gaining and holding territory, which Washington would later recognize was the key to the conduct of the war against Britain. This form of warfare involved far more than simply arraying troops for an attack; it required precise planning of every aspect of a campaign. Washington had observed how his generals Edward Braddock and especially John Forbes prepared their troops and led them in battle; how they paid careful attention to training, discipline, and order; how they mastered the details of provisioning and quartering their armies; and how they were able to support them on the move. Washington fully understood the military maxim that "amateurs study tactics, professionals study logistics," two centuries before the World War II general Omar Bradley reportedly uttered it.

Washington realized that both he and his men had to supplement their on-the-battlefield training with the study of military books and treatises, all of which came from Europe. At the top of his list was Humphrey Bland's *Treatise of Military Discipline,* the standard British manual of the duties of officers and soldiers, the conduct of drills, exercises, and reviews, and the establishment and deployment of fighting formations. He also bought translations of French-language works such as Turpin de Crissé's *Essay on the Art of War* and Jeney's *The Partisan,* both published during the Seven Years' War, which detailed the latest thinking regarding irregular warfare, such as laying and avoiding ambushes and interdicting enemy supply lines. Many of Washington's senior officers were equally well read; his chief of artillery, Henry Knox, had previously been a bookseller in Boston, and his shop on Cornhill carried treatises such as Maurice de Saxe's *Reveries on the Art of War,* which was avidly read by Knox's friend Nathanael Greene, who was later to become one of Washington's most gifted generals.

When Washington became commander in chief of American forces in July 1775, his first task had been to transform what had been a collection of various state militias into a coherent, professional Continental Army. "Discipline and subordination," he wrote to John Hancock, was the key to this professionalism. But discipline meant more than quickly following orders and adhering to strict daily routine. It also required the creation of a top-to-bottom hierarchy that did not exist in militias. From his exposure to European fighting practice and his reading of the latest in European military theory, Washington understood that he needed a general staff to assist him with strategic and tactical planning and to provide organizational and logistical support to the army as a whole. His staff officers would include adjutants who handled administrative duties; quartermasters and commissary officers in charge of training, arms, and supplies; and commissaries of muster and paymasters to handle enlistment and wages. In the first months and years of the war, Washington strove mightily to find fighting officers who also had the requisite managerial skills to handle these duties.

Most of all, Washington needed engineers and artillerists. Gaining and holding territory required intimate knowledge of fortification and laying sieges, which were the domain of the engineer, as well as the movement and emplacement of heavy weaponry, which were the province of the artillerist. In actual fact, there was always considerable overlap between the two professions—engineers learned about artillery, artillerists studied fortifications, and both were trained in mechanics, geometry, and surveying—so that one person, usually denoted as an engineer, might serve in both capacities. Regardless of their title, they were in short supply; a week after he assumed command of the troops outside Boston, Washington bluntly complained to the Continental Congress about the "disadvantages [under which] we labor; these consist in a want of engineers to construct proper works & direct the men." The Congress was equally direct in its response: "The want of engineers, I fear, is not to be supplied in America." There were few Americans who had even the most rudimentary engineering skills—as a former surveyor, Washington was one of them—much less any who had a military engineering background. Henry Knox, who was only twenty-five when the war began, originally gained his knowledge of engineering from the books in his shop, and was initially so inept a soldier that he had blown off his own fingers in a gun accident. Richard Gridley, an artillerist who had fortified Breed's Hill and became Washington's first chief of engineers, was perhaps the only American general officer with actual combat engineering experience—he was part of the colonial Massachusetts force that helped besiege and capture Louisbourg in 1745 during the War of the Austrian Succession—but he was now over sixty-five years old, well above the life expectancy of an adult male in the eighteenth century, and he could hardly be expected to endure the rigors of warfare for very long. Gridley's assistant Rufus Putnam, though younger and hardier, had only worked as a millwright before joining the army. America would clearly have to look abroad for its engineering talent.

The best engineers and artillerists, both Washington and the Congress already knew, had been trained in France under the Corps du génie (Engineering Corps) and the Corps de l'artillerie (Artillery Corps). These corps were born out of necessity during the almost incessant wars of the late 1600s under Louis XIV, when France was either attacking its Dutch, Spanish, and Germanic neighbors or defending its own borders from their incursions. During this time, its greatest military engineer, Sébastien Le Prestre de Vauban, perfected the art of fortification, creating the intricate star-shaped citadels that protected countless cities and harbors from attack. At the same time, Vauban established the "science" of siege warfare, which combined offensive trenches to approach enemy forts, the undermining of walls, and the use of heavy artillery to clear ramparts and destroy enemy positions. These corps were established under Vauban in the 1670s as professional bodies of army officers, the first of their kind in the world whose extensive education in mathematics and the sciences and practical training in military operations enabled them to build fortifications, forge artillery, and conduct sieges in the most efficient and effective ways possible. Training took place in several schools around the nation. Elite students attended the École royale du génie (Royal School of Engineering) at Mézières in northern France, where they underwent six grueling years of classroom instruction and practical military experience. The French system was quickly emulated throughout Europe; even Britain's Royal Military Academy at Woolwich, which trained both artillery and engineering officers, used translations of French works such as those of Vauban as its standard textbooks.

Washington's pleas to the Congress for engineers did not go unheeded. On December 2, 1775, three days after it was established, the Committee of Secret Correspondence resolved that its members would "find out and engage in the service of the United Colonies skillful engineers, not exceeding four, on the best terms they can." When the French agent Julien-Alexandre Achard de Bonvouloir et Loyauté met with the committee a few days later, he noted that although "everyone here is a soldier," they lacked for engineers to build fortifications. "France is fully capable of providing you two good engineers, and even more," he assured them, and made certain that Vergennes knew of this request. Soon after Bonvouloir's visit, committee members also wrote to its Dutch correspondent Charles Dumas: "We are in great want of good engineers," they said, "and wish you could engage and send us two able ones in time for the next campaign." Arthur Lee, who had already been instructed to communicate with Dumas, apparently learned of this request, for in April 1776 he pointedly told Beaumarchais that the Americans needed arms and gunpowder, "but above all we need engineers," a request that Beaumarchais also made known to Vergennes. Word of America's need for qualified engineers quickly spread in France, for when Silas Deane arrived in Paris that July he was inundated with "memorials from officers and engineers, offering their services in America," all anxious for a chance to fight the British overseas after the Treaty of Paris had left them no opportunity to fight them at home.

CANADA AND THE CARIBBEAN SUPPLY THE FIRST FRENCH VOLUNTEERS

The officers and engineers who approached Deane in July 1776 were not, in fact, the first Frenchmen to volunteer for the American cause. Before the United States was even a nation, French soldiers from the Caribbean colonies and Canada were already coming to the fight. One of the first was an Alsatian engineer of Irish descent, Louis O'Hicky d'Arundel, who had been a lieutenant of artillery in Saint-Domingue. It is not known how he came to Philadelphia in February 1776, nor why he signed his name Dohicky Arundel, but he was assigned to Williamsburg, Virginia, as an artillery captain under General Charles Lee, to help drive the Loyalist governor Lord Dunmore out of the state. D'Arundel thought the available artillery was inadequate to attack Dunmore's forces on Gwynn's Island, and, lacking a proper forge, he hastily constructed a mortar made from heavy wooden staves. During the Battle of Gwynn's Island on July 8, 1776, the mortar burst and killed its inventor, making him the first of many French soldiers who would give their lives to the cause of American independence.

While d'Arundel's service was tragically cut short, another engineer from the French Caribbean served throughout the war on both land and sea with great distinction. Antoine Félix Wuibert was born in Mézières on January 8, 1746, and though he never attended the École royale du génie in that city, he did go to Saint-Domingue, where he served as an engineer of fortifications. After his service, Wuibert came to Philadelphia to volunteer for the American cause, just as the Congress was taking up Richard Henry Lee's resolution for independence. In June 1776, Wuibert received the first official document ever bearing the term "the United States," commissioning him as a lieutenant colonel of engineering in the Continental Army. He was immediately dispatched to New York, where he worked under Colonel Rufus Putnam on the northern tip of Manhattan, building Fort Washington and an artillery redoubt at Jeffery's Hook, to prevent the British fleet from ascending the Hudson River. Despite Putnam's and Wuibert's best efforts, the solid bedrock made it almost impossible to erect the complex of ditches, casements, and earthworks required to fortify the strongholds against a British assault. After the Battle of Long Island in August, the American troops were pushed across Manhattan to White Plains and New Jersey, although George Washington decided to leave a large garrison to defend the Manhattan forts. On November 16, British and Hessian forces overran Fort Washington from three sides and captured almost three thousand troops, including Wuibert, who was sent to the notorious Forton Prison in Britain where he would languish for two years.

In October 1776, while Wuibert was helping build Fort Washington, "a number of French gentlemen, in the character of military officers," from Saint-Domingue arrived in Boston "to offer their services to the United States." Among them was Marie Louis Amand Ansart de Maresquelle, whose family forged cannon for the French army and who had himself been a military engineer under the famed Gribeauval. In 1771 his young wife and their newly born daughter died, and in his grief he departed France for the Caribbean. His decision to volunteer for the American cause was fortunate, for the Continental Army was just then trying to develop an indigenous artillery manufacture in addition to obtaining cannon from overseas. Within a month of his arrival, the Massachusetts Board of War commissioned Maresquelle as a colonel of artillery and placed him in charge of all state foundries. Like his competitor Jean Maritz back in France, Maresquelle employed the advanced technique of solid-casting bronze cannon and then drilling the bore, giving them greater power and accuracy, which he demonstrated to a local coppersmith, Paul Revere. Maresquelle quickly set up foundries at Bridgewater near Boston, and they became a major source of cannon for New England during the war. He also remarried but tragically lost his second wife soon thereafter.

One of the soldiers who accompanied Maresquelle from Saint-Domingue was already known in Boston. Pierre Benjamin Faneuil was a well-to-do cousin of Peter Faneuil, who had built Faneuil Hall. He and his companions had come in hopes of raising a regiment of French Canadian troops to serve in America, which they would personally outfit with "white coat, waistcoat, and breeches," and gold-embroidered hats for the officers. Faneuil passed away just a few months after his arrival, evidently not aware that French officers and engineers from Canada were already in the fight. When Richard Montgomery led the ill-fated invasion of Canada in June 1775, he found a sympathetic French engineer named Christophe Pélissier, director of the Saint-Maurice Ironworks in Trois-Rivières near Quebec City, who provided shot, bombs, and ammunition for the American forces. Pélissier left with the Americans when they departed the following year, and went on to serve as a lieutenant colonel of engineering, improving the defenses of Fort Ticonderoga after the Americans had captured it a few months earlier. While Montgomery was in Canada, he also directed the raising of two Canadian regiments from the French population in Quebec, though most of their officers were American. The First Canadian Regiment under James Livingston and the Second Canadian Regiment under Moses Hazen were small—neither was ever at its authorized strength of one thousand men—but they fought fiercely against the British at the Battle of Quebec, and would go on to serve in several more battles during the War of American Independence.

VOLUNTEERS BEGIN ARRIVING FROM FRANCE AND EUROPE

As volunteers from the Caribbean and Canada were fighting in the Continental Army, others were on their way from Europe. Among the first was Thaddeus Bonaventure Kosciuszko, born to a noble Polish family in February 1746. After training as an army cadet, in 1769 he enrolled in the Paris Academy of Painting and Sculpture in the Louvre, learning the elements of the arts as well as architecture. He returned to a newly partitioned Poland in 1774, but his dismal prospects there led him back to Paris a year later. There is no record of why he and several Polish and German companions decided at that point to go to America, but in June 1776 they sailed from Le Havre and were shipwrecked on the reefs of Martinique. After swimming to shore, they met a French artillery officer, Charles Noël François Romand de L'Isle, who had received permission to join the American forces from Robert d'Argout, the governor of Martinique who had been actively aiding the American colonists with arms and supplies. Together Kosciuszko, Romand de L'Isle, and their companions sailed in a fishing vessel up the coast of North America, arriving in Philadelphia in late August.

Romand de L'Isle may have come to America to flee an unhappy marriage; he had left his wife and two-year-old daughter in Martinique, and soon after receiving his commission as a major in the American artillery, he married an Irish immigrant while still married in Martinique (divorce was not possible in eighteenth-century Catholic France) and started another family. Kosciuszko also wanted a commission as an engineer or artillerist, but with no experience or training in either, he approached Benjamin Franklin to take an examination. Franklin offered to have him tested in geometry, which fortunately he had learned as part of his architectural training at the Paris Academy. Kosciuszko, having demonstrated his mathematical knowledge, was put to work alongside Romand de L'Isle in shoring up the river defenses at Billingsport and Red Bank (Fort Mercer) downriver from Philadelphia, which the Americans expected every day to come under attack by the British. Although this was Kosciuszko's first wartime engineering assignment in his life, he performed so well that in October he was appointed by Hancock as colonel of engineers in the Continental Army and sent to New York to serve under Horatio Gates.

Even as Franklin was examining Kosciuszko and other volunteers for American service, he did not know that his friend and correspondent Jacques Barbeu-Dubourg had already been busy recruiting officers and engineers in Paris, without any agreement or even requests from the Congress. In August 1775, soon after the news of Lexington and Concord broke, Barbeu-Dubourg dispatched a French cavalry officer who had served in the Prussian army, Frederick William, Baron de Woedtke. The Congress made him a brigadier general when he arrived the following spring, but his tenure was unremarkable, as he died later that year. Barbeu-Dubourg next sent an experienced Breton engineer named Gilles Jean Marie Barazer de Kermorvan in March 1776. The Congress made him a lieutenant colonel of engineers and set him to building ramparts, redoubts, land obstacles (abatis), and river obstacles (chevaux-de-frise) at Billingsport and Perth Amboy. In May, Barbeu-Dubourg recruited more officers, including René Gayault de Boisbertrand, to sail aboard his partner Pierre Penet's vessel carrying guns and ammunition to Robert Morris, but the ship was captured by American privateers en route, and only later was Boisbertrand released and given a commission. The following April, another Penet ship, *Morris,* also carrying guns and munitions, was blown up by British warships off Delaware; one of the escapees was the Breton cavalry officer Charles Armand Tuffin, Marquis de La Rouërie, who swam half-naked to shore and then walked to Philadelphia, where Congress commissioned him as a colonel. Neither Barbeu-Dubourg nor Penet had given any of these men any money to pay for their travel, merely the unauthorized assurances that they would "be received with gratitude by the Congress" and that they "would certainly be recompensed in America for their expenses."

Unknown to Barbeu-Dubourg, the Continental Congress was becoming increasingly unwilling to provide either gratitude or recompense to the influx of foreign volunteers, even when its own representative authorized their travel. Silas Deane had been sent to France by the Committee of Secret Correspondence to negotiate with the full authority of Congress. Although the committee had resolved to "find out and engage . . . skillful engineers" from overseas, it inexplicably failed to include those demands in its instructions to Deane. Thus, when he arrived in Paris in July 1776, Deane was taken aback by the "memorials from officers and engineers" which suddenly arrived on his desk, not knowing what the Congress intended and evidently not having given the matter much thought during his voyage. His greatest problem was that having had no military experience, he could not confidently judge the types of officers America needed, nor which applicants were up to the job.

Without any recourse to American advisers, Deane had little choice but to lean on those whom Franklin and Vergennes recommended, namely Barbeu-Dubourg and Beaumarchais. Both men insisted that America needed engineers and artillerists to properly employ the hundreds of cannon that Deane was about to purchase on credit. "I cannot satisfy your requests for such a large artillery train to depart France without drivers or even officers, as little is known in America of such tactics," explained Beaumarchais. "You ought not therefore to hesitate in adopting Mr. Arthur Lee's original plan, which I mentioned to you, of sending engineers and officers, in particular artillery officers." As to which officers to select, once again Barbeu-Dubourg and Beaumarchais were in agreement: Start with Philippe Charles Tronson du Coudray, Gribeauval's right-hand man. The minister of war, after all, had asked Coudray to personally select the artillery train that would go to America, and had already granted him leave to serve there. Deane became convinced of Coudray's worth to the United States, and in September concluded an agreement to send him there along with his artillery train, accompanied by ten engineering officers. Deane also selected, a few weeks later, an Irish-born infantry colonel named Thomas Conway to accompany the engineers. Deane may have thought that he had made sage decisions based on the best available counsel, but he had inadvertently set in motion another series of difficulties that rapidly cascaded out of his control.

The problems began soon after the agreement was concluded. When Beaumarchais arrived at Le Havre in December 1776 to inspect *Amphitrite* before departure, he expected to find Coudray, Conway, and the ten engineering officers Deane had agreed to, waiting to board the vessel as passengers for America. Instead, he was greeted with thirty engineering officers, nine infantry officers, and ten servants and volunteers, a total of forty-nine passengers, who would have to be housed, paid, and fed at Beaumarchais's expense on the voyage and at America's expense upon arrival. Some of the engineers were less experienced than Deane had been led to believe. One of them, the twenty-two-year-old Pierre Charles L'Enfant, had only just been commissioned a lieutenant of engineers, but was nothing of the sort. He was in fact an architect, the son of Pierre L'Enfant, who had painted the magnificent battle scenes in Vergennes's offices, and whose influence at Versailles had undoubtedly landed his son an officer's commission and a berth on *Amphitrite*. The younger L'Enfant had until recently attended the Paris Academy of Painting and Sculpture, and probably knew Kosciuszko, as their tenures overlapped. The events halfway across the world would bring them together again, this time not in a studio but in the fight for the same cause.

The problems continued after *Amphitrite* departed Le Havre on December 15, 1776. The ship had been victualed only for the crew and ten passengers Deane had agreed to, not the forty-nine who actually embarked. Just two weeks later the ship made a very public and humiliating return to resupply at Lorient. The minister of war, embarrassed by the whole affair, rescinded Coudray's leave and ordered him back to his garrison. Coudray disobeyed those orders and fled, first to Paris and then to Nantes, leaving most of his entourage at the quay. Jonathan Williams, Deane's agent in Nantes, had to scramble to get the remaining officers proper berths aboard *Amphitrite* and *Mercure,* another Beaumarchais ship, both of which arrived in Portsmouth, New Hampshire, a few months later. Deane was furious; in the space of just a month, he went from praising Coudray as "the first engineer of the kingdom" to excoriating him for the "disappointment, if not irreparable damage, to my country." That barb never reached Coudray; in late January he had secreted himself and four officers aboard a third Beaumarchais ship, *Seine,* which sailed to Martinique. There, both the officers and military cargo were offloaded onto schooners bound for Portsmouth, where in May 1777 they were reunited with the other passengers and cargo from *Amphitrite* and *Mercure.*

The problems did not end when the officers arrived in Portsmouth, for Deane had already committed a series of blunders that threatened to tear apart the fragile French-American coalition before it even began. Although the Congress had given Deane no instructions on volunteers nor any authority to grant military commissions, he had unilaterally appointed several of the volunteers to high-level positions that would make them answerable to no one but the commander in chief. He commissioned Coudray as a major general with "the direction of whatever relates to the Artillery and Corps of Engineers," while he told the Congress that in light of Thomas Conway's "long experience" in training troops, he should "fill the place of an Adjutant, or Brigadier General." Deane defended these commissions by arguing that in order to recruit any officer of merit, he had to offer "at least as good terms as he could have in his own country." His lack of military experience, though, apparently blinded him to the fact that Washington and the Congress needed to make such appointments, in order to maintain the "discipline and subordination" that was requisite for a professional army.

Nor was the situation aided by the lack of discretion in some of the French volunteers; almost as soon as Coudray landed, he waved Deane's commission that "he is to command all the Artillery and Engineers in the service of the United States" in front of Major General William Heath, himself an experienced artillery officer. It was a dilemma that could satisfy no one: As the number of volunteers multiplied, the financially strapped Congress found itself increasingly unable to provide their promised high-ranking commissions or pay their agreed-to salaries, while as Washington pointed out, promoting foreign officers over American ones "could not fail to occasion a general discontent" and "cause the resignation" of the American officers in line to advance in rank.

Washington's problems with foreign officers were still unknown back in Paris. Deane had yet to receive any instructions regarding volunteers, and his own letters requesting guidance would go unanswered for over a year. He continued to turn to Vergennes for trustworthy advisers, but by October 1776 both Barbeu-Dubourg and Beaumarchais were off that list. Instead, Vergennes apparently sent his longtime conspirator from the *Secret du Roi,* Charles-François de Broglie, to meet with Deane in order to sway his recruiting. De Broglie met with Deane twice in one day, on November 5, introducing him to Johann de Kalb as a prospective volunteer, and likely proposing Thomas Conway to him as well. De Kalb, who ten years earlier had gone to America as an agent for the French crown, had retired from service upon his return. He briefly came back to staff duty under de Broglie in 1775, and now was eager to reenter the military. Deane, impressed by de Broglie's recommendation and by the fact that de Kalb spoke English, was determined not to "let slip an opportunity of engaging a person of so much experience."

De Broglie's support for de Kalb was more than just helping a former comrade in arms. He was still determined to carry out the same policy of *revanche* against Britain he had helped create soon after the Seven Years' War. His plans for an invasion of England having been shelved, he foresaw America as the new battlefront, and had put forward both de Kalb and Bonvouloir as agents to assess the possibilities. With the war now under way, de Broglie was certain that the inexperienced Americans needed a strong European leader like himself to rally the troops. He likely had in mind the same kind of arrangement—an attempt to place a French leader on a foreign throne—under which the *Secret du Roi* had begun. Soon after de Kalb signed his agreement with Deane, de Broglie outlined his plan to have himself named the supreme commander of the new nation; de Kalb in turn proposed the plan to Deane; and Deane "suggested such a thought" to the Congress, where it disappeared without a trace. Reflecting the mood of the American public, which de Broglie, de Kalb, and even Deane failed to recognize, John Adams said later of this incident that he would not "voluntarily put on the chains of France, when I am struggling to throw off those of Great Britain." De Broglie never made it to the United States to assume his heroic mantle, but he was directly responsible for the arrival of the young French officer who would be hailed as a hero in both America and Europe.

Gilbert du Motier, Marquis de Lafayette, was born into wealth, but from an early age he was driven not by social status but by a "love of glory." In eighteenth-century France, that phrase meant something far different from fame-seeking; it merited its own entry in the celebrated *Encyclopédie* of Diderot and d'Alembert, where it was defined as the natural calling to high honor and reputation, a devotion to a noble cause and not to personal gain. For Lafayette, "glory" meant a military career like that of his father, who had been killed at the Battle of Minden during the Seven Years' War when the boy was just two years old. At age thirteen, Lafayette was commissioned as a sublieutenant in the Musketeers, then as a lieutenant in a cavalry unit at age fourteen. The following year he married into the aristocratic Noailles family, adding to his considerable fortune but also shackling him to the French court.

Lafayette was by most accounts happiest when he was with his regiment. In the summer of 1775, they were training on maneuvers in the garrison town of Metz, which was under de Broglie's command. On August 8, de Broglie's officers attended a dinner for an uncommon visitor en route to Italy, Prince William Henry, Duke of Gloucester and Edinburgh, who was King George III's younger brother. There, Prince William related the news that had just reached European shores of the revolts in New England, and the measures taken by the military to halt the rebellion. Johann de Kalb, who was at the time part of de Broglie's staff, likely heard the discourse, but it made an enormous impression on the young Lafayette seated at the table. As he recalled the events half a century later, his "curiosity was deeply excited by what he heard, and the idea of a people fighting for liberty had a strong influence upon his imagination. . . . Before he left the table the thought came into his head that he would go to America and offer his services to a people struggling for freedom and independence."

Despite Lafayette's insistence, de Broglie was at first reluctant to help him go to America, but in November 1776 he arranged for de Kalb

Marie Joseph Paul Yves Roch Gilbert du Motier,
Marquis de Lafayette (1757–1834).
Charles Willson Peale, after
Charles Willson Peale,
1779–1780, oil on canvas

to introduce him to Silas Deane. Deane, seeing the political influence that Lafayette could wield in France, commissioned him as a major general, though he was still a boy of nineteen having precisely two summers' worth of training under his belt. De Kalb and Lafayette, along with several other officers, made plans to sail on one of Beaumarchais's ships, but before the ship could depart it was detained by Vergennes after its secret cargo for America was revealed by Stormont.

Lafayette himself was also detained when his father-in-law found out about his imminent departure. Lafayette was now part of the Noailles family, meaning he had a duty to the court of Versailles, which also disapproved of his journey; besides, his wife, Adrienne, was expecting their second child. In February 1777, Lafayette was bundled off to London under the watchful eye of his wife's uncle Emmanuel Marie Louis, Marquis de Noailles, who was the French ambassador, presumably in order to shake off his republican fantasies. There he was introduced to Lieutenant General Henry Clinton, just back from the successful campaign to capture New York, and to George Germain, the newly appointed secretary of state for the colonies, who was now directing the military action in America; he was even presented to King George III.

For Lafayette, this trip was nothing more than a ruse; with de Broglie's help he had already bought *Victoire,* one of three merchant ships that had been outfitted by the firm Reculès de Basmarein et Raimbeaux to supply arms and volunteers to the rebels, in order to carry himself to America, along with de Kalb and fourteen other officers commissioned by Deane, as well as a cargo of muskets for sale to the insurgents. By mid-March all was ready. Lafayette hastily returned to Paris to collect de Kalb, and, eluding the agents of his family and the court, they rushed to the waiting *Victoire,* which set sail from Bordeaux at the end of the month. The vessel made a brief call in Los Pasajes, Spain, where Lafayette hurried back to France to post letters to his wife and to Versailles explaining his actions, and just as hurriedly returned to Spain disguised as a courier. The ship hoisted anchor on April 20, arriving in Charleston, South Carolina, in mid-June. There, the officers prepared to make their way to Philadelphia, not knowing that they would encounter a Congress already overwhelmed with foreign volunteers for whom they had run out of patience and funds.

SPANISH TROOPS PREPARE FOR WAR AND HELP THE AMERICANS IN THE WESTERN THEATER

Just as *Victoire* was coming into Charleston harbor in June 1777, a Spanish observer was in Pensacola, the British capital of West Florida, secretly taking notes on artillery, fortifications, and order of battle. The Spanish officials in Havana and New Orleans had been keeping a watchful eye on Florida since the end of the Seven Years' War, surreptitiously dispatching merchants and fishermen to keep tabs on military installations and fleet movements. Pensacola was the key to any Spanish attempt to retake Florida and return the Gulf of Mexico to Spain's control. Located within a vast bay accessible only by a narrow inlet, it was an ideal harbor for a British fleet to sortie against Spanish forces, then return to its protected waters. For all Pensacola's strategic importance, the observer—simply described in official dispatches as a "trusted man," to keep his identity secret—noted that its defenses were poorly planned, badly built, and inadequately provisioned and manned. The artillery primarily consisted of heavy naval guns, half of which lacked mounts and could not be repositioned in battle. The fortress walls could not stand up to repeated cannon fire. Many of the soldiers were considered "useless for service." They were short of foodstuffs. The governor of Pensacola, Peter Chester, also had spies in New Orleans and was well aware of the potential Spanish threat; however, his repeated requests to London for reinforcements, supplies, and ammunition had been to little avail. At the beginning of July, the Spanish agent returned to New Orleans to make his report.

The man to whom he reported, Bernardo de Gálvez y Madrid, had at the time been governor of Louisiana for only six months. He was the son of Matías de Gálvez y Gallardo, himself a fast-rising military officer, and nephew of José de Gálvez, the minister of the Indies. Just thirty-one at the time of his appointment, Bernardo de Gálvez had gained his position less through nepotism and more through competence, physical courage, and sheer force of will. He came from the little town of Macharaviaya in Málaga, and at age sixteen fought as a lieutenant in the failed Spanish invasion of Portugal during the Seven Years' War. In 1765 he accompanied his uncle on his inspection mission to New Spain. Four years later he was appointed captain of a series of expeditions to secure Spanish settlements against the Apache nations, who were noted for their ferocity and skill in war fighting. On one such expedition his troops, short on supplies, argued for turning back; but Gálvez, in a speech that presaged his most famous adage, said, "I alone will go if no one will accompany me." His men felt compelled to follow even through the hardships, and they achieved a surprising victory. During subsequent battles in both New Spain and the Old World, he showed himself to be an intrepid and courageous commander. In 1776 he arrived in New Orleans as colonel in command of the colony's professional regiment of soldiers, the Regimiento Fijo de La Luisiana (Fixed Regiment of Louisiana), which was supplemented by the militia. He was almost immediately called upon to replace Luis de Unzaga as governor of Louisiana, and soon thereafter endeared himself to the French Creole population by marrying one of their own, Marie Felice de Saint-Maxent d'Estrehan, with whom he had three children. He also earned the respect of his adversary Peter Chester when, upon learning from his agent of Pensacola's food shortages, he sent them 150 barrels of wheat.

Where Unzaga had been content to supply occasional arms and

money to the Americans, Gálvez was bolder in his support for the revolutionaries. Upon taking office on January 1, 1777, he clamped down on British smuggling, while at the same time opening the port of New Orleans to American trade and protecting American vessels from British capture. In May, he began a regular operation of consigning Spanish shipments of arms and munitions to Americans in the western theater of operations, using Oliver Pollock and the Beauregard family as go-betweens. His resolve was tested when an American raiding party led by James Willing turned up in New Orleans in March 1778. Willing was the younger brother of financier Thomas Willing (of Willing & Morris), and had himself done business with Pollock. Willing had departed Fort Pitt that January in a flat-bottomed boat dubbed *Rattle Trap,* with a captain's commission and instructions from the Congress to attack British outposts along the east bank of the Mississippi and to request additional supplies from Gálvez. His raids on and around Natchez were particularly brutal, and he also captured several British vessels, bringing all of his loot to New Orleans to be sold off. These acts prompted an outcry from Peter Chester, who demanded that Willing and his troops be handed over. Gálvez, though faced with a pair of British frigates that threatened to cannonade his city, professed strict neutrality and refused to turn over the Americans or their plunder. At the same time, he arranged with Pollock for Willing's troops to return up the Mississippi with three hundred muskets, ammunition, medicine, and cloth. Willing himself took a vessel to Philadelphia, but was captured by the British before he could arrive.

Pollock, as the agent for the Congress, had intended these supplies to go to the Continental Army, but instead they were appropriated in Saint Louis by George Rogers Clark, a lieutenant colonel in the Virginia militia. Clark was stationed at Fort Pitt, the American base of operations in the western theater and the main bulwark against British forces at Fort Detroit under Lieutenant Governor Henry Hamilton. Clark intended to use Pollock's supplies to continue his successful expeditions against British settlements along the Ohio and Mississippi Rivers in the Illinois Country, part of the still-contested Ohio Valley. If these operations were successful, it would place the strategically important trade route to New Orleans in American hands.

Clark left Fort Pitt in May 1778, provisioned with Pollock's supplies and the Spanish gunpowder that William Linn had brought from New Orleans the previous year. In July, a series of rapid, bloodless raids gave

Bernardo de Gálvez (1746–1786).
Attributed to Mariano Salvador Maella,
1784, oil on canvas

him control of the French-speaking towns of Kaskaskia, Cahokia, and Vincennes. Shortly thereafter he decamped to Saint Louis, where upon his insistence, Gálvez's lieutenant governor, Fernando de Leyba, turned over Pollock's military supplies to him. Within a few months, British forces from Fort Detroit retook Vincennes. Clark, determined to regain the settlement but unable to raise money from Virginia governor Patrick Henry, asked for more powder and guns from Pollock, who used his own personal credit to requisition them from Gálvez. Clark also drew upon Leyba and a local Italian-born merchant named Francis (Francesco) Vigo to obtain additional supplies on credit. In February 1779 he led 170 men almost two hundred miles through harsh winter wilderness to recapture

Vincennes and capture Henry Hamilton as well. Although Clark failed to extend his conquests to Fort Detroit, these victories—underpinned by Spanish arms, supplies, and munitions—helped secure the western theater against further British threats.

Back in Madrid, the Spanish court was also concerned about possible British threats in North America, but they saw the greatest danger not in the upper reaches of the Mississippi River but rather around the Gulf of Mexico. That threat was heightened at the beginning of 1778 when France decided to pursue an alliance with the United States without Spain. José de Gálvez, upon hearing the news of the impending treaty, advised Floridablanca that "we must see war as inevitable," and advised sending additional army regiments to reinforce Cuba, Puerto Rico, and New Spain. He also reassigned his older brother Matías de Gálvez to become president and captain-general of the *audiencia* of Guatemala, which was at the greatest risk of attack since the British already occupied logging settlements along the Mosquito Coast. One of Spain's primary fears was that the British would divide the Spanish Empire by seizing control of the vast Lake Nicaragua and using it to create a man-made waterway that would give them access from the Atlantic to the Pacific. When Matías de Gálvez arrived in June 1778, he set about rebuilding coastal and river fortifications, constructing a naval fleet on Lake Nicaragua, and ordering ten thousand muskets for the newly enlarged infantry and militia. Having a brother who was minister of the Indies meant that his demands were met with more alacrity than usual.

Matías's son Bernardo de Gálvez was equally busy preparing for war, but he was planning an offensive, not a defensive campaign. His goal would be the capture of British forts along the Gulf, notably Mobile and Pensacola, but for that he needed up-to-date intelligence on them. In February 1778, even before word reached him of the French-American alliance, he had dispatched army captain Jacinto Panis to Pensacola via Mobile, ostensibly to deliver a letter to Peter Chester complaining about "repeated insults committed on the Mississippi River by the English." In reality his mission was to spy upon the defenses and reinforcements of the cities and report back. The "insults" were real—Spanish traders were being fired upon as they journeyed downriver—but as Gálvez undoubtedly knew, Chester could do little about this. Panis's espionage mission went undetected; in July he reported back to Gálvez that although the inhabitants of Mobile had been unnerved by the news of James Willing's raids, they were doing little to protect against a possible American attack. "The fortifications are in a very bad condition" he noted, "and the barracks are in an equally bad state. The walls are going to ruin. Almost all of the artillery is dismounted, and the trenches in some places are choked up." In Pensacola, the situation was different; the Willing raids had spurred Chester to bring the fortifications back from the parlous state that Gálvez's "trusted man" had reported a year earlier. The fortress walls were being repaired and the artillery remounted. These reports gave Gálvez the information he needed to plan future assaults on Britain's Gulf outposts.

Any assaults by Gálvez would have to be supported from Havana, as the captain-general of Cuba, Diego José Navarro, already knew, and he needed his own sources of information on the British. Even though he had inherited from his predecessor Bucareli a network of fishermen, merchants, and clergy to act as observers, he also turned to Native Americans for assistance. Navarro selected Francisco Ruiz del Canto, a former Florida colonist who spoke several Indian languages, to live among the Yuchi nation in the Apalachee region of West Florida and learn about British activities in the area. The Yuchi regularly traded with Cuba, and Canto soon discovered that while the Yuchi leaders Tunapé and Tolope favored a closer alliance with Spain, other nations such as the Creek, Choctaw, and Cherokee actively supported the British. Canto encouraged the Yuchi to keep an eye on the military activities in Pensacola. When they reported to him, for example, that the garrison was running low on supplies or that Peter Chester had shifted troops to the Mississippi River in response to Willing's raids, Canto fed that information back to Cuba. Navarro also dispatched Juan Eligio de la Puente, the brother-in-law of Juan de Miralles, now in Philadelphia, to confer with the Yuchi around Saint Augustine as well as to draw up maps and plans of attack on the city. Gálvez and Navarro now had a well-established web of observers and spies across Florida to prepare them for Spain's entry into a war that had begun years before.

THE FRENCH VOLUNTEERS RECEIVE THEIR TRIAL BY FIRE

That war was already two years old when Lafayette and de Kalb arrived in Philadelphia in the summer of 1777, a city now awash with foreigners clamoring to join the fight. The earliest volunteers in the spring and summer of 1776 had appeared in dribs and drabs—Wuibert, Pélissier, Kosciuszko, Kermorvan—so the Congress could find them useful employment in the army. By the fall they were coming in a trickle of small groups, but were already straining army resources. George Washington endured seemingly endless petitions by the officers from Saint-Domingue "ignora[nt] of our language" who were planning to raise a regiment of French Canadian troops, without having given much thought to finance or logistics. "It has taken up half my time to hear their pretensions," he complained bitterly to Horatio Gates, "and explain to them the reasons why it is impossible for me to gratify them in their wishes—besides accommodations here is not to be had." By the spring of 1777, the Congress had established the Committee on Foreign Applications, chaired by Massachusetts representative James Lovell, one of the few who could speak French, to screen potential volunteers. Even this measure proved insufficient when the arrival of dozens of officers aboard Beaumarchais's ships *Amphitrite* and *Mercure,* and even more volunteers following afterward, turned that trickle into a torrent that would overwhelm Washington and the Congress.

The Congress felt it had to honor Deane's contracts for the Beaumarchais officers. The members were impressed with the English-speaking Thomas Conway, and on May 13 commissioned him brigadier general in command of the Third Pennsylvania Brigade. That was not the case with Tronson du Coudray, who arrived in Philadelphia a few days later bearing Deane's appointment of himself as major general in charge "of whatever relates to the Artillery and Corps of Engineers." That appointment had rankled Washington, who told the Congress that if Coudray were promoted over other American officers like Henry Knox, it would "confuse and unhinge" the entire artillery corps. The Congress, caught between denying Coudray's appointment altogether or risking the resignation of senior American officers, chose a middle ground by making Coudray a major general of the newly invented staff position of inspector general of ordnance and military manufactories, but without authority over other general officers. Coudray and his entourage, including Pierre Charles L'Enfant, were sent to work building up the defenses at Billingsport that had been started by Kosciuszko and Romand de L'Isle.

The Congress was still eager for experienced engineers. When Benjamin Franklin arrived in Paris the previous December, he had carried with him the Committee of Secret Correspondence's request for "four . . . skillful engineers," with which Vergennes quickly complied. The foreign minister selected as the leader Louis Lebègue Duportail, a thirty-four-year-old lieutenant colonel of engineers from Pithviers and graduate of the elite École royale du génie at Mézières, who had just finished rewriting the organizational instructions for the Corps of Engineers. With him were three other Mézières graduates, Louis des Hayes de La Radière, Jean-Baptiste de Gouvion, and Jean-Baptiste Joseph de Laumoy. With an appointment letter from Franklin and Deane they departed Nantes in March 1777 to Saint-Domingue, where they boarded a Beaumarchais vessel bound for North Carolina and thence overland to Philadelphia, arriving in early July. There they were heartily endorsed by Lovell and given commissions. Washington, knowing that there would be friction with the imperious Coudray, sent Duportail and his group to build up fortifications and chevaux-de-frise at Fort Mifflin, one of the Delaware River defenses opposite and upstream from Billingsport.

The situation changed as the year dragged on. With more and more foreign arrivals, the Congress's patience wore thin, even for those officers with special skills. Thus when a French cavalry officer named Augustin Mottin de La Balme arrived in the spring of that year, he was commissioned as inspector general of cavalry; however, when two other battle-hardened horsemen arrived soon after, Casimir Pulaski from Poland and Michael Kovats de Fabriczy from Hungary, their applications for commissions were denied, but they volunteered anyway. George Washington's own patience was already exhausted. Despite his recent victories at Trenton and Princeton, he was facing severe shortages of men and supplies, a series of small-scale defeats such as King's Bridge, New York, and Bound Brook, New Jersey, and the crippling loss of Fort Ticonderoga in July 1777. The political consequences of dealing with officers from a potential ally only added to his woes. "You cannot conceive what a weight these kind of people are upon the Service, and upon me in particular, few of them have any knowledge of the branches which they profess to understand, and those that have, are entirely useless as officers, from their ignorance of the English language," he wrote to the Congress. He could neither peremptorily dismiss them, for fear of offending France, nor grant them their wishes. He implored Franklin to stop sending more officers, or even to pen recommendations, so as not to encourage them to make the long and arduous voyage: "Either we must refuse to commis-

Louis Lebègue de Presle Duportail (1743–1802). Charles Willson Peale, probably from life, 1781–1784, oil on canvas

sion them at all . . . or we must commission them without being able to incorporate or employ them."

It was in this hostile climate that de Kalb, Lafayette, and their companions approached the Congress on July 28, 1777, the day after their arrival in Philadelphia. James Lovell, as the official in charge of foreign appointments, met them on the steps of the Pennsylvania State House but did not invite them in, rather "haranguing" them right there on the street in precise French, treating them "as mercenaries," as one of their group later recalled. Lovell revealed the source of the problem: Silas Deane, he claimed, had exceeded his powers by sending Coudray "with some supposed engineers who were not engineers at all, and artillery officers who had never served in the army." Coudray had further poisoned the well by taking a "lordly tone" upon his arrival, claiming that any aid to the Americans was due to himself alone, and "lashing out at all the other French [volunteers]." Lovell finished by stating that the four engineers

Franklin had sent over (Duportail and his colleagues) were the only ones the Americans had requested, and that they needed no more. With that he turned on his heel and went back inside.

Lovell's boorish behavior—a distinct departure from his earlier, warmer welcome of Duportail's group—did not sting nearly as much as the notion that they were "mercenaries," which they resented deeply. The Americans, of course, had used the word "mercenaries" in their Declaration of Independence to refer to the hated Hessian troops called into the war by George III, which was one of the catalysts for Congress to vote for independence. Apart from the Hessians, Americans had little experience with the idea of engaging foreign troops to fight, so at first they viewed these French volunteers with deep suspicion. This was not the case in France or in most of Europe in the eighteenth century. Many European nations had no standing armies, relying partly on the "proprietary system" where an officer was paid according to the number of troops he could muster, and also relying on foreign troops to fill the ranks. Serving under a foreign crown was not equivalent to being a mercenary, for these soldiers fought not just for pay but also for honor and prestige. In 1776, the French army included six regiments of Irish soldiers, known colloquially as "Wild Geese" (Thomas Conway was such a one), as well as Swiss, German, and Italian troops in its employ. The Spanish army included both Irish and French officers and troops. De Kalb and Lafayette had little reason to suppose that the situation in America would be any different, and they certainly did not expect their motives for volunteering to be questioned.

Volunteers came from all over Europe—Italian and German states, Poland, Hungary—but France was by far the largest source of volunteers who came to the war before the conflict widened in 1778. Then as now, those who volunteered in a foreign war had differing reasons to do so. Most came to America to fight the British; some came to fight for the United States. These were not the same things. Few of the more than four hundred volunteer applications that Franklin and the commissioners received during their tenure in Paris cited the political goal of *revanche* against Britain as their reason for wanting to come. But it was not necessary to bring up revenge, as this was already well understood; instead they spoke of duty and glory in the fight against their hated enemies. For some of those volunteers, the choice had already been made for them; fight the British in America or don't fight them at all. The devastating losses of the

Seven Years' War had prompted a series of reforms in the French army, notably in the proprietary system for officers. When Louis XVI came to the throne and in 1775 selected Claude Louis, Comte de Saint-Germain, as his minister of war, some of the minister's first reforms were to consolidate and eliminate corps and to create a system of advancement similar to that of Prussia, based on merit as opposed to how many troops an officer could purchase. Though these reforms were short-lived—Saint-Germain would be replaced by Montbarey in late 1777—the net effect was to place a number of officers on reserve status, where they would have almost no hope of going into battle. With the arrival of first Silas Deane and then Benjamin Franklin, many of these "reformed" officers, including Lafayette, leapt at the chance for duty and glory in America.

Other volunteers came because they were inspired by the image of the United States engaged in citizen warfare struggling for justice and independence against a tyrannical foe, in the same way the ancient Athenians and Spartans fought their enemies. That was the picture often presented in popular (but also government-controlled) newspapers like the *Gazette de France* and *Gazette de Leyde,* which compared George Washington to the "great men of antiquity." Even the term *"les insurgents"* was resurrected from history to describe the American revolutionaries. Many of Franklin's applicants waxed eloquent on the subject of United States independence; one Alsatian officer stated that he was ambitious to serve a nation so effectively defending the cause of liberty, while Mottin de La Balme professed "love of liberty" as his reason for joining the insurgents. Lafayette, writing to his wife while aboard *Victoire* in mid-Atlantic, expressed his yearning not only for glory but to defend "that liberty which I idolize" in the only way he could imagine: by "coming as a friend to offer my services to that most interesting republic." That a Frenchman born and raised in a monarchy could appreciate and even fight for the virtues of a republic came as a surprise to many Americans, even though the Declaration of Independence was inspired in part by French Enlightenment thinkers like Montesquieu and Voltaire. Pierre-Étienne du Ponceau related the following encounter that took place in Boston soon after his arrival in late 1777:

> I was then a stern Republican; I had been so from the first moment when I began to reflect. I shall never forget the compliment paid me by Samuel Adams on his discovering my

> Republican principles. "Where," said he to me, "did you learn all that?" "In France," replied I. "In France! that is impossible." Then, recovering himself, he added, "Well, because a man was born in a stable, it is no reason why he should be a horse."

Whatever their reasons for coming, these French and European officers surmounted many obstacles just to get into the fight. The harrowing experiences of Thaddeus Kosciuszko and Charles Armand Tuffin surviving their shipwrecks, yet still applying to the Congress as volunteers, were just two of many such stories that showed their determination. Upon arrival, many were at first treated with scorn by the Americans; after all, fewer than fifteen years earlier the French had been mortal enemies, and it was difficult to think of them now as allies. Nathanael Greene, whose formative years spanned the French and Indian War, considered French officers "as so many spies in our camp," and the label of mercenary continued to stick. With adversity also came culture shock. Some of the more aristocratic French volunteers had trouble adjusting to a nation where peasants treated them as peers. Many more were dismayed at the lack of American dedication to their fight for independence, which was often referred to in almost sacred terms as "The Cause." Duportail, in one of his first letters to Versailles, complained, "There is one hundred times more enthusiasm for this revolution in a single Parisian café than in all the colonies combined." This, he later explained, was especially disheartening to the French who were in the fight, for "in a certain sense, it is even more our Cause" than it was that of the Americans, since France's dignity was now bound up in the outcome, while the Americans could always return to the British fold. Duportail may have misread the depth of American commitment, but he astutely recognized how much the fate of France was now bound up with that of the United States.

The campaign of General William Howe to capture Philadelphia, and the subsequent rearguard action by the Continental Army, would prove the trial by fire for many of the newly arrived French and European officers, and dramatically change the opinions of both the Congress and the senior American officers toward them. The capital city was fairly swarming with foreign volunteers in July 1777, just as Howe's seventeen thousand British and Hessian troops were wallowing aboard over two hundred vessels in Perth Amboy across from Staten Island. The fleet cleared Sandy Hook on the twenty-fourth and then—from George

Washington's point of view—disappeared into the Atlantic. Howe briefly reappeared off the entrance to the Delaware River, but he had already been warned of the heavy defenses at Billingsport and Forts Mifflin and Mercer, and also was concerned that Washington could box him in if he arrived farther downstream. Instead he made his approach up the Chesapeake Bay, landing his troops at Head of Elk, Maryland, on August 25. The next day, Washington, Greene, and Lafayette reconnoitered the British positions. All three men wore the sashes of general officers, for the Congress had changed its mind about Lafayette the day after Lovell's "haranguing." Realizing the important political role he could play by inspiring the French court, they commissioned him as a major general, though without pay or command. Despite Lafayette's protests, the other officers, including de Kalb, were left to fend for themselves. Washington took Lafayette under his tutelage and carefully counseled him on character and conduct, as he did many of his younger officers. Intended or not, the young Gilbert saw this not simply as the mentoring of a senior leader, but rather as the affection of a "father and friend." In this he was far more prescient than his commanding officer, for their relationship would soon grow more familial than professional.

As Howe, with his generals Charles Cornwallis and Wilhelm von Knyphausen, advanced west toward Philadelphia, Washington deployed his troops on the east bank of Brandywine Creek in order to intercept them. Two of his brigades were commanded by French brigadier generals who came in Beaumarchais's ships, Thomas Conway and Philippe Hubert Preudhomme de Borre. Other French officers were scattered among the various regiments, including two engineers from Coudray's entourage, François-Louis Teissèdre de Fleury and Thomas Antoine de Mauduit du Plessis. On September 11, the two armies met. The early morning fog obscured Howe's maneuvers. He directed Knyphausen's smaller diversionary force to move toward the west bank opposite the main American body at the Chadd's Ford crossing, while at the rear he accompanied a much larger force under Cornwallis to outflank the American right by crossing the creek several miles farther north. On the American side, Major General John Sullivan dispatched Hazen's Second Canadian Regiment to guard other potential crossings against such a flanking maneuver. At midmorning, as Knyphausen paused opposite the American center to lob artillery shells across the river, Hazen sent word to Washington that his troops had sighted a large British contingent marching to cross the river farther north. Washington evaluated the report as uncorroborated and decided not to split his forces in the face of the enemy. By 2 p.m., Howe and Cornwallis had crossed the river and were poised on Osborne Hill, behind Washington's right flank. Sullivan wheeled his division, which included troops under Hazen; William Alexander, Lord Stirling; and John Stephens, to occupy the high ground at Birmingham Friends Meetinghouse in order to meet Howe head-on. At 4 p.m., Howe sent his redcoats marching down Osborne Hill, bayonets at the ready, smashing into Sullivan's wing.

The American troops had little experience facing bayonets, and their commanding officers had even less experience at maneuvering in difficult terrain. Some broke and ran—Preudhomme de Borre's Second Maryland Brigade was one—while others like Conway's Third Pennsylvania Brigade held their ground. Washington arrived at the Birmingham battle site accompanied by Lafayette, just in time to see Sullivan's line collapse. The commander in chief rode back to Chadd's Ford to rally Nathanael Greene's troops, while Lafayette stayed behind with Conway. As the American line was pushed farther back, Lafayette jumped off his horse and urged the men forward, ordering them to fix bayonets and physically pushing some by the shoulders. As the British line approached within twenty yards, a ball tore through Lafayette's left leg below the knee, and blood ran out of his boot. His aide Jean-Joseph Sourbader de Gimat helped him, weak with blood loss, remount his horse, and together they fled with the rest of the field into the woods before Lafayette received medical treatment.

Casimir Pulaski had also been following Washington during the battle, though without rank or command. As he watched Cornwallis plow into Sullivan's wing, he persuaded Washington to give him thirty mounted guards, and led this small cavalry unit against Cornwallis's left. This surprise attack halted the British advance long enough for Stirling and Stephens to fall back in an orderly fashion toward the town of Chester. Pulaski then led his impromptu cavalry unit against the flanks of Knyphausen's brigades, which had crossed Chadd's Ford and were pursuing Anthony Wayne, slowing them enough so that the American soldiers and their equipment trains were able to retreat intact as night fell.

Howe had decisively outmaneuvered Washington, and the best that Washington could report back to the Congress was that his army had survived to fight another day. Others were more charitable, one notably in a letter printed by the *Independent Chronicle* of Boston, which would find its way to Benjamin Franklin, who surely took pleasure touting it around Paris:

> A great number of French officers were in the action. The Marquis de Lafayette, that most accomplished youth, behaved with a bravery equal to his noble birth and amiable character. The Polish Count Pulaski with a party of light horse rode up to reconnoiter the enemy within pistol-shot of their front. The Chevalier du Plessis, who is one of General Knox's family, had three balls through his hat. Young Fleury's horse was killed under him. He showed so much bravery, and was so useful in rallying the troops, that the Congress have made him a present of another [horse]. I should not do justice if I did not add that the French officers in general behaved extremely well.

Apart from awarding Fleury a new horse, the Congress also changed its mind about the utility of foreign officers. The week after the Battle of Brandywine, it appointed Johann de Kalb as a major general (word reached him just as he was about to depart for Europe), and made Pulaski brigadier general in command of the cavalry over the higher-ranking Mottin de La Balme, who had not participated in the battle (whereupon the French officer resigned his commission, to eventually fight and die in the western theater). The congressional about-face was undoubtedly bolstered by the news that the thorn-in-both-sides Tronson du Coudray, on his way to unite with Washington's army, had just drowned after his horse bolted from a ferryboat and dragged him into the Schuylkill River. Neither the Americans nor the French mourned his passing; John Adams drily remarked, "This dispensation will save us much altercation," while Lafayette coldly labeled the drowning *"peut être un heureux accident"* (perhaps a fortunate accident).

The appointments of de Kalb and Pulaski were among the Congress's last actions before decamping for York. On September 26, Howe's army marched unopposed into Philadelphia. He had again outmaneuvered Washington, who was camped forty miles away guarding against an attack on the arsenal at Reading that never came. Howe's forces overwhelmed Anthony Wayne at the Battle of Paoli, and Washington suffered another defeat a week later at Germantown. But the Continental Army had not yet given up on the capital. The Delaware River would have to be the lifeline for the British garrison, as provisions could only come by ship. If the American forts could be held, the British would be starved out. Instead, Howe's troops easily captured the undermanned Billingsport, which was the farthest downstream, and began attacking the two forts closest to the capital. Fleury took charge of Fort Mifflin's defensive works, while Plessis did the same at Fort Mercer, and together they directed the daily gunfire that repelled British attacks for six weeks, while nightly repairing the damage from ships' guns and shore-based artillery. In mid-November, an all-out assault by Howe finally drove the Americans from their redoubts. Philadelphia was now firmly under British control.

Washington's army, which had started the year heartened by its showing at Trenton and Princeton, was now reduced to despondency. The defeats at Brandywine and Germantown, and the loss of Philadelphia, stood in stark contrast to the news of Horatio Gates's stunning victory at Saratoga. Rumblings of Washington's inadequacy began circulating in the Continental Army and in the Congress. An anonymous letter titled "Thoughts of a Free Man" appeared on the steps of the Pennsylvania State House, expressing general dismay at the state of the military. More pointed barbs from the Lee-Adams faction in the Congress suggested that Gates should replace Washington as commander in chief, a view that Gates himself thoroughly endorsed. A short-lived whisper campaign to unseat Washington later became known as the Conway Cabal, although Thomas Conway played only a minor role. Conway was only one of many officers, most notably the former quartermaster general Thomas Mifflin, who thought more highly of Gates than Washington. Conway's fault was that in an ill-conceived letter to Gates, he alluded to Washington as a "weak general." Washington got wind of this and directly confronted Conway, who denied writing those words and tendered his resignation. The Board of War, which the Congress had created to exert more administrative control over Washington and was now led by Gates and Mifflin, flexed its muscles by instead promoting Conway to major general and making him inspector general in charge of the training and organization of the Continental Army. Even though the Conway Cabal never amounted to more than a few gossipy letters, it nevertheless strained the relations between Washington and some of his most trusted generals, just at the time when his army was facing one of its greatest hardships—the winter at Valley Forge.

CREATING A PROFESSIONAL CONTINENTAL ARMY AT VALLEY FORGE

With the cold fast approaching, Washington had to decide quickly whether to prise Howe from Philadelphia or set up an encampment, and if he were to choose the latter, where to do so. On November 24, 1777, he called together a council of war with fifteen of his senior officers, including Knox, Greene, Sullivan, and Stirling. For the first time among them were Johann de Kalb and Louis Lebègue Duportail, the latter of whom had been serving as chief of engineers since July and had been promoted to major general just a few days earlier. Washington's purpose for the council that day was to have each officer provide his opinion regarding "the expediency of an attack upon Philadelphia." His army had almost no experience surrounding and taking a fortified city, which had been the hallmark of many European conflicts in the previous hundred years. He needed sound advice, not simply on the tactics, but also on the logistical and strategic implications of such an assault.

As Washington reviewed the written opinions that came back to him—only four were in support, eleven against—Duportail's rejection of the attack stood out for its command of the issues and precision of analysis. It not only reflected his years of training and experience in European-style warfare, but also marked him as that rare individual who could keep high-level strategy at the forefront while demonstrating a superb grasp of technical details. More important, Washington surely would have felt that moment *quand les grands esprits se rencontrent*—when great minds meet. The previous year, soon after the Battle of Long Island, Washington had explained to the Congress his Fabian strategy: "We should on all occasions avoid a general action, or put anything to the risk, unless compelled by a necessity, into which we ought never to be drawn." The subsequent war of posts had drawn loud criticism from the Congress and some of his generals, but had also kept the Continental Army intact. Now Duportail had independently come to the same conclusion, criticizing the notion of a frontal assault on Philadelphia without a viable route of retreat in case the assault failed. "To attack an enemy in their lines appears to me a very difficult and dangerous project . . . [which] exposes our army to a total defeat in case it does not succeed," he argued, asking rhetorically, "Should we stake the fate of America on a single action?" This was the very question Washington had been grappling with, and now he found someone with a sure and practiced eye to help him answer it. Here was a man Washington could and would lean upon for mature counsel as the war with Britain broadened and grew.

With the decision taken not to attack Philadelphia, Washington's next task was to establish a winter encampment, and once again he turned to his war council for advice. The area near Lancaster and Reading was rejected as being too far from the capital, for as Duportail presciently noted, "If war should be declared between France and England, and General Howe, from a dread of finding himself blocked up in the spring by a French fleet, should wish to quit Philadelphia," then the Continental Army would need to be within striking distance of the British retreat. Washington instead chose a heavily wooded plateau near the Schuylkill River called Valley Forge, named for the ironworks on the Valley Creek. Surrounded by hills that protected against surprise attack, near to farmland for foraging, and endowed with plenty of timber to build huts and make fires, it was a strategically sound location even though just twenty miles from Howe's forces. The twelve thousand soldiers and assorted camp followers marched onto the plateau on December 19, where Washington turned over the direction of building and fortifying the camp to Duportail. His first task was to construct shelter for the men. Although his English was still limited—John Laurens, son of the president of the Congress and Washington's aide-de-camp, translated for him—he quickly drew up maps and plans, crisply gave orders to the soldiers, and efficiently followed them through. "The [soldiers] appeared to me like a family of beavers; every one busy," noted Thomas Paine, who chanced to be at the encampment, "some carrying logs, others mud and the rest fastening them together." With over a thousand huts, what became America's fourth-largest city in terms of population took shape in the space of about six weeks.

With shelter assured, Duportail next set to fortifying the camp. The site had good natural defenses that he skillfully exploited. The north side of the camp backed to a deep and wide portion of the Schuylkill River, which he defended with a classic Vauban star-shaped redoubt. There was good high ground on three sides on which he created a series of barricades, entrenchments, and redoubts. Large military avenues crisscrossed the site, allowing for rapid deployment of troops. The winter at Valley Forge was not particularly harsh—average temperatures were actually above freezing—but with the quartermaster general's position vacant after

Mifflin's departure, the inability to obtain basic supplies like entrenching tools made even minor tasks maddeningly difficult. Work musters shrank as twenty-five hundred men were lost through disease and malnutrition, and another fifteen hundred through desertion. Despite these hardships, by late March 1778 Duportail reported to the Congress that the defenses were complete, well before the fighting season had begun. This was not merely conceit on the part of the French engineer; General Howe later explained that he did not go after Washington that winter or spring because "the entrenched situation of the enemy at Valley Forge did not . . . justify an attack upon that strong post [and] having good information that the enemy had strengthened the camp by additional works . . . I dropped all thoughts of an attack."

Duportail had laid out a substantial Grand Parade in the middle of Valley Forge for drilling and training soldiers, but at first it went largely unused. Pulaski had wanted to equip and train a cavalry corps there, but the forage was so poor that the horses were dying of starvation. Washington instead sent him to Trenton, where he and Kovats drilled a new cavalry squadron. Thomas Conway, who should have been marching the troops up and down the parade ground, found himself effectively shut out by Washington, who mistrusted both the new inspector general and the Board of War that had installed him. Even Conway's fellow countrymen did not forgive his role in the effort to discredit their commander in chief; Nathanael Greene reported, "The Marquis Lafayette, and all the other French gentlemen, will hardly speak to him."

Lafayette, who had been given a division by Congress after his conspicuous bravery at Brandywine and a few later skirmishes, should have been out training his troops, but he, Conway, and de Kalb were nowhere to be seen. Horatio Gates, as president of the Board of War, was convinced after defeating Burgoyne that Canada would now be easy pickings for conquest—this despite the fact that Montgomery and Arnold's invasion in 1775 had ended in disaster, and even after Benjamin Franklin, accompanied by Bonvouloir, had gone to Canada on a diplomatic mission in 1776 and singularly failed to win it over to the American cause. Without Washington's knowledge or consent, Gates ordered Lafayette to lead an invasion of the Canadian provinces. Lafayette at first refused to get caught in the tug-of-war between Gates and Washington—he respected Gates but was firmly allied with his "father and friend"—until Washington gave his approval. Lafayette departed in February for Albany, with de Kalb and Conway appointed as his subordinate commanders. There they were to lead an expedition composed of New England militia and Hazen's Second Canadian Regiment, but when they arrived later that month barely half the troops needed were fit for duty, and none of the supplies or equipment had arrived. With the invasion now abandoned, Lafayette and de Kalb returned to Valley Forge, while Conway, left behind at Albany in a backwater administrative position, again submitted his resignation. By late April it was accepted by the Congress, and Conway returned to France soon after.

The absence of an official inspector general was hardly felt back at Valley Forge, for Washington had just appointed a Prussian drillmaster to unofficially carry out those duties, and in doing so would transform his Continental Army from a demoralized rabble into a solidly professional body that achieved his ideals of "discipline and subordination." Friedrich Wilhelm, Baron von Steuben, was born in Magdeburg in 1730, and rose to captain of infantry in the Prussian army during the Seven Years' War. Steuben was granted the title of *Freiherr* (roughly, baron) while chamberlain in a minor German court, but by 1775 was out of work. In June 1777, he came to Paris to ask for a commission from his old comrade in arms Saint-Germain, but the minister of war's reforms were already placing many senior French officers out to pasture. Instead, Saint-Germain introduced Steuben to Beaumarchais, with the expectation that the Prussian officer could find useful employment in America. Beaumarchais in turn presented Steuben to Franklin and Deane, who agreed to provide him with letters of recommendation that greatly exaggerated his rank—they described him as a lieutenant general—and his accomplishments. In September, Steuben, accompanied by his idealistic seventeen-year-old aide-de-camp, Pierre-Étienne du Ponceau, and his dog, Azor, boarded Beaumarchais's ship *Flamand* in Marseilles, arriving at Portsmouth in December. In February 1778, they, along with Beaumarchais's agent, Théveneau de Francy, presented themselves to the Congress at York. With the backing of Horatio Gates, Steuben and du Ponceau were commissioned as captains and sent to Valley Forge, accompanied by Pierre Charles L'Enfant.

Washington was at first wary of Steuben, given his endorsement by Gates so soon after the collapse of the Conway Cabal. That was not the case for Washington's young French-speaking aides John Laurens and Alexander Hamilton, who delighted in Steuben's stories of military campaigns and shared his Enlightenment ideals. For several weeks they followed the portly German and his ever-present Azor around Valley Forge, happily translating for Washington his blunt pronouncements and commonsense recommendations. The Prussian military—"an army with a country"—was widely considered the finest in Europe, and Steuben had spent his entire career under its formation, so even if he had been just a captain, he knew exactly what he was looking at and what to do to improve it. By early March, the commander in chief was convinced he had found his man. He told Steuben that he was to be acting inspector general, since Conway up in Albany still held that official appointment, but otherwise he had full authority to command men and give orders.

Steuben's plan was to create a universal system of drill and maneuver by training a hundred-man company, each one handpicked from every brigade in the army, who would then be sent back to act as drill instructors for their units. The train-the-trainers approach was the only way to get the entire army ready for the fighting season, which was less than two

Frederick William Augustus, Baron von Steuben (1730–1794). Charles Willson Peale, after Charles Willson Peale, 1781–1782, oil on canvas

months away. On March 19, he formed the men up on the Grand Parade and started his instructions with the most basic exercise, how to march in formation. Instructions on loading and firing muskets, and fixing and unfixing bayonets, were broken down into the most basic steps and ceaselessly repeated. The European-style warfare that the Continental Army was now engaged in required men to form and maintain uniform lines of battle under fire and in the face of heavy casualties. Such discipline of movement could only be attained by constant practice of the most basic steps.

Each day new drills were added—slow march, quick march, oblique step, turns. Each day, Steuben barked a new set of orders at the troops. Hamilton, Laurens, and du Ponceau, along with his new staff members Teissèdre de Fleury and Benjamin Walker, struggled to keep up with the translation. As with Beaumarchais, Steuben's English was limited to the occasional "Goddam," but there was no mistaking his French and German invectives. At times he would beckon his aides to "come and swear for me in English, these fellows won't do what I bid them." After each new maneuver was learned in the morning, company commanders would separate and teach their units in the afternoon. By the third week Steuben had battalions and even entire regiments drilling up and down the Grand Parade in increasingly complex maneuvers—not just straight ahead but wheeling from column march (soldiers in a line like ants) to a line of battle (marching abreast). When Lafayette and de Kalb returned in April from their failed Canada expedition, they saw not merely a collection of soldiers, but an army that could drill and fight as a unit.

The opportunity to demonstrate that army's skill and discipline was soon in coming. The beginning of May brought two welcome pieces of news. Conway's resignation had been accepted, and Washington lost no time proposing Steuben to the post of inspector general with the rank of major general. The Congress quickly agreed, having believed Deane and Franklin's story about his previous rank. The second piece of news was the announcement of the long-awaited treaty of alliance with France, which spread through Valley Forge like a warm breeze after the winter's chill. The normally dignified Washington even allowed the effusive Lafayette—for whom he had instructed his doctors at Brandywine to "treat as if [he] were my own son, for I love him as such"—to clinch him in an embrace, acting more like a close family member than as his superior officer.

The commander in chief instructed an equally overjoyed Steuben to celebrate the alliance by preparing a Grand Review that would show off the army's newfound abilities. At nine o'clock on May 6, 1778, the cannon boomed as the ceremonies began. The troops dressed their lines and marched out by files onto the Grand Parade, feet and arms swinging in cadence, as brigade after brigade strode past Washington and his staff. Forming two lines of battle, they waited until the cannon salute—thirteen salvos from the artillery park past the far end of the parade ground—to raise their muskets to their shoulders and commence a rolling fire, known as a *feu de joie,* which rippled down each line and was repeated twice more until the smoke obscured the view. It was a remarkable display of precision, which John Laurens described to his father as "giving sensible pleasure to every one present. . . . The plan as formed by Baron von Steuben succeeded in every particular." The deprivations of winter were forgotten as the enlisted men were treated to an extra ration of rum, while the officers enjoyed "strong wine and other liquors." Their merriment would have been tempered with the knowledge that these parade-ground displays would soon be put to the test on the field of battle.

As the fighting season opened in May, Howe remained in Philadelphia, and Washington once again polled his general officers on whether they should attack. Duportail once again counseled caution, arguing that the Continental Army should remain at Valley Forge until the British came out, which they eventually must do as defense of the city was becoming untenable. He then went on to assert, in his halting English, "The more I reflect upon the matter . . . the more it seems to me impossible that the British can reduce America by arms, at least so long as the Americans behave himself properly. If there is any cause of reducing it, we should look for that cause in the American army itself." He had put his finger precisely on both the great hope and the profound dread in the three-year-old war. The United States was altogether too vast, and its population too dispersed, for the British army both to hold cities like New York and Philadelphia and still defeat the Continentals at every turn. However, the Continental Army had been suffering from want of arms, munitions, and men for much of that period, and a single decisive British victory, such as that which almost occurred at the Battle of Long Island, might destroy the military and political underpinnings of "The Cause," at least temporarily. That possibility had seemed very real when the troops had despondently marched into Valley Forge just a few months earlier.

The winter at Valley Forge had seen the Continental Army at its nadir. Yet with the spring came new hope. Troops began to fill the ranks once again, from a low of around 8,000 to almost 13,500. Steuben's intensive training was beginning to have its desired effect of creating discipline and order in those ranks. Those troops were now well armed with muskets and gunpowder, which Beaumarchais, Penet and Pliarne, Gardoqui, and many others supplied. They were also well clothed, as the uniforms manufactured in Montpellier, France, and Placencia, Spain, began arriving in New England ports and were immediately loaded onto wagons bound for Valley Forge, where they were received, undoubtedly with enormous gratitude, by the newly appointed quartermaster general, Nathanael Greene.

The spring's tidings brought additional good news. The British cabinet had just sent orders to Henry Clinton, Howe's replacement as commander in chief, to shift eight thousand troops to defend Florida and the West Indies, in response to the French entry into the war. Clinton was obliged to consolidate his remaining forces, and prepared to evacuate Philadelphia in order to avoid "finding himself blocked up by a French fleet," as Duportail had predicted. With no naval transport available for fear of being intercepted by French warships, Clinton was forced to march his ten thousand troops (out of the seventeen thousand that had arrived just nine months earlier) and accompanying wagon train overland to New York City. At 3 a.m. on June 18, they climbed into flat-bottomed boats that took them across the Delaware River to New Jersey, and began their trek north. Washington learned of the evacuation that afternoon and ordered advance brigades under Anthony Wayne and Charles Lee—who until recently had been a British prisoner of war, before being exchanged—to follow Clinton. Early the next morning, the first divisions under Lafayette (but without de Kalb, who was taken ill) marched out of Valley Forge, followed by Stirling and Greene.

On June 24, as the two armies moved toward a rendezvous, Washington called a council of war to decide whether to attack, or to let Clinton go and await the expected arrival of the French expeditionary force. Several of his generals, including Lee, argued for a continuation of the Fabian strategy. Duportail, who until now had counseled caution, thought that this was the right time to strike at the British, when they were on the move and vulnerable. Steuben agreed, as did Wayne and Greene. Washington compromised and ordered a small contingent to nip at Clinton's heels. Lafayette, who knew Clinton personally from his foray to London and undoubtedly wanted to meet him again on the battlefield, immediately wrote a letter to his commander in chief on behalf of Duportail and Steuben, expressing "how sorry, distressed they were to see that we were going to lose an occasion which may be reputed as one of the finest ever offered."

Whether he would attack or harass, Washington still needed to know when Clinton would be vulnerable, and dispatched Steuben and his aides to shadow his army. They barely left their saddles during three days and nights of scouting, enduring sweltering heat and torrential rains. By that time Washington had changed his mind and was determined to attack Clinton's vulnerable rear in force. Lee demanded to lead the advance charge in lieu of Lafayette, to which Washington agreed. Well before dawn on Sunday, June 28, Steuben reported back that the British, who were settled near the Monmouth Courthouse crossroads, had broken camp and were on the road. Lee sent his troops groping toward the British rear in the rising heat—by 9 a.m. it was already above ninety degrees—without adequate intelligence, knowledge of the terrain, or plan of battle. Nor did he know that Cornwallis's division, the best-trained of Clinton's army, was at his front. Cornwallis immediately ordered a flanking attack on Lee's right, where Lafayette's and Wayne's brigades were exposed. The American lines began to collapse. Lee, fearful of being surrounded, ordered a general retreat and asked Duportail to reconnoiter a defensible location.

As Lee fell back toward the main body of the American army, he found himself face-to-face with Washington, who dressed him down for his retreat and dismissed him from the field (he was later court-martialed from command). Taking charge of the battle, Washington quickly set up a defensive line along the Monmouth–Freehold road, with Greene on the right and Stirling on the left. In front of the line on high ground Greene placed Mauduit du Plessis and four cannon to provide enfilading fire. As Cornwallis came on to attack Greene's right wing, a steady cannonade and withering musket fire turned the renowned British general back. Stirling's left wing, with Lafayette in command of the second line, was assailed repeatedly by Clinton's elite 42nd Highland Regiment of Foot (the Black Watch), and each time it held its ground. Steuben raced between the rear and the front lines, skillfully feeding reinforcements to key positions. The battle raged back and forth under an unrelenting sun—perhaps half of the deaths in battle were due to heatstroke—before Clinton finally broke off the battle around 6 p.m. By the next morning the British had already slipped out under the cover of darkness and were heading to Sandy Hook, where two days later they were ferried to New York City.

The battle was a strategic defeat for the Americans but a tactical draw. More important, it gave the entire Continental Army, from George Washington right down to the infantry privates, a new sense of professionalism. Many of the same soldiers who had turned and run at Brandywine had now stood toe-to-toe with Britain's best troops and held their own under withering fire and bayonet charges. Even Alexander Hamilton, still a headstrong youth prone to criticism of the army, admiringly noted, "The behavior of the officers and men in general was such as could not easily be surpassed. Our troops, after the first impulse from mismanagement, behaved with more spirit & moved with greater order than the British troops." The difference between the soldiers at Brandywine and those same men at Monmouth was "discipline, which we understand by subordination or an obedience to orders." That newfound discipline was due entirely to Steuben's training and organization, and just as important for the Prussian officer, everyone recognized it.

That widespread recognition did not translate to a permanent field command, to Steuben's great disappointment. In truth, there was little he could have done in that position. The Battle of Monmouth would turn out to be one of the last major engagements in the North. The French fleet, which had arrived shortly after the battle, was unable to attack New York City, and would have little impact on the British forces at Newport, Rhode Island. During this relative lull in activity, the Continental Army began to lose some of its newly acquired discipline. Steuben saw that the training he had begun at Valley Forge was just the first step; the entire army needed a formalized set of rules and procedures, such as existed in all European armies, which could be universally applied. Washington agreed and ordered Steuben to carry out the task. As the leaves fell in the autumn of 1778 and the army camped at Middlebrook, New Jersey, Steuben all but locked himself in a home in Philadelphia with reams of paper and flocks of quills to write those regulations in the form of a drill manual. With his aides du Ponceau, Fleury, and Walker to translate and interpret his work, and L'Enfant to draw and etch the plates and figures, Steuben spent the winter of 1778–79 synthesizing and adapting Prussian and French army regulations into an abbreviated form that American soldiers could readily use. Much of their time was spent simplifying drills into their most basic elements—instead of requiring six steps to bring a musket from shoulder to at-rest, for example, it now required two steps. The *Regulations for the Order and Discipline of the Troops of the United States,* better known as the Blue Book for its sky-blue paperboard cover, was published in March 1779. Right away it became the benchmark by which Washington enforced discipline down the ranks, and remained the army's standard manual for the next thirty years.

At the same time as the Blue Book was being conceived, Duportail was trying to re-create another fixture of European armies, a corps of engineers. While wintering at Valley Forge, he drafted a plan for a unified command of engineers to enable coordinated planning of fortifications, defenses, and sieges. Washington strongly endorsed Duportail's plan, but the Congress demurred, leaving engineers to work without clear lines of discipline and authority. Complications with this ad hoc arrangement came to a head with the reinforcement of West Point on the Hudson River. The promontory was referred to as the "Gibraltar of the Hudson" and the "key to the continent," because its sharp bends and tidal currents made it a natural choke point to cut off any shipping traffic to the interior. After the Battle of Saratoga, the Congress directed Washington to fortify the Hudson River defenses against any attempts to follow Burgoyne's unsuccessful campaign to split the United States in two. Washington in turn assigned Duportail's second in command, Louis des Hayes de La Radière, to take charge of designing and building the stone fortifications at West Point, which he began in January 1778. Meanwhile, another engineer named Thomas Machin began fabrication of a great iron chain boom that would stretch across the river at the promontory, which would slow or stop enemy ships so that cannon on the heights above could take them under fire.

The problems with the lack of clear lines of authority began in March 1778. While La Radière was away from West Point, Horatio Gates sent *his* engineer, Thaddeus Kosciuszko, to take over construction of the works there. After leaving Philadelphia the previous year, Kosciuszko had been indispensable to Gates at Ticonderoga and most critically at Saratoga, where he identified Bemis Heights as the place to make a stand and supervised the placement of fortifications and cannon that kept Burgoyne in check. When La Radière returned to West Point, he was furious to find Kosciuszko directing the works he had begun. Even though the Conway Cabal had already collapsed, the two engineers were caught in the continuing power struggle between Washington and Gates. Egos also were in play on both sides, as the French engineer believed that Kosciuszko was an untrained dilettante, while the Polish engineer scoffed at what he saw as overly elaborate plans on the part of La Radière. Washington attempted to calm the situation by recalling La Radière but ordering Kosciuszko to follow Duportail's recommendations on the final design. Order was finally restored when another, more compatible member of Duportail's entourage, Jean-Baptiste de Gouvion, was assigned to assist Kosciuszko, and together they completed the works by the following spring.

The French engineers also found themselves the victims of another power struggle between the two congressional factions: the majority, which supported the French alliance, and the minority "party of the opposition," as the French ambassador Conrad Alexandre Gérard referred to the Adams-Lee faction, which attempted to stop or delay any foreign involvement. The original instructions from French minister of war Saint-Germain gave Duportail and his colleagues only a two-year leave of absence, which would end in the spring of 1779. The inability of the Congress to provide any clear direction or assurance of continued employment in the war led them to declare that they would return to France when their furloughs expired. Washington implored the Congress to finally take action on Duportail's plans, emphasizing how important it was for them to continue their work, and giving his personal endorsement of their abilities: "I have a high opinion of his merit and abilities, and esteem him . . . a man of sound judgment and real knowledge in military science. I have also a very favorable opinion of the other gentlemen." While the Congress mulled over its options, Gérard counseled patience to the disgruntled engineers. Finally on March 11, 1779, just as their furloughs were about to run out, the congressional majority managed to push through the creation of a Corps of Engineers, appointing Duportail as its first commandant while his countrymen filled out most of the ranks. As it happened, these actions were completed just in time, for a new British threat had just emerged that would require the expertise of Duportail's Corps of Engineers and the discipline found in Steuben's Blue Book to defeat.

On June 1, 1779, as the Congress feared, Clinton began a campaign to draw Washington into action along the Hudson River by capturing the Stony Point fort, just fifteen miles south of West Point. Washington ordered Anthony Wayne to recapture it. Attacking fortified positions was an integral part of an engineer's training, and Wayne assigned Teissèdre de Fleury, who had proved himself both a skillful engineer and an intrepid infantry commander, to lead the advance party. After identifying weaknesses in the fort's defenses, Washington and Wayne planned a daring night assault using handpicked troops. At midnight on July 16, Fleury's men scrambled up the rocky slope and enveloped the southern flank of the fort, while a diversionary attack commenced simultaneously to the north. Bayonets fixed, they chopped through the wooden outer works and rushed the defenders. Fleury was the first one over the inner wall, tearing down the British standard from the flagpole. The rest of Wayne's troops poured in, and by 1 a.m. the battle was over. With a loss of just 15 men, the Americans had captured the fort and its 624 defenders. Although it was too vulnerable to hold and defend—Washington followed Duportail's counsel and abandoned it just days later—the skill and discipline shown by the troops proved an enormous morale boost to the Continental Army. Just days after the battle, the Congress awarded Fleury a silver medal for having by his "personal achievements, exhibited a bright example to [his] brother soldiers." This was one of fewer than a dozen congressional medals awarded during the War of American Independence, and the only one given to a foreign officer.

SPANISH TROOPS BEGIN FIGHTING IN THE WAR WITH BRITAIN

On July 13, 1779, three days before the Battle of Stony Point and thirteen hundred miles to the south, Bernardo de Gálvez convened a *junta de generales* (war council) of his senior military officers to prepare for the defense of New Orleans against anticipated British attacks. Just weeks before, he had received the May 18 letter from his uncle José de Gálvez advising him of the Treaty of Aranjuez between France and Spain and the warning that war with Britain was to follow. That letter also instructed him to begin hostilities against British forces within two months of reception. The news of the imminent war had come as no surprise to Gálvez; his observers had already told him of the arrival in Florida of British and Loyalist troops from New York City, coming on the heels of their

Philadelphia evacuation. Other observers had already informed him of the state of British fortifications in the region. But the time for observations was now over, and mere protective measures were not what the pugnacious Gálvez had in mind. While his council made plans for New Orleans's defenses, Gálvez also prepared an offensive campaign against British outposts along the Mississippi and around the Gulf of Mexico that would rely upon speed and surprise, in the same way that George Rogers Clark took Kaskaskia, Cahokia, and Vincennes the year before.

On August 27, Gálvez and 667 troops of the Regimiento Fijo de La Luisiana and militia, including 9 American volunteers under Oliver Pollock, marched north out of New Orleans toward Fort Bute at Manchac on the shores of Lake Maurepas. They were not detected during their eleven-day march until they arrived at the gates of the fort, at which time Gálvez revealed to his men that he had received confirmation from Spain that war had been declared with Britain. By this time Manchac had been largely abandoned by the British, and the militia easily captured it without a loss.

The next target was just a short march away. Baton Rouge had been heavily fortified with cannon and over five hundred well-armed troops, so Gálvez decided against a direct assault and instead laid siege. Within two weeks his artillery was properly placed to fire directly into the fort, and on September 21, after a few hours of cannonade, the British surrendered Baton Rouge as well as the town of Natchez farther upriver. In the meantime, an American captain named William Pickles, aboard the schooner *Morris,* which had been provided to the Continental Navy by Gálvez, captured the brigantine sloop HMS *West Florida,* eliminating the British naval threat on Lake Pontchartrain. With a series of lightning campaigns that lasted fewer than thirty days, Gálvez had wrested complete control of the lower Mississippi from Britain. The next steps would be to drive the British from Mobile and Pensacola, which, as José de Gálvez noted, were "the keys to the Gulf of Mexico."

Even if Mobile and Pensacola were critical to the Spanish strategy of retaking the Gulf of Mexico, the British presence on the Mosquito Coast could not be ignored. Matías de Gálvez, recently appointed as president and captain-general of Guatemala, had received the same notice from his brother that war with Britain was coming, and he correctly divined their strategy of a two-pronged attack to cut the Spanish empire in half at the modern-day region of Honduras and Nicaragua. In September and October 1779, Jamaica governor John Dalling sent Captain William Dalrymple to capture the northern port of Omoa on the Gulf of Honduras, but the following month Matías de Gálvez counterattacked and recaptured it.

The British and Spanish next turned their attention to the south, where in April 1780, Dalling sent another force of a thousand men to capture the Inmaculada Concepción fortress on the San Juan River, which was the primary access to Lake Nicaragua. Disease and sickness took their toll on the troops, including a young navy lieutenant named Horatio Nelson who had taken the lead in the expedition before dysentery laid him low and forced him to return to Jamaica. After a two-week siege marked by both artillery salvos and hand-to-hand combat, the Spanish surrendered. Matías de Gálvez, meanwhile, had hastily constructed a new fort on Lake Nicaragua at the mouth of the San Juan River, effectively bottling up the British troops and preventing their planned assault across the isthmus. For the time being, Central America was at a stalemate.

After his lightning campaign on the Mississippi, Bernardo de Gálvez was also at a stalemate, although for much different reasons. Mobile and Pensacola were bigger and more heavily fortified than Manchac and Baton Rouge, and to lay siege would require direct naval support from Cuba. In January 1780, Gálvez sent his aide-de-camp Esteban Miró to Havana to petition Captain-General Navarro and his naval commander, Juan Bautista Bonet, for assistance. For Bonet, the 1763 capture of Havana was still an open wound, and he balked at sending valuable ships on what he saw as a useless expedition: "[Havana] is worth more than fifty Mobiles and Pensacolas," he argued, worried that a weakened navy could invite another British assault. Nor could Gálvez rely on the Americans for their long-promised help in diverting British forces. Continental Army and militia units from Georgia had made several desultory forays from 1776 to 1778 to capture Saint Augustine, but never advanced more than a few miles into East Florida before being turned back. Up in Philadelphia, the Spanish representative Juan de Miralles worked assiduously with the French ambassador, Luzerne, to convince the Congress to plan another assault on East Florida, to no avail. Even George Rogers Clark's Virginia militia, which had previously received considerable Spanish support, failed to come to the aid of Fernando de Leyba when he repelled British attacks on Saint Louis in 1780. Gálvez, it appeared, would have to carry out his campaign alone.

Without naval reinforcements from Havana, Gálvez knew he could not attack the British capital at Pensacola, but Mobile was within his grasp and its capture would at one blow provide Spanish soldiers with a considerable supply of cattle from its surrounding ranches, while also depriving the British of their primary source of meat. Calling upon his former spy Jacinto Panis to plan the attack based on his hard-won intelligence, on January 11, 1780, Gálvez embarked his army of thirteen hundred men aboard fourteen vessels, including the captured sloop HMS *West Florida,* which he had unabashedly rechristened *Galveztown.* Although Mobile was just a short distance from New Orleans, a devastating storm and inept navigation extended the voyage to almost two months, so it was only at the end of February that the Spanish troops were outside the walls of Fort Charlotte.

As the Spanish laid in a weeks-long siege, Gálvez and the British commander, Elias Durnford, exchanged some of the most chivalrous correspondence to be found during the entire War of American Independence. Gálvez, in French, began by reminding Durnford that he was vastly outnumbered and suggested he surrender to avoid casualties. Durnford, in English, politely refused the offer but thanked Gálvez for "the generosity of your excellency," perhaps referring to the shipment of wheat he had sent to the starving garrison at Pensacola. Gálvez's envoy Francisco Bouligny knew Durnford personally, and together they drank "a cheerful glass" to each other's sovereigns. Durnford sent Gálvez wine, mutton, and a dozen chickens; Gálvez responded with more wine, cigars, and oranges. Meanwhile, the two armies traded fire as part of the town of Mobile was reduced to ashes. An intense bombardment on March 12 finally convinced Durnford that his garrison could no longer hold out, and two days later the terms of surrender were agreed to. A promised relief column from Pensacola was still miles away, unable to advance through the marshy terrain, and it turned back upon hearing the news of the capitulation. A few weeks later, a fleet from Havana under a reluctant Bonet—who had finally been goaded into sailing by Navarro—arrived just in time to garrison the captured town. Gálvez appointed his old friend Colonel José Manuel de Ezpeleta of the Navarro Regiment to be the garrison commander and the town's governor.

It was already too late to conduct Gálvez's hoped-for campaign against Pensacola before the summer heat set in. Instead of returning with his troops to New Orleans, Gálvez instead sailed to Havana aboard his sloop *Galveztown,* arriving on August 2 to begin planning an attack on the British capital for later that year. Such an assault would require a large fleet to operate with confidence in the face of the British, and this in turn meant that the French and Spanish navies, working together, would have to divert the British navy to other regions. That diversion had already begun with a series of naval actions on each side of the Atlantic that echoed the Bourbon war plans developed over a decade earlier, and even now was changing the War of American Independence from a regional conflict into a global war.

CHAPTER 5

The Sailors

Vice Admiral Edward Vernon's attack in 1741 on Cartagena de Indias (in present-day Colombia) was at the time the largest amphibious assault in recorded history, and would remain so until the Gallipoli and Normandy campaigns of the twentieth century. During the British-Spanish War of Jenkins' Ear, so named for a British merchant who claimed that a Spanish officer had cut off one of his ears for smuggling, Vernon set out in March 1741 with 135 ships and thirty thousand men under arms for what he assumed would be an easy capture of Spain's richest port in the Americas, even minting commemorative medals to celebrate his presumed victory. He did not count on the tactical brilliance of the man commanding the city's defense, Admiral Blas de Lezo y Olavarrieta.

A generation before Horatio Nelson was born, Blas de Lezo, also having lost an eye and limbs in combat, was the most feared fighting admiral on the Atlantic. He understood siege warfare through a lifetime of experience attacking and defending cities. His plan was to have the three thousand men under his command—a tenth of what the British were bringing to bear—wage a delaying action against Vernon, using the city's extensive fortifications and natural defenses to wear down the attackers while gambling that the rainy season beginning in April would force them to retreat. Although Vernon's initial forays through the Boca Chica inlet were successful, the well-disciplined Spanish troops repeatedly repulsed British advances even as the incessant downpours made sieges increasingly difficult, and while diseases like malaria and yellow fever decimated the tightly packed shipboard crews. The British were now losing ten men for every Spanish casualty. By May 20, with two-thirds of his original force dead, wounded, or sick, Vernon withdrew to Jamaica. As for Blas de Lezo, his triumph would be short-lived, as he died four months later from the wounds his already ravaged body had suffered in the city's defense.

The Battle of Cartagena de Indias was the first time that American colonial troops were deployed outside their own borders. The four-thousand-man American Regiment, which included a twenty-two-year-old infantry captain named Lawrence Washington, was often relegated to menial tasks like digging trenches or carrying supplies. When given the opportunity, though, they proved themselves effective soldiers. As Vernon was attempting to force the Boca Chica strait, he determined to destroy the particularly troubling Varadero battery on the south side of the inlet. The night of March 29, six American companies, including Lawrence Washington's, overwhelmed the Spanish defenses and spiked the cannon (i.e., drove iron spikes into the touchholes to prevent further use), with the loss of just six men. Lawrence left little written record of his wartime experience—his one surviving letter home simply states that "war is horrid in fact but much more so in imagination"—but it so marked him that upon his return in 1743 he renamed his inherited plantation Mount Vernon, in honor of his admiral at Cartagena de Indias.

The young George Washington revered his older half brother, and must have hung on his stories of naval battles. When he was just fourteen, at the instigation of Lawrence, he was set on joining the British navy as a midshipman, only to be stopped at the last minute by his mother, who was fearful of the harsh conditions that would await him aboard ship. Several years later, his interest in the sea and ships was again piqued when he took his first, and only, set of ocean voyages, sailing to Barbados to accompany Lawrence, who was seeking respite from the tuberculosis that would kill him just a few years later. The few surviving fragments of his journal showed that George Washington quickly and enthusiastically learned the rudiments of seafaring and navigation. The lessons gained from Lawrence's tales of battle and from his own maritime experiences almost certainly underpinned the landlubberly soldier's remarkably clear-eyed understanding of both the importance of and the limits to sea power.

During the first campaigns of the War of American Independence, Washington saw at first hand the enormous value of British sea power in the conduct of army operations. In March 1776, he watched William Howe evacuate his troops from Boston to Halifax on British navy transports, only to see those same troops reappear in July at Staten Island where they assaulted and conquered New York City. In May 1776, a British naval squadron sailed through the ice-packed Saint Lawrence River to attack the Americans still camped outside the walls of Quebec after their failed assault the previous winter, driving them from the city and out of Canada. The following month, a British squadron led by Commodore Peter Parker and Lieutenant General Henry Clinton tried but failed to take Charleston, South Carolina. Six months later, the two leaders regrouped their forces to lead a textbook amphibious descent on Newport, Rhode Island, which provided the British with a secondary naval base. In 1777, Richard Howe ferried his brother's army from New York City to Head of Elk, Maryland, in order to capture Philadelphia. Washington, in a letter mixing admiration and anxiety, admitted to John Hancock that "the amazing advantage the enemy derive from their ships and the command of the water, keeps us in a state of constant perplexity." His alarm was due in no small part to the fact that after two years of war, while his army and militia could claim several victories against the vaunted British army, he still could not muster an effective maritime response to British naval mastery.

Even as he contemplated with awe the importance of sea power as displayed by Britain, Washington also recognized the limitations he faced in creating a military force with comparable capabilities for combined land-sea operations. He had thus far been reasonably successful in creating an effective Continental Army in part because he could draw on the tradition of colonists fighting alongside British regulars, most recently during the French and Indian War. By contrast, the Americans had almost no tradition of fighting overseas in extended operations; the last time they had done so in strength was more than thirty years earlier, when Lawrence Washington and his American Regiment fought in the War of Jenkins' Ear, and when Richard Gridley with a colonial Massachusetts force helped capture Louisbourg during the War of the Austrian Succession.

Neither did the American colonies have any extensive naval tradition upon which to base a strategy of *guerre d'escadre,* or fleet against fleet, to counter the British threat. Such a strategy required the construction, operation, and maintenance of large ships of the line that could fight in a line of battle, each ship carrying from 60 to 110 cannon and accommodating up to a thousand men. The actual construction of warships was not the problem; there was plenty of suitable timber, and American shipbuilders had been building warships for the British navy for almost a century. But the fledgling nation still lacked adequate gun foundries and powder mills to supply naval cannon, and had no dockyard facilities to maintain large, complex warships. Nor could it support and train the enormous numbers of men necessary to keep a fleet ready for combat at sea. While the Baron von Steuben had demonstrated that he could go a long way to turning callow farmhands into well-ordered troops while overwintering at an encampment, naval gun discipline and seamanship (handling lines, sails, and capstans) could only be learned by continuous practice at sea over extended periods of time. As Britain, France, and Spain had already discovered over the previous two centuries, creating and provisioning a navy ready to fight at sea required a powerful, centralized government that could raise and spend large sums of money. Given the parlous and disjointed state of Continental finances, neither the individual colonies nor the fractious Congress could possibly create a European-style navy.

Instead, Washington decided to make use of that oldest of American maritime traditions, smuggling, to form the strategic basis for his first navy. The previous century of defying the Navigation Acts had honed shipbuilders' skills in creating small, fast vessels, and also sharpened the ability of ship's masters to slip past blockades and revenue cutters. These speedy merchant ships, properly manned and armed with light cannon, were ideal for waging an entirely different naval strategy—*guerre de course,* or commerce raiding. *Guerre de course* had long been the preferred strategy of smaller navies that could not afford to maintain large fleets of specialized ships of the line. Instead, schooners, sloops, and frigates (warships typically carrying between eight and forty-four cannon, used for patrol and escort) as well as converted merchant vessels would be employed in attacking an enemy's commercial shipping in order to destroy their supply lines, confiscate war materiel, and put a dent in their economy.

In the summer of 1775, with the Continental Army lacking the arms and gunpowder to sustain its siege of Boston, Washington asked the colonies of Massachusetts and Rhode Island to charter a fleet of armed schooners to wage *guerre de course* by capturing British storeships that were resupplying Howe's troops, and by raiding arsenals in Britain's island colonies. These privateers—private individuals carrying letters of marque authorizing the capture of enemy vessels and assets—were at first reasonably successful in resupplying Washington's soldiers. A raid on Bermuda seized over 100 barrels of gunpowder, the schooner *Lee* captured a wayward British transport carrying 2,000 muskets and 30 tons of shot, and the schooner *Franklin* brought in another transport hauling 10 cannon, 1,000 muskets, and 150,000 pounds of powder. As the British navy ramped up its patrols and blockades, though, these powder cruises became less and less effective.

Meanwhile, in October 1775, the Continental Congress authorized the creation of the Continental Navy with the purpose, as John Adams explained, of "distressing the enemy, supplying ourselves, and beginning a system of maritime and naval operations." It would never resemble a European navy with large numbers of ships of the line; the largest vessels in the Continental Navy would be the thirteen frigates the Congress ordered later that year. The Congress also issued letters of marque and commissioned naval officers like Lambert Wickes and John Paul Jones, both of whom had previously served as merchant shipmasters, and later authorized Benjamin Franklin in Paris to also hand out commissions (one of which he awarded to the former privateer Gustavus Conyngham). Finally, the Congress authorized the creation of the Continental Marines, tasked with protecting the officers and crew of the ships, but more importantly to serve as sharpshooters in the rigging during ship-to-ship engagements. Meanwhile, most of the individual colonies and states, including Rhode Island, Massachusetts, Georgia, and South Carolina, created their own navies to protect their coastlines, waterways, and harbors.

In practice, the Continental Navy acted much the way privateers did, carrying out *guerre de course* assaults on shipping and raids on British outposts, like the March 1776 powder raid on Nassau in the Bahamas. As the war expanded, officers like Jones, Wickes, and Conyngham traveled farther afield to attack British shipping in European waters. Adams was convinced that commerce raiding was a "short, easy, and infallible method of humbling the English," but this was based more on wishful patriotism than on actual fact. The Continental Navy never represented much of a threat to Britain's conduct of the war. It was almost always outgunned—most American ships carried six-, nine-, or twelve-pound cannon, while British escorts were generally armed with larger cannon, all the way to eighteen-pounders. It was also outnumbered—at its peak in 1777 it had just 34 vessels in operation compared with a British fleet numbering over 260 warships; and of the original 13 frigates, 10 were captured or destroyed in their first two years of operation, while only one survived the war. Nor were the privateers particularly damaging to the British economy. It was true that the insurance company Lloyds of London estimated that the nation lost 2,200 vessels to American privateers out of 3,400 total lost in the war. It was also true that, due to privateering, Britain had to divert its warships to escort merchantmen. Because of these factors, freight rates and shipping expenses increased. But to put this in perspective, these losses were proportionally half those of the War of the Grand Alliance in the 1690s, in which the French navy had also adopted a *guerre de course* strategy against the superior British fleet. In that war as in the War of American Independence, Britain simply absorbed the damage by building or capturing ships faster than it lost them, without suffering any public outcry or demands by Parliament for action. Against the most powerful navy and merchant fleet on earth, the Continental Navy and its supporting privateers would prove to be little more than annoyances. America needed a much larger naval force to turn the tide of the war against Britain, and for that it would have to look across the Atlantic.

THE FRENCH NAVY ENTERS THE WAR

Both Washington and the Congress knew that America could not afford to take on the British navy by itself. That was apparent as far back as 1775, when Bonvouloir reported after meeting with Franklin and his colleagues that the Americans "are convinced they cannot defend themselves without a seafaring nation to protect them, and the only two powers which are able to help are France and Spain." Two years later, on October 11, 1777, after the British had occupied Philadelphia and the war seemed at its nadir, Johann de Kalb reported to his patron Charles-François de Broglie that the Americans were intent upon driving the British from the continent, except that "one obstacle remains which exceeds all others—the absence of a navy. Without assistance from abroad they will never get one." What de Kalb did not know was that even as he was writing his letter, Horatio Gates was surrounding the British at Saratoga, and that Burgoyne's surrender a week later would give Vergennes the pretext to form an alliance with the Americans and finally send them the navy they so desperately needed.

When Washington received word of the treaty of alliance in May 1778, his first thoughts were of his pressing manpower problems; he hoped that the prospect of arms, money, and troops would not lead to complacency but would rather cause the states to "be stimulated to complete their battalions." He would only later fully realize that it was the presence of French warships, not additional arms or men, that would change the fundamental nature of the war. The British, by contrast, understood far more quickly the naval ramifications of the French-American alliance. Until then, the British commander in chief, William Howe, had been free to position his forces up and down the former colonies and resupply them by sea as he saw fit, with little to fear from naval attacks. Now that France was sending ships of the line across the Atlantic, his replacement, Henry Clinton, would have to consolidate his troops and fortify his maritime supply lines. Back in London, Prime Minister North and his cabinet realized that their navy did not have the strength to simultaneously cover the enormous American coast and also protect their vital interests in the West Indies and Florida. For this reason, they ordered the evacuation of their troops in Philadelphia, using them to reinforce New York and also to shore up the defenses at Pensacola and in the West Indies. Further, the fear of a possible invasion of Britain meant that only the minimum number of ships could be detached from European waters. With the coming of the French fleet, the British navy for the first time in the war would be on the defensive.

Two months would pass from the news of the alliance before Washington even learned that France had sent a fleet to his assistance. On July 13, he received intelligence from the Congress that a large fleet under the Comte d'Estaing had arrived off the mouth of the Delaware River and was heading to New York. His letter to d'Estaing found him already at anchor off Sandy Hook, New Jersey, where he had just missed Clinton's evacuation of troops to New York City. While the two men would never meet in person—Washington sent his aides-de-camp John Laurens and Alexander Hamilton as his envoys, and d'Estaing sent his own aide-de-camp André Michel Victor, Marquis de Choin, as his—the tone of their correspondence marked an immediate and profound respect on both sides. D'Estaing referred to Washington as the "deliverer of America," while Washington lauded d'Estaing's "distinguished talents, experience and reputation." Before d'Estaing departed Toulon, the king had given him sealed orders to "attack the enemy in the place where I shall be able to inflict the most damage . . . in the Delaware [and] not only up to New York but also at any other port of North America." At the same time, d'Estaing was also directed to keep his fleet intact in order to defend the French colonies in the West Indies. Washington would not have been privy to the specifics of those orders, but he knew that the primary French objective was to destroy or drive out the British. Based on d'Estaing's renown and that of his officers, he had every reason to believe they would be successful.

Charles-Henri, Comte d'Estaing, born in 1729 into a long line of army officers and raised alongside Louis XVI's father, was groomed from a young age to serve in the highest echelons of the military. He was aide-de-camp to Marshall Maurice de Saxe during the War of the Austrian Succession, led major reforms of the French infantry, served with distinction in India during the Seven Years' War, and subsequently was promoted to lieutenant general. He then moved into the naval service, commanding a small squadron in the East Indies before being vaulted to the position of *chef d'escadre* (roughly, rear admiral). He profited from his royal connections, his career having included a stint in the diplomatic service in London and governorship of Saint-Domingue. Though he was physically brave as well as being a gifted and intelligent tactician, d'Estaing's extraordinarily rapid rise through the ranks, coupled with his arrogance and the fact that he was an army interloper into naval service, nevertheless earned him the enmity of many junior officers.

In the eighteenth-century *La Royale* (the French Royal Navy), the highest-ranking officers were the two elderly vice admirals in charge of the Mediterranean and Atlantic fleets. In 1777, Louis XVI authorized Sartine to create a third post, vice admiral of Asia and the Americas, specifically for the forty-eight-year-old d'Estaing. During the opening phase of the war with Britain, when Vergennes and Sartine decided to send a seventeen-ship squadron to America (which also carried Silas Deane and Conrad Alexandre Gérard to their new posts), d'Estaing was naturally placed in command. His officers were a veritable who's who of French naval luminaries. Aboard his eighty-gun flagship *Languedoc* was

Charles-Henri, Comte d'Estaing (1729–1794).
Charles Étienne Gaucher,
after François Sablet, engraving

Jean-Charles de Borda, who like d'Estaing had jumped from army to navy service, and was already famous for having perfected marine chronometers and several precision navigational instruments. Another army turned navy officer, Louis-Antoine de Bougainville, was the first French explorer to circumnavigate the globe (and have the tropical vine *Bougainvillea* named for him in the process) and commanded the seventy-four-gun *Guerrier*. Most of the other captains, such as Pierre André de Suffren and Jacques-Melchior, Comte de Barras, were well experienced in fighting the British during previous wars. D'Estaing apparently believed this would be an epic campaign, for he brought not just a printing press to publicize his achievements, but also one of France's most talented marine artists, Pierre Ozanne, who would capture the battles in exquisite ink-and-wash drawings.

D'Estaing had decent intelligence on Richard Howe's fleet that awaited him in New York. He knew that the sixty-four-gun flagship

HMS *Eagle* (which two years earlier had survived the attack by the Continental submersible *Turtle*), five other sixty-fours, and nine other vessels would be outgunned by his squadron. Upon his arrival at Sandy Hook, d'Estaing received word that a squadron of reinforcements under Rear Admiral John Byron had departed Portsmouth and was in pursuit across the Atlantic. True to his nickname, "Foul Weather Jack," Byron's fleet was dispersed by storms and would only straggle into American ports much later than planned. D'Estaing, unaware of this delay, grew more concerned with each passing day and resolved to attack Howe's fleet while it was still vulnerable in harbor.

As the French ships stood at anchor off Sandy Hook, d'Estaing could see Howe's ships moored in a defensive line inside the bay, just a mile or two away—yet he could not attack. The entrance to New York harbor, he learned from the American pilots whom Washington sent his way, was obstructed by a shallow sandbar just three and one-half fathoms deep (about twenty-one feet) at low tide. This explained why Richard Howe had elected to bring only the smallest ships of the line, sixty-four-gun ships, to New York. They drew just twenty-one feet of water and could come and go at high tide. Meanwhile, d'Estaing's bigger ships of the line, including his eighty-gun flagship *Languedoc,* drew twenty-five feet at the stern and could only clear the bar if they offloaded their heavy cannon, which of course would leave them vulnerable to destruction by the British fleet and shore batteries. After almost two weeks of trying but failing to cross the bar, d'Estaing ordered his fleet to weigh anchor on July 22 and make for Newport, Rhode Island.

The city of Newport, at the southern end of Aquidneck Island, commands the entrance of Narragansett Bay. It had been in British hands since 1776, its six thousand soldiers now under the overall command of Major General Robert Pigot, with a squadron of ten small warships under Captain John Brisbane's pennant. They were in theory surrounded by Americans, though in reality Major General John Sullivan, headquartered in Providence, had fewer than two thousand troops at his disposal. D'Estaing, with his one thousand embarked soldiers and a large contingent of sailors who would act as marine infantry, intended to help the Americans defeat and capture the British forces at Newport, which he knew was also the desire of both Washington and the Congress. When Washington received confirmation of d'Estaing's intent, he dispatched Lafayette with two brigades to reinforce Sullivan, and requested that militia from the surrounding states be called up. The Continental Congress also ordered several Continental Navy warships to assist d'Estaing's fleet, though none ever did. Meanwhile, contrary winds and a circuitous course intended (as on his transatlantic voyage) to throw the British off his scent meant that d'Estaing took over a week to make the short journey.

On July 29, d'Estaing arrived at Newport and promptly blockaded the entrance to Narragansett Bay. The following day Sullivan met with him aboard *Languedoc,* with John Laurens, who had ridden from New Jersey, acting as translator. The two commanders agreed to a pincer strategy in which American troops would land on the eastern side of Aquidneck Island while French troops would simultaneously land on the western side. Sullivan, however, asked to wait for the militia to form and for Lafayette's brigades to arrive. In the interim, Laurens arranged for d'Estaing's ships to be watered and provisioned, even as they deployed to seal off the British squadron from escape.

Brisbane, anxious to prevent the French from landing and not wanting his ships to be captured, began scuttling some vessels as blockships and blowing others up. Among the scuttled ships was the prison hulk *Lord Sandwich,* formerly HMS *Endeavour* on which James Cook had embarked for his celebrated around-the-world voyage in 1768, just when Bougainville was nearing completion of his own circumnavigation. The French captain almost certainly was unaware of this coincidental encounter as he watched, undoubtedly with astonishment, as four British warships exploded, one after the other, raining books, paper, and debris for three miles around. With Brisbane's squadron now gone, it certainly appeared that the British position was untenable and that Pigot would soon have to capitulate.

By this time, Lafayette's brigades had arrived, as had militia and state regiments from around New England. The officers preparing for the assault upon Newport included many of the leading lights of the War of American Independence to date: Nathanael Greene, released from his quartermaster-general duties by Washington in order to support his home state; John Hancock, lately president of the Congress and now a general in the Massachusetts militia; Paul Revere, a lieutenant colonel in the Massachusetts State Artillery Regiment; Moses Hazen with his Second Canadian Regiment; and François-Louis Teissèdre de Fleury, at Lafayette's side. Massachusetts sent almost forty cannon and mortar, most of them likely forged in the Bridgewater foundries established by Marie Louis Amand Ansart de Maresquelle, who was also present at the battle as Sullivan's aide-de-camp. Five hundred muskets from the Springfield Armory, many doubtlessly from Beaumarchais's shipments, were distributed to the militia. Both Sullivan and d'Estaing were wary of the militia, due to their inexperience and the fact that their terms of enlistment were very short to allow them to harvest their crops. Lafayette, whose Steuben-trained and battle-tested soldiers were some of the best in the Continental Army, attempted to calm d'Estaing's fears by assuring him that "this militia would at least rattle the enemy while the French troops did the damage."

On August 8, d'Estaing led a heavy squadron into Narragansett Bay to cannonade British positions, then anchored in preparation for the planned combined descent on Aquidneck Island in two days' time. On August 9, d'Estaing allowed his troops to debark, for the first time in almost four months, on the adjacent Conanicut Island in order to give them the chance to exercise and prepare for battle. As they were milling about, Fleury rode up with a message from Sullivan: That morning he had learned that Pigot was already withdrawing British outposts back to the main lines at Newport, and though Sullivan had not consulted with d'Estaing before ordering his attack on the suddenly vulnerable enemy positions, he was now requesting French assistance. It was a prudent move, and Sullivan certainly had alerted his French counterpart as soon as possible, but nonetheless d'Estaing and his officers felt they were losing their chance for battle. D'Estaing, who was well known for having a temper "so violent that nothing approaches it," reportedly lashed out at Fleury for being more American than French. Just as quickly as he had exploded, he returned to being a leader and ordered his four thousand sailors and troops to link up with Lafayette's brigades already on Aquidneck Island. Shortly after 11:30 a.m., a sailor aboard *Languedoc* spotted sails to the southwest: one ship, then two, then a dozen, finally thirty-six. Richard Howe, his squadron reinforced with the first of Byron's ships from across the Atlantic, had arrived at the mouth of Narragansett Bay and was now threatening to bottle up the French fleet. Within an hour d'Estaing had passed the order to the French troops still on Conanicut Island to return to the ships "with all haste." At an evening conference that included Lafayette, d'Estaing and his officers concluded that the danger of being bottled up by the prevailing winds was too great to continue supporting the landings, as it put the fleet at risk from shore bombardment and fireships (of which Richard Howe had three), potentially preventing it from carrying out that other vital mission, to protect the French West Indies. Instead, the fleet would sail out to meet Howe on the open ocean. D'Estaing dispatched Fleury with a promise to Sullivan that he would return.

The following morning, August 10, the French warships slipped their anchors, leaving the hawsers tied to buoys to be retrieved later, took a pummeling as they sailed in a line ahead past the British shore batteries, and aimed directly for Howe's fleet. D'Estaing had the weather gage, meaning he was upwind and therefore had the advantage for maneuvering. Howe wisely kept his distance, hoping for a change in winds that would give him the tactical advantage. The next morning, as the two fleets jockeyed for position, heavy seas and darkening skies in the southwest signaled the onset of foul weather. They did not realize until late afternoon that it was in fact a massive, fast-moving hurricane, one that had already devastated Charleston, South Carolina, the day before. For two days the winds wreaked destruction on ships and scattered them across the Atlantic seaboard all the way to Cape May, New Jersey. *Languedoc* suffered the worst damage, losing first its bowsprit, which provides the primary structural foundation for the standing rigging, after which all the masts tumbled like dominoes. It then lost its rudder. With no stabilization or helm, the once proud flagship came sideways into the waves and rolled uncontrollably, heavy cannonballs smashing across the decks. The next day, d'Estaing feared he and his crippled vessel would be captured by the much smaller HMS *Renown,* until six intact French vessels drove it away. After *Languedoc* and other damaged ships were fitted with jury-rigged masts, the remains of the fleet arrived, just as d'Estaing had promised Sullivan, at their former Newport anchorages—still marked by their buoys—on August 20.

D'Estaing may have promised Sullivan that he would return, but he never vowed that he would remain. With his fleet shattered and Richard Howe certain to return with even more reinforcements from Byron, he and his officers elected to sail straight to the more protected harbor of Boston, which the king's orders had already directed them to do in the face of a superior enemy, and where the fleet could be repaired and made ready to depart for the West Indies. They would not stay to assist the American assault, despite imploring from Greene, Hancock, and even Lafayette to remain just two days more to complete the siege. To d'Estaing's practiced eye, Sullivan had done little to advance his position on Aquidneck Island against the British since the French departure ten days earlier, and it seemed doubtful that another forty-eight hours would result in a victory. Now it was Sullivan's turn to lash out in one of his famous rants, penning letters and even general orders that called French honor into question and accused France of "refus[ing] to assist" its ally. D'Estaing silently bore the insults, as on August 22 he once again slipped the anchors and made for Boston—though this time the hawser buoys were severed by Pigot's men, leaving the anchors lost at the bottom of the bay. Unknown to the French at the time, Richard Howe would choose d'Estaing's departure as his own signal to return to Britain.

A week later, as Sullivan was withdrawing his troops from Aquidneck Island, Pigot attacked in force on several fronts. As at the Battle of Monmouth, the Continental Army demonstrated its newfound discipline by continuing its rearguard action in an orderly manner. Greene directed a regiment with a series of skillful maneuvers into a gap in the Hessian lines, causing them to uncharacteristically retreat to a more defensible position. Other troops charged and captured British cannon. By August 30, the Americans had gotten off the island largely intact, leaving Newport in British hands.

By then, d'Estaing's fleet had limped into Boston harbor, where resentment against his troops flared up into a riot that left two French sailors dead. It took all of Washington's diplomatic savoir faire to smooth the ruffled feathers on all sides, to the satisfaction of Ambassador Gérard and especially that of d'Estaing, who continued to admire above all other Americans a man he would never meet. During d'Estaing's two-month stay in Boston while his ships were refitted, John Hancock presented him with a full-length portrait of Washington, which d'Estaing proudly hung in his cabin. Lafayette told his friend and commander, "I never saw a man so glad of possessing his sweetheart's picture, as the admiral was to receive yours."

Soon after this first, failed joint operation by France and America, Washington received word of the French and British declarations of war, and of the opening of hostilities at the indecisive Battle of Ouessant. Washington was already well aware that France was now officially in the fight, and the events of the past several months had convinced him how much the war hinged on naval support. At the same time, he understood that France alone might not have the naval power necessary to bring an end to the conflict. As he noted to Henry Laurens in November, "The truth of the position will entirely depend on naval events. If France and Spain should unite, and obtain a decided superiority by sea . . . France might throw in what number of land forces she thought proper, [while] England . . . could give no effectual aid to oppose them." He had no way of knowing that even as he wrote this letter, peace negotiations between Spain and Britain had ground to a halt, and that the Treaty of Aranjuez was in the offing. France and Spain would indeed unite their fleets, just not in the place where Washington expected it.

THE SPANISH NAVY ENTERS THE WAR; THE FRENCH AND SPANISH ARMADA FAILS TO INVADE GREAT BRITAIN, BUT GIVES RISE TO AN AMERICAN LEGEND

With France now officially at war with Britain and no further American exploits in his immediate future, in October Lafayette petitioned the Congress for a furlough to allow him to return home. "I made it my pride and pleasure to fight under American colors," he explained. "Now . . . that France is involved in a war, I am urged by a sense of my duty as well as patriotic love, to present myself before the king and know in what manner he judges proper to employ my services." The Continental Congress, hoping that Lafayette's presence in France would spur Louis XVI to offer more assistance, granted him leave and ordered him to Boston to meet the ship that would take him home. The newly commissioned frigate *Alliance*—renamed from *Hancock* in honor of the French-American treaty—soon after arrived in Boston with its captain, Pierre Landais, who had the previous year brought the Beaumarchais ship *Flamand* into Portsmouth with Steuben aboard. In the interim, the Congress had confirmed Landais's commission from Silas Deane, and the state of Massachusetts had granted him citizenship. While in Boston, he may have met his old commander Bougainville, with whom he had sailed around the world ten years earlier. *Alliance* weighed anchor on January 11, 1779, mooring at Brest the following month. On February 11, Lafayette arrived unannounced in Versailles at a midnight ball, where he was fêted as a hero. After a week's house arrest to atone for his disobedience to the king by going to America, he was back in the good graces of the court. He was even allowed to buy a colonel's commission in the French army, a promotion from his previous office as captain but certainly a step down from his American generalship.

Lafayette's American exploits opened doors for him that would normally be closed to a twenty-one-year-old aristocrat who was not even a general officer. He hunted with the king, met with Maurepas and Vergennes about the American alliance, discussed strategy with Navy Minister Sartine and Minister of War Montbarey, and became a frequent guest of Franklin and Chaumont at Passy. He was a whirlwind of ideas, proposing any number of expeditions, which he of course would lead. With Franklin's assistance he stumped for a renewed invasion of Canada, which Washington had already rejected before his departure, and which Vergennes firmly opposed. To the Swedish ambassador he proposed that King Gustav III send a fleet of ships to America that he would underwrite. With John Paul Jones, fresh from his raids on Ireland and Scotland and now arming, at Chaumont's expense, a converted merchant ship under the new name *Bonhomme Richard,* Lafayette proposed a series of descents along the Irish Sea, including a raid on Liverpool, with himself leading the troops while Jones commanded the squadron. None of these proposals came to fruition, despite the fact that France sorely needed a *coup de pouce* (a shot in the arm) in its war against Britain.

France had now been in the war almost a year, with little to show for it. D'Estaing's retreat from Newport had allowed Clinton to redeploy his troops from New York to support operations in the American South and in the West Indies, where French forces from Martinique, under its new governor-general, François Claude de Bouillé, had already captured the British island of Dominica. On November 4, 1778—the same day d'Estaing's fleet left Boston—Clinton sent a squadron with five thousand troops to support a descent on the French island of Saint Lucia, just south of Martinique, France's primary base in the eastern Caribbean. In a decisive attack on December 13, the local commander, Rear Admiral Samuel Barrington, seized the French strongholds and prepared his defenses. The following afternoon, d'Estaing, who had just arrived on station and learned of the attack only that morning, arrived with superior numbers of ships and men. After two halfhearted naval attacks and several ineffectual land assaults, he departed, leaving the strategically important island in British hands. Meanwhile, Clinton also detached an amphibious force under Lieutenant Colonel Archibald Campbell to capture Savannah,

which he did on December 29. The following month Campbell extended his conquests across the state of Georgia, claiming that he would be "the first officer . . . to take a stripe and star from the rebel flag of Congress," which was proved true when Georgia was restored under British rule several months later. Only the recapture in January 1779 of Fort Saint-Louis, a French slaving port in Senegal taken by the British during the Seven Years' War, helped buoy spirits back in France.

In truth, France needed more than a *coup de pouce;* it required a *coup de main*—a swift, decisive victory. It was just at this time that the secret negotiations on the Treaty of Aranjuez were reaching their conclusion, as Floridablanca maneuvered Vergennes into accepting his own plan for a *golpe de mano,* which would be a joint invasion of Britain that echoed the war plans first laid out by Choiseul and Grimaldi back in 1767. Those plans, along with the *revanche* strategy that underpinned them, had fallen out of favor in the French court after the fall of Choiseul in 1770. Louis XVI's wholesale rejection of the *Secret du Roi* upon his coronation certainly appeared to seal the fate of any invasion of Britain. Vergennes himself was not enamored of the idea, which would have required diverting the British navy with minor attacks overseas while directing the main attack across the Channel. All through 1778, the navy had been carrying out Vergennes's opposite strategy, actually developed by Sartine's right-hand man the Comte de Fleurieu, which was to probe close to home with a series of feints, such as d'Orvilliers at Ouessant, while actually sending a powerful fleet commanded by the navy's highest-ranking officer, the Comte d'Estaing, across the Atlantic to carry out the primary strikes in America and the West Indies.

Even so, several plans for invading Britain had already emerged, many of which resembled the schemes originally submitted to Choiseul. An army officer, Charles François Dumouriez, worked with the military engineer La Rozière, who had personally scouted out landing sites a decade earlier and submitted a plan that called for the occupation of the Isle of Wight as a jumping-off point to invade Portsmouth. A renegade British officer named Robert Mitchell Hamilton, who had joined the French navy in 1778, seconded this plan and provided intelligence that Portsmouth and the adjacent naval base at Gosport had only a thousand men garrisoned and could be easily captured. Finally, Charles-François de Broglie dusted off his 1765 plan of invasion and sent it directly to Louis XVI. It differed from other plans in that it envisioned an assault not on

Portsmouth but instead on London, where the financial and economic chaos would bring the nation to its economic knees. Despite the effort put into each, for some time those plans sat on the shelves in the ministerial archives.

Vergennes's own, earlier invasion scheme for Britain had been an effort, ultimately unsuccessful, to prevent Spain from attacking Portugal, so as to keep the various Continental alliances in check. These new invasion schemes, by contrast, carried the risk that a newly resurgent France could be seen as a threat by the Continental powers. For some time Vergennes was able to ignore them as he continued to peddle the narrative that Britain, not France, was the aggressor in this conflict. By March 1779, with the Aranjuez negotiations under way, he was forced to reconsider them and choose the one least likely to cause a diplomatic rift. Even if vengeance were not the goal of Vergennes and Floridablanca, the invasion plans had all the hallmarks of the Bourbon *revanche* strategy of their predecessors Choiseul and Grimaldi. An attack on London was considered too costly and likely to frighten France's allies. Vergennes instead settled on the Isle of Wight/Portsmouth strategy, on the grounds that it would weaken Britain both militarily and economically without provoking a major political backlash from Europe. Montbarey and Sartine, aided by Fleurieu, drew up plans for a joint attack in which thirty French and twenty Spanish ships of the line would rendezvous in mid-May at the northern coast of Spain before turning toward Britain. Once sea control had been established in the Channel, smaller vessels would transport a twenty-thousand-strong Army of Invasion from Brittany and Normandy for the amphibious descent, during which they would occupy the Isle of Wight and Gosport, then destroy the British fleet at Portsmouth. The final plans were sent to Spain by the end of March. The Conde de Aranda in Paris had been kept on the sidelines throughout these negotiations, but he was fully aware of what was happening and sent to Carlos III his own plan of assault on London, apparently based on a copy of de Broglie's plan that he somehow had obtained in secret. Floridablanca, who continued to be at odds with his ambassador, instead approved the Portsmouth strategy. In April, the Treaty of Aranjuez was signed, and the two navies began preparations for the campaign, even as the Marqués de Almodóvar was presenting Spain's final demands for a truce to the court of George III.

While France and Spain sent spies to Portsmouth and Gosport,

where they found undermanned garrisons and weak defensive works, they also stepped up dockyard activities to get their ships into service. Spain was actually the more prepared of the two. Minister of the Navy González de Castejón and his chief shipbuilder, Jean-François Gautier, had overhauled and improved the Spanish dockyard system, so that fast warships based on French design principles were steadily coming off the slipways. Back in France, however, Sartine was rushing to achieve the number of ships that back in 1776 he had determined were needed for the proposed naval campaigns. Most of the dockyards' efforts were directed at refitting older vessels, which averaged just half the cost of a new-construction ship—the 90-gun *Ville de Paris,* for example, was being refitted to carry 104 guns in order to face British three-deckers like the 100-gun HMS *Victory.*

Meanwhile, shipbuilders were so harried to complete the new-build warships still needed to meet Sartine's goals that in their haste to get the ships to sea they made disastrous mistakes. In 1778, François Guillaume Clairan-Deslauriers, one of the first shipbuilders to be trained in the new scientific methods of ship design pioneered by the French mathematician Pierre Bouguer, made an "unpardonable error in calculation," according to one naval officer, of the stability for three seventy-four-gun ships, *Pluton, Hercule,* and *Scipion,* so that when they went to sea they almost capsized. Shortages of timber—a perennial difficulty for all navies—also pushed back the timetable to have the fleet ready for action. Soon after the signing of the Treaty of Aranjuez, it was obvious that the proposed date of May 15 for the opening of the campaign was hopelessly optimistic, and a chagrined Vergennes informed the Spanish that the rendezvous would have to be postponed several weeks.

In truth, both navies were delayed by an even larger problem that afflicted even the vaunted British navy—lack of manpower. Under the flag of Lieutenant General (a naval rank similar to a rear admiral) d'Orvilliers, the hero of the Battle of Ouessant, the French fleet of twenty-eight ships of the line, plus frigates and other vessels, assembled in early June at Brest. The fleet was short four thousand sailors, which d'Orvilliers had to supplement with inexperienced army men drafted at the last moment, many of whom boarded the ships already ill from an epidemic that was just beginning to grip the French nation. On June 3 they set sail, arriving a week later at their rendezvous point at the Sisargas Isles just off the coast of Galicia in Spain. The thirty-nine Spanish ships of the line at Ferrol and Cádiz, under the overall command of Captain-General (admiral equivalent) Luis de Córdova y Córdova, who had served the *Real Armada* (Royal Spanish Navy) almost as long as its sixty-five-year existence, also faced delays due to lack of qualified officers and the need to quickly draft inexperienced hands from the local population. The Cádiz fleet sailed in late June, but due to contrary winds did not reach the rendezvous until July 23. By then, Carlos III had issued his de facto declaration of war against Britain. With the campaign now in motion, all sides girded for battle.

France and Spain had prepared meticulously for this invasion as far back as 1765, when Choiseul and Grimaldi first envisioned a combined Bourbon fleet, and had exchanged shipbuilders and artillery engineers so

Luis de Córdova y Córdova (1706–1796).
Anonymous, eighteenth century, oil on canvas

that their ships and weapons could operate side by side. It was therefore astonishing, even by the standards of the day, that these preparations had not extended to developing a common system of communications between the fleets. The problem lay not in the language—all of the Spanish officers spoke French—but in the signal flags. In the age of sail, each fleet commander developed his own system of signals to pass messages and instructions down the line of battle, which could extend for several miles. Smoke from artillery, fog, and spray often obscured the line of sight, so signal flags had to be as simple and visible as possible. Signal books were distributed among the ships to code and decode the flags.

D'Orvilliers was fortunate to have Jean-François du Cheyron, Chevalier du Pavillon, as his chief of staff. Pavillon was the author of several highly respected books on naval signals and tactics, as well as being the officer who drew up the French fleet's official signal book. A copy had been sent to Madrid back in March, but it did not reach Pavillon's counterpart, José de Mazarredo y Salazar, Córdova's chief of staff and a brilliant theoretician in his own right, until shortly before the Cadiz fleet weighed anchor. "I was very surprised to learn that the signal books had not been printed in Spanish, and that M. Mazarredo was obliged to copy them by hand since his departure from Cadiz," complained d'Orvilliers to Sartine. "I assure you that never before have two squadrons at sea had to improvise their signals, but that is what I have been forced to do." As soon as the Spanish fleet arrived, Pavillon set to work with Mazarredo, producing ten signal books in one week to distribute to the rest of the ships. Unfortunately, that left the French and Spanish commanders no time to train and exercise together before entering into battle.

With the two fleets joined into a single armada, they were arranged into seven squadrons. D'Orvilliers was in overall command of the fleet as well as leader of one combined French/Spanish squadron, while two French flag officers, Luc Urbain du Bouëxic, Comte de Guichen, and Charles-Auguste Levassor de Latouche-Tréville, and the Spanish lieutenant general Miguel José Gastón, led the other combined squadrons. Córdova, aboard his massive 112-gun flagship *Santísima Trinidad,* led an all-Spanish "squadron of observation" that would operate in reserve to attack the British during battle. Two more squadrons, led by Antonio de Ulloa and Juan de Lángara, would patrol the Azores to protect Spanish convoys returning from the Americas. On July 29 the combined armada of 150 vessels, larger even than the 128 ships of the original Spanish Armada of 1588, left the Sisargas Isles bound for the English Channel.

As the ships were under way, a nervously impatient Lafayette received a summons from Versailles that he was to participate in the Army of Invasion as a staff member to Lieutenant General Noël Jourda, Comte de Vaux, who had just been appointed in overall command of the expedition. Many reformed and retired officers were already clamoring to rejoin the army to finally give battle to their British enemy; even the Chevalier d'Éon volunteered, without success, to trade his dresses for an army uniform. Lafayette jumped at the chance for glory, even though the position was far beneath his previous generalship. He quickly found his post at Le Havre in Normandy, where about half of the thirty-one thousand troops—the other half were at Saint-Malo, Brittany—were waiting to board transports once d'Orvilliers had gained control of the Channel.

That number was well above the original twenty thousand men planned for the expedition, and comprised some of the best-trained soldiers in France. In September of the previous year, Minister of War Montbarey had ordered a massive exercise in Vaussieux, Normandy, in anticipation of an attack on England. There two different armies composed of four divisions each were pitted against each other in an elaborate set of maneuvers to determine whether tactics using "thin" (*ordre mince*) columns that emphasized firepower and movement were superior, as many of Gribeauval's theorists argued, to "deep" (*ordre profond*) columns that emphasized shock. Championing the *ordre profond* tactics was the decorated Lieutenant General Victor François, Duc de Broglie (Charles-François's brother), while leading the charge for the *ordre mince* was Lieutenant General Jean-Baptiste-Donatien de Vimeur, Comte de Rochambeau, inspector general for infantry and a gifted tactician in his own right. After two weeks of combined maneuvers, Rochambeau's *ordre mince* was judged to be superior. Six months later, when it came time to select the generals for the Army of Invasion, the Duc de Broglie was sidelined, while Rochambeau would lead these same divisions intended to spearhead the assault upon Britain.

While the men on shore under the Comte de Vaux waited anxiously for their orders to debark, the men at sea under d'Orvilliers were being steadily decimated by disease; within a few days, 80 were dead and 1,500 ill. The doctors were at a loss to explain it, some pointing to scurvy as the cause. It was in fact part of a massive dysentery epidemic, one of the largest on record until that time, which would ultimately kill 175,000 in western France—there were more burials than baptisms that year—and then spread through Kent in Britain, even leaping the Atlantic to attack the Americas. The soldiers whom d'Orvilliers had conscripted in Brest at the last minute were undoubtedly the primary vectors, though such epidemics typically spread with astonishing speed via many routes. One of the first to die was d'Orvilliers's only son, a twenty-two-year-old lieutenant who served with his father aboard his flagship, *Bretagne.* D'Orvilliers, who had seen more than his share of death in the War of the Austrian Succession and the Seven Years' War, was devastated by the loss of his son. "The Lord has taken from me all I had in this world," he wrote to Sartine the morning of August 2, "but He left me the strength to finish this campaign." His attempt at bravado fooled no one. Córdova later reported to Madrid that the tragedy rendered d'Orvilliers "incapable of carrying out any action," leaving all decisions to his chief of staff, Pavillon. The wind had been knocked from d'Orvilliers's sails, both metaphorically and literally; it took the armada two weeks fighting calms and contrary winds to round the Brittany peninsula, finally entering the English Channel on August 16.

The British navy was already well aware that a combined invasion fleet was in the offing, though at first they were unsure where the landings would take place. William Eden's spy network continued to operate in France even after Ambassador Stormont left the country the previous year, and provided a stream of intelligence that also pointed to preparations for war. Part of this intelligence leak was due directly to Lafayette, Franklin, and Vergennes. As the invasion fleet was forming, Vergennes wanted to stoke a rebellion in Catholic Ireland as a distraction for the British government. In June 1779, on the advice of Lafayette and Franklin, he sent on that mission Edward Bancroft, who would never be uncovered as one of Eden's spies during their lifetime. Bancroft returned several weeks later dismissing the idea of a rebellion to Vergennes, but undoubtedly providing his handlers in London with the clues that a military action was in the works but that it would not involve Ireland. Another clue for the British was the abortive French invasion of the Channel island of Jersey in May of that year, which was easily repelled but alerted the nation to prepare for hostilities. By June 12, the government learned that d'Orvilliers had left Brest nine days earlier. On June 16, the twenty-eight ships of the line in the Channel Fleet, Britain's "wooden walls," departed Portsmouth under Vice Admiral Charles Hardy's flag, which flew above HMS *Victory*. Like the French and Spanish, the British ships were undermanned and their crews sickly, but they nevertheless sped west to the Scilly Isles to intercept d'Orvilliers before he could enter the Channel.

The long-anticipated showdown between the Bourbon and British fleets never came. Hardy's fleet patrolled back and forth for a month, though it was too far west to catch sight of d'Orvilliers when he arrived. When the armada was finally sighted off Plymouth on August 16, the coastal towns immediately girded for an invasion, issuing arms and calling up militia, while back in London stocks dropped sharply on the news. But the Bourbon fleet was steadily losing its ability to threaten the British population. Their resupply ships never made their rendezvous, leaving the armada increasingly short of victuals and water. Meanwhile, dysentery continued to ravage the crews. Guichen's newly renovated flagship, *Ville de Paris,* saw three hundred men fall ill, one-quarter of its crew of eleven hundred, necessitating that a frigate be stripped of much of its crew just to keep the flagship operational. Even the commander in chief, de Vaux, was laid low by the disease.

On August 18, a gale from the east blew the armada out of the Channel. A week later they finally encountered Hardy's fleet. D'Orvilliers attempted to engage the Channel Fleet. Hardy knew he was overmatched, but his chief of staff, Captain Richard Kempenfelt, had long thought about the concept of a "fleet in being," in which an inferior fleet, by staying in a defensive role even if it is far removed from the site of a potential battle, can dictate the conditions of battle to the superior fleet. Accordingly, Hardy avoided combat but continued to lead the armada back east toward the safety of Portsmouth, where on September 3 he moored to reprovision for battle. The same day, d'Orvilliers received orders from Versailles to end the campaign and return to Brest. The armada entered port a week later with eight thousand sick and dying sailors aboard, but with only one captured British ship to show for its efforts. Sartine and the other members of the French court immediately denounced d'Orvilliers's failure to engage Hardy's fleet, but Pavillon leapt to his defense, pointing out that "the French vessels . . . were really more hospitals than ships of war." D'Orvilliers, his spirit broken by the death of his son, resigned and took retirement. Gastón's Spanish squadron overwintered at Brest, Córdova departed with the rest of the fleet for Cádiz, and Lafayette returned to his home. De Vaux sent his soldiers to their winter quarters while clamoring for another invasion, but Vergennes refused his request. The French-Spanish armada, which had been the centerpiece of the entire Bourbon strategy and the culmination of a fifteen-year naval buildup, had simply fizzled out.

Back in the United States, only a handful of newspapers such as the *Pennsylvania Packet* and the *Independent Ledger* carried one-paragraph accounts of the Channel cruise of d'Orvilliers and Córdova, which were generally consigned to page three of the broadsides. Instead, more than two hundred lengthy articles appeared on the front pages of dozens of newspapers, telling and retelling the tale of what was supposed to be a footnote to the great armada: John Paul Jones's epic three-hour battle on September 23, 1779, in which he lost his ship *Bonhomme Richard* but captured HMS *Serapis*. The story began earlier in June, when Jones was despondently casting about for a mission after Lafayette's latest schemes had come to naught. Chaumont had already paid to outfit a small squadron of French and American ships to be placed under the command of Jones, with assurances from Sartine that he would be reimbursed. In addition to the converted forty-gun frigate *Bonhomme Richard* (named in honor of Benjamin Franklin's *Poor Richard's Almanac*), the squadron that lay idle at Lorient in Brittany consisted of three French warships detached from service, and Pierre Landais's frigate *Alliance*, which Franklin authorized to be included. Just as d'Orvilliers's fleet was departing Brest, Sartine approached Jones and Chaumont with a mission for their little squadron: Cruise around the British Isles to attack British shipping, in order to distract the Channel Fleet from the actual invasion, in the same way Bancroft's foray to Ireland was intended to sidetrack Parliament from the real danger. Jones readily agreed to this mission, although his first cruise was cut short when *Bonhomme Richard* and *Alliance* collided, both requiring extensive repairs. On August 14, just as d'Orvilliers's armada was preparing to enter the English Channel, Jones's squadron once again departed the roadstead at Lorient to sail around the British Isles, in an attempt to draw off the Channel Fleet from its real target.

Neither Hardy nor any other admiral was foolish enough to send ships after Jones, but the American did cause localized panic around Edinburgh when his squadron pulled into the Firth of Forth in a failed attempt to land his troops there. Sartine's instructions to Jones, endorsed by Franklin, specifically called for commerce raiding on the high seas and made no mention of landings, but Jones obviously had other ideas. To support his intended amphibious raids, he embarked 137 marines aboard *Bonhomme Richard* instead of the usual 60 that would be assigned to a frigate of that size to provide security and musketry support. These were not Continental Marines but rather members of France's Irish Regiment of Walsh-Serrant, whose motto *Semper et Ubique Fidelis* (Always and Everywhere Faithful) would later serve as inspiration for the United States Marines. Jones would soon have cause to be grateful for having a surfeit of these Wild Geese.

One of the five officers in charge of this regiment was the engineer Antoine Félix Wuibert, who had been captured by the British at Fort Washington back in 1776 and spent two years at Forton Prison near Portsmouth, before Benjamin Franklin arranged for him to be part of a prisoner exchange in January 1779. Arriving penniless in Paris but anxious to return to fight for America, Wuibert beseeched Franklin for help, who most likely recommended him, along with several other Forton exchangees, to Jones. By May, Wuibert was at Lorient as *Bonhomme Richard* was fitting out, where he met John Adams still waiting for his passage back to America. Adams, who was certain he could read a person's character simply by studying his appearance, was mistakenly unimpressed with the man who had already proved his mettle more than once fighting for the American cause: "[He] has something little in his face and air, and makes no great discovery of skill or science." Adams would be proved wrong in the coming months.

On the afternoon of September 23, Jones's squadron was cruising off Flamborough Head on the Yorkshire coast, just south of Scarborough, when they spotted a large merchant convoy of timber-carrying ships, escorted by the frigate HMS *Serapis* and a smaller armed merchant ship, *Countess of Scarborough*. Jones immediately set out toward the convoy while ordering the crew to their combat stations. Wuibert was in charge of *Bonhomme Richard*'s principal battery, the twenty-eight twelve-pound guns on the upper deck, which were to fire into *Serapis*'s rigging in order to disable it. The Irish marines were sent to the poop deck and fighting tops (the highest parts of the masts) to fire down upon the enemy ship. Aboard *Serapis,* Captain Richard Pearson made similar preparations, while he signaled the convoy to seek safety under Scarborough Castle's guns and moved to intercept the enemy squadron. His ship was less than six months old, with a fast, sturdy hull and armed with forty-four cannon, almost half of which were eighteen-pounders. *Bonhomme Richard* was an elderly thirteen years old, with a slower, more fragile merchant hull and fewer, much lighter guns. There seemed no chance that Jones could prevail.

Night was falling when the two ships closed to within hailing distance—about one hundred yards—then ran up their colors while simultaneously firing broadsides. Wuibert's twelve-pounders were cutting up *Serapis*'s masts and spars, but the British ship still outsailed the American to achieve better firing positions. Pearson's better-trained crew could also reload and fire more quickly, which coupled with the heavier weight of shot, meant that *Serapis* was tearing apart *Bonhomme Richard* at a faster rate than the American could damage its opponent. Jones saw that his only chance was to have his crew grapple and lash the two ships together, so that Pearson could no longer run out some of his cannon. As night fell, the two ships drifted northwest lashed side by side, *Serapis*'s stern hove up against *Bonhomme Richard*'s bow. Some of *Serapis*'s batteries still managed to blast away, silencing the rest of the American's guns. *Countess of Scarborough* stood off from the action, its captain unwilling to fire at the American ship for fear of also hitting *Serapis*. Pierre Landais aboard *Alliance* showed no such reserve, firing into *Serapis* three times while part of each broadside also scythed into *Bonhomme Richard*, killing and wounding British and American sailors alike. After over two hours of battle, the gun duel was clearly going in Pearson's favor. He called to Jones, "Have you struck?" Jones fired back, "I may sink, but I'm damned if I'll strike!" It was clear indeed that *Bonhomme Richard* was settling lower in the water and that time was running short.

If the British were to succeed, they would have to get clear of the Americans and finish them off with gunfire. If the Americans were to win before they sank, they would have to kill and maim as many of *Serapis*'s crew as possible. With his cannon disabled or destroyed, Wuibert, wounded in the thigh and arm, undoubtedly rejoined the marines under his command as they rained musket balls on the British sailors trying to cut away the grappling hooks. Every British seaman who reached the bulwarks was hit; the fire from the Irish regiment was so accurate that the British thought they were using rifles. By now the belowdecks of the American ship was almost uninhabitable due to flooding and cannon fire, while the British sailors dared not venture abovedeck. Half of each ship's crew lay dead or wounded. Just then, one of Jones's sailors crawled out along *Bonhomme Richard*'s yards and threw grenades onto *Serapis*'s deck, one of which bounced through a hatch and ignited gun cartridges below. The resulting explosion and deflagration ran the length of the gun deck, killing or wounding fifty of the men crammed there and putting the rest of the guns out of action. At 10:30 p.m., Pearson decided to strike his colors. The convoy he was assigned to protect was safely at Scarborough, and while offering one's sword to the commander of a sinking ship might be a disgrace, he believed he could honorably surrender to *two* warships, one of which, *Alliance,* was still an active threat. Further bloodshed was unwarranted, a decision later upheld when Pearson was knighted for saving the convoy.

John Paul Jones transferred his command to *Serapis* the next day, as *Bonhomme Richard* gradually sank beneath the waves. A week later the squadron was at Texel in the Dutch Republic, where Jones was warmly welcomed by Franklin's correspondent Charles Dumas.

The news—and legend—of John Paul Jones arrived in both France and America soon after. Even though Jones had not carried out the mission directed by Sartine, Franklin assured the naval captain that "scarce anything was talked of at Paris and Versailles but your cool conduct and persevering bravery during that terrible conflict." His defeat of the larger and better armed *Serapis* served as a powerful metaphor for the fight between the United States and Great Britain, providing a needed boost to America's morale. Although he never held another major command in the United States, Jones's courageous action in battle stood as a lasting inspiration for the nascent American navy. As for Antoine Félix Wuibert, whose own actions—and those of his Irish marines—had been partly responsible for the victory, he asked Jones for permission to "return as soon as possible to America . . . to renew my service as an engineer." Jones reluctantly granted him leave, but with the highest regard for his abilities. While he was bound for Philadelphia in March 1780, Wuibert's vessel was captured by the frigate HMS *Greyhound.* He was once again made prisoner of the British and sent to Jamaica.

THE EUROPEAN THEATER OF NAVAL OPERATIONS

In late 1779, in the wake of the failed French-Spanish attempt to invade Britain, each nation reassessed its plans for the upcoming year. All of them saw the strategically and economically vital West Indies as the focus of their future campaigns. In London, the British cabinet, realizing that another invasion was improbable in the near future, decided to send five thousand troops and ten ships of the line to reinforce the squadron based at Jamaica, stripping five ships from the Channel Fleet. Secretary of State for the Colonies George Germain wanted to send even more ships, but First Lord of the Admiralty John Montagu, Earl of Sandwich, was already concerned that this would leave Britain dangerously undefended; while the war could only be won in the Americas, it could be lost in the Channel. In Madrid, Floridablanca had not given up hope of renewing the assault on Britain, but with Vergennes's refusal to embark upon another costly campaign without first obtaining a firm commitment from the Spanish to provide additional funding for the operation, the possibility of another amphibious operation faded away. Instead, Spain now pledged to send at least ten ships of the line and ten thousand troops to the West Indies. This placed Vergennes in a diplomatic bind. Fleurieu insisted that even if the failed invasion attempt of Britain demonstrated the enormous problems inherent in joint operations, France still needed the Spanish navy's assistance to win the war, given the huge numerical disparity with the British fleet. In order to keep Spain from reneging on its obligations, Sartine pledged at least ten ships of the line to aid the Spanish fleet in the West Indies.

The other strategic focus, in the eyes of Britain and Spain, was the "pile of rocks called Gibraltar," as Floridablanca had so dismissively called it. It had been in British hands since it was captured from Spain in 1704 during the War of the Spanish Succession, allowing them to control the shipping and naval traffic between the Atlantic and the Mediterranean. Since that time, the two nations had fought and negotiated over its return, but after the Seven Years' War both sides seemed resigned to the status quo, and had even developed a sort of camaraderie at the front lines. British mail to the colony would regularly arrive via the Spanish post, while the British governor and commander at Gibraltar, George Elliott, and his Spanish counterpart Joaquin Mendoza, in the adjacent town of San Roque, would often exchange visits and invite each other to official celebrations. Therefore, when no mail arrived early on June 21, 1779—the day Carlos III issued his de facto declaration of war—Elliott knew he was now under a naval blockade, as Mendoza unenthusiastically admitted later that day. Elliott immediately sent word to London to send a relief convoy, for even with severe rationing, the near-uncultivable and water-poor promontory could only hold out for a few months.

The task of resupplying the colony fell to Vice Admiral George Brydges Rodney, the very model of a fighting sailor who had just been brought out of retirement in October to become commander in chief of the Leeward Islands. On Christmas Day 1779, as his orders from Sandwich instructed, Rodney sailed from Portsmouth with twenty-two ships of the line, ten frigates, and almost two hundred other ships to deliver stores and victuals to Gibraltar and Minorca, before proceeding to his post in the West Indies. The Spanish navy was incapable of massing a fleet with sufficient force to prevent Rodney's mission, for it was in bad shape after the failed invasion attempt of Britain and was scattered among several far-flung harbors. Gastón was still at Brest with twenty ships, while Córdova had arrived at Cádiz with just eleven of his fifteen ships—four had to divert to Ferrol in desperate need of repairs—and most of the remaining ships were in refit at the Carraca dockyard in the Bay of Cádiz. Only fifteen vessels under Lángara, who had recently returned from the Azores to Cartagena, were in any condition to counter the massive fleet that was headed toward Gibraltar.

Whatever Rodney's strengths as a naval commander or weaknesses with his personal finances, he was inordinately possessed of the one trait that Napoleon would famously value in his officers above all others—Rodney was lucky, and moreover he had the skill to transform that luck into victory. On January 8, off the coast of Portugal, he spotted a Spanish merchant convoy bound for Cádiz. Leaving his own merchants under the protection of a frigate, he signaled his warships to a general chase—meaning to go straight at the enemy without forming a line of battle—and soon swarmed the convoy, which quickly struck its colors in the face of an overwhelming enemy. Rodney had captured seven warships and fifteen merchant ships of the Royal Guipuzcoan Company of Caracas, richly laden with naval stores and provisions, which he incorporated into his fleet bound for the relief of Gibraltar. On January 16, 1780, as he was passing between Cape Saint Vincent and Cape Santa María off southern Portugal, he sighted Lángara's squadron and gave chase. Despite having two frigates that were supposed to scout ahead, Lángara was caught unawares and turned south in a disorderly attempt to escape. Rodney's much faster ships overtook them and picked them off one by one. The Moonlight Battle, as it became known, lasted well past midnight and resulted in the capture or destruction of five of Lángara's ships, including his eighty-gun flagship, *Fénix*.

Two days later Rodney's fleet began pulling into Gibraltar harbor, unmolested by the surrounding Spanish forces. It took a month to offload supplies, granting the besieged colony another year of survival, before he was able to resume his journey to the West Indies. In addition to the relief of Gibraltar, Sandwich noted, Rodney had "taken more line-of-battle ships than had been captured in any one action of either the last preceding wars." All of Britain was delighted with this unprecedented string of victories, especially the financiers in the City of London, whose renewed confidence in the government allowed Prime Minister North to raise an additional $150 billion equivalent at favorable interest rates. The Spanish, too, respected the strength of Rodney's forces, for when he passed Cádiz on the way to the West Indies, Córdova's fleet, still undergoing repairs, remained in the bay rather than sortie to meet him in battle.

Not all of Rodney's fortune was due to luck and skill. He was able to overtake the Spanish ships in both engagements because every one of his warships was sheathed in copper below the waterline, which made them much faster than their uncoppered Spanish counterparts. Copper sheathing—thin plates nailed to the underwater part of the ship—prevented shipworms from boring holes into the wooden hulls, and also stopped barnacles and seaweed from attaching themselves to the hull (copper is poisonous to marine life). Preventing shipworms and reducing hull fouling on a near-permanent basis meant that copper-sheathed ships could sail faster, turn more quickly, and stay at sea for much longer periods than uncoppered ones, which had to come into port at regular intervals to be careened and scraped. Copper sheathing would turn out to be the single most important maritime technology to emerge from the War of American Independence.

The practice of coppering hulls was first tried by the British navy during the Seven Years' War, and though it was enormously successful at keeping the hulls free from fouling—"the finest invention in the world," claimed one officer—the galvanic interaction of copper plates with the ships' iron fasteners would cause the iron to corrode, loosening planks and timber and putting the ships at risk of leaking and flooding. The British navy had consequently dropped its coppering program, but reinstated it in 1778 due to France's entry into the war. By then, a short-term solution to the corrosion problem had been found—layers of tarred paper placed between the iron fasteners and the copper plates would insulate them and reduce the galvanic action. The fleet, already stretched thin by having to fight in several theaters at once, clamored for the fix. "For God's sake and our country's, send out copper-bottomed ships to relieve the fouled and crippled ones," wrote one officer to the controller of the navy, Charles Middleton. "With those, everything will be done; if you do not, nothing but misery and distress must ensue." Britain had the industrial might to manufacture copper plates in large quantities, but the cost would be enormous, coming on top of a naval buildup that was now averaging 27 new ships every year. Together, Sandwich and Middleton convinced the king and Parliament to authorize the expense, so that almost the entire navy, 331 ships in all, were coppered at a total cost of £400,000, equivalent to $4.5 billion, the cost of a modern British aircraft carrier.

Both France and Spain saw the same advantages to coppering as did the British. When the French navy sent the Chevalier d'Oraison to spy on British shipyards in 1764 (as well as others after him), it was partly to gain intelligence on coppering; and the Spanish navy was well aware that Lángara could not escape Rodney because the British ships were copper-bottomed. The problem was that neither nation had the industrial capacity to produce copper plates in the quantities needed. Where in Britain almost every major dockyard was engaged in coppering, in France only the Brest dockyard was able to do so, outfitting barely half the fleet by war's end. In Spain, the situation was even direr, with fewer than one in ten ships coppered. The failure of France and Spain to copper their warships would put them at a tactical and strategic disadvantage, even when luck favored them.

Luck certainly favored Luis de Córdova y Córdova in the summer of 1780, and like Rodney he also had the skill to use it, despite the protestations of the French ambassador, Montmorin, that the seventy-three-year-old mariner was "senile." If Spain had been ineffective at blockading Gibraltar, then Britain's Channel Fleet had been equally unsuccessful at bottling up the French Atlantic ports of Brest and Rochefort. Over the course of 1780, ten French ships of the line from those ports, along with another six from Toulon, entered Cádiz, where they joined Córdova's newly repaired ships to make several combined sorties into the Atlantic in order to intercept the Channel Fleet, which was cruising off the Spanish coast.

One of those sorties departed Cádiz on July 31, 1780, with twenty-four Spanish and six French ships. Owing to good intelligence passed to him by Floridablanca, Córdova knew that a massive, lightly escorted convoy was en route to the East and West Indies, and went in search of it. In the predawn darkness of August 9, Spanish frigates glimpsed a cannon flash and heard a boom one minute later, which Córdova's chief of staff, Mazarredo, argued must be the convoy just ten miles away, and not the Channel Fleet. Córdova duped the convoy into following him by using the stern lamp of *Santísima Trinidad*, which the convoy mistook for its own escort, the seventy-four-gun HMS *Ramillies*. Dawn saw the fifty-five merchantmen under the guns of the combined fleet, while the copper-bottomed *Ramillies* was able to outrun its pursuers, much to the dismay of the French captains whose uncoppered ships were left in its wake.

The Spanish-French convoy returned to Cádiz with an enormous haul. It was the single largest loss of ships the British mercantile fleet would experience in the war, and with over three thousand soldiers, eighty thousand muskets, and uniforms for dozens of regiments now in Spanish hands, it put an enormous dent in Rodney's West Indies campaign. The financial loss—£1.6 million in gold and silver, about $17 billion today—also wiped out much of the goodwill that Rodney had generated in the financial markets just a few months earlier. The perception that the British navy could no longer control the seas drove freight insurance rates up 25 percent, not a crippling figure, but coming on top of higher shipbuilding costs meant that the government felt increasing pressure from public opinion to end the conflict.

Córdova's capture of the convoy also closed off one potential route to ending the conflict, however feeble, which was a series of secret negotiations between an Irish-Spanish priest named Thomas Hussey and Richard Cumberland of the Parliament's Board of Trade. The Spanish and British governments had sent these two men to open an alternate channel for dialogue about a truce, but gave neither man full authority to negotiate. The only outcome of the Hussey-Cumberland mission was to confirm that Spain and Britain remained as far apart as ever on the crucial question of Gibraltar. Vergennes, however, was sufficiently worried by the possibility of a separate peace that he alerted the Americans to the talks, and was undoubtedly relieved when they effectively collapsed in October 1780, soon after news of the capture of the convoy arrived.

THE AMERICAN THEATER OF NAVAL OPERATIONS

The French and British navies had been building up their fleets in the West Indies for a year before they decided, in late 1779, that it would become the focus of their future campaigns. D'Estaing had been at his base at Fort Royal (today Fort-de-France) in Martinique since the 1778 campaigns of Dominica and Saint Lucia, and was bolstered shortly thereafter to nineteen ships by the arrival of François Joseph Paul, Comte de Grasse, recently promoted to *chef d'escadre*. Meanwhile, Barrington at Saint Lucia was relieved in January 1779 when Byron arrived from Newport with his reconstituted fleet, bringing the British strength to twenty-four ships. For six months, d'Estaing and Byron watched each other's comings and goings—Martinique and Saint Lucia are just twenty miles apart and visible from each other's coasts—with almost no action. On May 25, 1779, Byron left harbor to escort a large homeward-bound convoy from nearby Saint Kitts until it was out of reach of the French cruisers. D'Estaing profited from Byron's absence by ordering the recapture of the nearby sugar island Saint Vincent, which had been in French hands until the Treaty of Paris ceded it to Britain. The island fell in just one day.

In late June, a large, armed convoy arrived from France under the flag of *Chef d'Escadre* Toussaint Guillaume Picquet, Comte de La Motte, more commonly known as La Motte-Picquet. The accompanying squadron included the Beaumarchais ship *Fier Roderigue,* which had returned to France with a cargo of Virginia tobacco in partial repayment for the Roderigue Hortalez munitions, and was now rearmed with sixty cannon to serve as escort for the outbound convoy. D'Estaing now had twenty-six ships of the line, outnumbering Byron, and once again took the initiative to recapture another former French sugar colony, Grenada. This time, the battle took two days, with the British forces capitulating on July 4. Sartine's orders for d'Estaing had been to protect French commerce and to destroy British strongholds, but not to occupy them. The former army man, however, saw the gaining and holding of territory as the primary strategy in the conduct of war against Britain, just as did George Washington, whose portrait hung on the wall of his cabin. The two islands would stay in French hands if d'Estaing could help it.

While d'Estaing was en route to Grenada, Byron had returned to Saint Lucia and received the news about Saint Vincent. On July 3 he put to sea, and upon learning of Grenada, continued on to confront d'Estaing. Storms and a hurricane had conspired to prevent the two men from engaging off Newport a year earlier, but they would be no impediment now. D'Estaing's fleet was anchored in Saint George's Bay when they were informed of Byron's approach, just a day after the British forces had surrendered. In the early morning hours of July 6, he formed his ships into a line of battle and sailed northward to meet Byron. The British admiral, not yet realizing he was outnumbered, ordered a general chase. As the battle progressed and Byron saw the true nature of the situation, he hastily ordered his ships to draw into a line of battle, but not before many had already been crippled, their rigging and masts destroyed by accurate French gunfire. At 3 p.m., d'Estaing's fleet tacked into the British and delivered a series of broadsides that put an end to the battle and forced Byron to withdraw. It was a stunning naval victory, adroitly executed by a man who was often disparaged for being more of a landlubber than a seaman. He did not, however, see the capture of warships in the same light as the capture of territory, so did not capitalize on his triumph by pursuing the remains of Byron's fleet. Instead, he put into Saint George's to repair his ships—*Fier Roderigue* had suffered the most damage—before returning to Martinique. His pugnacious captain Suffren, lamenting the lost opportunity to have destroyed a significant part of the British presence in the Caribbean and thus shift the balance of power, said of his commander that "if his seamanship had equaled his bravery, we never would have allowed four dismasted English warships to escape." Despite Suffren's criticisms, Grenada and Saint Vincent would remain in French hands for the rest of the war.

The strategic victories at Grenada and Saint Vincent were due to d'Estaing's violating Sartine's direct orders not to capture any islands, but there was one order from the navy minister that he could not disobey: to return to France. He would, however, stretch out that command to include another amphibious descent before returning. He first brought his fleet to Saint-Domingue, where he was instructed to pick up a homeward-bound convoy and embark assault troops. Learning that Spain had now entered the war, he put aside a proposed attack on the main British base in Jamaica—that would have to be a future joint operation—and began reading the letters that awaited him at Cap François. South Carolina's governor, John Rutledge; the French consul, Jean Plombard; and other dignitaries all gave him the same grim news: The British brigadier general Augustine Prévost had left Saint Augustine to assume command at Savannah earlier in the year, and in response to American incursions into Georgia had launched an attack on Charleston, which Major General Benjamin Lincoln, commander of the Continental Army's Southern Department, had barely repulsed. The Congress and Washington were unable to send any troops except a combined infantry and cavalry legion, consisting of French, German, Italian, Swedish, Polish, and American volunteers, under the command of Casimir Pulaski and Michael Kovats. None of the other states were willing to spare their own forces. D'Estaing was their only hope. One French cavalry volunteer put the situation in the starkest of terms: "Never has this country been in greater need of help . . . in truth she has no-one but yourself, Monsieur Le Comte, to save her from peril." D'Estaing's choice was clear. Just as prying Grenada from the British erased the stain of losing Saint Lucia, chasing them from Savannah might make amends for Newport.

On August 16, 1779, d'Estaing's fleet departed Cap François with four thousand troops aboard, among which were the Chasseurs-Volontaires de Saint-Domingue, a corps of 750 *"gens de couleur"* (free men of color, meaning both black and mixed-race) who were intended to support the regular troops in the same way that Lawrence Washington's American Regiment was supposed to dig trenches and carry supplies at Cartagena de Indias. After dispatching the merchant convoy to France, d'Estaing believed that his remaining twenty-two ships of the line and ten frigates would be more than enough to dislodge the few British vessels around Prévost and force his surrender. With colonial troops already acclimated to the southern environment, and with the best of the French navy at his disposal—Bougainville, de Grasse, La Motte-Picquet, and Suffren were among his officers—he was looking for a quick victory; they were at the height of hurricane season, and he did not wish to risk creating another tempest at Versailles by arriving overdue in France. He sent word of his arrival in Savannah to Charleston via fast frigate, and on September 4 a coordinated attack was planned. Two days later the first of Lincoln's two thousand troops marched from Charleston, led by Pulaski's Legion. D'Estaing appeared off the mouth of the Savannah River on September 8, catching by surprise Prévost and his twenty-four hundred troops garrisoned in the city. The British general immediately sent dispatches to John Byron, hoping for relief to come from the West Indies, not knowing that the rear admiral had already departed for Britain under a cloud. Prévost's requests to Henry Clinton in New York would also go unfulfilled. Help would have to come from eight hundred troops under Colonel John Maitland, stationed fifty miles away in Beaufort.

Following the advice of local residents, d'Estaing began debarking on September 12 at the landing of Beaulieu, a dozen miles south of Savannah. Four days later he had surrounded the city with two thousand troops and heavy artillery. With Lincoln still a day's march away, there would be no question which nation should claim this victory. D'Estaing dispatched a summons to Prévost, imperiously demanding his capitulation *"aux Armes de Sa Majesté Le Roy de France."* Prévost asked for twenty-four hours to consider the surrender, stalling for time until reinforcements could arrive. D'Estaing, who thought that Lincoln's army had blocked Maitland's approach via the inland waterways, agreed. It was a grievous error. Maitland entered the city the following day and immediately began shoring up the defenses, while Prévost now politely declined the surrender, saying that "the King, my master pays these men to fight, and they must fight." Lincoln's army marched in later that day, swelling the total allied force to fifty-five hundred regulars and militia. D'Estaing and Lincoln agreed to lay in a siege instead of attacking, and more heavy cannon were brought from the ships to pummel the city.

Listening to the dull thuds of cannon in the distance were the men aboard d'Estaing's ships, temporarily bereft of artillery, running low on water and provisions, and becoming increasingly stricken with the dreaded dysentery that at this very same moment was also laying low the French-Spanish armada attempting to invade Britain. D'Estaing's vaunted officer corps were left with nothing to do except run the occasional patrol and gripe about their commander. The monotony only was broken on September 24 when the ship of the line *Sagittaire* captured HMS *Experiment* off Hilton Head, netting £650,000 in coin, victuals to restock the ships, and British army uniforms, which some of the officers took to wearing when they returned to France. Meanwhile, five days of bombardment had devastated the city but failed to dislodge the troops. With time running out before the French fleet needed to depart, d'Estaing met with his officers and laid out his plan for an all-out assault, but "all of them [the officers] were opposed to this disastrous attack." With the same volcanic temper he had displayed at Newport, d'Estaing peremptorily overruled them, citing the need to honor their commitment to the Americans and to France, and end the siege with a "vigorous blow." Lincoln had little choice but to agree, as the French were his final resort.

The main assault was launched in the early morning hours of October 9 on the Spring Hill redoubt, just southwest of the city, which the allies thought was manned only with militia. Prévost evidently had been forewarned and fortified the emplacements with regular troops. As the French soldiers scrambled up the sides of the redoubts, their white uniforms made them highly visible targets for the British through the morning fog. Canister shot and chain mowed down more soldiers. As d'Estaing, who was seriously wounded in the arm and the right leg, described it, a "frightful carnage" ensued. Nevertheless the French troops pressed forward. One column led by the Swedish officer Curt von Stedingk planted a flag on the emplacements, but they were driven back with a bayonet charge that left half of them dead or wounded. Charles Romand de L'Isle, the French artillery officer who had left Philadelphia to serve in Georgia, led another charge that was also repulsed. Lincoln's American troops fought well despite suffering terrible casualties. Pulaski, leading many of those troops into the thick of the fighting before the Spring Hill redoubt, was mortally wounded by canister shot. An hour after the assault began, d'Estaing and Lincoln ordered a general retreat. As the allied soldiers fell back toward the east, Maitland sortied his troops for a counterattack. When they came to the Jewish Burial Ground, the Chasseurs-Volontaires de Saint-Domingue, who had been placed there in reserve, held their ground at great cost to allow the orderly withdrawal of the French and American forces.

The Siege of Savannah was a rout—almost 1,000 French and Americans killed, wounded, or captured, compared with 150 British. Savannah would remain British until near the end of the war. Yet recriminations between the French and Americans were few. D'Estaing praised the "great bravery" of the American officers, and even lauded the performance of the Charleston militia, which he found a far cry from what he had witnessed at Newport. Lincoln, in turn, told the Congress that d'Estaing "has the interest of America much at heart," and laid the blame for the failure to "the uncertain events of war." Only d'Estaing's own officers continued to criticize him, with Bougainville saying that he had left Georgia in "chaos."

Despite further entreaties from Rutledge and others to remain, d'Estaing's fleet began pulling away from the South Carolina coast on

October 25, leaving in the care of the Americans dozens of men too wounded or sick to survive the ocean crossing. While de Grasse and La Motte-Picquet peeled off to resume their patrols in the Caribbean, the flagship *Languedoc* battled storms to anchor in Brest on December 5. Certain he was arriving in disgrace, he was astonished to find himself showered with praise from all quarters. The French people spoke of his French victories in the West Indies, not of his American defeats at Newport and Savannah. Unlike the attempted French-Spanish invasion of Britain that had only recently ended in disgrace, d'Estaing had shown that *La Royale* could stand toe-to-toe against the Royal Navy. "D'Estaing is the first to have placed a laurel wreath upon my crown," said King Louis XVI, referring to the twin prizes of Grenada and Saint Vincent.

Lieutenant General Comte de Guichen may have had visions of laurel wreaths when he departed Brest in February 1780, just two months after d'Estaing's return. His sixteen ships of the line escorted a convoy bound for Martinique, from where he hoped to add Saint Lucia and Barbados to Louis XVI's crown. He arrived safely on March 22, just a few days before Vice Admiral Rodney, the man who would prevent Guichen's reveries from being realized, came on station to take over from Rear Admiral Hyde Parker as commander in chief of the Leeward Islands. Guichen wasted little time in preparing for his attack, sailing from Martinique on April 13 in order to draw Rodney out from his base on Saint Lucia. The two fleets made contact a few days later, and on the morning of April 17 they drew into their lines of battle. They were almost equally matched in numbers, twenty British warships versus twenty-two for the French. A sailing line of battle was usually arranged in three squadrons: van (front), center, and rear. Rodney's idea was to avoid a slugging match where each ship engaged its opposite number, and instead achieve victory by shortening his battle line to focus on just the rear of the French line, which he would destroy before the French van and center could wear (turn completely around) to support their overwhelmed companions. Such tactics required not only clear signals but also a complete understanding of intention between Rodney and his captains, which Rodney had failed to communicate during his maneuvers with the fleet two weeks earlier.

Rodney was heading north and Guichen south when Rodney signaled his fleet to turn toward the rear of Guichen's line. Rodney's captains read the signals correctly but misinterpreted the intent, aiming (as was traditional) for their opposite number in the French line instead of focusing many British ships on a smaller number of French ones. Guichen deduced Rodney's plan and wore his ships around to head north, foiling the action. The battle turned into the very ship-to-ship slugging match that Rodney had sought to avoid, and after 4 p.m. the two fleets withdrew with inconclusive results. Rodney was furious with his captains at the missed opportunity to destroy the French fleet. Impatient for a rematch, he ordered repairs at sea and chased Guichen, who was also making repairs, to Guadeloupe. In May the two fleets were back at sea and in sight of one another for almost three weeks, but apart from two tentative skirmishes they remained out of range. By then their supplies had been exhausted and they returned to their respective ports. With Guichen's plan for capturing the British islands thwarted, he wrote to Sartine to be relieved of command in the West Indies and return home.

The West Indies had thus far been the focus of attention of France and Britain, but Spain had yet to turn its attention there, despite Floridablanca's pledge to Vergennes at the end of 1779 of ten ships and ten thousand troops. The notices of d'Estaing's successes were certainly heartening, but of greater importance to Carlos III and Floridablanca was the news from New Orleans and Havana. The Gálvez family, father and son, were succeeding—or at least not failing—in the Gulf coast theater against Britain. Matías de Gálvez had achieved a stalemate in Central America, while his son Bernardo de Gálvez now occupied the Mississippi River and Mobile. A strong push could drive Britain from the Mosquito Coast and place Pensacola in Spanish hands. In Cádiz, a fleet of 146 merchantmen and 12,400 troops set sail on April 8, 1780, for Havana to provide support for that push.

Escorting that massive convoy were just fourteen ships of the line and two frigates, a meager number given that if the convoy were captured, it could potentially knock Spain out of the war. The navy was counting on the ability of naval brigadier general José Solano y Bote to bring them to safety. Solano was a competent sailor but a master charlatan. As a young officer, he and his comrade Jorge Juan y Santacilia had accomplished a daring feat of industrial espionage, sneaking into London under assumed names, spending a year spying on British shipyards and arsenals, capturing plans and technical information, and managing to spirit away eighty British shipbuilders to work in Spanish shipyards (which explains why the builder of the Spanish flagship *Santísima Trinidad* was named Matthew Mullan). Solano knew the British better than any other Spanish admiral. Therefore when he spied an unidentified sail en route, he correctly guessed that it was one of Rodney's frigates looking for him. He diverted the convoy far to the north to pass around Guadeloupe, where Guichen escorted him in unharmed on June 9. For having outmaneuvered the formidable Rodney, Solano later was granted the royal title of *Vizcondado previo del Feliz Ardid* (Former Viscount of the Clever Ruse).

Guichen had hoped to make use of the Spanish ships and troops to try, one more time, to recapture Saint Lucia, but Solano firmly stuck to his orders to go to Havana. Guichen had already received his own instructions to return to France. Leaving behind *Chef d'Escadre* François-Aymar, Chevalier de Monteil, with a squadron of nine warships, Guichen formed an escort squadron with his senior officers La Motte-Picquet, de Grasse, and Suffren that took Solano's convoy to the easternmost point of Cuba before turning for home. Solano arrived at Havana on August 4,

José Solano y Bote, Marqués del Socorro (1726–1806).
Anonymous, eighteenth century, oil on canvas

1780, two days after Bernardo de Gálvez sailed into harbor aboard his self-christened sloop *Galveztown,* and together they would begin planning the final phases of the Spanish domination of the Gulf.

While out to sea, Guichen opened Sartine's orders and learned that his destination was Cádiz, where he arrived on October 23 to regroup with the main French fleet. The combined French-Spanish operations under Córdova over the course of 1780 had been successful in bringing in large hauls from captured British convoys, but in the eyes of the court at Versailles they had done little of strategic importance. The forty French ships of the line now in Cádiz were needed back in France for a much more ambitious campaign, and to underscore its importance, the Comte d'Estaing had been sent to Spain to convey them home. They arrived in Brest on January 3, 1781, where the pieces for a new campaign were already coming together, one that might bring the war to an end.

CHAPTER 6

The Pieces Converge

The pivotal campaign in the War of American Independence traced its beginnings to a meeting at West Point on September 16, 1779, when Ambassador-Select Anne-César de La Luzerne asked George Washington "whether it would be agreeable to the United States . . . to send directly from France a squadron and a few regiments attached to it," and Washington replied that it would be "very advantageous of the common cause." That seemingly offhand exchange had in fact been orchestrated months before by the Comte de Vergennes, much as he had orchestrated the entire French involvement in the war. From arming the insurgents to forming an alliance with the new nation, to dispatching a fleet under the Comte d'Estaing, Vergennes had been the driving force behind every major initiative taken by France during the war. But those actions were always undertaken with European politics at the forefront of Vergennes's thinking, for like any state leader worthy of the title, he would not commit his country to go to war in support of a foreign power except when it furthered France's own interests. The arms and munitions that flowed to the Americans through Beaumarchais's fleet were aimed first and foremost at preventing a distant war between Portugal and Spain from erupting on the European continent. The Treaty of Alliance was intended to prevent America from unilaterally suing for reconciliation with Britain and thereby threatening the French and Spanish possessions in the West Indies. D'Estaing's fleet was meant to disrupt and divide British forces in order to prevent them from destroying Washington's army and reestablishing control over America. The stability of Europe under French supremacy, not the creation of an independent nation across the Atlantic, was Vergennes's primary goal throughout the War of American Independence.

Vergennes had come to these views through a lifetime of diplomacy working outside of France. Being so distant from the court at Versailles, he also came to exhibit a strong independence of mind, taking strategic actions based on his interpretation of France's geopolitical interests and its military and economic limitations, as well as those of its allies. He most notably demonstrated this while ambassador to the Ottoman Empire, where initially he balked at then–foreign minister Choiseul's orders to encourage the Porte (the Ottoman government) to declare war on Russia in order to put a brake on its growing influence in northern Europe. In his view, neither the Porte nor the Ottoman army was ready, a judgment later confirmed when Sultan Mustafa III, in response to Vergennes's eventual halfhearted urging, launched an ill-conceived campaign against Russia that resulted in a stunning series of defeats and the near collapse of the Porte.

Vergennes, as Louis XVI's foreign minister, showed the same independent streak as he did while ambassador, while at the same time closely working with his king and Maurepas to rationally calculate France's interests and limitations before taking any action. To account for America's interests and limitations, Vergennes depended on firsthand observations or reliable intelligence to include in his calculations. Thus Bonvouloir's report was crucial to his decision to send arms and munitions to the insurgents in 1776; Deane's and Franklin's steady stream of reports about Washington's army in 1777 gave Vergennes the rationale he needed to propose a treaty with the Americans; and Gérard's reports during 1778 helped shape the strategy that Vergennes and Sartine developed for d'Estaing's campaign after Newport. Up until this point, the French strategy in the war closely followed the outline that Vergennes had mapped out years earlier.

In June 1779, the French-Spanish armada that Floridablanca had forced upon Vergennes threatened to upend the plans the French minister had made thus far. In his view, the two nations, instead of fighting the British in the Americas as he had foreseen, were now embarked upon an ill-considered attempt to invade Britain that could potentially cause a backlash among France's European allies. Even as d'Orvilliers was preparing to depart from Brest, Vergennes was casting about for a new way to regain the initiative and take the fight back across the Atlantic. The poor showing by d'Estaing and Sullivan at Newport was evidence that well-trained and well-equipped French troops fighting alongside the Americans, and not just another naval squadron, were needed to turn the tide of battle. Vergennes certainly could not commit to sending troops without knowing whether they would be seen as an allied force or as an invading army. Since at that time Luzerne was in Lorient preparing to board the frigate *Sensible* to take over as ambassador in Philadelphia, it was vital that, as one of his first actions, he be instructed to sound out the Americans on whether sending "a few regiments" would be acceptable.

Even before Luzerne had his fateful meeting with Washington and reported back to Vergennes, the impatient foreign minister was already planning for this new expedition. In July, while the French fleet stood at anchor at the Sisargas Isles off Spain and the Army of Invasion waited on the French coast, Vergennes sent a query to Lafayette at his camp in Le Havre for "some ideas on an expedition to America." Lafayette enthusiastically answered on July 18 that such an expedition was "more than ever necessary," as the ravages of war had devastated America's trade and commerce and left its ability to continue the fight in a precarious state. He cautioned, however, that too large a contingent would likely be rejected by the Americans, proposing instead that a force of about forty-three hundred men, plus horses and artillery, be sent first to Newport, and then deployed farther south for a campaign in Virginia. Now having some idea of how the American allies would react, Vergennes immediately sounded out his Spanish allies by proposing to his ambassador Montmorin that "perhaps we should resolve that the major blows should be landed less in Europe than in America." Montmorin's reply, that the Spanish court did not take a keen interest in an American expedition, was made before the extent of the armada's disaster became apparent.

By late autumn 1779 the situation had changed, as Spain shifted its focus from Britain to the West Indies, removing a potential obstacle to Vergennes's new strategy. At just that time, several additional pieces of intelligence arrived from the United States that confirmed the acceptability of sending French troops to America: Luzerne's report of his West Point meeting with Washington; a subsequent letter from Washington to Lafayette, intimating that "a corps of gallant French" would be welcomed on American shores; and a memorandum from the recently returned hero of Stony Point, François-Louis Teissèdre de Fleury, arguing that in order to prevent America from making a separate peace with Britain, France needed to send "clothes, arms, money, or even still more, effective aid." Even if Benjamin Franklin could offer no advice on the matter—he had "no orders to request troops," as he told Lafayette, and complained to John Jay that he knew "nothing of the sentiments of Congress on the subject of introducing foreign troops"—Vergennes now had sufficient information to propose to his king a *"projet particulier"* (special project), a new expedition to America.

Events moved quickly after the New Year. On January 29, 1780, as Guichen's squadron was preparing to set sail for Martinique, Vergennes informed Montmorin that the king had authorized a squadron of six ships with three to four thousand troops to be placed at Washington's disposal. On February 2, Sartine appointed *Chef d'Escadre* Charles-Henri-Louis d'Arsac, Chevalier de Ternay, to command the squadron and sent him to Brest to oversee its organization. Three days later Vergennes wrote to Luzerne to inform him that the *Expédition Particulière* (Special Expedition), as it was now known, was on its way, and ordered the ambassador to tell only Washington and the president of the Congress so as to maintain secrecy. Two weeks later Lafayette learned that he was to leave for America to prepare for the expedition's arrival. He would be allowed to serve once more as an American general under George Washington, but not, as he had hoped, at the head of the French forces. That position, Minister of War Montbarey decided, would be entrusted to "a learned, dedicated general officer who was one of the most fit to lead troops"—Lieutenant General Rochambeau, the man who had been ready just months earlier to lead the assault on Britain. Vergennes's instructions to Rochambeau were clear: He and his troops were to serve "under the high command" of General Washington, and fight at the side of the Continental Army.

As Rochambeau prepared for the voyage, Lafayette impressed upon him the need for his army to be entirely self-sufficient, as the Americans were poor in everything needed to feed and clothe an army. Thus the ships must carry not only war materiel like musket flints and harnesses, but also flour, bricks to build bread ovens, leggings, shirts, leather for shoes, fabric for making clothing, and even needles and thread. Lafayette also suggested that the expedition bring d'Estaing's barely used printing press from his Newport campaign, on the grounds that it would be "handy for proclamations and joint relations with allies." Most important, Rochambeau must bring plenty of hard currency in silver to pay for everything. Lafayette, meanwhile, would travel with an officer from the French commissary service, Lieutenant Colonel Louis Éthis de Corny, to make advance arrangements to secure supplies for the expedition.

On March 11, the newly built frigate *Hermione*, commanded by Louis-René Madeleine Le Vassor, Comte de Latouche-Tréville (nephew of one of d'Orvilliers's flag officers in the armada), departed Rochefort with Lafayette and Corny aboard. They arrived in Boston on April 28, and by May 10 Lafayette was at Washington's encampment at Morristown with the news of the *Expédition Particulière*, which even now was under way from Brest. Ternay and Rochambeau had set sail without a clear idea of their destination, since the latest news from America was almost six months old. For the time being they would head for the Chesapeake Bay or perhaps Charleston, where they could receive updated intelligence on the British and American dispositions, and if necessary support Spanish operations by menacing Saint Augustine. Neither man knew that the British had already evacuated Newport, or that Charleston was now in British hands.

THE SOUTHERN STRATEGY BRINGS CHARLESTON AND SOUTH CAROLINA UNDER BRITISH CONTROL

D'Estaing's two-year campaign had failed to wrest Newport and Savannah from British control, but the presence of the French fleet in North American waters had robbed the commander in chief, Henry Clinton, of the freedom to quickly move his troops from one conflict to another by sea. This was Kempenfelt's "fleet in being" writ large—not only did the lesser French fleet dictate the conditions of battle to the superior British fleet, but its entire strategy as well. Some fifty-five thousand British and Hessian soldiers now lay in isolated pockets from Quebec to the West Indies to the Gulf of Mexico. Clinton was unable to send troops from his primary base in New York City to support an assault on New Orleans, as Secretary of State for the Colonies Germain had suggested. Dalling's and Dalrymple's calls for help from Central America went unanswered, leaving them in an uneasy stalemate with Matías de Gálvez. Newport was particularly vulnerable to another French attack, even with its five thousand troops and six warships. Clinton, worried that a potential capture could be seen as a second Saratoga, ordered the garrison's evacuation to New York. In the evening hours of October 25, 1779, the soldiers boarded transports and sailed out of sight, in their haste leaving behind forage and horses for the Americans who arrived the next morning.

The very day the British withdrew from Newport, d'Estaing's fleet departed Savannah to return to France. Clinton received the news at the end of November, and decided that with the North American coast temporarily clear of French warships, he could continue the long-considered Southern Strategy. As far back as 1776, British campaign plans had called for conquering the southern states, starting with Georgia and South Carolina, which were generally seen as more Loyalist than the northern states. Burgoyne's defeat at Saratoga had elevated the importance of this strategy. Burgoyne himself had returned to London deeply skeptical of the size and strength of Loyalist support in the former colonies; nevertheless, from Germain down to the generals and royal officials in America, the notion that overwhelming Loyalist forces in the South would be on hand to subdue the traitorous Continentals was accepted almost as gospel. If the thinly populated southern states could be subdued and brought back under the Crown, the thinking went, the British navy could blockade the northern states into submission without another, more costly ground offensive. The capture of Savannah and the restoration of British rule in Georgia were the first major steps in this new strategy, and having routed d'Estaing's forces, Clinton was now free to extend his conquests to Charleston.

New York City was already in the grip of the remorseless winter of 1779–80 that also plagued the Continental Army's Jockey Hollow encampment at Morristown, some thirty miles away. For the first and so far only time in recorded history, all saltwater estuaries along the entire northeastern seaboard were frozen solid. In early December, Washington's spies reported the extraordinary sight of cannon and supplies being hauled by sleigh across the frozen Hudson River to a hundred-ship fleet anchored at Paulus Hook, New Jersey, under the command of Vice Admiral Mariot Arbuthnot, recently arrived from Britain. Almost seven thousand British, Hessian, and Loyalist troops fought through shifting ice floes and high winds just to get aboard the ships. Clinton himself boarded one frigate, Cornwallis another, while Knyphausen was left in command of the city. The first sortie on December 10 turned back after ice and waves destroyed seven transports. On December 26, they finally were able to clear Sandy Hook, only to battle five weeks of mountainous seas and frigid winds before assembling off the Georgia coast at the end of January 1780.

Major General Lincoln had by then returned from Savannah to Charleston. Determining the city's defenses to be inadequate, he charged his two French engineers, Colonel Jean-Baptiste de Laumoy of Duportail's original company, and another recruit, Lieutenant Colonel Louis Antoine Cambray-Digny, to oversee their reinforcement. They were assisted by L'Enfant, who was still recuperating from the wounds he had received at Savannah. After receiving word in mid-January of Clinton's departure from New York, Lincoln called on Washington, the Congress, and the states of North Carolina and Virginia to send more troops to supplement the thirty-six hundred regulars and militia under his authority. A number of French volunteers were under Lincoln's command, including sixty from d'Estaing's fleet who had stayed behind after Savannah or were left behind because of their wounds. They were incorporated into a militia company commanded by Charles François Sevelinges, Marquis de Bretigny, a volunteer from Martinique who had been captured en route to America by the British and brought to Saint Augustine, but escaped to Philadelphia from the dungeon of Fort Saint Marks by disguising himself as a British sailor. The remains of Pulaski's cavalry, commanded by Major Pierre-François Vernier, would help defend the city's supply lines across the Cooper River. There was even a Spanish volunteer from Minorca, Jordi (Jorge) Ferragut Mesqueda, who had anglicized his name to George Farragut when he arrived as a merchant sailor in 1776, before joining the South Carolina navy as a lieutenant and commanding one of Charleston's war galleys.

Meanwhile, Arbuthnot had managed to reassemble and replenish the storm-tossed fleet, and sailed north to begin the assault. After landing thirty miles south of Charleston on February 11, 1780, British and Hessian troops slogged through the marshy terrain to begin surrounding the city. As Charleston is situated at the end of a peninsula, the key to the siege was to cut off the lines of supply and communication on the single landward side, while maintaining a naval blockade on the seaward sides. By late March, Clinton, bolstered with troops from Savannah to a strength of ten thousand men, had captured Fort Johnson south across the harbor from Charleston and sent Cornwallis northward to surround the city. Arbuthnot's fleet easily cut off any access to the Atlantic, forcing the Continental and South Carolina navies to sink their vessels as blockships to prevent closer intrusion to the city. Farragut and his naval comrades now served as artillery officers, having dismantled and remounted their cannon in shore batteries. The first of the Continental reinforcements from North Carolina and Virginia began arriving about this time, though they would only amount to fifteen hundred men, far fewer than the six thousand Lincoln had hoped to see. On April 1, the British and Hessian forces arrived at the northern neck of the city and began laying "parallels," or siege lines consisting of trenches and breastworks, slowly advancing on the city walls.

While the engineers were laying their siegeworks, Lieutenant Colonel Banastre Tarleton and his British Legion—a cavalry and infantry unit primarily composed of Loyalist troops—targeted a supply train for the Virginia Continentals. They set their sights on the Cooper River crossing near Moncks Corner, guarded by an American detachment under Brigadier General Isaac Huger, which included the Pulaski Legion under Vernier, and a Continental cavalry regiment under Lieutenant Colonel William Washington, a cousin of the commander in chief. In a lightning 3 a.m. raid on April 14, Tarleton's Legion routed the Americans, killing Vernier and several other Pulaski cavaliers, while Washington and Huger managed to escape into the swamps with most of their men and horses. Not only did Tarleton's victory net him a considerable quantity of arms and munitions at the expense of the Continentals, but it also cut off the only major escape route available to Lincoln. The American army was now trapped inside Charleston and running out of supplies. Despite these grim notices, Lincoln refused Clinton's offer of surrender.

British and Hessian engineers continued to advance their siege lines despite murderous fire from the Americans. On April 25, just as they began to erect their third parallel of trenches and redoubts, Bretigny's militia attacked in force, "yelling at the same time *avance, tue,* [advance and kill] which so filled our workmen and their guard with terror that the former ran away and the latter withdrew to the second parallel," reported one Hessian officer. This setback was only temporary, for as Colonel Laumoy, the only man in Charleston with significant siege experience, pointed out to Lincoln, the city's defenses would never be able to hold against the relentless advance, and advised capitulation. His view was confirmed with the arrival of the commandant of the Corps of Engineers Duportail, who had slipped through enemy lines after having been dispatched by George Washington a month earlier. A quick tour confirmed Laumoy's grim assessment: He found the "town in a desperate state, almost entirely invested [surrounded] by the British army and fleet," as he later reported to Washington, with surrender "unavoidable unless an army came to her assistance, which then did not appear likely."

With Charleston's citizens against surrender but the officers generally for it, Lincoln bartered with Clinton for terms of surrender until May 9, when the British commander unleashed a barrage of artillery that finally brought the Americans to terms. On May 12, 1780, Charleston's forces set down their arms. Most civilians were pardoned, and the militia, including Bretigny's company, were paroled, but over three thousand regulars were made prisoners of war, the single largest capture of American forces during the war. Duportail, who had arrived only days earlier, now found himself imprisoned several miles from Charleston at Haddrell's Point. He, along with other senior American officers, including Charleston's native son John Laurens, would be exchanged several months later for their British counterparts in the Convention Army of Saratoga. Many others, including Laumoy and L'Enfant, would not be paroled until 1782, almost at the end of the war.

With Georgia already under British rule and Charleston now in British hands, Clinton believed he had a clear path to subduing the rest of the South. So certain was he of an easy victory that, taking forty-five hundred soldiers and most of the heavy artillery back to New York City to protect against an expected French assault, he left Cornwallis in charge of three thousand men to consolidate power and put down any remaining resistance. Cornwallis wasted little time in carrying out his Southern Strategy, pursuing stray rebels and establishing Loyalist strongholds in the South Carolina backcountry. One of the first encounters took place on May 29 at Waxhaw Creek near the North Carolina border. Cornwallis had sent Tarleton's Legion in pursuit of a Continental force that had turned back after learning of Charleston's capture. After a three-day, 150-mile ride that left many horses dead from exhaustion, Tarleton's Loyalist Americans surrounded the Patriot Americans and unleashed a furious saber and bayonet attack that continued even when the Patriots asked for quarter, ultimately killing or wounding almost 80 percent of the rebels.

The British commander later stated that he had been unable to stop the carnage, but "Tarleton's quarter," the notion that British and Loyalist troops would kill insurgents rather than take them prisoner, became the rallying cry for Patriot forces to justify their own brutal actions against the Loyalists. The Revolution in the South became one of the war's bloodiest campaigns, and the most internecine. It was, in fact, a civil war that had as much to do with personal retribution between Patriots and Loyalists as with the question of national sovereignty. In South Carolina alone, more than one hundred battles were fought between Patriot and Loyalist Americans, with few British regulars even present. Generals in both the Continental and British armies often were powerless to halt the destruction that expended men and munitions to no strategic advantage for either side.

Into this chaotic cauldron Washington had sent some of his most trusted foreign volunteers, who he surely hoped would be able to bring some European discipline to bear. After learning of Pulaski's demise at Savannah, Colonel Charles Armand Tuffin, who had been conducting cavalry raids in New York and New England, asked to be transferred to the South. Washington and the Congress agreed, sending his legion to South Carolina where it would incorporate what was left of Pulaski's Legion after the fall of Charleston. Washington also dispatched Johann de Kalb, who had spent the last year inspecting troops without seeing battle, at the head of Continental regiments from Maryland and Delaware to relieve Charleston. De Kalb learned of Lincoln's capitulation while he was still in Virginia, but nevertheless continued through North Carolina in order to take command of the remaining forces. The Congress had other ideas, and instead selected Horatio Gates as head of the Southern Department. On July 25, de Kalb turned over command to Gates near the South Carolina border. The "Grand Army," as Gates called it, which incorporated de Kalb's regiments, three companies of artillery, and Armand's Legion, now marched south toward Camden, South Carolina, where Gates hoped to destroy one of Cornwallis's most important garrisons. Along the way he picked up two thousand militia, giving him an effective force of three thousand against Cornwallis's two thousand troops.

Each side was hoping to surprise the other when their lead cavalry elements clashed near Camden in the predawn hours of August 16, 1780, where Tarleton's Legion got the better of Armand's Legion in a pistol-and-sword fight before each one withdrew. As dawn approached, both sides formed their battle lines astride the Camden Road. Both generals followed the traditional British practice of placing their strongest troops in the post of honor on the right wing. In practice this meant that Cornwallis's finest troops, the 23rd and 33rd Regiments of the Foot, were face-to-face with raw North Carolina and Virginia militia on the American left. De Kalb, who as Gates's most experienced officer commanded the American right wing, faced Tarleton's foot soldiers and a Loyalist regiment from North Carolina on the British left. American field guns thundered the opening shots, and within a few minutes both lines were ablaze with musket and cannon fire. The British right fired one volley and then charged with bayonets into the American left. The inexperienced militia broke and ran under the onslaught.

De Kalb's right wing held its own against repeated attacks and even managed several successful counterattacks, until Cornwallis swung his own right and center through the fleeing American militia and flanked the American right wing. De Kalb's horse was shot out from under him, and in hand-to-hand fighting his skull was laid open by a saber. Still, the sixty-year-old Bavarian shook off the wound that would have stopped a man half his age, and rallied his troops for another counterattack. It took eleven musket balls to finally drop him, and even with his grievous wounds he lived another three days before he succumbed. By that time the Americans were in full flight from the enemy. Armand's Legion attempted to cover the retreat and save the American supply train at Rugeley's Mill, but was chased off by Tarleton's Legion. Gates, seeing that another rally at Rugeley's was impossible, left his troops behind and galloped all the way to Hillsborough, North Carolina, he later said, in order to reorganize his army. In actual fact, only eight hundred troops joined up with him, and two months later the Congress relieved him of command.

The Battle of Camden was a rout, the fighting over before the sun had barely cleared the horizon. With two major American defeats in as many months and with Gates effectively removed from command, the American forces in the South were leaderless and in disarray. There appeared to be nothing to stop Cornwallis's march into North Carolina and on toward Virginia. That is, until a contingent of 940 Patriots slogged through a driving rain on October 7 to attack an equal force of Loyalists guarding Cornwallis's left flank, who were perched atop Kings Mountain at the border between South and North Carolina. The battle was nasty, brutish, and short, as was the aftermath. The Patriot forces did not immediately accept the proffered surrender of the Loyalists, shouting "Tarleton's quarter" while they continued firing for several minutes after the white flag was shown. When Cornwallis learned of the battle, he was forced to abandon his push north and fell back through South Carolina. The British general did not realize at the time that this crucial delay would allow the American forces in the South to regroup into an army that would drive him toward his downfall; nor could he have even suspected that the torrential downpours that had enveloped Kings Mountain the morning of the battle were in fact the remnants of the first of a series of devastating hurricanes, striking far to the south in the Caribbean, which would reorder the balance of naval power there and make the end of the war possible.

On June 30, 1780, Alexander Hamilton, learning of John Laurens's parole in Philadelphia, and despondent over the loss of Charleston, poured out his anxieties to him: "If we are saved France and Spain must save us." Hamilton did not realize as he penned these lines that in less than a fortnight the French saviors he had wished for would arrive at Newport, and that in less than a year his hoped-for Spanish saviors would drive the British from Pensacola, laying the foundations for the victory that would indeed save the United States.

THE ARRIVAL OF THE *EXPÉDITION PARTICULIÈRE* AT NEWPORT

On May 10, 1780, the same day that Lafayette informed Washington of the approach of Ternay's *Expédition Particulière,* a British frigate docked in Charleston carrying the same news for Henry Clinton. That hard-won intelligence, gleaned from Britain's extensive spy network in France, was the reason Clinton had departed so quickly for New York. He was concerned that the five ships of the line in Arbuthnot's fleet would be no match for the twelve French ships that British intelligence had reported were on their way. London had the same misgivings, so at the same time as they dispatched a frigate to warn Clinton, they also ordered a squadron of six ships of the line to set out immediately under Rear Admiral Thomas Graves. A series of mishaps and a mutiny forced him to delay departure until May 17, two weeks after the fleet under Ternay had sailed from Brest.

Ternay did not have a dozen ships of the line, as Britain feared, nor was he able to obtain the large number of merchant ships needed to accommodate Rochambeau's demands for troops, munitions, and supplies. The *Expédition Particulière* had been laid on at a particularly bad time for the port of Brest. When the orders to fit out the new fleet came in February 1780, the dockyard already had its hands full repairing d'Estaing's battle-weary squadron that had just arrived two months earlier from Charleston, while at the same time outfitting Guichen's fleet, which was just about to sail to the West Indies. The naval commander in charge of the port, Charles Jean, Comte d'Hector, stripped other vessels in the region of their fittings to ready just seven ships of the line and twelve smaller warships, while only thirty-two merchant ships could be located to carry more troops, plus the guns, munitions, and accompanying engineers and artillery officers. With such limited cargo space, Rochambeau had to settle for taking only a thousand men from each of the four regiments, Bourbonnais, Saintonge, Soissonnais, and Royal Deux-Ponts, which he had trained at Vaussieux and originally had hoped to lead in the invasion of Britain. Another six hundred foreign volunteers would serve in the legion of the flamboyant Armand Louis de Gontaut, Duc de Lauzun, who had already seen action in Africa. The rest of the troops and supplies would have to sail in a second expedition as soon as enough vessels could be appropriated. On May 2, the fleet departed the Brest roadstead, formed into three divisions, and sailed toward America.

Ternay and Rochambeau had originally intended to make for Charleston or the Chesapeake Bay, but news from a passing merchant ship informed them that Charleston had fallen the previous month, and they mistook a fleet of merchant ships near the Chesapeake for British warships. With supplies running low and no other viable ports of call, they made for Newport. Early on July 11, through a dissipating fog they sighted a pair of white-and-gold Bourbon flags at the entrance to Narragansett Bay, the signals that Lafayette had placed to assure Ternay's fleet that Newport was now in friendly hands. The fleet came to anchor later that morning and the officers began debarking. Rochambeau's first official action ashore was political, not military, writing to Washington on July 12, "We are now, sir, under your command." Rochambeau was of course following the instructions of Vergennes, but the fact that he had set the tone for their relationship so early and unequivocally—the French would fight alongside the Americans, but always as subordinate to the American commander in chief—confirmed Montbarey's wisdom in selecting Rochambeau as a general who understood that war is always a continuation of politics by other means.

Jean-Baptiste-Donatien de Vimeur, Comte de Rochambeau (1725–1807).
Joseph-Désiré Court, eighteenth century, oil on canvas

The Americans who watched the arrival of the French fleet were understandably nervous. They had just been occupied by a military force—the British—scarcely nine months earlier. Now a new group of soldiers was coming ashore, and even if the French were America's allies, it would have been hard to forget that just fifteen years earlier they had been the enemy during the French and Indian War. One of the French artillery officers, Jean-François-Louis, Comte de Clermont-Crèvecoeur, recorded that the town was empty when they arrived. "The shops were closed, and the local people . . . would have preferred to see at that moment their enemies rather than their allies. We inspired the greatest terror in them." That all changed when Rochambeau met with the citizens of the town. His son and aide-de-camp Donatien-Marie-Joseph de Vimeur, Vicomte de Rochambeau, noted that the crowd was reserved and somber while he explained that the army was there at Washington's request and that the soldiers would be well disciplined, but when they were told that the French would pay for what they needed in silver coin, "their countenances brightened . . . at this mention of hard money." With inflation rampant—the Congress had just stopped issuing paper money, which was now worth just one-fortieth of the face value—the French were welcome as never before.

The next tasks for Ternay and Rochambeau were to establish defensive positions, find encampments for the troops and lodging for his officers, and ensure that all were provisioned. The French commissary officer Éthis de Corny was already working with Luzerne and his first secretary, François Barbé-Marbois, to secure food and transport for the troops. Corny had brought the modern equivalent of $300,000 in specie, but this was not enough to pay for the hundreds of wagons and teams of horses, thousands of head of livestock, and tons of foodstuffs that were needed, so they arranged for loans with the merchant John Holker, who took out credit under his account with Chaumont to cover the remainder. While these supplies were located and warehoused, Washington assigned Major General William Heath to coordinate the overall logistics needs for the French. He quickly established hospital facilities at Providence, which were almost immediately full as fifteen hundred French soldiers and sailors suffering from scurvy and dysentery were carried off the ships. Heath also arranged for the troop encampments on the island's central ridge east of the town, mapped out defenses, and called in militia from across New England to guard the allied forces as they disembarked. In four days the army troops were encamped, no doubt to the relief of the sailors, who now had more room on their ships where they remained quartered. Thanks to French engineers like Mathieu Dumas, in two weeks defenses were erected and artillery was in place. The town's leaders offered up their homes to the senior officers, with Rochambeau making his headquarters in the home of the merchant William Vernon, who also oversaw the Continental Navy's business in the region. Meanwhile, Ternay anchored his vessels in a defensive line against possible attacks by Arbuthnot, who was now patrolling the waters off Newport and whose fleet had just been reinforced with the arrival of Thomas Graves.

Any initial fears that the French were an invading force were quickly dispelled by their unfailing politeness. It was more than just that they brought hard cash to an ailing economy. One merchant commented that the French officers "are the most civilized men I ever met. They are temperate, prudent, and extremely attentive to duty." Heath, who had had an unfortunate experience several years before with the French engineer

Coudray, nevertheless stated, "I was always fond of our allies, but I assure you I never was more pleased than with the officers now here."

Those officers had come to America for a variety of reasons—most because they were under orders, but others having volunteered expressly for this expedition. Teissèdre de Fleury and Mauduit du Plessis, who had previously served as volunteers in the Continental Army and returned to France, jumped at the opportunity to fight the British again as part of the French army. Some had more personal motives: One was "tormented" by the desire for glory in combat; another wished to escape the unnamed "grief" he had suffered. Louis Marie, Vicomte de Noailles, having watched his brother-in-law Lafayette attain glory in America, had volunteered for the Soissonnais regiment. Hans Axel von Fersen, a wealthy Swedish count and confidant of Queen Marie Antoinette, had interrupted his social ascent in the French court to volunteer as a colonel. Louis-Alexandre Berthier, the son of the architect who had designed the Hôtels de la Guerre, Marine, et des Affaires Étrangères at Versailles and had continued in the family profession as a military surveyor, had such a strong "taste for a profession of which I had seen only the reflection" that after being rejected by Ternay for the initial voyage, he caught a frigate bound for Martinique and made his way to Newport, where after arriving in September he was attached to the Soissonnais regiment. Most of the officers were highly literate—one, Major-General François Jean, Marquis de Chastellux, was a member of the Académie française—and kept meticulous diaries and journals of their campaigns, some of which were later published.

The rank-and-file soldiers and noncommissioned officers represented a typical cross section of France's regions and social classes, from peasants to artisans to minor nobility. Most were single men between eighteen and thirty, although the oldest was sixty-one and the youngest was a four-year-old drummer boy. Unlike some of the officers, they were not volunteers for the fight in America—few of them even knew their destination was the United States until they were almost at the Chesapeake—but since most were illiterate or barely literate, almost none left any record of their thoughts and observations during the campaigns. One exception was Private Georg Daniel Flohr of the Royal Deux-Ponts, which in fact was a mostly German-speaking regiment from the Alsace and Zweibrücken under the command of Guillaume, Comte de Deux-Ponts. Flohr's journal was filled with insightful descriptions of towns and their inhabitants, but almost nothing about the American cause for which he was about to fight. If he paid little attention to the notion of political freedom, Flohr was greatly impressed with the religious and social freedoms he saw around him.

As the French forces settled into their new quarters, discussion turned to the strategy the two armies should jointly pursue. Lafayette, Washington's emissary to Rochambeau, left his camp at Dobbs Ferry and arrived at Newport on July 24, where he immediately urged an attack on New York City. He was well aware that the recapture of New York had been Washington's goal since he had been driven out in 1776, and believed that such an attack was a military and political necessity for the combined French-American forces. Rochambeau and Ternay did not disagree with that judgment, but told him that with many of their troops still convalescing and supplies only slowly coming in, they simply lacked the means to do so. They were also appalled at the state of the Continental Army and militia, who were arriving at their own camps scarcely able to fend for themselves; Rochambeau referred to the whole war effort as "a cord stretched to the limit." Washington certainly would have agreed with that assessment; back in February, in response to a French request for the Americans to provide more troops for the upcoming fighting season, he had informed Luzerne that after the deprivations of the terrible winter at Morristown "our force is so reduced by the expiration of the terms [of enlistment] for which a considerable part of it was engaged . . . as scarcely to suffice for the exigence of the service." Washington had also learned from d'Estaing's campaigns that without naval superiority, any assault on the city would be futile, and Ternay's fleet was at the moment bottled up at Newport by Arbuthnot.

The conference ended without reaching a conclusion. Back at Dobbs Ferry, Lafayette continued to press for an attack on New York, as he wrote in a twelve-page missive to Rochambeau and Ternay. "I assure you that action is important in this campaign," he asserted, arguing that inaction would be fatal to their cause. Rochambeau was furious; he complained bitterly about the extravagance of these demands to Luzerne, who was everyone's confidant in this dispute. To Lafayette he was gentler, but he still put the younger man firmly in his place: "My dear marquis, allow an old father to reply to you as a dear son," he wrote on August 27; Lafayette was two years younger than his own son. "You know me well enough to believe that I have no need to be spurred, and that at my age when a decision is reached . . . all the incitements possible cannot make me change without a positive order from my general [Washington]. It is always good to think the French invincible, but I am going to tell you a secret learned from forty years' experience. There are no easier men to defeat than those who have lost confidence in their leaders, and they lose it at once when they have been endangered through personal and selfish ambition." Lafayette knew he had gone too far, and he begged for forgiveness from all quarters.

Lafayette's importuning had at least persuaded Washington and Rochambeau to meet face-to-face in Hartford, Connecticut, halfway between the two camps. Leaving their seconds in command, Antoine Charles du Houx, Baron de Vioménil, and Charles Sochet, Chevalier des Touches, in charge, Rochambeau and Ternay set out by carriage, which had to be repaired along the way. They brought in tow several young officers, including Fersen, Dumas, and the Vicomte de Rochambeau, to serve as interpreters and aides-de-camp. Washington, meanwhile, had Henry Knox by his side, along with Lafayette, Alexander Hamilton, and Jean-Baptiste de Gouvion, his acting chief engineer while Duportail was languishing in Charleston under British arrest. Late in the morning of September 21, 1780, Washington and Rochambeau met for the first time in front of the state capitol building at Hartford. Washington, standing six feet two inches and broad in the shoulders, had an "air of sadness," as Fersen later reported. Rochambeau, stocky with an aura of calm self-possession, was, at age fifty-five, seven years older than his American counterpart and the veteran of many more wars. Yet as they clasped hands, each man would have seen in the other a sober, competent leader upon whom he could rely. Introductions made, they walked a few blocks to the home of Jeremiah Wadsworth, a commissary agent who had been helping Corny with provisioning the French forces. There, the three senior officers retired to a room, accompanied only by Lafayette, who acted as interpreter and scribe.

Over the course of the next two days, Rochambeau, Ternay, and Washington agreed on a few strategic points. The first was that "naval superiority" was essential for any operations; at that moment, they were hoping for the arrival of Guichen and his fleet, not knowing that he had already left the West Indies and was on his way to Cádiz. The second was that once command of the sea was established, "New York should become the object of the combined operations." Third, both armies needed reinforcements, between twenty and thirty thousand more troops than they currently had under arms. Washington was noncommittal about the Congress being able to supply half these troops, bluntly stating that given the weakened state of the American forces and the growing strength of the British navy, Louis XVI "should add to our many other obligations and to other proofs of his generous interest, that of assisting the United States of America by sending them more ships, more men, and more money," an assessment with which both Rochambeau and Ternay agreed. Until such assistance was sent, there could be no hope for an offensive push against the British.

At the end of the Hartford conference, Lafayette and Hamilton made clean copies of the report and requests for French troops and money. These were given to the Vicomte de Rochambeau to hand-deliver to Vergennes, along with instructions to memorize them in case he was captured and had to destroy them. The following month he boarded the frigate *Amazone* commanded by Jean-François de La Pérouse. A massive hurricane that had already wrecked a Spanish naval fleet in the Gulf of Mexico now scattered Arbuthnot's blockading fleet, allowing *Amazone* to break out and arrive in France in November. The Congress, meanwhile, sent John Laurens to Paris with a similar request to carry to Vergennes, asking for 25 million livres in new loans. This was only the latest in a series of ultimately futile moves by the Congress to circumvent Franklin's diplomacy. John Adams had arrived unannounced in Paris back in February 1780, appointed as minister plenipotentiary to negotiate a peace treaty with Britain, except that with the war continuing to rage, there was no peace to be negotiated, so he moved to Amsterdam to obtain recognition for the American republic. A month earlier John Jay had arrived in Madrid in an attempt to open diplomatic negotiations with the Spanish court, but Spain had entered the war solely as an ally of France and would not recognize the United States until the War of American Independence had ended. Henry Laurens, John's father, had left the American coast in August 1780 to obtain loans from the Dutch Republic, but his ship was captured at sea the following month and he was imprisoned in the Tower of London. When John Laurens arrived in Paris in February 1781 to ask for more money, Franklin, who had already been attempting to secure a new loan from the French court, decided that he had had enough and offered his resignation to the Congress, which was refused.

Back at Newport, with no possibility for an offensive campaign until at least the spring of 1781, the French settled into winter life. There were, to be sure, disciplinary problems brought on by boredom, but on the whole the soldiers got on well with the locals. They took English lessons, attended dances, and had even established something of a French community, using their printing press to circulate a local newspaper, *Gazette Françoise,* that summarized the American press as well as local news. Their daily routines were marred by the death on December 15 of Ternay, whose illness—likely typhoid fever—had begun back at Hartford. Command of the squadron was turned over to des Touches.

Washington and his aides also thought they would be returning from the Hartford conference to their daily routines at their winter headquarters in New Windsor, New York, on the Hudson River. On September 25, they decided to pay a visit to Benedict Arnold, now the commander at West Point. Unbeknownst to them, Arnold, who after the Battle of Saratoga felt increasingly misused and ill-treated by Washington and the Congress, had been conspiring with Clinton's adjutant-general, Major John André, to arrange for the British to capture West Point, which would have put the entire Hudson River under British control and split the nation in two. Just as Lafayette's aide arrived at Arnold's home to inform them of Washington's arrival, Arnold received news that André had been captured with incriminating papers that revealed his traitorous plot. Leaving his wife behind, Arnold quickly fled to the sloop HMS *Vulture* moored in the Hudson River. Washington, Knox, Lafayette, and Hamilton arrived at the house shortly afterward, took a quick tour of West Point, and returned to find Arnold still unaccountably absent. Their puzzlement turned to anxiety and then rage when they were shown the papers that revealed Arnold's "blackest treason," which might have also resulted in Washington's own capture. By then Arnold was safely aboard the British warship, which brought him straight to Clinton in New York City, who commissioned him as a brigadier general. André was summarily hanged, but Washington's bitter hatred for Arnold would soon be shared by Lafayette, who took to heart the betrayal of his father figure and commander in chief. He would soon attempt to capture or kill the turncoat, only to find himself pursued by Cornwallis across the backwoods of Virginia.

THE RACE TO THE CHESAPEAKE

The defection of Benedict Arnold, and his subsequent assignment by Clinton to invade Virginia as a diversion for Cornwallis's campaign in the South, proved to be a harbinger of the cruel winter of 1780–81. It was not as severe in terms of cold as the previous winter, where the incessant snowfalls and bitter temperatures so reduced the availability of forage and supplies that the soldiers at the Morristown encampment quite literally ate their own shoes. It was, however, Washington's harshest winter in terms of morale. The defeats at Charleston and Camden had shaken the confidence of the Continental Army to its core. Food and clothing were in short supply, as was the supply of money; a horse that sold for $40,000 in the spring now cost $150,000 in the hyperinflated currency of the time, which mattered little since Congress was incapable of raising funds for the army. Salaries went unpaid for months and years, and Washington's communications with Rochambeau came to an almost complete halt when he ran out of funds to pay his couriers. The nadir occurred in January 1781, when Anthony Wayne's Pennsylvania Continentals mutinied over lack of pay, followed by the New Jersey brigade. The mutinies were suppressed by a mix of negotiation and punishment, but not before Washington worried to the Congress of "an end to all subordination in the Army, and indeed to the Army itself." The French troops were also short of money and supplies, and incapable of sortieing from Newport to resupply in the West Indies, since their seven ships of the line were blockaded by Arbuthnot's ten ships patrolling between Narragansett Bay and the eastern end of Long Island. That Clinton and Arbuthnot could not agree on a strategy to assault Newport was one of the few apparent bright spots for the French and American allies.

And yet the tide of the war was, almost imperceptibly at first, beginning to turn. Back in October, when the Congress had removed Horatio Gates from command of the Southern Department, Washington immediately nominated—and the Congress approved—Nathanael Greene to replace him. Washington also appointed his old Valley Forge drillmaster Friedrich Wilhelm von Steuben as Greene's second in command. Greene, who once spoke of foreign officers "as so many spies in our camp," was now grateful for their presence. Greene and Steuben were still in Philadelphia when they heard of the American victory at Kings Mountain, surely a promising omen. As they marched through Virginia, Greene left Steuben in the capital, Richmond, to take command there and organize recruits and supplies for the army, while Greene took command from Gates at Hillsborough, North Carolina, in December. Greene knew he could not defeat Cornwallis head-to-head as his predecessor had tried to do at Camden. Instead, he divided his forces in his campaign through South Carolina so as to split Cornwallis's army. While Greene went southeast, Brigadier General Daniel Morgan went southwest. Meanwhile, Greene assigned Thaddeus Kosciuszko, as his newly appointed engineer, to build a flotilla of boats that would enable his armies to fall back through North Carolina and across the Dan River into Virginia. Cornwallis reacted exactly as Greene had hoped, splitting his forces three ways and sending Banastre Tarleton after Morgan. On January 17, Morgan led Tarleton into a trap at Cowpens, luring him into charging his militia in the center while springing a flanking cavalry attack by William Washington. The battle resulted in the death or capture of most of Tarleton's troops, though Tarleton himself escaped after shooting William Washington's horse from under him. In early February, Greene and Morgan linked back up, then outran Cornwallis's determined pursuit to board Kosciuszko's hastily built boats and cross the Dan River into the relative safety of southern Virginia.

Southern Virginia may have been a safe haven for the Continentals, but that was not true of the state's central region. British naval forces had recently entered the Chesapeake Bay and attacked Portsmouth and Suffolk at the mouth of the James River, before suddenly departing. Since the James is a tidal estuary navigable by smaller seagoing ships almost all the way to Richmond, Steuben knew that another British invasion could endanger the capital and the surrounding munitions foundries. He proposed to Virginia governor Thomas Jefferson to build a small fort on a bend in the river at Hood's Landing to forestall such an attack. Jefferson brushed those plans aside, arguing that such an attack was implausible, and in any event the militia required to build and man it were needed elsewhere. On December 29, 1780, Arnold and his sixteen hundred men appeared in the Chesapeake Bay. A week later his frigates and sloops sailed past Hood's Landing and dropped anchor at Westover, just twenty-five miles from the capital. As Jefferson and the rest of the population fled, Arnold torched Richmond and destroyed or captured arms and munitions before withdrawing to Portsmouth to establish and fortify a new British base of operations, followed closely by Steuben.

Washington was gripped with the need to stop Arnold at any cost. It was more than just personal—Arnold's troops stood in the way of resupplying Greene's army in the Carolinas. A light infantry force could conceivably capture him, but Arnold's escape route had first to be cut off by sea. Even if regular couriers no longer ran between Newport and New Windsor, some mail still got through, including Washington's request to Rochambeau and des Touches for a squadron to stopper the Chesapeake Bay. Fortunately for the French, the British blockade was temporarily lifted when a powerful nor'easter tore through the region on the evening of January 22, 1781. It scattered Arbuthnot's fleet, destroying one ship of the line and crippling two more. Suddenly, the French and British had nearly equal ship numbers. Wasting little time, des Touches assigned Captain Armand Le Gardeur de Tilly to take a small squadron to attack Arnold's isolated position in Portsmouth. Arriving in mid-February, Tilly made several attempts to burn Arnold's fleet, but his deeper-draft ships could not ascend the Elizabeth River. On his return he captured a British convoy, bringing the forty-four-gun HMS *Romulus* into his fleet and capturing 7,000 guineas (just over $1 million today) in specie. The same day Tilly returned to Newport, February 25, another 1.5 million livres ($10 million) in coin came into Boston aboard the frigate *Astrée,* which had almost been dismasted in the same nor'easter that wrecked Arbuthnot's fleet. Its commander, La Pérouse, who had just a few months earlier conveyed the report of the Hartford conference to Vergennes, carried back word that the young Vicomte de Rochambeau remained in Versailles while the court continued its deliberations over what to do about its American ally, but had no instructions for Lieutenant General Rochambeau regarding the 1781 campaign.

When the sputtering mail system alerted Washington to the news of Tilly's expedition—though minus important details like the size of the invading force—he determined to detach from his main army a light infantry column and send it to Virginia in order to counter Arnold's invasion. As a symbol of what he hoped would be a joint French-American operation, on February 20 he ordered Lafayette to take command of the twelve hundred men now gathering in Peekskill, New York. His three battalions were themselves led by a mix of French volunteer and American officers, with Gouvion leading the engineers. Washington's orders left no doubt as to their mission: "Do no act whatever with Arnold that . . . may screen him from the punishment due to his treason and desertion, which if he should fall into your hands, you will execute in the most summary way." The expedition moved quickly, arriving on March 3 at Head of Elk, Maryland, at the top of the Chesapeake Bay, and a week later at Annapolis, where they were blockaded into inaction by a British squadron. Lafayette nevertheless took a barge with a small contingent of soldiers to Yorktown. There he and Steuben attempted with little success to request that Jefferson marshal enough militia to crush Arnold's forces, while a second French naval expedition would once again attempt to prevent his escape.

The second French naval expedition to capture Arnold was planned in haste almost immediately upon Tilly's return. Rochambeau, having learned from captured dispatches of the importance of Arnold's forces to Cornwallis's campaign, sent his aide Ludwig von Closen from the Royal Deux-Ponts to courier a message to Washington that they would be sending a fleet to the Chesapeake under des Touches, with a force of eleven hundred light and heavy infantry under Vioménil, to assist Lafayette. Closen covered the two hundred miles in three days, and was rewarded with the news that Washington would return with him to Newport to review the French troops. He arrived on March 6 to great acclaim. The fully manned warships were dressed in flags and gave him a thirteen-gun salute, while French troops in dress uniforms lined the streets as he marched past under honors normally reserved for a full marshal of France. As he met with the senior officers aboard the flagship *Duc de Bourgogne,* it certainly appeared that any memory of Washington as the instigator of the now-distant Battle of Jumonville Glen had either been long erased or long forgiven.

The ten warships in des Touches's fleet weighed anchor just before sunset on March 8. With the exceptions of the frigates *Hermione* and *Amazone,* ships of the line *Neptune* and *Éveillé,* and the captured *Romulus* they were uncoppered, and having been idle at anchor for the past six months, they were heavily fouled with barnacles and seaweed that greatly slowed them down. Des Touches, aboard *Neptune,* had to frequently heave to and wait for the slowest ships to catch up during the laborious voyage to the Chesapeake, made more so by having to travel far outside the normal shipping lanes to avoid detection by Arbuthnot. The British commander, anchored at Gardiner's Island off the eastern end of Long Island, did not learn of des Touches's sailing until the morning of March 10. He immediately led his fleet of eleven coppered warships around Montauk Point and into the Atlantic in pursuit. Coppering made all the difference—despite a thirty-six-hour handicap, Arbuthnot arrived at the Chesapeake just ahead of the French fleet on the morning of March 16. The ensuing daylong Battle of Cape Henry belonged to des Touches in terms of tactics and maneuvering, but in strategic terms Arbuthnot had won before the first shot was fired. By arriving in second place at the Chesapeake, des Touches realized, he could never accomplish his mission of debarking the troops while under fire from the British fleet. He turned for Newport the next day to repair the damage, while Arbuthnot entered the Chesapeake to form a protective cordon against further French incursions. Learning of Arbuthnot's success, Clinton sent two thousand troops to reinforce Arnold, and they began arriving on March 25.

Lafayette was heartbroken at the lost opportunity to capture and presumably hang the traitor he had once considered a friend, but his emotions were more complex when he learned that the reinforcements would be led by Major General William Phillips, who took over command of the British forces from Arnold. Lafayette's father, he was always reminded while growing up, had died in a hail of artillery fire during the Battle of Minden. That artillery battery was commanded by then-captain Phillips. If *revanche* were the natural response to the intelligence he had just received, he kept it in check when he asked Greene to be allowed to lead the troops against this new British force, saying, "I will now only mention that General Phillips's battery, at Minden, having killed my father, I should have no objection to contract the latitude of his plans."

Lafayette made that request of Greene because per Washington's orders he was now part of the Southern Department and subordinate to Greene. After Greene had escaped from Cornwallis across the Dan River, he had been sufficiently reinforced to return to North Carolina and confront Cornwallis. The British general sortied from his headquarters at Hillsborough to meet Greene head-on. At the hamlet of Guilford Courthouse on March 15, Cornwallis won a Pyrrhic victory so costly that he was forced to withdraw to Wilmington, North Carolina. Greene pursued Cornwallis for several days before breaking off, determined to retake South Carolina. Now, so as to keep Cornwallis from linking up with Arnold and Phillips, he assigned Lafayette to harass the latter while he kept the former occupied in the Deep South. The plan was "a great piece of generalship," Lafayette admitted to Greene, and he hastened to comply. By April 19, Lafayette was back with his troops who were now in Baltimore, and he led them on a forced march through the springtime heat to Richmond, leaving behind baggage, tents, artillery, and anything else that would encumber them. Time was of the essence; Arnold and

Phillips were moving up the James River, and had defeated Steuben to capture Petersburg, just twenty-five miles south of Richmond. On April 29, Lafayette and his bedraggled troops slogged into the capital just in time to stave off an attack by Phillips, who fumed and "swore vengeance against me," he reported to Washington.

Lafayette's forced march certainly had saved what was left of Richmond, but just days later he learned that Cornwallis had directed his second in command, Francis Rawdon, to go after Greene in South Carolina, while he and Tarleton were on their way north to Virginia to link up at Petersburg with Arnold and Phillips. Lafayette attempted to forestall that on May 10 by marching on Petersburg and shelling Phillips's positions, a sort of Battle of Minden in reverse. Phillips did die in front of Lafayette's guns, though not from a shell—instead, he grew weaker and lapsed into a coma from an undiagnosed fever, succumbing several days later. If retribution of sorts had been meted out for one of Lafayette's enemies, it would escape the other. Arnold was only briefly in command before Cornwallis arrived to take the reins from him. He had in fact been ordered by Clinton to return to New York. Benedict Arnold, once again and for the final time, had slipped from Lafayette's grasp.

With Greene occupied in retaking South Carolina, Washington gave the young French general free rein. Lafayette now had the major independent command he had longed for, for the first and what would turn out to be the only time in his career. To his own surprise, independent command made him timorous where as a subordinate he would have been bold. His caution was well placed, the mark of a seasoned leader. As he set about reorganizing his corps, he realized that he had just twelve hundred regulars, another forty cavalry from Armand's Legion, and two thousand Virginia militia, or just over three thousand ill-equipped men facing seventy-two hundred experienced troops under Cornwallis. As Cornwallis began to sally forth from Petersburg, Lafayette abandoned Richmond, while Jefferson and the rest of the Virginia government decamped to Charlottesville. Now began the cat-and-mouse game between the two generals. Cornwallis had become a soldier the very year Lafayette was born, and even if he never wrote the phrase "the boy cannot escape me," as Lafayette himself later claimed, the British general had little doubt about his opponent's lack of ability or the outcome of the chase. Lafayette, for his part, adopted the same Fabian strategy that his commander in chief had perfected earlier in the war, and told him so directly: "I am determined to skirmish, but not engage too far," he admitted to Washington on May 24. "We are not strong enough even to get beaten."

Lafayette's instructions from Washington were to keep north of Cornwallis, in order to protect his own lines of communication as well as the American supply depots at Fredericksburg, where Lafayette also hoped to link up with Anthony Wayne's reconstituted Pennsylvania Continentals. Cornwallis passed up the opportunity to capture Richmond in order to give chase to Lafayette and at the same time to hobble Greene's operations by wrecking his sources of supplies and recruits in Virginia. The British general picked up additional reinforcements at Westover on the James River, then moved north and west while destroying or capturing enemy depots, manufactures, and government institutions along the way. He dispatched Tarleton to raid Jefferson's home at Monticello, barely missing the fleeing governor. On June 6, Loyalists captured a crucial supply depot at Point of Fork on the James River, which Steuben, outgunned and outnumbered, was unable to defend. Shortly thereafter, Wayne and his eight hundred Continentals joined up with Lafayette. By mid-June, with further reinforcements from Steuben and Virginia militia, he had five thousand troops under his command.

Cornwallis had realized by this point that his enemy's force was considerably enlarged and no longer worth the effort to run to ground. He was also running out of supplies and forage himself, so he determined to move east to the British base at Portsmouth, raiding farms and plantations and sacking what was left of Richmond along the way. By early June he was near Williamsburg. Lafayette had chased him along the way, looking for an opportunity to engage him with his enlarged force. On July 6, he saw the opportunity to attack Cornwallis's rear guard while they attempted to cross the James River toward Portsmouth. Cornwallis had anticipated this and set an ambush close to the Green Spring Plantation, which nearly trapped Wayne's advance guard before he managed to fall back after a bayonet charge. While Lafayette withdrew his forces to a strong defensive position near Richmond, Cornwallis arrived at Portsmouth. There he found dispatches from Clinton, pointing out that since Portsmouth was too shallow to accept deep-draft British warships, Cornwallis needed to establish a deepwater port in the region for overwintering the fleet. Based on his engineers' reports, Cornwallis moved his troops on August 1 to Yorktown, a tobacco port on the York River, and Gloucester Point just opposite, where he began fortifying the sites and ensuring that the wharves below the town could accommodate British warships. Lafayette repositioned his forces to guard against any potential breakout, while reporting back to Washington that for the time being, Cornwallis was fixed at Yorktown. The first pieces in the endgame were now in place.

While Lafayette and Cornwallis had been chasing each other across Virginia, back in New England several other pieces were also moving into position. Some of those pieces were put into motion soon after des Touches's disappointing return from the Chesapeake. There was a sense among both the French and American leaders that further action against the British was needed, and at the Hartford conference they had already agreed that New York should be the objective. In late March, Rochambeau wrote Washington that he would be ready to come to New York when the American general opened his campaign. Washington told Rochambeau that such action would not be needed for some time yet, but asked him to begin preparations. Rochambeau complied by ordering his quartermaster general, Pierre-François de Béville, to survey the roads between Newport and New York, and contracting with Jeremiah Wadsworth to buy horses, oxen, and wagons for transport and to build up campsites and supply depots for the campaign.

On May 10, 1781, the French frigate *Concorde* arrived in Newport, carrying important passengers, cargo, and dispatches that hastened the progress of the endgame. Back in France, the political landscape had changed considerably from when Ternay and Rochambeau had departed exactly one year before. The death in December 1780 of Maria Theresa of Austria had not only plunged Versailles into mourning, it had also placed all of Europe on tenterhooks. Marie Antoinette's brother Joseph II, now on the Austrian throne and something of an unknown quantity, was likely to seek an alliance with Russia, the repercussions of which might place France on a war footing. Meanwhile, Spain was certain to ask France for more help in recovering Gibraltar, and the arrival of the large British fleet in the Caribbean under Vice Admiral Rodney put the French colonies there at risk. All of these uncertainties had to be dealt with by a new council of ministers at Versailles, which was itself something of an unknown quantity. In October 1780, Sartine had been replaced as minister of the navy by Charles de La Croix, Marquis de Castries, a highly decorated army general and a friend of Finance Minister Jacques Necker. In December in another palace shake-up, the minister of war, Montbarey, was replaced by another general and friend of Necker, Philippe Henri, Marquis de Ségur. Necker, now at the apogee of power, released his famous *Compte rendu au roi* (Statement of Accounts to the King) in January 1781, which for the first time revealed to the public the actual financial state of the French government with details of revenue and expenditures, a practice long observed in the British Parliament. While the *Compte rendu* indicated that there was "a surplus sufficient to pay for loans needed for the campaign of 1781," the credit balance amounted only to 10 million livres and would have to be carefully husbanded. As the king's new council looked out over the foreign policy landscape for the upcoming year, the American war still stood at the center, but France's interests in preserving the Bourbon Alliance and maintaining its rich West Indies colonies would have to take precedence if the war dragged on too much longer.

The debates over American independence that took place in the halls of Versailles during the early part of 1781 were every bit as careful and deliberate as those that rang through the halls of the Pennsylvania State House, and would have equal if not greater ramifications for the year ahead. The dispatches brought by the Vicomte de Rochambeau "were thoroughly examined and discussed in the king's council." Memoranda on France's strategic alternatives were prepared by the *commis* and argued over by the ministers. Much of the focus was on the second expedition that had been promised to Rochambeau to bring his additional troops and supplies, and to the reinforcements that both Washington and Rochambeau had asked for at Hartford. That demand, the ministers noted, was based on the thin promise that Washington "might" have ten to fifteen thousand troops available. Even if France sent another ten thousand men to the United States, they further argued, then Britain would do so as well and the entire war would just escalate. Additionally, those same troops might be needed to meet the increased threat in the Caribbean and new demands from Spain. Finally, the cost of sending that second expedition and those troops to America would amount to 30 million livres; even if Vergennes was beginning to disavow Necker's financial policies, he could hardly ignore that this sum was far greater than the very public budget surplus that the *Compte rendu* revealed. It would be much cheaper simply to underwrite the cost of maintaining the American army, which was calculated as 670,000 livres for twelve thousand troops. So when John Laurens came before Vergennes almost brandishing his sword to demand more money, it simply provided the foreign minister the pretext to further finance the Americans, a decision to which he had already come.

The dispatches that *Concorde* carried back to Newport outlined Versailles's intentions for the upcoming campaign and also explained its unexpected passengers and cargo. One of the first to debark would have been the Comte de Barras, who had been with d'Estaing during the 1778 expedition and now took command of the naval squadron from a disappointed des Touches. Rochambeau was heartened to see his son the Vicomte de Rochambeau return, but was discouraged that the second expedition he had been promised would not arrive. Instead, Louis XVI had promised Franklin and John Laurens another 6 million livres, not the 25 million that the Congress had wanted, but this would be a gift, not a loan. *Concorde* carried 1 million of that sum, which amounted to almost five tons of coin carried in barrels. A second convoy under the escort of the fifty-gun *Sagittaire* was due to arrive in Boston in June with another 2.5 million livres, as well as six hundred troops and artillery. John Laurens would be given the final 2.5 million livres, minus expenses for war materiel, when he departed for the United States later that summer.

The most important news by far was conveyed by two almost identical letters, one from Ségur and the other from Castries, telling Rochambeau that a fleet of twenty ships of the line and thirty-two hundred troops, bound for the defense of the Caribbean, had already set sail in late March under the flag of the newly promoted Lieutenant General Comte de Grasse. While these were not the dedicated reinforcements for the *Expédition Particulière* that Rochambeau had hoped for, he learned that de Grasse, after his scheduled arrival in Martinique in July or August, would be able to pick up another ten ships there and then sail north to temporarily support Rochambeau's operations on the American coast. When combined with the eight ships already at Newport, the French would have an overwhelming naval advantage over the British, but only for a brief window of time. Ségur made no specific recommendations as to what those "operations" might be; it was up to Rochambeau to make those plans with Barras, Washington, and eventually de Grasse himself. There was absolutely no time to waste; de Grasse could be anywhere on the East Coast in a matter of weeks. The next morning, May 11, a courier sped off to New Windsor to ask Washington for an urgent meeting. Washington responded immediately, proposing to meet on May 21 at Wethersfield, a small town in Connecticut just south of Hartford. Washington brought Henry Knox and his engineer, Duportail, who had recently been paroled from Charleston. Anxious to avoid delays, Rochambeau and his aide Chastellux rode on horseback to the meeting instead of taking a breakdown-prone carriage.

The two parties met at the handsome three-storied timber-framed home of Joseph Webb, the next-door neighbor of Silas Deane. In stark contrast to the French king's council, which deliberated under gilded arches and sumptuous oil paintings, or the Second Continental Congress, whose debates occurred in grand, high-ceilinged chambers, the most consequential meeting of the entire war took place in a sparely decorated parlor whose plank floors creaked underfoot. The Wethersfield conference started on the afternoon of the twenty-first and continued until the following day. Both generals were far too experienced to make definitive plans in the face of so many unknowns—how many troops each would bring, what were the British intentions, and, most important, what de Grasse's timetable would be. Instead, they would draw the grand outline and fill in the details later, as information became available. Rochambeau was under orders to keep Washington in the dark about the details of de Grasse's fleet, but through letters from Chastellux, Washington was at least certain it would arrive. The leaders discussed two possible sites for an attack—the original objective of New York, or the British forces gathering in Virginia. Both men agreed that Virginia was the least attractive alternative; Barras's fleet was too small to transport the troops and equipment needed, wagons and beasts of burden might be hard to come by, and a march overland in the brutal southern summer heat would be devastating to both armies. New York remained the logical choice, but for either operation they needed de Grasse's fleet to ensure "naval superiority," as Washington noted in his diary. Rochambeau agreed to send dispatches to de Grasse, advising him of the situation and urging him to the American coast; but what was left unclear was the destination, as Washington wanted de Grasse to come directly to New York, while Rochambeau believed in leaving that decision to de Grasse. For the time being, Rochambeau would begin moving his troops to New York while awaiting de Grasse's reply as to his decision and destination. The meeting ended on that note.

Rochambeau penned several letters to de Grasse explaining the situation and requesting his assistance. On May 28 he said:

François Joseph Paul, Comte de Grasse (1722–1788).
Jean-Baptiste Mauzaisse, 1842, oil on canvas

> America and especially her Southern states are in a very grave crisis. The arrival of the Count de Grasse can save her. . . . There are two points to act offensively against the enemy: the Chesapeake and New York. The southwest winds and the troubles in Virginia will probably make you prefer the Chesapeake Bay, and this will be where we think you can render the greatest service, especially as it only takes you two days to come from there to New York.

Sagittaire docked in Boston on June 10 with letters from de Grasse to Rochambeau. The French general learned that de Grasse would arrive that summer and was requesting instructions on where to land, and also needed pilots who were familiar with American waters to be brought to his base at Cap François in Saint-Domingue. De Grasse cautioned that his ships might have difficulty passing the shallow Sandy Hook bar at the entrance to New York harbor, and further warned that he could only stay a short while. Rochambeau's reply to de Grasse underlined the urgency of the situation: "I cannot hide from you, Monsieur, that the Americans are at the end of their resources." So was he; his army was desperately short of funds, so he asked de Grasse to obtain another 1.2 million livres in specie from the intendant at Cap François. Rochambeau then told de Grasse that he was about "to join the General [Washington] to attempt, by threatening New York, to create a diversion in favor of Virginia." He asked that de Grasse bring ships and troops to "help us destroy their establishments in Portsmouth," before moving on to attack New York. He admitted that Washington preferred a direct attack on New York, without striking first in Virginia, but warned that the British fleet appeared to be ready to sail for the South. At Barras's request, he also included a note from Luzerne, who appealed for de Grasse to bring ships and troops to relieve Lafayette in Virginia. He ended the letter asking de Grasse to immediately let him know "the time and place of your arrival." Even if it appeared that Rochambeau was placing in the hands of de Grasse the final decision on where to attack, the trail of hints and suggestions left no doubt that he was all but shouting for de Grasse to meet him at the Chesapeake.

Twelve American pilots boarded the frigate *Concorde,* and the packet of Rochambeau's letters to de Grasse was handed to its captain, Louis-Marie, Chevalier de La Tanouarn. By foresight and perhaps by fortune, *Concorde* was one of France's newest, fastest, and most seaworthy warships. Like its sister ship *Hermione,* it was copper-clad and built according to the latest scientific theories of hydrodynamics by Jean-Denis Chevillard, a graduate of France's unique École du génie maritime (School of Naval Engineering). *Concorde* sortied from Boston on June 20 for its fateful rendezvous at Cap François. The future of the entire campaign, it is no exaggeration to state, rode on the speed and surety of this ship.

By then, Rochambeau's army had already departed Newport and was marching overland. His planning with his quartermaster general, Béville, and the Continental commissary agent Wadsworth now paid off. The route was carefully marked, supply depots and campsites were already established, with bread ovens and water already in place, so that the forty-three hundred men, plus another thousand servants, were able to march about twelve to fifteen miles a day without deviation or foraging for supplies. Every part of the march had been meticulously thought out beforehand. Troops were awakened at 2 a.m. and on the road by 4 a.m., so they could reach the next camp before noon to avoid the worst of the summer heat. The four main regiments were spaced one day apart so that each camp was not overwhelmed: Bourbonnais first, commanded by Rochambeau, then Royal Deux-Ponts, Soissonnais, and finally Saintonge. Each regiment and corps wore different uniforms—Bourbonnais and Saintonge had white lapels, Royal Deux-Ponts blue, Soissonnais red—so that from afar the roads on which they marched appeared to be slowly moving, multicolored ribbons.

Rochambeau's army joined the sixty-three hundred troops under Washington at Westchester County, New York, on July 6, and in the following days the two men reviewed the troops in the company of Luzerne. Rochambeau's aide Closen was particularly struck by the largely black regiment from Rhode Island, which he stated was the "most neatly dressed, the best under arms and the most precise in its maneuver." Still lacking any word from de Grasse, in late July Washington and Rochambeau started reconnoitering New York, with Duportail estimating the troops and materiel needed for an assault. By then, Arbuthnot had departed for Britain, leaving Graves in command of the squadron, which had five ships of the line. Clinton's forces numbered ten thousand soldiers who could be considered effective for combat. Duportail's report, sent July 25, indicated that a successful assault on the city would be feasible only with large-scale naval support and double their current troop numbers.

That doubling of the troop numbers was not only infeasible, it soon was no longer necessary. On August 14, Rochambeau and Washington received the long-awaited letter from de Grasse. *Concorde* had reached Cap François in the rapid time of eighteen days, arriving a week before de Grasse's appearance on July 16. Upon opening and reading Rochambeau's packets, de Grasse could not ignore the obvious indications that he was needed most urgently at the Chesapeake Bay, "the location which it seems to me that you, Washington, Luzerne, and Barras indicated would be the surest place to carry out the object proposed," as he stated in his reply. After several crucial meetings with the Spanish, he began preparations for the campaign. On July 28 he sent *Concorde* back to Newport with the pivotal news that he would set sail for the Chesapeake within a few days, with twenty-nine ships of the line and thirty-two hundred troops. On that crucial return trip *Concorde* beat its outbound passage by sailing almost twice as fast as other similar warships, requiring just fourteen days to arrive at Newport on August 11. Barras's courier reached the camp in Westchester three days later.

Rochambeau had kept Washington fully informed of his correspondence with de Grasse, so Washington knew that it had been Rochambeau, not himself, who had decided the place and time of the great battle that might determine the outcome of the War of American Independence; yet there was never a question of resentment. He was naturally disappointed to "give up all idea of attacking New York," but wasted no time in changing his plans to suit the new situation. The generals soon learned from Lafayette's reports that Cornwallis was fortifying Yorktown, and that they would have to corner him there. Washington quickly selected veteran troops from New Jersey, New York, and New England, as well as Hazen's Second Canadian Regiment, as the American force. Dispatches flew by courier to de Grasse for when he arrived at the Chesapeake Bay, to Barras ordering him to load his fleet with the artillery siege train and set sail to meet de Grasse there, and to Lafayette cautioning him to keep Cornwallis bottled up. Duportail, meanwhile, was sent to meet with the fleet and organize the activities of the land and sea forces. Washington and Rochambeau now had to coordinate three separate armies and two fleets across hundreds of miles in the face of unknown enemy resistance to arrive simultaneously at one location, and to do so in just six weeks.

On the American and French sides, most of the pieces of the endgame were now in place. But in order for the upcoming campaign to be successful, British power in the Gulf of Mexico and the West Indies would have to be at least temporarily neutralized, and that could only happen if Spain were to have a commanding presence there. The Spanish pieces of the endgame had been gathering far to the south in Havana, arrayed to descend on the British stronghold at Pensacola. But just as they were prepared to attack, a series of massive hurricanes, including the most destructive on record, would scatter those pieces across the Gulf of Mexico and threaten the whole enterprise.

CHAPTER 7

The Endgame

Before Columbus's second voyage to the West Indies in 1494, no modern European had ever witnessed or even imagined the sustained fury of a hurricane, where winds can blow upwards of 100 knots, wiping away entire landscapes, and where waves of phenomenal height can reduce ships to kindling. Hurricanes, we now understand, start when hot, dust-laden air from the Sahara forms clusters of thunderstorms off the coast of Africa. Combining and growing as they cross the Atlantic, they may pass through the Caribbean into the Gulf of Mexico or swing north along the North American coast. The Spanish word *huracán* came from an approximation of what the indigenous Taíno people of the Caribbean called the storms, which the French transliterated into *ouragan* and the English into "hurricane." As Spain and other nations established colonies in the New World, they gradually learned how to plan naval movements to avoid the worst months of hurricane season (generally September and October, around the time of the autumn equinox), which was why d'Estaing had been in such a hurry to depart Savannah in October 1779.

When Bernardo de Gálvez and José Solano met in Havana in August 1780 to plan the attack on Pensacola, the dangers of operating during the height of hurricane season were very well known. The 1780 season was already shaping up to be particularly destructive; one hurricane had already swept through Puerto Rico in June, and another one in August had devastated New Orleans. However, the orders that Solano had brought from Madrid to capture the British capital made no allowance for the weather. The military leader of Cuba, Captain-General Navarro, held five *juntas de generales* (war councils) during the course of the next month to agree on the strategy for the assault. Gálvez argued for an immediate, large-scale amphibious descent, based on intelligence about the British fortification gathered two years earlier by his spy Jacinto Panis, and recently updated by Mobile governor José de Ezpeleta from accounts by British deserters. The narrow entrance to Pensacola Bay, they reported, was guarded by a battery at the top of the Barrancas Coloradas (Red Cliffs) and naval forces below, but the battery was almost devoid of cannon and the small naval force could be reduced by a sustained attack from Spanish warships. Gálvez was supported by Solano, who would provide escort for the invasion fleet, and by General Juan Manuel de Cagigal, who had recently arrived in Cuba after participating in the siege of Gibraltar and would lead part of the ground assault. Navarro, along with his naval commander, Juan Bautista Bonet, had little faith in the plan and worried that a rumored British fleet could threaten the convoy and Havana. Solano immediately sortied to look for the British fleet, but found nothing. At the beginning of October, two more *juntas* laid to rest the fears of Navarro and Bonet. Now Solano wanted to wait several days, as his sea sense told him that the meteorological and tidal conditions pointed to a dangerous impending storm. The landlubberly Gálvez would brook no more delays, and under his continued pressure the *junta* voted on October 15 for the convoy to depart the next morning.

Solano had good reason to fear the weather. At the beginning of October, the first of a series of powerful hurricanes swept through the Caribbean. Known as the Savanna-la-Mar Hurricane, it pummeled Jamaica on October 3, leveling several towns and destroying five warships in Vice Admiral Peter Parker's fleet at Port Royal. The next day it passed over central Cuba before skirting the American eastern seaboard—this was the hurricane that dropped torrents of rain on Patriot and Loyalist troops at Kings Mountain in South Carolina. A week later on October 10, a second, even more massive hurricane rolled into the Caribbean through the Leeward Islands. Known today as the Great Hurricane of 1780, it created a trail of devastation three thousand miles long that left over twenty thousand people dead—by far the most destructive hurricane ever recorded. With estimated winds of 200 knots, it first laid Barbados to waste—every tree on the island was flattened, and not one home, building, or fort was left intact. Saint Lucia was next, where six thousand people perished, and every home save two was destroyed in the port city of Castries. In the harbor, eight British warships were sunk or wrecked, with one being bodily lifted by the incoming waves and dropped atop the city's hospital. Martinique lost nine thousand people, the highest single death toll of the storm, but of the French naval fleet only the frigate *Junon* was lost. The storm continued unabated through the island chain—Guadeloupe, Dominica, Puerto Rico, Santo Domingo—and then passed into the Atlantic, where it heaped its final fury on Bermuda before disappearing off Newfoundland.

The news of this massive sequence of annihilation had not reached Havana, almost a thousand miles away, when Solano's fleet of fourteen warships, escorting fifty transports carrying four thousand troops, set sail on October 16 under a freshening breeze that carried it into the Gulf of Mexico. Solano's instinct was soon proved correct; that very evening the wind gained strength, and by next day the third great hurricane of October came roaring over Havana and smashed into the fleet. Solano's Hurricane, as it became known, moved slowly through the warm Gulf waters, maintaining its strength for almost a week before passing over Florida, and several days later scattering the British blockading fleet under Arbuthnot at Newport. For eighty hours Solano's fleet was pummeled by wind and waves and scattered from Florida to Mexico. His flagship, *San Juan Nepomuceno,* was dismasted, so Solano ordered its captain to return the jury-rigged ship to Cuba. Meanwhile, he transferred his flag to the frigate *Santa Rosalía* in order to gather up the remaining ships and press on with the attack. Despite his valiant efforts, it proved to be a fruitless endeavor. He found only a few ships near the rendezvous point off Mobile, not enough to carry out an assault, and was forced to return to Havana. It would turn out that, despite the storm's violence, only one ship was sunk and another was destroyed on shore, though most of the remaining ships were badly damaged. Many vessels had taken refuge in the Yucatán; some ended up in New Orleans, others at Mobile. Gálvez's own frigate encountered several other ships of the fleet, but despite his protests, the captains took stock of their dwindling supplies and elected to return to Havana, managing to capture two British frigates en route. The dockyard workers at Havana, who had been steadily rebuilding the Spanish fleet since the end of the Seven Years' War, were now furiously patching and repairing the storm-tossed vessels as they limped into port.

On November 30, another *junta de generales* was assembled to determine "if there ought to be and could be a new attempt at Pensacola." The combative Gálvez emphasized the need for an immediate attack; the enemy garrison there was also badly affected by the storm, he said, as was the British base at Jamaica. Had the Spanish lost their vaunted "military virtue," he asked scornfully, or "will we retreat upon suffering a single setback?" While the *junta* was still deliberating—once again, Navarro and Bonet opposed Gálvez's plans—word came from José de Ezpeleta that Mobile was under threat of a British assault from Pensacola. Gálvez's confident assertion that the British garrison at Pensacola had been weakened was wrong and dangerously misguided; in fact, its commanders had been emboldened by the assumed destruction of the Spanish invasion fleet to attempt a recapture of Mobile. Gálvez promptly convinced the *junta* to send five hundred troops to aid in the defense, but before they could arrive in Mobile, a combined land and naval force attacked an outpost called the Village on January 7, 1781. Although Ezpeleta had only two hundred troops there to counter the seven hundred men that Pensacola had sent against them, they repelled the attacks with deadly musket volleys. Ezpeleta could not contain his pride when he reported to Gálvez that "our troops are acquiring a certain superiority over the enemy, which may be very useful in the future," alluding to the hoped-for assault on Pensacola.

"Superiority over the enemy" certainly applied to the disposition of Spanish and French naval forces in the Caribbean, as Vice Admiral Rodney, the British commander in chief of the region, discovered there on his return from New York. Back in August 1780, soon after the inconclusive Battle of Martinique, he learned of Ternay's fleet en route to North America. On his own authority he took thirteen ships to New York to help convince Clinton and Arbuthnot to take offensive action against the French at Newport, but the two men continually rebuffed him. When news of the hurricanes reached him, Rodney returned to his base in December to be greeted by almost complete destruction. Barbados was nothing but mud, debris, and decaying corpses of men and beasts. The mainstay of the island's economy, its sugarcane crop and mills, was gone. The scene repeated itself on the other islands. Food and water, never plentiful, were now dangerously scarce and barely capable of sustaining his fleet, which itself was much reduced. Of the twenty-seven British warships that had been deployed around the Caribbean stations before the October hurricanes, almost half were destroyed and the rest damaged, some severely. By comparison, the Spanish had lost just two warships and the French just one, leaving them with, respectively, twenty and twenty-seven warships. It would have been obvious to Rodney that the naval balance of power in the West Indies had shifted to the Bourbon empires, but events four thousand miles away in the Dutch Republic would soon draw his attention elsewhere.

"YO SOLO"... PERO NO SOLAMENTE YO: GÁLVEZ AND SOLANO CAPTURE PENSACOLA

The importance to Spain of recapturing Pensacola was far out of proportion to its apparent lack of value to British military leaders. Even after the outbreak of the War of American Independence, it only had a colonial governor, Peter Chester, until it belatedly received a military commander, Brigadier General John Campbell, who arrived in January 1779 with Loyalist troops recently evacuated from Philadelphia. Campbell was faced with the difficult task of organizing a disparate group of defenders against the determined attacks by the Spanish. Of his roughly two thousand troops, fewer than half were professional soldiers from the British army, navy, and Loyalist contingents. In addition to militia, Campbell also had a substantial force of enslaved Africans, as well as Native Americans from the Choctaw and Creek nations, who fought in the belief that their interests were better served by the British than by the colonials. Campbell had little else to draw upon to defend his own territory, much less to carry out the attack on New Orleans that Secretary of State for the Colonies Germain requested soon after Campbell had assumed command. With the American brigadier general George Rogers Clark now at Vincennes and the Spanish occupying Natchez, there was no hope for reinforcements from British settlements farther up the Mississippi. Nor could he count upon much assistance from Jamaica; Peter Parker's main concerns were to defend the British sugar colonies and convoys from attack against a resurgent French presence in the West Indies, and to support his governor, John Dalling, in his campaign against Matías de Gálvez in Central America.

Parker's ability to reinforce Pensacola had been crippled by the devastating hurricanes of October 1780, but it was Britain's war over trade with the Dutch Republic, and specifically Rodney's actions as a result of it, that placed any naval assistance to the beleaguered fortification beyond Campbell's reach. That trade war had its roots in the declaration in March 1780 by Catherine II that Russia would establish an armed fleet of twelve ships of the line and five frigates to protect the rights of neutral nations to trade with belligerents on both sides of the war, on the internationally recognized maxim that neutral ships are assumed to carry neutral cargo—"free ships make free goods." This maxim was more honored in the breach than the observance during wartime. For several years, Britain in particular, but also France and Spain, had been detaining a number of ships from neutral countries like Russia, Denmark, Sweden, and the Dutch Republic, which were trading with their adversaries. Catherine wanted to put a stop to that, so she invited other neutral nations to join her League of Armed Neutrality, as it was known. Denmark and Sweden quickly signed on. The British government fumed, but, not wanting to antagonize Russia, it could do little to interfere—that is, until the Dutch Republic sought membership in the league. Of all the neutral nations, the Dutch Republic represented the gravest threat to Britain's war effort, as it supplied the greatest quantity of war materiel to its enemies. Since 1774, the Dutch Republic had tacitly allowed its merchants to supply the American colonials with munitions and gunpowder, and since 1778 it had openly permitted them to provide naval stores and timber to France. The British government could not tolerate these practices under Russia's protection, so it decided to go to war to forestall the agreement. London therefore manufactured a pretext of Dutch nonneutrality, based on the discovery of an old draft of a commercial treaty between the United States and Amsterdam that was in the possession of Henry Laurens, who had been captured at sea in September 1780 while he was en route to negotiate loans with the Dutch Republic. With those documents in hand, Britain declared war before the Dutch government could sign on to the league.

The two nations had already gone to war over trade three times since 1652; on December 20, 1780, the Fourth Anglo-Dutch War was declared, with orders sent that same day to Rodney to capture Sint Eustatius, the hub of contraband trade in the Caribbean. He received those orders at the end of January 1781, shortly after his depleted squadron had been reinforced with eight ships of the line under Rear Admiral Samuel Hood. On February 3, Rodney descended "as sudden as a clap of thunder" on the Dutch island, which was largely defenseless and unaware that it was even at war, taking it without a fight. The value of goods contained in its hundreds of ships and warehouses was estimated at £3 million, close to $40 billion today. Expecting to receive a very handsome reward, Rodney remained on the island for several months to personally account for all the captured wealth, while sending Hood with a large squadron to blockade four French warships in Fort Royal, Martinique, and dispatching two sloops to bloodlessly capture the sugar colonies in Dutch Guiana (Suriname). Rodney also used up more warships to escort the treasure convoy home, although it was captured with all its plunder by the French *chef d'escadre* La Motte-Picquet just before it made landfall in Britain. With calls for help coming from all corners of the Caribbean and Gulf of Mexico, Parker could scarcely find any vessels to aid the Pensacola garrison.

By contrast, Field Marshal Bernardo de Gálvez—he had just received word of his promotion—was prepared to throw everything he had at the British capital in order to secure its capture. His *junta* compatriots Navarro and Bonet were initially unwilling to commit to a major assault so soon after the disastrous hurricane, until the sudden appearance of Carlos III's personal envoy, Francisco Saavedra de Sangronis, changed their minds. At the time, Saavedra was fourth secretary to Minister of the Indies José de Gálvez, and although just a step up from *covachuelista* was already in charge of the ministry's financial affairs. His presence in Havana stemmed from reports sent to Madrid back in mid-1780 about the disagreements between Gálvez, Navarro, and Bonet over the early campaigns against Mobile and Pensacola. Upon hearing of the obstacles his nephew faced, José de Gálvez confided in Saavedra that Havana needed a man from Madrid who could "communicate to the military leaders with the voice of the Court, bring them into agreement [and] arrange for the payment of funds." Saavedra immediately volunteered for that duty, and with direct orders from Carlos III embarked in August 1780. A British warship captured his vessel in November, but he went unrecognized as a court official and was released from Jamaica at the New Year, arriving at Havana on January 22, 1781.

Saavedra immediately began taking stock of the situation, speaking individually with the members of the *junta de generales* and with the French commander Chevalier de Monteil, who had recently arrived to careen and scrape his nine warships at the Havana dockyard. Saavedra got on well with Bernardo de Gálvez, not only because they were about the same age and came from the same province of Andalusia, but also because they agreed on the urgency to take Pensacola. The other members of the *junta,* he discovered, supported the operation to varying degrees, but they also had to support Matías de Gálvez in Nicaragua as well as plan for a future attack on the main British stronghold at Jamaica; their concerns about overstretching their limited manpower, money, and supplies were very real. Monteil, he found, was eager to assist the Spanish fleet, and anxious to go into action before he was forced to return to the Windward Islands to protect French commerce from British attacks.

On February 1, Navarro called the first of six *juntas,* which included the "voice of the Court." Saavedra made it clear to them that their king demanded nothing less than the "total expulsion of the English from the Gulf of Mexico," and desired the immediate execution of the assault against Pensacola. Saavedra's presence animated a sea change in the *junta* members; where before many saw only impediments, they now all vowed that they were "ready to execute the royal intention." Over the course of the next two weeks the *junta* debated strategy and tactics. They agreed that, despite their having just one-third the number of troops that had embarked the previous October, Pensacola should be attacked immediately. Saavedra knew that the Spanish invasion force would be undermanned, and promised Gálvez that he would secure more ships and troops to bolster his position should the British send reinforcements. Meanwhile, Ezpeleta would be ordered to march his troops overland from Mobile to Pensacola, and more reinforcements were called in from New Orleans. Only after Pensacola fell would Havana obtain additional funds from Mexico and provide reinforcements to Nicaragua; the planned assault on Jamaica would have to wait until the following year. The fleet was ready to sail on February 21, two days after the final *junta,* but the weather did not cooperate for another week. On February 28, just after midnight, two of Monteil's warships briefly sortied from Havana to sweep the sea lanes of any danger; two hours before sunrise, thirty-two Spanish ships carrying just fifteen hundred troops made sail; and by noon they had disappeared over the horizon.

Pensacola Bay is one of the largest and most defensible anchorages on the northern Gulf coast, which was why Spain first occupied it and why the British made it their capital of West Florida. The Santa Rosa barrier island protects it from waves and storm surges, while its only entrance is through a shallow, narrow inlet requiring a sharp turn to gain access, a difficult maneuver under sail that in practice would leave an enemy ship nearly immobile and vulnerable to the Red Cliffs shore battery, which the Spanish learned had lately been reinforced with heavy cannon. Soon after departure from Havana, Gálvez called his commanders aboard the sixty-four-gun flagship *San Ramón* to explain his strategy. First, they would seize the western end of Santa Rosa overlooking the inlet and install cannon there to drive away blockading British warships; they would then sail the fleet into Pensacola Bay to await the reinforcements from Mobile and New Orleans, before laying siege to Fort George and its redoubts just north of Pensacola proper. On March 9, the fleet approached Santa Rosa, waiting until the cover of night before landing troops ashore. But the British had already spotted the fleet, and Campbell, too, waited until nightfall the next day before dispatching his copper-bottomed sloop HMS *Childers* to slip past the Spanish and send for help from Parker at Jamaica.

The landings went unopposed, as did the construction of a Spanish battery at the end of Santa Rosa Island on March 11 that drove the British warships deep into the bay. Just after midnight under a full moon, the Spanish fleet attempted to force the entrance, but *San Ramón* went aground on a sandbar. The fleet commander, José Calvo de Irazábal, ordered the ship to be lightened, and upon freeing it withdrew the squadron. Gálvez wrote a note to Calvo demanding that he try to force the straits again; Calvo and his senior officers refused his orders, replying indignantly that it was too dangerous to sail under the Red Cliffs battery. After several days of argument, during which time a Spanish landing party attempting to storm the Red Cliffs was repelled by Campbell's Choctaw warriors, Gálvez resolved to force the strait himself.

Early on Sunday, March 18, Gálvez prepared to board his personal sloop *Galveztown*, which had joined the fleet from Havana a few days earlier, to show the rest of the Spanish fleet that the strait was indeed passable. In an echo of the ultimatum that he had made a decade earlier to his troops fighting the Apache nation, he sent Calvo and his officers a sharply worded challenge: "He who has honor and valor, follow me. I am going ahead on the *Galveztown* to take away your fear." The fleet commander fired back that Gálvez "was the real coward, who had his cannon ass-backwards." Gálvez ignored the insult, and at 2:30 p.m. boarded *Galveztown* and ordered it through the inlet. With the flag pennant flown so the British knew exactly who was aboard, *Galveztown* and three other vessels tacked through the dangerous turns while staying close to Santa Rosa Island. The British cannon on Red Cliffs let fly, and while some of the heavy shot tore through sails and rigging, most splashed harmlessly around the ships. Gálvez's intuition had been correct; after closely examining the Red Cliffs redoubt, he had realized it was too high and too far away to accurately range the whole inlet, so that the probability of a hit was minimal. Now safely inside the bay, he exulted to his assembled crews, "I alone went to sacrifice myself so as not to expose any soldier or member of my army," overlooking the obvious fact that they also had been "sacrificed." He then waited for the rest of the fleet to follow. The next day Calvo ordered the other warships into the bay, where they too had sails and rigging torn by cannon fire but suffered no major damage and no casualties. By afternoon they were all safely anchored under the protection of the Spanish cannon on Santa Rosa Island. Calvo himself remained aboard *San Rámon* anchored outside the bay, as it was too deep to traverse the inlet. In any event, he could no longer serve with Gálvez, electing instead to return to Havana. Now bereft of their most powerful warship, the Spanish invasion force could only hunker down and await reinforcements.

The next day Gálvez began a train of correspondence with Campbell and Governor Chester that was every bit as chivalrous as that with Durnford at Mobile. "We partake in this war because of duty, not because of hatred," Gálvez reminded them, setting out the conditions for the conduct of hostilities, exchange of prisoners, and protection of civilians. Fighting would be limited to Fort George and the outlying redoubts; the town of Pensacola would be spared. Gálvez was firm but polite, the British commander equally so: We will "defend this post to the last," Campbell assured him. While the exchange of letters was going on, Ezpeleta arrived from Mobile with nine hundred troops, managing to evade detection along the way. Gálvez immediately sent his troops from Santa Rosa Island to link up with them on the mainland. Scarcely had they broken their first bivouac the following day when they sighted sixteen sails from New Orleans, loaded with cannon, munitions, and sixteen hundred troops. Gálvez now had about four thousand men under arms, enough to begin planning their attack.

On March 26, Gálvez began moving his troops closer to Pensacola. For several days they resisted deadly attacks by mostly Choctaw warriors, before securing camp around the Bayou Chico. Too far from Fort George to lay siege, but unable to advance, they had now reached a stalemate. Gálvez wrote to Havana for more aid, now unsuspectingly in the same position as Campbell, who was still waiting for word from Jamaica. On April 12, the British launched a major assault that caught the Spanish by surprise. After a short but fierce battle the British withdrew, but Gálvez was wounded by a ball through his left hand that struck his abdomen. Handing over command to Ezpeleta, he was treated in the hospital while the stalemate continued. On April 18, his convalescence was surely quickened when he received news from Havana that his father, Matías de Gálvez, had recaptured the Inmaculada Concepción fortress in Nicaragua and had pushed the British back to the coast.

The following day saw another arrival from Havana: twenty ships under the flag of José Solano, including eight French warships under Monteil, who had agreed to postpone an assault on a British blockade in South America to join the invasion. The combined fleet had been hastily formed ten days earlier by the *junta* after receiving reports from fishermen who sighted what they thought was a British convoy sailing for Pensacola, and determined to carry out Saavedra's earlier promise to send reinforcements if the British attempted to do so. In fact, the sloop HMS *Childers* had brought word of the assault to the British at Jamaica, but the governor was only able to release two warships carrying a regiment of ex-prisoners, which in the event never actually bothered to reach Pensacola. It was apparent that Campbell would never be reinforced, and that with a total of seventy-six hundred troops, Gálvez now had overwhelming superiority; for the moment his biggest worry appeared to be where he would billet the almost four thousand men who waded ashore.

Solano's fleet had arrived just when it was needed most. Supplies were running low; the Spanish troops were down to three ounces of beans per day. The fleet also brought cannon, mortars, siege tools, and gunpowder. Most welcome were the battle-hardened troops under the leadership of Gibraltar veteran Juan Manuel de Cagigal, whose previous command of the Pensacola invasion forces had been scattered to the winds. His assistant Francisco de Miranda, a native of Caracas in colonial Venezuela, had participated in the siege of Melilla in North Africa several years earlier. The Spanish forces included French-speaking troops from Flanders, members of the Irish Hibernia Regiment, and Gálvez's own Regimiento Fijo de La Luisiana. One of the brigade commanders was Jerónimo Girón y Moctezuma, a ninth-generation descendant of the Aztec leader Moctezuma whose reign was brutally ended by the conquistador Hernán Cortés in 1520. On the French side, most of the soldiers from its five regiments had been at the Siege of Savannah or in the conquests of Saint Vincent and Grenada. Finally, Saavedra himself accompanied the fleet aboard Solano's seventy-four-gun flagship, *San Luis,* which remained outside Pensacola Bay, along with the other deep-draft ships of the line, to stand guard against any possible counteroffensive from Jamaica.

On April 24, with troops and artillery now offloaded, the combined Spanish-French army began its siege. The first objective was a large hill just to the west of Fort George, which also overlooked the Prince of Wales' and Queen's Redoubts. Gálvez, now recovered and back in command, was certain that the key to the British position was the northernmost Queen's Redoubt. After a three-day struggle to take the overlooking hill, he ordered his men to extend their siege trenches around the north side of the redoubts. Campbell countered with intense artillery fire and several flanking attacks, but over the course of a week the Bourbon siege lines were extended, and their own artillery kept the British at bay. By May 6, Gálvez's position was becoming desperate. He confided to Saavedra that his supply of shot was almost exhausted, despite offering his soldiers one peso for every four British cannonballs recovered. The French commander, also realizing their precarious position, reminded Gálvez that he had postponed a campaign to assist him, and threatened to withdraw if Campbell did not soon surrender. Almost desperate, Gálvez ordered Girón and Ezpeleta to attempt a nighttime assault on the Queen's Redoubt, but they withdrew when the approaching dawn eliminated the element of surprise. Now the only chance for success lay with the Spanish artillery that had been emplaced just two hundred yards from the British fortification.

With time and supplies almost running out, a lucky shot ended the siege. About 9 a.m. on May 8, one of the two newly placed Spanish howitzers lobbed a six-inch fused grenade into the Queen's Redoubt, which just cleared the top of the powder magazine and detonated at the open door that faced to the rear. The resulting explosion of powder and munitions leveled much of the redoubt and instantly killed over one hundred British troops. As soon as Gálvez and his officers heard the blast and witnessed its devastating effects, they ordered a general charge into the ruined fort and overwhelmed it. They then brought in cannon and howitzers and began firing on the Prince of Wales' Redoubt, which fell silent about midday. An intense artillery duel with Fort George, the last British stronghold, continued until 3 p.m., when Campbell raised the white flag and dispatched an envoy to request a cease-fire. Gálvez firmly rejected any delay and sent the envoy back with terms of surrender that he had already prepared. Campbell returned the terms with additional articles. Negotiations continued until after midnight, when the surrender was agreed to, in which Campbell and Chester ceded all of West Florida to the Spanish. At 2 p.m. the next day, May 9, a clean copy of the surrender was signed. On May 10, Spanish troops occupied the town. Arturo (Arthur) O'Neill, one of the Wild Geese of the Hibernia Regiment, was named governor, while Gálvez and Solano returned to Havana. Campbell, Chester, and most of the troops were released from captivity, but Gálvez did not remand them to Havana, where they would be a burden on a city already overstretched with soldiers and sailors, nor did he parole them to Jamaica, which he fully intended to attack in the near future. Instead, Gálvez paroled them to the British base in New York City. By his calculation this was the most expedient action, since Spain was not directly allied with the United States; but it also meant that the British soldiers could once again take up arms against the Americans.

The victory of Gálvez and Solano at Pensacola was the culmination of a two-year struggle to return the Gulf of Mexico to Spanish rule. The remaining British forces in East Florida, and those in Central America still in battle with Matías de Gálvez, were of minor strategic consequence. For his service to the Spanish Empire, Carlos III granted Gálvez the title Conde de Gálvez in 1783, and allowed him to place the words *Yo Solo* (I Alone) on his coat of arms, in commemoration of his single-handedly forcing the strait at Pensacola. The following year the king also acknowledged that the victory was not only Gálvez's (*pero no solamente "yo"*), but also belonged to the men who fought with him, by granting the newly promoted Captain-General José Solano y Bote the title Marqués de Socorro for the aid (*socorro*) he provided to Gálvez at the crucial moment.

To American leaders in the Congress and on the front lines, the siege of Pensacola appeared but a sideshow to their own battles. Part of this dismissiveness was due to the death of Juan de Miralles a year earlier. Miralles, who had carried out with aplomb his duties as Spain's informal

The Capture of Pensacola: Explosion of Queen's Redoubt Magazine, May 8, 1781. Nicolas Ponce, after Berteaux Lausan [1784?], engraving

ambassador, had been a well-respected figure in Philadelphia and had even been invited to witness Washington's troops in review at their Morristown encampment in April 1780. While there, the aged diplomat had contracted "pulmonic fever" (likely pneumonia), and despite the ministrations of Washington's own doctor, he died on April 28 in the commander in chief's residence. Miralles's secretary Francisco de Rendón succeeded him, but with Spain already at war in places far removed from Philadelphia, there was little need for local intelligence or helping with covert aid. Rendón's duties and interactions were much curtailed, primarily focused on obtaining commercial contracts to ship flour and foodstuffs to hurricane-ravaged Havana. Washington took little notice when Rendón informed him of the Spanish victory at Pensacola, writing only a cursory reply: "[I] congratulate you in the success of His Catholic Majesty's Arms at Pensacola, and I have no doubt but a recital of the particulars will reflect much honor upon General Don Gálvez and the troops under his command." In spite of Washington's offhandedness, it would soon become apparent that Spain's newly won dominion over the Gulf of Mexico gave America's French allies the liberty to array all of their naval forces against the British at the most critical moment of the war, the battles of the Chesapeake and Yorktown. It would become obvious later still that Spain's driving out the British from West Florida, thus eliminating both its menace and influence, had secured the nation's southern border and helped ensure its future as a sovereign power.

THE BATTLE OF THE CHESAPEAKE

François Joseph Paul, Comte de Grasse, had decided at an early age to become a naval officer. Born in 1722 in Provence, he was eleven years old when he joined the Order of the Knights of Saint John of Jerusalem, also known as the Knights of Malta. As one of the Catholic Church's oldest military orders, it had long been associated with the French navy and counted among its members some of its highest-ranking officers; de Grasse's contemporaries Ternay and Suffren also had belonged to the order. After joining the navy at age eighteen, de Grasse steadily rose through the ranks in the War of Austrian Succession and the Seven Years' War. When France entered the war of American Independence, he held increasingly high-level commands at the Battle of Ouessant and in the campaigns of d'Estaing and Guichen in the West Indies. He was tall, physically courageous, and beloved by his sailors, who said of him, "The Comte de Grasse stands six foot four, and six foot five on days of battle."

De Grasse had been part of the forty-ship fleet that sailed from Cádiz to Brest in January 1781. He returned that winter to an empty château, as his second wife, Catherine—whose immense plantations in Saint-Domingue he had added to his own—had died while he was on campaign. He did not have to endure the echoes for long, for the new minister of the navy, Castries, called him to Versailles a few weeks later to promote him to lieutenant general and give him command of one of three fleets that were to carry out the campaigns of 1781. De Grasse would take the first and largest fleet to the West Indies, with the mission of defending the French islands and assisting the Spanish in their conquest of the primary British base at Jamaica. Depending upon the needs of the Spanish, as an alternate mission he would go to the American coast to cooperate with Rochambeau and Washington. Barras was assigned to take command of the *Expédition Particulière* fleet in Newport. Pierre André de Suffren would take the third fleet, really a squadron, to help the Dutch defend Cape Town against the British, then go to India to recover Pondicherry and other French and Dutch possessions that the British had captured shortly after France allied with America in 1778.

On March 22, 190 ships departed Brest harbor, with de Grasse leading in his flagship, *Ville de Paris*. A week later, Suffren detached from this fleet with a squadron of five ships of the line and a dozen merchant ships bound for the Cape of Good Hope. The following day, *Sagittaire* and its convoy separated from the main fleet and made for Boston. De Grasse arrived at Martinique on April 28, to find Hood's squadron blockading Fort Royal. Hood was caught entirely off guard by de Grasse's arrival; back in London, First Lord of the Admiralty Sandwich had sent an alert to Rodney and Hood about the French convoy at almost the same time de Grasse sortied, but the message went aboard HM Sloop *Swallow,* which did not reach the Caribbean until mid-May. On April 29, Hood and de Grasse engaged in the short, sharp Battle of Fort Royal, with most of the gunfire ineffectually exchanged at long range, before Hood, who was outgunned and outmaneuvered, broke free and left the pursuing French fleet in his wake. De Grasse brought his convoy intact into harbor, but complained to Castries that he could not press his advantage because "British ships are faster than ours," not for the last time bemoaning Britain's advantage in coppering. Hood was equally dissatisfied with the result: "Never," he wrote of the engagement, "was more powder and shot thrown away on one day before."

The French fleet now had at least temporary numerical superiority in the Caribbean, and could range more or less at will, in May attacking Saint Lucia and capturing Tobago, before proceeding to their main base at Cap François. Meanwhile, de Grasse wrote to the Spanish officials in Havana to inquire about their combined campaign for 1781. The leadership in Cuba had changed since the Spanish victory at Pensacola; Gálvez was now captain-general, Cagigal was now governor, and Solano head of the naval forces. Gálvez asked Saavedra to meet with de Grasse, knowing that further action in the Caribbean later in the hurricane season would be infeasible. Saavedra traveled with Monteil's squadron, which was returning to Cap François, arriving shortly before de Grasse.

On July 18 aboard *Ville de Paris,* Saavedra and de Grasse discussed the upcoming campaign. De Grasse explained that the dispatches he had just received from Rochambeau made it urgent that he depart immediately for the Chesapeake with troops and as many ships as possible, and asked Saavedra if the Spanish could supply several vessels as he needed to leave a few ships behind to guard the commerce at Cap François. No Spanish campaigns were in the offing that required the French forces, but Saavedra demurred on providing ships for the combined French-American operation—"Spain had not yet formally recognized the independence of the Anglo-Americans." Instead, he offered to send four Spanish warships to guard the French port and its shipping while de Grasse was away. Saavedra was only able to make this promise because Gálvez's victory at Pensacola had already assured Spanish naval domination of the Gulf of Mexico. De Grasse was pleased with this elegant compromise, and they came to a formal agreement in which he promised Saavedra to return to the West Indies the following spring, after their campaign against Cornwallis was successfully ended, in order "to expel [the English] from the Windward Islands . . . and to conquer Jamaica, its center of wealth and power." Saavedra also agreed to release some of the French troops under Claude-Anne de Rouvroy, Marquis de Saint-Simon, which Versailles had put under Spanish command, many of whom had just fought at Pensacola. Monteil's squadron, although also battle-weary from Pensacola, would nevertheless also sail with de Grasse. On July 24, both men signed the agreement, and four days later *Concorde* sailed for Newport with de Grasse's response to Rochambeau.

De Grasse prepared his convoy for departure, which was reduced by two ships that had accidentally caught fire and burned. There remained a larger problem that Saavedra ingeniously resolved. Rochambeau had asked de Grasse to bring 1.2 million livres in specie to pay his troops, but the intendant of Saint-Domingue protested that such funds were not available, even when de Grasse promised to mortgage his plantations on that island. With time running short, de Grasse approached Saavedra for a loan from the Spanish government, and though the envoy from Madrid could not authorize a direct advance, he once again came up with an inspired solution. De Grasse's great convoy of twenty-six ships of the line, two fifties, four frigates, and fifteen merchant transports carrying thirty-three hundred troops set sail from Cap François on August 5. Saavedra, in the fast frigate *Aigrette,* pulled ahead of the fleet to secure the funds in Cuba. Arriving ten days later in Havana, he discovered that the treasury was empty of hard currency. He knew, however, that ever since

Spain entered the war, its colonial subjects had been asked to contribute to it. The following day, with the backing of Cagigal, two French officers went to the landowners and merchants of Havana requesting contributions that would be repaid from the Spanish treasury at 2 percent interest. In six hours they raised 500,000 pesos (which was worth somewhat more than the required 1.2 million livres) from twenty-eight contributors. The very next day, August 17, *Aigrette* brought the six tons of silver coin to the French fleet, where it was distributed among all the ships for redundancy. With Saavedra having provided the necessary funds to pay the French troops, and on his promise of four warships to guard Cap François in their absence—a promise that was barely kept—de Grasse's fleet rode the Gulf Stream north through the channel between Florida and the Bahamas, toward the Chesapeake. Now the final pieces of the endgame were in motion.

Rodney had received word in early July of de Grasse's departure from Fort Royal, and suspected that he might be heading to the American coast, though he could not be sure if the destination was the Chesapeake Bay, New York, or Newport. He dispatched HM Sloop *Swallow* to New York City to alert the naval commander there. Rodney had by then decided that he was too ill to stay overseas, so he departed for Britain and turned over command to Hood, but only after ordering Hood to take a squadron of ten ships of the line and four smaller warships to look for de Grasse and to reinforce the New York fleet. *Swallow* once again failed to deliver its message when needed; on August 15, Connecticut privateers drove it ashore at Fire Island off Long Island and burned it before the dispatches could reach Graves in time to warn him of the danger. Meanwhile Hood, along with Rear Admiral Francis Samuel Drake, departed Antigua on August 10 and went directly to New York, completely bypassing the Chesapeake Bay even though it was a potential landing site for the French. Arriving at Sandy Hook on August 28, he turned command of the combined fleet over to Graves, who was the senior rear admiral of the two. Graves and Clinton had been planning an attack upon Newport, but after Hood gave them the news of de Grasse's fleet—two weeks after *Swallow* was supposed to have delivered it—the British determined to proceed south to intercept the French. Graves would soon discover that it was already too late.

Meanwhile, de Grasse's fleet had been making slow headway along the coast. By 1781 almost half the French fleet had been copper-sheathed, including *Ville de Paris* and many warships in the convoy, but that still meant they had to travel at the speed of the slowest uncoppered ships. By the evening of August 29, the fleet had anchored just outside the mouth of the Chesapeake, and the next morning they filed past Cape Henry into the bay, anchoring at Lynnhaven Roads. The small British squadron in the Chesapeake Bay fled to the York River under the guns of Cornwallis, who had not budged from Yorktown since he had arrived a month earlier. By then Duportail had arrived with instructions from Washington, so he and Lafayette's aide Jean-Joseph Sourbader de Gimat went aboard *Ville de Paris* to coordinate with de Grasse and Saint-Simon. Together they decided that an immediate assault would be too hazardous, opting instead to wait for Washington and Rochambeau, to whom they dispatched couriers. Meanwhile, de Grasse ordered his frigates to bottle up the British ships, while at Jamestown, Saint-Simon began landing his troops, which Lafayette consolidated with his own and those of Anthony Wayne. Cornwallis was now trapped by de Grasse's systematic closure and control of the bay, but he made no attempt to harass or prevent the landings. This did not stop some of the soldiers under Tarleton from taking out their rage on the locals before retreating; Karl Gustaf Tornquist, who was one of the dozen or so Swedish officers serving in de Grasse's fleet, came upon the body of a pregnant woman slaughtered in her bed, and scrawled above the canopy was, "You shall never give birth to a rebel."

Graves and Hood had left Sandy Hook on September 1 with nineteen ships of the line and eight smaller warships, but they were not sure where the French might be or what to expect. Their ships stationed off the Delaware Bay had no information as they groped their way south. The morning of September 5, the scouting frigate HMS *Solebay* signaled that enemy ships were at anchor inside Cape Henry, but the observers could not be certain of the size of the fleet. The French frigate *Aigrette* saw the British fleet at about the same time, but at first its observers thought it was Barras's convoy from Newport carrying the siege train, which they were expecting daily. About nineteen hundred French crew and officers were at that moment moving Saint-Simon's troops and equipment ashore, so by midmorning when the signals identified that the sails were indeed British, de Grasse had to make some quick but difficult decisions to prepare for combat. There was not enough time to recover the crews and boats, so the ships would have to go into battle severely undermanned. The remaining sailors slipped the anchor cables and tied them to buoys as de Grasse ordered the ships to form a *ligne de vitesse,* or rapid line ahead, meaning the ships ignored their normally assigned fleet positions to create a fighting line as quickly as possible. Leaving four vessels behind to maintain the blockade of Cornwallis, de Grasse took just over half an hour to form his twenty-four ships into a line of battle. Just after midday they sortied past Cape Henry, headed straight toward the nineteen ships under Graves and Hood bearing down on them. De Grasse took the center and Monteil had the rear, while Bougainville aggressively went for the forwardmost part of the line, pulling so far ahead of the rest of the fleet that wide gaps started to form in the French battle line.

Graves and Hood were outnumbered, but each ship was fully manned and therefore better prepared for combat. Having the advantage of the weather gauge—the wind was behind them—they brought their ships into a line ahead, with Hood in the van, Graves at the center, and Drake in the rear, sailing on a parallel but opposite tack from the French. Around 2 p.m. as they came abreast of the French line, Graves ordered the line to wear, a maneuver that requires a large number of expert sailors to quickly and precisely adjust sails and yards. Now Drake was in the van with the fleet on roughly the same course as the French, slowly closing the range between the two lines. Given that so many of the French ships were desperately short of hands—*Citoyen* did not have enough to man any of its upper-deck guns—de Grasse had to limit his own maneuvers to just simple changes of heading. The two fleets were now advancing at a shallow angle, so that the vans were within firing range but the centers and rears were not. At 3:45 p.m., Graves hoisted the signal for "line ahead," meaning the British line should continue on its parallel course but draw closer to the French line.

By now the fleets had been maneuvering for over six hours without a shot fired, and daylight would be fading in just a few more hours. At 4:03 p.m., Graves decided to engage directly with the enemy by turning sharply at right angles into their line of battle, a maneuver called "bear down and engage close." He hoisted this signal, but in a moment of misunderstanding that would cause endless analyses and recriminations, he continued to let fly the "line ahead" signal. These two signals are completely contradictory, as they tell the fleet to move in entirely different directions. Hood interpreted the "line ahead" command as taking prece-

Battle of the Virginia Capes [Battle of the Chesapeake], September 5, 1781.
V. Zveg (Vladimir Zvegintzov), 1969, oil on canvas

dence, so he did not turn into the French line. The resulting engagement was confused. Drake's van fiercely engaged Bougainville's, which fought just as hard, and both bore the brunt of the damage during engagement. The two centers exchanged gunfire at long range, about half a mile distant from each other, while Hood remained too far away—about three-quarters of a mile—to engage Monteil. Both fleets drifted southeast, the gunfire waning as the sun began to set. There was damage to both sides but no clear tactical victory for either.

It was now clear that Saavedra's offer to have Spain guard the French shipping—which was only made possible by Gálvez's victory at Pensacola—had allowed de Grasse to take all of his ships north, thus giving him the overwhelming numerical superiority needed to stave off the British. De Grasse knew he did not have to defeat Graves, just keep him from entering the Chesapeake. Graves believed he had gotten the worst of the battle and did not think he was in any position to press on for another fight. For the next four days the fleets drifted southeast, never engaging. On September 9, de Grasse received word that Barras had been sighted approaching Cape Henry. Barras had departed Newport back on August 27 with eight ships of the line and a convoy of artillery and supplies, but had taken a circuitous route to avoid Graves. De Grasse immediately brought his ships back to the bay, arriving on September 12. Graves sent a frigate to reconnoiter the Chesapeake, which returned with the news that now thirty-six ships of the line were barring the entrance to the bay. The following day, Graves and his admirals held a council of war and decided that because of the "state of the position of the enemy, the present condition of the British fleet, the season of the year so near the equinox [i.e., the height of hurricane season], and the impracticability of giving any effectual succor to General Earl Cornwallis in the Chesapeake," that they would return to New York to refit as best they could. Graves returned to New York on September 20, and almost immediately began planning with Clinton a rescue of Cornwallis's beleaguered army. It would be too little, far too late. The tactical stalemate of the Battle of the Chesapeake would turn out to be the crucial strategic victory that allowed the French and American forces to envelop and dominate Cornwallis in just a few weeks.

THE SIEGE OF YORKTOWN

On September 5, just as de Grasse's fleet was sortieing from the Chesapeake Bay to take on Graves and Hood, some two hundred miles north Rochambeau's troops were marching toward Chester, Pennsylvania. They and the American troops had been on a forced march since they left Westchester in mid-August, taking three parallel routes through New York and New Jersey on their way toward Yorktown. A casual observer might have been forgiven for thinking they were all of the same army; the Americans carried the same 0.69 caliber muskets as the French, and though they were not as well shod or turned out as their French counterparts, many of their uniforms were noticeably French-made, brought over in the cargoes of Beaumarchais and Chaumont. That day, as the French troops passed through Philadelphia, Rochambeau and his entourage went by boat to see the Billingsport and Fort Mercer fortifications that Mauduit du Plessis had supervised some years earlier. As they returned to the dock at Marcus Hook near Chester, his aide Ludwig von

Closen recounted that "we discerned in the distance General Washington, standing on the shore and waving his hat and a white handkerchief joyfully. There was good reason for this; for he informed us as we disembarked that M. de Grasse had arrived in Chesapeake Bay." Washington, known as a stoic among his own troops, in the presence of his French compatriots was somehow more permissive and openly expressive of his emotions, for as Closen next reported, "MM. de Rochambeau and Washington embraced *warmly* on the shore." The dispatches Rochambeau and Washington received that morning told them that de Grasse's ships had blocked Cornwallis by sea, and his troops were already reinforcing Lafayette to prevent his escape over land. But the dispatches also came with a warning: De Grasse told them he could only stay until October 15 due to his obligation to join the Spanish in an attack on Jamaica, so it was necessary, he said, "to use me promptly and efficiently."

The march south had been organized in haste and had to balance speed with secrecy. To throw Clinton off the scent by making him think New York City was the target, carpenters built boats in Staten Island to make an invasion look plausible; masons built bread ovens in New Jersey to simulate campsites to stage an assault; fake contracts and messages pointing to an imminent attack were scattered among merchants and couriers like so many bread crumbs, in the expectation that British spies would intercept them. The real French encampments along the actual route had not been prepared beforehand as they were while crossing Connecticut, so engineers and supply officers under Louis-Alexandre Berthier went a day or two ahead of the lead regiment to locate campsites, secure water and forage, and map out the route with remarkable precision and detail. As in Connecticut, each camp was occupied by different regiments on successive days. The American troops were also foraging off the land, but were again on the verge of mutiny due to lack of pay. Washington arranged with Robert Morris to borrow half of Rochambeau's silver coin to disburse directly to the men, the first time they had ever been paid in specie instead of paper notes.

On September 8 at Head of Elk, Maryland, some of the French and American troops under the Baron de Vioménil and Benjamin Lincoln began boarding boats and watercraft to transport them to the battlefront. More were embarked at Baltimore, while others marched farther south to Annapolis, where de Grasse and Barras had already arranged for more ships to carry troops and field artillery. Supply wagons, cattle, and beasts of burden continued overland all the way to Yorktown. Washington and Rochambeau rode ahead with their staffs, stopping first at Mount Vernon, overlooking the wide Potomac River. This was Washington's first visit since the war began six years earlier, and the fact that de Grasse now had Cornwallis bottled up undoubtedly allowed the American commander the leisure to spend a few days taking care of his estate and showing it to his French colleagues. Rochambeau was likely reminded of his own estate at Thoré-la-Rochette in central France, on the banks of the much narrower Loir River. On September 12, they continued together on their journey south, Rochambeau undoubtedly speaking directly to Washington in his much-improved English. They arrived in Williamsburg on the fourteenth, where Lafayette, with Steuben now at his side, had billeted his troops along with those of Saint-Simon and Anthony Wayne. On learning of his commander in chief's arrival, Lafayette left his sickbed—he had been stricken with a violent fever—to embrace Washington "with an ardor not easily described." Washington's famous reserve once again seemed to disappear before his French compatriots.

Cornwallis was busily reinforcing Yorktown, as was Tarleton at Gloucester Point, with defensive ramparts, breastworks, ditches, abatis, and redoubts. He did not yet appreciate the size of the French and American armies now encircling him and was still unaware that de Grasse had him blockaded by sea. He also fully expected that Clinton, who by early September had recognized where Washington and Rochambeau were heading, would follow through on his promise to send a relief expedition by October 5, so Cornwallis did not want to risk losing men and equipment by sallying forth from his ramparts to attack the allied forces. Washington, meanwhile, knew that he had but little time to besiege and capture Cornwallis's army. The day after his arrival at Williamsburg he sent a request to de Grasse for a conference. On September 17, de Grasse dispatched the sloop *Queen Charlotte,* recently captured from the British with Cornwallis's former second in command Francis Rawdon aboard, to transport Washington's party down the river to *Ville de Paris,* now at anchor in Lynnhaven Roads. The party included Washington's aides Knox and Duportail, along with Rochambeau and his aide Chastellux, while Lafayette remained behind, feverish in bed. The party arrived about noon, and as Washington ascended to the quarterdeck, de Grasse "flew to embrace him, imprinting the French salute upon each cheek." For a third time Washington's reserve seemed to melt away, but his bewildered staff were momentarily delighted when de Grasse, who at six feet four inches stood two inches taller than Washington, "hugged him in his arms, exclaiming '*mon petit général!*'"

The meeting was rather more professional in nature than were the introductions, and set the stage for the battle that was to come. Washington had arrived with a set of questions, which de Grasse answered one by one. How long could the French fleet stay? De Grasse had originally fixed October 15 as the date he needed to depart to support the Spanish, but he could conceivably extend that to the end of the month. Could de Grasse spare another two thousand men for the campaign? Yes, but only in a final *coup de main*. Could he supply cannon and gunpowder? Cannon yes, gunpowder not much. If the campaign were successful, could he detach vessels to retake Charleston or Wilmington? No, he could not. The meeting ended on a friendly note, and after dinner and a tour of the ship, Washington and his companions departed around sunset to the sounds of a thirteen-gun salute. They embarked aboard *Queen Charlotte,* but for five days its commanding officer, Lieutenant Jean Audubon, had to battle contrary winds, then no winds, to return them the short distance to their camp on September 22.

Washington came away from the conference with a profound respect for de Grasse, whom he referred to as a "Great Mind," and that respect was returned in full. There was some minor consternation when intelligence revealed that a British squadron under Admiral Robert Digby was expected in New York, and though de Grasse gave some thought to sallying forth to meet that threat, the idea was voted down in a council of his general officers. Washington now knew he had forty days to besiege and capture Cornwallis. The American and French supply officers were already busy provisioning for the siege. The French commissary general Claude Blanchard gratefully received de Grasse's 500,000 pesos from Havana to pay for his troops' salaries and their supplies, but the great weight of the coin caused the storeroom floor to collapse into the cellar. The first elements of the Continental Army began arriving at Williamsburg on September 19, a few days after the arrival of six hundred French troops under Brigadier General Claude Gabriel de Choisy, whom Barras had transported from Newport. The rest of the troops arrived over the course of the next five days.

At 4 a.m. on September 28, preparations for the Battle of Yorktown got under way. The entire combined army marched out from its encampment at Williamsburg along the sandy roads toward Yorktown, twelve miles away. The heat was oppressive, and even the generals dismounted to walk their horses. As they came within sight of the ramparts, the single column split into three: Americans on the right, French at the center and left. By 6 p.m. they had fully invested (surrounded) the town. The British quickly fled their indefensible outer redoubts, which French engineers captured and reused for their own offensive campaign. Meanwhile, de Grasse detached eight hundred of his marines to Choisy, who took them under his command at Gloucester Point, where eleven hundred Virginia militia were already in place under Brigadier General George Weedon, and later reinforced by six hundred men in Lauzun's Legion. The great French siege guns remained aboard Barras's ships until the wagon trains with oxen and horses finally began arriving from October 3 to 6. As each herd came to the landings, guns were debarked, hitched, and pulled to their siege lines, so that by October 9 all of the batteries were in place.

Yorktown would be a classic European siege, one with which both the British and French were very familiar during the Seven Years' War, and comparable in size. The Siege of Kassel, which preceded the peace negotiations in late 1762, had pitted twelve thousand German and British troops against five thousand French troops garrisoned inside the city. At Yorktown the situation was almost exactly reversed; Cornwallis had behind the ramparts seven thousand British, German, and Loyalist troops, which included Tarleton's detachment of a thousand men at Gloucester Point, while in front of them were eighteen thousand French and American troops. At Yorktown on the right were eight thousand Continental and militia forces, consisting of Lafayette's light division (which included battalions under Alexander Hamilton and John Laurens, as well as Hazen's Second Canadian Regiment), Lincoln's and Steuben's divisions, plus Armand's Legion and Knox's artillery regiments. The French left and center consisted of Saint-Simon's regiments, including a number of soldiers in the Agenois and Gâtinais who just six months earlier had besieged Pensacola; the Saintonge and Soissonnais regiments under Rochambeau's second in command, Antoine Charles, Baron de Viomé-nil; the Royal Deux-Ponts and Bourbonnais regiments under Antoine's brother Charles Joseph, Vicomte de Viomènil; and the artillery batteries under Lieutenant Colonel François Marie d'Aboville. At Gloucester Point were twenty-five hundred men arrayed with Weedon's militia on the right, Lauzun's Legion in the center, and de Grasse's marines on the left. At anchor around Hampton Roads and the Chesapeake Bay were almost twenty-nine thousand French sailors and marines under de Grasse's standard.

The Battle of Yorktown, like most sieges, would be an artillery duel fought at increasingly shorter ranges, as the investing force of French and Americans dug siege trenches to move their guns closer to the British defensive lines. Although Cornwallis was outmanned two and a half to one, he outgunned the French and Americans, 244 pieces to 155 pieces. Knox had fewer than half the allied artillery, 60 field guns in all, some of them from the original Beaumarchais shipments back in 1777. All of the heavy siege guns, which did most of the damage by destroying ramparts and fortifications, were in the batteries of d'Aboville, which also included a mix of the older Vallière and newer Gribeauval field guns. The first week of the siege saw little action on the allied side, as the French and Americans, under the overall direction of Duportail, began digging the first parallel of trenches, six hundred yards from the ramparts and about fifteen hundred yards long, and preparing the sites for the Grand Batteries. Cornwallis kept up an artillery barrage in an attempt to disrupt the trenchwork and battery emplacement, but with little effect. On October 4 across the river, Lauzun's Legion caught Tarleton's Legion out foraging near Gloucester Point. The Duc de Lauzun charged directly for Tarleton, who was about to meet the approach when Tarleton's horse was knocked to the ground by another dueling pair of riders. Tarleton dashed off to escape, leaving Lauzun with his horse as a prize. Tarleton never left his fortification again until the end of the siege.

By October 9 the French and American Grand Batteries were prepared and ready. At 3 p.m. the French guns opened up on the left, followed at 5 p.m. by the American right. Cornwallis was forced to withdraw the outer pieces that had been continuously firing during the previous week. The allied barrage continued into the night and the following day. Both Knox and d'Aboville boasted highly trained gun crews who could place shot, shell, and bombs very accurately, and do so at the comparatively high rate of nine rounds per hour. With 155 allied guns firing from dawn to well past dusk, that averaged one shot fired every three seconds. The noise would have been deafening, almost drowning out the commands *Load! Ram! Fire!* at the American battery, *Chargez! Bourrez! Feu!* at the French battery. The evening of the tenth, the French battery began lobbing red-hot shot at the British frigate HMS *Charon* at anchor in the

York River, setting it and several other ships ablaze with "a fire that was superb to see; all the sky was reddened by it," as Closen reported.

It was harder for the allies to see the effects of their bombardment inside the town, but the almost immediate silence of Cornwallis's guns, despite his having more of them, spoke to the accuracy and destructive power of the allied fire—British gun crews could barely fire their own cannon for the incessant pounding and explosions, day and night. American civilians whom Cornwallis let depart from the town told of massive damage: "Our bombardment produced great effects in annoying the enemy [the British] and destroying their works. . . . Lord Cornwallis has built a sort of grotto [at the foot of the cliffs] where he lives underground." Diaries of the soldiers under the bombardment tell similar stories: "The heavy fire forced us to throw our tents into the ditches. . . . We could find no refuge in or out of town. . . . Many were killed by bursting bombs. . . . The greater part of the town lies in ashes, and two batteries have been completely dismantled." But artillery alone could not finish off the British: For the siege to be successful, the allied forces had to get much closer to the ramparts in order to support a final troop assault. The evening of October 11, Washington ordered the second parallel trench be dug at four hundred yards out, but its right flank was blocked by two British redoubts: Number 10 near the York River, and Number 9 about a quarter mile inland. These redoubts, which were heavily fortified with palisades and sharp abatis, were the key to the assault, for if they were left occupied by the British, they would bring enfilading fire into the allied trenches. Washington planned the attack upon the redoubts for the night of October 14.

Lafayette's division was immediately opposite Redoubt 10, so he selected his aide-de-camp Jean-Joseph Gimat to lead the charge. Hamilton protested that since he was officer of the day in the trenches, he should be given the command, a decision upheld by Washington. The Baron de Vioménil was given the task of neutralizing Redoubt 9. Vioménil, who was openly skeptical of Lafayette's American troops, selected the Comte de Deux-Ponts to lead the French charge. For maximum surprise and effect, the American and the French assault troops would attack simultaneously. At 8 p.m., six cannon shots boomed, the signal for the charge. Hamilton's four hundred men surrounded their redoubt, which had seventy British soldiers inside. Instead of waiting for sappers to clear away the obstacles, the men rushed past the defenses and,

Siege of Yorktown, September 28–October 19, 1781.
Jean-Mathias Fontaine, after Auguste Couder, engraving.

despite murderous fire, attacked only with bayonets, overwhelming the defenders. Within six minutes of the cannon sounding, Redoubt 10 was in American hands.

Five hundred yards away at Redoubt 9, the Comte de Deux-Ponts was having a much rougher time of it. He sent his sappers forward to first cut down the abatis and breach the palisades. During those precious minutes the 120 British defenders unleashed volley after volley into the French troops below. Despite heavy losses, they continued to climb. Then, as the Comte de Deux-Ponts later described,

> our fire was increasing, and making terrible havoc among the enemy, who had placed themselves behind a kind of entrenchment of barrels, where they were well massed, and where all our shots told. We succeeded at the moment when I wished to give the

> order to leap into the redoubt and charge upon the enemy with the bayonet; then they laid down their arms, and we leaped in with more tranquility and less risk. I shouted immediately the cry of *Vive le Roi,* which was repeated by all the grenadiers and chasseurs who were in good condition, by all the troops in the trenches, and to which the enemy replied by a general discharge of artillery and musketry. I never saw a sight more beautiful or more majestic.

During the agonizing minutes that Deux-Ponts's troops were trapped below the abatis, Lafayette dispatched a messenger to Vioménil asking "if he required some American help." The French general sent no reply, but after the redoubt was taken, Vioménil graciously praised Lafayette's "intrepidity and intelligence" in his after-action report to Rochambeau, and acknowledged that the American infantry appeared "like [French] grenadiers accustomed to difficult things."

The capture of Redoubts 9 and 10, followed by the completion of the second parallel trench, made further defense of Yorktown untenable. Cornwallis would receive no help from Clinton; the British commander in chief was unable to formulate any response to the situation in Virginia, other than to send Benedict Arnold on a diversionary raid to burn down his hometown of New London, Connecticut. Digby's long-awaited reinforcement turned out to be just three ships, so the relief squadron for Cornwallis would only have twenty-five ships of the line, not enough to overcome the thirty-six French ships in the bay; and by the time Graves had it ready to sail on October 17, it was already too late. That same day some three hundred miles south, a drummer boy mounted the parapets of Yorktown at ten o'clock in the morning and beat a parley. The incessant cannon fire from the newly opened second parallel trench made it impossible to hear, but the officer waving the white handkerchief next to him was unmistakable. Cornwallis would surrender.

The following day, John Laurens and the Vicomte de Noailles negotiated the terms of surrender with the British, which lasted well into the night. On the morning of October 19, the final Articles of Capitulation were signed by Washington, Rochambeau, and Barras for de Grasse, who stayed aboard *Ville de Paris* to prepare for the imminent arrival of Graves's fleet. Cornwallis signed the articles later that morning, and at 2 p.m. the British troops filed out of the town, marching between parallel lines of French troops on the left and American troops on the right. One of Rochambeau's aides, the engineer Mathieu Dumas, had been sent to lead Cornwallis to present his surrender, but instead his second in command Brigadier General Charles O'Hara came out, representing Cornwallis, who was indisposed. As O'Hara reached the commanders, he began to turn left toward Rochambeau. This was neither a mistake nor an insult to the Americans; the British simply saw Yorktown as a French military victory, a sentiment borne out by the fact that the French lost twice as many men as did the Americans during the battle. Though the victory was certainly as much France's as it was America's, the French general was well aware to whom belonged the moment. Rochambeau wordlessly pointed across the lane to Washington, who in turn had Benjamin Lincoln, his own second in command, accept the surrender. The British troops then marched to an open field, grounded their arms and flags, and returned to Yorktown. The same actions were repeated at Gloucester Point. With the ceremonies ended, the surrender was complete.

A few hours after the ceremonies, Washington signed a letter that was a marvel of understatement: "I have the honor to inform Congress that a reduction of the British Army . . . is most happily effected." Washington's natural caution—not a defeat but a "reduction," with more fighting likely ahead—was not universally echoed in London. Upon learning the news of Yorktown on Sunday afternoon, November 25, Prime Minister North reacted "as he would have taken a ball in the breast . . . exclaiming wildly, 'Oh God! it is all over!'" North was only partially correct—there would be no more major campaigns fought by the Americans, but the French and Spanish would fight on against the British for another year.

CHAPTER 8

The Road to Peace

For once, news from America arrived at Paris before it got to London. The afternoon of November 19, 1781, after a speedy transatlantic voyage, the Duc de Lauzun arrived at Versailles with dispatches from Rochambeau detailing the French-American victory at Yorktown exactly one month earlier. He first went to Maurepas, who was barely conscious on his deathbed but received Lauzun and the notice "in the most touching manner." The king and queen were "overjoyed." Vergennes sent off a courier to Benjamin Franklin, who arrived at Passy with the news just before midnight. Franklin, with "infinite pleasure," spent the night making duplicates of Vergennes's note on his newfangled letter copying press, just patented by the British inventor James Watt, and flooded Paris with the announcement of the "important Victory at York." Many came to Passy to wish Franklin well; others waited until confirmation of the news.

Rochambeau had already taken the precaution of sending two coppered frigates, the second of which had the Comte de Deux-Ponts aboard. It had been delayed for a few days by the arrival of Graves's fleet off the Chesapeake, which turned around after learning of Cornwallis's defeat through British deserters and after seeing the strength of the French fleet in the bay. Deux-Ponts's frigate also made a fast journey, and he arrived at Versailles with updated news just days after Maurepas's death and a few hours before Lord North received word.

The news from Yorktown was followed by French officers returning from the battlefield. With no prospect for further campaigns that season, several officers including Lafayette and Duportail asked for and were granted a leave of absence to return to France. Lafayette in particular promised to request money, ships, and troops for the upcoming 1782 campaign. After departing their regiments at the end of October, they went to Boston to board the trustworthy frigate *Alliance*, now under the command of John Barry. A fast voyage that started on Christmas Day brought them to Lorient, then Versailles, by the end of January 1782. Lafayette was publicly fêted as a hero, honored with audiences with the king, standing ovations at the opera, and fireworks to celebrate both "his" victory at Yorktown and the recent birth of the dauphin, Louis Joseph. Privately, Vergennes was worried about the viability of America as a nation and also was increasingly concerned that it depended too much on France, telling Lafayette, "I am not marvelously pleased with the country you have just left. I find it barely active and very demanding." Franklin and Lafayette did not assuage his concerns when they asked for another loan of 6 million livres, on top of the 6 million that John Laurens had received the previous year. Vergennes granted the request, along with a promise to send more troops for Rochambeau's army, but France's war chest was rapidly emptying.

By 1781, the expense of the American theater had become a small part of what was now a global war that was depleting French finances. Yorktown was just one battle in a string of conflicts. Vergennes told Lafayette, shortly after receiving news of the victory, that peace was not yet at hand: "It is not in the English character to give up so easily." And he was correct: Britain was still fighting France and Spain in the Caribbean, Asia, and Europe. Most of these engagements were either at sea or involved amphibious assaults, and the British navy was hardly a spent force after the Battle of the Chesapeake. If anything it was increasing in power; shipbuilding was at its height, with twenty-eight ships built in 1781, another twenty-eight on the ways for 1782, and the vessels in service were in good repair. With the future of the French and Spanish campaigns still uncertain, the question of how much longer the United States could be kept afloat by Versailles also remained unresolved.

THE WAR DRAWS TO A CLOSE IN THE CARIBBEAN

When Washington and de Grasse met aboard *Ville de Paris* in September, the French commander told Washington that his commitments to support the Spanish in the Caribbean required him to depart by the end of October 1781. As that date was now drawing near, Washington asked for assistance for an expedition to either Wilmington or Charleston, which de Grasse was ready to undertake if it met his schedule. When it became apparent that Washington could not gather the needed stores and troops in that time, they both agreed to consider a campaign for the following summer. On November 4, de Grasse's fleet majestically sortied from the Chesapeake for what would turn out to be the last time, to return to his base at Martinique. A week later, Hood departed New York with his fleet of seventeen ships of the line and three smaller warships, expecting that his arrival at Barbados in December would even out the balance of power in the Caribbean. Graves also departed New York to serve under Peter Parker in Britain's most important Caribbean base, Jamaica, which they already anticipated would be the target of the French and Spanish fleets for the following spring.

De Grasse arrived at Fort Royal on November 25 to find that the governor-general, François Claude de Bouillé, was absent; a few days later he learned that Bouillé had just retaken the Dutch colony of Sint Eustatius and the sugar plantations of Dutch Guiana from the British, just months after Rodney had left to treat his illness in Britain. These would be the first in a series of lightning assaults around the West Indies during the months after the Battle of Yorktown. Before that battle, de Grasse had agreed with Francisco Saavedra to join with the Spanish fleet in March 1782. From their base in Cap François, they would conduct a "vigorous attack" against the biggest prize, Jamaica. This plan was first envisioned by the Comte d'Estaing, who as vice admiral of Asia and the Americas took charge of naval strategy in the Caribbean. It was subsequently approved by the courts at Versailles and Madrid. That left de Grasse just enough time to refit his fleet and go after smaller prizes, while awaiting a convoy from France to reinforce him. His first forays against Barbados during December had to turn back due to foul weather. In January 1782 he set his sights on Saint Kitts (Saint Christopher) and Nevis, two small islands almost swimming distance from Sint Eustatius. De Grasse landed Bouillé's troops, who besieged the British garrison at Brimstone Hill. When Hood learned of the attack, he sortied immediately, hoping to achieve a victory by surprising de Grasse's larger fleet while still at anchor. De Grasse slipped anchors to get sea room for a line of battle, but the squadron under Monteil missed the signals and failed to attack Hood's line. Hood thereby was able to anchor his fleet near to where de Grasse had just left. The French could neither dislodge nor destroy the British. Hood's tactical success did not bring victory on land, for his landing force could not unseat the French siege troops, and after a monthlong assault the British garrison at Brimstone Hill capitulated. By mid-February, Hood had departed, and Saint Kitts and Nevis were in French hands. A few days later the Comte de Barras captured the nearby island of Montserrat, after which he and Monteil returned to France aboard the frigate *Concorde*.

By February 1782, the only islands Britain had left in the Caribbean were Saint Lucia, Antigua, Barbados, and Jamaica. It certainly would have appeared to de Grasse that the rest of the British colonies were about to fall, but when the long-awaited transports from France arrived with just a fraction of the expected reinforcements, that certainty was shaken. *Chef d'Escadre* Louis Philippe de Rigaud, Marquis de Vaudreuil, had departed Brest on December 10 with five ships of the line and a hundred merchantmen carrying thousands of troops, escorted by the Comte de Guichen. Lying in wait for them off the Island of Ouessant was the British strategic genius Richard Kempenfelt, his rear-admiral flag hoisted above HMS *Victory*. Guichen had mistakenly positioned his escorting warships leeward (downwind) of the convoy, so that two days after their departure when Kempenfelt attacked suddenly, Guichen could not beat upwind to help. Many of the French ships that managed to escape were then scattered and devastated by a winter storm. Only two ships of the line and twenty merchantmen in Vaudreuil's squadron made it to Martinique, although a second convoy arriving a month later added three more ships and much-needed munitions and gunpowder. Meanwhile, Rodney, who had recovered from the illness that forced him from the Caribbean, and was now promoted to vice admiral, had left Portsmouth in January with seventeen ships of the line to take command from Hood at the end of February.

The balance of power in the Caribbean appeared to have shifted to Britain's favor, thirty-six ships of the line versus France's thirty-three. But those numbers ignored the eleven Spanish ships of the line under José Solano. By 1782, after several years of trial and error, the French and Spanish navies were beginning to operate as a combined Bourbon fleet. The original idea of Jerónimo Grimaldi just after the Seven Years' War, of "French and Spanish vessels as forming a single Armada," was finally coming to fruition. Thanks in large part to Grimaldi's standardization,

French and Spanish ships were regularly operating from one another's ports and being refitted in each other's dockyards, in both Europe and the Caribbean. The problems of signals and tactics that had plagued the combined armada against Britain had long since been ironed out. As the capture of the British convoy in 1780 and that of Pensacola the following year demonstrated, the two fleets now operated together routinely, with French captains taking orders from Spanish fleet commanders and vice versa. De Grasse, as the senior officer, was preparing to take command of the combined Bourbon fleet, which he fully expected would outnumber Rodney and conquer Jamaica. But first he had to get to Cap François for his rendezvous with Solano.

At daybreak on April 8, de Grasse set sail from Martinique for Cap François. The convoy of 150 merchantmen and three thousand soldiers was escorted by his entire battle fleet, with Bougainville in the van, de Grasse in the center, and Vaudreuil at the rear. At Cap François (which the Spanish called Guárico), Saavedra, Gálvez, and Solano were waiting with the Spanish fleet and nine thousand troops for the amphibious assault of Jamaica. Rodney, anticipating de Grasse's move, was moored near Martinique at Saint Lucia. His chain of scouting frigates witnessed the French departure and within hours passed the signal to him. By noon, Rodney was clear of the harbor, and by nightfall the two fleets had made contact. Over the next two days the two fleets maneuvered for position in the strait between Dominica and Guadeloupe known as the Saintes. On the morning of April 12, de Grasse's progress northward was blocked by unfavorable winds, so he reversed course and doubled back on Rodney's fleet. As the two fleets were passing on opposite tacks and exchanging broadsides, a sudden change of wind caused the center of de Grasse's battle line to slow down and separate, and a gap opened up between two ships. At the prodding of his flag captain, Rodney gave commands for his flagship, *Formidable,* to turn quickly to starboard and break through the French line at that gap, followed by five of his ships. Farther to the rear, Hood's squadron did the same thing. By breaking the French line, Rodney and Hood were able to slow the French fleet's momentum, at the same time allowing their heavy guns to pour murderous fire into the relatively unprotected bows and sterns of the French ships while sustaining little damage themselves. The fight soon turned into a rout, with Rodney and Hood eventually capturing seven French ships, including *Ville de Paris* with de Grasse aboard. Vaudreuil, senior to Bougainville, now took command of the French fleet and brought it to Cap François. De Grasse was brought to London as a prisoner, where he blamed his subordinates, his ships, and even the lack of coppering for his defeat. The Battle of the Saintes soon became one of the most analyzed naval engagements ever, with Rodney's pioneering tactic of the breaking of the line an inspiration for future commanders, most notably Horatio Nelson in 1805 at the Battle of Trafalgar.

Vaudreuil's fleet began limping into Cap François eight days after the battle. "Their hulls were all riddled from cannon shot, as were their sails," recorded Saavedra; "their masts and rigging were in terrible shape; the ship with the fewest casualties counted 127 killed and wounded." The morale of the officers and crews was also shot through with "despair." On April 26, Saavedra, Gálvez, Solano, and Vaudreuil held a *junta de generales.* Despite the heavy casualties at the Saintes, Saavedra and Gálvez thought at first it was just a setback, and that after repairs the campaign against Jamaica could still go forward. After all, West Florida was now in Spanish hands, British East Florida was merely an annoyance, and in the Honduras, Matías de Gálvez had won important victories at Caribe and Roatán and had successfully swept the main British forces from the mountains and the coasts.

But the wretched state of the French fleet compared with that of Rodney's was too great to ignore. The *junta* ultimately agreed that "it was impossible to attack Jamaica given that the English had superior maritime forces," and until the French and Spanish courts developed a new strategy, they would continue to carefully observe the British. Meanwhile, Saavedra would go to Versailles to discuss the new campaign plans, Solano would return to Havana, some of the French warships would escort two major sugar convoys bound for Europe, and Vaudreuil would remain at Cap François to refit his fleet for a new expedition to North America. It certainly appeared to the *junta,* at least for the 1782 fighting season, that there were no more campaigns in the offing against the British West Indies.

The very day the *junta de generales* met in Cap François, a combined Spanish-American fleet had already left Havana and was heading for the Bahamas. Back in January, while Solano and Gálvez had been preparing for the invasion of Jamaica, the governor of Havana, Juan Manuel de Cagigal, was planning an attack on the capital of the British Bahamas at Nassau, on the island of New Providence. He had both troops and transports, but Solano could not spare any warships to escort him. At just that time, an American merchant and naval officer named Alexander Gillon sailed into Havana aboard the principal warship of the South Carolina navy, the frigate *South Carolina.* The ship, originally named *Indien,* had been built in Amsterdam in 1778 at the request of the American commissioners Deane, Franklin, and Lee, with their banker, Ferdinand Grand, paying for it through money loaned by the French government. When the Americans could no longer afford the vessel, a French aristocrat took control of it and in 1780 leased it to Gillon, who at the time was in Europe as commodore of the South Carolina navy, looking for loans and ships for his state. An arrangement was quickly reached swapping the ship for a share of any prize money, and it was renamed *South Carolina.* Gillon attempted to return to the ship's namesake state, only to find the Union Jack flying over Charleston harbor, so he headed to Havana for resupply.

Cagigal immediately saw that *South Carolina* could provide the escort he needed for the Nassau expedition, and Gillon saw payment for his work and prize money in the future. The Spanish governor obtained agreement for his plan from Gálvez and Saavedra, both of whom left for Cap François shortly afterward. Cagigal and Gillon spent the next several weeks equipping the twenty-four hundred troops, loading the forty Spanish transports, and arming the dozen or so American merchantmen that Gillon had recruited in Havana to serve as the fleet escort alongside his flagship. On April 22, the convoy left harbor. Cagigal had just missed Gálvez's new order to abort the expedition, which he had sent immediately upon his learning of the Battle of the Saintes, and this would later cause a falling-out between the two Spanish officers.

The voyage took just two weeks, during which time Cagigal's aide Francisco de Miranda acted as interpreter and occasional mediator for the two leaders, who often found themselves arguing over prize money and the status of future British prisoners. The arguments came to a head on May 5, when the fleet arrived before Nassau harbor, but within twenty-four hours Miranda had convinced the two to present a united front to their opponent. On May 6, Miranda went ashore to hand the terms of surrender to the British governor, John Maxwell. The inhabitants had been dreading such an invasion since the Continental Navy powder raid of 1776, and neither they nor Maxwell wanted a useless fight against an overwhelming enemy. Cagigal's terms were generous—no private property would be taken, only weapons and public property—so the surrender was agreed to without so much as a musket being shouldered. The Spanish and Americans departed Nassau just a few days later leaving only a small occupying garrison and a Spanish flag flying where the Union Jack used to be.

The lack of any prize money reignited the row between the American and Spanish leaders, so Gillon went north empty-handed, while Cagigal went south with the British troops as prisoners but without an armed escort. The capture of the Bahamas would turn out to be the only time during the entire war that large numbers of Spanish and American forces operated jointly in a major campaign, albeit without the knowledge or sanction of the leaders in Philadelphia or Madrid. It was also the last significant naval operation in and around the West Indies before the war's end.

THE WAR DRAWS TO A CLOSE IN ASIA

The West Indies and the East Indies refer to lands on opposite sides of the globe. The reason for this confusing terminology is that for many years after the voyages of Columbus to the Caribbean (1492) and Vasco da Gama to Asia (1497), it was assumed that both explorers and their followers had reached the same Indies, but from different directions. It was not until after Magellan's circumnavigation in 1522 that mapmakers gradually realized that these were in fact two distinct and unconnected regions, and therefore gave them their separate designations. The West Indies and Caribbean (the two terms describe regions that largely overlap), being far closer and therefore easier to organize in trade and military networks, was an important economic and strategic center for many European nations, including France and Great Britain, both of which fought continuously to gain the upper hand in territory as well as commerce. The ambitions of France and Britain toward the East Indies in Asia were quite different from one another. This was especially notable after the Seven Years' War, in which the Treaty of Paris reduced France's formerly substantial territorial presence in India to just five trade outposts, or *comptoirs,* of which Pondicherry was the largest. Soon after the war the monopoly trade of the Compagnie des Indes (French East India Company) was suspended. By contrast, Great Britain augmented the monopoly power of the East India Company (EIC) by investing it with the governance of large swaths of territory around the Bay of Bengal, and the port of Bombay (Mumbai) on the western coast of the subcontinent. The EIC controlled this territory using its own hired army, which included Hessian troops, and a navy known as the Bombay Marine, which regularly shared its support and repair facilities with Britain's Royal Navy.

French policy in the East Indies was an outgrowth of France's European goals, and therefore was largely a mirror image of its policies in America and the West Indies: Reduce British influence in those regions in order to diminish its power in Europe, allowing France to return to its rightful place at Europe's center. The means to achieve this were also roughly similar to France's strategy toward the nascent United States; rather than confronting Britain head-to-head, France would aim to restore power to the original rajahs and sultans of the Indian states that the British had appropriated and ally them against Britain, while at the same time diminishing the influence of the pro-British rulers. This was clearly stated in the king's instructions to Guillaume Léonard de Bellecombe, who was sent to become governor of Pondicherry in 1776: "The principal object of our politics in India, is to reunite the princes in our favor, and detach from the side of our rivals those who have embraced English interests." Versailles hoped, as with the United States, that with French backing the Indian nations would eventually revolt and expel Britain and the EIC from their territories.

Bellecombe made his strongest alliance with Hyder Ali, the sultan of the Kingdom of Mysore and one of India's most powerful opponents of British colonial rule. He had already fought one war against the EIC back in 1768 (today called the First Anglo-Mysore War) that ended in a shaky truce between the two former belligerents. In July 1778, word of the declaration of war between France and Britain reached the EIC base in Calcutta (Kolkata) well before it reached the French forces, because Britain had recently struck a deal with Egyptian rulers that gave it the use of a shortcut across the Nile River and the Red Sea as a faster means of communication than sending ships around Africa. Having the element of surprise, the British launched lightning attacks against all of France's *comptoirs*. Bellecombe had fewer than fifteen hundred French and sepoy troops to resist the EIC's twenty thousand soldiers, and even though Hyder Ali had committed his own troops to the defense of the *comptoirs*, they were quickly overrun by the British. Pondicherry was captured in October 1778 after a seven-week siege, and the port of Mahé in March

1779, after which Bellecombe and his men were paroled to France. India now was a battleground of the far distant War of American Independence and Hyder Ali one of the associated combatants. With no more French troops in all of India, the closest assistance available to Hyder Ali was located in the two French outposts in the Indian Ocean, Île Bourbon and Île de France (Réunion and Mauritius, respectively), almost three thousand miles away.

The French navy, aware of the situation but already stretched thin with d'Estaing's expedition and the planned invasion of Britain, dispatched only two small squadrons to Île de France, one in 1779 under Brigadier General Thomas d'Orves and the other in 1780 under Captain René Joseph Bouvet. Aboard Bouvet's flagship was the recently commissioned Lieutenant Bonvouloir, who had been Vergennes's agent in Philadelphia back in 1775, and had since then departed America in order to fulfill his dream of fighting for France against the British. By the time the squadrons arrived, Hyder Ali had assembled a confederacy with eighty thousand troops and opened hostilities against the British. The governor of Île de France, while negotiating a treaty with the sultan, ordered d'Orves to assist the army with a show of naval force. D'Orves arrived off the Indian coast in February 1781, where Hyder Ali asked him to blockade the port of Cuddalore and cut off the EIC troops from resupply. D'Orves, short of supplies and lacking troops, abandoned the coast after just three weeks to return to Île de France. Hyder Ali subsequently lost the Battle of Porto Novo, a defeat for which he deeply mistrusted his supposed French allies.

Hyder Ali's mistrust of the French all but disappeared when Pierre André de Suffren appeared off the Indian coast in February 1782. Suffren's expedition, which had departed Brest back in March 1781 alongside de Grasse's fleet, had been the brainchild of the newly appointed Minister of the Navy Castries. In a major shift from his predecessor Sartine, Castries saw the East Indies theater of operations as being of a "more important nature" than the West Indies, a view shaped in part from his having been a member of the board of directors of the Compagnie des Indes. The portly, pugnacious, and tactically brilliant Suffren was also Castries's choice to lead the expedition. "Admiral Satan," as the British called him, showed his skill and determination long before he arrived at India. Just a month out of Brest he came upon a British squadron at Porto Praya in Cape Verde. Like Suffren, they were bound for the Dutch colony of Cape Town before heading to India. Since the Fourth Anglo-Dutch War had just broken out, the British fleet was trying to capture the colony, while the French fleet was trying to protect the Dutch, now their de facto ally in the face of a common British enemy. Suffren surprised and damaged the British squadron while at anchor in Porto Praya and then withdrew, beating them to Cape Town by several weeks. He successfully reinforced his Dutch allies against further British assault, then arrived at Île de France in October.

Joining their squadrons together, d'Orves and Suffren were approaching the Indian coast near Pondicherry in February 1782 when d'Orves died suddenly at sea. Suffren now took command of the ten ships of the line plus transports, intending to land at the British base in Madras (Chennai). A squadron of eight ships under the command of Rear Admiral Edward Hughes was already there, so Suffren, as was his wont, went on the attack. The Battle of Sadras, like each of the five battles that Suffren and Hughes would fight in Indian waters over the next sixteen months, was tactically indecisive. Suffren inflicted more damage upon Hughes's squadron, but of greater importance was that Suffren was able to land his troops at Porto Novo in support of Hyder Ali, where together they captured Cuddalore. Hyder Ali, whose trust in the French had now been somewhat restored by Suffren's timely assistance, met with him to plan strategy for the next campaigns. Suffren let his ally know that more French reinforcements were on their way, while he went off to fight Hughes again. He failed in July to dislodge Hughes from the formerly Dutch-controlled port of Negapatam (Nagapattinam), but in September he recaptured Trincomalee in Ceylon (Sri Lanka), which Hughes had captured a few months earlier from the Dutch East India Company, and which the French could now use as a base of support.

The promised French reinforcements under Brigadier General Charles Joseph Patissier de Bussy did not arrive in India until March 1783, where they joined with the Mysore army under Tipu Sultan, who had succeeded his father, Hyder Ali, upon his death a few months earlier. None of the belligerents yet knew that peace talks between France and Britain were under way at Versailles, and that a preliminary accord had already been signed. The last major engagements of the war between French and British forces were the Siege of Cuddalore in June 1783, in which the EIC surrounded a garrison of French and Mysorean troops, and the concurrent naval Battle of Cuddalore, the last fought between

Suffren and Hughes, which was once again indecisive. The siege was lifted at the end of June when the British frigate HMS *Medea* arrived carrying news of the preliminary peace accord. The cessation of hostilities between France and Britain also resulted in the end of the Second Anglo-Mysore War, with Tipu Sultan dictating terms of the peace to the EIC, but this did not cause the expulsion of Britain from the subcontinent. The fact that French support for Mysore was far too little to change the balance of power on the subcontinent, and that the political conditions there were markedly different than for the United States, meant there would never be an Indian equivalent of the Battle of Yorktown. As François Emmanuel de Montigny, the incoming French envoy to the neighboring Maratha Empire, ruefully admitted to Bussy, "The revolution which we had every right to expect in India and was already well planned, will not take place."

By the time the fighting ended, far more troops on both sides were dead or dying of disease than from battle wounds. Among those who had passed away from an "epidemic" in April 1783 at the French military hospital of Mangicoupan (Manjakuppam) in Cuddalore was one Lieutenant Julien-Alexandre Achard de Bonvouloir et Loyauté, age thirty-four. His meetings eight years earlier in the darkened rooms of Carpenters' Hall had helped induce France to support a breakaway republic, and would turn a minor civil revolt into a major war, that before it was over would involve half a dozen nations and span the globe.

THE WAR DRAWS TO A CLOSE IN EUROPE

Of the six nation-states that fought in the War of American Independence, four of them—France, Spain, Great Britain, and the Dutch Republic—were in Europe, and it was in European waters that some of the fiercest fighting occurred during and after the campaign at Yorktown. Catherine II's formation of the League of Armed Neutrality in 1780, with the promise of an armed fleet to protect the shipping rights of neutral nations, had done nothing to stop Britain from preemptively declaring war on the Dutch Republic in December 1780, nor had the league come to the Dutch Republic's aid after it joined in February 1781. Britain moved quickly to neutralize what it saw as the Dutch threat, seizing Sint Eustatius in a lightning raid, blockading the Dutch coast, and sealing off the approaches from the North Sea and English Channel. The few Dutch ships that attempted to break the blockade were generally captured and brought into British naval service, which was what happened in January 1781 when the fifty-gun *Rotterdam* was taken by HMS *Warwick*.

In late July 1781, now–Vice Admiral Hyde Parker was escorting a British convoy returning from the Baltic when he received a dispatch warning that a large Dutch breakout was under way at Texel. Seven months of blockade had crippled the Dutch economy, so desperate measures were called for. Dutch rear admiral Johan Zoutman led sixteen warships and seventy merchantmen into the North Sea, where on August 5, sailing over a shallow patch known as Dogger Bank, they were intercepted by Hyde Parker's seven ships of the line. Neither side fired a shot until the ships were within two hundred yards of each other, at which point they opened up their broadsides at point-blank range. The two fleets fought gunport-to-gunport for over three hours, inflicting enormous damage on one another. Each side counted about five hundred casualties when they withdrew. In naval gun battles during the age of sail, warships were often disabled by riddling the topsides above the waterline, but they rarely sank bodily. The gunfire at the Battle of Dogger Bank was so fierce that the Dutch ship of the line *Holland* was discovered the next day sitting on the bottom in sixty feet of water, only its topgallant masts standing above the surface, its pennant still flying. Tactically the battle was a draw—both sides claimed the other withdrew first, no warships were captured, both convoys escaped, and both the Dutch and British sailors were lauded for their bravery. But Britain maintained its blockade and no Dutch fleet ventured out of port again until the end of the war.

Catherine's League of Armed Neutrality, while incapable of defending the Dutch Republic, had the effect of further isolating Great Britain from any potential allies during the War of American Independence. Denmark and Sweden had joined the league almost immediately in 1780, the Dutch Republic, Austria, and Prussia the following year, and even Britain's erstwhile partner Portugal joined before the war's end. Bereft of any other avenues for a coalition against the Bourbon powers, David Murray, Viscount Stormont, who became the secretary of state for the Northern Department after his return from Paris, developed the idea late in 1780 that Russia could somehow be bribed into an alliance. He ordered James Harris, his ambassador to Saint Petersburg, to offer the island of Minorca as an inducement to join the war on Britain's side. Catherine's longtime lover and favored minister Grigory Potemkin was taken with the notion of a Mediterranean stronghold from which they could dominate the Ottoman Empire. Negotiations dragged on until March 1781, when Catherine finally decided to reject the offer on the grounds that obtaining Minorca would forever keep her indebted to Britain to protect against any invasions from Spain or France.

Catherine's rationale for rejecting the offer was prescient, for Spain and France had already agreed to the recapture of Minorca in the still-secret 1779 Treaty of Aranjuez. Spain's chief minister, Floridablanca, considered the island under British rule to be a "nest of pirates" that preyed on Spanish shipping. More important, its capture would "get rid of a resource for Gibraltar" as a supply base for the British garrison on the Rock. Even after almost twenty years of British rule, as Floridablanca learned through his spies, the inhabitants very much considered themselves Spanish and would not help the governor, Lieutenant General James Murray, with the island's defenses. His planning for an invasion was already under way when, through his ambassador in Saint Petersburg and from French intelligence, he learned of Harris's offer of Minorca to Russia. This spurred both more urgency and greater secrecy to the preparations.

In the spring of 1781, Floridablanca proposed to Vergennes that the two nations jointly attack Minorca. Vergennes and Castries agreed to send a fleet from Brest to assist the Spanish invasion. Guichen arrived in Cádiz in early July to link up with Córdova, with whom he had already sailed during the attempted invasion of Britain two years earlier. Meanwhile, Floridablanca appointed Louis des Balbes de Berton, Duc de Crillon, to lead the amphibious force. Crillon was an ideal choice to lead a joint campaign; he had been a French lieutenant general in the first part of the Seven Years' War, before transferring with the same rank into Spanish service in 1762. As Crillon, Córdova, and Guichen made their final preparations for the assault, word came of the victory of another combined Spanish-French campaign, the capture of Pensacola, which was celebrated with a twenty-one-gun salute. On July 21, the massive fleet began departing the Bay of Cádiz, fifty-eight ships of the line and seventy-five transports carrying eight thousand troops. Britain's navy was at that time spread across the English Channel, the North Sea, New York, the West Indies, and the East Indies; it had no more ships left to confront such a massive fleet, or to reinforce Murray's garrison on Minorca.

Even if the British navy was spread thin, it was still a force to be reckoned with. Córdova and Guichen took a long, roundabout route to disguise their ultimate objective; London did not know that it would be Minorca until just days before the force landed near the capital of Mahón, on August 20, and Murray was caught so off guard that his twenty-seven hundred troops barely had time to retreat to the citadel of Fort San Felipe. Crillon, accompanied by his American aide-de-camp, Lewis Littlepage, established a blockade of the city, while further Spanish and French reinforcements arrived in October. Crillon now had fourteen thousand men to occupy the entire island and lay siege to San Felipe, whose garrison endured months of almost constant bombardment while succumbing to diseases like scurvy. When Murray finally hoisted a white flag in February 1782, only six hundred men were fit enough to walk out unaided. The victors were appalled by the near-skeletons they had to carry out of the citadel and nurse back to health; the vanquished boasted that their captors could take little credit for seizing a hospital.

With the fall of Minorca, the only British stronghold left in the Mediterranean was Gibraltar, and now the Spanish and French turned their attention to concluding the four-year-long blockade and siege by its capture. Rodney's resupply of January 1780 had allowed the British garrison under George Elliott to maintain its strength and morale, as did the convoy of one hundred stores ships that arrived in April 1781 under Vice Admiral George Darby. Smaller supply convoys from Portugal, Morocco, and Minorca, carrying food and much-needed citrus fruits to ward off scurvy, easily penetrated the porous naval blockade of Lieutenant General Antonio Barceló, who never had more than a third of the ships he thought necessary to seal off the Rock and starve out the garrison. The constant Spanish bombardment and cannonade from both land and sea, averaging two hundred rounds daily, destroyed the town of Gibraltar and some shoreside fortifications, but not the batteries higher up the cliffs. The long duration of the siege also led to the adoption of some innovative technologies by the British, including the construction of long siege tunnels behind the northern face of the Rock, bored by hand through the limestone, and depressing gun carriages that could aim cannon downward from on high at Spanish artillery positions.

The French and Spanish also had developed their own technical innovation to break the deadlock. Soon after Rodney's relief squadron departed Gibraltar in 1780, a French engineering colonel named Jean Le Michaud d'Arçon sent a proposal for floating, heavily armored gun batteries to Spain's ambassador in Paris, the Conde de Aranda, which he forwarded to Madrid. The idea of such floating batteries was not new, and many similar proposals were also submitted to the Spanish court, including a plan for twelve armored batteries by Spain's French-born chief shipbuilder, Jean-François Gautier. D'Arçon's proposal found particular favor in both Versailles and Madrid, and he was sent to Spain as one of seven French advisers to assist Crillon. While there, he spent much of his time visiting Gibraltar and drawing up plans for the floating batteries. The concept was simple if also farsighted: Since the most vulnerable part of the fortification was its western side, facing the Bay of Algeciras, the Spanish should build the naval equivalent of the Grand Batteries at Yorktown to pummel the British defenses and open up a breach for an amphibious assault to follow. D'Arçon did not limit himself to the drawings of the floating batteries, but, like any Mézières-trained engineer, developed a complete operational plan and timetable for a grand assault. Versailles agreed to support the plan with additional ships, while Spain brought ten merchant-ship hulks to the port of Algeciras to be converted into the floating batteries.

The fall of Minorca in February 1782 freed up many thousands of Spanish and French troops to join the siege of Gibraltar and prepare for the grand assault. In June, the Duc de Crillon was back in Madrid to accept his commission and receive his orders to lead the assault against Gibraltar, when he was shown d'Arçon's proposal. Even though Crillon was highly doubtful the proposal could work—he believed the floating batteries could not be brought close enough to shore to do significant damage, and left a sealed letter absolving himself of all responsibility in case of failure—he nevertheless took overall command of the operation and placed his naval commander from Minorca, Lieutenant General Buenaventura Moreno, in charge of the floating batteries. Through the summer months the hulks were fitted with naval cannon on the port side, while the ships' decks were roofed over and heavily reinforced with layers of wood, rope, and hide to protect against red-hot shot. Perhaps d'Arçon's most innovative concept was a series of pump-fed seawater pipes that ran the length of the ship, "like the blood in the veins of animals," to continually wet down the wooden structures in order to prevent them from catching fire.

By September 1782, over thirty-five thousand Spanish and French troops surrounded Gibraltar. On September 12, the combined Bourbon fleet of Córdova and Guichen moored across the bay in Algeciras with thirty-nine ships of the line. The *junta de generales* that took place that evening was heated. Crillon wanted to launch the attack right away, but d'Arçon was very concerned that while the floating batteries were finished, they had never properly test-fired the guns or tried out the seawater piping systems, and other critical preparations had not even started. According to d'Arçon's carefully prepared timetable, they were still twelve days away from the final assault. On the other hand, Crillon knew that a British relief convoy for Gibraltar was being prepared, and any delay in his attack could jeopardize the whole operation. Ultimately, military and political considerations prevailed over technical ones; the threat of imminent British reinforcements was considered too great, but perhaps of equal consideration was that the Spanish had already set up well-appointed grandstands in front of Algeciras for the nobles and aristocrats who had come from as far away as France—including Louis XVI's younger brother, Charles Philippe, Comte d'Artois—to watch the assault. Meanwhile, on the hills above the town, eighty thousand people gathered to witness the spectacle. The grand assault was set for the following morning.

On Friday, September 13, 1782, at 7 a.m., the spectators were greeted by the sight of Moreno leading the ten floating batteries into a line opposite Gibraltar's western fortifications. By 10 a.m. they had moored about a thousand yards out—as Crillon had recognized, too far to inflict heavy damage. Both the Spanish land and floating batteries now opened up, while the British fired back from behind their fortified walls and tunnels, and with their depressing guns aiming directly into Spanish trenches. The most concentrated fire was between the Spanish floating batteries and the British shore batteries. At first, neither side did much damage; the Spanish shot battered the walls but did not silence the guns, while the red-hot British artillery bounced off the sloping roofs without setting anything ablaze.

As the afternoon wore on the battle began to turn against the Spanish floating batteries. Some began to catch fire as the seawater pipes ran dry, while their crews were unable to maneuver out of harm's way. Great clouds of smoke covered the ships. Across the bay, Córdova, the senior naval commander, watched intently but took no action, unwilling to bring his forty-seven ships into battle—at first because he did not want to expose his highly flammable ships to the red-hot shot, then because

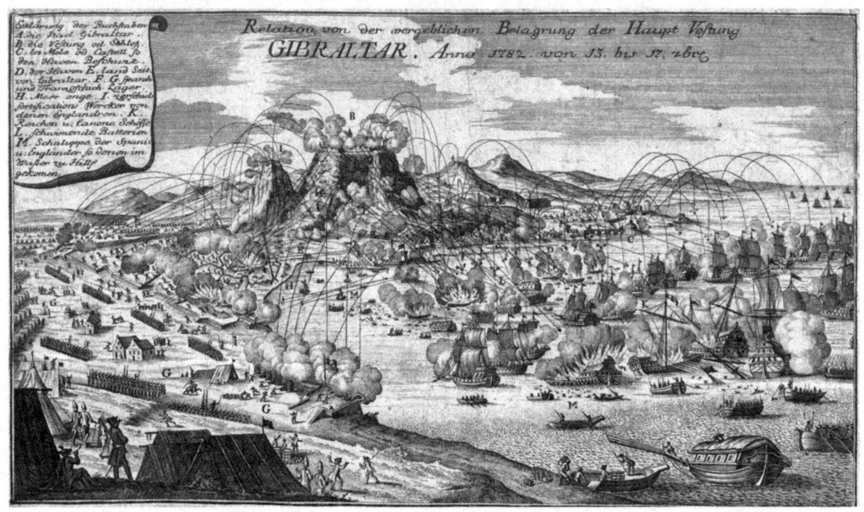

Siege of the Mountain Fortress of Gibraltar, September 13, 1782.
Johann Martin Will, c. 1782, engraving

the wind was wrong, then because it became too late to assist. Neither was there an attempt at an amphibious assault; despite months of careful planning, the actual operation was rushed and uncoordinated. By late afternoon the floating batteries had all but ceased fire, as had the Spanish land batteries, which ran out of ammunition. At midnight, Córdova ordered the floating batteries to be burned so as not to fall into enemy hands. At 5 a.m. the flames began reaching their powder magazines, and one by one they blew up, the eruptions lofting enormous mushroom clouds a thousand feet into the sky. The next day, seven hundred bodies from the floating batteries began washing up on the Gibraltar shoreline, half the casualties of the battle. The September 13 assault on Gibraltar had been one of the fiercest of the entire war—forty thousand artillery rounds expended, almost one for every second of the battle. Yet when the smoke and wreckage cleared, the British garrison at Gibraltar remained intact, and would do so through the end of the war.

Just as Crillon had feared, the British navy had been preparing another convoy to supply the Gibraltar garrison, but unknown to him, its departure had been delayed by weather and accidents. On September 11, 1782, thirty-four ships of the line and thirty-one transports bound for Gibraltar left Portsmouth. Above HMS *Victory* flew the flag of Admiral Richard Howe, recently promoted and appointed as the commander of the Channel Fleet. The fleet weathered storms en route, but as it approached Algeciras on the night of October 10, a particularly violent gale blew in from the southwest. When dawn came it was clear that the French and Spanish ships would be unable to stop the British from entering the bay; many had broken their moorings and were scattered about, with some hove up on shore. Howe's fleet had remained intact and came unopposed into harbor to offload the much-needed provisions.

A week later, Howe's thirty-four ships departed Gibraltar. By then, Córdova and Guichen had collected thirty-six ships intact, and gave chase. Although Córdova's flagship, *Santísima Trinidad*, was coppered, most of the Bourbon fleet was uncoppered, and this greatly slowed it down. Even worse, the difference in performance meant that Córdova's formation was ragged, as the faster coppered ships tried to match speeds with the slower uncoppered ones. By contrast, Howe's fully coppered fleet was able to solidly maintain its formation, and at first he was so confident in his ability to control the battle that he intentionally slowed down to engage his adversaries. When the two met off Cape Spartel in Morocco on October 20, they exchanged a few desultory rounds before Howe decided that engaging Córdova's larger force presented too great a gamble—after all, he had already accomplished his mission of resupplying Gibraltar—so he ordered a general retreat. Howe's coppered ships were able to open the gap between the two fleets as night fell, and by daybreak the combined Bourbon fleet was twelve miles behind and unable to catch up. The last major European battle of the war ended with a whimper, not a bang. Howe returned to Britain unscathed, while Córdova returned to Spain, where he forced the navy to finally admit that "uncoppered ships are worthless."

As the two fleets disengaged, they would have been able to see, across the Strait of Gibraltar on the horizon to their north, a Spanish cape named Trafalgar. Twenty-three years in the future, many of these same men and ships that had sparred at the Battle of Cape Spartel would meet again at Cape Trafalgar, in a battle that would change the course of history.

THE WAR DRAWS TO A CLOSE IN AMERICA

In the months before the last artillery rounds echoed across the fields of Yorktown, America was already acting like a triumphant nation and not a defeated colony, even though the military was in a parlous state. Its barely surviving the harsh winter at Morristown, the mutinies of the Pennsylvania and New Jersey Continentals, and the raids of Benedict Arnold in Virginia had all sapped the morale of soldiers and officers alike. The economy also was in shambles. When Robert Morris was selected by the Congress in February 1781 as superintendent of finance, he inherited what today is called hyperinflation. A year after the Congress had stopped issuing paper money, the worth of a paper dollar dropped to seven hundred times less than its face value, with angry mobs threatening to escalate their protests into full-blown riots. Yet in the midst of these crises of confidence, in March 1781 the thirteen states had ratified the Articles of Confederation, which for the first time gave the United States a formal, if flawed, constitution that established the rules for its government to function. The Articles represented the last in the three-step process toward nationhood laid out by Richard Henry Lee back in June 1776: Declare independence, develop a model treaty for foreign alliances, and establish a plan of confederation. This last step actually had been completed in 1777, but it was not until four years later that the plan was ratified. That this was accomplished although military victory was far from assured spoke to the confidence the founders had in the eventual success of their new nation.

Even after the Battle of Yorktown, victory was by no means a sure thing for the Continental Army and its French allies. Cornwallis had been defeated, but Clinton certainly was not. He had lost seven thousand troops in Virginia, but he could still call upon another forty thousand men in North America and the West Indies, of whom fifteen thousand were in New York City and another nine thousand in South Carolina and Georgia. Even so, Clinton had to consolidate his forces in the face of the victorious American and French armies. Just a few weeks after Yorktown, the remaining British and Loyalist troops in Wilmington, North Carolina, were evacuated to Charleston, where they were surrounded by a renewed southern Continental Army under Greene. Washington, unable to mount a new offensive without French naval support, established his new headquarters at Newburgh, New York, on the Hudson River, in order to keep an eye on Clinton. He left Rochambeau encamped in Williamsburg to take charge in Virginia, and to provide a link between himself and Greene. The three leaders would remain in that disposition—Washington in the North, Greene in the South, and

Rochambeau in the center—for the next eight months, without any major strategic action taking place.

The absence of major strategic actions did not equate to no fighting. In the year between the Battle of Yorktown and the British evacuation of New York, another hundred battles would be fought, with five hundred casualties between them. Many of these engagements really were skirmishes between Patriots and Loyalists, raids on remote British outposts, or frontier conflicts with Native American nations. Fort Pitt, as the headquarters for the Continental Army's western department, was the jumping-off point for several of these raids and expeditions under men like George Rogers Clark. In the spring of 1782, Antoine Felix Wuibert reported to Fort Pitt as its chief engineer. Wuibert had had a tumultuous career in the service of his adopted nation since its birth in 1776, when he was one of the earliest French volunteers and the very first officer ever commissioned in the name of "the United States." Later that year he had fought at Fort Washington in New York, was imprisoned at Forton for two years, and then in 1779 led the Irish Regiment aboard *Bonhomme Richard* to capture HMS *Serapis*. He was captured at sea in March 1780, paroled from Jamaica, and then found passage home from the Caribbean aboard the Continental Navy frigate *Confederacy*. That ship was captured in April 1781, and Wuibert was imprisoned for a third time aboard the notorious New York harbor prison ship HMS *Jersey*—nicknamed "Hell"—before he was released in September 1781 and resumed his old post as a lieutenant colonel of engineers. His commanding officer, Duportail, who described him as "brave" but inexperienced given how much time he had been a prisoner of war, recommended his assignment to Fort Pitt. Wuibert had just married the widow Altathea Garrison in February 1782, but the following month he left her in Philadelphia while he decamped to Fort Pitt, where he would spend several years in charge of its defenses.

By the summer of 1782 it was clear that the war was drawing to a close. The government in London had changed hands to a political party more inclined toward peace, the new British general in New York City had called for a truce, and British troops were evacuating Savannah to consolidate at Charleston and New York. At just that time Rochambeau received a message from Vaudreuil, still at Cap François, that he was on his way to Boston to refit his fleet, which was still damaged from the Battle of the Saintes. Rochambeau, Vaudreuil said, should be prepared to meet him in Boston in the fall, so that the fleet could transport his troops to the West Indies in order that Spain and France might carry out their assault on Jamaica the following year. Rochambeau had by then been idle for eight months and was coming down to "his last penny." With no more campaigns in the offing, Rochambeau's army broke camp on July 1 and began the journey toward Boston, using much the same route and in the same manner—awake at 2 a.m., march until noon—as their forced march to Yorktown the year before. Now their cadence was much slower, and they had time to appreciate the country whose independence they had just saved. Rochambeau's bookish aide Chastellux took the opportunity to pen a travelogue of his journey, *Voyages dans l'Amérique septentrionale* (Travels in North America), which became something of a bestseller in both its French and English versions.

Rochambeau had received Vaudreuil's note from another squadron of French ships that had left Cap François back in May for a daring expedition to Hudson Bay in Canada, and that had passed close to the Chesapeake Bay in order to deliver the message. The expedition was the brainchild of Jean-François de La Pérouse, who commanded the fifteen-ship squadron. The targets were the fur trading posts of the Hudson's Bay Company, a major source of income and power for the British Empire in Canada. La Pérouse was unopposed when he entered the Hudson Bay in August and in back-to-back raids captured the Prince of Wales Fort and York factory, making off with enough fur and trade goods to badly damage the company's finances for almost a decade. The expedition was something of a Pyrrhic victory; the ships and men suffered greatly in the cold, icy bay so far north, and returned to Europe in very bad condition.

Rochambeau, meanwhile, was continuing his stately march to Boston. On July 19, Washington met him in Philadelphia to see if there was one more campaign they might carry out together. Rochambeau demurred, politely but firmly, when Washington suggested an invasion of Canada; Vergennes, the French general knew, had always been against any further territorial conquests, and had ordered him not to be drawn into any American offensives outside the thirteen states. Washington dropped the subject, and the two parted as amicably as ever. On September 14, Rochambeau was invited to review the Continental Army at Verplanck, New York. In large part thanks to Steuben's original training, that army had performed admirably at Yorktown, but even then the men were often bereft of proper uniforms and equipment, and their military discipline was not as polished as the soldiers under Rochambeau. At Verplanck, the change was nothing short of dramatic; these were highly disciplined, well-turned-out troops the equal of any European army. Rochambeau, who always was candid with his friend Washington, turned to him and said, "You must have formed an alliance with the King of Prussia. These troops are Prussians." It was the highest possible compliment he could give. After a farewell dinner on October 19, the anniversary of their victory at Yorktown, Rochambeau's troops continued their march to Boston, while Washington prepared to return to his winter camp at Newburgh.

The French army arrived at Boston on December 6, and immediately boarded Vaudreuil's ships. His squadron of fourteen vessels had arrived in Boston back in August, but upon entering the harbor, the seventy-four-gun *Magnifique* smashed into rocks off Lovell's Island and foundered. The Continental Congress immediately voted to give the French navy its only ship of the line, the seventy-four-gun *America* still building in Kittery, Maine, in compensation, which France accepted. By late December, the repairs to Vaudreuil's fleet were complete, and it set sail for a rendezvous with Solano's fleet the following February in Venezuela, from where they intended to carry out their attack on Jamaica. Rochambeau would not go with his troops; they would be under his former second in command, Baron de Vioménil. Rochambeau visited with Washington one more time before journeying to Annapolis, from whence in January 1783 he left America to return home. He would enjoy an unexpectedly short period of peace before France once more was at war; but this time, it would not start as a war with Britain but as a war with itself.

THE PEACE TREATIES

Prime Minister North may have believed "it is all over" when he heard the news of Yorktown, but that sentiment was certainly not shared by everyone. His counterpart Vergennes—who after the death of Maurepas was effectively Louis XVI's principal minister—was perceptive in noting that accepting defeat was "not in the English character." That character was nowhere more in evidence than in King George III. Upon receiving word of Cornwallis's defeat just hours after North did, he reacted with none of his prime minister's despair. The news changed his outlook on the war not a whit. He simply demanded that the speech he was to give at Parliament's opening in two days' time acknowledge that while Cornwallis's defeat was "very unfortunate," it was merely a temporary setback. He was convinced, he told Parliament, of the "justice of his cause," and he would continue to prosecute the war. For him, holding on to America was a matter of existential importance; worried that if America fell to independence, so too would Ireland, the West Indies, Canada, and India, he vowed to "do what I can to save the empire."

Despite his misgivings about continuing the war, North managed to hold his government together for several more months. The only vocal proponent for the war, Secretary of State for the Colonies George Germain, stepped down in February 1782. North was now caught between a king who wanted to continue the fight and a cabinet that did not, and he resigned his position at the end of March. The new prime minister, Charles, Marquess of Rockingham, was committed to ending the war, and he immediately enacted a number of changes to facilitate this. Major General Guy Carleton was sent to New York to replace Clinton as commander in chief, with orders to evacuate the troops from across the United States and send them to the West Indies. The old Southern and Northern Departments were combined into one secretary of state for foreign affairs, Charles Fox, which would place multilateral negotiations for peace under one authority. His new secretary of state for home and colonial affairs, William, Earl of Shelburne, had been active in opposing the war ever since the Battle of Saratoga, and was committed to achieving a peace with the Americans. He was also a very old acquaintance of Benjamin Franklin.

By happenstance, Franklin, not yet knowing that Shelburne had attained that position, had dashed off an unrelated personal note to him just hours after his nomination. "Great affairs sometimes take their rise from small circumstances," Franklin would later say, for that one note began a flurry of negotiations that would result in a permanent set of treaties that ended the war. In mid-April, just over a week after Shelburne read Franklin's note, came a ringing of the front bell at the Hôtel de Valentinois in Passy. Richard Oswald, one of Shelburne's advisers, had been sent to broach the subject of a general peace with the American commissioner. Franklin showed cautious interest in the idea, bringing Oswald to Versailles, where Vergennes too expressed cautious interest. Oswald returned to Shelburne with the clear understanding that the next moves were up to him.

Despite their caution, both Franklin and Vergennes were anxious for peace. For Vergennes, the reasons were financial as well as political and military. By 1782 the French government was nearing insolvency. Soon after the publication of his *Compte rendu* the year before, which showed a budget surplus, Necker resigned amid accusations of malfeasance and treason. The new finance minister, Jean François Joly de Fleury, was instead faced with a budget shortfall of 400 million livres (well over $200 billion today), the navy was begging for more funds, and Franklin and Lafayette had just wrangled another 6 million livre loan. On the political front, a resurgent Russia was threatening yet another war with the Ottoman Empire over a dispute in Crimea, and until the American war ended, France would be hamstrung in its ability to support its Ottoman ally. Finally, France's military successes at the Chesapeake and Yorktown were not matched by substantial victories in India and the Caribbean, which both Castries and Vergennes recognized as of greater importance to France's stature in Europe.

Franklin looked at America's balance sheet and realized that almost all the entries were on the debit side. Beaumarchais, who had been operating Roderigue Hortalez throughout the war, reminded Franklin that the almost 3 million livres of credit he had extended back in 1779 for goods sold was now due, payable by the Congress. Franklin's landlord Chaumont also insisted on payment for a variety of goods and services. There was little on the credit side of the ledger. John Jay had spent two years in Madrid with nothing to show for it. John Adams had been in Amsterdam for just as long, but apart from diplomatic recognition of the United States by the Dutch Republic, all he could obtain was a small loan that mainly went to pay French creditors. And all that Robert Morris had to offer was paper money that literally was worth more as tinder than as legal tender. Franklin was well aware that the mutinies of the Pennsylvania and New Jersey Continentals over lack of pay could happen again at any time. Peace could not come too soon.

For the moment, Franklin was the only American in Europe who could negotiate a peace treaty. He sent appeals to his fellow peace commissioners who had been nominated the previous year by the Congress—John Adams, John Jay, Henry Laurens (out on parole in London), and Thomas Jefferson—but Jefferson declined, and it would be some time before the others could arrive in Paris. By contrast, in early May there were two separate peace envoys from London. In addition to Oswald as Shelburne's representative, Charles Fox sent a young diplomat named

Thomas Grenville to negotiate. Franklin and Vergennes met both envoys, then had to decide whether to choose Fox or Shelburne as their counterpart for negotiations. That decision was largely made for them on July 1, when Rockingham died from influenza and Shelburne became prime minister, leading to Fox's resignation. Shelburne took direct, personal control of the treaty process and sent Oswald to finalize the negotiations, not just with America and France, but also with Spain and the Netherlands. The goal was to end the worldwide conflict all at once.

In order to speed the treaty process, Vergennes told Franklin that he could negotiate separately with Oswald as long as he worked hand in hand with Vergennes and as long as both nations signed their treaties on the same day. Such action would not be seen as a violation of the 1778 French-American treaty that forbade each side from a separate peace. On July 10, Franklin presented Oswald with a list of "necessary" articles of peace, which included full recognition of the independence of the United States, and "advisable" articles, which included the transfer of Canada to America. By the end of the month, Shelburne had decided to conclude the terms based solely on the "necessary" articles. Shortly thereafter Franklin was laid low by kidney or bladder stones, and the unfortunate John Jay took over negotiations for a critical six weeks. Jay, who was never able to realize, as Franklin did, that France had always fought the war and negotiated the peace out of its own self-interest, learned that Vergennes was negotiating with Shelburne and accused France of treachery against the United States, almost snatching defeat from the jaws of victory.

The "treachery" against which Jay so wrongly railed was nothing of the sort. Vergennes and Franklin had already agreed to separately pursue peace talks with Britain, and the French minister was responding to an overture by Shelburne to restart their dialogue, which had been stalled for months while the American-British talks continued. The overture was actually due to the Comte de Grasse, who had met Shelburne in London after he had been paroled in August after being captured at the Battle of the Saintes. Rodney's stunning victory at that battle, which gave Britain naval superiority in the West Indies, had placed Shelburne in a strong position to start peace negotiations. When he outlined for de Grasse specific proposals—full recognition of American independence, restitution of Gibraltar to Spain, and the exchange of various Caribbean islands—de Grasse recognized that he was being asked to take to Vergennes the message that the British were ready to negotiate, and he did so immediately upon his return to Versailles. Vergennes dispatched his *premier commis,* Rayneval, to meet with Shelburne at his country estate in mid-September, after Vergennes had received approval from Spain to negotiate on its behalf. The weeklong discussions were very detailed and established a firm level of trust between the two negotiators, reinforced by Shelburne's argument that France and Britain were "not natural enemies . . . but they have interests which bring them together." Vergennes, hearing Rayneval's report at the end of the month, was still wary but saw the advantage of having Britain by France's side as a counterweight to Russia.

Soon after the initial Rayneval-Shelburne discussions were complete, Adams arrived from Amsterdam, with Henry Laurens coming soon afterward. Together with Franklin and Jay, they began hammering out the final terms of the peace treaty with Oswald. The main points of full recognition of the independence of the United States and Britain's removal of its soldiers had already been agreed to; negotiations dragged on for weeks about the northern and western boundaries of the United States, access to the Mississippi River, and fishing rights off Newfoundland. On November 30, pushed by the other American commissioners over Franklin's objections, they signed the preliminary articles of peace. When Franklin told Vergennes of the signing of the articles, the French minister was appalled, as Franklin knew he would be; this violated their agreement to coordinate their negotiations and sign their separate treaties on the same day. Moreover, it completely undercut the second round of negotiations that Rayneval and Shelburne had almost completed. Britain had been ready to give up Gibraltar in exchange for a combination of French and Spanish possessions in America and Europe that Vergennes and the Spanish ambassador Conde de Aranda had also agreed to. The loss of America might be acceptable to Parliament, Shelburne realized, but losing both America and Gibraltar at the same time never would be accepted, especially after the news that just weeks earlier, the British garrison at the Rock had successfully fended off the grand assault. Instead, Shelburne now backed away from that commitment to the Spanish.

Time was of the essence on all sides to complete the peace treaty. Both Vergennes and Aranda knew that d'Estaing was currently in Cádiz, waiting to take command of the massive Bourbon fleet—forty ships of the line—that was preparing to rendezvous with Vaudreuil and Solano in early 1783 to finally capture Jamaica. It would be a futile gesture that would prolong a war no one wanted. On December 16 on his own authority and in direct violation of orders from Floridablanca, Aranda agreed to accept Minorca and the Floridas in lieu of Gibraltar. This cleared the way for final peace talks to begin, since Floridablanca, after he calmed down, reluctantly agreed to the deal rather than restart the war. Vergennes took the opportunity to negotiate on behalf of the Dutch Republic, though initially without its consent.

America's agreement was largely unchanged from the November 30 draft, although some details like navigation rights along the Mississippi River would not be clarified for another decade. In the French agreement, France retained fishing rights off Newfoundland, exchanged with Britain several captured Caribbean islands, and regained territory in India. Spain got Minorca and East and West Florida, returned the Bahamas to Britain, and, in a separate treaty not finalized until 1786, pushed all British settlements out of Central America except for the tiny enclave of Belize in the Honduras. Based on the last available news from Suffren's campaign in Asia, the Dutch Republic lost Negapatam in India but regained Trincomalee in Ceylon. The Dutch would not finalize their treaty with Britain until 1784.

On Monday, January 20, 1783, at 10 a.m., Franklin and Adams arrived in Versailles at the Aile des Ministres Nord and mounted the stairs to Vergennes's apartment. At 11 a.m., Aranda and the minister plenipotentiary for Great Britain, Alleyne FitzHerbert, Baron Saint Helens, arrived. Together the ministers signed and exchanged their preliminary agreements of peace and armistices. Rayneval, exhausted from his labors, pronounced the agreements "a miracle." Adams, writing to his wife, Abigail, was more somber: "Thus drops the curtain upon this mighty tragedy. It has unraveled itself happily for us." Though the curtain had fallen, the encores had yet to play out.

Word of the preliminary agreements and notification of the end of hostilities was sent as quickly as possible around the globe. It reached d'Estaing in Cádiz in just days, Vaudreuil in Venezuela by March 24, and Suffren in India by the end of June. In New York, Carleton heard the news long after he had already evacuated Savannah and Charleston. By the beginning of 1783 he had twenty thousand soldiers in New York City ready to depart. They would be leaving not for the West Indies on a new campaign, but for Portsmouth and Plymouth, and then to their homes. It took almost a year to find enough shipping to accommodate this migration of men and supplies, and also of the Loyalist families who chose to move to Britain and Canada. In both East and West Florida, however, a number of British citizens chose to live under Spanish rule.

The preliminary peace accords agreed to by the diplomats largely ignored public sentiment. The British people wanted the war to end but demanded some form of vengeance, not conciliation. The French ministers wanted a greater presence in India, and the Spanish, of course, wanted Gibraltar. Still, only Shelburne would pay a political price for his deeds. The concessions he had negotiated were roundly condemned by Parliament as far too generous, and he was forced to resign just weeks after the preliminary agreements were signed. He was replaced by Charles Fox as prime minister, who in turn appointed his own negotiators to conclude the talks: George Montagu, Duke of Manchester, to treat with France and Spain; and to negotiate with America, David Hartley, an old acquaintance of Franklin. A separate treaty was arranged with the Dutch Republic. The final terms of the treaties were negotiated during the exceptionally cold summer of 1783, the result of a massive series of lava flows from the Laki volcano in Iceland, an event Franklin noted caused a "constant fog over all Europe."

The final treaties for America and the Bourbon powers were signed on the same day, September 3, 1783, but in separate locations. At 9 a.m., the American ministers Franklin, Jay, and Adams joined David Hartley at his temporary residence on the second floor of one of the few English-speaking lodgings in Paris, the Hôtel d'York at 56 rue Jacob. This was just three blocks from the Duke of Bedford's old residence where the 1763 Treaty of Paris had been signed that ended the Seven Years' War. With a few strokes of a pen, this 1783 Treaty of Paris put an end to another war that had begun on the American continent. A courier brought the news to Vergennes's apartment, where he, Aranda, and the Duke of Manchester affixed their signatures to the Treaty of Versailles before 3 p.m., thus ending the global conflagration that had followed the American outbreak.

That year and into 1784, fireworks lit the night sky several times in Madrid's Parque del Buen Retiro to celebrate the peace treaty. Spain certainly had reason to celebrate. Of all the nations that fought in the War of American Independence, it came closest to achieving the goals it originally had set out—recovering Minorca, recapturing the Floridas, and driving Britain from Central America and the Gulf of Mexico. Only the prized Gibraltar remained elusive. Spain's recovery of Florida had also secured the southern border of the United States against British incursions or influence that could have stymied its political and economic sway over the region in future years. Britain still retained Canada to the north, which suited Vergennes as a counterweight to keep the new nation in check against expansion or aggression against its own territories in the region.

The Treaty of Paris arrived in the United States in November, but it was not until January 14, 1784, that the Congress finally ratified it at its temporary location in Annapolis. Philadelphia was still the commercial and spiritual capital of the nation, and a massive fireworks display was planned there for the night of January 22. Just at dusk, one of the decorations caught fire and set off the entire display, causing the fireworks to detonate prematurely, killing and injuring several people.

France's territorial gains were minor, largely *status quo ante bellum*. It had achieved, at least in the short term, its primary goals of returning to the center of European power and of weakening British influence; Vergennes could be comforted by Joseph II of Austria's assertion that Britain would "no longer be considered one of the premier powers of Europe." Soon after the treaties had been signed, fireworks lit the heavens above Paris's Hôtel de Ville. But another sight also filled the Paris skies in late 1783—men first began to ascend in hot-air and hydrogen-gas balloons. The most celebrated of these aeronauts were Joseph and Étienne Montgolfier, who had been inspired to develop their balloon after hearing accounts of the siege of Gibraltar and initially were trying to devise a way to assault the Rock from the air. Benjamin Franklin was there to watch many of those flights, and upon being asked, "What is the good of these experiments?" responded with his now-famous quote (or something very near to it), "What is the good of a newborn babe?"

"A NEWBORN BABE"

If the United States were also a newborn babe, then Franklin most assuredly considered France, in the personage of King Louis XVI, to be its father. As France was providing yet another loan in June 1782 to help the newborn babe get to its feet, Franklin wrote to Robert Morris, "These repeated instances of [Louis XVI's] goodness towards us, make me consider and respect and love him as our father." He used that same language to Vergennes a few months later, when he referred to the king as "our friend and father." Franklin might have been forgiven for never having referred to the Spanish monarch, if not as a father then perhaps, say, as a kindly uncle. His focus had been almost wholly on Versailles, after all, and the shiploads of munitions and uniforms by Diego de Gardoqui, as well as the great victories by Luis de Córdova, Bernardo de Gálvez, and José Solano, were carried out beyond the sight of most Americans.

It would have been harder to forgive some of Franklin's fellow commissioners and statesmen for their hostility toward their allies, which began almost as soon as the news of the peace treaties arrived on American shores. Samuel Osgood, a Massachusetts representative to the Congress, wrote to John Adams accusing France of a nefarious "system of influence" that began when the "United States were reduced to the most deplorable situation. . . . At this fatal moment the eagle-eyed politician of our great ally [i.e., Vergennes], discovered the absolute importance of the aid of his master [Louis XVI], and the critical situation of the United States. It was then he ventured to propose that Congress should subject their peace commissioners to the absolute control of a foreign court." John Adams did nothing to dissuade Osgood from this sentiment, and in fact supported the idea that America had somehow done France a favor by bringing it into the war; France, he claimed, derived "immense advantages" from the war, and "has raised herself by it from the deepest prostration in the dust, to the highest elevation she ever obtained." Their churlish sentiments, however, were not widespread among the American public. As Samuel Adams reminded his cousin John soon after the news of the definitive treaties reached American shores, "I will say it for my countrymen, they are, or seem to be, very grateful. All are ready freely to acknowledge our obligation to France for the part she took in our late contest. . . . America with the assistance of her faithful ally has secured and established her liberty and independence."

The United States, as John Adams noted, was born from "mighty tragedy" and the outcome had never been certain. There were more than a half dozen paths that Britain could have taken to avoid the war before its outbreak in 1775, including a return to salutary neglect or pulling back from hostilities after Lexington and Concord. Once war had broken out, Britain could have won the war in any of a dozen ways, from a military victory at the Battle of Long Island to giving up Gibraltar in 1778 in order to ensure that Spain stayed out of the conflict. Instead, over the course of seven years, the war grew beyond the British public's ability and willingness to support. By the time of the Battle of Yorktown in October 1781, Great Britain was at war with five separate nation-states: the United States, France, Spain, the Dutch Republic, and the Kingdom of Mysore. Fighting on multiple fronts was not new for Britain—during the Seven Years' War it had faced down an equal number of opponents and prevailed—but this was the first time it was doing so alone, without allies. While the Seven Years' War had the 1759 annus mirabilis early enough so that there was general support during the conflict, during the War of American Independence the arc of British public sentiment continually bent downward; the only person to be universally praised by the British press was George Washington. After Yorktown, the popular support for the war collapsed so completely that the North government itself had to be replaced by one committed to peace. In the end, Britain was simply overwhelmed, both militarily and politically.

Even if Britain could have won a military victory on the American continent, it is highly doubtful that it could have also won a political victory there. The British government and its military had continually overestimated the level of Loyalist support in America, and continually underestimated the popularity of independence. By contrast, the French who came to fight side by side with the Americans saw this very clearly. Duportail had observed, as far back as 1778, that it was "impossible that the English can reduce America by arms." Much later in 1782, as peace talks were being proposed, Vioménil's aide-de-camp, Joseph-Frédéric, Baron de Brentano, noted to a friend of Charles Fox that "although the people of America might be conquered by well-disciplined European troops, the country of America was unconquerable."

Even so, America could never have gained its independence from Britain when it did without the support of the "well-disciplined European troops," and especially the naval forces, of France and Spain. The war was won not by American marksmen firing from behind trees, but by the combined might of many nations against a common foe. "Victories," Vergennes reminded Lafayette shortly after Yorktown, "are decided by the great battalions." There were certainly great battalions and also great fleets, but it is hard to estimate the numbers who fought and died in support of the United States during the war that gave America its independence. Americans of course bore the greatest burden; between 250,000 and 380,000 fought, and 25,000 died, in "The Cause."

No complete accounting of the contributions by France and Spain has yet been made. A list compiled in 1903 for the Library of Congress by the French Foreign Ministry listed over 40,000 French soldiers and sailors who fought in the United States and territorial waters, a later enumeration listed 2,112 who died there, and several other works provided biographical details of French officers. These compilations do not fully account for the French who fought in Europe, the Caribbean, and Asia; worldwide, over 100,000 French fought during the war, and over 5,000 perished. For Spain, no thorough compilations yet exist. Even a partial accounting of the major engagements would likely push the total number involved to over 100,000; at Gibraltar alone more than 60,000 soldiers and sailors fought, and over 3,700 men died during the four-year siege. Dutch and Mysorean soldiers and sailors also numbered in their thousands during the war, as yet unenumerated and, so far, little remembered.

The Americans and French were intent upon remembering those who fought in the war. In the wake of the Newburgh Conspiracy of March 1783, in which Continental Army officers nearly mutinied against the Congress over back pay before Washington put an end to their movement by insisting that they respect the civilian authority of the Congress, Henry Knox revisited his old idea to firmly bond those officers in a fraternal organization. In April 1783, he drafted articles for the Society of the Cincinnati, which he pointedly named for the fifth-century BCE Roman general Lucius Quinctius Cincinnatus, who after being granted dictatorial powers to win stunning victories turned his power back over to the civilian Senate and returned to his farm. In May 1783 the society, dedicated to charitable functions and preserving the memory of the Revolution, was formally instated at Steuben's headquarters, and the following month Washington became its first president. Within a few months, chapters of the Society of the Cincinnati, consisting of officers who had served during the war, had formed in all thirteen states. In December 1783, Pierre Charles L'Enfant, who had designed its insignia, was in Paris and helped form the French branch, the Société des Cincinnati, which was approved by Louis XVI and initially presided over by the Comte d'Estaing. For several years there were exchanges between the members of the societies, notably when Lafayette came to the United States in 1784 to see Washington at Mount Vernon and visit old friends and comrades.

Washington by then had retired his generalship, in the manner of Cincinnatus, and returned to the life of a plantation owner. In February 1784, shortly after he had come back to Mount Vernon, he wrote to his old friend Rochambeau, who likewise was enjoying the river views from the windows of his own estate in France. Washington told his friend of seeing the British fleet ready to depart New York City the previous December, and wished him a future free of the cares they had endured together. Benjamin Franklin may have thought of France and the French in fatherly terms, but Washington had the fraternal ideals of the Cincinnati more in mind when he penned his valediction to Rochambeau: "I shall recollect with pleasure, that we have been contemporaries and fellow laborers in the cause of liberty, and that we have lived together as brothers should do, in harmonious friendship." It was a fine sentiment that nevertheless would be sorely tested as the two nations went their separate ways in the decades and centuries to follow.

CHAPTER 9

The Legacy

The very day that the two peace treaties were signed, Vergennes took up his pen to write to his ambassador in Madrid about his sentiments on the occasion. Those sentiments would sound familiar to any modern diplomat who had just concluded a multilateral accord; Vergennes was not so much proud of the agreements he had so carefully wrought as he was simply worried about the next crisis that landed on his desk. European affairs had not stopped during the war. All the while he was coping with an America clamoring for more aid and a recalcitrant Spain with its own diplomatic agenda, Vergennes was also juggling conflicting interests on the Continent. His biggest concern was still Russia, which had continued to threaten France's ally the Ottoman Empire, having recently annexed the former Ottoman possession of Crimea. Vergennes was busy trying, without success, to coax Austria and Prussia into stopping Catherine II's ambitions before they led to yet another war. "I do not feel tranquil in spirit seeing that the affairs of the Levant [Ottoman Empire] will replace those of America," he told Montmorin.

Even though France was once more at the center of European power, its relationship with the United States was already on the wane. A Maryland delegate to the Congress, James McHenry, argued in 1783 that since both nations entered into their alliance, each for its own political motives, solely to defeat Britain, "the alliance is therefore completed and terminated, without leaving . . . any permanent connection between them."

At almost exactly the same time, the Chevalier de Luzerne predicted to Vergennes that "natural interests" between Britain and the United States, notably language and long-established trade networks, would supplant French commerce. His prediction was entirely correct; trade between France and the United States plummeted sharply after 1781, while American trade with Britain rose.

Vergennes saw no need to interfere with this process, as France had not considered the improvement of trade with America as a primary goal for going to war: "We have never based our policy towards the United States upon their gratitude," he explained to Luzerne. Instead, he was now focused on cementing France's position in Europe, notably by building upon the rapprochement with Britain that had stumbled into being during the peace negotiations. He and his *premier commis* Rayneval worked with William Eden, now one of the Lords of Trade, to negotiate a commercial treaty between the two nations in 1786, which though favoring British interests, lowered tariffs on both sides of the Channel. At the same time, Vergennes negotiated another dozen treaties around the Continent, including a long-sought-after commercial treaty with Catherine II at the beginning of 1787, which he hoped would promote European stability by loosening Britain's grip on Russian trade and at the same time strengthening French commercial influence over Russia without the need for an entangling political alliance.

The Russian treaty would be Vergennes's last diplomatic achievement. In late January 1787, he developed a fever, fatigue, and dark skin blotches that Louis XVI thought were due to "overwork" but that more likely pointed to septicemia (blood infection). Three weeks later, on the night of February 13, 1787, he was dead at age sixty-nine. The king was "overcome" by his passing, as he had lost his most trusted mentor and confidant. Vergennes did not live to see that his Russian treaty never had the chance to succeed, as Russia and Austria went to war against the Ottoman Empire within just a few months, and that France would be powerless to stop it. Nor would he see that his ultimate goal of affixing France as the dominant power in a peaceful Europe—the reason he had committed to the War of American Independence in the first place—would be derailed, not by outside powers but by France's own internal politics. The subsequent French Revolution, with the concurrent civil wars and Revolutionary and Napoleonic Wars across Europe, would strengthen Great Britain almost beyond measure, strip Spain of its empire, reshape the map of Europe, and give the nascent United States a foothold to expand across the entire North American continent.

AMERICA AFTER THE WAR OF INDEPENDENCE

Back in 1784 when Washington wrote his farewell to Rochambeau, he was looking forward to the "tranquil walks of domestic life" as plantation owner, landholder, and gentleman farmer, but that would last fewer than three years. By 1787 he was back in the public sphere, and after a new federal Constitution had been ratified to replace the old Articles of Confederation, he was elected as the first president of the United States on April 6, 1789. By then New York City was the capital of the new nation, and the inauguration was scheduled to take place there at the end of the month. When Washington arrived at the city on April 23, he was greeted by a fifteen-gun salute from the Spanish war sloop *Galveztown*. This was not the same ship that had brought Bernardo de Gálvez to victory at Pensacola. In 1785, when he became viceroy of New Spain in Mexico City, Gálvez ordered a new ship to replace his old one, which had become worn out in use. The vessel was built in New York City and had entered Spanish service in 1787, the year after Gálvez had died at age forty after a brief, unspecified illness.

At noon on April 30, Washington's military escort arrived at his residence on Cherry Street and brought him to Federal Hall, newly redesigned by Pierre Charles L'Enfant, which would serve as the inaugural venue and the capitol building. In the Senate chamber, in the very first set of rows right next to the senators and cabinet officials, sat Diego María de Gardoqui, Spain's ambassador, and his French counterpart Elénor-François-Élie, Comte de Moustier. After a signal by the master of ceremonies, Washington went to the second-floor balcony facing the street to take the oath of office. He was joined on the balcony by his secretary of war, Henry Knox, and his old drillmaster Friedrich Wilhelm von Steuben, now an American citizen. After he took the oath, the cry "Long live George Washington, President of the United States!" went out, answered by a roar from the crowd and a booming fifteen-gun salute from *Galveztown,* the sole foreign warship at the event. Returning to the Senate chamber, Washington read out his inaugural address, in which he pledged that the new nation would "command the respect of the world."

That evening, the skies were lit by fireworks and the streets illuminated by dramatic candlelight displays at the homes of the French and Spanish ambassadors.

Upon the signing of the Treaty of Versailles, the Spanish court had named Gardoqui, who had been central to Spain's provisioning of America during the war, as the first plenipotentiary minister to the United States, where he arrived in 1785 to take over from Rendón. Similarly, the Comte de Moustier in 1787 had taken over from Luzerne as ambassador. As the representatives of the two nations that had supported the war even before it had started, and that ultimately saved American independence, these two men had been accorded the highest places of honor at the inauguration, and were among the first to call upon President Washington the following day. They were witness not only to the spectacle of a new nation in the throes of creation, but also to the legacy that France and Spain would confer. The United States did not simply fight side by side with its allies; it readily adopted their ideas and philosophies, and frequently welcomed their people as immigrants. Even before the Revolution, America had been a prime destination for immigration, not merely because of its high standard of living, but also because, unlike almost any other nation, it adapted itself to its new immigrants just as much as the immigrants adapted to their new country. America, in short, continually changed as a result of the constant influx of new individuals and new ideas.

In the years after Lexington and Concord, this tradition of adopting individuals and adapting ideas from abroad had only intensified. "The history of the American Revolution," noted John Adams, "is indeed the history of mankind during that epoch." This was especially evident in the changes made to the American army after the war. Over its entire existence, the Continental Army had absorbed volunteers, weapons, troops, and training from France, Spain, and across Europe, which transformed it from an undisciplined and uncoordinated collection of militias to a model of military efficiency. After the war, Washington, Knox, and their successors built upon that experience—admittedly in fits and starts—to refine that model. Steuben's Blue Book continued to be the official regulations for the various incarnations of the American army that succeeded the Continental Army, and would remain in use until after the War of 1812. The French 0.69 caliber musket, often referred to as the "Charleville" even though it had been manufactured in many locations, had become the standard weapon during the war. In 1794, when the Springfield Armory became America's first industrial arms manufacturer, it settled on the French musket rather than the British Brown Bess as the model of choice, and this model continued to be the standard produced at the Springfield and Harpers Ferry arsenals until just before the American Civil War.

Not only did America use the French musket, but it also adopted Gribeauval's manufacturing system to produce weapons with standardized parts, and adapted it to create a system where those parts became truly interchangeable. This system was actually introduced to the United States by Thomas Jefferson, who in 1785 succeeded Benjamin Franklin as the minister to France. While there, he met Gribeauval's successor, Honoré Blanc, who had greatly improved the process of standardization, and sought to bring Blanc to the United States. When that did not happen, Jefferson made Knox aware of Blanc's improvements. In 1798, the War Department contracted with two private firms under Eli Whitney and Simeon North to produce large numbers of muskets, and they in turn began employing Blanc's standardization methods to create uniform piece parts in their gun manufacture. As this process spread to agricultural, transportation, household, and other products, it became known as the American system of manufacturing. True interchangeability did not happen for several decades, but by that time standardization and interchangeability was already evolving into the system of mass production that spurred American industrial growth in the nineteenth century.

Thomas Jefferson was also responsible for bringing another French concept to realization, the establishment of a military academy for the United States Army. Louis Lebègue Duportail had actually put together the first proposal for such an establishment back in 1783, when he and his compatriot Gouvon had returned from France for a brief stay. The Continental Army, along with the original Corps of Engineers, was then in the process of being mustered out of service after Yorktown. Duportail saw the need for the establishment of a permanent Corps of Artillery and Engineers, and just before returning to France he wrote a memorandum for George Washington detailing its composition. "The necessity of an academy," he noted, "to be the nursery of the Corps, is too obvious to be insisted upon." The proposal lay unheeded for a decade, until Congress in 1794 established a small Corps of Artillerists and Engineers to be established at West Point, with one of Duportail's fellow engineers, Lieutenant Colonel Étienne (Stephen) Rochefontaine, appointed as the first chief engineer. Another decade would pass before Congress authorized President Thomas Jefferson in 1802 to "organize and establish a Corps of Engineers . . . [which] shall be stationed at West Point and shall constitute a military academy." For years, textbooks and many of the professors at the academy were from France, and when in 1812 Colonel Jonathan Williams, West Point's first superintendent, developed the insignia still in use today for the Army Corps of Engineers, he chose the castle at Verdun and the motto *Essayons* (We Shall Try) in honor of its origins in France's Corps du génie.

By contrast to the close ties formed between the French and American militaries, only in a few instances—notably at Baton Rouge and the Battle of Nassau—did Spanish and American forces directly operate together. In consequence, Spain had comparatively little impact on the United States due to its participation in the war. Even so, the Battle of Nassau would have unintended repercussions for both nations that would echo down the next century. After jointly capturing the island in May 1782, Juan Manuel de Cagigal and Francisco de Miranda had parted on very bad terms with Alexander Gillon. Matters did not improve for Cagigal and Miranda when they returned to Havana, where Bernardo de Gálvez was furious that they had disobeyed his orders (which they had never received) to abandon the expedition. With his family connections back in Madrid, Gálvez had Cagigal demoted, arrested, and sent back to Cádiz on trumped-up charges. Miranda was to face a similar fate, but in June 1783 he fled Cuba for the United States. His persecution at the hands of the Gálvez family turned him forever against Spain, but he would not know what form that rebellion would take until he went to America.

Miranda's visit to America transformed him from a loyal colonist who had fought for his mother country into a revolutionary who dreamed of freeing his native Venezuela from Spanish rule. During his two-year visit up and down the eastern seaboard, he visited the battlefields of Brandywine and Bunker Hill, and he absorbed the lessons of the great battles from luminaries of the Revolution he met, who included George Washington, Thomas Paine, Samuel Adams, Thomas Jefferson, and Henry Knox. As he grew to understand how America threw off its own shackles, he formed his plans to create a South America independent from Spain. Though he would not begin to act on those plans for another two decades, the seeds of revolution had been sown.

Alexander Gillon's grievances bore much different fruit. He had brought *South Carolina* back from Nassau to the United States victorious but empty-handed, and always maintained that Cagigal had promised him payment that never materialized. His investors in Charleston went to the Congress to seek remuneration, and they in turn sent a request in May 1784 to the American envoy in Spain to handle the matter. William Carmichael had been Silas Deane's secretary in Paris before being assigned to accompany John Jay during his unhappy two-year stay in Madrid. Upon Jay's departure in 1782, Carmichael was appointed as chargé d'affaires, and unlike Jay he was both welcomed at the court and understood the language and culture. Carmichael approached the Conde de Floridablanca for assistance with reparations. It happened that at the same time, George Washington was looking to obtain for his plantation some male (jack) Andalusian jackasses, widely reputed to be some of the largest and strongest donkeys in the world, which he intended to breed with female horses to produce mules. As partial compensation for the *South Carolina* affair, Floridablanca, with Carlos III's blessing, ordered Diego de Gardoqui (prior to his ambassadorship) to ship a pair of Andalusian jackasses to America, which he did via his firm Casa Joseph Gardoqui e hijos. Only one animal survived the ocean voyage to Boston, and Royal Gift, as it was named, was cautiously transported overland to Mount Vernon, where it arrived with its Spanish handler in December 1785.

Washington immediately began putting Royal Gift to stud. An experienced breeder, he first created a new line of donkey, known as the American Mammoth, by mating Royal Gift with jennies (female donkeys), so that within a year he had a line of American Mammoth donkey sires. The second step was to mate Royal Gift and the other jacks with mares to produce mules, which were preferred over either horses or donkeys as draft animals.

Washington's Mammoth jacks were in great demand, and since each jack could sire a thousand offspring a year, by 1810 over eight hundred thousand American Mammoth mules were working the farms and pulling loads across the South and beyond the Allegheny frontier. The descendants of Spain's Royal Gift, interbred with other European stock, would become America's preferred beasts of burden as the nation expanded westward. They were raised in their tens of millions to haul supplies during the Civil War and pull army supply wagons and commercial stagecoaches along the Oregon Trail. In World War I, nearly a million American Mammoth mules with "US" branded on their hindquarters would be sent to Europe as the new warhorses of that conflict.

FRANCE AND SPAIN IN REVOLUTION

Alexander Gillon's difficulties in obtaining wartime payments were echoed, with less productive outcomes, by the postwar travails of Pierre-Augustin Caron de Beaumarchais and Jacques-Donatien Le Ray de Chaumont. After the Battle of Yorktown, British land operations had come to a virtual halt, but that was not true of the British naval blockade, which actually tightened. By 1782, the blockade had all but cut off Robert Morris's access to hard currency from France and Cuba, and it greatly reduced trade and thus income. With bills coming in from creditors both in Europe and America, Morris doubted he could cover the debt of almost 3 million livres owed to Beaumarchais, which was due in June 1782. After receiving assurances from Luzerne that the bills could wait, he wrote to Franklin to ask him to hold off on payment. The letter arrived too late; Beaumarchais had already anticipated that Morris might renege, so he sold his letters of credit, at a loss, to a number of his own creditors. Franklin might be able to avoid paying one merchant, but he could not do so to a whole slew of them without risking the good faith and credit of the United States. Franklin's account with Morris was now overdrawn, but Beaumarchais also reminded the Americans that he was owed even more money; the total value of all the goods and services supplied by Roderigue Hortalez et Compagnie during the war, his detailed invoices showed, amounted to more than 6 million livres.

Morris, who could not even cover Franklin's first payment, had no way to cover the additional amount. He was given an excuse not to pay when the Congress ordered an audit of Beaumarchais's account. Arthur Lee, who had been shunted aside by Silas Deane in his dealing with Beaumarchais, had subsequently returned to the Congress attacking the arms dealer and claimed that he was bilking the Americans for payment of munitions that the French government had supplied for free. Deane had unintentionally bolstered Lee's claim when he had originally told the Congress that "everything [Beaumarchais] says, writes, or does, is in reality the action of the Ministry." In fact, the French government had already made clear to Franklin that the arms Beaumarchais had provided back in 1777 were never a gift of the king, but always were intended to be repaid to Beaumarchais. Even so, the Congress continued to balk at paying, even after the peace treaties were signed. For several more years Beaumarchais approached Thomas Jefferson and the Marquis de Lafayette for assistance, all to no avail. By 1789 the French Revolution had made any further action almost impossible, and when Beaumarchais died in 1799, the claims were still pending. It would turn out that the case would drag on through another three presidential administrations and numerous courts until 1837, when after sixty years, Beaumarchais's heirs were finally awarded a payment of $150,000, about one-tenth of the amount originally owed.

Beaumarchais's commercial rival Chaumont suffered a similar fate, but not through the direct refusal of the Congress to repay its debts. In fact, almost all of Chaumont's invoices for clothing, arms, and other materiel had been properly paid to his agent, John Holker. The problem was, those payments had been made in paper money, and after the Congress stopped issuing paper in 1780, its value plummeted sharply and the payments became almost worthless. Chaumont, who had lost money in other financial speculations as well, declared bankruptcy shortly afterward. After the war ended, Chaumont sent his son, also named Jacques, to the United States to collect on what he saw as the Congress's moral obligation to compensate French merchants like himself who had taken enormous financial risks to support the war. Jacques Chaumont fils spent five years arguing the case until 1790, when Alexander Hamilton, Washington's secretary of the treasury, settled the account for pennies on the dollar. After becoming an American citizen during his stay—and thereafter referring to himself as James LeRay—he returned to France with $9,000 and a new American bride. They would soon revisit America to participate in a land speculation scheme in an attempt to recoup their losses.

The debts that Beaumarchais and Chaumont had run up during the War of American Independence were minor compared with the 18 million livres that the United States owed the French government at the end of the war (a debt that Hamilton sold to a private investor in 1795), and paled in comparison to France's overall wartime debt. By the end of the conflict, the total cost to France was 1 billion livres, about a half trillion dollars today, most of it going to the navy and almost all of it financed through loans. Even though Necker was a banker, he could not get the

5 percent rate that the Bank of England could obtain in the European markets; Necker was paying closer to 10 percent because of the shoddy state of French finances, so that by 1786 almost half of France's budget was spent on covering debt interest payments. By itself this debt was not calamitous; during the same period Britain's wartime expenditure was double that of France, yet it was able to pay down its debt fairly quickly through a variety of prudent fiscal measures, including raising taxes and the establishment of a reformed sinking fund, a type of financial reserve in which any budget surplus was appropriated directly to debt repayment instead of going to some minister's pet project. France had previously been able to pay off its debt after the Seven Years' War through a combination of tax increases, reduced tax exemptions, and improved collections. The prospects for stable finances in a postwar France therefore looked reasonably good.

It was peacetime fiscal policy, more than indebtedness from fighting the war for America, that plunged France into the financial crisis that led to the French Revolution, even though the American war was certainly an exacerbating factor. The finance ministers who came after Necker, most notably Charles Alexandre de Calonne, lost control of state finances by reinstating the system of using "tax farmers" and other private corporations to collect taxes on behalf of the government. Royal expenditures and borrowing costs increased, revenues decreased, and Callone, who did not repeat Necker's experiment with the very public *Compte rendu,* allowed the debts to pile up in secret. France soon reached a point where drastic reforms were needed to stem the fiscal hemorrhaging. The calamitous state of France's finances came as a shock to the Assembly of Notables, composed of members of the high-ranking First and Second Estates of clergy and nobility, which Calonne convened in 1786 and 1787 to offer a series of fiscal reforms. Even in the face of financial catastrophe, they rejected all his proposals, such as a land tax on all levels of society, where previously only the Third Estate of commoners had been subject to taxation. The assembly insisted that tax matters had to be submitted to the Estates General, which comprised members from all three estates but which had not been convened since 1614.

With the French state essentially bankrupt, Louis XVI convoked the Estates General at Versailles in May 1789. His goal was to find a general resolution to the fiscal crisis. The goals of the Third Estate, by contrast, were to specifically address the immediate problem of famine brought about by recent harvest failures, and the broader underlying problems of social inequality. This disparity in priorities led to the Third Estate breaking away from the Estates General in June and forming a National Constituent Assembly. The storming of the Bastille on July 14 by Third Estate partisans in search of munitions forced the king to accept the National Constituent Assembly as a legitimate legislative body. July 14 marks the traditional beginning of the French Revolution, as it also unleashed a wave of peasant revolts that spread throughout the nation and led to the abolition of the old feudal system, the adoption of the Declaration of the Rights of Man and of the Citizen, and the establishment of a constitution for the French First Republic.

The Revolution also led to the yearlong Reign of Terror, the apogee of France's bloody civil wars, during which time ordinary citizens were beaten to death by mobs and revolutionaries executed each other in the tens of thousands. These deaths paled in comparison to those of the French Revolutionary Wars that began in 1792 with the Battle of Valmy, pitting France against a series of coalitions that included Austria, Prussia, and Great Britain, all of whom saw intervention against the new French Republic as vital to maintaining their own monarchies. Even as its armies were marching to victories across Europe, France was steadily losing allies on the Continent and across the Atlantic.

In 1798, France engaged in the undeclared Quasi-War with the United States, fought in part over neutral trading rights, and whose end in 1800 also marked the termination of the French-American alliance. The French Revolutionary Wars ended temporarily in 1802 with the Treaty of Amiens, only to be reignited the following year when Britain declared war on France as a result of treaty violations by the French dictator, soon to be emperor, Napoleon Bonaparte. The even bloodier Napoleonic Wars ultimately would involve two dozen nations across the entire globe, resulting in five million civilian and military deaths by its end in June 1815 at the Battle of Waterloo. The Congress of Vienna, which marked the political end of the wars even though the treaty was signed a few days before Waterloo, established the international framework for the European great powers that would last until World War I. By then, Great Britain was firmly in place as the global hegemonic power for the rest of the nineteenth century.

Just as France's debts from the War of American Independence contributed to, but were not the catalyst for, its 1789 fiscal crisis, the ideology of the American Revolution was a contributory but not causal factor in the French Revolution. Books, newspapers, and pamphlets extolling the virtuous Americans in their fight for liberty became widespread, but it was the fact that they had successfully fought and won that liberty, rather than their political philosophy, that inspired. Neither were the French veterans who had returned from the war responsible for spreading the gospel of revolution. Only a handful of memoirs about the war were published by those soldiers before 1789, and they generally described the American nation and its people rather than its political ideals. Instead, the root cause of the French Revolution lay in the tensions between the different estates that had been brewing for many years, and in fact had given rise to the same Enlightenment ideals of Voltaire and Montesquieu that had inspired Jefferson's Declaration of Independence.

Although not directly caused by it, the French Revolution featured many of the same luminaries who had shone brightly during the American Revolution. Some supported the people's revolt. Lafayette was appointed to the Assembly of Notables, was elected to the Estates General, and, in consultation with Thomas Jefferson, drafted the Declaration of the Rights of Man and of the Citizen. He also became leader of the French National Guard, a citizen militia, which included members of Rochambeau's *Expédition Particulière* such as Louis-Alexandre Berthier, Louis Éthis de Corny, and several officers from the Soissonnais regiment. In Saint-Domingue, the Haitian Revolution that began in 1791 to overthrow the French colonial government and slavery, creating the independent nation of Haiti in 1804, counted numerous members of the Chasseurs-Volontaires who had fought at Savannah. Most veterans of the American war, however, remained loyal to the king, and because of their time in service and experience held higher ranks in the French military. Rochambeau, for example, commanded the Army of the North against the Austrians in 1792, Charles Armand Tuffin led a Royalist counterrevolt in Brittany, while Duportail served as minister of war from 1790 to 1791. As the French Revolutionary and Napoleonic Wars spread, those veterans from the American conflict would be faced with war on a far vaster scale than they had previously known. At the 1809 Battle of Wagram, over three hundred thousand troops clashed; four years later, a half million combatants were engaged at the Battle of Leipzig. By contrast, the battles of Saratoga and Yorktown each had fewer than twenty-five thousand soldiers in total on the field. As Lafayette explained to Napoleon's brother Joseph Bonaparte, during the War of American Independence "the world's most important consequences were decided by encounters between patrols."

The French Revolutionary Wars coincided with the Reign of Terror, which began a few months after Louis XVI's execution on January 21, 1793. The members of the Committee of Public Safety could order the punishment—including execution—of anyone judged to be an enemy of the Revolution, even if they had wholeheartedly supported the principles of liberty. Officers of the French navy were imprisoned, guillotined, shot, or exiled in disproportionate numbers compared with their army counterparts. Naval officers were generally not only from the hated aristocracy, but also part of the scientific and technological elite in a revolution that "had no need of intellectuals," as was reportedly said when France's leading chemist, Antoine Lavoisier, was guillotined. Vice Admiral d'Estaing was the most notable victim; as the navy's highest-ranking officer, who had also demonstrated his attachment to the Revolution by joining the National Guard, he was nevertheless convicted in 1794 of "conspiring" with the royal family and guillotined. Before he was executed, he reportedly told his captors, "When you take off my head, send it to the English, they will pay dearly for it." The loss of so many experienced naval officers would play havoc with the French navy during its decade-long fight against the British navy, from its defeat in 1794 at the Glorious First of June, to its drubbing in 1798 at the Battle of the Nile, and finally to its near decimation, along with that of the Spanish navy, at the Battle of Trafalgar in 1805.

Spain, which had been joined at the hip with France during the War of American Independence, had not originally been its ally during the French Revolutionary Wars. After the Treaty of Versailles was signed in 1783, the paths of the two nations had diverged radically. Unlike France, Spain had kept a tight rein on its fiscal policy and even created new financial structures to manage its wartime debt. The increase in military spending, mostly due to naval expenditures, was funded through a combination of tax increases and the establishment of a national bank, the Bank of San Carlos, founded by the French financier François Cabarrus, which provided short-term credit by issuing promissory notes. Spain also had the advantage of a strong colonial economy. The Viceroyalty of New Spain (today's Mexico and Central America) actually increased silver production throughout the war, enabling Gálvez and Solano to fund their expeditions, and Mexico even served as the arsenal and breadbasket for other Spanish colonies around the region. Spain's economy was strong enough to finance a total direct contribution to the United States, through Beaumarchais, Pollock, and Gardoqui, of about 400,000 pesos (close to $1 billion equivalent), according to the invoice that Gardoqui submitted to John Jay in 1794, and that Alexander Hamilton repaid to the Spanish government in full. The next year the two nations followed up the repayment of the debt with the Treaty of San Lorenzo that formalized Spain's recognition of the United States and finalized navigation rights along the Mississippi River.

Spain also avoided France's revolutionary fervor through ruthless crackdowns where it was most vulnerable, the Spanish American colonies. Every decade or so since the conquistadores had overpowered the Americas, there had been uprisings up and down the continent, from Mexico to Venezuela to Peru. These were almost always led by the indigenous populations, rebelling against loss of autonomy, onerous taxes, and the brutal working conditions imposed by the Spanish landowners. Each of these rebellions had been crushed by the army and local militia. Fear of providing further inspiration for these rebellions was a crucial factor in Spain's rejection of a direct alliance with the United States in 1778 and 1779, and news of the American revolt was continually blocked from reaching the colonies. Even so, the two largest indigenous uprisings, led by José Gabriel Túpac Amaru in Cuzco and Andrés Túpac Katari in La Paz, took place in 1780–81, coinciding with the Battle of Pensacola at the height of Spain's involvement in the American War. Spain was so fearful of the revolution spreading even further that its executions of those rebellion leaders were not only intentionally gruesome—beheading and quartering by horses—but their body parts were then sent around the Viceroyalty of Peru to be displayed as a warning to any would-be rebels.

After the Haitian Revolution and the execution of Louis XVI, the Spanish government was also fearful that the French Revolution would spread across the Pyrenees and to its own Caribbean colonies. In 1793 it broke with its hereditary ally, France, and instead sided with its erstwhile enemy Great Britain in a coalition against the French First Republic. By then, the former architects of the Bourbon alliance were gone; Carlos III had died in 1788, succeeded by his son Carlos IV, while Floridablanca and then Aranda were ousted as prime ministers in 1792, to be replaced with the aggressive Manuel Godoy. Spain fought against France for two years, then, finding itself on the losing end of the conflict, switched sides in 1796 to join France in its fight against Britain. Spain's navy, which had reached its apogee under men like Córdova and Solano, was already on the decline; it lost the Battle of Saint Vincent in 1797, despite outnumbering the British almost two to one. As in the previous war, the French and Spanish navies would have to combine into a single Bourbon fleet to have any chance of defeating Britain.

They would have that chance in 1805, soon after the French Revolutionary Wars had resumed with France and Spain once again united against Britain. Spain had already ceded Louisiana to France, and Napoleon had instructed his finance minister, François Barbé-Marbois, Luzerne's former secretary, to sell the entire territory to the Americans in order to pay for the new war effort. A major part of that effort would be a planned invasion of Britain, drawn in part from Charles-François de Broglie's assault plan of 1765 and from the lessons of the failed attempt of 1779. In order for the assault to proceed, a combined French-Spanish fleet would have to first take control of the English Channel, before a flotilla of invasion barges could cross the narrow stretch to land in Kent. While Napoleon's plan broadly resembled the previous ones, the scale would be vastly different; where the 1779 invasion had twenty thousand troops on shore, Napoleon had mustered ten times that number between Boulogne and Bruges for his invasion.

The naval element of the assault failed before the invasion flotilla could even get under way. The two navies had learned some lessons from their previous experience but forgotten others. By now all ships were coppered, but as with the invasion attempt twenty-six years earlier, the French and Spanish fleets had not trained together to perform complex battle maneuvers. In early 1805, Napoleon developed a complicated and ultimately unworkable strategy to have the fleets break out from their ports on the Atlantic and Mediterranean, evade the British blockade, race across the Atlantic to rendezvous in the Caribbean, then race back to the English Channel to support the invasion flotilla. As the spring and summer progressed, only the Toulon fleet was able to accomplish its breakout, and by August the necessary fleet rendezvous with the invasion flotilla had failed. In the fall, Napoleon ordered the combined Bourbon fleet to depart its base at Cádiz to transport troops for a planned invasion of Naples. Under French vice admiral Pierre Charles Silvestre de Villeneuve and Spanish captain-general Federico Gravina, thirty-three ships of the line sortied from Cádiz on the evening of October 20 and headed for the Strait of Gibraltar. Waiting for them in the offing were twenty-seven ships under the flag of Admiral Horatio Nelson.

As the two fleets closed near Cape Trafalgar the morning of October 21, several officers in both fleets would have recognized the scene. The Battle of Cape Spartel, the final European battle of the War of American Independence, had been fought within sight of Trafalgar twenty-three years earlier. Robert Moorsom and Philip Durham had been junior officers at Spartel, and now commanded their own British ships of the line. In the Spanish fleet, Spartel veterans Federico Gravina, Antonio de Escaño, José Gardoqui, and Ignacio María Álava were now flag officers, while Cosme Damián Churruca and Francisco Asedo commanded ships. The sense of déjà vu would have been all the stronger, as the flagships HMS *Victory* and *Santísima Trinidad,* along with HMS *Britannia, Rayo,* and *San Justo,* fought in both battles. But there the comparisons ended. Where the Battle of Cape Spartel was inconclusive, the Battle of Cape Trafalgar was an overwhelming British victory. Using the breaking-of-the-line tactic that had been pioneered by Rodney and Hood at the Battle of the Saintes, Nelson decisively cut the French-Spanish battle line in two places and destroyed it piecemeal. By the end of the day, the British fleet had captured or wrecked two-thirds of the French and Spanish ships, while Nelson was fatally wounded and died a national icon. Napoleon was thereafter reduced to Continental operations as he could no longer count on his navy to carry out any major overseas campaigns. The British victory at Trafalgar went far beyond the European sphere and indelibly marked the century to come—after the battle, Britannia unquestionably "ruled the waves" across the entire globe for the next hundred years, until the outbreak of World War I, as no other navy would contest its command of the ocean.

Luis de Córdova, who had become the director-general of the Spanish navy, did not live to see the Battle of Trafalgar. His colleague José Solano, who died soon after the battle, did not witness Trafalgar's devastating and widespread effects, as it paved the way for the independence of its Spanish American colonies and the breakup of its once mighty empire. Spain was left with only twenty ships of the line, and no more would be built for another fifty years. The remaining officers and sailors were too demoralized to be effective. The Spanish nation as a whole was reeling under the weight of the ongoing war. In 1807, Godoy allowed Napoleon to march through Spain in order to invade Portugal, and Napoleon returned the favor by occupying Spain and replacing the Spanish monarch with his brother Joseph Bonaparte. The Spanish people both on the Iberian Peninsula and in the Spanish American colonies rose up against the foreign invader. On the peninsula, the combined armies of Spain, Portugal, and Britain eventually drove out the French in 1814. For several decades afterward, Spain was governed by regents, including Floridablanca and Saavedra, until Queen Isabella II directly ruled as monarch in 1843.

In Spanish America, Napoleon's invasion and the French usurpation of the throne had transformed the colonial uprisings against the travesties of Spanish rule into full-blown wars of independence. Not only did the colonials no longer believe that they were bound to the government in Madrid, which had abdicated, but they were also emboldened by the fact that Spain's grip on the American continent was grievously weakened after Trafalgar, as the navy was no longer a force that could quickly transport troops to and around it. While the colonials girded for rebellion, the American Revolution and the Declaration of Independence loomed large in the minds of the patriotic societies that sprang up across Spanish America, as the more liberalized press carried articles and essays on Enlightenment ideals and the North American experience. *El primer grito,* the first cry of freedom, was heard in 1809, in the Manifesto of the People of Quito, which borrowed directly from the Declaration of Independence: "When in the course of human events, it becomes necessary for one people to dissolve the political bands which have connected them with one another . . ." was liberally translated as *"Cuando un pueblo, sea el que fuere, muda el orden de un gobierno establecido largo tiempo . . ."* Similar declarations were produced across Spanish America: Colombia, 1810; Venezuela, 1811; Mexico, 1813.

These Spanish American declarations of independence, as with the United States, were the prelude to war. One of the first military leaders was Francisco de Miranda, who after leaving the United States had fought on the side of France in the French Revolutionary Wars. In 1811 he struck his blow against Spain by leading the creation of the First Republic of Venezuela, only to see it fall to Spanish forces the following year. The mantle was picked up by Simón Bolívar in the northern parts of the South American continent, and José de San Martín in the south. Similar struggles occurred in Mexico and Central America. Even after the Spanish government was restored to power in 1814, its colonies continued the fight. By the 1820s Spain was exhausted and politically weakened. It had already ceded Florida to the United States, and could no longer maintain its vast empire. By 1825 the American hemisphere, which had been simply an extension of European powers just fifty years earlier, was home to two dozen independent nations groping their way toward a hopeful but uncertain future.

AMERICA WELCOMES FRENCH AND EUROPEAN EXILES

For the French soldiers and sailors who had returned from the American Revolution and the War of Independence, only to come face-to-face a few years later with the French Revolution and their own civil war, the future looked neither hopeful nor certain. Even before the Reign of Terror had begun, many of them fled France to find refuge in the American nation they helped create. They were accompanied by thousands more nobility and aristocrats, most from France but some from other European nations, who escaped a gruesome fate at the hands of the revolutionaries. Some would stay in exile only a short time, to return to their mother country once the civil war subsided. Others remained permanently and put down roots, raising families and sometimes dynasties that left indelible legacies in American society.

Some of those soldiers had made a home in the United States even before the War of American Independence ended. Antoine Felix Wuibert, after his tumultuous career on land, at sea, and in prison, settled in the Philadelphia area in 1786 after his final posting at Fort Pitt and a brief foray to his former home in Saint-Domingue. In 1788 he divorced his wife, Altathea, and in 1805 married the widow Jeanne Marie Magdalene Pourcent (née Moreau), adopting her two children and having two more by her. Wuibert had seen the consequences of slavery firsthand in Saint-Domingue, and became an active member of the Pennsylvania abolitionist movement. His record disappears after 1806, except for the marriage of his daughter Jeanne Adelaide Marie in 1833. Another early volunteer, Charles Romand de L'Isle, had married Letitia Ingraham in Philadelphia shortly after his arrival in 1776. Letitia apparently did not know of his wife Rose Anne and family back in Martinique, nor vice versa. In fact, he somehow allowed his American family to believe that he had died shortly after his participation in the Siege of Savannah in 1779, when in fact

he had been captured by the British, paroled, and returned to the West Indies to serve as a French artillery officer. He died of illness aboard ship returning to France in 1784, leaving behind families in both Martinique and Philadelphia. His Martinique family eventually moved to France, while his Philadelphia family left a long line of descendants in the Midwest, who founded the Lisle Corporation in Iowa, still in operation today. Steuben's aide Pierre-Étienne du Ponceau also remained in Philadelphia, changing his name to Peter Stephen Du Ponceau. After leaving military service he worked for the American government for several years, then entered law practice in 1785. He had a long and distinguished legal career, while simultaneously becoming one of America's foremost linguists and contributing greatly to the understanding of Native American languages.

When Rochambeau's troops departed the United States in 1782 and 1783, about four hundred men were left behind. They were either deserters or had been discharged, yet for the most part it was not cowardice or fear but rather the charms of their newfound country that led them to remain. In a number of cases, those charms were women with whom they had fallen in love. Nicolas Anciaux of the Royal Deux-Ponts, for example, resigned his commission in 1781 to marry Linda Richardson from Georgia. Absent any journals it is hard to know other reasons for staying, but given that the majority of those who remained came from the Germanic regiments of Royal Deux-Ponts and Lauzun's Legion, it is likely that some of them found the conditions in America more to their liking than did their French comrades.

As the Reign of Terror unfolded, many of those comrades loyal to France would change their minds about the relative merits of America. Georg Daniel Flohr of the Royal Deux-Ponts, one of the few enlisted men who left behind a journal, had returned to France to study medicine. He was in Paris the day Louis XVI was executed in 1793, when a mob brutally murdered an unnamed individual next to him, such that "a part of [his] mangled body was cast against Mr. Flohr." The incident turned him from medicine to religion, and from France to America. Later that year, apparently, the traumatized Flohr was studying theology in Virginia, then went on to become a well-respected preacher in the southwestern part of the state for many years.

Another of the many soldiers who fled the horrors of the Revolution was Louis Lebègue Duportail. His service as minister of war had put him at odds with the revolutionary tribunals, and in August 1792 he was con-

victed by Georges Danton, one of the early leaders of the movement, of "having conspired against liberty and the sovereignty of the people." He went into hiding to avoid a certain death sentence. By 1795 he had come to the United States and bought a plantation in Swede's Ford, Pennsylvania (present-day Bridgeport and Norristown), along the Schuylkill River. For several years he led a bucolic existence, cultivating rye and oats and establishing a shad fishery on the river, while leaving legal matters to his attorney, Du Ponceau. In 1801, the call of his mother country—more particularly, that of Napoleon, who recalled him to duty—proved stronger than his desire for a peaceful retirement. He sold his plantation and embarked from New York aboard the vessel *Sophia,* but died suddenly at sea, possibly from a burst appendix, on August 11, 1801, leaving no descendants in either France or the United States.

One man who did leave his trace in America was François Joseph Paul, Comte de Grasse. After his parole as a British prisoner of war, he was court-martialed and acquitted for losing the Battle of the Saintes, after which he went into retirement. He died in 1788, leaving a son and four daughters behind. Having learned of the gruesome fate of their father's colleague d'Estaing, they managed to escape to Charleston, South Carolina, where Congress granted them a pension and where they established themselves as community leaders. With property in America, the West Indies, and France, their descendants moved between the regions. One of those descendants, Altima deGrasse, was born in 1897 on the British island of Nevis. Her grandson Neil deGrasse Tyson became the director of the Hayden Planetarium in New York City and one of the most celebrated astrophysicists of the early twenty-first century.

While the United States opened its doors to the men and their families who had fought for American independence, talent and skill even among noncombatants was also a passport to citizenship. As the French (and others) fled the Revolutionary and Napoleonic Wars raging across the European continent, as well as the Haitian Revolution in Saint-Domingue, many found homes up and down the American continent. Their destinations were predominantly the urban centers of Philadelphia and New York City, and several French settlements that were established in Pennsylvania, Ohio, and upstate New York. Philadelphia, then the capital of the United States, was the most cosmopolitan of them all, and the favored way station for French royalty and aristocracy who came to live in, or just pass through, America.

The little bookstore at 84 Front Street at the corner of Walnut Street was the gathering place for this group of exiles. Its owner, Médéric-Louis-Élie Moreau de Saint-Méry, had been the Martinique representative to the National Constituent Assembly; his friend Charles Maurice de Talleyrand-Périgord had been a representative for the clergy; Louis Marie, Vicomte de Noailles, had been another assemblyman after returning home from Yorktown. These were among the men who formed the nucleus of the French community in exile from 1793 to 1798, which at its height made up almost 10 percent of Philadelphia's population. Many visitors were short-term: Several members of the royal family passed through the city as they moved from place to place while in exile; Talleyrand returned to France in 1796 to become Napoleon's foreign secretary, where he initiated the Louisiana Purchase and subsequently became one of the chief architects of the Congress of Vienna; while Thaddeus Kosciuszko briefly came to Philadelphia in 1797 after leading a failed Polish uprising against Russia, then returned to resume the fight. Other visitors remained in the region and established American dynasties, the most notable being Éleuthère Irénée du Pont de Nemours, who had studied gunpowder manufacture under Antoine Lavoisier and in 1801 built a gunpowder factory on Brandywine Creek in Wilmington, Delaware, which evolved to become the chemical manufacturing giant E. I. du Pont de Nemours and Company, better known today as DuPont. Meanwhile, French jewelers, furniture makers, and chefs catered to the political and social elite of the nation's capital, restyling the American aesthetic.

Some of the former aristocrats sought to recoup their lost wealth by speculating in land purchases on the expanding American frontier. The French aristocrats were following the trend of land speculation that was widespread in postwar America. The Ohio Lands were particularly rife with unscrupulous deals. After the war they had been divided into a number of conflicting territories, some granted by Congress and the states (for example, military districts reserved for war veterans in lieu of pensions), others by private companies and individuals for sale to pioneers, such as the Kanawha Tracts owned by George Washington. Deeds to these lands were often in dispute or falsified outright, as happened with the Scioto Company, formed in 1787 by William Duer, who later was imprisoned for life in a separate fraud case. The Scioto Company investors in Paris—which included Minister of War Duportail—offered thousands of acres of land optioned by the Ohio Company to prospective French settlers, with pamphlets promising rich harvests and a mild climate. In 1791 a group of five hundred French settlers arrived in the United States, only to find that the promises made by the company were empty. No transportation awaited to take them to Ohio, and the ones who did arrive at the hamlet of Gallipolis on the Ohio River learned that the Scioto Company had never made good on its options and so did not own the Ohio Company shares. When they finally settled into farming, they learned that the soil was poor and the weather harsh. With the help of Congress and the Ohio Company, the French settlers who remained were able to purchase their tracts and managed to carve out an existence, eventually creating a thriving township that exists to this day.

The smaller French settlement of Azilum in northern Pennsylvania had a more fortunate beginning but proved far shorter-lived. In 1793 Robert Morris, who was an avid land speculator himself, sold sixteen hundred acres to a Philadelphia consortium of French aristocrats headed by the Vicomte de Noailles. Unlike Gallipolis, which was pitched to average Frenchmen, Azilum was intended, as the name implied, as an asylum or refuge for a small number of French elite who had escaped the Terror. Noailles set about creating an elegant planned town on a horseshoe bend of the Susquehanna River, complete with a central market, shops, taverns, a schoolhouse, theater, chapel, and a large cabin destined—they hoped—for the French royalty who would surely emigrate. Louis Philippe, who would later become king of France, did in fact visit, but there was never any real prospect of the French monarchy setting up court overseas. Both buyers and investors turned out to be scarce—Talleyrand had a look but never invested in it—and the town never had more than about fifty homes. The soil turned out to be inadequate for profitable farming, and the few settlers began departing around 1800. Within a decade the remains of the town were barely visible to passersby.

The Company of New York was one of several land speculation schemes that attempted to resell large tracts of land in upstate New York that had been confiscated from Native American nations and Loyalist estates. In 1792 a group of investors in Paris, including James LeRay, bought about a thousand square miles of land along the Black River in order to resell to French settlers. The speculators called the territory Castorland (*castor* means beaver in French), and in 1793 sent two representatives, Simon Desjardins and Pierre Pharoux, to survey the territory. One of their fellow passengers, Marc Isambard Brunel, was fleeing the Terror, and upon landing in New York City, he agreed to accompany them on their survey of Castorland, as he was already bursting with ideas about canals and waterways for New York State. The survey showed the land to be far different and less manageable than they had been led to believe. Even when James LeRay left France in 1802 to join his family and recoup his previous financial losses by personally overseeing Castorland, the French settlers failed to make a go of it, and the colony foundered a few years later. LeRay nevertheless established a mansion there, became a prominent local figure, and even managed to sell property to a second wave of French émigrés who fled France after the downfall of Napoleon.

After helping survey Castorland, Brunel had moved back to New York City in 1795, where a French exile community was already thriving. Gaining American citizenship, he established a "manufactory" and began submitting designs for competitions on canals, theaters, and civil engineering works, most notably working with Pharoux to win at least part of the design for the Park Theater. New York City was fertile ground for Brunel, as French engineers and architects had earned a stellar reputation during the war and were highly sought after by military and civilian authorities. Around 1793 a fellow French émigré named Joseph-François Mangin arrived in New York City, worked as an army assistant engineer and then engineer in chief to fortify its port defenses, and in 1796 was appointed as surveyor of the city. A few years earlier, L'Enfant, who had designed monuments, banquet halls, and pavilions in the city, had been given the commission to renovate Federal Hall where Washington was inaugurated.

All three Frenchmen went on to illustrious careers. Shortly after Washington's inauguration, L'Enfant was appointed by the president to plan the new federal city that was to rise on the banks of the Potomac River. His commission lasted just over a year before Washington dismissed him over conflicts with government officials. Nevertheless, L'Enfant's plan for a city grid crisscrossed by grand avenues was largely adopted, with revisions, as the basis for the District of Columbia. Magnin remained in New York City and established an architectural firm, where among the many now-historic buildings he designed were the New York City Hall and the original Saint Patrick's Cathedral in lower Manhattan. Brunel's legacy, by contrast, lay outside the United States. While dining at the home of Alexander Hamilton in 1798, he was made aware of a major problem that the British navy was having in manufacturing ships' pulley blocks in large quantities. Having developed a new system of mass production, the next year he brought it to Britain, where it was adopted at the Portsmouth Dockyard Block Mills. With the engineering and manufacturing skills he acquired in New York, the French émigré Marc Brunel now became a well-respected British engineer, but it was his more famous son Isambard Kingdom Brunel who would go on to introduce so many innovations in tunnels, bridges, railroads, and steamships that he became known as a founding father of the Industrial Age.

George Farragut was another émigré whose son became his best-known legacy, and in some ways also helped bring to a close what his father had started. The Spanish-born sailor had fought at the Siege of Charleston, was captured and paroled, and fought again at Cowpens before turning to civilian life. In 1807, Farragut and his family moved to New Orleans. After his wife died, he placed his son, David, in the care of close friends, the family of naval captain David Porter, who introduced the younger Farragut to navy life. The America that George Farragut had adopted after the War of American Independence was still divided by slavery. When the Civil War broke out in 1861 his son, David Glasgow Farragut, became one of the Union navy's most aggressive officers, the first to be promoted to full admiral. His victories over the Confederate navy in the Gulf of Mexico and at Mobile Bay—where he shouted, "Damn the torpedoes!" to press home an attack—helped ensure that more than eighty years after its creation, the American nation would become truly united.

"LAFAYETTE, WE ARE HERE!"

From 1824 to 1825, midway between the end of the War of American Independence and the beginning of the Civil War, Gilbert du Motier, Marquis de Lafayette, toured the United States. He was then in his midsixties, an age when nostalgia can exert a powerful grip. He had not yet reached twenty years of age when "love of glory" had propelled him aboard *Victoire* to America in 1777, and was just thirty-two when he joined the Estates General. Despite being the author of the Declaration of the Rights of Man and of the Citizen, he was labeled an enemy of the Revolution in 1792 and hounded out of the country. Arrested by Austrian troops, he spent the next five years in prison, while his son, Georges

Washington Lafayette, was smuggled to the United States to stay with his namesake at Mount Vernon. After being released and returning to France, Lafayette spent his middle years staying out of the public eye during Napoleon's regime, having lost his wife, Adrienne, in 1807. The fall of Napoleon and the restoration of the Bourbon monarchy in 1814 led him back into politics, but naturally on the side of the liberals and antiroyalists.

In late 1823, he learned of the death of Joseph Bloomfield, an officer with whom he had served at the Battle of Brandywine. In a letter to President James Monroe, who also had fought in the War of American Independence, he declared a deep sadness at the loss of his "brother in arms" and expressed a profound longing "to rejoin the friends with whom I can once more enjoy the sweetest memories and visit the happy shores of an adopted land which has so fulfilled my very first desires." The letter reached Monroe just over a month later, and the president immediately asked Congress to extend an official invitation. Despite the fact that the upcoming 1824 election was already proving partisan and divisive, Congress passed a joint resolution expressing its "ardent desire to receive" Lafayette. He wasted little time accepting the invitation, bringing with him his son Georges Washington and his secretary, Auguste Levasseur, who would record the journey in detail. Lafayette, as both an American war veteran and a French elder statesman from the Revolution, was equally loved on both sides of the Atlantic; a throng bade him farewell when his ship departed Le Havre on July 13, 1824, and another greeted him at his arrival in New York City on August 16. The city officials had planned Lafayette's visit down to the minute; for four days he was shuttled between admiring crowds, long-winded speeches, gala dinners, and demonstrations of technological wonders—New York City's firemen put on an unintentionally impressive show when they doused an actual fire. On August 20, Lafayette's retinue was escorted with a military guard as they made their way to Boston.

The same scenes would be repeated over and again for the next thirteen months as Lafayette wound his way through all twenty-four states, from north to south and back. The dinners, festivals, and galas that greeted him at every turn were the preliminaries for the nation's jubilee. In 1826 the United States would turn fifty, and the last of its founding fathers and war heroes were dead or dying. America, like Lafayette, was gripped with a fierce nostalgia for the days of revolution, and grappling with the meaning of its legacy. People still referred to the country as "these United States," and the divisions between North and South—more specifically between free and slave—were every bit as deep as those that had divided Patriot and Loyalist a half century earlier.

For the benefit of Lafayette, however, the nation temporarily united and put on its grandest pageants. The nation had changed dramatically since his last visit in 1784. There were double the number of states, and the general prosperity appeared to have increased over the already high levels it had known. Steam technology was far more widespread in the United States than on the Continent; although one of the first steamboats was actually invented in Lyon, they were still rare in France, while steamboats took Lafayette's entourage almost everywhere they went. In October, after he visited Mount Vernon and wept at George Washington's tomb, a steamer brought him to the battlefield at Yorktown, forty-three years to the day after the battle was won. Little had changed from when he left Cornwallis's stronghold a smoldering rubble; all they could see, according to Levasseur, were "houses in ruins, blackened by fire or riddled with bullet holes."

Lafayette stopped at Point Breeze, Pennsylvania, to pay a visit to Joseph Bonaparte. In 1816, after his brother's downfall, Joseph had bought the estate twenty miles from Philadelphia, where until 1832 he would entertain other exiled Frenchmen who had been loyal to Napoleon's cause, and in the summers would stay at his hunting lodge in upstate New York that he purchased from James LeRay. Lafayette went on to meet Jefferson at Monticello; visited the French settlement at Gallipolis; was fêted by Congress in Washington, D.C., on New Year's Day 1825; in March visited Fayetteville, North Carolina, which had been so named in 1783 in his honor; and in May was in Louisville, Kentucky, named in 1780 for his former king. By July he was at Brandywine, the site of his first trial by fire, where veterans of the battle and their children walked the battlefield with him, remembering actions and pointing out landmarks from a half century before. In August and September, as he prepared to return to France, he stopped for a final time at Mount Vernon, then met the newly elected president, John Quincy Adams. After the president and Congress awarded him a large stipend for his services, which would go to clearing the enormous debts the once rich marquis had accumulated back in France, they presented him with an apt memento: America's newest forty-four-gun frigate was renamed USS *Brandywine,* in honor of Lafay-

General Lafayette at the Anniversary of the Battle of York Town, October 19, 1824.
William Russell Birch after Ary Scheffer, c. 1824–1834, enamel on copper

ette's first battle, and on its maiden voyage in September 1825 it returned Lafayette and his party to France. Lafayette lived another decade, and upon his death on May 20, 1834, he was interred at the Picpus Cemetery in Paris, with soil he had brought back from Bunker Hill covering his grave. He became known on both sides of the Atlantic as "the hero of two worlds," the most recognizable icon of the alliance that brought victory and assured independence to the American republic.

By the time of the jubilee celebrations the year after Lafayette's departure—indelibly marked by the stunning coincidence of Thomas Jefferson and John Adams dying within five hours of each other on the fiftieth anniversary of the signing of the Declaration of Independence, July 4, 1826—enough time had passed for Americans, even as they contemplated their own legacies of the Revolution and independence, to also start thinking about them in historical terms. In the years after the jubilee, speeches and articles exhorting Americans to live up to revolutionary ideals portrayed that revolution and the war in the language of American exceptionalism. "The American Revolution is the greatest political event in history," stated one newspaper. It "marks a new era in the history of man" and was "the dividing point in the history of mankind," avowed orators across the country marking the anniversary.

These narratives, and many which came long after that, were infused with the notion that the progress toward a democratic republic was a uniquely American undertaking, derived from its exceptional nature. American exceptionalism had always been different from that of other nations. Instead of being rooted in soil, ancestry, or cultural identity, from the beginning Americans believed they were an exceptional nation because of their distinctive ideologies of republicanism and liberalism, or as it was more often expressed, liberty and equality. John Winthrop's famous admonition that America would be as a "city upon a hill" served as the exceptionalist ideal, that America's struggle to free itself from European corruption would be an inspiration for the world.

Americans' views of the Revolution and the War of American Independence were most powerfully shaped by George Bancroft's magisterial ten-volume *History of the United States from the Discovery of the Continent,* published from 1834 to 1874, the last volume of which came out just as America was preparing to celebrate its centennial. Bancroft's *History* would underpin the work of many popular histories, and served as the touchstone to define the American experience for generations to come. His narrative followed the exceptionalist model: Since the time of their arrival in the New World, Americans had moved inexorably away from European domination and toward freedom and independence. Written in an age when the notion of Manifest Destiny was used to justify America's relentless western expansion, this narrative was strongly individualistic with little room for outside influence or help, especially from European powers like France and Spain, which in the mind-set of that era represented the antithesis of American ideals. In Bancroft's account and countless others that followed, Lafayette became the main character who represented French interests in the prosecution of the war, until Rochambeau and de Grasse arrived at the end to defeat Cornwallis at Yorktown. Otherwise, the Americans fought the rest of the war themselves. And if the French got short shrift, the Spanish got no shrift at all; there was no mention of Gardoqui, one passing reference to Gálvez, and the battles of Pensacola and Gibraltar were all but ignored. In more modern times, popular histories, textbooks, film, television, and other media have made only perfunctory references to French contributions, and to Spain they make almost no reference at all.

The creation myth that America bootstrapped itself from colony to nation, that it fought the war and gained independence all by itself, was never correct and was never a good fit. France and Spain had supported the War of American Independence before it had started, even before the Americans themselves knew that their revolution would lead to war. John Adams made that connection in 1815 when he wrote to Jefferson, "What do we mean by the revolution? The war? It was only an effect and consequence of it." As Adams explained it, the Revolution began with Britain's mishandling of America after the Seven Years' War, and the War of American Independence was its inevitable outgrowth. Yet France and Spain understood this long beforehand. As soon as the 1763 Treaty of Paris was signed, their ministers saw that America's dissatisfaction with British rule would set the stage for the next war, and they used their spies and observers to keep close tabs on the brewing revolution even as they built up their navies and armed forces in preparation for the fight with Britain.

When war finally broke out, France and Spain were present at every step, even before the Declaration of Independence invited them to do so. Both nations had allowed clandestine aid to flow from private merchants to the Americans at the beginning of the war, and then covertly funded shipments to the rebels as the conflict intensified. Volunteers and arms from France began arriving even before the Declaration of Independence was drafted, while Spain kept munitions and supplies flowing to the western theater of operations. Ultimately, over 90 percent of the arms used by the Americans came from overseas, while close to $30 billion equivalent in direct monetary aid from France and Spain kept the sinews of war from unravelling. But their role in winning the war went far beyond providing money and weapons. The French-American alliance of 1778 removed Britain's naval advantage in American waters, and when Spain joined the fight in 1779, it turned a regional conflict into a global war that sapped Britain's military strength and political will, eventually forcing its surrender.

Gardoqui, Beaumarchais, Vergennes, Lafayette, Rochambeau, de Grasse, Córdova, Gálvez—these brothers at arms who saved American independence did so in the interest of their own nations, but along the way they made the American cause their own. America has honored them with place-names like Fayetteville, North Carolina; Louisville and Bourbon County, Kentucky; Cordova, Alaska; Vergennes, Vermont; Pulaski, Virginia; Kosciusko County, Indiana; and Galveston, Texas. It has also bestowed monuments and memorials like that of Gardoqui in downtown Philadelphia, and the Army Corps of Engineers de Fleury Medal. Countless streets, parks, and byways also bear the names of these Revolutionary heroes. In recent times Congress has declared the Marquis de Lafayette, Casimir Pulaski, and Bernardo de Gálvez to be honorary citizens of the United States. Spain and France have returned the favor: Avenida Washington in Málaga, the capital of Gálvez's home province; rue Benjamin Franklin, the Paris street that crosses his old neighborhood of Passy. And when Versailles was extensively renovated after the treaty that ended World War I, the street in front of Vergennes's old Hôtel des Affaires Étrangères, where the day-to-day work of forging alliances was carried out, was ceremoniously renamed rue de l'Indépendance américaine.

Instead of the myth of heroic self-sufficiency, the real story is that the American nation was born as the centerpiece of an international coalition, which together worked to defeat a common adversary. America could never have won the war without France, and France could never have succeeded without Spain. Through their actions, France and Spain became America's first brothers at arms, and they continue to be to this day. As between all brothers, their relationship has been tumultuous. They have fought a few times—the Quasi-War with France in 1798 and the Spanish-American War of 1898—but as those nations matured and their political and military interests aligned, they have come to each other's aid many times more. In 1917, the American Expeditionary Force under General John J. Pershing arrived in France to join the fight against the Central Powers during World War I. On July 4, his aide-de-camp Colonel Charles E. Stanton stood before Lafayette's grave at the Picpus Cemetery to give a ten-minute speech explaining why the Americans were there. In English, he reminded the crowd that Lafayette had come to America's side and that "America defaults no obligations." He pledged "our heart and honor" to victory, then ended on the rousing note, "Lafayette, we are here!" The speech was inspirational, yet it was also off the mark. For these nations, it has never been a mere question of repaying an obligation in time of need. Between brothers, the bonds of sacred honor run far deeper.

Acknowledgments

First and foremost, to Keith Goldsmith, my editor at Knopf, who guided this work with insight and grace.

Next, to my agent, Michelle Tessler, who provided the impetus for this work and shepherded it to exactly the right editor.

I owe thanks to many individuals and institutions both for assistance in my research and for critique of the first drafts of this work. I list the most significant ones here, alphabetically and by nation. Even with their assistance, all analyses as well as any errors in fact or translation are mine alone.

BELGIUM

Marion Huibrechts

FRANCE

Château de Versailles; École navale, Brest; Musée de l'Armée, Paris; Société des Cincinnati, Paris.

Pascal Beyls; Olivier Chaline; Raynald, Duc de Choiseul Praslin; Patrice Decencière; Jean-Marie Kowalski; Jean Langlet; Pierre Lévêque; Élisabeth Maisonnier; Christophe Pommier; Charles-Philippe Gravier, Marquis de Vergennes; Laurent Veyssière; Patrick Villiers.

GREAT BRITAIN

Robert Gardiner; Peter Hore; Andrew Lambert; Munro Price; Sam Willis.

MEXICO

Iván Valdez-Bubnov

NETHERLANDS

Alan Lemmers

SPAIN

Asociación Bernardo de Gálvez, Málaga; Museo Naval, Madrid; Patrimonio Nacional, Madrid.

José María Blanco Núñez; Reyes Calderón Cuadrado; José Luis Cano de Gardoqui; Francisco Fernández González; Agustín Guimerá Ravina; Juan Hernández Franco; Sylvia Hilton; Lorena Martínez García; Valentín Moreno Gallego; Manuel Olmedo Checa; Gonzalo Quintero Saravia; Agustín Ramón Rodríguez González; José María Sánchez Carrión; Juan Torrejón Chaves; José Yaniz.

UNITED STATES OF AMERICA

Army Center of Military History, Washington, DC; Daughters of the American Revolution, Washington, DC; Fred W. Smith National Library, Mount Vernon, VA; Naval History and Heritage Command, Washington, DC; National Park Service; Regimiento Fijo de la Luisiana Española (Fixed Regiment of Spanish Louisiana); Smithsonian Institution, National Museum of American History, Washington, DC; Society of the Cincinnati, Washington, DC; Sons of the American Revolution, Louisville, KY.

Joshua Beatty; Eliud Bonilla; Michael Carroll; Thomas Chávez; Ellen Clark; John Cloud; Douglas Comer; Dennis M. Conrad; Michael Crawford; James Delgado; Héctor Díaz; Richard Doty; Jonathan Dull; James Garner; Martha Gutiérrez-Steinkamp; John Hattendorf; John T. Kuehn; Karen Lee; Cliff Lewis; Darren Lickliter; John R. Maass; Albert "Durf" McJoynt; David Miller; Brian Morton; Sarah Myers; Charles Neimeyer; Julia Osman; Elaine Protzman; Ray Raphael; Eric Schnitzer; Emily Schulz; Robert A. Selig; Donald Spinelli; Albert "Skip" Theberge; Anthony Tommell; Samuel Turner; Robert Whitaker; Glenn F. Williams.

Notes

NAMES, TITLES, AND GRAMMAR

I have used the Biblioteca Nacional de España (National Library of Spain) and the Bibliothèque nationale de France (National Library of France) as the sources for the accepted spellings of proper names. Where the person's title changes over the years (e.g., from marquis to duc), I have generally tried to use the person's best-known designation for consistency.

I have followed the guidelines of the Académie française (French Academy) and the Real Academia Española (Royal Spanish Academy) for style and grammar. The most noticeable example is the Académie française guideline that "de" is to be included in family names with only one syllable, but excluded when it has two or more syllables. Thus, François Joseph Paul, comte de Grasse, is referred to as "de Grasse," but Charles Gravier, comte de Vergennes, is simply "Vergennes."

Most navies of the era were royal, not just the British (e.g., France's La Royale and Spain's Real Armada), so I refer to all navies by their national designation.

Just as I translate original French and Spanish quotations into modern English, I have also updated spelling and punctuation to make it readable to the audience.

CURRENCY

I often translate the currencies of the era into modern equivalents to make their value understandable to the audience. This is a more fraught process than it would appear, as the economies of the late eighteenth century were vastly different than those of the early twenty-first century—horses versus cars, for example, and the fact that the relative cost of commodities like foodstuffs was far higher back then than today.

Nevertheless, economists have developed several ways of comparing the value of money across time. I have used two broad comparators depending upon what is being measured. When I am discussing the price of individual goods, outlays, and salaries, I use the real price comparator that measures consumer goods and services and is based on the consumer price index (CPI). When I am discussing large national outlays like government projects, loans, and major arms deals, I use the economy cost comparator that is based upon the national gross domestic product (GDP) deflator. These give very different modern values, as GDP growth has been much faster than CPI growth over the past 240 years.

In general I have used 1775 as the basis year, on the grounds that it was the last year that prices were relatively stable in all nations, before the effects of the war resulted in varying inflation rates and instability in exchange rates. All exchange rates between currencies are based upon the values for that year: £1 (Britain) = $5 (American) = 23.5 livres (French) = 6.3 pesos (Spanish).

Finally, all modern prices are keyed to the year 2010, and converted to U.S. dollars using purchasing power parity rates.

NATION	CURRENCY	REAL PRICE COMPARATOR	ECONOMY COST COMPARATOR
United States	Dollar ($)	$29.40	$77,500 (1790 basis)
Great Britain	Pound (£)	$149.00	$13,127
France	Livre	$6.30	$560
Spain	Peso	$24	$2,083

Sources:

McKusker, John J. *Money and Exchange in Europe and America, 1600–1775: A Handbook.* Chapel Hill: University of North Carolina Press, 1978.

Maddison, Angus. "Historical Statistics for the World Economy: 1–2003 AD," http://www.ggdc.net/maddison/oriindex.htm.

Measuring Worth: www.measuringworth.com.

OECD PPP: Organisation for Economic Co-operation and Development (OECD) Purchasing Power Parities (PPP) Data: http://www.oecd.org/std/prices-ppp/purchasingpowerparitiespppsdata.htm.

INTRODUCTION

xvi **hired regiments from the German states**: Phillips, *1775*, 387–91.

xvi **"to declare the colonies in a state of independent sovereignty"**: Cited in Ferling, *Almost a Miracle*, 114.

xvi **"immediately to cast off the British yoke"**: Cited in Ketcham, *James Madison: A Biography,* 70.

xvi **"the Army had not five rounds of powder a man"**: *PBF,* 23:237–38.

xvii **The standard account regarding the Declaration of Independence**: Here I synthesize writings from my children's primary and secondary school curricula and textbooks from the Commonwealth of Virginia and the Department of Defense Dependents Schools; university-level textbooks; and several online encyclopedias.

xvii **The Declaration was not meant**: Garry Wills makes similar arguments in his *Inventing America,* 325.

xvii **"is manifestly carried on"**: Bobrick, *Angel in the Whirlwind,* 156.

xvii **the Corsican Republic; the Act of Abjuration**: Armitage, *The Declaration of Independence,* 41–45; Lucas, "The 'Plakkaat van Verlatinge': A Neglected Model for the American Declaration of Independence."

xvii **Stemming from British legal practice**: Maier, *American Scripture,* 51; Armitage, *The Declaration of Independence,* 31.

xviii **adopted a series of declarations and resolves**: See Shain, ed., *The Declaration of Independence in Historical Context,* 190–250, for a thorough accounting and analysis.

xviii **Declaration of the Causes and Necessity of Taking Up Arms; Olive Branch Petition**: Ibid., 274–93.

xviii **Thomas Paine; *Common Sense***: Liell, *46 Pages;* Ferling, *Independence,* 217–23; additional thanks to Ray Raphael for pointing out the coincidence with the arrival of George III's speech.

xix **"Every thing that is right or natural"**: Liell, *46 Pages,* 174.

xix **"Nothing can settle our affairs so expeditiously"**: Ibid., 196.

xx **the scientific experiments of Benjamin Franklin**: See Shachtman, *Gentlemen Scientists and Revolutionaries,* 47–63.

xxi **Calls for independence**: Ferling, *Independence,* 258–77; Shain, ed., *The Declaration of Independence in Historical Context,* 438–59.

xxi **"America may yet owe her salvation"**: Potts, *Arthur Lee,* 148.

xxi **"I am clearly of opinion"**: Wills, *Inventing America,* 328.

xxi **"danger . . . may be prevented"**: Lee and Ballagh, eds., *The Letters of Richard Henry Lee,* 1:176–79.

xxi **"to concur with the delegates of the other Colonies"**: Alden, *The South in the Revolution,* 211.

xxi **"declare the united colonies free and independent states"**: Shain, ed., *The Declaration of Independence in Historical Context,* 462–64.

xxii **"We should be driven to the Necessity"**: Adams, ed. Adams, *The Works of John Adams,* 2:503.

xxii **"It is not choice then"**: Lee and Ballagh, eds., *The Letters of Richard Henry Lee,* 1:198.

xxii **three interconnected resolutions**: Shain, ed., *The Declaration of Independence in Historical Context,* 461–62; Maier, *American Scripture,* 41–46. Ferling, *Independence,* 3–7; Wills, *Inventing America,* 325–33.

xxiii **"entangle us in future wars in Europe"**: Adams, ed. Adams, *The Works of John Adams,* 2:505.

xxiv **John Hancock, officially used the term "The United States"**: Nettles, "A Link in the Chain of Events Leading to American Independence," 36–37.

xxiv **The revised draft of the Declaration**: Ellis, ed., *What Did the Declaration Declare?,* 15–21.

xxiv **a copy of the Declaration aboard a ship**: Kite, "How the Declaration of Independence Reached Europe," 410.

xxv **He was reaching instead**: Bailyn, *The Ideological Origins of the American Revolution,* 26–27.

xxv **"We hold these truths"**: Shain, ed., *The Declaration of Independence in Historical Context,* 490–93. For a comparison of Jefferson's text with George Mason's Virginia Declaration of Rights, from which he borrowed heavily, see Raphael, *Founding Myths,* 125–29.

CHAPTER ONE THE ROAD TO WAR

3 **On the surprisingly warm evening**: *Gazette de France,* no. 13 (February 14, 1763); Bedford, *Correspondence of John, Fourth Duke of Bedford,* 3:190–96, 208; Evans, "The Embassy of the 4th Duke of Bedford to Paris, 1762–1763." Bedford's residence, the Hôtel de Grimberghen, 16 rue Saint Dominique, was demolished in the 1870s as part of Baron Haussmann's renovation of Paris. Its original site is now occupied by French government ministry offices at 244 boulevard Saint-Germain.

4 **"supremely gifted in the art of reconciling political agreement"**: Bourguet, *Le duc de Choiseul et l'alliance espagnole,* 187.

4 **"sensible, laborious"**: Bedford, *Correspondence of John, Fourth Duke of Bedford,* 149.

4 **"gives balls every week"**: Gibbon, *Private Letters of Edward Gibbon,* 1:28–29.

4 **"stateliness and avarice"**: Ibid.

4 **"a very good man"**: Blampignon, *Le duc de Nivernais,* 119.

5 **"a system of equilibrium"**: Grivel, "Balance politique" (quote at 279). On balance of power in theory and practice, see Black, "The Theory of the Balance of Power in the First Half of the Eighteenth Century."

6 **"as he wished to conduct the peace"**: Voltaire, *Siècle de Louis XV,* 1:209.

6 **The Seven Years' War**: Among the many accounts of the Seven Years' War, I have made particular use of: Dull, *The French Navy and the Seven Years' War;* Baugh, *The Global Seven Years War;* Anderson, *Crucible of War;* Szabo, *The Seven Years' War in Europe;* and Waddington, *La guerre de Sept Ans: Histoire diplomatique et militaire.*

7 **"preventing them from coming there"**: Waddington, *Louis XV et le renversement des alliances,* 21.

7 **"I do not think myself obliged to obey it"**: Anderson, *Crucible of War,* 45.

7 **"in case of resistance"**: Ibid., 51.

8 **"a few acres of snow"**: Although Voltaire most famously trotted out this phrase in chapter 23 of his novella *Candide,* he used variations of it in several letters and essays.

8 **"Diplomatic Revolution"**: Black, "Essay and Reflection: On the 'Old System' and the 'Diplomatic Revolution' of the Eighteenth Century," 314–16; Szabo, *The Seven Years' War in Europe,* 12–15; Anderson, *Crucible of War,* 128–29.

9 **"was not a country with an army"**: Quote from Prussian minister Friedrich von Schrötter, cited in Szabo, *The Seven Years' War in Europe,* 21.

9 **Prussia became a highly militarized society**: Corvisier, *Armies and Societies in Europe,* 113–14.

11 **Choiseul . . . assumed that role in all but name**: Waddington, *La guerre de Sept Ans,* 3:447.

12 **outbuilt and outcaptured France's navy**: Glete, *Navies and Nations,* 1:272.

12 **Choiseul now proposed to Spain a combined amphibious invasion**: Fernández Duro, *Armada española,* 7:53–58.

12 **built more warships than any shipyard in Spain**: Harbron, *Trafalgar and the Spanish Navy,* 15.

12 **"Since we do not know how to make war"**: Flassan, *Histoire générale et raisonnée diplomatie française,* 5:376.

13 **"Does the king of Spain want war or peace?"**: Blart, *Les rapports de la France et de l'Espagne,* 33.

13 **The three men negotiated the final terms**: Rashed, *The Peace of Paris 1763,* 159–200.

14 **trained roughly one-third of the navy's sailors**: Dull, *The French Navy and the Seven Years' War,* 249.

14 **"an uninhabited country"**: Gipson, *The British Empire before the American Revolution,* 8:307.

14 **"succeed greatly beyond my expectations"**: Bedford, *Correspondence of John, Fourth Duke of Bedford,* 190.

14 **spectacular fireworks display**: These are the subject of a series of watercolors in *BNF* Stamps and Photographs, LI–72 and QB–201.

15 **prices and trade quickly returned to prewar levels**: Riley, *The Seven Years' War and the Old Regime in France,* 12, 106.

15 **"not to spend more money"**: Playstowe, *The Gentleman's Guide,* title page.

15 **"anglomania"**: See Grieder, *Anglomania in France 1740–1789.*

15 **"London abounds in French"**: Lennox, *The Life and Letters of Lady Sarah Lennox,* 212.

15 **Jean-Jacques Rousseau . . . immersed himself in botanical science**: Damrosch, *Jean-Jacques Rousseau,* 472.

15 **Jérôme Laland and Charles-Marie de La Condamine**: Lalande, *Journal d'un voyage en Angleterre.*

15 **"We had drubbed those fellows"**: Boswell, *The Life of Samuel Johnson,* 1:419.

16 **Bourbon strategy of *revanche*:** Abarca, "Bourbon 'Revanche' Against England."

16 **"constant information from you"**: Wickham Legg, *British Diplomatic Instructions,* 86.

17 **"Everything is closed to civilians and foreigners"**: Oraison, "Mémoire sur l'Amirauté anglaise."

17 **military spies were reconnoitering**: Morison, "The Duc de Choiseul and the Invasion of England."

17 **"It was at Deal where Julius Caesar"**: Stanhope, *History of England,* 5:363–64.

17 ***Secret du Roi*:** See Perrault, *Le secret du roi.*

18 **De Broglie . . . also hit upon the idea**: De Broglie, "Plan de guerre contre l'Angleterre"; Lacour-Gayet, *La marine militaire de la France sous le règne de Louis XV,* 430–55; Patterson, *The Other Armada,* 6–12; Kates, *Monsieur d'Éon Is a Woman,* 91–94; Das, *De Broglie's Armada,* 4–21.

18 **Finally, after years of inaction on the king's part**: Perrault, *Le secret du roi,* 2:173–75.

19 **France had only forty-seven ships of the line**: Abarca, "Bourbon 'Revanche' Against England," 459; Dull, *The French Navy and the Seven Years' War,* 245–48.

19 **the portion of revenues**: Riley, *The Seven Years' War and the Old Regime in France,* 231.

19 **Choiseul issued a sweeping Naval Ordinance**: Ferreiro, *Ships and Science,* 286–87.

20 **"My duty is to regard French and Spanish vessels"**: Sánchez Carrión, *De constructores a ingenieros de marina,* 236.

20 **Jean Maritz**: Valdez-Bubnov, *Poder naval y modernización del estado,* 312–19.

20 **The war plan that was agreed to by both nations**: Das, *De Broglie's Armada,* 18–20; Abarca, "Classical Diplomacy and Bourbon 'Revanche' Strategy, 1763–1770"; Scott, "The Importance of Bourbon Naval Reconstruction to the Strategy of Choiseul after the Seven Years' War."

20 **Choiseul . . . a memorandum to Louis XV**: Soulange-Bodin, *La diplomatie de Louis XV et le pacte de famille,* 236–53.

21 **"This peace is a remarkable epoch"**: Rain, *La diplomatie française d'Henri IV à Vergennes,* 257.

21 **Pontleroy de Beaulieu**: Agay, *La Provence au service du roi,* 2:582.

21 **"Americans were never more British than in 1763"**: Shy, "The American Colonies in War and Rebellion, 1748–1783," 308.

22 **For generations Britain had taken**: Calloway, *The Scratch of a Pen,* 12.

23 **Pontleroy reported that the American colonies**: ANF Marine, B4 106 folio 144, 1763; B4 107 folio 92, 1764; B4 folio 4, 1766. See also Lacour-Gayet, *La marine militaire de la France sous le règne de Louis XV,* 415; and Van Tyne, "French Aid before the Alliance of 1778," 24–26.

23 **the Stamp Act and the Quartering Act**: Anderson, *Crucible of War,* 641–51, 664–76. Additional thanks to Michael Crawford for his insights into the nature of colonial taxation.

24 **selling barrels of "choice prime" Madeira**: *PGW,* 7:458–59.

24 **he was furiously taking notes**: "Journal of a French Traveller in the Colonies, 1765"; Beatty, "The 'French Traveller,' Patrick Henry, and the Contagion of Liberty." The anonymous journal was unearthed in the Paris archives of the French navy in the early twentieth century, but the identity of the traveler as Charles Murray was not uncovered until 2011 with some particularly insightful sleuthing by Joshua Beatty.

25 **Johann de Kalb**: Perrault, *Le secret du roi,* 3:241–47; Kapp, *The Life of John Kalb,* 46–73; Zucker, *General de Kalb,* 65–79.

26 **"There is no doubt"**: Kapp, *The Life of John Kalb,* 288.

27 **North America was a continent on the move**: Calloway, *The Scratch of a Pen,* 57–61, 164.

27 **British efforts to populate the two Florida colonies**: Raab, *Spain, Britain and the American Revolution in Florida, 1762–1783,* 7–92.

27 **the French population of Canada**: See Imbeault, Vaugeois, and Veyssière, *1763: le traité de Paris bouleverse l'Amérique.*

28 **a network of observers**: Cummins, *Spanish Observers and the American Revolution,* 6–26.

29 **he dispatched Jean Surriret**: Ibid., 22–24. On Surriret's militia service (where his name is sometimes spelled Juan Suriray), see Churchill, *Spanish Records,* 1:49, 93, 96, 114, 121, 123, 130, and 2:326.

30 **"the destruction of the tea"**: Adams, ed. Adams, *The Works of John Adams,* 2:323.

30 **"accommodation of our differences"**: Skemp, *The Making of a Patriot,* xi.

CHAPTER TWO THE MERCHANTS

32 **The American insurrection; the Jacobite rising**: Black, *War for America,* 13–18.

32 **act in unison against their common adversary**: Among the many histories of,

and guides to, the War of American Independence, I have made particular use of: Boatner, *Encyclopedia of the American Revolution;* Bobrick, *Angel in the Whirlwind;* Dupuy and Dupuy, *An Outline History of the American Revolution;* Ferling, *Almost a Miracle;* Mackesy, *The War for America;* Middlekauff, *The Glorious Cause;* and Middleton, *The War of American Independence.*

33 **The Pennsylvania Committee of Safety**: Brown, *Firearms in Colonial America,* 306.

33 **a number of the militia volunteers**: Lindgren and Heather, "Counting Guns in Early America," 1835; Churchill, "Gun Ownership in Early America," 626; Phillips, *1775,* 296.

33 **the colonists' access to local stockpiles of arms and powder**: Raphael and Raphael, *The Spirit of '74,* 146–59; Bunker, *An Empire on the Edge,* 306–7; Russell, *The American Revolution in the Southern Colonies,* 52–53.

34 **gunsmiths . . . across the thirteen colonies**: Moller, *Colonial and Revolutionary War Arms,* 99–105; Brown, *Firearms in Colonial America,* 347–55. Additional information thanks to David Miller, associate curator in the Division of Armed Forces History, Smithsonian Institution National Museum of American History. Free population from Selesky and Boatner, eds., *Encyclopedia of the American Revolution,* 2:922.

34 **no cannon forges . . . not a single mill**: Gordon, *American Iron, 1607–1900,* 202; Stephenson, "The Supply of Gunpowder in 1776," 271.

34 **"a prodigious amount for exportation"**: Fitzmaurice, *Life of William Earl of Shelburne,* 1:404.

34 **little in the way of manufacturing**: Peskin, *Manufacturing Revolution,* 56–57; McCusker, "British Mercantilist Policies and the American Colonies," 346, 352.

35 **with an average household income**: Lindert and Williamson, "American Incomes before and after the Revolution," 757–58.

35 **Americans were in fact richer**: McCusker, "British Mercantilist Policies and the American Colonies," 352.

35 **"they experience neither famine nor barren harvests"**: Kapp, *The Life of John Kalb,* 292.

35 **colonial merchants focused on domestic procurement and trade**: Peskin, *Manufacturing Revolution,* 58.

35 **"everybody has property"**: Marshall, "Travellers and the Colonial Scene," 20.

35 **"By riches I do not mean gold"**: Crèvecoeur, *Letters from an American Farmer,* 39.

35 **The colonies had no mints**: Lasser, *The Coins of Colonial America,* 1–5; Mossman, *Money of the American Colonies and Confederation,* 35–36, 58, 63, 93–94. Additional information thanks to Karen Lee and the late Richard Doty, curators in the National Numismatic Collection, Smithsonian Institution National Museum of American History.

36 **American farmers**: Buel, *In Irons,* 8–10.

37 **"do not come into this port"**: Schulte Nordholt, *The Dutch Republic and American Independence,* 35.

37 **Robert Crommelin, William Hodshon, and Isaac van Dam**: Matson, *Merchants and Empire,* 147.

37 **the Montaudouin firm**: Rouzeau, "Aperçus du rôle de Nantes," 234; Martin, "Commercial Relations between Nantes and the American Colonies," 821.

37 **Casa Joseph Gardoqui e hijos**: Magra, *The Fisherman's Cause,* 166.

37 **In the summer and autumn of 1774**: Huibrechts, "Swampin' Guns and Stabbing Irons," 147–48.

37 **"such a dangerous traffic"**: Ibid., 174–75.
38 **one hundred pounds of gunpowder**: Schulte Nordholt, *The Dutch Republic and American Independence,* 35.
38 **"would sell arms and ammunition"**: Huibrechts, "Swampin' Guns and Stabbing Irons," 174–75.
38 **some of the finest gunpowder in the world**: Spooner, *Risks at Sea,* 99–100.
38 **in the principality of Liège**: Huibrechts, "Swampin' Guns and Stabbing Irons," 306–24; Moller, *Colonial and Revolutionary War Arms,* 372–78.
38 **Liège muskets accounted**: Moller, *Colonial and Revolutionary War Arms,* 484–85.
38 **"our traders"**: Huibrechts, "Swampin' Guns and Stabbing Irons," 320, 544.
39 **"Pro Libertate"**: Ibid.
39 **Munitions were sent**: Ibid., 363–64, 444–52.
39 **Arthur and Jean-Gabriel Montaudoin**: Rouzeau, "Aperçus du rôle de Nantes"; Martin, "Commercial Relations between Nantes and the American Colonies."
39 **Bilbao appeared to be**: Lamikiz, *Trade and Trust in the Eighteenth-Century Atlantic World,* 17.
39 **Joseph Gardoqui y Mezeta**: Calderón Cuadrado, *Empresarios españoles,* 192–96.
40 **Cabot and Gardoqui**: Lydon, *Fish and Flour for Gold,* 87, 97; Basurto Larrañaga, "Linajes y fortunas mercantiles de Bilbao," 356.
40 **Provincial Congress; Committee of Supplies**: Magra, *The Fisherman's Cause,* 162–68; Bunker, *An Empire on the Edge,* 339–43.
41 **"each of the minutemen"**: Huibrechts, "Swampin' Guns and Stabbing Irons," 66–67.
41 **Gardoqui replied**: *NDAR,* 1:401. Gardoqui stated that Jeremiah Lee's letter was dated December 16. However, he received it on December 23, and it would have been impossible for an eighteenth-century sailing vessel to have made the voyage from Marblehead to Bilbao, a distance of over thirty-three hundred nautical miles, in just seven days. Four weeks would have been considered an exceptionally fast voyage.
41 **the Spanish government apparently knew**: Calderón Cuadrado, *Empresarios españoles,* 142; Chávez, *Spain and the Independence of the United States,* 235.
42 **"new Spanish guns"**: *Muster and Pay Rolls of the War of the Revolution,* 185–87.
42 **Thomas Gage had sent his own dispatches**: Bunker, *An Empire on the Edge,* 343–65.
42 **On the evening of April 18**: Boatner, *Encyclopedia of the American Revolution,* 620–32.
42 **laying siege to the city**: Ibid., 95–97, 120–30.
43 **The devastating want of gunpowder**: Phillips, *1775,* 297; Risch, *Supplying Washington's Army,* 339; Stephenson, "The Supply of Gunpowder in 1776," 272–73.
43 **Benjamin Franklin; his Conciliatory Proposal**: O'Shaughnessy, *The Men Who Lost America,* 56.
44 **"The General was so struck"**: Risch, *Supplying Washington's Army,* 340.
44 **Washington requested**: Knox, *The Naval Genius of George Washington,* 7–11.
44 **"prohibiting the needless expense of gunpowder"**: *AA,* 3:325.
44 **supply Washington's proposed twenty-thousand-man army**: Risch, *Supplying Washington's Army,* 341–51.
44 **"good pistol and cannon powder"; "friendship of foreign factors"**: *NDAR,* 1:818.
44 **Americans were facing trouble paying**: Harlow, "Aspects of Revolutionary Finance," 47; Sumner, *A History of American Currency,* 44; Buel, *In Irons,* 159.
44 **agricultural surpluses available for export**: Buel, *In Irons,* 30–49.

45 **had been living in precarious exile in London**: Kates, *Monsieur d'Éon Is a Woman,* 119–36, 182–88.

45 **Their solution was straightforward**: Ibid., 216–19.

46 **Pierre-Augustin Caron de Beaumarchais**: Among the almost two hundred biographies of Beaumarchais, I have found two English-language works particularly useful: Morton and Spinelli, *Beaumarchais and the American Revolution,* and Lever, *Beaumarchais: A Biography,* a single-volume synopsis of his three-volume French work *Pierre-Augustin Caron de Beaumarchais.*

47 **on the calle de Hortaleza**: Corral, *La Gran Vía: historia de una calle,* 32–33, 40.

47 **Beaumarchais, encouraged by his discussions**: Lever, *Beaumarchais: A Biography,* 21–30.

47 **"D'Éon's secret"**: Kates, *Monsieur d'Éon Is a Woman,* 220. Beaumarchais actually quoted a sum of 100,000 écus, equivalent to $2 million today.

48 **"about the situation in America"; "not one farmer"**: *BC,* 2:140; Morton and Spinelli, *Beaumarchais and the American Revolution,* 24.

48 **untrained but capable farmers**: Philbrick, *Bunker Hill,* 242.

49 **introduce him to Arthur Lee**: Wilkes, ed. and Eagle, *The Diaries of John Wilkes,* 86; Morton and Spinelli, *Beaumarchais and the American Revolution,* 33, 50; Paul, *Unlikely Allies,* 134–41; Cash, *John Wilkes,* 319–21; Potts, *Arthur Lee,* 151–55.

49 **Gardoqui had already shipped muskets**: Calderón Cuadrado, *Empresarios españoles,* 15. No correspondence between Gardoqui and Hayley exists today to determine whether they remained in contact after Gardoqui's apprenticeship (acknowledgments to Dr. José Luis Cano de Gardoqui for searching the Gardoqui family archives).

49 **Beaumarchais addressed the proposal**: *DP,* 1:100–15; *NDAR,* 3:525–30; Beaumarchais, *For the Good of Mankind,* 38–39, 75–81.

50 **The Perfect Merchant**: Savary, *Le parfait négociant,* 76–80; Dussert, *La machinerie Beaumarchais,* 278.

50 **Beaumarchais had just been named**: Johnson, *Climate and Catastrophe,* 128–29.

50 **All of the information on the American crisis**: *DHPF,* 1:253.

50 **De Broglie likely received news**: Perrault, *Le secret du roi,* 3:179–82.

50 **"make a faithful account"**: *DHPF,* 1:153–59. On Bonvouloir, see Hamon, *Le chevalier de Bonvouloir.*

51 **invasion of Canada**: Dupuy and Dupuy, *An Outline History of the American Revolution,* 29–33.

51 **"colonies are in open and avowed rebellion"; "manifestly carried on"**: Bobrick, *Angel in the Whirlwind,* 156.

51 **Secret Committee of Trade**: See Nuxoll, *Congress and the Munitions Merchants.*

51 **Pierre Penet and Emmanuel de Pliarne**: Rappleye, *Robert Morris,* 48–49.

51 **"for the sole purpose of corresponding"**: *AA,* 3:1936.

52 **"elderly lame gentleman"; "[they] shall have it"**: Jay, ed., *The Life of John Jay,* 1:39–40.

52 **"the writing would only appear"**: *DHPF,* 1:266.

52 **Bonvouloir began his report**: Ibid., 1:267–69, 1:287–92; *NDAR,* 3:279–85.

53 **The committee had already sent letters**: *PBF,* 22:287, 296, 298, 369–74.

53 **"Peace or War"**: *BC,* 2:171–76.

54 **"consider the best means"**: *DHPF,* 1:370–71.

54 **"must always be cloaked"**: *DHPF,* 1:284.

54 **"I received from M. Duvergier"**: *BC,* 2:219.

54 **Beaumarchais became a whirlwind of activity**: Morton and Spinelli, *Beaumarchais and the American Revolution,* 46–49, 75; Lever, *Pierre-Augustin Caron de Beaumarchais,* 2:181–86.

55 **"On your part"; "This is not a commercial transaction"**: *DP,* 3:296–98.

55 **Beaumarchais was in Bordeaux**: Morton and Spinelli, *Beaumarchais and the American Revolution,* 53–54.

55 **Jacques Barbeu-Dubourg**: See Aldridge, "Jacques Barbeu-Dubourg," and Schaeper, *Edward Bancroft.*

56 **Edward Bancroft**: Ibid.

56 **Deane arrived in Paris**: Schiff, *A Great Improvisation,* 7.

56 **"purchase a large quantity"**: *DP,* 1:198–202.

56 **"the quietest man in France"**: *BC,* 2:235.

57 **"everything he says, writes, or does"**: *DP,* 1:217.

57 **"perpetually shrouded [it] in coal smoke"**: Alder, *Engineering the Revolution,* 163.

57 **most commonly used muskets**: Moller, *Colonial and Revolutionary War Arms,* 291–363; Alder, *Engineering the Revolution,* 163–220. Additional information thanks to Robert A. Selig.

58 **In September 1776 the minister of war sent Coudray**: *PCC,* Roll 176, 626–27; Nardin, *Gribeauval,* 291–92. Additional information from Christophe Pommier, Musée de l'Armée, Paris.

58 **Although the Congress gave him no authority**: Schiff, *A Great Improvisation,* 12; Morton and Spinelli, *Beaumarchais and the American Revolution,* 80.

58 **Deane signed the contract**: Alder "Forging the New Order," 51–58; Huibrechts, "Swampin' Guns and Stabbing Irons," 303–5; Morton and Spinelli, *Beaumarchais and the American Revolution,* 67–76; Rouzeau, "Aperçus du rôle de Nantes," 226, 243–44. Additional information thanks to Donald Spinelli.

59 **"not to attempt to buy cannons or other arms"**: *BC,* 3:13.

59 **Deane also met with Chaumont**: Schaeper, *France and America in the Revolutionary Era,* 77–79.

59 **Bancroft returned to London**: Schaeper, *Edward Bancroft,* 52–64, 94–106, 124–33, 147–48.

60 **brick-red carriages**: Smithsonian military history collection, French M1732 four-pounder field cannon, Catalog #12182 Accession #54996.

60 **loaded only at night**: Morton and Spinelli, *Beaumarchais and the American Revolution,* 80–88; Lever, *Beaumarchais: A Biography,* 152–54; *BC,* 2:238; *NDAR,* 10:937–38. Additional information thanks to Donald C. Spinelli and Robert A. Selig.

60 **"I am at a loss"**: *NDAR,* 6:560.

61 **News of Franklin; "We look only to heaven"**: Morton and Spinelli, *Beaumarchais and the American Revolution,* 92; Schiff, *A Great Improvisation,* 7, 29.

61 **Gardoqui's shipments to New England**: Calderón Cuadrado, *Empresarios españoles,* 211.

62 **With Pollock translating**: Cummins, *Spanish Observers and the American Revolution,* 49–53; James, *Oliver Pollock,* 61–70 (dollar mark "$," 356–59).

62 **those reports taken together helped**: Chávez, *Spain and the Independence of the United States,* 28–32.

62 **"to encourage the insurgents"**: Yela Utrilla, *España ante la independencia de los Estados Unidos,* 2:25–26.

63 **ordered Unzaga to send a new observer**: Cummins, *Spanish Observers and the*

American Revolution, 44–51. An abstract of Beauregard's report indicated that he met with members of the Congress, but the original reports have been lost, and I have not found his name mentioned in the correspondence of the members of the Continental Congress.

63 **devastating series of droughts**: Johnson, *Climate and Catastrophe,* 95–96, 131–37.

63 **deliver supplies to the American rebels**: Thomson, *Spain: Forgotten Ally,* 135–40; Cummins, *Spanish Observers and the American Revolution,* 51–53, 78–81; Chávez, *Spain and the Independence of the United States,* 92; Yaniz, "The Role of Spain in the American Revolution," 50–51.

64 **he wrote a long dispatch**: Thomson, *Spain: Forgotten Ally,* 36–41.

64 **"cease working with that man"**: Vergennes, ed. Hardman and Price, *Louis XVI and the Comte de Vergennes,* 239.

64 **John Adams's Plan of Treaties:** *PJA,* 4:290–302.

64 **they met the Spanish ambassador**: Emmanuelli, "Spanish Diplomatic Policy," 64.

65 **the American commissioners expanded their wish list**: Dull, *A Diplomatic History of the American Revolution,* 55–56, 75–78; Murphy, *Charles Gravier, Comte de Vergennes,* 243–44; Schiff, *A Great Improvisation,* 31–32; Granet, *Images de Paris,* 59.

65 **Pierre Penet and Emmanuel de Pliarne**: *DHPF,* 1:506–9; *NDAR,* 6:524–25, 7:1000–1003; Shomette, *Shipwrecks, Sea Raiders, and Maritime Disasters,* 59–65; Crout, "The Diplomacy of Trade," 130–31. Hedges, *The Browns of Providence Plantations,* 230–33.

65 **some of their muskets burst during proofing tests**: *PGW,* 10:152–53.

65 **"one of those fortune seekers"**: *NDAR,* 6:399–400.

66 **"to house for free"**: *SFME,* 23:245–50.

66 **he would act as the commissioners' gatekeeper**: Schaeper, *France and America in the Revolutionary Era,* 92–107, 156–65; Schiff, *A Great Improvisation,* 50–53.

66 **uniforms . . . began arriving in New England in the spring of 1778**: *PGW,* 15:29–30; Risch, *Supplying Washington's Army,* 293–95.

66 **Rodolphe-Ferdinand Grand**: Lüthy, *La banque protestante en France,* 339, 452–55, 612–19.

67 **Grimaldi now instructed Lee**: Potts, *Arthur Lee,* 167–72; Beerman, *España y la independencia de Estados Unidos,* 27–35; Thomson, *Spain: Forgotten Ally,* 48–62; Chávez, *Spain and the Independence of the United States,* 61–63. Acknowledgments to Reyes Calderón Cuadrado for additional information regarding Gardoqui's smuggling activities.

68 **to Elbridge Gerry in New England**: *NDAR,* 10:1130–33; Moller, *Colonial and Revolutionary War Arms,* 404–5. Spanish muskets had been built to the same 0.69 caliber as French muskets ever since the War of the Spanish Succession (1701–14) created a Bourbon family dynasty: see Chartrand and Rickman, *The Spanish Army in North America,* 41.

68 **Howe gradually cleared out Washington's troops**: Mackesy, *The War for America,* 89–91.

68 **Battle of Trenton [and Princeton]**: Middleton, *The War of American Independence,* 60–63; Selesky and Boatner, eds., *Encyclopedia of the American Revolution,* 2:933–37, 1161–65.

69 **at least ten thousand muskets and close to one million pounds of gunpowder**: Estimated from Moller, *Colonial and Revolutionary War Arms,* 484, and Stephenson, "The Supply of Gunpowder in 1776," 277–78.

69 **his own musket and sixty rounds**: McCullough, *1776,* 274.

69 **survey of shot recovered**: Selig et al., "Archaeology, Computer Technology, and the

Battle of Princeton as a Cross-Cultural, Trans-Atlantic Encounter," in Comer, ed., *The Archaeology of Interdependence,* 27–33.

69 **their larger plan for dividing the American forces**: Middleton, *The War of American Independence,* 69–80.

69 **Philadelphia**: Dupuy and Dupuy, *An Outline History of the American Revolution,* 80–96.

70 **Ticonderoga**: Ibid.

70 **Beaumarchais's ships were on their way to America**: Morton and Spinelli, *Beaumarchais and the American Revolution,* 97–112, 207.

70 ***Mercure* was the first to arrive**: Ibid., 125–27; *PGW,* 9:336–37, 440–44.

71 **to the Springfield Armory**: *PGW,* 9:579–80, 10:152–53; Smith, "A Veritable . . . Arsenal of Manufacturing," 2–5. Acknowledgments to Anthony Tommell for additional information.

71 **newspapers . . . carried stories**: Morton and Spinelli, *Beaumarchais and the American Revolution,* 128.

71 **dispatch more cannon to the front lines**: Elting, *The Battles of Saratoga,* 88; Ketchum, *Saratoga,* 334; *PGW,* 10:152–53, 216–18. Acknowledgments to Eric Schnitzer, National Park Service Saratoga, for additional information.

71 **arrival of Beaumarchais's arms**: Carroll, "New Hampshire Marked French Revolutionary War Muskets."

72 **Orders flowed out of Gates's camp**: Luzader, *Saratoga,* 189–92.

72 **the first Battle of Saratoga**: Elting, *The Battles of Saratoga,* 48–67; Luzader, *Saratoga,* 201–96.

73 **"The first opportunity"**: Stark, *Memoir and Official Correspondence,* 357.

73 **loss of nearly a quarter of Britain's forces**: Mackesy, *The War for America,* 524–25.

73 **"courage and obstinacy"**: Ketchum, *Saratoga,* 369.

74 **Beaumarchais learned of Saratoga**: Schiff, *A Great Improvisation,* 109; Beaumarchais, *For the Good of Mankind,* 254; Morton and Spinelli, *Beaumarchais and the American Revolution,* 130.

74 **saw their losses mount**: Schaeper, *France and America in the Revolutionary Era,* 196–98; Buel, *In Irons,* 60–61.

74 **received naval salutes**: Tuchman, *The First Salute,* 5–7.

CHAPTER THREE THE MINISTERS

75 **"Sir, *is* Philadelphia taken?"**: Schiff, *A Great Improvisation,* 109–10.

75 **"was received in France"**: Franklin, *Memoirs of the Life and Writings of Benjamin Franklin,* 2:59.

75 **the accounts published in French newspapers**: Censer, *French Press in the Age of Enlightenment,* 176–77; Ascoli, "The French Press and the American Revolution."

76 **Similarly in Spain**: García Melero, *La independencia de los Estados Unidos de Norteamérica a través de la prensa española; Gaceta de Madrid,* December 30, 1777, 512–15; *Mercurio Histórico y Político,* March 1778, 226–30.

76 **absolute, if enlightened, monarchs**: See Scott, ed., *Enlightened Absolutism.*

76 **Carlos III**: Domínguez Ortiz, *Carlos III y la España de la Ilustración;* Vaca de Osma, *Carlos III;* Hull, *Charles III and the Revival of Spain.*

77 **Carlos III and his court led a peripatetic existence**: My thanks to Lorena Martínez García and Valentín Moreno Gallego, both of the Spanish Patrimonio Nacional (National Heritage) for providing Carlos III's annual itinerary.

78 **a handful of administrative secretaries**: Acknowledgments to Lorena Martínez García and Juan Hernández Franco for their knowledge and assistance.

78 ***covachuelistas***: See López-Cordón, "Administración y política en el siglo XVIII." My thanks to José María Blanco Núñez, Agustin Guimerá, and José María Sánchez Carrión for uncovering and explaining this underreported aspect of Spanish diplomatic history.

78 **Floridablanca; Castejón; Ricla; Gálvez**: Chávez, *Spain and the Independence of the United States*, 9–10; Cummins, *Spanish Observers and the American Revolution*, 7–8, 31; Blanco Núñez, *La Armada española en la segunda mitad del siglo XVIII*, 109–10. On Floridablanca, see Pardos, *El modernizador*.

80 **Under Floridablanca, these ministers created a new approach**: Emmanuelli, "Spanish Diplomatic Policy," 28–44, 50.

80 **Louis XVI**: See Lever, *Louis XVI;* Hardman, *Louis XVI*.

81 **the king himself so seldom visited Paris**: Manceron, *Twilight of the Old Order*, 408.

81 **Louis XVI traveled**: Hardman, *French Politics, 1774–1789*, 254–56.

81 **"two oiled billiardballs"**: Lever, *Louis XVI*, 146.

81 **The ministers lived and worked**: See Baudez, Maisonnier, and Pénicaut, *Les hôtels de la Guerre et des Affaires Étrangères à Versailles*, 85–93, 112–13. Additional information thanks to Élisabeth Maisonnier.

82 **Necker had replaced**: Hardman, *Louis XVI*, 57–64; Harris, *Necker: Reform Statesman of the Ancien Régime;* Dull, *The French Navy and American Independence*, 14–15, 108; Villiers, *La marine de Louis XVI*, 19–24; Castex, *Les idées militaires de la marine du XVIIIme siècle*, 164.

83 **Vergennes**: See Murphy, *Charles Gravier, Comte de Vergennes*, and Labourdette, *Vergennes*.

83 **with assistance from the Grand family**: Schaeper, *France and America in the Revolutionary Era*, 98.

83 **"put a brake on"**: Bonneville de Marsangy, *Le chevalier de Vergennes: Son ambassade en Suède*, 64.

83 **"I chat with M. de Maurepas"**: Murphy, *Charles Gravier, Comte de Vergennes*, 345.

84 **"honesty and restraint"**: Hardman, *Louis XVI*, 93.

84 **"arrived at Versailles"**: Murphy, *Charles Gravier, Comte de Vergennes*, 211.

84 **his four long-serving *premiers commis***: *Almanach Royal*, 1777, 218, 1779, 219. Biographies: Hudson, *The Minister from France;* Luraschi, *Conrad-Alexandre Gérard*.

84 **Noailles**: *Recueil des instructions données aux ambassadeurs*, vol. 12 bis, 359–67; Vergennes, ed. Hardman and Price, *Louis XVI and the Comte de Vergennes*, 28–30.

84 **"an honest gentleman"**: That earlier diplomat was Henry Wotton, 1568–1639.

84 **Ossun; Montmoris**: *Recueil des instructions données aux ambassadeurs*, vol. 12 bis, 359–67; Vergennes, ed. Hardman and Price, *Louis XVI and the Comte de Vergennes*, 28–30.

85 **For some time France had used its influence**: Murphy, *Charles Gravier, Comte de Vergennes*, 211–21; Labourdette, *Vergennes*, 89–90; Vergennes, ed. Hardman and Price, *Louis XVI and the Comte de Vergennes*, 157–59, 166.

85 **"restless and greedy"**: Labourdette, *Vergennes*, 89.

85 **Spain was less troubled**: Domínguez Ortiz, *Carlos III y la España de la Ilustración*, 95–115; Batista González, *España estratégica*, 366–76; García Diego, *Jano en Hispania*, 400–442; Chávez, *Spain and the Independence of the United States*, 33–44.

86 **the Spanish navy added thirty new ships**: Kuethe and Andrien, *The Spanish Atlan-*

tic World in the Eighteenth Century, 332, 350–52; Harbron, *Trafalgar and the Spanish Navy,* 168–71; Glete, *Navies and Nations,* 1:271–76.

86 **France was supposed to increase**: Glete, *Navies and Nations,* 1:271–76; Dull, *The French Navy and American Independence,* 11–13.

87 **Spain and Portugal had been disputing**: Hernández Franco, "El gobierno español ante la independencia de los Estados Unidos," 171; Hull, *Charles III and the Revival of Spain,* 221–25; Kuethe and Andrien, *The Spanish Atlantic World in the Eighteenth Century,* 290–91; Alden, "The Marquis of Pombal and the American Revolution"; Walker, "Atlantic Dimensions of the American Revolution," 261–63.

88 **"War is inevitable"**: Murphy, *Charles Gravier, Comte de Vergennes,* 222–31; Labourdette, *Vergennes,* 96–97. Grimaldi's dispatch of October 18, 1775, and Vergennes's response of November 29, are reprinted in *DHPF,* 1:299–312.

88 **His missives to Grimaldi**: Labourdette, "Vergennes et le Portugal," 180.

88 **his richly inlaid Brazilian hardwood desk**: Louvre Atlas database, inventory number OA 6600, bureau plat dit "de Vergennes."

88 **For Vergennes, it must have been**: Murphy, *Charles Gravier, Comte de Vergennes,* 239; Vergennes, ed. Hardman and Price, *Louis XVI and the Comte de Vergennes,* 223.

89 **Vergennes sent Grimaldi a letter**: *DHPF,* 1:370–71; Murphy, *Charles Gravier, Comte de Vergennes,* 239.

89 **"Considerations"; "Reflections"**: Murphy, *Charles Gravier, Comte de Vergennes,* 232–41; Labourdette, *Vergennes,* 96–97; Meng, "A Footnote to Secret Aid in the American Revolution"; Dull, *The French Navy and American Independence,* 30–65; Dull, *A Diplomatic History of the American Revolution,* 57–65, 70. The text of the memoranda are in *DHPF,* 1:243–49, 273–86.

90 **one of the coldest winters in living memory**: Manceron, *Twilight of the Old Order,* 274.

90 **Louis XVI quickly made several critical pronouncements**: *DHPF,* 1:345–46.

90 **the navy budget**: Villiers, *La marine de Louis XVI,* 66; Villiers, "La stratégie de la marine française," 215. The modern French navy budget is about €7.7 billion: see French Navy Information File 2011.

90 **The king also replaced Turgot**: *DHPF,* 2:261.

91 **The ship that had set sail**: Kite, "How the Declaration of Independence Reached Europe." The text of Garnier's letter to Vergennes is in *DHPF,* 1:585–86.

91 **"Considerations on the position France should take"**: Murphy, *Charles Gravier, Comte de Vergennes,* 240–41; Labourdette, *Vergennes,* 97–98; Gérard et al. *Despatches and Instructions of Conrad Alexandre Gérard,* 64–65. The text of the memorandum and the one outlining an amphibious assault are in *DHPF,* 1:567–77 and 2:158–70.

92 ***attente expectative:*** Gérard and Vergennes, *Despatches and Instructions of Conrad Alexandre Gérard,* 65–66.

92 **The Spanish court debated:** Yela Utrilla, *España ante la independencia de los Estados Unidos,* 1:72–95; Kuethe and Andrien, *The Spanish Atlantic World in the Eighteenth Century,* 290–91.

92 **Carlos III sent a fleet of nineteen warships and nine thousand soldiers**: Chávez, *Spain and the Independence of the United States,* 42–43; Blanco Núñez, *La Armada española en la segunda mitad del siglo XVIII,* 115–17.

93 **decided that an invasion of Portugal**: *DHPF,* 2:228.

93 **Vergennes . . . was once again petitioned**: Dull, *A Diplomatic History of the American Revolution,* 79; Schiff, *A Great Improvisation,* 65.

94 **left the American commissioners perplexed**: Dull, *A Diplomatic History of the American Revolution,* 75–88; Schiff, *A Great Improvisation,* 81–93; Patton, *Patriot Pirates,* 163–84.

95 **"to reciprocally bind ourselves"**: *PBF,* 23:412.

95 **Rayneval drew up plans**: Dull, *A Diplomatic History of the American Revolution,* 90; Dull, *The French Navy and American Independence,* 84–85.

95 **"The time has come to decide"**: Dull, *A Diplomatic History of the American Revolution,* 90–91; Labourdette, *Vergennes,* 99–100. Text of Vergennes's memorandum: *DHPF,* 2:460–69. Text of Floridablanca's response: Yela Utrilla, *España ante la independencia de los Estados Unidos,* 2:122–29.

95 **was determined to forge an alliance with the United States**: Dull, *A Diplomatic History of the American Revolution,* 91–96; Dull, *The French Navy and American Independence,* 89–92.

96 **somewhat optimistic reports**: Murphy, "The Battle of Germantown and the Franco-American Alliance of 1778," 60–64.

96 **"no doubt of the ability"**: Lee, *Life of Arthur Lee,* 1:357.

96 **"uncommon politeness"**: Ibid., 358–60; Schiff, *A Great Improvisation,* 137.

97 **Vergennes tried one last time**: Dull, *The French Navy and American Independence,* 92–96; text of the dispatches *DHPF,* 2:637–67.

97 **"the most interesting conjunction"; "nothing can justify"**: *DHPF,* 2:645, 666.

97 **"it was determined to acknowledge"**: *PBF,* 25:305; Luraschi, *Conrad-Alexandre Gérard,* 210.

97 **Floridablanca's reply**: Chávez, *Spain and the Independence of the United States,* 75–76; text of the reply, Yela Utrilla, *España ante la independencia de los Estados Unidos,* 2:165–70.

97 **On January 8 they opened negotiations**: Dull, *The French Navy and American Independence,* 95; Schiff, *A Great Improvisation,* 126–28.

98 **"my brother [monarch] and uncle"; "the destruction of Burgoyne's army"**: Vergennes, ed. Hardman and Price, *Louis XVI and the Comte de Vergennes,* 255–56.

98 **the dispatches arrived at El Pardo**: Yela Utrilla, *España ante la independencia de los Estados Unidos,* 1:247–303; text of the disptaches and memoranda, 2:165–223.

98 **"His whole body trembled"**: *DHPF,* 2:751.

98 **Floridablanca's irate response**: Corwin, *French Policy and the American Alliance of 1778,* 106; Chávez, *Spain and the Independence of the United States,* 76–77.

99 **a treaty of amity and commerce**: For the text of the treaty, see *A Century of Lawmaking,* 8–31.

99 **The signing was delayed**: Hudson, *The Minister from France,* 77–79.

99 **"the ambassadors of the Thirteen United Provinces"; "wisest, most reserved conduct"**: Castries, *La France et l'indépendance américaine,* 187; Croÿ-Solre, *Journal inédit du duc de Croÿ,* 4:78.

99 **in actual fact they had had little influence**: Dull, *A Diplomatic History of the American Revolution,* 95–96.

100 **Edward Bancroft had already given it to them**: Schaeper, *Edward Bancroft,* 115.

100 **While the Paris aristocracy; Vergennes quickly deployed the French and European press**: Censer, *The French Press in the Age of Enlightenment,* 177; Osman, "American Nationality: A French Invention?"

100 **Silas Deane's brother Simeon**: *DP,* 2:465–66.

100 **Weymouth's stunned reaction**: Castries, *La France et l'indépendance américaine,* 186.

100 **Gérard issued his passports so promptly**: Hudson, *The Minister from France,* 80–81.

101 **Simeon Deane landed in Falmouth**: *NDAR,* 12:121–22; Stinchcombe, *The American Revolution and the French Alliance,* 14–15.

101 **"I believe no event"**: *PGW,* 15:5.

101 **"Long Live the King of France"**: Fleming, *Washington's Secret War,* 248–50.

101 **"America is at last saved"**: Stinchcombe, *The American Revolution and the French Alliance,* 14.

101 **The civilian reaction to the alliance**: Ibid., 14–17.

102 **"articles of entangling alliance"**: McCullough, *John Adams,* 161.

102 **the Second Continental Congress had been divided**: Henderson, *Party Politics in the Continental Congress,* 164–71.

102 **Deane recalled on unspecified charges**: Potts, *Arthur Lee,* 194–95; Van Vlack, *Silas Deane,* 158–62; McCullough, *John Adams,* 196.

103 **Vergennes further gilded these tributes**: Schiff, *A Great Improvisation,* 151.

103 **The seventeen ships**: Dull, *The French Navy and American Independence,* 109–12; Hudson, *The Minister from France,* 82–85, 217–20; Gérard and Vergennes, *Despatches and Instructions of Conrad Alexandre Gérard,* 125–30.

104 **the Carlisle Commission**: Giunta, ed., *Documents of the Emerging Nation,* 68–73.

104 **"You have come to our rescue"**: Gérard and Vergennes, *Despatches and Instructions of Conrad Alexandre Gérard,* 175; Hudson, *The Minister from France,* 91–93.

105 **Samuel Adams had met; Adams was also opposed to a congressional resolution**: Stinchcombe, *The American Revolution and the French Alliance,* 34–35; Gérard and Vergennes, *Despatches and Instructions of Conrad Alexandre Gérard,* 98–99.

105 **"will not conclude peace or truce"**: *DP,* 3:257.

105 **Gérard believed that the competing interests**: Gérard and Vergennes, *Despatches and Instructions of Conrad Alexandre Gérard,* 92–95; Hudson, *The Minister from France,* 138–41; Stinchcombe, *The American Revolution and the French Alliance,* 41–43.

105 **the Congress held multiple hearings:** Henderson, "Congressional Factionalism and the Attempt to Recall Benjamin Franklin"; Potts, *Arthur Lee,* 228–39; Van Vlack, *Silas Deane,* 168–71; Hudson, *The Minister from France,* 139–40.

105 **"Why should we bind"**: Gérard and Vergennes, *Despatches and Instructions of Conrad Alexandre Gérard,* 571.

106 **negotiations with the Congress:** Gérard and Vergennes, *Despatches and Instructions of Conrad Alexandre Gérard,* 96–115, 480, 561.

106 **a home on Chestnut Street**: Hudson, *The Minister from France,* 94–96.

106 **"many frivolous & unwarrantable applications"**: *PGW,* 16:338.

107 **While Francy waited for the Congress to take action**: Morton and Spinelli, *Beaumarchais and the American Revolution,* 129–31, 145–62, 178–85, 229–35.

108 **John Holker**: Schaeper, *France and America in the Revolutionary Era,* 200–203; Gallagher, "Private Interest and the Public Good."

108 **Juan de Miralles**: Cummins, *Spanish Observers and the American Revolution,* 105–51; Böttcher, "Juan de Miralles"; McCadden, "Juan de Miralles and the American Revolution"; Ribes-Iborra, "Nuevos datos biográficos sobre Juan de Miralles"; Ribes-Iborra, "La era Miralles."

109 **The two men were even invited**: Cummins, *Spanish Observers and the American Revolution,* 124.

110 **"one man of inflexible integrity"**: McCullough, *John Adams,* 174.

110 **Adams noted that the countryside was calm**: McCullough, *John Adams,* 188–213; Schiff, *A Great Improvisation,* 154–58, 183–202.
111 **For Vergennes, it was critical**: Murphy, "The View from Versailles," 122–23.
111 ***Belle Poule* returned fire**: Dull, *The French Navy and American Independence,* 118–22.
111 **"show the French flag in all its glory"**: Villiers, *La marine de Louis XVI,* 88.
111 **Battle of Ouessant**: Tunstall, *Naval Warfare in the Age of Sail,* 136–40; Villiers, *La marine de Louis XVI,* 88–89, 95–98, 109–12.
111 **"secure naval superiority"**: McCullough, *John Adams,* 210–14.
112 **Adams gratefully left**: Ibid.
112 **Their conversations, like their correspondence**: Stockdale, *The Parliamentary Register,* 12:446.
112 **Spain could mediate a peaceful solution**: Hernández Franco, "El gobierno español ante la independencia de los Estados Unidos," 177–80; Dull, *The French Navy and American Independence,* 114, 126–35.
113 **"I have no doubt"**: Fortescue, *The Correspondence of King George the Third,* 4:208.
113 **"this pile of rocks called Gibraltar"**: Danvila y Collado, *Reinado de Carlos III,* 5:33–39.
113 **"a most fortunate fleet"**: Blanco Núñez, *La Armada española en la segunda mitad del siglo XVIII,* 117–20.
114 **a sudden invasion of Britain might yield territorial gains**: Patterson, *The Other Armada,* 40.
114 **Floridablanca now proceeded**: Chávez, *Spain and the Independence of the United States,* 126–36; Dull, *A Diplomatic History of the American Revolution,* 108–9; Patterson, *The Other Armada,* 39, 47.
114 **his special agent Francisco Gil y Lemos**: Gil Aguado, "Francisco Gil y Lemos: Marino, virrey y ministro," 131–67.
114 **Vergennes was appalled**: *DHPF,* 3:760–67.
114 **"gigantic"**: Vergennes, ed. Hardman and Price, *Louis XVI and the Comte de Vergennes,* 269–70.
114 **double the navy's funding**: Dull, *The French Navy and American Independence,* 135.
115 **The Treaty of Aranjuez**: Hernández Franco, *Aspectos de la política exterior de España en la época de Floridablanca,* 178–79.
115 **Louis XVI thanked his "brother and uncle"**: *DHPF,* 3:773.
115 **wrote letters to his viceroys**: Dull, *The French Navy and American Independence,* 135–39, 150; Yela Utrilla, *España ante la independencia de los Estados Unidos,* 1:359–60.
115 **Britain had in effect sacrificed the United States**: Chávez, *Spain and the Independence of the United States,* 81, 132, 135.
116 **Anne-César de La Luzerne**: O'Donnell, *The Chevalier de La Luzerne,* 42–46.
116 **"whether it would be agreeable"**: *DCAR,* 3:321.

CHAPTER FOUR THE SOLDIERS

118 **a matter of numbers:** British troop numbers: Mackesy, *The War for America,* 524–25; American troop numbers: Upton, *The Military Policy of the United States,* 20.
118 **wage war both offensively and defensively**: Anderson, *Crucible of War,* 103.
119 **Washington had observed**: Wright Jr., *The Continental Army,* 26; Brumwell, *George Washington: Gentleman Warrior,* 125–26; Kelly, *Band of Giants,* 6–7; Lengel,

General George Washington: A Military Life, 64, 78; Middlekauff, *Washington's Revolution,* 52.

119 **military books and treatises**: Starkey, *War in the Age of Enlightenment,* 195; Brumwell, *George Washington: Gentleman Warrior,* 219–20; Lengel, *General George Washington: A Military Life,* 79; Kelly, *Band of Giants,* 15.

119 **"Discipline and subordination"**: Lengel, *General George Washington: A Military Life,* 106–7.

120 **general staff**: Risch, *Supplying Washington's Army,* 8–10; Wright Jr., *The Continental Army,* 25–40. Additional acknowledgments to John T. Kuehn, U.S. Army Command and General Staff College.

120 **"disadvantages [under which] we labor"; "The want of engineers"**: *PGW,* 1:85–97, 145–51.

121 **well above the life expectancy of an adult male in the eighteenth century**: The life expectancy of an adult American male who had survived childhood diseases was about sixty-three years. See Pope, "Adult Mortality in America before 1900," 280.

121 **The best engineers and artillerists . . . had been trained in France**: For accessible histories of French military engineers and artillerists, see Langins, *Conserving the Enlightenment,* and Vérin, *La gloire des ingénieurs*. Additional information thanks to Glenn F. Williams and Joseph Seymour, U.S. Army Center of Military History.

121 **Corps du génie**: Note that the French word *génie* can be translated as both "engineering" and "genius."

121 **"find out and engage"**: *RDC,* 2:63.

121 **"everyone here is a soldier"**: *DHPF,* 1:269.

122 **"France is fully capable"**: Ibid.

122 **"We are in great want of good engineers"**: *PBF,* 22:287.

122 **"but above all we need engineers"**: *BC,* 2:190.

122 **"memorials from officers and engineers"**: *DP,* 1:202.

122 **Louis O'Hicky d'Arundel**: *DOAR,* 366; Gill Jr., "Dohicky's Folly."

123 **Antoine Felix Wuibert**: The spelling of his family name had many variants. At birth it was Wibert; the Congress commissioned him as Weibert; it was reported at various times as Wybert, Wuybert, Vibert, and Viebert; and later in life he went by the spelling Wuibert. Sources: birth certificate, ADA microfilm 5Mi 15 R 8 323 (acknowledgments to Jacques de Trentinian for discovering it); general biography, Kilbourne, *Virtutis Praemium,* 2:1004–7 (thanks to Cliff Lewis of the Society of the Cincinnati for alerting me to it).

123 **Fort Washington**: Walker, *Engineers of Independence,* 140–45.

123 **"a number of French gentlemen"**: *AA,* 2:1108–9.

123 **Marie Louis Amand Ansart de Maresquelle**: Maresquelle genealogy notes, IIC 4.1.7.1; Smith Jr., *The French at Boston during the Revolution,* 23–29; Martello, *Midnight Ride, Industrial Dawn,* 87–88.

124 **Pierre Benjamin Faneuil**: *AA,* 2:1109–10; Faneuil, Last Will and Testament (thanks to Sarah Myers at the Fred W. Smith National Library for the Study of George Washington for discovering it).

124 **Pélissier; the First Canadian Regiment**: Walker, *Engineers of Independence,* 96–97; Wright Jr., *The Continental Army,* 59–60.

124 **Thaddeus Bonaventure Kosciuszko**: Kajencki, *Thaddeus Kosciuszko;* Storozynski, *The Peasant Prince.*

125 **Romand de L'Isle**: ANOM COL E 356 bis, Romand de L'Isle, François, capitaine

d'artillerie des colonies à Saint-Domingue; *DOAR,* 410; Lisle, *The Lisle (de Lisle) Family in America,* 1–2; Beyls, "Un Dauphinois dans la guerre d'Indépendance des États-Unis." Additional information thanks to Pascal Beyls.

125 **Barbeu-Dubourg had already been busy**: Aldridge, "Jacques Barbeu-Dubourg," 349–51; Butterfield, "Franklin, Rush, and the Chevalier de Kermorvan"; *DOAR,* 23–24, 216.

126 **Charles Armand Tuffin**: Carrer, *La Bretagne et la guerre d'Indépendance américaine,* 171–98.

126 **"be received with gratitude"; "would certainly be recompensed"**: *SFME,* 23:51–56.

126 **"I cannot satisfy your requests"**: *BC,* 3:13–14.

127 **As to which officers to select**: *DP,* 1:229–32, 1:380–81.

127 **passengers for America**: Morton and Spinelli, *Beaumarchais and the American Revolution,* 91–92.

127 **Pierre Charles L'Enfant**: Caemmerer, *The Life of Pierre Charles L'Enfant,* 9, 37–38; Berg, *Grand Avenues,* 29.

128 **Coudray disobeyed those orders; "first engineer of the kingdom"; "disappointment"**: Morton and Spinelli, *Beaumarchais and the American Revolution,* 102, 125–26; *DP,* 1:213, 468–69; *NDAR,* 9:275.

128 **"the direction of whatever"; "fill the place of an Adjutant"; "at least as good terms"**: *DP,* 1:218, 229, 381.

128 **"he is to command"**: *PGW,* 9:472–73.

129 **"could not fail to occasion"**: *PGW,* 10:647–48.

129 **Deane had yet to receive any instructions**: Schiff, *A Great Improvisation,* 56, 72.

129 **Vergennes apparently sent**: Perrault, *Le secret du roi,* 3:247–48.

129 **likely proposing Thomas Conway**: Charles-François de Broglie was a cousin of Elzéar Marie Joseph Charles, Vicomte de Broglie, who had been the commander of the Regiment of Aquitaine in which Thomas Conway served. Given that Deane selected Conway shortly after his meeting with de Broglie, it seems likely that de Broglie had recommended him to Deane, based on Conway's service to his cousin.

129 **"let slip an opportunity"**: *DP,* 1:342.

129 **de Broglie outlined his plan**: Stillé, "Comte de Broglie, the Proposed Stadtholder of America"; Zucker, *General de Kalb,* 94–107.

130 **"voluntarily put on the chains"**: Adams, ed. Adams, *The Works of John Adams,* 3:147.

130 **Gilbert du Motier, Marquis de Lafayette**: Of the almost two hundred biographies of Lafayette, I have primarily relied on the following: Gottschalk, *Lafayette in America;* Bernier, *Lafayette, Hero of Two Worlds;* Chatel de Brancion and Villiers, *La Fayette: Rêver la gloire;* Taillemite, *La Fayette;* and Auricchio, *The Marquis.*

130 **"love of glory"**: La Fayette, *Mémoires,* 1:6; Diderot and d'Alembert, eds., *Encyclopédie,* 2:409. Additional thanks to Patrick Villiers for further clarification on the role of "glory" in eighteenth-century thought.

130 **"curiosity was deeply excited"**: *SWGW,* 5:445; Villiers, "La Fayette and the Passage of the Ship *La Victoire* in 1777."

131 **Lafayette himself was also detained**: The cat-and-mouse game that Lafayette and de Kalb played to get to America is detailed in: Gottschalk, *Lafayette in America,* book 1, 83–142; Manceron, *Twilight of the Old Order,* 240–44, 391–96; Bernier, *Lafayette, Hero of Two Worlds,* 23–41; Chatel de Brancion and Villiers, *La Fayette: Rêver la gloire,* 60–73; Auricchio, *The Marquis,* 28–35; Kapp, *The Life of John Kalb,* 80–110; Zucker, *General de Kalb,* 108–19.

132 **a Spanish observer was in Pensacola**: Gold, "Governor Bernardo de Gálvez and Spanish Espionage in Pensacola, 1777."

133 **Bernardo de Gálvez**: Caughey, *Bernardo de Gálvez in Louisiana,* remains his most accessible biography (**"I alone,"** 63). A far more extensive study of his life is Quintero Saravia, "Bernardo de Gálvez y América a finales del siglo XVIII."

134 **Gálvez was bolder; an American raiding party**: James, "Spanish Influence in the West during the American Revolution"; Abbey, "Peter Chester's Defense of the Mississippi after the Willing Raid"; Neimeyer, "Continental Marines: The 1778 Willing Expedition."

134 **George Rogers Clark; successful expeditions against British settlements**: Nester, *George Rogers Clark,* 65–154.

136 **"we must see war as inevitable"**: Yela Utrilla, *España ante la independencia de los Estados Unidos,* 2:204.

136 **One of Spain's primary fears**: Chávez, *Spain and the Independence of the United States,* 119–21; Fernández Duro, *Armada española,* 7:284; Floyd, *The Anglo-Spanish Struggle for Mosquita,* 128, 142. The British did intend to divide the empire and construct a road to connect the two oceans, but had no interest in building a canal. Acknowledgments to Andrew Lambert for his insights into the British campaign strategy.

136 **his mission was to spy upon the defenses**: Caughey, "The Panis Mission to Pensacola, 1778."

137 **Navarro . . . needed his own sources of information**: Cummins, *Spanish Observers and the American Revolution,* 95–98.

138 **"ignora[nt] of our language"; "It has taken up half my time"**: *PGW,* 8:377–78, 381–83.

138 **Thomas Conway; Tronson du Coudray**: Freeman, *George Washington: A Biography,* 4:421–24, 454–57.

139 **Louis Lebègue Duportail**: Kite, *Brigadier-General Louis Lebègue Duportail;* Le Pottier, *Duportail ou le génie de George Washington.*

139 **Augustin Mottin de La Balme**: Magnin, *Mottin de La Balme.*

139 **Casimir Pulaski**: Kajencki, *Casimir Pulaski;* Kajencki, *The Pulaski Legion.*

139 **Michael Kovats de Fabriczy**: Lyons, *Foreign-Born American Patriots,* 133–40.

139 **"You cannot conceive"**: *PGW,* 9:453–54.

139 **"Either we must refuse to commission them at all"**: *PBF,* 24:440–43.

140 **It was in this hostile climate**: Zucker, *General de Kalb,* 132–38; *DHPF,* 3:218–19.

141 **"mercenaries"**: Ferling, *Almost a Miracle,* 114.

141 **Americans had little experience**: Hatch, *The Administration of the American Revolutionary Army,* 48; Zucker, *General de Kalb,* 9–11.

141 **"Wild Geese"**: McLaughlin and Warner, *The Wild Geese: The Irish Brigades of France and Spain.*

141 **Few of the more than four hundred volunteer applications**: Prelinger, "Less Lucky Than Lafayette," 267.

142 **a series of reforms in the French army**: Blaufarb, *The French Army, 1750–1820,* 29–32; Gottschalk, *Lafayette in America,* book 1, 53–54, 157–58.

142 **"great men of antiquity"**: Osman, "The Citizen Army of Old Regime France," 168–80.

142 ***"les insurgents"***: Prevost, *Manuel lexique,* 1:580.

142 **one Alsatian officer**: Prelinger, "Less Lucky Than Lafayette," 267.

142 **"love of liberty"**: Magnin, *Mottin de La Balme,* 252.
142 **"that liberty which I idolize"; "coming as a friend"**: Bernier, *Lafayette, Hero of Two Worlds,* 36.
142 **"I was then a stern Republican"**: Du Ponceau and Whitehead, "The Autobiography of Peter Stephen Du Ponceau," part 1, 201.
143 **"as so many spies in our camp"**: Gottschalk, *Lafayette in America,* book 2, 25.
143 **Some of the more aristocratic French volunteers**: Seeber, trans., *On the Threshold of Liberty,* 104; Echeverria and Murphy, "The American Revolutionary Army: A French Estimate in 1777," 158.
143 **"The Cause"**: Ellis, *Revolutionary Summer,* x.
143 **"There is one hundred times more enthusiasm"; "in a certain sense"**: Le Pottier, *Duportail ou le génie de George Washington,* 62; Kite, *Brigadier-General Louis Lebègue Duportail,* 59.
143 **The campaign of General William Howe . . . and subsequent rearguard action**: The general outlines are from Boatner, *Encyclopedia of the American Revolution,* 104–10, 426–30, 856–65; Lengel, *General George Washington,* 211–65; and Middlekauff, *Washington's Revolution,* 140–65.
144 **"father and friend"**: Gottschalk, *Lafayette in America,* book 2, 25.
144 **Second Canadian Regiment**: Everest, *Moses Hazen and the Canadian Refugees in the American Revolution,* 52–54.
145 **Lafayette stayed behind with Conway**: Gottschalk, *Lafayette in America,* book 2, 44–47.
145 **Casimir Pulaski had also been following**: Kajencki, *The Pulaski Legion,* 18–21.
146 **"A great number of French officers"**: *PBF,* 25:244.
146 **"This dispensation will save us much altercation"**: Adams, ed. Adams, *The Works of John Adams,* 2:437–38.
146 ***"peut être un heureux accident"***: Lasseray, *Les Français sous les Treize Étoiles,* 2:452.
147 **Howe's troops easily captured**: Walker, *Engineers of Independence,* 157–74.
147 **the Conway Cabal**: Selesky and Boatner, eds., *Encyclopedia of the American Revolution,* 1:266–68; Lengel, *General George Washington,* 277–78; Freeman, *George Washington: A Biography,* 4:555–60; Middlekauff, *Washington's Revolution,* 175–77.
148 **"We should on all occasions"**: *PGW,* 6:248–51.
148 **Now Duportail had independently come to the same conclusion**: Ford, "Defences of Philadelphia in 1777," 20:95–115; Walker, *Engineers of Independence,* 177–83; Kite, *Brigadier-General Louis Lebègue Duportail,* 35–43; Le Pottier, *Duportail ou le génie de George Washington,* 67–75.
149 **"The [soldiers] appeared to me"**: *PBF,* 26:478–89.
149 **With over a thousand huts; America's fourth-largest city**: Fleming, *Washington's Secret War,* 9, 129, 160; Bureau of the Census, *A Century of Population Growth,* 11.
149 **average temperatures were actually above freezing**: Brier, "Tolerably Comfortable," 2–3.
150 **"the entrenched situation of the enemy"**: *RDC,* 1:286.
150 **Pulaski had wanted to equip and train**: Kajencki, *Casimir Pulaski,* 45–61.
150 **"The Marquis Lafayette"**: Cited in Gottschalk, *Lafayette in America,* book 2, 109.
150 **Benjamin Franklin, accompanied by Bonvouloir**: Hamon, *Le chevalier de Bonvouloir,* 56–68.
150 **an invasion of the Canadian provinces**: Everest, *Moses Hazen,* 56–59; Zucker, *General de Kalb,* 156–58; Bernier, *Lafayette, Hero of Two Worlds,* 61–68.

151 **Friedrich Wilhelm, Baron von Steuben**: See Lockhart, *The Drillmaster of Valley Forge,* for a thorough and engaging biography.
153 **Each day new drills were added**: Lockhart, *The Drillmaster of Valley Forge,* 95–113.
153 **"come and swear for me in English"**: Du Ponceau and Whitehead, "The Autobiography of Peter Stephen Du Ponceau," part 1, 219.
154 **"treat as if [he] were my own son"**: La Fayette, *Mémoires,* 1:105.
154 **clinch him in an embrace**: Auricchio, *The Marquis,* 61.
154 **a Grand Review**: Lockhart, *The Drillmaster of Valley Forge,* 114–16; Fleming, *Washington's Secret War,* 250–52.
154 **"The more I reflect upon the matter"**: Kite, *Brigadier-General Louis Lebègue Duportail,* 70–71.
154 **a single decisive British victory**: My analysis follows that of Mackesy in *The War for America,* 510–15, and Black, *War for America,* 246–47.
155 **Troops began to fill the ranks**: Middlekauff, *The Glorious Cause,* 426.
155 **They were also well clothed**: Risch, *Supplying Washington's Army,* 293.
155 **The British cabinet had just sent orders**: Mackesy, *The War for America,* 214.
156 **"how sorry, distressed they were"**: *PGW,* 15:529.
156 **settled near the Monmouth Courthouse crossroads**: Boatner, *Encyclopedia of the American Revolution,* 716–25; Middlekauff, *The Glorious Cause,* 427–34; Papas, *Renegade Revolutionary,* 235–55; Fleming, *Washington's Secret War,* 311–24; Lockhart, *The Drillmaster of Valley Forge,* 141–68; Gottschalk, *Lafayette in America,* book 2, 204–33.
157 **"The behavior of the officers and men"; "discipline"**: *PAH,* 1:497–501, 513–14.
158 **the Blue Book**: Lockhart, *The Drillmaster of Valley Forge,* 169–96.
158 **a corps of engineers**: Walker, *Engineers of Independence,* 34–49, 203–52; Kite, *Brigadier-General Louis Lebègue Duportail,* 79–135; Le Pottier, *Duportail ou le génie de George Washington,* 97–151; Kajencki, *Thaddeus Kosciuszko,* 61–119; Storozynski, *The Peasant Prince,* 52–93.
159 **"I have a high opinion"**: *PGW,* 18:168–69.
160 **capturing the Stony Point fort**: Selesky and Boatner, eds., *Encyclopedia of the American Revolution,* 2:1116–20.
160 **Bernardo de Gálvez convened a *junta de generales***: Caughey, *Bernardo de Gálvez in Louisiana,* 149–53; Chávez, *Spain and the Independence of the United States,* 110, 134–35.
161 **Manchac; Baton Rouge; Natchez; Lake Pontchartrain**: Caughey, *Bernardo de Gálvez in Louisiana,* 153–62; Beerman, *España y la independencia de Estados Unidos,* 52–59.
161 **"the keys to the Gulf of Mexico"**: Haarmann, "The Spanish Conquest of British West Florida," 108.
162 **The British and Spanish next turned their attention**: Beerman, *España y la independencia de Estados Unidos,* 237–46; Chávez, *Spain and the Independence of the United States,* 150–57.
162 **Horatio Nelson**: Lambert, *Nelson: Britannia's God of War,* 10–11.
162 **"[Havana] is worth more"**: Chávez, *Spain and the Independence of the United States,* 174.
162 **Continental Army and militia units from Georgia**: Raab, *Spain, Britain and the American Revolution in Florida,* 97–112.
162 **Juan de Miralles worked assiduously**: Cummins, *Spanish Observers and the American Revolution,* 156–59.

162 **Even George Rogers Clark's Virginia militia**: Chávez, *Spain and the Independence of the United States,* 179–81.
163 **Mobile was within his grasp**: DuVal, *Independence Lost,* 167–68.
163 **HMS *West Florida; Galveztown***: Fernández González, "El bergantín *Galveztown.*"
163 **Spanish laid in a weeks-long siege**: Medina Rojas, *José de Ezpeleta, gobernador de La Mobila,* 1–30; Caughey, *Bernardo de Gálvez in Louisiana,* 177–88; Wright Jr., *Florida in the American Revolution,* 79–82; Thomson, *Spain: Forgotten Ally of the American Revolution,* 208–14.

CHAPTER FIVE THE SAILORS

165 **Vice Admiral Edward Vernon's attack in 1741 on Cartagena de Indias**: Harding, *Amphibious Warfare in the Eighteenth Century,* 83–122; Blanco Núñez, *La Armada española en la primera mitad del siglo XVIII,* 139–83.
166 **American Regiment; Lawrence Washington**: Jones, "The American Regiment in the Carthagena Expedition"; Lengel, *General George Washington: A Military Life,* 3–6; Brumwell, *George Washington: Gentleman Warrior,* 21–26. Many British accounts of the assault on Varadero give the Julian calendar date of March 18.
166 **The young George Washington**: Lengel, *General George Washington: A Military Life,* 12–16; Brumwell, *George Washington: Gentleman Warrior,* 29–34.
167 **Washington saw at first hand:** Knox, *The Naval Genius of George Washington,* 24–25; Gardiner, ed., *Navies and the American Revolution,* 24–29, 42–45, 62–63.
167 **"the amazing advantage"**: *PGW,* 10:410.
168 **The actual construction of warships**: Miller, *Sea of Glory,* 205.
168 **naval gun discipline and seamanship**: Rodger, *The Wooden World,* 42.
168 **The previous century of defying the Navigation Acts**: Chapelle, *The Search for Speed under Sail,* 4, 5, 79.
168 ***Guerre de course:*** Gardiner, ed., *Navies and the American Revolution,* 66–71.
168 **Washington asked the colonies of Massachusetts and Rhode Island**: Patton, *Patriot Pirates,* 25–45.
169 **"distressing the enemy"**: Adams, ed. Adams, *The Works of John Adams,* 3:7–8.
169 **"short, easy, and infallible method"**: Ibid., 7:258.
169 **The Continental Navy never represented much of a threat**: Miller, *Sea of Glory,* 372, 379; NHHC, "Vessels of the Continental Navy"; Glete, *Navies and Nations,* 1:278, 2:778.
170 **Nor were the privateers particularly damaging**: Crawford, "The Privateering Debate in Revolutionary America," 223–24; Gardiner, ed., *Navies and the American Revolution,* 69. Note that in the 1690s, England and Scotland were still separate nations, so while I use the word "British" in the text for consistency, it would be more accurate to state that the French adopted a *guerre de course* strategy against the superior *English* fleet.
170 **"are convinced they cannot defend themselves"**: *DHPF,* 1:288; *NDAR,* 3:280.
170 **"one obstacle remains"**: Kapp, *The Life of John Kalb,* 128.
171 **"be stimulated to complete their battalions"**: Freeman, *George Washington: A Biography,* 5:3; Knox, *The Naval Genius of George Washington,* 39–45.
171 **The British . . . understood far more quickly**: Dull, *The French Navy and American Independence,* 105–7; Brown, "The Anglo-French Naval Crisis, 1778."

172 **"deliverer of America"; "distinguished talents"**: *PGW,* 16:38–39, 88–89.

172 **"attack the enemy"**: *DHPF,* 3:237–39.

172 **Charles-Henri, Comte d'Estaing**: See Calmon-Maison, *L'Amiral d'Estaing (1729–1794);* Michel, *La vie aventureuse et mouvementée de Charles-Henri, comte d'Estaing;* and Taillemite, "Les officiers généraux de la guerre d'Indépendance américaine."

172 ***La Royale:*** See especially Vergé-Franceschi, *La marine française au XVIIIe siècle.*

172 **the highest-ranking officers**: The title of admiral, the rank above vice admiral, was honorific and given to a member of the royal household. Acknowledgments to Patrice Decencière for this information.

174 **a squadron of reinforcements under Rear Admiral John Byron**: O'Shaughnessy, *The Men Who Lost America,* 335.

174 **The entrance to New York harbor . . . was obstructed**: Des Barres, *The Atlantic Neptune,* 4: "A Chart of New York Harbour." Acknowledgments to John Cloud, James Delgado, and Albert "Skip" Theberge of the National Oceanic and Atmospheric Administration (NOAA) for additional hydrographic information.

174 **only the smallest ships**: For the drafts of British vessels, see Gardiner, ed., *Navies and the American Revolution,* 54. For those of French vessels, see Demerliac, *La marine de Louis XVI,* 15–16. All measurements have been converted to modern English units.

174 **The city of Newport:** I have made particular use of McBurney, *The Rhode Island Campaign;* Hattendorf, *Newport, the French Navy and American Independence;* and Crawford, "The Joint Allied Operation at Rhode Island, 1778."

176 **Maresquelle . . . as Sullivan's aide-de-camp**: Smith Jr., *The French at Boston during the Revolution,* 23–24.

176 **"this militia would at least rattle the enemy"**: Murphy, "The French Professional Soldier's Opinion of the American Militia in the War of the Revolution," 195; Doniol, "Correspondance inédite de La Fayette," 416.

176 **"so violent that nothing approaches it"**: Michel, *La vie aventureuse et mouvementée de Charles-Henri, comte d'Estaing,* 199.

176 **"with all haste"**: *DHPF,* 3:376.

178 **"refus[ing] to assist"**: McBurney, *The Rhode Island Campaign,* 153.

178 **"I never saw a man so glad"**: *PGW,* 16:461–64.

178 **Washington received word**: Ibid., 17:68–72.

179 **"The truth of the position"**: Ibid., 18:149–52.

179 **"I made it my pride and pleasure"**: Gottschalk, *Lafayette in America,* book 2, 290.

179 **Pierre Landais**: Balch, *The French in America during the War of Independence of the United States,* 2:158; Lasseray, *Les Français sous les Treize Étoiles,* 1:255–64.

179 **Lafayette arrived unannounced in Versailles**: Bernier, *Lafayette, Hero of Two Worlds,* 81–83.

180 **He was a whirlwind of ideas**: Gottschalk, *Lafayette in America,* book 3, 7–19; Schaeper, *France and America in the Revolutionary Era,* 232–38.

180 **captured the British island of Dominica; Saint Lucia**: Mahan, *The Major Operations of the Navies in the War of American Independence,* 99–104.

181 **"the first officer"**: Mackesy, *The War for America,* 234.

181 **Vergennes himself was not enamored**: Pritchard, "French Strategy and the American Revolution," 90.

181 **plans for invading Britain**: Patterson, *The Other Armada,* 12–20.

182 **Montbarey and Sartine . . . drew up plans for a joint attack**: Perugia, *La tentative*

d'invasion de l'Angleterre de 1779, 71–73; Patterson, *The Other Armada,* 46–53; Dull, *The French Navy and American Independence,* 142–50.

182 **The Conde de Aranda . . . sent to Carlos III his own plan of assault**: Blanco Núñez, *La Armada española en la segunda mitad del siglo XVIII,* 123.

183 **had overhauled and improved the Spanish dockyard system**: Sánchez Carrión, *De constructores a ingenieros de marina,* 118.

183 **Most of the dockyards' efforts**: Villiers, "Sartine et la préparation de la flotte de guerre française 1775–1778."

183 **"unpardonable error in calculation"**: Ferreiro, *Ships and Science,* 242.

183 **both navies were delayed**: I have drawn from the accounts in: Patterson, *The Other Armada,* 160–229; Dull, *The French Navy and American Independence,* 143–58; Villiers, "La tentative franco-espagnole de débarquement en Angleterre de 1779"; Lacour-Gayet, "La campagne navale de La Manche en 1779"; Perugia, *La tentative d'invasion de l'Angleterre de 1779,* 75–176; Fernández Duro, *Armada española,* 7:233–47; Blanco Núñez, *La Armada española en la segunda mitad del siglo XVIII,* 125–27; Alsina Torrente, *Una guerra romántica 1778–1783,* 142–49.

183 **Lieutenant General . . . d'Orvilliers**: *Lieutenant-général des armées navales* (lieutenant general of the naval armies) was an *ancien régime* flag rank that has no real equivalent in modern terms. It was similar to rear admiral in operational terms, but unlike for admiral ranks, these men had little influence in naval planning. See Pritchard, *Louis XV's Navy, 1748–1762,* 58.

184 **Captain-General . . . Luis de Córdova y Córdova; the *Real Armada;* sixty-five-year existence**: *Capitan general de la Armada* was a Spanish naval rank generally equivalent to admiral. The *Real Armada* was formed when the Bourbon dynasty took power in 1714 and combined nine separate fleets into one centralized navy. See Blanco Núñez, *La Armada española en la primera mitad del siglo XVIII,* xix–xx. In Spanish, the word *armada* can signify both the entire navy as well as a fleet of ships.

185 **communications between the fleets; signal flags**: Tunstall, *Naval Warfare in the Age of Sail,* 135–45. It is worth pointing out that in the twentieth and twenty-first centuries, joint military force organizations like NATO focus extensively on training and communications as the primary means of interoperability, while spending comparatively few resources on creating common weapons systems between nations.

185 **"I was very surprised"**: Chevalier, *Histoire de la marine française pendant la guerre de l'indépendance américaine,* 161.

186 **a nervously impatient Lafayette received**: Gottschalk, *Lafayette in America,* book 3, 29–34.

186 **even the Chevalier d'Éon volunteered**: Patterson, *The Other Armada,* 153–54.

186 **a massive exercise in Vaussieux**: Alder, *Engineering the Revolution,* 113–17.

186 **It was in fact part of a massive dysentery epidemic**: Kohn, *Encyclopedia of Plague and Pestilence,* 133–34.

187 **"The Lord has taken from me"**: Lacour-Gayet, "La campagne navale de La Manche en 1779," 1653.

187 **"incapable of carrying out any action"**: Perugia, *La tentative d'invasion de l'Angleterre de 1779,* 159.

187 **The British navy was already well aware**: Schaeper, *Edward Bancroft,* 188–90; Syrett, *The Royal Navy in European Waters during the American Revolutionary War,* 66–69; Patterson, *The Other Armada,* 74–76, 96–100.

188 **the Bourbon fleet was steadily losing**: Perugia, *La tentative d'invasion de l'Angleterre de 1779*, 104–7.

188 **"fleet in being"**: Corbett, *Some Principles of Maritime Srategy*, 199; Hattendorf, "The Idea of a 'Fleet in Being' in Historical Perspective."

188 **d'Orvilliers received orders**: Patterson, *The Other Armada*, 208–11.

188 **"the French vessels"**: Villiers, "La tentative franco-espagnole de débarquement en Angleterre de 1779," 28.

189 **more than two hundred lengthy articles**: Search results from *America's Historical Newspapers, 1690–1922*, conducted July 2013.

189 **Jones readily agreed to this mission**: Out of several hundred books on these subjects, I have relied on two: Boudriot, *John Paul Jones and the* Bonhomme Richard; and Schaeper, *John Paul Jones and the Battle of Flamborough Head*.

190 **France's Irish Regiment; Wuibert**: Kilbourne, *Virtutis Praemium*, 2:1004–7; Smith, *Marines in the Revolution*, 227–35. On Wuibert and Forton Prison, see Cohen, *Yankee Sailors in British Gaols*, 128. Additional thanks to Charles Neimeyer for clarifying the roles of the marines aboard Jones's ships.

190 **"[He] has something little in his face and air"**: *PJA*, 2:364–79.

191 **"I may sink, but I'm damned if I'll strike!"**: These words, or words to that effect, were recorded in contemporary accounts of the battle. The apocryphal "I have not yet begun to fight!" was only cited almost a half century later by one of Jones's officers, Richard Dale. See Boudriot, *John Paul Jones and the* Bonhomme Richard, 82.

191 **Wuibert, wounded in the thigh and arm:** *Mercure de France*, Saturday, December 18, 1779, 187–88.

192 **Jones was warmly welcomed**: See Enthoven, "Sir, I Have Not Yet Begun to Fight!"

192 **"scarce anything was talked of"**: *PBF*, 30:537.

192 **"return as soon as possible"**: Ibid., 30:511.

192 **He was once again made prisoner**: Kilbourne, *Virtutis Praemium*, 2:1005.

193 **the British cabinet . . . decided**: Mackesy, *The War for America, 1775–1783*, 327–28; Syrett, *The Royal Navy in European Waters during the American Revolutionary War*, 83–84; Knight, "The Royal Navy's Recovery after the Early Phase of the American Revolutionary War," 11.

193 **Floridablanca had not given up hope**: Blanco Núñez, *La Armada española en la segunda mitad del siglo XVIII*, 136–38; Dull, *The French Navy and American Independence*, 163–69; Pritchard, "French Strategy and the American Revolution," 97; Villiers, *Marine royale, corsaires et trafic dans l'Atlantique*, 2:582–83; Lacour-Gayet, *La marine militaire de la France sous le règne de Louis XVI*, 305.

193 **"pile of rocks called Gibraltar"**: Danvila y Collado, *Reinado de Carlos III*, 5:33–39.

193 **George Elliott; Joaquin Mendoza**: McGuffie, *The Siege of Gibraltar*, 35–47.

194 **The Spanish navy was incapable of massing a fleet**: Fernández Duro, *Armada española*, 7:253–55; Alsina Torrente, *Una guerra romántica 1778–1783*, 149–50.

194 **Rodney was lucky; the relief of Gibraltar; The Moonlight Battle**: Blanco Núñez, *La Armada española en la segunda mitad del siglo XVIII*, 130–33; Syrett, *The Royal Navy in European Waters during the American Revolutionary War*, 84–89; McGuffie, *The Siege of Gibraltar*, 48–62.

195 **"taken more line-of-battle ships"**: Cited in Mahan, *The Major Operations of the Navies in the War of American Independence*, 124–25.

195 **whose renewed confidence in the government allowed**: Middleton, *The War of American Independence*, 162.

195 **Copper sheathing**: See Ferreiro, "Development and Tactical Advantages of Copper Sheathing."
195 **"the finest invention in the world"**: Cock, "The Finest Invention in the World," 453.
196 **"For God's sake and our country's"**: Barham and Laughton, ed., *Letters and Papers of Charles, Lord Barham,* 1:55.
196 **coming on top of a naval buildup**: Knight, "The Royal Navy's Recovery after the Early Phase of the American Revolutionary War," 19–20.
196 **equivalent to $4.5 billion, the cost of a modern British aircraft carrier**: To put the enormous cost of the coppering program into a modern naval perspective, £400,000 is equivalent to $4.5 billion today, which is the cost for the British aircraft carrier *Queen Elizabeth*. See Ferreiro, "Development and Tactical Advantages of Copper Sheathing."
196 **"senile"**: *DHPF,* 4:447.
196 **One of those sorties departed Cádiz**: Blanco Núñez, *La Armada española en la segunda mitad del siglo XVIII,* 134–36; Syrett, *The Royal Navy in European Waters during the American Revolutionary War,* 136–37.
197 **The perception that the British navy could no longer control the seas**: Sutton, *The East India Company's Maritime Service,* 137–38.
197 **the Hussey-Cumberland mission**: See Bemis, *The Hussey-Cumberland Mission and American Independence.*
198 **For six months, d'Estaing and Byron watched each other's comings and goings**: Michel, *La vie aventureuse et mouvementée de Charles-Henri, comte d'Estaing,* 190–91.
198 ***Fier Roderigue:*** Morton and Spinelli, *Beaumarchais and the American Revolution,* 229–35.
198 **recapture another former French sugar colony**: Michel, *La vie aventureuse et mouvementée de Charles-Henri, comte d'Estaing,* 203–9.
198 **upon learning of Grenada continued on to confront**: Mahan, *The Major Operations of the Navies in the War of American Independence,* 106–10.
199 ***Fier Roderigue* had suffered the most damage**: Morton and Spinelli, *Beaumarchais and the American Revolution,* 237.
199 **"if his seamanship had equaled his bravery"**: Villiers, *La marine de Louis XVI,* 121.
199 **[D'Estaing] began reading the letters that awaited him at Cap François**: Michel, *La vie aventureuse et mouvementée de Charles-Henri, comte d'Estaing,* 221–24.
200 **"Never has this country"**: *DHPF,* 4:297.
200 **chasing them from Savannah**: Boatner III, *Encyclopedia of the American Revolution,* 982–85.
201 ***"aux Armes de Sa Majesté Le Roy de France"*; "the King, my master"**: Lawrence, *Storm over Savannah,* 35, 57.
201 ***Sagittaire* captured HMS *Experiment:*** Michel, *La vie aventureuse et mouvementée de Charles-Henri, comte d'Estaing,* 235.
201 **"all of them"; "vigorous blow"**: Lawrence, *Storm over Savannah,* 93.
202 **Charles Romand de L'Isle**: Sheftall, Mordecai Sheftall papers, 1777–1778, Subseries IX: Provision Returns for the Artillery, 1771–1778, has over two hundred provision returns for the artillery unit of the Continental Army of Georgia, primarily signed by Captain Romand de L'Isle.
202 **Lincoln's American troops fought**: Boatner III, *Encyclopedia of the American Rev-*

olution, 985–87; Lawrence, *Storm over Savannah,* 100–112; Kajencki, *The Pulaski Legion in the American Revolution,* 205–19.

202 **Chasseurs-Volontaires de Saint-Domingue**: Rhodes, "Haitian Contributions to American History."

202 **"great bravery"; "has the interest"; "the uncertain events of war"; "chaos"**: Lawrence, *Storm over Savannah,* 108, 135.

203 **"D'Estaing is the first"**: Michel, *La vie aventureuse et mouvementée de Charles-Henri, comte d'Estaing,* 244.

203 **Rodney was heading north and Guichen south**: Mahan, *The Major Operations of the Navies in the War of American Independence,* 128–45; Gardiner, ed., *Navies and the American Revolution,* 108–9; Villiers, *La marine de Louis XVI,* 129–34; Tunstall, *Naval Warfare in the Age of Sail,* 165–67.

204 **In Cádiz, a fleet**: Chávez, *Spain and the Independence of the United States,* 141–44.

204 **Solano was a competent sailor**: Santaló Rodriguez de Viguri, *Don José Solano y Bote,* 110.

205 ***Vizcondado previo del Feliz Ardid:*** *Vizcondado previo* (former viscount) was a noble title granted when the higher-ranking titles of conde or marqués were simultaneously conferred.

206 **The forty French ships of the line now in Cádiz**: Mahan, *The Major Operations of the Navies in the War of American Independence,* 158; Lewis, *Admiral de Grasse and American Independence,* 95.

CHAPTER SIX THE PIECES CONVERGE

207 **"whether it would be agreeable"**: *DCAR,* 3:321.

208 **He most notably demonstrated this**: Murphy, *Charles Gravier, Comte de Vergennes,* 151–54. See also Bonneville de Marsangy, *Le chevalier de Vergennes: Son ambassade à Constantinople.*

208 **rationally calculate France's interests and limitations**: Hardman, *French Politics, 1774–1789,* 123; Murphy, "The View from Versailles," 111; Vergennes, ed. Hardman and Price, *Louis XVI and the Comte de Vergennes,* 60.

209 **"some ideas on an expedition"; "more than ever necessary"**: *SFME,* 17:57–116.

209 **"perhaps we should resolve"**: *DHPF,* 4:276, 323.

209 **Luzerne's report of his West Point meeting with Washington**: *DHPF,* 4:329.

209 **"a corps of gallant French"**: *PGW,* 22:557–62.

210 **"clothes, arms, money"**: *SFME,* 17:167–97.

210 **"no orders to request troops"; "nothing of the sentiments"**: *PBF,* 30:424, 470.

210 ***"projet particulier":*** *DHPF,* 4:283.

210 ***Expédition Particulière:*** *DHPF,* 4:352; Stinchcombe, *The American Revolution and the French Alliance,* 134–35. Kennett, *The French Forces in America,* 10–11.

210 **"a learned, dedicated general officer"**: Montbarey, *Mémoires autographes de M. le prince de Montbarey,* 2:339.

210 **"under the high command"**: *DHPF,* 4:282–83.

210 **Lafayette impressed upon him**: *DHPF,* 5:315–16; Whitridge, *Rochambeau,* 74; Gottschalk, *Lafayette in America,* book 3, 69.

211 **Ternay and Rochambeau had set sail**: Kennett, *The French Forces in America,* 12–13; Gottschalk, *Lafayette in America,* book 3, 71.

211 **Some fifty-five thousand British and Hessian soldiers**: Mackesy, *The War for America,* 274–76.

212 **Southern Strategy**: Ibid., 110, 157–59, 267; O'Shaughnessy, *The Men Who Lost America,* 162–63, 186–92, 229–30.

212 **all saltwater estuaries . . . were frozen solid**: Raphael, *Founding Myths,* 108–9.

212 **Almost seven thousand British, Hessian, and Loyalist troops**: Russell, *The American Revolution in the Southern Colonies,* 130–31.

213 **They were assisted by L'Enfant**: Berg, *Grand Avenues,* 47.

213 **including sixty from d'Estaing's fleet**: Murdoch, "A French Account of the Siege of Charleston, 1780," 144.

213 **Marquis de Bretigny . . . escaped**: Raab, *Spain, Britain and the American Revolution in Florida,* 126.

213 **Jordi (Jorge) Ferragut Mesqueda**: Caleo, "'A Most Serious Wound': The Memorial of George Farragut"; Lyons, *Foreign-Born American Patriots,* 91–95.

213 **Charleston**: Borick, *A Gallant Defense: The Siege of Charleston, 1780.*

214 **"yelling at the same time"**: Uhlendorf, ed. and trans., *The Siege of Charleston,* 70–71.

215 **"town in a desperate state"**: Kite, *Brigadier-General Louis Lebègue Duportail,* 172.

215 **the single largest capture of American forces during the war**: Lumpkin, *From Savannah to Yorktown,* 49; Boatner III, *Encyclopedia of the American Revolution,* 212–13.

215 **Cornwallis wasted little time**: Lumpkin, *From Savannah to Yorktown,* 49–56; Russell, *The American Revolution in the Southern Colonies,* 148–61.

216 **The Revolution in the South became**: Raphael, *Founding Myths,* 228–39.

216 **Charles Armand Tuffin; Johann de Kalb**: Zucker, *General de Kalb,* 197–231; Carrer, *La Bretagne et la guerre d'Indépendance américaine,* 184–86.

216 **post of honor on the right wing**: Spring, *With Zeal and with Bayonets Only,* 95–96.

217 **The Battle of Camden**: Lumpkin, *From Savannah to Yorktown,* 57–67; Russell, *The American Revolution in the Southern Colonies,* 162–75.

217 **Kings Mountain**: Lumpkin, *From Savannah to Yorktown,* 91–104; Russell, *The American Revolution in the Southern Colonies,* 176–96.

218 **"If we are saved"**: *PAH,* 2:347–49.

218 ***Expédition Particulière:*** In addition to the references cited below, I made extensive use of the *W3R: Washington-Rochambeau Revolutionary Route* website (with enormous gratitude to its chief historian, Robert A. Selig), and the Xenophon Group website (with equal gratitude to its webmaster, Albert "Durf" McJoynt).

218 **Thomas Graves; Ternay**: Kennett, *The French Forces in America,* 14–35; Hattendorf, *Newport, the French Navy and American Independence,* 42–61.

219 **they sighted a pair of white-and-gold Bourbon flags**: Blanchard, *The Journal of Claude Blanchard,* 38–39.

219 **"We are now, sir, under your command"**: *SWGW,* 7:511.

219 **war is always a continuation of politics by other means**: This dictum was most famously expressed by Carl von Clausewitz in his 1832 book *On War.*

220 **"The shops were closed"**: Rice Jr. and Brown, trans. and ed., *The American Campaigns of Rochambeau's Army,* 1:17.

221 **"their countenances brightened"**: Weelen, *Rochambeau, Father and Son,* 205.

221 **the Congress had just stopped issuing paper money**: Ferguson, *The Power of the Purse,* 46–47.

221 **The next tasks for Ternay and Rochambeau**: Kennett, *The French Forces in America,* 36–47; Hattendorf, *Newport, the French Navy and American Independence,* 62–67.

221 **Any initial fears that the French were an invading force**: Stinchcombe, *The American Revolution and the French Alliance,* 136–37.

222 **"tormented"; "grief"**: Kennett, *The French Forces in America,* 22.

222 **"taste for a profession"**: Berthier, *Alexandre Berthier,* 15; Rice and Brown, trans. and ed., *The American Campaigns of Rochambeau's Army,* 1:221.

222 **The rank-and-file soldiers and noncommissioned officers**: Scott, *From Yorktown to Valmy,* 6–12.

222 **Georg Daniel Flohr**: Selig, "A German Soldier in America, 1780–1783: The Journal of Georg Daniel Flohr."

223 **Lafayette, Washington's emissary to Rochambeau**: Kennett, *The French Forces in America,* 50–52; Auricchio, *The Marquis,* 88–89.

223 **"a cord stretched to the limit"**: *DHPF,* 5:354.

223 **"our force is so reduced"**: *RDC,* 3:498.

223 **"I assure you that action is important"**: Lafayette, *Mémoires,* 1:248–49.

223 **"My dear marquis"**: Weelen, *Rochambeau, Father and Son,* 89–90; *DHPF,* 4:380–81.

224 **"air of sadness"**: Fersen, *Lettres d'Axel de Fersen à son père,* 31.

224 **Rochambeau, stocky with an aura of calm self-possession**: Whitridge, *Rochambeau,* 87.

224 **the home of Jeremiah Wadsworth**: The site is now occupied by the Wadsworth Atheneum.

224 **Over the course of the next two days**: The Hartford conference took place on September 21 and 22, 1780. See Izerda, ed., *Lafayette in the Age of American Revolution,* 3:175–76; Hattendorf, *Newport, the French Navy and American Independence,* 69–70; Manceron, *The Wind from America,* 300–302; Gottschalk, *Lafayette in America,* book 3, 121–34.

224 **"naval superiority"; "New York should become the object"**: *WGW,* 20:79.

225 **"should add to our many other obligations"**: Tower, *The Marquis de La Fayette in the American Revolution,* 2:162.

225 **John Jay had arrived in Madrid**: On John Jay's failed mission to the Spanish court, see: Brecher, *Securing American Independence: John Jay and the French Alliance,* 145–58; Rodriguez, *La Revolución americana de 1776 y el mundo hispánico,* 116–50.

225 **When John Laurens arrived in Paris**: Stinchcombe, *The American Revolution and the French Alliance,* 140–41; Schiff, *A Great Improvisation,* 262–77.

225 **Back at Newport**: Hattendorf, *Newport, the French Navy and American Independence,* 72–76.

226 ***Gazette Françoise:*** Poulin and Quintal, eds. and trans., *"La Gazette Françoise," 1780–1781.*

226 **Benedict Arnold; John André; Lafayette**: Manceron, *The Wind from America,* 303–7; Gottschalk, *Lafayette in America,* book 3, 134–42.

227 **quite literally ate their own shoes**: Raphael, *Founding Myths,* 110.

227 **a horse that sold for $40,000 in the spring now cost $150,000**: Lengel, *General George Washington,* 326.

227 **ran out of funds to pay his couriers**: Hattendorf, *Newport, the French Navy and American Independence,* 79.

227 **"an end to all subordination in the Army"**: Lengel, *General George Washington,* 327.

227 **That Clinton and Arbuthnot could not agree**: Syrett, *The Royal Navy in American Waters,* 145–47.

227 **"as so many spies in our camp"**: Gottschalk, *Lafayette in America,* book 2, 25.

228 **The Battle of Cowpens and the crossing of the Dan River**: Boatner III, *Encyclopedia of the American Revolution,* 291-301; Lockhart, *The Drillmaster of Valley Forge,* 234–37; Storozynski, *The Peasant Prince,* 129–37.

228 **Arnold torched Richmond**: Lockhart, *The Drillmaster of Valley Forge,* 238–45; Russell, *The American Revolution in the Southern Colonies,* 217–18; Maass, *The Road to Yorktown,* 29–31.

229 **des Touches assigned Captain Armand Le Gardeur de Tilly**: Hattendorf, *Newport, the French Navy and American Independence,* 80–83; Mahan, *The Major Operations of the Navies in the War of American Independence,* 169–70.

229 **Washington . . . determined to detach**: Freeman, *George Washington: A Biography,* 4:255–63; Maass, *The Road to Yorktown,* 42–58; Gottschalk, *Lafayette in America,* book 3, 189–208.

229 **"Do no act whatever with Arnold"**: *WGW,* 21:255.

230 **Washington would return with him to Newport**: Closen, *The Revolutionary Journal of Baron Ludwig von Closen,* 59–64; Kennett, *The French Forces in America,* 98; Hattendorf, *Newport, the French Navy and American Independence,* 83–86.

230 **The ten warships in des Touches's fleet weighed anchor:** Mahan, *The Major Operations of the Navies in the War of American Independence,* 170–74; Kennett, *The French Forces in America,* 98–100; Hattendorf, *Newport, the French Navy and American Independence,* 88–91; Ferreiro, "Development and Tactical Advantages of Copper Sheathing of French, British and Spanish Ships during the War of American Independence."

231 **"I will now only mention"**: Johnson, *Sketches of the Life and Correspondence of Nathanael Greene,* 2:52.

231 **"a great piece of generalship"**: Gottschalk, *Lafayette in America,* book 3, 215.

232 **"swore vengeance against me"**: Ibid., book 3, 223.

232 **Phillips did die in front of Lafayette's guns**: Davis, *Where a Man Can Go,* 179–80.

232 **Lafayette now had the major independent command he had longed for**: Gottschalk, *Lafayette in America,* book 3, 232–33; Russell, *The American Revolution in the Southern Colonies,* 255–56.

232 **"the boy cannot escape me"**: This myth is debunked in Gottschalk, *Lafayette in America,* book 3, 431–32.

232 **"I am determined to skirmish"**: Lafayette, *Memoirs, Correspondence and Manuscripts,* 3:417.

233 **Lafayette's instructions**: Maass, *The Road to Yorktown,* 57–147. Acknowledgments to John Maass for additional insights.

233 **supply depots**: For an overview of provisioning French troops during the campaign, see Bodle, "La logistique et l'Armée française en Amérique."

234 **Joseph II . . . something of an unknown quantity**: Kennett, *The French Forces in America,* 89–90; Dull, *A Diplomatic History of the American Revolution,* 131–32.

234 **Sartine had been replaced as minister of the navy**: Caron, *La guerre incomprise ou la victoire volée: Bataille de la Chesapeake, 1781,* 359–65; Dull, *The French Navy and American Independence,* 194–202.

235 ***Compte rendu au roi:*** Harris, *Necker: Reform Statesman of the Ancien Régime,* 217–35.

235 **"a surplus sufficient"**: Ibid., 225; Manceron, *The Wind from America,* 321–32.

235 **The debates over American independence**: Caron, *La guerre incomprise ou la victoire volée: Bataille de la Chesapeake, 1781,* 367–73; Weelen, *Rochambeau, Father and Son,* 99–100, 214–17; Whitridge, *Rochambeau,* 127–34; Kennett, *The French Forces in America,* 89–111; Stinchcombe, *The American Revolution and the French Alliance,* 145–46.

235 **"were thoroughly examined and discussed"**: *DHPF,* 4:585.

235 **So when John Laurens came**: Schiff, *A Great Improvisation,* 274; Massey, *John Lau-*

rens and the American Revolution, 277. Laurens told Vergennes that he might be "compelled to draw [his sword] against France, as a British subject" if the loan were not granted.

236 **The dispatches that *Concorde* carried**: Kennett, *The French Forces in America,* 104–5.

236 **The most important news by far**: Bonsal, *When the French Were Here,* 81–82; Kennett, *The French Forces in America,* 104–5.

237 **The Wethersfield conference**: Freeman, *George Washington: A Biography,* 4:284–90; Kennett, *The French Forces in America,* 105–6; Whitridge, *Rochambeau,* 135–41.

237 **"naval superiority"**: *DGW,* 3:369.

237 **Rochambeau penned several letters**: Lewis, *Admiral de Grasse and American Independence,* 117–26; Antier, *L'Amiral de Grasse,* 189–94; O'Donnell, *The Chevalier de La Luzerne,* 176–79; Kennett, *The French Forces in America,* 106–9. Transcripts of the correspondence are in *DHPF,* 5:475–90.

239 **Twelve American pilots boarded the frigate *Concorde*:** This was the number that the Spanish official Francisco de Saavedra counted when *Concorde* arrived at Cap François. Reparaz, *Yo solo,* 248; Reparaz, *I Alone,* 248.

239 **The future of the entire campaign**: On *Hermione* and *Concorde,* see Villiers and Lemineur, *L'*Hermione, *La Fayette, Latouche-Tréville;* Lemineur and Villiers, *L'*Hermione, *frégate de 12;* Kalbach and Gireaud, *L'*Hermione *au vent de la Liberté.* On Chevillard and the École du génie maritime, see Ferreiro, *Ships and Science.*

239 **By then, Rochambeau's army had already departed**: Selig, *The March to Victory,* 13–23; Scott, *From Yorktown to Valmy,* 53–58; Chartrand and Back, *The French Army in the American War of Independence,* 20–34.

240 **"most neatly dressed"**: Closen, *The Revolutionary Journal of Baron Ludwig von Closen,* 59–64.

240 **Clinton's forces numbered ten thousand soldiers**: Mackesy, *The War for America, 1775–1783,* 410.

240 **Duportail's report**: Kite, *Brigadier-General Louis Lebègue Duportail,* 200–202.

240 **"the location which it seems to me"**: *DHPF,* 4:651, 5:520–21; Lewis, *Admiral de Grasse and American Independence,* 138–39.

240 **sailing almost twice as fast as other similar warships**: *Concorde*'s average speed over ground of four knots was double that achieved by Arbuthnot's squadron between Long Island and the Chesapeake in March 1781.

241 **"give up all idea of attacking New York"**: *DGW,* 3:410.

CHAPTER SEVEN THE ENDGAME

242 **Before Columbus's second voyage in 1494**: Neely, *The Great Hurricane of 1780,* 56–60.

243 ***juntas de generales*:** Chávez, *Spain and the Independence of the United States,* 180–81; Reparaz, *Yo solo,* 46; Reparaz, *I Alone,* 46; Medina Rojas, *José de Ezpeleta, gobernador de La Mobila,* 399–413; Medina Rojas, "José de Ezpeleta and the Siege of Pensacola," 108–9; Santaló Rodriguez de Viguri, *Don José Solano y Bote,* 109–10.

243 **the Great Hurricane of 1780**: Neely, *The Great Hurricane of 1780,* 102–8, 122–34; Gardiner, ed., *Navies and the American Revolution,* 109; Alsina Torrente, *Una guerra romántica 1778–1783,* 228–30. Additional assistance thanks to Patrick Villiers.

244 **Solano's Hurricane**: Neely, *The Great Hurricane of 1780,* 102–34; Santaló Rodriguez

de Viguri, *Don José Solano y Bote,* 111–12; Beerman, "José Solano and the Spanish Navy at the Siege of Pensacola," 126–29.

245 **"will we retreat upon suffering a single setback?"**: Reparaz, *Yo solo,* 48–49; Reparaz, *I Alone,* 48–49.

245 **attempt a recapture of Mobile**: Medina Rojas, *José de Ezpeleta, gobernador de La Mobila,* 521–54 (quote, 551–52); Medina Rojas, "José de Ezpeleta and the Siege of Pensacola," 113; Wright Jr., *Florida in the American Revolution,* 84–85.

245 **Rodney returned to his base**: Tuchman, *The First Salute,* 217; Neely, *The Great Hurricane of 1780,* 127–30.

246 **By comparison**: Blanco Núñez, *La Armada española en la segunda mitad del siglo XVIII,* 139; Villiers, "La stratégie de la marine française," 232.

246 **The importance to Spain of recapturing Pensacola**: Odom, *The Longest Siege of the American Revolution: Pensacola,* 45, 67; Wright Jr., *Florida in the American Revolution,* 74–76.

247 **League of Armed Neutrality**: Madariaga, *Britain, Russia and the Armed Neutrality of 1780;* Gilje, "Ideology and Interest: Free Trade, the League of Armed Neutrality, and the American Revolution"; Willis, *The Struggle for Sea Power,* 399–407.

247 **the Fourth Anglo-Dutch War; capture Sint Eustatius**: Edler, *The Dutch Republic and the American Revolution,* 95–187; Jameson, "St. Eustatius in the American Revolution"; Breen, "Sir George Rodney and St. Eustatius in the American War: A Commercial and Naval Distraction, 1775–81"; Alsina Torrente, *Una guerra romántica 1778–1783,* 266.

248 **"communicate to the military leaders"**: Saavedra, *Diario de Don Francisco de Saavedra,* 46; Saavedra, *Journal of Don Francisco Saavedra de Sangronis,* 11.

249 **"total expulsion of the English"; "ready to execute the royal intention"**: Saavedra, *Diario de Don Francisco de Saavedra,* 45, 137; Saavedra, *Journal of Don Francisco Saavedra de Sangronis,* 10, 112.

249 **Pensacola**: Reparaz, *Yo solo;* Reparaz, *I Alone;* Odom, *The Longest Siege of the American Revolution.*

250 **"had his cannon ass-backwards"**: Reparaz, *Yo solo,* 87. This is the closest translation of the original, *"que tenía los cañones por culata."*

251 **"I alone"**: Quintero Saravia, "Bernardo de Gálvez y América a finales del siglo XVIII," 475.

251 **"We partake in this war"; "defend this post to the last"**: Reparaz, *I Alone,* 87, 103.

252 **had recaptured the Inmaculada Concepción fortress**: Chávez, *Spain and the Independence of the United States,* 157.

252 **The combined fleet had been hastily formed**: Saavedra, *Journal of Don Francisco Saavedra de Sangronis,* 143–45.

252 **never actually bothered to reach Pensacola**: Mackesy, *The War for America,* 416.

252 **The Spanish forces**: Chartrand and Rickman, *The Spanish Army in North America, 1700–1793,* 14–24.

253 **He confided to Saavedra**: Saavedra, *Journal of Don Francisco Saavedra de Sangronis,* 168–69.

255 **Miralles's secretary Francisco de Rendón succeeded him**: Cummins, *Spanish Observers and the American Revolution,* 160–86.

255 **"[I] congratulate you"**: *WGW,* 22:243.

256 **Spain's driving out the British from West Florida**: Dull, *The Miracle of American Independence,* 141–42.

256 **François Joseph Paul, Comte de Grasse**: Lewis, *Admiral de Grasse and American Independence;* Antier, *L'Amiral de Grasse.*

256 **"The Comte de Grasse stands six foot four"**: Droz, *Histoire du règne de Louis XVI,* 128. The original text read, *"Le comte de Grasse a six pieds, et six pieds un pouce les jours de combat."* One *pied* was an *ancien régime* measurement equating to about one foot and three-quarter inches.

257 **On March 22**: Dull, *The French Navy and American Independence,* 222–24; Antier, *L'Amiral de Grasse,* 173–79; Lewis, *Admiral de Grasse and American Independence,* 106–16.

257 **"British ships are faster than ours"**: Chevalier, *Histoire de la marine française pendant la guerre de l'indépendance américaine,* 227.

257 **"Never . . . was more powder and shot thrown away"**: Mahan, *The Major Operations of the Navies in the War of American Independence,* 165.

258 **"Spain had not yet formally recognized"; "expel [the English]"**: Saavedra, *Journal of Don Francisco Saavedra de Sangronis,* 192–209; Reparaz, *Yo solo,* 247–52; Reparaz, *I Alone,* 247–52.

258 **de Grasse approached Saavedra for a loan**: Lewis, "Las Damas de la Havana, El Precursor, and Francisco de Saavedra"; Tejera, *La ayuda de España y Cuba a la independencia norteamericana,* 187–228; Gutiérrez-Steinkamp, *Spain: The Forgotten Alliance,* 191–92. One of the legends that subsequently arose from this incident was that de Grasse had received his loan from "las damas de la Havana," who sold their jewelry to finance the American Revolution. In actual fact only one of the twenty-eight contributors was a woman (Bárbara Santa Cruz, Marquesa de Cárdenas), and none of the contemporary accounts makes any mention of her selling her jewelry to raise the contribution.

259 **a promise that was barely kept**: It would turn out that despite Saavedra's constant badgering, Solano did not release the four promised Spanish warships to protect Cap François until November, and then only for a week before returning to Havana. See Saavedra, *Journal of Don Francisco Saavedra de Sangronis,* 272.

259 **Rodney; dispatched HM Sloop *Swallow;* ordering Hood**: Syrett, *The Royal Navy in American Waters,* 185–86; Graves, *The Graves Papers,* 33, 44–45, 52.

259 **completely bypassing the Chesapeake Bay**: On August 30, after his arrival in New York, Hood reported to the Admiralty that he had "made the land" at Cape Henry on August 25 and, "finding no enemy had appeared either in the Chesapeake or Delaware," sailed for Sandy Hook (Graves, *The Graves Papers,* 58). Graves never believed that story, and he was correct. The logbooks of two ships in Hood's fleet, HMS *Alfred* and HMS *Shrewsbury,* showed that the fleet never approached closer than forty miles from Cape Henry, well over the horizon. (NAUK Admiralty 52/2125 and 51/905. Personal communication by Michael Crawford, November 2015.)

259 **By 1781 almost half the French fleet had been copper-sheathed**: Ferreiro, "Development and Tactical Advantages of Copper Sheathing of French, British and Spanish Ships during the War of American Independence."

260 **Saint-Simon began landing his troops**: Larrabee, "A Neglected French Collaborator in the Victory of Yorktown, Claude-Anne, Marquis de Saint-Simon."

260 **"You shall never give birth to a rebel"**: Tornquist, *The Naval Campaigns of Count de Grasse,* 57. This account was substantially verified by a French officer of the Royal Deux-Ponts, Jean-Baptiste de Verger (Rice and Brown, trans. and eds., *The American Campaigns of Rochambeau's Army,* 1:137).

260 **The morning of September 5**: The Battle of the Chesapeake was also called the Battle of the Chesapeake Capes, the Battle of the Virginia Capes, and the Battle of the Capes. In addition to biographies of de Grasse, Hood, and Graves, as well as more general histories of the Yorktown campaign, I have found the following works to be particularly useful: Tornquist, *The Naval Campaigns of Count de Grasse;* Shea, *The Operations of the French Fleet under the Count de Grasse in 1781–2;* Larrabee, *Decision at the Chesapeake;* Société en France des Fils de la Révolution Américaine, *La glorieuse campagne du comte de Grasse;* McGee, *The French Victory in the Battle of the Chesapeake.*

261 **a maneuver that requires a large number of expert sailors:** Willis, *Fighting at Sea in the Eighteenth Century,* 45–46.

261 **endless analyses and recriminations**: See, for example, Breen, "Graves and Hood at the Chesapeake," and Sulivan, "Graves and Hood."

263 **"state of the position of the enemy"**: Graves, *The Graves Papers,* 83–84.

263 **"we discerned in the distance General Washington"**: Closen, *The Revolutionary Journal of Baron Ludwig von Closen,* 123; Selig, "The Washington-Rochambeau Revolutionary Route in the State of Delaware," 76.

264 **"to use me promptly and efficiently"**: *DHPF,* 5:521.

264 **The march south had been organized in haste**: Selig, *The March to Victory; W3R: Washington-Rochambeau Revolutionary Route* website; and many long conversations with Bob Selig, to whom I am utterly grateful.

264 **Louis-Alexandre Berthier; map out the route**: Berthier's maps, which exist today at Princeton University, are remarkable for their precision and clarity; they can be laid over modern georeferenced aerial photographs with almost no distortion, and archeological sites have been accurately identified based upon them. See Berthier, Louis-Alexandre Berthier Collection; and Comer, "Phase I and II Archaeological Investigations at the Rochambeau Campsite." My thanks to Doug Comer for showing me the archeological site at Colchester, Virginia, and highlighting for me the importance of Berthier's maps.

265 **Loir River**: Not to be confused with the larger Loire River, of which the Loir is a tributary.

265 **his much-improved English**: In his *Mémoires,* Rochambeau describes two conversations with a wheelwright in Connecticut who repaired his coach, with every indication that he conducted them directly in English without interpreters. Rochambeau, *Mémoires militaires,* 1:251–52.

265 **"with an ardor not easily described"**: Gottschalk, *Lafayette in America,* book 3, 305.

265 **He did not yet appreciate**: O'Shaughnessy, *The Men Who Lost America,* 279.

265 **de Grasse dispatched the sloop *Queen Charlotte*:** Trentinian, "Washington, de Grasse et la *Reine Charlotte.*"

266 **"'*mon petit général!*'":** Custis, *Recollections and Private Memoirs of Washington, by his Adopted Son, George Washington Parke Custis,* 236.

266 **The meeting was rather more professional in nature**: Washington and Comte de Grasse, *Correspondence of General Washington and Comte de Grasse,* 34–42; Lewis, *Admiral de Grasse and American Independence,* 174–75; Freeman, *George Washington: A Biography,* 4:333–38.

266 **Lieutenant Jean Audubon**: Four years after the Battle of Yorktown, he would become the father of America's foremost naturalist, John James Audubon.

266 **"Great Mind"**: Washington and Comte de Grasse, *Correspondence of General Washington and Comte de Grasse,* 54.

266 **the great weight of the coin caused the storeroom floor to collapse**: Blanchard, *The Journal of Claude Blanchard,* 143.

266 **Brigadier General Claude Gabriel de Choisy**: Rice and Brown, trans. and eds., *The American Campaigns of Rochambeau's Army,* 1:137–38.

266 **the Battle of Yorktown**: In addition to standard histories of the War of American Independence and biographies of the principal participants, I have made particular use of: Bonsal, *When the French Were Here;* Grainger, *The Battle of Yorktown, 1781;* Rice and Brown, trans. and eds., *The American Campaigns of Rochambeau's Army;* Ketchum, *Victory at Yorktown;* Selig, *The March to Victory;* and *W3R: Washington-Rochambeau Revolutionary Route* website.

267 **the wagon trains**: Selig, "Revolutionary War Route and Transportation Survey in the Commonwealth of Virginia, 1781–1782," 454, 488.

267 **Yorktown would be a classic European siege; Siege of Kassel**: Wright, "Notes on the Siege of Yorktown in 1781"; Szabo, *The Seven Years' War in Europe,* 376.

268 **The Battle of Yorktown, like most sieges**: Selig, "Artillery at Yorktown: A Statistical Overview."

268 **high rate of nine rounds per hour; *Load! Ram! Fire!*:** Greene, *The Guns of Independence,* 472. The official gun commands were longer, but in the heat and noise of battle they could be truncated to single words. I extend my gratitude to the Regimiento Fijo de La Luisiana Española (Fixed Regiment of Spanish Louisiana), especially Héctor Díaz, James Garner, and Eliud Bonilla, for allowing me to participate as part of the artillery crew during several battlefield reenactments in Maryland and Virginia.

269 **"a fire that was superb to see"**: Closen, *The Revolutionary Journal of Baron Ludwig von Closen,* 146–47. While the shot was heated to red-hot in a pit or over a brazier, the gun barrel was packed with powder and then with sod or damp hay to act as insulation to keep the powder from igniting when the hot shot was rammed into the barrel; the moment the shot was in place, the gun was fired. Greene, *The Guns of Independence,* 373.

269 **"Our bombardment produced great effects"; "The heavy fire"**: Grainger, *The Battle of Yorktown, 1781,* 128–29.

270 **"our fire was increasing"**: Deux-Ponts, *My Campaigns in America,* 59, 146.

271 **"if he required some American help"**: La Fayette, *Mémoires, correspondance et manuscrits,* 1:279.

271 **"intrepidity and intelligence"; "accustomed to difficult things"**: Deux-Ponts, *My Campaigns in America,* 67, 157.

271 **Clinton . . . was unable to formulate any response**: Syrett, *The Royal Navy in American Waters,* 192, 210, 216, 217.

272 **the French lost twice as many men as did the Americans**: Washington and Comte de Grasse, *Correspondence of General Washington and Comte de Grasse,* 127. France lost 253 killed or wounded, the Americans 135.

272 **Rochambeau wordlessly pointed**: Bonsal, *When the French Were Here,* 164; Freeman, *George Washington: A Biography,* 4:389–91; Grainger, *The Battle of Yorktown, 1781,* 148–49.

272 **"I have the honor to inform Congress"**: *SWGW,* 8:182–83.

272 **"as he would have taken a ball"**: O'Shaughnessy, *The Men Who Lost America,* 2–3.

CHAPTER EIGHT THE ROAD TO PEACE

273 **For once, news from America**: Lauzun, *Mémoires de M. le duc de Lauzun,* 375–76; Deux-Ponts, *My Campaigns in America,* 154–55; *PBF,* 36:79; Fleming, *The Perils of Peace,* 79–80; Schiff, *A Great Improvisation,* 289; Syrett, *The Royal Navy in American Waters,* 217.

273 **The news from Yorktown**: Gottschalk, *Lafayette in America,* book 3, 329–56. Washington and Comte de Grasse, *Correspondence of General Washington and Comte de Grasse,* 145–47.

274 **"I am not marvelously pleased"**: Gottschalk, *Lafayette in America,* book 3, 353.

274 **"It is not in the English character to give up so easily"**: *DHPF,* 4:688.

274 **the British navy was hardly a spent force**: Knight, "The Royal Navy's Recovery after the Early Phase of the American Revolutionary War."

275 **Washington asked for assistance**: Washington and Comte de Grasse, *Correspondence of General Washington and Comte de Grasse,* 121–59.

275 **de Grasse's fleet majestically sortied; Hood departed; Graves also departed**: Syrett, *The Royal Navy in American Waters,* 219.

275 **These would be the first in a series of lightning assaults**: Lewis, *Admiral de Grasse and American Independence,* 208–21; Mahan, *The Major Operations of the Navies in the War of American Independence,* 195–96.

275 **"vigorous attack"**: Chávez, *Spain and the Independence of the United States,* 205; Fernández Duro, *Armada española,* 7:292.

276 **he and Monteil returned to France**: Lacour-Gayet, *La marine militaire de la France sous le règne de Louis XVI,* 426; Monteil, Chevalier de Monteil logbook.

276 **Vaudreuil, had departed Brest**: Mahan, *The Major Operations of the Navies in the War of American Independence,* 195–96; Alsina Torrente, *Una guerra romántica 1778–1783,* 289. The Marquis de Vaudreuil's younger brother Louis de Rigaud, Comte de Vaudreuil, commanded the seventy-four-gun *Sceptre* in the Battle of the Chesapeake and in the Battle of the Saintes. See Villiers, *La marine de Louis XVI,* 277.

276 **Rodney . . . had left Portsmouth in January**: Mackesy, *The War for America,* 446–57.

276 **"French and Spanish vessels"**: Sánchez Carrión, *De constructores a ingenieros de marina,* 236.

277 **the strait . . . known as the Saintes**: For the Battle of the Saintes, see: Saavedra, *Journal of Don Francisco Saavedra de Sangronis,* 306–15; Santaló Rodriguez de Viguri, *Don José Solano y Bote,* 122; de Grasse, *Mémoire du comte de Grasse sur le combat naval du 12 avril 1782;* Tornquist, *The Naval Campaigns of Count de Grasse,* 91–109; Mackesy, *The War for America,* 458–59; Lewis, *Admiral de Grasse and American Independence,* 230–54.

278 **blamed . . . the lack of coppering for his defeat**: First Lord of the Admiralty Sandwich claimed that in intercepted letters of de Grasse, he attributed his loss to the improved maneuverability that coppering afforded Hood's ships: "[De Grasse] expressly says that he should have annihilated Admiral Hood's fleet if it had not been for his ships being coppered, which enabled him to maneuver as he thought proper, and take any advantage that wind or weather might give him to avoid an action if he judged it advisable to do so." Sandwich, *The Private Papers of John, Earl of Sandwich,* 4:286.

278 **The Battle of the Saintes soon became**: See, for example, Mahan, *The Major Oper-*

ations of the Navies in the War of American Independence, 206–26; Tunstall, *Naval Warfare in the Age of Sail,* 179–84; and Trew, *Rodney and the Breaking of the Line.*

278 **"Their hulls were all riddled from cannon shot"**: Saavedra, *Diario de Don Francisco de Saavedra,* 301; Saavedra, *Journal of Don Francisco Saavedra de Sangronis,* 321.

278 **Matías de Gálvez had won important victories at Caribe and Roatán**: Chávez, *Spain and the Independence of the United States,* 161–65; Beerman, *España y la independencia de Estados Unidos,* 243–46.

278 **"it was impossible to attack Jamaica"**: Saavedra, *Diario de Don Francisco de Saavedra,* 305; Saavedra, *Journal of Don Francisco Saavedra de Sangronis,* 325.

278 **French warships would escort two major sugar convoys**: Tornquist, *The Naval Campaigns of Count de Grasse,* 109–13.

278 **Cagigal, was planning an attack**: See Lewis, *Neptune's Militia;* Beerman, "The Last Battle of the American Revolution."

280 **The West Indies; the East Indies**: *[The] Present State of the West-Indies,* 3.

280 **the East India Company**: Willis, *The Struggle for Sea Power,* 267–68.

281 **"The principal object of our politics in India"**: Das, *Myths and Realities of French Imperialism in India,* 1–19, 129–217 (quote, 151). See also Ruggiu, "India and the Reshaping of the French Colonial Policy (1759–1789)," and Haudrère, "La Révolution de l'Inde n'aura pas lieu."

281 **a shortcut across the Nile River and the Red Sea**: Willis, *The Struggle for Sea Power,* 269–71.

282 **Lieutenant Bonvouloir**: Hamon, *Le chevalier de Bonvouloir,* 94–107.

282 **Castries saw the East Indies theater of operations**: Haudrère, "La Révolution de l'Inde n'aura pas lieu," 153. On Castries, see also: Montbarey, *Mémoires autographes de M. le prince de Montbarey,* 2:243; Dull, *The French Navy and American Independence,* 263–64; Das, *Myths and Realities of French Imperialism in India,* 154–55.

282 **The portly, pugnacious, and tactically brilliant Suffren; "Admiral Satan"**: Several recent, accessible biographies of Suffren are: Cavaliero, *Admiral Satan;* Klein, *Mais qui est le bailli de Suffren Saint-Tropez?;* and Monaque, *Suffren: Un destin inachevé.*

283 **the five battles that Suffren and Hughes would fight**: Tunstall, *Naval Warfare in the Age of Sail,* 185–87; Dupuy, Hammerman, and Hayes, *The American Revolution: A Global War,* 236–62.

284 **"The revolution which we had every right to expect"**: Haudrère, "La Révolution de l'Inde n'aura pas lieu," 168.

284 **Among those who had passed away**: Hamon, *Le chevalier de Bonvouloir,* 108–9.

284 **nor did the league come to the Dutch Republic's aid**: Madariaga, *Britain, Russia and the Armed Neutrality of 1780,* 292, 308–12.

285 **the fifty-gun *Rotterdam***: Winfield, *British Warships in the Age of Sail, 1714–1792,* 161.

285 **the Battle of Dogger Bank**: Syrett, *The Royal Navy in European Waters during the American Revolutionary War,* 129–32; Edler, *The Dutch Republic and the American Revolution,* 191–93. Additional information courtesy of Alan Lemmers.

285 **Stormont; ordered James Harris**: Madariaga, *Britain, Russia and the Armed Neutrality of 1780,* 239–63, 295–302.

286 **"nest of pirates"; "get rid of a resource"**: Blanco Núñez, *La Armada española en la segunda mitad del siglo XVIII,* 147.

287 **Crillon, accompanied by his American aide-de-camp**: Brecher, *Securing American Independence,* 155.

287 **lay siege to San Felipe**: For the campaign and capture of Minorca, see: Chávez, *Spain and the Independence of the United States,* 145–47; Beerman, *España y la independencia de Estados Unidos,* 249–60; Blanco Núñez, *La Armada española en la segunda mitad del siglo XVIII,* 145–50; Dull, *The French Navy and American Independence,* 232–36; Mackesy, *The War for America,* 436–38.

288 **"like the blood in the veins of animals"**: D'Arçon, *Mémoire pour servir à l'histoire du siège de Gibraltar,* 11.

288 **Gibraltar**: For the siege of Gibraltar, see: McGuffie, *The Siege of Gibraltar, 1779–1783,* 83–167; Chartrand and Courcelle, *Gibraltar, 1779–83,* 57–87; Fernández Duro, *Armada española,* 7:309–28; Blanco Núñez, *La Armada española en la segunda mitad del siglo XVIII,* 154–60. Additional information thanks to Agustín Ramón Rodríguez González.

291 **When the two met off Cape Spartel:** For the Battle of Cape Spartel, see: McGuffie, *The Siege of Gibraltar, 1779–1783,* 168–75; Fernández Duro, *Armada española,* 7:329–44; Blanco Núñez, *La Armada española en la segunda mitad del siglo XVIII,* 160–63.

291 **"uncoppered ships are worthless"**: Juan-García Aguado, *José Romero Fernández de Landa,* 188.

291 **America was already acting like a triumphant nation**: Fleming, *The Perils of Peace,* 106–14.

292 **Clinton . . . could still call upon another forty thousand men**: O'Shaughnessy, *The Men Who Lost America,* 360–61; Raphael, *Founding Myths,* 244–46.

293 **another hundred battles . . . five hundred casualties**: See Peckham, ed., *The Toll of Independence.*

293 **Antoine Felix Wuibert reported to Fort Pitt**: Kilbourne, *Virtutis Praemium,* 2:1006–7.

294 **"his last penny"**: Whitridge, *Rochambeau,* 243.

294 ***Voyages dans l'Amérique septentrionale:*** Chastellux, *Voyages de M. le marquis de Chastellux dans l'Amérique septentrionale;* Chastellux, *Travels in North-America.*

294 **a daring expedition to Hudson Bay**: Alsina Torrente, *Una guerra romántica 1778–1783,* 302–6.

295 **"You must have formed an alliance"**: Thacher, *A Military Journal during the American Revolutionary War,* 386.

295 **Vaudreil's fleet; Rochambeau visited with Washington**: Whitridge, *Rochambeau,* 240–51; Dull, *The French Navy and American Independence,* 299–301.

295 **Vergennes . . . was effectively Louis XVI's principal minister**: Dull, *A Diplomatic History of the American Revolution,* 123.

296 **"very unfortunate"; "do what I can to save the empire"**: O'Shaughnessy, *The Men Who Lost America,* 4, 41; Fleming, *The Perils of Peace,* 102.

296 **By happenstance; "Great affairs"**: Schiff, *A Great Improvisation,* 295–97.

296 **began a flurry of negotiations**: I have used the following works to construct the account of the peace negotiations: Morris, *The Peacemakers;* Fleming, *The Perils of Peace;* Stockley, *Britain and France at the Birth of America;* Dull, *A Diplomatic History of the American Revolution.*

297 **a budget shortfall of 400 million livres**: Dull, *The French Navy and American Independence,* 279–80, 297–98.

297 **Beaumarchais . . . reminded Franklin**: Morton and Spinelli, *Beaumarchais and the American Revolution,* 275.

297 **all he could obtain was a small loan:** Edler, *The Dutch Republic and the American Revolution,* 214.

298 **John Jay took over negotiations:** Stockley, *Britain and France at the Birth of America,* 71–72; Morris, *The Peacemakers,* 308–10; Schiff, *A Great Improvisation,* 310–11.

298 **The overture was actually due to the Comte de Grasse:** Lewis, *Admiral de Grasse and American Independence,* 275–79.

299 **"not natural enemies":** Fitzmaurice, *Life of William Earl of Shelburne,* 2:180–81.

300 **On Monday, January 20, 1783; "a miracle"; "Thus drops the curtain":** Morris, *The Peacemakers,* 408–10. Additional information thanks to Élisabeth Maisonnier of the Château de Versailles.

300 **Vaudreuil in Venezuela by March 24:** Tornquist, *The Naval Campaigns of Count de Grasse,* 123.

300 **By the beginning of 1783:** Syrett, *The Royal Navy in American Waters,* 225–26.

301 **In both East and West Florida:** Wright Jr., *Florida in the American Revolution,* 145.

301 **The preliminary peace accords:** Dull, *The French Navy and American Independence,* 293–94.

301 **"constant fog over all Europe":** Franklin, *Memoirs of the Life and Writings of Benjamin Franklin,* 3:288.

301 **the Hôtel d'York at 56 rue Jacob:** Jouve, Jouve, and Grossman, *Paris: Birthplace of the U.S.A.,* 42–44. The building has now been occupied for over a century by the engraving and typography company Firmin Didot.

301 **fireworks lit the night sky:** Sambricio, "Fiestas en Madrid durante el reinado de Carlos III."

302 **a massive fireworks display was planned:** Barber and Voss, *Blessed Are the Peace Makers,* 44.

302 **"no longer be considered":** Stockley, *Britain and France at the Birth of America,* 206.

302 **fireworks lit the heavens:** These are the subject of a series of watercolors in BNF Stamps and Photographs, folio QB–201.

302 **Joseph and Étienne Montgolfier; "What is the good of a newborn babe?":** Chapin, "A Legendary *Bon Mot*? Franklin's 'What Is the Good of a Newborn Baby?'"

302 **"These repeated instances":** *PBF,* 37:539–44, 38:289–90.

303 **"our friend and father":** Ibid.

303 **"system of influence"; "immense advantages":** *PJA,* 15:398–414; 16:126–29.

303 **"I will say it for my countrymen":** *PJA,* 15:342.

303 **Britain could have won the war:** See Dull, *The Miracle of American Independence.*

304 **the only person to be universally praised:** O'Shaughnessy, *The Men Who Lost America,* 358–59.

304 **continually overestimated the level of Loyalist support:** Ibid., 186–93.

304 **"impossible that the English can reduce America by arms":** Kite, *Brigadier-General Louis Lebègue Duportail,* 70–71.

304 **"although the people of America might be conquered":** Mackesy, *The War for America,* 510.

304 **"Victories . . . are decided by the great battalions":** *DHPF,* 4:688.

304 **the numbers who fought and died:** Boatner III, *Encyclopedia of the American Revolution,* 264; Peckham, ed., *The Toll of Independence,* 130.

305 **A list compiled in 1903:** Ministère des Affaires étrangères, *Les combattants français de la guerre américaine, 1778–1783;* Dawson, "Les 2112 Français morts aux États-Unis." See also *DOAR;* La Jonquière, *Les marins français sous Louis XVI;* Lasseray, *Les Français sous les Treize Étoiles;* Balch, *The French in America during the War of*

Independence of the United States; Trentinian, "France's Contribution to American Independence."

305 **For Spain, no thorough compilations yet exist**: Lists of Spanish soldiers who served in North America during the War of American Independence are: Hough and Hough, *Spanish Borderland Studies;* and Martinez, *From across the Spanish Empire.* My estimates for Spain's global contribution is based on secondary sources, and include engagements where there was likely to be little or no overlap of the participating soldiers and sailors, for example, concurrent battles in Europe and the West Indies.

305 **at Gibraltar alone**: Chartrand and Courcelle, *Gibraltar 1779–83,* 80, 86.

305 **Society of the Cincinnati**: See Gardiner, *The Order of the Cincinnati in France;* Myers, *Liberty without Anarchy;* Hünemörder, *The Society of the Cincinnati.* The Society of the Cincinnati went dormant on both sides of the Atlantic through much of the nineteenth century, but was reconstituted by the beginning of the twentieth.

306 **"I shall recollect with pleasure"**: *WGW,* 27:317.

CHAPTER NINE THE LEGACY

307 **"I do not feel tranquil"**: Morris, *The Peacemakers,* 455–56.

307 **"the alliance is therefore completed"**: Stinchcombe, *The American Revolution and the French Alliance,* 200–203.

308 **"natural interests"**: Ibid.

308 **"We have never based our policy"**: Morris, *The Peacemakers,* 454.

308 **he was now focused on cementing France's position in Europe**: Murphy, *Charles Gravier, Comte de Vergennes,* 432–72.

308 **developed a fever; "overwork"; septicemia**: Vergennes, *Louis XVI and the comte de Vergennes,* 390; Murphy, *Charles Gravier, Comte de Vergennes,* 473; Bachaumont, *Mémoires secrets pour servir à l'histoire de la République des Lettres en France,* 34:71. His condition was described as *dissolution de sang,* "dissolution of the blood," indicating granularity and clotting, which are also symptoms of septicemia.

309 **"tranquil walks of domestic life"**: *WGW,* 27:317.

309 **the Spanish war sloop *Galveztown*:** Fernández González, "El bergantín *Galveztown*"; Olmeda Checa, "El *Galveztown.*" Gálvez had sent the order for the new ship to Diego de Gardoqui, who contracted with New York City shipbuilder James Seaman, via the merchant firm of Dominick Lynch and Thomas Stoughton, for its construction. The new *Galveztown* subsequently participated in the Spanish-American wars of independence.

309 **At noon on April 30**: Bowen, ed., *The History of the Centennial Celebration of the Inauguration of George Washington as First President of the United States.*

310 **the Spanish court had named Gardoqui**: Garteiz-Aurrecoa, "El embajador Don Diego María de Gardoqui y la Independencia de los EE.UU," 188–89.

310 **"The history of the American Revolution"**: Adams, *The Works of John Adams,* 5:494.

310 **Steuben's Blue Book**: Lockhart, *The Drillmaster of Valley Forge,* 301.

311 **Springfield Armory; settled on the French musket**: Whittlesey, "The Springfield Armory: A Study in Institutional Development," 166–67.

311 **the American system of manufacturing**: Hounshell, *From the American System to Mass Production, 1800–1932,* 25–30.

311 **"The necessity of an academy"**: Kite, *Brigadier-General Louis Lebègue Duportail,* 269.

311 **West Point**: See Ambrose, *Duty, Honor, Country;* McDonald, ed., *Thomas Jefferson's Military Academy.*

312 **the castle at Verdun and the motto *Essayons*:** Vogel, "Engineer Buttons and Castle."

312 **Matters did not improve for Cagigal and Miranda**: Chávez, *Spain and the Independence of the United States,* 208–9; Beerman, *España y la independencia de Estados Unidos,* 182–83.

312 **Miranda's visit to America**: Racine, *Francisco de Miranda,* 24–66.

313 **Royal Gift**: Beerman, "The Last Battle of the American Revolution: Yorktown. No, the Bahamas!" 93–95; Chávez, *Spain and the Independence of the United States,* 1–2; Buck, *The Oregon Trail,* 32–35.

314 **the postwar travails of Pierre-Augustin Caron de Beaumarchais**: Morton and Spinelli, *Beaumarchais and the American Revolution,* 183–84, 275–325; Rappleye, *Robert Morris,* 240–42, 317–19; Buel Jr., *In Irons,* 230–34. Beaumarchais's detailed invoices are shown in Morris, *The Papers of Robert Morris, 1781–1784,* 5:322–25.

314 **"everything [Beaumarchais] says, writes, or does"**: *DP,* 1:217.

315 **Chaumont suffered a similar fate**: Schaeper, *France and America in the Revolutionary Era,* 290–326.

315 **the 18 million livres that the United States owed the French government**: *PBF,* 37:633–38.

315 **a debt that Hamilton sold**: The debt was bought by Boston financier James Swan and resold on secondary markets. See Rice, "James Swan: Agent of the French Republic, 1794–1796," 478.

315 **the total cost to France was 1 billion livres**: Price, *The Road from Versailles,* 22.

316 **It was peacetime fiscal policy . . . that plunged France into the financial crisis**: Harris, "French Finances and the American War, 1777–1783"; White, "Was There a Solution to the *Ancien Régime*'s Financial Dilemma?"

317 **five million civilian and military deaths**: Bell, *The First Total War,* 7.

318 **it was the fact that they had successfully fought and won that liberty**: Library of Congress, *The Impact of the American Revolution Abroad,* 11–13.

318 **Neither were the French veterans**: Scott, *From Yorktown to Valmy,* 120–21.

318 **French National Guard; included members of Rochambeau's *Expédition Particulière*:** Ibid., 138–40.

318 **In Saint-Domingue, the Haitian Revolution . . . , counted numerous members of the Chasseurs-Volontaires**: Rhodes, "Haitian Contributions to American History." One of the leaders of the Haitian Revolution was Henry Christophe, who was twelve years old when he served at Savannah.

318 **Most veterans . . . remained loyal; Duportail served as minister of war**: Le Pottier, *Duportail ou le génie de George Washington,* 255–74; Scott, *From Yorktown to Valmy,* 136–37.

319 **"the world's most important consequences"**: Lafayette, *Mémoires, correspondance et manuscrits,* 5:167; Taillemite, *La Fayette,* 404.

319 **Officers of the French Navy**: Vergé-Franceschi, "Marine et Révolution: Les officiers de 1789 et leur devenir."

319 **"When you take off my head"**: Calmon-Maison, *L'Amiral d'Estaing (1729–1794),* 431.

319 **Spain had kept a tight rein on its fiscal policy**: Lancho Rodríguez, "La ayuda financiera española a la independencia de EE.UU."; Sánchez, "Possibilities and Limits: Testing the Fiscal-Military State in the Anglo-Spanish War of 1779–1783"; Kuethe and Andrien, *The Spanish Atlantic World in the Eighteenth Century*, 306–11; Lewis, "New Spain during the American Revolution, 1779–1783," iii–v; Glascock, "New Spain and the War for America, 1779–1783," 277–78.

320 **two largest indigenous uprisings**: See Walker, *The Tupac Amaru Rebellion*.

321 **drawn in part from Charles-François de Broglie's assault plan of 1765**: Das, *De Broglie's Armada*, xi.

322 **The sense of déjà vu would have been all the stronger**: Rodríguez González, *Trafalgar y el conflicto naval Anglo-Español del Siglo XVIII;* Hore, *Nelson's Band of Brothers*. My thanks to the authors Agustín Rodríguez and Peter Hore, as well as Pierre Lévêque, for the help in locating the ships and men who fought both at Cape Spartel and at Cape Trafalgar.

322 **Trafalgar's devastating and widespread effects**: Dull, *The Age of the Ship of the Line*, 178; Harbron, *Trafalgar and the Spanish Navy*, 173.

323 **In Spanish America**: For an overview of the wars of independence, see McFarlane, *War and Independence in Spanish America*. For an examination of its most charismatic character, see Arana, *Bolívar: American Liberator*.

323 **the more liberalized press carried articles and essays**: Novales, "La independencia de América en la conciencia española."

323 **Manifesto of the People of Quito; Similar declarations**: Keeding, *Surge la nación*, 618–19; Armitage, *The Declaration of Independence*, 145–49.

324 **Antoine Felix Wuibert**: Kilbourne, *Virtutis Praemium*, 2:1006–7; Wuibert, Correspondence 1788–1803.

324 **Charles Romand de L'Isle**: Beyls, "Un Dauphinois dans la guerre d'Indépendance des États-Unis"; Lisle, "The Lisle (de Lisle) Family in America."

325 **Pierre-Étienne du Ponceau**: Tieck, "In Search of Peter Stephen Du Ponceau."

325 **When Rochambeau's troops departed the United States**: Scott, *From Yorktown to Valmy*, 103–7.

325 **Georg Daniel Flohr**: Selig, "Private Flohr's Other Life."

325 **Louis Lebègue Duportail**: Le Pottier, *Duportail ou le génie de George Washington*, 269–79; Kite, *Brigadier-General Louis Lebègue Duportail*, 278–86. Note that Duportail's farm is not the same as the Duportail House, still extant, which served as a headquarters in 1777–78 near Valley Forge.

326 **Comte de Grasse; Neil deGrasse Tyson**: Lewis, *Admiral de Grasse and American Independence*, 308–9; Tyson, *The Sky Is Not the Limit*, 23.

326 **While the United States opened its doors**: On French exiles in Philadelphia, see: Furstenberg, *When the United States Spoke French;* Harsanyi, *Lessons from America*.

328 **Gallipolis; Azilum**: Rosengarten, *French Colonists and Exiles in the United States;* Murray, *The Story of Some French Refugees and Their "Azilum."*

328 **Castorland**: Desjardins and Pharoux, *Castorland Journal;* Schaeper, *France and America in the Revolutionary Era*, 337–39.

329 **New York City . . . where a French exile community was already thriving**: Kennedy, *Orders from France;* Caemmerer, *The Life of Pierre Charles L'Enfant;* Berg, *Grand Avenues;* Belhoste, "Les Brunel père et fils"; Bagust, *The Greater Genius?*, 17–21.

330 **George Farragut**: Caleo, "'A Most Serious Wound': The Memorial of George Farragut"; Lyons, *Foreign-Born American Patriots,* 91–95.

331 **"brother in arms"; "to rejoin the friends"**: Lafayette, *Mémoires, correspondance et manuscrits,* 6:160–61.

331 **asked Congress to extend an official invitation**: On Lafayette's visit to America, see: Levasseur, *Lafayette in America;* Burstein, *America's Jubilee,* 8–33; Auricchio, *The Marquis,* 295–303. For a lighthearted look at Lafayette's trip, see Vowell, *Lafayette in the Somewhat United States.*

332 **one of the first steamboats was actually invented in Lyon**: Claude François Dorothée, Marquis de Jouffroy d'Abbans, developed the steamboat *Pyroscaphe* in Lyon in 1783.

332 **"houses in ruins, blackened by fire"**: Levasseur, *Lafayette in America,* 199.

332 **Lafayette stopped at Point Breeze**: Stroud, *The Man Who Had Been King.*

333 **speeches and articles exhorting Americans**: Bercovitch, *The American Jeremiad,* 143–44.

334 **American exceptionalism had always been different**: Greenfeld, *Nationalism,* 447; Kagan, *Dangerous Nation,* 42; Deconde, "Historians, the War of American Independence, and the Persistence of the Exceptionalist Ideal."

334 **Bancroft's *History* . . . served as the touchstone**: Bancroft, *History of the United States from the Discovery of the Continent;* Raphael, *Founding Myths,* 249, 258, 292–93.

335 **"What do we mean by the Revolution?"**: Adams, ed. Adams, *The Works of John Adams,* 10:172.

335 **90 percent of the arms . . . close to $30 billion equivalent in direct monetary aid**: Moller, *American Military Shoulder Arms,* 1:103; Schaeper, *France and America in the Revolutionary Era,* 156. The direct aid included 47 million livres from France and 400,000 pesos from Spain.

336 **rue de l'Indépendance américaine**: Many thanks to Élisabeth Maisonnier for this information.

336 **"America defaults no obligations"; "Lafayette, we are here!"**: Gilmer, "Lafayette, We Are Here!" manuscript, chapter 3.

Bibliography

ABBREVIATIONS

AA: American Archives: Documents of the American Revolutionary Period, 1774–1776. 9 vols. Compiled by Peter Force. Northern Illinois University Libraries, http://dig.lib.niu.edu/amarch/.

ADA: Archives départementales des Ardennes (Ardennes Departmental Archives). Charleville-Mézières, France.

AGI: Archivo General de Indias (General Archive of the Indies). Seville, Spain.

ANF: Archives nationales de France (National Archives of France). Paris.

ANOM: Archives nationales d'outre-mer (National Overseas Archives). Aix-en-Provence, France.

BC: Beaumarchais: Correspondance [Beaumarchais: Correspondence]. Compiled by Brian N. Morton and Donald C. Spinelli. 5 vols. Paris: Éditions A.-G. Nizet, 1969–2010.

BNE: Biblioteca Nacional de España (National Library of Spain). Madrid.

BNF: Bibliothèque nationale de France (National Library of France). Paris.

DCAR: *The Diplomatic Correspondence of the American Revolution.* 12 vols. Compiled by Jared Sparks. Boston: N. Hale and Gray and Bowen, 1829–30.

DGW: *The Diaries of George Washington.* 6 vols. Compiled by Donald Jackson and Dorothy Twohig. Charlottesville: University of Virginia Press, 1978.

DHPF: Doniol, Henri. *Histoire de la participation de la France à l'établissement des États-Unis d'Amérique* [History of the French participation in the establishment of the United States]. 6 vols. Paris: Imprimerie nationale, 1886–99.

DOAR: Bodinier, Gilbert. *Dictionnaire des officiers de l'armée royale qui ont combattu aux États-Unis pendant la guerre d'Indépendance* [Dictionary of royal army officers who fought in the United States during the War of Independence]. Vincennes: Service historique de l'armée de terre, 1982.

DP: The Deane Papers, 1774–1790, by Silas Deane. 5 vols. Compiled by Charles Isham. New York: New-York Historical Society, 1887–91.

IIC: Ingram Industrial Collection, Stonehill College, Easton, MA.

NAUK: National Archives of the United Kingdom, Kew, Richmond, Surrey.

NDAR: Naval Documents of the American Revolution. 12+ vols. Washington, DC: Government Printing Office, 1964–.

NHHC: Naval History and Heritage Command website, http://www.history.navy.mil/.

PAH: The Papers of Alexander Hamilton. 27 vols. Compiled by Harold C. Syrett. New York: Columbia University Press, 1961–87.

PBF: The Papers of Benjamin Franklin. 40+ vols. Compiled by Yale University. http://franklinpapers.org/.

PCC: Papers of the Continental Congress: The Correspondence, Journals, Committee Reports, and Records of the Continental Congress (1774–1789). NARA Microfilm Publication, M247, 204 rolls. National Archives and Records Administration, College Park, MD.

PGW: The Papers of George Washington Digital Edition, Revolutionary War Series. 22+ vols. Compiled by Theodore J. Crackel et al. Charlottesville: University of Virginia Press, Rotunda, 2007. Founders Online, National Archives, http://founders.archives.gov.

PJA: Papers of John Adams. 17+ volumes. Compiled by Robert J. Taylor. Cambridge, MA: Belknap Press of Harvard University Press, 1977–. Adams Papers Digital Editions, http://www.masshist.org/publications/apde2/.

RDC: The Revolutionary Diplomatic Correspondence of the United States. 6 vols. Compiled by Frances Wharton. Library of Congress, http://memory.loc.gov/ammem/amlaw/lwdc.html.

RHM: Revista de Historia Militar [Journal of Military History]. Madrid, 1957–.

RHN: Revista de Historia Naval [Journal of Naval History]. Madrid, 1983–.

SFME: B. F. Stevens' Facsimiles of Manuscripts in European Archives Relating to America, 1773–1783: With Descriptions, Editorial Notes, Collations, References and Translations. 25 vols. Compiled by Benjamin Franklin Stevens. Wilmington, DE: Mellifont Press, 1970.

SWGW: Sparks' Writings of George Washington. 12 vols. Compiled by Jared Sparks. Boston: American Stationers' Company, John B. Russell, 1834–37.

WGW: The Writings of Washington from the Original Manuscript Sources, 1745–1799. 39 vols. Compiled by John C. Fitzpatrick. Washington, DC: Government Printing Office, 1931–44.

PRIMARY SOURCES

Adams, John. *The Works of John Adams.* Edited by Charles Francis Adams. 10 vols. Boston: Little, Brown, 1850–56.

Almanach Royal [Royal almanac]. Paris: Houry/Le Breton, 1700–1792.

America's Historical Newspapers, 1690–1922, http://www.readex.com/content/americas-historical-newspapers.

d'Arçon, Jean Le Michaud. *Mémoire pour servir à l'histoire du siège de Gibraltar, par l'auteur des batteries flottantes* [Memoir to serve as the history of the siege of Gibraltar, by the inventor of the floating batteries]. Cádiz: Chez Hermil frères, 1783.

Bachaumont, Louis Petit de. *Mémoires secrets pour servir à l'histoire de la République des Lettres en France depuis 1762 jusqu'à nos jours* [Secret memoirs serving as a history of the Republic of Letters in France from 1762 until today]. 36 vols. London: James Adamson, 1777–89.

Barham, Charles Middleton, and John Laughton, eds. *Letters and Papers of Charles, Lord Barham, Admiral of the Red Squadron, 1758–1813.* 3 vols. London: Navy Records Society, 1907–11.

Beaumarchais, Pierre-Augustin Caron de. *For the Good of Mankind: Pierre-Augustin Caron de Beaumarchais Political Correspondence Relative to the American Revolution.* Translated and edited by Antoinette Shewmake. Lanham, MD: University Press of America, 1987.

Bedford, John Russell, Fourth Duke of. *Correspondence of John, Fourth Duke of Bedford.* 3 vols. London: Longman, Brown, Green & Longmans, 1842–46.

Berthier, Louis-Alexandre. *Alexandre Berthier: Journal de la campagne d'Amérique, 10 mai 1780–26 août 1781* [Alexandre Berthier: American campaign diary, May 10, 1780–August 26, 1781]. Edited by Gilbert Chinard. Easton, PA: American Friends of Lafayette, 1952.

———. Louis-Alexandre Berthier Collection. Princeton, NJ: Princeton University Library, Department of Rare Books and Special Collections, Manuscripts Division, call number C0022.

Blanchard, Claude. *The Journal of Claude Blanchard.* Translated by William Duane, edited by Thomas Balch. Albany, NY: J. Munsell, 1876; New York: Arno Press, 1969.

Boswell, James. *The Life of Samuel Johnson.* 2 vols. London: Baldwin, 1799.

Brier, Marc A. "Tolerably Comfortable: A Field Trial of a Recreated Soldier Cabin at Valley Forge." National Park Service, Valley Forge National Historical Park, 2004.

de Broglie, Charles-François. "Plan de guerre contre l'Angleterre" [War plan against England]. ANF Marine, B4 132 folio 13 and B4 135 folio 3, 1777.

Bureau of the Census. *A Century of Population Growth.* Washington, DC: Government Printing Office, 1909.

A Century of Lawmaking for a New Nation: U.S. Congressional Documents and Debates, 1774–1875. Library of Congress, http://www.memory.loc.gov.

Chastellux, François Jean, Marquis de. *Voyages de M. le marquis de Chastellux dans l'Amérique septentrionale, dans les années 1780, 1781 & 1782* [Travels of Marquis de Chastellux in North America in the years 1780, 1781 & 1782]. Paris: Chez Prault, 1786.

———. *Travels in North-America, in the Years 1780, 1781, and 1782.* Translated by George Grieve. London: Printed for G. G. J. and J. Robinson, 1787.

Churchill, Charles Robert. *Spanish Records: List of Men under General Don Bernardo de Galvez in His Campaigns against the British, 1779–1783* (also titled *SAR Spanish Records, Spanish-English War, 1779–1783. Men under Gen. Don Bernardo de Galvez and Other Records from the Archives of the Indies, Seville, Spain*). Typed manuscript. 2 vols. Washington, DC: Daughters of the American Revolution Library, 1925.

Clausewitz, Carl von. *On War.* Translated and edited by Michael Eliot Howard and Peter Paret. Princeton, NJ: Princeton University Press, 1989.

Closen, Ludwig von. *The Revolutionary Journal of Baron Ludwig von Closen, 1780–1783.* Translated and edited by Evelyn M. Acomb. Chapel Hill: University of North Carolina Press, 1958.

Crèvecoeur, John Hector St. John (Michel Guillaume Jean) de. *Letters from an American Farmer.* London: Thomas Davies & Lockyer Davis, 1782.

Croÿ-Solre, Emmanuel, Duc de. *Journal inédit du duc de Croÿ* [Unpublished journal of the Duc de Croÿ]. 4 vols. Paris: Flammarion, 1906–7.

Custis, George Washington Parke. *Recollections and Private Memoirs of Washington, by His Adopted Son, George Washington Parke Custis.* New York: Derby & Jackson, 1860.

Des Barres, Joseph F. W. *The Atlantic Neptune.* 4 vols. London: The Admiralty, 1777.

Desjardins, Simon, and Pierre Pharoux. *Castorland Journal: An Account of the Exploration and Settlement of New York State by French Émigrés in the Years 1793 to 1797.* Translated and edited by John A. Gallucci. Ithaca, NY: Cornell University Press, 2010.

Deux-Ponts, Guillaume, Comte de. *My Campaigns in America: A Journal Kept by Count*

William de Deux-Ponts, 1780–81. Translated by Samuel A. Green. Boston: J. K. Wiggin & Wm. Parsons Lunt, 1868.

Diderot, Denis, and Jean Le Rond d'Alembert, eds. *Encyclopédie ou dictionnaire raisonné des sciences des arts et des métiers* [Encyclopedia or systematic dictionary of science, arts and industries]. 28 vols. Paris: Briasson, 1751–72.

Doniol, Henri. "Correspondance inédite de La Fayette: Lettres écrites au comte d'Estaing du 14 juillet au 20 octobre 1778" [Unpublished correspondence of La Fayette: Letters written to Comte D'Estaing from 14 July to 20 October 1778]. *Revue d'Histoire Diplomatique* [Diplomatic history review] 6 (1892): 395–448.

Du Ponceau, Peter Stephen (Pierre-Étienne), and James L. Whitehead. "The Autobiography of Peter Stephen Du Ponceau." 5 parts. *Pennsylvania Magazine of History and Biography* 63 (1939): 189–227, 311–43, 432–61; 64 (1940): 97–120, 243–69.

Faneuil, Pierre Benjamin. Last will and testament of Colonel Pierre Benjamin Faneuil, Boston, Mass., 1777. Ithaca, NY: Cornell University Library, Division of Rare and Manuscript Collections, Guide to the Legal Documents—Massachusetts, New York, Pennsylvania, 1777–1851. Collection Number: 4779, Box 1, Folder 1.

Fersen, Hans Axel von. *Lettres d'Axel de Fersen à son père, pendant la guerre de l'Indépendance d'Amérique* [Letters of Axel de Fersen to his father, duirng the War of American Independence]. Paris: Firmin-Didot et cie, 1929.

Fitzmaurice, Edmund. *Life of William Earl of Shelburne*. 2 vols. London: Macmillan, 1875–76.

Fortescue, John. *The Correspondence of King George the Third from 1760 to December 1783*. 6 vols. London: Macmillan, 1927–28.

Franklin, William Temple. *Memoirs of the Life and Writings of Benjamin Franklin*. 3 vols. London: Henry Colburn, 1818.

French Navy Information File 2011, www.defense.gouv.fr/marine.

Gaceta de Madrid. Madrid, 1697–1936.

Gazette de France. Paris, 1631–1792.

Gérard, Conrad Alexandre, and Charles Gravier, Comte de Vergennes. *Despatches and Instructions of Conrad Alexandre Gérard, 1778–1780: Correspondence of the First French Minister to the United States with the Comte de Vergennes*. With an historical introduction and notes by John J. Meng. Baltimore: Johns Hopkins University Press, 1939.

Gibbon, Edward. *Private Letters of Edward Gibbon (1753–1794)*. 2 vols. London: J. Murray, 1896.

Giunta, Mary A., ed. *Documents of the Emerging Nation: U.S. Foreign Relations, 1775–1789*. Wilmington, DE: Scholarly Resources, 1998.

de Grasse, François Joseph Paul, Comte. *Mémoire du comte de Grasse sur le combat naval du 12 avril 1782* [Memoir of the Comte de Grasse on the naval combat of April 12, 1782]. 1782.

Graves, Thomas. *The Graves Papers and Other Documents Relating to the Naval Operations of the Yorktown Campaign, July to October, 1781*. Edited by French Ensor Chadwick. New York: Navy History Society, 1916.

Grivel, Guillaume. "Balance politique." In *Encyclopédie méthodique. Économie politique et diplomatique* [Methodological encyclopedia: Political economy and diplomacy]. 4 vols. Edited by Jean-Nicolas Démeunier. Paris: Panckoucke, 1784–88.

Izerda, Stanley J., ed. *Lafayette in the Age of American Revolution: Selected Letters and Papers, 1776–1790*. 5 vols. Ithaca, NY: Cornell University Press, 1977–83.

Jay, William, ed. *The Life of John Jay*. 2 vols. New York: J. & J. Harper, 1833.

Johnson, Sherry. *Climate and Catastrophe in Cuba and the Atlantic World in the Age of Revolution*. Chapel Hill: University of North Carolina Press, 2011.

"Journal of a French Traveller in the Colonies, 1765." *American Historical Review* 26, no. 4 (July 1921): 726–47, and 27, no. 1 (October 1921): 70–89.

Lafayette, Gilbert du Motier de. *Mémoires, correspondance et manuscrits du général La Fayette, publiés par sa famille* [Memoirs, correspondence and manuscripts of General La Fayette, published by his family]. 6 vols. Paris: Fournier l'aîné, 1837–38.

———. *Memoirs, Correspondence and Manuscripts of General Lafayette*. 3 vols. London: Saunders & Otley, 1837.

Lalande, Joseph Jérôme Le Français de. *Journal d'un voyage en Angleterre: 1763* [Journal of a voyage in England, 1763]. Edited by Hélène Monod-Cassidy. Oxford: Voltaire Foundation at the Taylor Institution, 1980.

Lauzun, Armand Louis de Gontaut, Duc de. *Mémoires de M. le duc de Lauzun*. Paris: Chez Barrois l'aîné, 1822.

Lee, Richard Henry. *Life of Arthur Lee*. 2 vols. Boston: Wills & Lilly, 1829.

Lee, Richard Henry, and James Curtis Ballagh, eds. *The Letters of Richard Henry Lee*. 2 vols. New York: Macmillan, 1911–14.

Lennox, Sarah. *The Life and Letters of Lady Sarah Lennox, 1745–1826*. London: J. Murray, 1901.

Levasseur, Auguste. *Lafayette in America in 1824 and 1825: Journal of a Voyage to the United States*. Translated by Alan R. Hoffman. Manchester, NH: Lafayette Press, 2006.

Lisle, James. *The Lisle (de Lisle) Family in America*. Microfilm. Salt Lake City: Genealogical Society of Utah, 2001.

Louvre Atlas database, http://cartelen.louvre.fr/.

Mercure de France [Mercury of France]. Paris, 1672–1825.

Mercurio Historico y Politico [Historical and political mercury]. Madrid, 1738–84.

Montbarey, Alexandre Marie Léonor de Saint Mauris (prince de). *Mémoires autographes de M. le prince de Montbarey: Ministre secrétaire d'état au Département de la guerre sous Louis XVI* [Autobiography of M. the Prince of Montbarey, minister of war under Louis XVI]. 3 vols. Paris: Alexis Eymery, 1826–27.

Monteil, François-Aymar, Chevalier de. Chevalier de Monteil logbook, May 20, 1781–March 21, 1782. Ann Arbor: University of Michigan, William L. Clements Library, Manuscripts Division.

Morris, Robert. *The Papers of Robert Morris, 1781–1784*. Edited by E. James Ferguson. 9 vols. Pittsburgh: University of Pittsburgh Press, 1973–99.

Muster and Pay Rolls of the War of the Revolution, 1775–1783. New York: New-York Historical Society, 1914.

Oraison, Henri Fulque d'. "Mémoire sur l'Amirauté anglaise" [Memorandum on the English Admiralty]. ANF Marine B7 475 folio 11, 1764.

Playstowe, Philip. *The Gentleman's Guide, in His Tour through France*. London: Kearsley, 1766.

Poulin, Eugena, and Claire Quintal, eds. and trans. *"La Gazette Françoise," 1780–1781: Revolutionary America's French Newspaper*. Newport, RI: Salve Regina University, 2007.

[The] Present State of the West-Indies: Containing an Accurate Description of What Parts Are Possessed by the Several Powers in Europe. London: R. Baldwin, 1778.

Prevost, Antoine François. *Manuel lexique, ou dictionnaire portatif des mots françois* [Lexical manual, or portable French dictionary]. 2 vols. Paris: Libraires associés, 1788.

Recueil des instructions données aux ambassadeurs et ministres de France depuis les traités de

Westphalie jusqu'à la Révolution (1648–1789) [Collection of instructions given to the ambassadors of France from the Treaties of Westpahlia until the Revolution, 1648–1789]. 31+ vols. Paris: Alcan, 1884–present.

Rice, Howard C. Jr., and Anne S. K. Brown, trans. and eds. *The American Campaigns of Rochambeau's Army, 1780, 1781, 1782, 1783*. 2 vols. Princeton, NJ: Princeton University Press, 1972.

Rochambeau, Jean-Baptiste-Donatien de Vimeur, Comte de. *Mémoires militaires, historiques et politiques de Rochambeau: Ancien maréchal de France, et grand officier de la Légion d'honneur* [Military, historical and political memoirs of Rochambeau: Former marshall of France, and grand officer of the Legion of Honor]. 2 vols. Paris: Fain, 1809.

Saavedra, Francisco de. *Diario de Don Francisco de Saavedra* [Journal of Mr. Francisco de Saavedra]. Edited by Francisco Morales Padrón. Seville: Universidad de Sevilla, 2004.

———. *Journal of Don Francisco Saavedra de Sangronis during the Commission Which He Had in His Charge from 25 June 1780 until the 20th of the Same Month of 1783*. Edited by Francisco Morales Padrón; translated by Aileen Moore Topping. Gainesville: University of Florida Press, 1988.

Sandwich, John Montagu, Earl of. *The Private Papers of John, Earl of Sandwich*. 4 vols. London: Navy Records Society, 1932–38.

Savary, Jacques. *Le parfait négociant* [The perfect merchant]. Paris: Jean Guignard fils, 1675.

Scots Magazine. Edinburgh, 1739–1826.

Seeber, Edward Derbyshire, trans. *On the Threshold of Liberty: Journal of a Frenchman's Tour of the American Colonies in 1777*. Bloomington: Indiana University Press, 1959.

Shain, Barry Alan, ed. *The Declaration of Independence in Historical Context: American State Papers, Petitions, Proclamations, and Letters of the Delegates to the First National Congresses*. New Haven, CT: Yale University Press, 2014.

Shea, John D. G. *The Operations of the French Fleet under the Count de Grasse in 1781–2 as Described in Two Contemporaneous Journals*. New York: Bradford Club, 1864.

Sheftall, Mordecai. Mordecai Sheftall papers, 1777–1778. American Jewish Historical Society, New York.

Smithsonian military history collection, http://amhistory.si.edu/militaryhistory/collection/.

Stanhope, Philip Henry (Lord Mahon). *History of England*. 7 vols. Leipzig: Tauchnitz, 1853–54.

Stark, Caleb. *Memoir and Official Correspondence of Gen. John Stark*. Concord, NH: G. Parker Lyon, 1860.

Stockdale, John. *The Parliamentary Register*. 17 vols. London: T. Gillet, 1802.

Thacher, James. *A Military Journal during the American Revolutionary War, from 1775 to 1783*. Boston: Richardson & Lord, 1823.

Tornquist, Karl Gustaf. *The Naval Campaigns of Count de Grasse during the American Revolution, 1781–1783*. Translated by Amandus Johnson. Philadelphia: Swedish Colonial Society, 1942.

Tower, Charlemagne, ed. *The Marquis de La Fayette in the American Revolution: With Some Account of the Attitude of France toward the War of Independence*. 2nd ed. 2 vols. Philadelphia: J. B. Lippincott, 1901.

Uhlendorf, Bernhard A., ed. and trans. *The Siege of Charleston: Capts. Johann Ewald, Johann Hinrichs, and Maj. Gen. Johann Christoph von Huyn*. New York: Arno, 1968.

Vergennes, Charles Gravier, Comte de. *Louis XVI and the Comte de Vergennes: Correspondence, 1774–1787*. Edited by John Hardman and Munro Price. Oxford: Voltaire Foundation, 1998.

Voltaire (François-Marie Arouet). *Candide, ou l'optimisme* [Candide, or optimism]. Paris: Sirène, 1759.

———. *Siècle de Louis XV* [Louis XV's century]. 2 vols. Geneva: Cramer, 1769.

Washington, George. *The Papers of George Washington. Colonial Series*. 10 vols. Edited by William Wright Abbot and Dorothy Twohig. Charlottesville: University of Virginia Press, 1983–95.

Washington, George, and François Joseph Paul, Comte de Grasse. *Correspondence of General Washington and Comte de Grasse, 1781, August 17–November 4*. Washington, DC: Government Printing Office, 1931.

Wickham Legg, Leopold George. *British Diplomatic Instructions, 1689–1789*, vol. 7, *France, Part IV, 1745–1789*. London: Royal Historical Society, 1934.

Wilkes, John. *The Diaries of John Wilkes, 1770–1797*. Edited by Robin Eagle. Woodbridge, UK: Boydell & Brewer, 2014.

Wuibert, Antoine Felix. Correspondence, 1788–1803. MSC 156. Bucks County Historical Society, Mercer Museum Research Library, Doylestown, PA.

SECONDARY SOURCES

Abarca, Ramon E. "Bourbon 'Revanche' against England: The Balance of Power, 1763–1770." PhD dissertation, University of Notre Dame, 1965.

———. "Classical Diplomacy and Bourbon 'Revanche' Strategy, 1763–1770." *Review of Politics* 32, no. 3 (June 1970): 313–37.

Abbey, Kathryn T. "Peter Chester's Defense of the Mississippi after the Willing Raid." *Mississippi Valley Historical Review* 22, no. 1 (June 1935): 17–32.

Agay, Frédéric d'. *La Provence au service du roi (1637–1831): Officiers des vaisseaux et des galères. Dictionnaire* [Provence in the service of the king: Officers of ships and galleys. Dictionary]. 2 vols. Paris: Honoré-Champion, 2011.

Alden, Dauril. "The Marquis of Pombal and the American Revolution." *The Americas* 17, no. 4 (April 1961): 369–76.

Alden, John Richard. *The South in the Revolution, 1763–1789*. Baton Rouge: Louisiana State University Press, 1957.

Alder, Ken. "Forging the New Order: French Mass Production and the Language of the Machine Age, 1763–1815." PhD dissertation, Harvard University, 1991.

———. *Engineering the Revolution: Arms and Enlightenment in France, 1763–1815*. Chicago: University of Chicago Press, 1997.

Aldridge, Alfred Owen. "Jacques Barbeu-Dubourg, a French Disciple of Benjamin Franklin." *Proceedings of the American Philosophical Society* 95, no. 4 (August 17, 1951): 331–92.

Alsina Torrente, Juan. *Una guerra romántica 1778–1783. España, Francia e Inglaterra en la mar: Trasfondo naval de la independencia de Estados Unidos* [A romantic war, 1778–1783: Spain, France and England on the sea: The naval backdrop of the independence of the United States]. Madrid: Ministerio de Defensa, Instituto de Historia y Cultura Naval, 2006.

Ambrose, Stephen E. *Duty, Honor, Country: A History of West Point*. Baltimore: Johns Hopkins University Press, 1966.

Anderson, Fred. *Crucible of War: The Seven Years' War and the Fate of Empire in British North America, 1754–1766*. New York: Alfred A. Knopf, 2000.

Antier, Jean-Jacques. *L'Amiral de Grasse: Héros de l'Indépendance américaine* [Admiral de Grasse: Hero of American Independence]. Paris: Plon, 1965.

Arana, Marie. *Bolívar: American Liberator*. New York: Simon & Schuster, 2013.

Armillas Vicente, José A. "Ayuda secreta y deuda oculta, España y la independencia de los Estados Unidos" [Secret aid and hidden debt, Spain and the independence of the United States]. In *Norteamérica a finales del siglo XVIII: España y los Estadoes Unidos* [North America at the end of the 18th century: Spain and the United States], edited by Eduardo Garrigues López-Chicheri, 171–96. Madrid: Marcial Pons, 2008.

Armitage, David. *The Declaration of Independence: A Global History*. Cambridge, MA: Harvard University Press, 2007.

Ascoli, Peter M. "The French Press and the American Revolution: The Battle of Saratoga." In *Proceedings of the Fifth Annual Meeting of the Western Society for French History*, edited by Joyce Duncan Falk, 46–55. Santa Barbara, CA, 1978.

Augur, Helen. *The Secret War of Independence*. New York: Duell, Sloan & Pearce, 1955.

Auricchio, Laura. *The Marquis: Lafayette Reconsidered*. New York: Alfred A. Knopf, 2014.

Bagust, Harold. *The Greater Genius?: A Biography of Marc Isambard Brunel*. Hersham, Surrey: Ina Allan Publishing, 2006.

Bailyn, Bernard. *The Ideological Origins of the American Revolution*. Cambridge, MA: Belknap Press of Harvard University Press, 1967.

Balch, Thomas. *The French in America during the War of Independence of the United States, 1777–1783. A Translation of "Les Français en Amérique pendant la guerre de l'indépendance des États-Unis."* Translated by Thomas Willing Balch, Edwin Swift Balch, and Elise Willing Balch. 2 vols. Philadelphia: Porter & Coates, 1891–95.

Bancroft, George. *History of the United States from the Discovery of the Continent*. 10 vols. Boston: Little, Brown, 1834–74.

Bancroft, George, and Adolphe de Circourt. *Histoire de l'action commune de la France et de l'Amérique pour l'indépendance des États-Unis* [History of the common action of France and America for the Independence of the United States]. 3 vols. Paris: F. Vieweg, 1876.

Barber, James, and Frederick Voss. *Blessed Are the Peace Makers: A Commemoration of the 200th Anniversary of the Treaty of Paris*. Washington, DC: Smithsonian Institution Press, 1983.

Barthélemy, Édouard de. "Le Traité de Paris entre la France et l'Angleterre" [The Treaty of Paris between France and England]. *Revue des Questions Historiques* 43 (1888): 420–88.

Basurto Larrañaga, Román. "Linajes y fortunas mercantiles de Bilbao del siglo XVIII" [Lineages and fortunes in 18th century Bilbao]. *Itsas Memoria: Revista de Estudios Marítimos del País Vasco* 4 (2003): 343–56.

Batista González, Juan. *España estratégica: Guerra y diplomacia en la historia de España* [Strategic Spain: War and diplomacy in the history of Spain]. Madrid: Sílex, 2007.

Baudez, Basile, Élisabeth Maisonnier, and Emmanuel Pénicaut. *Les Hôtels de la Guerre et des Affaires Étrangères à Versailles* [The bureaus of war and foreign affairs at Versailles]. Paris, Nicolas Chaudun, 2010.

Baugh, Daniel A. *The Global Seven Years War, 1754–1763: Britain and France in a Great Power Contest*. New York: Longman, 2011.

Beatty, Joshua. "The 'French Traveller,' Patrick Henry, and the Contagion of Liberty." 2011. http://lemonadeandinformation.wordpress.com/2011/03/26/french-traveller/.

Beerman, Eric. "José Solano and the Spanish Navy at the Siege of Pensacola." In *Anglo-Spanish Confrontation on the Gulf Coast during the American Revolution,* edited by William S. Coker and Robert E. Rea, 125–44. Pensacola, FL: Gulf Coast History and Humanities Conference, 1982.

———. "The Last Battle of the American Revolution: Yorktown. No, the Bahamas!: The Spanish-American Expedition to Nassau in 1782." *The Americas* 45, no. 1 (July 1988): 79–95.

———. *España y la independencia de Estados Unidos* [Spain and the independence of the United States]. Madrid: Editorial MAPFRE, 1992.

Belhoste, Jean-François. "Les Brunel père et fils: Deux célèbres ingénieurs anglais 'Made in France'"[The Brunels father and son: Two famous British engineers made in France]. *Documents pour l'Histoire des Techniques* 19 (December 2010): 131–52.

Bell, David A. *The First Total War: Napoleon's Europe and the Birth of Modern Warfare as We Know It.* New York: Houghton Mifflin, 2007.

Bemis, Samuel Flagg. *The Hussey-Cumberland Mission and American Independence: An Essay in the Diplomacy of the American Revolution.* Princeton, NJ: Princeton University Press, 1931.

———. *The Diplomacy of the American Revolution.* Bloomington: Indiana University Press, 1957.

Bercovitch, Sacvan. *The American Jeremiad.* Madison: University of Wisconsin Press, 1978.

Berg, Scott W. *Grand Avenues: The Story of the French Visionary Who Designed Washington, D.C.* New York: Pantheon, 2007.

Bernier, Olivier. *Lafayette, Hero of Two Worlds.* New York: E. P. Dutton, 1983.

Beyls, Pascal. "Un Dauphinois dans la guerre d'Indépendance des États-Unis" [A Dauphiné resident in the War of Independence of the United States]. *Généalogie & Histoire, Revue Trimestrielle du Centre d'Études Généalogiques Rhône-Alpes* [Genealogy and History, Quarterly Journal of the Center of Genealogical Studies of Rhône-Alps], no. 129 (March 2007): 38–41.

Black, Jeremy. "The Theory of the Balance of Power in the First Half of the Eighteenth Century: A Note on Sources." *Review of International Studies* 9, no. 1 (January 1983): 55–61.

———. "Essay and Reflection: On the 'Old System' and the 'Diplomatic Revolution' of the Eighteenth Century." *International History Review* 12, no. 2 (May 1990): 301–23.

———. *War for America: The Fight for Independence, 1775–1783.* Stroud, UK: Sutton, 1991.

Blampignon, Émile-Antoine. *Le duc de Nivernais, ou un grand seigneur au XVIIIe siècle* [The Duke de Nivernais, or a nobleman of the 18th century]. Paris: Perrin, 1888.

Blanco Núñez, José María. *La Armada española en la primera mitad del siglo XVIII* [The Spanish navy in the first half of the 18th century]. Madrid: IZAR Construcciones Navales, 2001.

———. *La Armada española en la segunda mitad del siglo XVIII* [The Spanish navy in the second half of the 18th century]. Madrid: IZAR Construcciones Navales, 2004.

Blart, Louis. *Les rapports de la France et de l'Espagne après le pacte de famille jusqu'à la fin du ministère du duc de Choiseul* [The relations between France and Spain after the family compact until the end of the ministry of the Duke de Choiseul]. Paris: Alcan, 1915.

Blaufarb, Rafe. *The French Army, 1750–1820: Careers, Talent, Merit*. Manchester: Manchester University Press, 2002.

Boatner III, Mark M. *Encyclopedia of the American Revolution*. Mechanicsburg, PA: Stackpole, 1994.

Bobrick, Benson. *Angel in the Whirlwind: The Triumph of the American Revolution*. New York: Simon & Schuster, 1997.

Bodle, Wayne. "La logistique et l'Armée française en Amérique" [Logistics and the French army in America]. In *La France et l'Indépendance américaine* [France and American Independence], edited by Olivier Chaline, Philippe Bonnichon, and Charles-Philippe de Vergennes, 99–113. Paris: Presses de l'université Paris-Sorbonne, 2008.

Bonneville de Marsangy, Louis. *Le chevalier de Vergennes: Son ambassade à Constantinople* [The chevalier de Vergennes: His embassy at Constantinople]. 2 vols. Paris: E. Plon, Nourrit, 1894.

———. *Le chevalier de Vergennes: Son ambassade son ambassade en Suède, 1771–1774* [The chevalier de Vergennes: His embassy in Sweden 1771–1774]. 2 vols. Paris: E. Plon, Nourrit, 1898.

Bonsal, Stephen. *When the French Were Here*. Garden City, NY: Doubleday, Doran & Co., 1945.

Borick, Carl P. *A Gallant Defense: The Siege of Charleston, 1780*. Columbia: University of South Carolina Press, 2003.

Böttcher, Nikolaus: "Juan de Miralles: Un comerciante cubano en la guerra de independencia norteamericana" [Juan de Miralles: A Cuban businessman in the North American War of Independence]. *Anuario de Estudios Americanos* [Yearbook of American studies] 62, no. 1 (2000): 171–94.

Boudriot, Jean. *John Paul Jones and the* Bonhomme Richard: *A Reconstruction of the Ship and an Account of the Battle with HMS* Serapis. Translated by David H. Roberts. Annapolis, MD: Naval Institute Press, 1987.

Bourguet, Alfred. *Le duc de Choiseul et l'alliance espagnole* [The Duke of Choiseul and the Spanish alliance]. Paris: Librairie Plon, 1906.

Bowen, Clarence Winthrop, ed. *The History of the Centennial Celebration of the Inauguration of George Washington as First President of the United States*. New York: D. Appleton, 1892.

Brecher, Frank W. *Securing American Independence: John Jay and the French Alliance*. Westport, CT: Praeger, 2003.

Breen, Kenneth. "Graves and Hood at the Chesapeake." *The Mariner's Mirror* 66, no. 1 (1980): 53–65.

———. "Sir George Rodney and St Eustatius in the American War: A Commercial and Naval Distraction, 1775–81." *The Mariner's Mirror* 84, no. 2 (1998): 193–203.

Brown, Gerald S. "The Anglo-French Naval Crisis, 1778: A Study of Conflict in the North Cabinet." *William and Mary Quarterly,* Third Series, 13, no. 1 (January 1956): 3–25.

Brown, Martin L. *Firearms in Colonial America, 1492–1792*. Washington, DC: Smithsonian Institution, 1980.

Brumwell, Stephen. *George Washington: Gentleman Warrior*. New York: Quercus, 2012.

Buck, Rinker. *The Oregon Trail: A New American Journey*. New York: Simon & Schuster, 2015.

Buel, Richard Jr. *In Irons: Britain's Naval Supremacy and the American Revolutionary Economy*. New Haven, CT: Yale University Press, 1998.

Bunker, Nick. *An Empire on the Edge: How Britain Came to Fight America.* New York: Alfred A. Knopf, 2014.

Burstein, Andrew. *America's Jubilee: How in 1826 a Generation Remembered Fifty Years of Independence.* New York: Alfred A. Knopf, 2001.

Butterfield, Lyman Henry. "Franklin, Rush, and the Chevalier de Kermorvan: An Episode of '76." *American Philosophical Society Library Bulletin* (1946): 33–44.

Caemmerer, Hans Paul. *The Life of Pierre Charles L'Enfant.* New York: Da Capo, 1970.

Calderón Cuadrado, Reyes. *Empresarios españoles en el proceso de independencia norteamericana: La Casa Gardoqui e hijos de Bilbao* [Spanish businessmen in the process of American independence: The House of Gardoqui and Sons of Bilbao]. Madrid: Unión Editorial, 2004.

Caleo, Robert L. "'A Most Serious Wound': The Memorial of George Farragut." *Journal of East Tennessee History* 79 (2007): 63–79.

Calloway, Colin G. *The Scratch of a Pen: 1763 and the Transformation of North America.* Oxford: Oxford University Press, 2006.

Calmon-Maison, Jean Joseph Robert. *L'Amiral d'Estaing (1729–1794).* Paris: Calmann-Lévy, 1910.

Caron, François. *La guerre incomprise ou la victoire volée: Bataille de la Chesapeake, 1781* [The misunderstood war or the stolen victory: the Battle of the Chesapeake]. Vincennes: Service historique de la Marine, 1989.

Carrer, Philippe. *La Bretagne et la guerre d'Indépendance américaine* [Brittany and the War of American Independence]. Rennes: Les Portes du Large, 2005.

Carroll, Michael R. "New Hampshire Marked French Revolutionary War Muskets." *Bulletin of the American Society of Arms Collectors* 100 (September 2009): 35–46.

Cash, Arthur. *John Wilkes: The Scandalous Father of Civil Liberty.* New Haven, CT: Yale University Press, 2008.

Castex, Raoul. *Les idées militaires de la marine du XVIIIme siècle. De Ruyter à Suffren* [Naval strategic thought of the 18th century, from Ruyter to Suffren]. Paris: L. Fournier, 1911.

Castries, René de La Croix, Duc de. *La France et l'Indépendance américaine: Le livre du bicentenaire de l'Indépendance* [France and American Independence: The book of the bicentennial of the Independence]. Paris: Perrin, 1975.

Caughey, John Walton. "The Panis Mission to Pensacola, 1778." *Hispanic American Historical Review* 10, no. 4 (November 1930): 480–89.

———. *Bernardo de Gálvez in Louisiana, 1776–1783.* Berkeley: University of California Press, 1934.

Cavaliero, Roderick. *Admiral Satan: The Life and Campaigns of Suffren.* London: I. B. Tauris, 1994.

Censer, Jack. *The French Press in the Age of Enlightenment.* New York: Routledge, 2002.

Chaline, Olivier, Philippe Bonnichon, and Charles-Philippe de Vergennes, eds. *La France et l'Indépendance américaine* [France and American Independence]. Paris: Presses de l'université Paris-Sorbonne, 2008.

———. *Les marines de la guerre d'Indépendance américaine, 1763–1783: I. L'instrument naval* [The navies of the War of American Independence, 1763–1783: I. The naval apparatus]. Paris: Presses de l'université Paris-Sorbonne, 2013.

Chapelle, Howard. *The Search for Speed under Sail, 1700–1855.* New York: Bonanza Books, 1967.

Chapin, Seymour L. "A Legendary *Bon Mot*? Franklin's 'What Is the Good of a Newborn

Baby?'" *Proceedings of the American Philosophical Society* 129, no. 3 (September 1985): 278–90.

Chartrand, René. *Louis XV's Army*. 5 vols. London: Osprey, 1996–98.

Chartrand, René, and Francis Back. *The French Army in the American War of Independence*. London: Osprey, 1991.

Chartrand, René, and Patrice Courcelle. *Gibraltar, 1779–83: The Great Siege*. London: Osprey, 2008.

Chartrand, René, and David Rickman. *The Spanish Army in North America, 1700–1793*. London: Osprey, 2011.

Chatel de Brancion, Laurence, and Patrick Villiers. *La Fayette: Rêver la gloire* [La Fayette: To dream of glory]. Saint-Rémy-en-L'Eau, France: Éditions Monelle Hayot, 2013.

Chávez, Thomas E. *Spain and the Independence of the United States: An Intrinsic Gift*. Albuquerque: University of New Mexico Press, 2002.

Chevalier, Louis Édouard. *Histoire de la marine française pendant la guerre de l'indépendance américaine* [History of the French Navy during the War of American Independence]. Paris: Hachette, 1877.

Churchill, Robert H. "Gun Ownership in Early America: A Survey of Manuscript Militia Returns." *William and Mary Quarterly,* Third Series, 60, no. 3 (July 2003): 615–42.

Cock, Randolph. "The Finest Invention in the World: The Royal Navy's Early Trials of Copper Sheathing, 1708–1770." *The Mariner's Mirror* 87, no. 4 (2001): 446–59.

Cohen, Sheldon S. *Yankee Sailors in British Gaols: Prisoners of War at Forton and Mill, 1777–1783*. Newark: University of Delaware Press, 1995.

Coker, William S., and Robert E. Rea, eds. *Anglo-Spanish Confrontation on the Gulf Coast during the American Revolution*. Pensacola, FL: Gulf Coast History and Humanities Conference, 1982.

Comer, Douglas C. "Phase I and II Archaeological Investigations at the Rochambeau Campsite in the BLM [Bureau of Land Management] Meadowood Special Recreation Management Area." Lorton, VA: U.S. Department of the Interior, Bureau of Land Management, 2012.

———, ed. *The Archaeology of Interdependence: European Involvement in the Development of a Sovereign United States*. New York: Springer, 2013.

Corbett, Julian S. *Some Principles of Maritime Strategy*. London: Longmans, Green, 1918.

Corral, José del. *La Gran Vía: Historia de una calle* [The great road: History of a street]. Madrid: Sílex, 2002.

Corvisier, André. *Armies and Societies in Europe, 1494–1789*. Translated by Abigail T. Siddall. Bloomington: Indiana University Press, 1979.

Corwin, Edward S. *French Policy and the American Alliance of 1778*. Princeton, NJ: Princeton University Press, 1916.

Crawford, Michael J. "The Privateering Debate in Revolutionary America." *The Northern Mariner/Le Marin du Nord* 11, no. 3 (July 2011): 219–34.

———. "The Joint Allied Operation at Rhode Island, 1778." In *New Interpretations in Naval History: Selected Papers from the Ninth Naval History Symposium,* edited by William R. Roberts, 227–42. Annapolis, MD: Naval Institute Press, 1991.

Crout, Robert R. "The Diplomacy of Trade: The Influence of Commercial Considerations on French Involvement in the Angloamerican War of Independence 1775–78." PhD dissertation, University of Georgia, 1977.

Cummins, Light Townsend. *Spanish Observers and the American Revolution, 1775–1783*. Baton Rouge: Louisiana State University Press, 1991.

Cunat, Charles. *L'histoire de Bailli de Suffren* [The history of Bailli de Suffren]. Rennes: Marteville et Lefas, 1852.

Curtis III, George M. "The Goodrich Family and the Revolution in Virginia, 1774–1776." *Virginia Magazine of History and Biography* 84, no. 1 (January 1976): 49–74.

Damrosch, Leo. *Jean-Jacques Rousseau: Restless Genius*. New York: Houghton Mifflin Harcourt, 2007.

Danvila y Collado, Manuel. *Reinado de Carlos III* [Reign of Carlos III]. 6 vols. Madrid: El Progreso Editorial, 1894.

Das, Sudipta. *Myths and Realities of French Imperialism in India, 1763–1783*. New York: Peter Lang, 1992.

———. *De Broglie's Armada: A Plan for the Invasion of England, 1765–1777*. Lanham, MD: University Press of America, 2009.

Daubigny, Eugène Théodore. *Choiseul et la France d'outre-mer après le traité de Paris: Étude sur la politique coloniale au XVIIIe siècle* [Choiseul and the French colonies after the Treaty of Paris: A study in 18th century colonial politics]. Paris: Hachette, 1892.

Davis, Robert P. *Where a Man Can Go: Major General William Phillips, British Royal Artillery, 1731–1781*. Westport, CT: Greenwood Press, 1999.

Dawson, Warrington. "Les 2112 Français morts aux États-Unis de 1777 à 1783 en combattant pour l'indépendance américaine" [The 2,112 French who died in the United States from 1777–1783 in fighting for American independence]. *Journal de la Société des Américanistes* 28, no. 1 (1936): 1–154.

Deconde, Alexander. "Historians, the War of American Independence, and the Persistence of the Exceptionalist Ideal." *International History Review* 5, no. 3 (August 1983): 399–430.

Demerliac, Alain. *La marine de Louis XVI: Nomenclature des navires français de 1774 à 1792* [Louis XVI's Navy: Nomenclature of French ships from 1774 to 1792]. Nice: Éditions Omega, 1996.

Domínguez Ortiz, Antonio. *Carlos III y la España de la Ilustración* [Carlos III and Enlightenment Spain]. Madrid: Alianza Editorial, 1988.

Droz, Joseph. *Histoire du règne de Louis XVI* [History of the reign of Louis XVI]. Brussels: A. Wahlen, 1839.

Dull, Jonathan R. *The French Navy and American Independence: A Study of Arms and Diplomacy, 1774–1787*. Princeton, NJ: Princeton University Press, 1975.

———. *A Diplomatic History of the American Revolution*. New Haven, CT: Yale University Press, 1985.

———. *The French Navy and the Seven Years' War*. Lincoln: University of Nebraska Press, 2005.

———. *The Age of the Ship of the Line: The British and French Navies, 1650–1815*. Barnsley, UK: Seaforth Publishing, 2009.

———. *The Miracle of American Independence: Twenty Ways Things Could Have Turned Out Differently*. Lincoln: University of Nebraska Press, 2015.

Dupuy, Richard Ernest, and Trevor N. Dupuy. *An Outline History of the American Revolution*. New York: Harper & Row, 1975.

Dupuy, Richard Ernest, Gay Hammerman, and Grace P. Hayes. *The American Revolution: A Global War*. New York: David McKay Co., 1977.

Dussert, Gilles. *La machinerie Beaumarchais*. Paris: Riveneuve Éditions, 2012.

DuVal, Kathleen. *Independence Lost: Lives on the Edge of the American Revolution*. New York: Random House, 2015.

Echeverria, Durand, and Orville T. Murphy. "The American Revolutionary Army: A French Estimate in 1777." *Military Affairs* 27 (Spring/Winter 1963): 2–6, 155–61.

Edler, Friedrich. *The Dutch Republic and the American Revolution*. Baltimore: Johns Hopkins University Press, 1911.

Ellis, Joseph J. *Revolutionary Summer: The Birth of American Independence*. New York: Alfred A. Knopf, 2013.

Ellis, Joseph J., ed. *What Did the Declaration Declare?* Boston: Bedford St. Martin's, 1999.

Elting, John R. *The Battles of Saratoga*. Monmouth Beach, NJ: Philip Freneau Press, 1977.

Emmanuelli, Loliannette. "Spanish Diplomatic Policy and Contribution to the United States Independence, 1775–1783." PhD dissertation, University of Massachusetts, 1990.

Enthoven, Victor. "'That Abominable Nest of Pirates': St. Eustatius and the North Americans, 1680–1780." *Early American Studies: An Interdisciplinary Journal* 10, no. 2 (Spring 2012): 239–301.

———. "'Sir, I Have Not Yet Begun to Fight!'": John Paul Jones' Friends in the Dutch Republic, 1779–1780." Paper presented at the conference *The Marquis de Lafayette and the European Friends of the American Revolution,* Mount Vernon, VA, June 13–15, 2015.

Evans, Joan. "The Embassy of the 4th Duke of Bedford to Paris, 1762–1763." *Archaeological Journal* 113 (1956): 137–56.

Everest, Allan S. *Moses Hazen and the Canadian Refugees in the American Revolution*. Syracuse, NY: Syracuse University Press, 1976.

Ferguson, Elmer James. *The Power of the Purse: A History of American Public Finance, 1776–1790*. Chapel Hill: University of North Carolina Press, 1961.

Ferling, John. *Almost a Miracle: The American Victory in the War of Independence*. Oxford: Oxford University Press, 2009.

———. *Independence: The Struggle to Set America Free*. New York: Bloomsbury, 2011.

Fernández Duro, Cesáreo. *Armada española desde la unión de los Reinos de Castilla y Aragón* [The Spanish navy from the union of the kingdoms of Castille and Aragon]. 9 vols. Madrid: Imprenta Real, 1894–1903.

Fernández González, Francisco. "El bergantín *Galveztown:* Reconstitución del barco de 1781" [The brigantine *Galveztown:* Reconstruction of the ship of 1781]. *Revista de Historia Naval* 118 (2012): 9–42.

Ferreiro, Larrie D. *Ships and Science: The Birth of Naval Architecture in the Scientific Revolution, 1600–1800*. Cambridge, MA: MIT Press, 2007.

———. "Development and Tactical Advantages of Copper Sheathing of French, British and Spanish Ships during the War of American Independence." *Les Marines de la guerre d'Indépendance américaine: Aspects opérationnels* [Navies of the War of American Independence: Operational aspects]. Paris: École militaire, February 7–8, 2013.

Flassan, Gaétan de Raxis de. *Histoire générale et raisonnée de la diplomatie française* [General and rational history of French diplomacy]. 6 vols. Paris: Lenormant, 1809.

Fleming, Thomas. *Washington's Secret War: The Hidden History of Valley Forge*. New York: HarperCollins, 2005.

———. *The Perils of Peace: America's Struggle for Survival after Yorktown*. New York: Collins, 2007.

Floyd, Troy S. *The Anglo-Spanish Struggle for Mosquita*. Albuquerque: University of New Mexico Press, 1967.

Ford, Worthington C. "Defences of Philadelphia in 1777." *Pennsylvania Magazine of History and Biography* 18–21 (1894–96).

Freeman, Douglas Southall. *George Washington: A Biography*. 7 vols. New York: Charles Scribner's Sons, 1948–57.

Furstenberg, François. *When the United States Spoke French: Five Refugees Who Shaped a Nation*. New York: Penguin Press, 2014.

Gallagher, Mary A. Y. "Private Interest and the Public Good: Settling the Score for the Morris-Holker Business Relationship, 1778–1790." *Pennsylvania History* 69, no. 2 (Spring 2002): 179–209.

García Diego, Paulino. *Jano en Hispania: Una aproximación a la figura y obra de Jerónimo Grimaldi (1739–1784)* [Janus in Spain: An approach to the life and work of Jerónimo Grimaldi, 1739–1784]. Madrid: CSIC, 2014.

García Melero, Luis Angel. *La independencia de los Estados Unidos de Norteamérica a través de la prensa española: "Gaceta de Madrid y Mercurio" histórico y político: Los precedentes 1763–1776* [The Independence of the United States according the the Spanish press: *Gaceta de Madrid* y *Mercurio histórico y político*; precedents 1763–1776]. Madrid: Ministerio de Asuntos Exteriores, Dirección General de Relaciones Culturales, 1977.

Gardiner, Asa Bird. *The Order of the Cincinnati in France*. Providence: Rhode Island State Society of the Cincinnati, 1905.

Gardiner, Robert, ed. *Navies and the American Revolution, 1775–1783*. Annapolis, MD: Naval Institute Press, 1996.

Garteiz-Aurrecoa, Javier Divar. "El embajador Don Diego María de Gardoqui y la independencia de los EE.UU" [Ambassador Diego María de Gardoqui and the Independence of the United States]. *JADO: Boletín de la Academia Vasca de Derecho* 9, no. 20 (December 2010): 183–99.

Gil Aguado, Iago. "Francisco Gil y Lemos: Marino, virrey y ministro: Una vida al servicio de la Monarquía española" [Francisco Gil y Lemos: Sailor, viceroy and minster: A life in the service of the Spanish monarchy]. PhD thesis, UNED (Madrid), 2012.

Gilje, Paul A. "Ideology and Interest: Free Trade, the League of Armed Neutrality, and the American Revolution." Paper presented at the conference *The Marquis de Lafayette and the European Friends of the American Revolution,* Mount Vernon, VA, June 13–15, 2015.

Gill, Harold B., Jr. "Dohicky's Folly." *Colonial Williamsburg: The Journal of the Colonial Willamsburg Foundation* 15, no. 4 (Summer 1993): 44–46.

Gilmer, Albert Hatton. "Lafayette, We Are Here!" Manuscript, Lafayette, We Are Here! Collection, 1917–1951, Folder 1, Skillman Library, Lafayette College, Easton, PA.

Gipson, Lawrence Henry. *The British Empire before the American Revolution*. 15 vols. New York: Alfred A. Knopf, 1939–70.

Glascock, Melvin Bruce. "New Spain and the War for America, 1779–1783." PhD dissertation, Louisiana State University, 1969.

Glete, Jan. *Navies and Nations: Warships, Navies and State Building in Europe and America, 1500–1860*. 2 vols. Stockholm: Academitryck AB Edsbruk, 1993.

Gold, Robert L. "Governor Bernardo de Gálvez and Spanish Espionage in Pensacola, 1777." In *The Spanish in the Mississippi Valley, 1762–1804,* edited by John Francis McDermott, 87–99. Urbana: University of Illinois Press, 1974.

Gordon, Robert B. *American Iron, 1607–1900*. Baltimore: Johns Hopkins University Press, 1996.

Gottschalk, Louis. *Lafayette in America*. Arveyres, France: L'Esprit de Lafayette Society, 1975.

Grainger, John. *The Battle of Yorktown, 1781: A Reassessment*. Woodbridge, UK: Boydell & Brewer, 2005.

Granet, Solange. *Images de Paris: La place de la Concorde*. Paris: Gallimard, 1963.

Greene, Jerome A. *The Guns of Independence: The Siege of Yorktown, 1781*. New York: Savas Beattie, 2009.

Greenfeld, Liah. *Nationalism: Five Roads to Modernity*. Cambridge, MA: Harvard University Press, 1992.

Grieder, Josephine. *Anglomania in France, 1740–1789: Fact, Fiction, and Political Discourse*. Geneva: Librairie Droz, 1985.

Gutiérrez-Steinkamp, Martha. *Spain: The Forgotten Alliance. Independence of the United States*. CreateSpace, 2013.

Haarmann, Albert W. "The Spanish Conquest of British West Florida, 1779–1781." *Florida Historical Quarterly* 39, no. 2 (October 1960): 107–34.

Hamon, Joseph. *Le chevalier de Bonvouloir, premier émissaire secret de la France auprès du Congrès de Philadelphie avant l'indépendance américaine* [The chevalier de Bonvouloir, first secret emissary from France as seen by the Philadelphia Congress before American Independence]. Paris: Jouve, 1953.

Harbron, John D. *Trafalgar and the Spanish Navy*. Annapolis, MD: Naval Institute Press, 1988.

Harding, Richard. *Amphibious Warfare in the Eighteenth Century: The British Expedition to the West Indies, 1740–1742*. Woodbridge, UK: Boydell & Brewer, 1991.

Hardman, John. *Louis XVI*. New Haven, CT: Yale University Press, 1993.

———. *French Politics, 1774–1789: From the Accession of Louis XVI to the Fall of the Bastille*. London: Longman, 1995.

Harlow, Ralph V. "Aspects of Revolutionary Finance, 1775–1783." *American Historical Review* 35, no. 1 (October 1929): 46–68.

Harris, Robert D. "French Finances and the American War, 1777–1783." *Journal of Modern History* 48, no. 2 (June 1976): 233–58.

———. *Necker: Reform Statesman of the Ancien Régime*. Berkeley: University of California Press, 1979.

Harsanyi, Doina Pasca. *Lessons from America: Liberal French Nobles in Exile, 1793–1798*. University Park: Pennsylvania State University Press, 2010.

Hatch, Louis Clinton. *The Administration of the American Revolutionary Army*. New York: Longmans, Green & Co., 1904.

Hattendorf, John B. *Newport, the French Navy and American Independence*. Newport, RI: Redwood Press, 2005.

———. "The Idea of a 'Fleet in Being' in Historical Perspective." *Naval War College Review* 26, no. 1 (Winter 2014): 43–61.

Haudrère, Philippe. "La Révolution de l'Inde n'aura pas lieu" [The Indian Revolution will not happen]. In *La France et l'Indépendance américaine* [France and American Independence], edited by Olivier Chaline, Philippe Bonnichon, and Charles-Philippe de Vergennes, 153–68. Paris: Presses de l'université Paris-Sorbonne, 2008.

Hedges, James B. *The Browns of Providence Plantations: The Colonial Years*. Providence, RI: Brown University Press, 1968.

Henderson, H. James. "Congressional Factionalism and the Attempt to Recall Benjamin Franklin." *William and Mary Quarterly* 27, no. 2 (April 1970): 246–67.

———. *Party Politics in the Continental Congress.* New York: McGraw-Hill, 1974.

Hernández Franco, Juan. "El gobierno español ante la independencia de los Estados Unidos. Gestión de Floridablanca, 1777–1783" [The Spanish government confronted with the independence of the United States: The administration of Floridablanca, 1777–1783]. *Anales de Historia Contemporánea* [Annals of contemporary history] 8 (1991): 163–85.

———. *Aspectos de la política exterior de España en la época de Floridablanca* [Aspects of Spain's external politics in the era of Floridablanca]. Murcia: Real Academia Alfonso X El Sabio, 1992.

Holmes, Jack D. L. "French and Spanish Military Units in the 1781 Pensacola Campaign." In *Anglo-Spanish Confrontation on the Gulf Coast during the American Revolution,* edited by William S. Coker and Robert E. Rea, 145–57. Pensacola, FL: Gulf Coast History and Humanities Conference, 1982.

Hore, Peter. *Nelson's Band of Brothers: Lives and Memorials.* Barnsley, UK: Seaforth Publishing, 2015.

Hough, Granville W. and Nancy C. Hough. *Spanish Borderland Studies.* 8 vols. Midway City, CA: SHHAR Press, 1998–2001.

Hounshell, David A. *From the American System to Mass Production, 1800–1932: The Development of Manufacturing Technology in the United States.* Baltimore: Johns Hopkins University Press, 1984.

Hudson, Ruth S. *The Minister from France: Conrad-Alexandre Gerard, 1729–1790.* Euclid, OH: Lutz, 1994.

Huibrechts, Marion. "Swampin' Guns and Stabbing Irons: The Austrian Netherlands, Liège Arms and the American Revolution, 1770–1783." PhD dissertation, Catholic University of Leuven, 2009.

Hull, Anthony. *Charles III and the Revival of Spain.* Washington, DC: University Press of America, 1980.

Hünemörder, Markus. *The Society of the Cincinnati: Conspiracy and Distrust in Early America.* New York: Berghahn Books, 2006.

Imbeault, Sophie, Denis Vaugeois, and Laurent Veyssière. *1763: Le traité de Paris bouleverse l'Amérique* [1763: The Treaty of Paris turns America upside down]. Québec: Septentrion, 2013.

James, James Alton. "Spanish Influence in the West during the American Revolution." *Mississippi Valley Historical Review* 4, no. 2 (September 1917), 193–208.

———. *Oliver Pollock: The Life and Times of an Unknown Patriot.* New York: D. Appleton–Century Company, 1937.

Jameson, John Franklin. "St. Eustatius in the American Revolution." *American Historical Review* 8, no. 4 (July 1903): 683–708.

Johnson, William. *Sketches of the Life and Correspondence of Nathanael Greene, Major General of the Armies of the United States, in the War of the Revolution.* 2 vols. Charleston, SC: A. E. Miller, 1822.

Jones, E. Alfred. "The American Regiment in the Carthagena Expedition." *Virginia Magazine of History and Biography* 30, no. 1 (January 1922): 1–20.

Jouve, Daniel, Alice H. Jouve, and Alvin Grossman. *Paris: Birthplace of the U.S.A.: A Walking Guide for the American Patriot.* Paris: Gründ, 1995.

Juan-García Aguado, José María de. *José Romero Fernández de Landa: Un ingeniero de marina en el siglo XVIII* [José Romero Fernández de Landa: A naval engineer in the 18th century]. La Coruña: Universidade da Coruña, 1998.

Kagan, Robert. *Dangerous Nation*. New York: Alfred A. Knopf, 2006.

Kajencki, Francis Casimir. *Thaddeus Kosciuszko: Military Engineer of the American Revolution*. El Paso, TX: Southwest Polonia Press, 1998.

———. *Casimir Pulaski, Cavalry Commander of the American Revolution*. El Paso, TX: Southwest Polonia Press, 2001.

———. *The Pulaski Legion in the American Revolution*. El Paso, TX: Southwest Polonia Press, 2004.

Kalbach, Robert, and Jean-Luc Gireaud. L'Hermione *au vent de la Liberté, 1780–1990 . . .* [*Hermione* before the winds of freedom, 1780–1990 . . .] La Roche-Rigault: Éditions en marge, 1999.

Kapp, Friedrich. *The Life of John Kalb, Major-General in the Revolutionary Army*. New York: Henry Holt, 1884.

Kates, Gary. *Monsieur d'Eon Is a Woman: A Tale of Political Intrigue and Sexual Masquerade*. New York: Basic Books, 1995.

Keeding, Ekkehart. *Surge la nación. La Ilustración en la Audiencia de Quito (1725–1812)* [Emerging nation: The Enlightenment in the Audiencia of Quito]. Quito: Banco Central del Ecuador, 2005.

Kelly, Jack. *Band of Giants: The Amateur Soldiers Who Won America's Independence*. New York: Palgrave Macmillan, 2014.

Kennedy, Roger G. *Orders from France: The Americans and the French in a Revolutionary World, 1780–1820*. New York: Alfred A. Knopf, 1989.

Kennett, Lee. *The French Forces in America, 1780–1783*. Westport, CT: Greenwood Press, 1977.

Ketcham, Ralph. *James Madison: A Biography*. Charlottesville: University of Virginia Press, 1990.

Ketchum, Richard M. *Saratoga: Turning Point of America's Revolutionary War*. New York: Henry Holt, 1999.

———. *Victory at Yorktown: The Campaign That Won the Revolution*. New York: Henry Holt, 2004.

Kilbourne, John D. *Virtutis Praemium: The Men Who Founded the State Society of the Cincinnati of Pennsylvania*. 2 vols. Rockport, ME: Picton Press, 1998.

Kite, Elizabeth S. "How the Declaration of Independence Reached Europe." *Daughters of the American Revolution Magazine* 62, no. 5 (July 1928): 405–13.

———. *Brigadier-General Louis Lebègue Duportail, Commandant of Engineers in the Continental Army, 1777–1783*. Baltimore: Johns Hopkins University Press, 1933.

Klein, Charles Armand. *Mais qui est le bailli de Suffren Saint-Tropez?* [But who is the Bailli de Suffren Saint-Tropez?]. Barbentane, France: Equinoxe, 2000.

Knight, Roger J. B. "The Royal Navy's Recovery after the Early Phase of the American Revolutionary War." In *The Aftermath of Defeat: Societies, Armed Forces, and the Challenge of Recovery*, edited by George J Andreopoulos and Harold E. Selesky, 10–25. New Haven, CT: Yale University Press, 1994.

Knox, Dudley W. *The Naval Genius of George Washington*. Boston: Houghton Mifflin, 1932.

Kohn, George C. *Encyclopedia of Plague and Pestilence: From Ancient Times to the Present*. New York: Facts on File, 2008.

Kuethe, Allan F., and Kenneth F. Andrien. *The Spanish Atlantic World in the Eighteenth Century: War and the Bourbon Reforms, 1713–1796*. Cambridge: Cambridge University Press, 2014.

Labourdette, Jean-François. "Vergennes et le Portugal, 1774–1787" [Vergennes and Portugal, 1774–1787]. In *Histoire du Portugal, histoire européenne* [Portuguese history, European history], 175–201. Paris: Centre Cultural Portuguese, 1987.

———. *Vergennes: Ministre principal de Louis XVI* [Vergennes: Principal minister of Louis XVI]. Paris: Desjonquères, 1990.

Lacour-Gayet, Georges. "La campagne navale de La Manche en 1779" [The naval campaign in the Channel of 1779]. *Revue Maritime* 150 (July 1901): 1629–73.

———. *La marine militaire de la France sous le règne de Louis XV* [The French navy under the reign of Louis XV]. Paris: Honoré Champion, 1902.

———. *La marine militaire de la France sous le règne de Louis XVI* [The French navy under the reign of Louis XVI]. Paris: Honoré Champion, 1905.

La Jonquière, Christian de. *Les marins français sous Louis XVI: Guerre d'Indépendance américaine* [French sailors under Louis XVI: The War of American Independence]. Issy-les-Moulineaux: Muller, 1996.

Lambert, Andrew. *Nelson: Britannia's God of War.* London: Faber & Faber, 2004.

Lamikiz, Xabier. *Trade and Trust in the Eighteenth-Century Atlantic World: Spanish Merchants and Their Overseas Networks.* Woodbridge, UK: Boydell & Brewer, 2013.

Lancho Rodríguez, José María. "La ayuda financiera española a la independencia de EE.UU" [Spanish financial aid to the independence of the United States]. In *España y la independencia norteamericana* [Spain and American Independence], edited by the Instituto de Historia y cultura naval, 101–18. 44th Conference, October 2014, Cuaderno monográfico 70. Madrid: Ministerio de Defensa, 2015.

Langins, Jānis. *Conserving the Enlightenment: French Military Engineering from Vauban to the Revolution.* Cambridge, MA: MIT Press, 2004.

Larrabee Harold A. "A Neglected French Collaborator in the Victory of Yorktown, Claude-Anne, Marquis de Saint-Simon (1740–1819)." *Journal de la Société des Américanistes* 24, no. 2 (1932): 245–57.

———. *Decision at the Chesapeake.* New York: Clarkson N. Potter, 1964.

Lasser, Joseph R. *The Coins of Colonial America: World Trade Coins of the Seventeenth and Eighteenth Centuries.* Williamsburg, VA: Colonial Williamsburg Foundation, 1997.

Lasseray, André. *Les Français sous les Treize Étoiles, 1775–1783* [The French under the Thirteen Stars]. 2 vols. Paris: Désiré Janvier, 1935.

Lawrence, Alexander A. *Storm over Savannah: The Story of Count d'Estaing and the Siege of the Town in 1779.* Athens: University of Georgia Press, 1951.

Lemineur, Jean-Claude, and Patrick Villiers. *L'Hermione, frégate de 12* [*Hermione,* 12-Pounder frigate]. Nice: Ancre, 2015. English-language edition: *Hermione, Frigate of the American War of Independence, 1779–1793.* Nice: Ancre, 2016.

Lengel, Edward G. *General George Washington: A Military Life.* New York: Random House, 2005.

Le Pottier, Serge. *Duportail ou le génie de George Washington* [Duportail, or the engineering genius of George Washington]. Paris: Economica, 2011.

Lever, Évelyne. *Louis XVI.* Paris: Fayard, 1985.

Lever, Maurice. *Pierre-Augustin Caron de Beaumarchais.* 3 vols. Paris: Fayard, 1999–2004.

———. *Beaumarchais: A Biography.* Translated by Susan Emanuel. New York: Farrar, Straus & Giroux, 2009.

Lewis, Charles Lee. *Admiral de Grasse and American Independence.* Annapolis, MD: Naval Institute Press, 1945.

Lewis, James A. "New Spain during the American Revolution, 1779–1783: A Viceroyalty at War." PhD dissertation, Duke University, 1975.

———. *Neptune's Militia: The Frigate* South Carolina *during the American Revolution.* Kent, OH: Kent State University Press, 1999.

Lewis, James H. "Las Damas de la Havana, El Precursor, and Francisco de Saavedra: A Note on the Spanish Participation in the Battle of Yorktown." *The Americas* 37 (July 1980): 83–99.

Library of Congress. *The Impact of the American Revolution Abroad: Papers Presented at the Fourth Symposium, May 8 and 9, 1975.* Washington, DC, 1976.

Liell, Scott. *46 Pages: Thomas Paine, "Common Sense," and the Turning Point to American Independence.* Philadelphia: Running Press, 2003.

Lindert, Peter H., and Jeffrey G. Williamson. "American Incomes before and after the Revolution." *Journal of Economic History* 73, no. 3 (September 2013): 725–64.

Lindgren, James, and Justin L. Heather. "Counting Guns in Early America." *William and Mary Law Review* 43, no. 5 (2002): 1777–1842.

Lockhart, Paul. *The Drillmaster of Valley Forge: The Baron de Steuben and the Making of the American Army.* New York: HarperCollins, 2008.

López-Chicheri, Eduardo Garrigues, ed. *Norteamérica a finales del siglo XVIII: España y los Estados Unidos* [North America at the end of the 18th century: Spain and the United States]. Madrid: Marcial Pons, 2008.

López-Cordón, María Victoria. "Administración y política en el siglo XVIII: Las secretarías del despacho" [Administration and politics in the 18th century: The departments of state]. *Chronica Nova* 22 (1995): 185–209.

Louis, William Roger, ed. *The Oxford History of the British Empire.* 5 vols. Oxford: Oxford University Press, 1998–99.

Lucas, Stephen E. "The 'Plakkaat van Verlatinge': A Neglected Model for the American Declaration of Independence." In *Connecting Cultures: The Netherlands in Five Centuries of Transatlantic Exchange,* edited by Rosemarijn Hofte and Johanna C. Kardux, 187–207. Amsterdam: VU University Press, 1994.

Lumpkin, Henry. *From Savannah to Yorktown: The American Revolution in the South.* Columbia: University of South Carolina Press, 1981.

Luraschi, Christophe. *Conrad-Alexandre Gérard (1729–1790): Artisan de l'indépendance américaine* [Conrad-Alexandre Gérard (1729–1790): craftsman of the American Independence]. Biarritz: Séguier, 2008.

Lüthy, Herbert. *La banque protestante en France, de la révocation de l'Édit de Nantes à la Révolution* [The Protestant Bank in France, from the revocation of the Edict of Nantes to the Revolution]. Paris: SEVPEN, 1961.

Luzader, John. *Saratoga: A Military History of the Decisive Campaign of the American Revolution.* New York: Savas Beatie, 2010.

Lydon, James G. *Fish and Flour for Gold, 1600–1800.* Philadelphia: Library Company of Philadelphia, 2008.

Lyons, Renée Critcher. *Foreign-Born American Patriots: Sixteen Volunteer Leaders in the Revolutionary War.* Jefferson, NC: McFarland & Co., 2013.

Maass, John R. *The Road to Yorktown: Jefferson, Lafayette and the British Invasion of Virginia.* Charleston, SC: History Press, 2015.

McBurney, Christian N. *The Rhode Island Campaign: The First French and American Operation in the Revolutionary War.* Yardley, PA: Westholme Publishing, 2011.

McCadden, Helen Matzke. "Juan de Miralles and the American Revolution." *The Americas* 29, no. 3 (January 1973): 359–75.

McCullough, David. *John Adams.* New York: Simon & Schuster, 2001.

———. *1776.* New York: Simon & Schuster, 2005.

McCusker, John J. "British Mercantilist Policies and the American Colonies." In *The Cambridge Economic History of the United States,* vol. 1, *The Colonial Era,* edited by Stanley L. Engerman and Robert E. Gallman, 337–62. Cambridge: Cambridge University Press, 1996.

McDonald, Robert M. S., ed. *Thomas Jefferson's Military Academy: Founding West Point.* Charlottesville: University of Virginia Press, 2004.

McFarlane, Anthony. *War and Independence in Spanish America.* New York: Routledge, 2014.

McGee, Peter R. "The French Victory in the Battle of the Chesapeake: The Emerging French Perspective." Honors paper, U.S. Naval Academy, 2014.

McGuffie, Tom Henderson. *The Siege of Gibraltar, 1779–1783.* London: B. T. Batsford, 1965.

Mackesy, Piers. *The War for America, 1775–1783.* Cambridge, MA: Harvard University Press, 1964.

McLaughlin, Mark G., and Christopher Warner. *The Wild Geese: The Irish Brigades of France and Spain.* London: Osprey, 1980.

Madariaga, Isabel de. *Britain, Russia and the Armed Neutrality of 1780.* London: Hollis & Carter, 1962.

Magnin, Frédéric. *Mottin de La Balme: Cavalier des deux mondes et de la liberté* [Mottin de La Balme: Knight of the two worlds and of liberty]. Paris: L'Hartmattan, 2005.

Magra, Christopher P. *The Fisherman's Cause: Atlantic Commerce and Maritime Dimensions of the American Revolution.* Cambridge: Cambridge University Press, 2009.

Mahan, Alfred Thayer. *The Major Operations of the Navies in the War of American Independence.* Boston: Little, Brown, 1913.

Maier, Pauline. *American Scripture: Making the Declaration of Independence.* New York: Alfred A. Knopf, 1997.

Manceron, Claude. *The Age of the French Revolution.* Vol. 1, *Twilight of the Old Order.* Translated by Patricia Wolf. New York: Alfred A. Knopf, 1977.

———. *The Age of the French Revolution.* Vol. 2, *The Wind from America.* Translated by Nancy Amphoux. New York: Alfred A. Knopf, 1978.

Marshall, Peter. "Travellers and the Colonial Scene." *Bulletin of the British Association for American Studies,* New Series, no. 7 (December 1963): 5–28.

Martello, Robert. *Midnight Ride, Industrial Dawn: Paul Revere and the Growth of American Enterprise.* Baltimore: Johns Hopkins University Press, 2010.

Martin, Gaston. "Commercial Relations between Nantes and the American Colonies during the War of Independence." *Journal of Economic and Business History* 4 (1932): 812–29.

Martinez, Leroy. *From across the Spanish Empire: Spanish Soldiers Who Helped Win the American Revolutionary War, 1776–1783: Arizona, California, Louisiana, New Mexico, and Texas Military Rosters.* Baltimore: Clearfield Company, 2015.

Massey, Gregory D. *John Laurens and the American Revolution.* Columbia: University of South Carolina Press, 2000.

Matson, Cathy. *Merchants and Empire: Trading in Colonial New York.* Baltimore: Johns Hopkins University Press, 2002.

Medina Rojas, Francisco de Borja. *José de Ezpeleta, gobernador de La Mobila, 1780–1781.* Seville: Escuela de Estudios Hispano-Americanos de Sevilla, 1980.

———. "José de Ezpeleta and the Siege of Pensacola." In *Anglo-Spanish Confrontation on the Gulf Coast during the American Revolution,* edited by William S. Coker and Robert E. Rea, 106–24. Pensacola: Gulf Coast History and Humanities Conference, 1982.

Meng, John J. "A Footnote to Secret Aid in the American Revolution." *American Historical Review* 43, no. 4 (July 1938), 791–95.

Michel, Jacques. *La vie aventureuse et mouvementée de Charles-Henri, comte d'Estaing, 1724–1794* [The adventurous and eventful life of Charles-Henri, comte d'Estaing, 1724–1794]. Paris: J. Michel, 1976.

Middlekauff, Robert. *The Glorious Cause: The American Revolution, 1763–1789.* New York: Oxford University Press, 2005.

———. *Washington's Revolution: The Making of America's First Leader.* New York: Alfred A. Knopf, 2015.

Middleton, Richard. *The War of American Independence: 1775–1783.* Harlow, UK: Pearson, 2012.

Miller, Nathan. *Sea of Glory: The Continental Navy Fights for Independence, 1775–1783.* New York: David McKay Co., 1974.

Ministère des Affaires étrangères (French Foreign Ministry). *Les combattants français de la guerre américaine, 1778–1783* [French combatants in the American war, 1778–1783]. Paris: Ancienne maison Quantin, Libraries-imprimeries reúnies, Motteroz, Martinet, 1903.

Moller, George D. *American Military Shoulder Arms.* Vol. 1, *Colonial and Revolutionary War Arms.* Albuquerque: University of New Mexico Press, 2011.

Monaque, Rémi. *Suffren: Un destin inachevé* [Suffren: An unfulfilled destiny]. Paris: Tallandier, 2009.

Morison, Margaret Cotter. "The Duc de Choiseul and the Invasion of England, 1768–1770." *Transactions of the Royal Historical Society,* Third Series, 4 (1910): 83–115.

Morris, Richard B. *The Peacemakers: The Great Powers and American Independence.* New York: Harper & Row, 1965.

Morton, Brian N., and Donald C. Spinelli, *Beaumarchais and the American Revolution.* Lanham, MD: Lexington Books, 2003.

Mossman, Philip L. *Money of the American Colonies and Confederation: A Numismatic, Economic and Historical Correlation.* New York: American Numismatic Society, 1993.

Murdoch, Richard K. "A French Account of the Siege of Charleston, 1780." *South Carolina Historical Magazine* 67, no. 3 (July 1966): 138–54.

Murphy, Orville T. "The Battle of Germantown and the Franco-American Alliance of 1778." *Pennsylvania Magazine of History and Biography* 82, no. 1 (January 1958): 55–64.

———. "The French Professional Soldier's Opinion of the American Militia in the War of the Revolution." *Military Affairs* 32, no. 4 (February 1969): 191–98.

———. "The View from Versailles: Charles Gravier Comte de Vergennes's Perceptions of the American Revolution." In *Diplomacy and Revolution: The Franco-American Alliance of 1778,* edited by Ronald Hoffman and Peter J. Albert, 107–49. Charlottesville: University of Virginia Press, 1981.

———. *Charles Gravier, Comte de Vergennes: French Diplomacy in the Age of Revolution, 1719–1787.* Albany: State University of New York Press, 1982.

Murray, Louise Welles. *The Story of Some French Refugees and Their "Azilum."* Athens, PA: Tioga Point Historical Society, 1903.

Myers, Minor. *Liberty without Anarchy: A History of the Society of the Cincinnati.* Charlottesville: University of Virginia Press, 2004.

Nardin, Pierre. *Gribeauval: Lieutenant général des armées du roi, 1715–1789* [Gribeauval: Lieutenant general of the King's armies, 1715–1789]. Paris: Fondation pour les études de défense nationale, 1982.

Neely, Wayne. *The Great Hurricane of 1780: The Story of the Greatest and Deadliest Hurricane of the Caribbean and the Americas.* Bloomington, IN: iUniverse, 2012.

Neimeyer, Charles. "Continental Marines: The 1778 Willing Expedition." *Leatherneck* 91, no. 9 (September 2008): 58–62.

Nester, William R. *George Rogers Clark: "I Glory in War."* Norman: University of Oklahoma Press, 2012.

Nettles, Curtis P. "A Link in the Chain of Events Leading to American Independence." *William and Mary Quarterly,* Third Series, 3, no. 1 (January 1946): 36–47.

Novales, Alberto Gil. "La independencia de América en la conciencia española, 1820–1823" [American Independence in the Spanish conscience, 1820–1823]. *Revista de Indias* 39 (January 1979): 235–65.

Nuxoll, Elizabeth Miles. *Congress and the Munitions Merchants: The Secret Committee of Trade during the American Revolution, 1775–1777.* New York: Garland, 1985.

Odom, Wesley S. *The Longest Siege of the American Revolution: Pensacola.* Pensacola, FL: W. S. Odom, 2009.

O'Donnell, William Emmett. *The Chevalier de La Luzerne, French Minister to the United States, 1779–1784.* Bruges: Desclée De Brouwer, 1938.

Olmeda Checa, Manuel. "El *Galveztown.*" *Pendulo: Revista de Ingeniería y Humanidades* 20 (2009): 200–228.

Oltra, Joaquín, and María Ángeles Pérez Samper. *El Conde de Aranda y los Estados Unidos* [The Conde de Aranda and the United States]. Barcelona: PPU, 1987.

O'Shaughnessy, Andrew Jackson. *The Men Who Lost America: British Leadership, the American Revolution, and the Fate of the Empire.* New Haven, CT: Yale University Press, 2013.

Osman, Julia. "The Citizen Army of Old Regime France." PhD dissertation, University of North Carolina, 2010.

———. "American Nationality: A French Invention?" Paper presented at the conference *The Marquis de Lafayette and the European Friends of the American Revolution,* Mount Vernon, VA, June 13–15, 2015.

Papas, Phillip. *Renegade Revolutionary: The Life of General Charles Lee.* New York: New York University Press, 2014.

Pardos, José Luis. *El modernizador: Una aproximación a Floridablanca* [The modernizer: An approach to Floridablanca]. Murcia: Editum, 2012.

Patterson, Alfred Temple. *The Other Armada: The Franco-Spanish Attempt to Invade Britain in 1779.* Manchester: Manchester University Press, 1960.

Patton, Robert H. *Patriot Pirates: The Privateer War for Freedom and Fortune in the American Revolution.* New York: Pantheon, 2008.

Paul, Joel Richard. *Unlikely Allies: How a Merchant, a Playwright, and a Spy Saved the American Revolution.* New York: Riverhead, 2009.

Pavía y Pavía, Francisco de Paula. *Galeria biografica de los generales de marina, jefes y per-*

sonajes notables que figuraron en la misma corporación desde 1700 á 1868 [Biographical encyclopedia of naval admirals, leaders and notable persons who figured in the same organization from 1700 to 1868]. 4 vols. Madrid: J. Lopez, 1873–74.

Peckham, Howard H., ed. *The Toll of Independence: Engagements and Battle Casualties of the American Revolution.* Chicago: University of Chicago Press, 1974.

Perrault, Gilles. *Le secret du roi* [The king's secret]. 3 vols. Paris: Fayard, 1992–96.

Perugia, Paul del. *La tentative d'invasion de l'Angleterre de 1779* [The attempted invasion of England of 1779]. Paris: Alcan, Presses universitaires de France, 1939.

Peskin, Lawrence A. *Manufacturing Revolution: The Intellectual Origins of Early American Industry.* Baltimore: Johns Hopkins University Press, 2003.

Philbrick, Nathaniel. *Bunker Hill: A City, a Siege, a Revolution.* New York: Viking, 2013.

Phillips, Kevin. *1775: A Good Year for Revolution.* New York: Viking, 2012.

Pope, Clayne L. "Adult Mortality in America before 1900: A View from Family Histories." In *Strategic Factors in Nineteenth Century American Economic History: A Volume to Honor Robert W. Fogel,* edited by Claudia Goldin and Hugh Rockoff, 267–96. Chicago: University of Chicago Press, 1992.

Potts, James M. *French Covert Action in the American Revolution.* Lincoln, NE: iUniverse, 2005.

Potts, Louis W. *Arthur Lee: A Virtuous Revolutionary.* Baton Rouge: Louisiana State University Press, 1981.

Prelinger, Catherine M. "Less Lucky Than Lafayette: A Note on the French Applicants of Benjamin Franklin for Commissions in the American Army, 1776–1785." *Proceedings of the Western Society for French History* 4 (1976): 263–76.

Price, Munro. *The Road from Versailles: Louis XVI, Marie Antoinette, and the Fall of the French Monarchy.* New York: St. Martin's, 2014.

Pritchard, James. *Louis XV's Navy, 1748–1762: A Study of Organization and Administration.* Kingston, ON: McGill–Queen's University Press, 1987.

———. "French Strategy and the American Revolution: A Reappraisal." *Naval War College Review* 47, no. 4 (Autumn 1994): 83–108.

Quintero Saravia, Gonzalo M. "Bernardo de Gálvez y América a finales del siglo XVIII" [Bernardo de Gálvez and America at the end of the 18th century]. PhD thesis, Universidad Complutense de Madrid, 2015.

Raab, James W. *Spain, Britain and the American Revolution in Florida, 1762–1783.* Jefferson, NC: McFarland & Co., 2008.

Racine, Karen. *Francisco de Miranda: A Transatlantic Life in the Age of Revolution.* Wilmington, DE: Scholarly Resources Books, 2003.

Rain, Pierre. *La diplomatie française d'Henri IV à Vergennes* [French diplomacy from Henri IV to Vergennes]. Paris: Librairie Plon, 1945.

Raphael, Ray. *Founding Myths: Stories That Hide Our Patriotic Past.* New York: New Press, 2014.

Raphael, Ray, and Marie Raphael. *The Spirit of '74: How the American Revolution Began.* New York: New Press, 2015.

Rappleye, Charles. *Robert Morris: Financier of the American Revolution.* New York: Simon & Schuster, 2010.

Rashed, Zenab Esmat. *The Peace of Paris, 1763.* Liverpool: University Press of Liverpool, 1951.

Reparaz, Carmen de. *Yo Solo: Bernardo de Gálvez y la toma de Panzacola en 1781* [I alone:

Bernardo de Gálvez and the taking of Pensacola in 1781]. Madrid and Barcelona: Serbal/ICI, 1986.

———. *I Alone: Bernardo de Gálvez and the Taking of Pensacola in 1781.* Translated by Walter Rubin. Madrid: ICI, 1993.

Rhodes, Leara. "Haitian Contributions to American History: A Journalistic Record." In *Slavery in the Caribbean Francophone World: Distant Voices, Forgotten Acts, Forged Identities,* edited by Doris Y. Kadish, 75–90. Athens: University of Georgia Press, 2000.

Ribes-Iborra Vincent. "Nuevos datos biográficos sobre Juan de Miralles" [New biographical information about Juan de Miralles]. *Revista de Historia Moderna* 16 (1997): 363–74.

———. "La era Miralles: El momento de los agentes secretos" [The Miralles era: The moment of the secret agents]. In *Norteamérica a finales del siglo XVIII: España y los Estados Unidos* [North America at the end of the 18th century: Spain and the United States], edited by Eduardo Garrigues López-Chicheri, 143–69. Madrid: Marcial Pons, 2008.

Rice, Howard C. "James Swan: Agent of the French Republic, 1794–1796." *New England Quarterly* 10, no. 3 (September 1937): 464–86.

Riley, James C. *The Seven Years' War and the Old Regime in France: The Economic and Financial Toll.* Princeton, NJ: Princeton University Press, 1986.

Risch, Erna. *Supplying Washington's Army.* Washington, DC: Government Printing Office, 1981.

Rodger, Nicholas A. M. *The Wooden World: An Anatomy of the Georgian Navy.* Annapolis, MD: Naval Institute Press, 1986.

Rodriguez, Mario. *La Revolución americana de 1776 y el mundo hispánico* [The American Revolution of 1776 and the Spanish world]. Madrid: Éditorial Tecnos, 1976.

Rodríguez González, Agustín Ramón. *Trafalgar y el conflicto naval Anglo-Español del siglo XVIII* [Trafalgar and the English-Spanish naval conflict of the 18th century]. Madrid: Editorial Actas, 2005.

Rosengarten, Joseph George. *French Colonists and Exiles in the United States.* Philadelphia: J. B. Lippincott, 1907.

Rouzeau, Léon. "Aperçus du rôle de Nantes dans la guerre d'Indépendance d'Amérique (1775–1783)" [Insights on the role of Nantes in the War of American Independence, 1775–1783]. *Annales de Bretagne* 74, no. 2 (1967): 217–78.

Ruggiu, François-Joseph. "India and the Reshaping of the French Colonial Policy (1759–1789)." *Itinerario* 35, no. 2 (August 2011): 25–43.

Russell, David Lee. *The American Revolution in the Southern Colonies.* Jefferson, NC: McFarland & Co., 2000.

Sambricio, Carlos. "Fiestas en Madrid durante el reinado de Carlos III" [Festivals in Madrid during the reign of Carlos III]. In *Carlos III, Alcalde de Madrid,* 575–629. Madrid: Ayuntamiento de Madrid, 1988.

Sánchez, Rafael Torres. "Possibilities and Limits: Testing the Fiscal-Military State in the Anglo-Spanish War of 1779–1783." In *War, State and Development: Fiscal-Military States in the Eighteenth Century,* edited by Rafael Torres Sánchez, 437–60. Pamplona: EUNSA, 2007.

Sánchez Carrión, José María. *De constructores a ingenieros de marina: Salto tecnológico y professional impulsado por Francisco Gautier* [From constructors to naval engineers: The technological and professional leap driven by Francisco Gautier]. Madrid: Fondo Editorial de Ingeniería Naval, 2013.

Santaló Rodriguez de Viguri, José Luis. *Don José Solano y Bote, primer Marqués del Socorro, capitán general de la Armada* [Sir José Solano y Bote, first Marqués del Socorro, captain-general of the Armada]. Madrid: Instituto Histórico de Marina, 1973.

Schaeper, Thomas J. *John Paul Jones and the Battle of Flamborough Head: A Reconsideration.* New York: Peter Lang, 1989.

———. *France and America in the Revolutionary Era: The Life of Jacques-Donatien Leray de Chaumont, 1725–1803.* Providence, RI: Berghahn Books, 1995.

———. *Edward Bancroft: Scientist, Author, Spy.* New Haven, CT: Yale University Press, 2011.

Schiff, Stacy. *A Great Improvisation: Franklin, France and the Birth of America.* New York: Henry Holt, 2005.

Schulte Nordholt, Jan Willem. *The Dutch Republic and American Independence.* Translated by Herbert H. Rowen. Chapel Hill: University of North Carolina Press, 1982.

Scott, Hamish M. "The Importance of Bourbon Naval Reconstruction to the Strategy of Choiseul after the Seven Years' War." *International History Review* 1, no. 1 (January 1979): 17–35.

———, ed. *Enlightened Absolutism: Reform and Reformers in Later Eighteenth-Century Europe.* Ann Arbor: University of Michigan Press, 1990.

Scott, Samuel F. *From Yorktown to Valmy: The Transformation of the French Army in an Age of Revolution.* Niwot: University Press of Colorado, 1998.

Selesky, Harold E., and Mark M. Boatner III, eds. *Encyclopedia of the American Revolution: Library of Military History.* 2nd ed. 2 vols. Detroit: Charles Scribner's Sons, 2006.

Selig, Robert A. "A German Soldier in America, 1780–1783: The Journal of Georg Daniel Flohr." *William and Mary Quarterly,* Third Series, 50, no. 3 (July 1993): 575–90.

———. "Private Flohr's Other Life." *American Heritage* 4, no. 6 (October 1994): 94–95.

———. "The Washington-Rochambeau Revolutionary Route in the State of Delaware: A Historical and Archeological Survey." Dover: State of Delaware, 2003.

———. *The March to Victory: Washington, Rochambeau, and the Yorktown Campaign of 1781.* Washington, DC: U.S. Army Center of Military History, 2007.

———. "Revolutionary War Route and Transportation Survey in the Commonwealth of Virginia, 1781–1782: An Historical and Architectural Survey." Richmond: Commonwealth of Virginia, Department of Historic Resources, 2009.

———. "Artillery at Yorktown: A Statistical Overview." *Brigade Dispatch: Journal of the Brigade of the American Revolution* 40, no. 3 (2010): 2–11, and 40, no. 4 (2010): 26–32.

Shachtman, Tom. *Gentlemen Scientists and Revolutionaries: The Founding Fathers in the Age of Enlightenment.* New York: Palgrave MacMillan, 2014.

Shomette, Donald. *Shipwrecks, Sea Raiders, and Maritime Disasters along the Delmarva Coast, 1632–2004.* Baltimore: Johns Hopkins University Press, 2007.

Shy, John. "The American Colonies in War and Rebellion, 1748–1783." In *The Oxford History of the British Empire,* vol. 2, *The Eighteenth Century,* edited by P. J. Marshall, 300–323. Oxford: Oxford University Press, 1998.

Skemp, Sheila L. *The Making of a Patriot: Benjamin Franklin at the Cockpit.* New York: Oxford University Press, 2013.

Smith, Charles R. *Marines in the Revolution: A History of the Continental Marines in the*

American Revolution, 1775–1783. Washington, DC: Government Printing Office, 1975.

Smith, Fitz-Henry Jr. *The French at Boston during the Revolution*. Boston: Privately printed, 1913.

Smith, Robert F. "'A Veritable . . . Arsenal of Manufacturing': Government Management of Weapons Production in the American Revolution." PhD dissertation, Lehigh University, 2008.

Société en France des Fils de la Révolution Américaine. *La glorieuse campagne du comte de Grasse* [The glorious campaign of the comte de Grasse]. Paris: SPM, 2010.

Soulange-Bodin, André. *La diplomatie de Louis XV et le pacte de famille* [The diplomacy of Louis XV and the Family Pact]. Paris: Perrin 1894.

Spooner, Frank C. *Risks at Sea: Amsterdam Insurance and Maritime Europe, 1766–1780*. Cambridge: Cambridge University Press, 1983.

Spring, Matthew H. *With Zeal and with Bayonets Only: The British Army on Campaign in North America, 1775–1783*. Norman: University of Oklahoma Press, 2012.

Starkey, Armstrong. *War in the Age of Enlightenment, 1700–1789*. Westport, CT: Praeger, 2003.

Stephenson, Orlando W. "The Supply of Gunpowder in 1776." *American Historical Review* 30, no. 2 (January 1925): 271–81.

Stillé, Charles J. "Comte de Broglie, the Proposed Stadtholder of America." *Pennsylvania Magazine of History and Biography* 11, no. 4 (January 1888): 369–405.

Stinchcombe, William C. *The American Revolution and the French Alliance*. Syracuse, NY: Syracuse University Press, 1969.

Stockley, Andrew. *Britain and France at the Birth of America: The European Powers and the Peace Negotiations of 1782–1783*. Exeter: University of Exeter Press, 2001.

Storozynski, Alex. *The Peasant Prince: Thaddeus Kosciuszko and the Age of Revolution*. New York: St. Martin's, 2009.

Stroud, Patricia Tyson. *The Man Who Had Been King: The American Exile of Napoleon's Brother Joseph*. Philadelphia: University of Pennsylvania Press, 2005.

Sulivan, J. A. "Graves and Hood." *The Mariner's Mirror* 69, no. 2 (1983): 175–94.

Sumner, William G. *A History of American Currency*. New York: Henry Holt, 1874.

Sutton, Jean. *The East India Company's Maritime Service, 1746–1834: Masters of the Eastern Seas*. Woodbridge, UK: Boydell & Brewer, 2010.

Syrett, David. *The Royal Navy in American Waters, 1775–1783*. Aldershot, UK: Scolar Press, 1989.

———. *The Royal Navy in European Waters during the American Revolutionary War*. Columbia: University of South Carolina Press, 1998.

Szabo, Franz A. J. *The Seven Years' War in Europe, 1756–1763*. New York: Pearson/Longman, 2008.

Taillemite, Étienne. *La Fayette*. Paris: Fayard, 1989.

———. "Les officiers généraux de la guerre d'Indépendance américaine" [General officers in the American War of Independence]. In *Les marines de la guerre d'Indépendance américaine, 1763–1783*, edited by Philippe Bonnichon, Charles-Philippe de Vergennes, and Ovilier Chaline, 381–89. Paris: Presses de l'université Paris-Sorbonne, 2013.

Tejera, Eduardo J. *La ayuda de España y Cuba a la independencia norteamericana: Una historia olvidada* [Spanish and Cuban aid to American Independence: A forgotten story]. Santo Domingo, Dominican Republic: Editorial Luz de Luna, 2009.

Thomson, Buchanan Parker. *Spain: Forgotten Ally of the American Revolution*. North Quincy, MA: Christopher Publishing House, 1976.

Tieck, William A. "In Search of Peter Stephen Du Ponceau." *Pennsylvania Magazine of History and Biography* 89, no. 1 (January 1965): 52–67, 69–78.

Trentinian, Jacques de. "Washington, de Grasse et la *Reine Charlotte*." *L'Alliance franco-américaine, Bulletin de la Société en France des fils de la Révolution Américaine* 24 (Spring 2013): 15–17.

———. "France's Contribution to American Independence." Xenophon Group, http://xenophongroup.com/issues/contribution.htm.

Trew, Peter. *Rodney and the Breaking of the Line*. Barnsley, UK: Pen & Sword Military, 2006.

Tuchman, Barbara W. *The First Salute*. New York: Alfred A. Knopf, 1988.

Tunstall, Brian. *Naval Warfare in the Age of Sail: The Evolution of Fighting Tactics, 1650–1815*. Annapolis, MD: Naval Institute Press, 1990.

Tyson, Neil deGrasse. *The Sky Is Not the Limit: Adventures of an Urban Astrophysicist*. Amherst, NY: Prometheus Books, 2010.

Upton, Emery. *The Military Policy of the United States*. Washington, DC: Government Printing Office, 1917.

Vaca de Osma, José Antonio. *Carlos III*. Madrid: Ediciones Rialp, 1997.

Valdez-Bubnov, Ivan. *Poder naval y modernización del estado: Política de construcción naval española (siglos XVI–XVIII)* [Naval power and state modernization: The politics of Spanish naval construction, 16th–18th centuries]. Madrid: Iberoamericana, 2011.

Van Tyne, Claude H. "French Aid before the Alliance of 1778." *American Historical Review* 31, no. 1 (October 1925): 20–40.

Van Vlack, Milton C. *Silas Deane, Revolutionary War Diplomat and Politician*. Jefferson, NC: McFarland & Co., 2013.

Vergé-Franceschi, Michel. *La marine française au XVIIIe siècle: Guerres, administration, exploration* [The French navy in the 18th century: wars, administration, exploration]. Paris: SEDES, 1996.

———. "Marine et Révolution: Les officiers de 1789 et leur devenir" [Navy and revolution: The officers of 1789 and their fates]. *Histoire, Économie et Société* 9, no. 2 (1990): 259–86.

Vérin, Hélène. *La gloire des ingénieurs: L'intelligence technique du XVIe au XVIIIe siècle* [The glory of the engineers: Technical intelligence from the 16th through the 18th centuries]. Paris: Albin Michel, 1993.

Villiers, Patrick. *La marine de Louis XVI: De Choiseul à Sartine* [Louis XVI's navy: From Choiseul to Sartine]. Grenoble: J. P. Debbane, 1985.

———. *Marine royale, corsaires et trafic dans l'Atlantique, de Louis XIV à Louis XVI* [Royal Navy, pirates and smuggling in the Atlantic, from Louis XIV to Louis XVI]. 2 vols. Dunkirk: Sociéte Dunkerquoise d'Histoire et d'Archéologie, 1991.

———. "La tentative franco-espagnole de débarquement en Angleterre de 1779" [The attempted French-Spanish landings in England in 1779]. In *Revue du Nord* [Northern review], *Le Transmanche et les Liaisons Maritimes XVIIIe–XXe Siècle* [Cross-Channel and maritime liaisons 18th–20th centuries], Hors-série n° 9 (1995): 13–29.

———. "La stratégie de la marine française de l'arrivée de Sartine à la victoire de la Chesapeake" [The French naval strategy from the arrival of Sartine until the victory of the Chesapeake]. In *Les marines de guerre européennes: XVIIe–XVIIIe siècles* [European navies: 17th to 19th centuries], edited by Martine Acerra, José Merino, Jean Meyer, and Michel Vergé-Franceschi, 211–52. Paris: Presses de l'université Paris-Sorbonne, 1998.

———. "Sartine et la préparation de la flotte de guerre française 1775–1778: Refontes ou constructions neuves?" [Sartine and the preparation of the French naval fleet, 1775–1778: Refit or new construction?] In *Les marines de la guerre d'Indépendance américaine, 1763–1783* [The navies of the War of American Independence, 1763–1783], edited by Philippe Bonnichon, Charles-Philippe de Vergennes, and Olivier Chaline, 65–75. Paris: Presses de l'université Paris-Sorbonne, 2013.

———. "La Fayette and the Passage of the Ship *La Victoire* in 1777: New Interpretations." Paper presented at the conference *The Marquis de Lafayette and the European Friends of the American Revolution,* Mount Vernon, VA, June 13–15, 2015.

Villiers, Patrick, and Jean-Claude Lemineur. *L'Hermione, La Fayette, Latouche-Tréville.* Nice: Ancre, 2015. English-language edition: *Hermione, Lafayette's Frigate at the Service of the American Independence.* Nice: Ancre, 2015.

Vogel, Herbert. "Engineer Buttons and Castle." *The Military Engineer* 33, no. 188 (March–April 1941): 103.

Vowell, Sarah. *Lafayette in the Somewhat United States.* New York: Riverhead, 2015.

W3R: Washington-Rochambeau Revolutionary Route website, http://www.w3r-us.org/.

Waddington, Richard. *Louis XV et le renversement des alliances: Préliminaires de la guerre de Sept Ans, 1754–1756* [Louis XV and the reversal of alliances: Preliminaries in the Seven Years' War, 1754–1756]. Paris: Firmin-Didot, 1896.

———. *La guerre de Sept Ans: Histoire diplomatique et militaire* [The Seven Years' War: Diplomatic and military history]. 5 vols. Paris: Firmin-Didot, 1899–1914.

Walker, Charles F. *The Tupac Amaru Rebellion.* Cambridge, MA: Belknap Press of Harvard University Press, 2014.

Walker, Paul K. *Engineers of Independence: A Documentary History of the Army Engineers in the American Revolution, 1775–1783.* Washington, DC: Government Printing Office, 1981.

Walker, Timothy. "Atlantic Dimensions of the American Revolution: Imperial Priorities and the Portuguese Reaction to the North American Bid for Independence (1775–83)." *Journal of Early American History* 2 (2012): 247–85.

Weelen, Jean-Edmond. *Rochambeau, Father and Son: A Life of the Marechal de Rochambeau, and the Journal of the Vicomte de Rochambeau.* Translated by Lawrence Lee. New York: Henry Holt, 1936.

White, Eugene Nelson. "Was There a Solution to the *Ancien Régime*'s Financial Dilemma?" *Journal of Economic History* 49, no. 3 (September 1989): 545–68.

White, Kenton. "The Ordnance Board and Arms Production, 1750–1815: Did an Industrial Revolution Take Place in Birmingham Arms Manufacture?" MA thesis, University of Reading, 2013.

Whitridge, Arnold. *Rochambeau.* New York: Collier, 1974.

Whittlesey, Derwent S. "The Springfield Armory: A Study in Institutional Development." PhD dissertation, University of Chicago, 1920.

Williams, Basil. *The Life of William Pitt, Earl of Chatham.* 2 vols. London: Longmans, Green, 1913.

Willis, Sam. *Fighting at Sea in the Eighteenth Century.* Woodbridge, UK: Boydell & Brewer, 2008.

———. *The Struggle for Sea Power: A Naval History of the American Revolution*. New York: W. W. Norton, 2015.

Wills, Garry. *Inventing America: Jefferson's Declaration of Independence*. Garden City, NY: Doubleday, 1978.

Winfield, Rif. *British Warships in the Age of Sail, 1714–1792: Design, Construction, Careers and Fates*. Barnsley, UK: Seaforth Publishing, 2007.

Wright, James Leitch Jr. *Florida in the American Revolution*. Gainesville: University Press of Florida, 1975.

Wright, John W. "Notes on the Siege of Yorktown in 1781 with Special Reference to the Conduct of a Siege in the Eighteenth Century." *William and Mary Quarterly*, Second Series, 12, no. 4 (October 1932), 239–52.

Wright, Robert K. Jr. *The Continental Army*. Washington, DC: Government Printing Office, 1983.

Xenophon Group: http://www.xenophongroup.com/mcjoynt/ep_web.htm.

Yaniz, José L. "The Role of Spain in the American Revolution: An Unavoidable Strategic Mistake." MA thesis, Marine Corps University, 2009.

Yela Utrilla, Juan Francisco. *España ante la independencia de los Estados Unidos* [Spain confronted with the Independence of the United States]. 2 vols. Lérida, Spain: Gráficos Academia Marina, 1925.

Zucker, Adolf Eduard. *General de Kalb: Lafayette's Mentor*. Chapel Hill: University of North Carolina Press, 1966.

Zylberberg, Michel. *Capitalisme et catholicisme dans la France moderne: La dynastie Le Couteulx* [Capitalism and christianity in modern France: The Couteulx dynasty]. Paris: Publications de la Sorbonne, 2001.

Index

A NOTE ABOUT THE AUTHOR

Larrie D. Ferreiro received his PhD in the history of science and technology from Imperial College London. He teaches history and engineering at George Mason University in Virginia and the Stevens Institute of Technology in New Jersey. He has served for more than thirty-five years in the U.S. Navy, U.S. Coast Guard, and Department of Defense, and was an exchange engineer in the French navy. He is the author of *Measure of the Earth: The Enlightenment Expedition That Reshaped Our World* and *Ships and Science: The Birth of Naval Architecture in the Scientific Revolution, 1600–1800*. He lives with his wife and their sons in Virginia.

A NOTE ON THE TYPE

This book was set in a modern adaptation of a type designed by the first William Caslon (1692–1766). The Caslon face, an artistic, easily read type, has enjoyed more than two centuries of popularity in the English-speaking world. This version with its even balance and honest letterforms was designed by Carol Twombly for the Adobe Corporation and released in 1990.

Composed by North Market Street Graphics,
Lancaster, Pennsylvania

Printed and bound by Berryville Graphics,
Berryville, Virginia